THE FINANCE OF HIGHER EDUCATION:
Theory, Research, Policy, and Practice

THE FINANCE OF HIGHER EDUCATION:
Theory, Research, Policy, and Practice

Edited by
Michael B. Paulsen
University of New Orleans

and

John C. Smart
University of Memphis

AGATHON PRESS
A division of Algora Publishing
New York

The principal portions of the following chapters in this book were originally published in the
specified volumes of *Higher Education: Handbook of Theory and Research,* and were copyrighted in the year of publication by Agathon Press; the Epilogues were provided for this volume by the original authors and are covered by this copyright notice: "Costs and Productivity
in Higher Education: Theory, Evidence and Policy Implications," by Darrell R. Lewis and
Halil Dundar," Vol. XIV, 1999; "Economic Perspectives on Rising College Tuition," by
Michael B. Paulsen, Vol. XV, 2000; "The Paradox of Growth in Federal Aid for College Students, 1960-1990," by James C Hearn, Vol. IX, 1993; "State Efforts to Keep Colleges
Affordable in the Face of Fiscal Stress," by Michael Mumper, Vol. XIII, 1998; "State Policy
and Private Higher Education" by William Zumeta, Vol. XII, 1997; "College and University
Budgeting: What Do We Know? What Do We Need to Know?" by William F. Lasher and
Deborah L. Greene, Vol. IX, 1993.

Library of Congress Cataloging in Process Information
The finance of higher education : theory, research, policy, and practice
/ edited by Michael B. Paulsen and John C. Smart.
p. cm.
Includes bibliographical references and index.
ISBN 0-87586-135-0 (alk. paper)
1. Education, Higher--United States--Finance. 2. Universities and
colleges--United States--Finance. I. Paulsen, Michael B. II. Smart,
John C.
LB2342 .F475 2001
338.4'737873--dc21
2001003740

CONTENTS

THE CONTRIBUTORS

ERIC H. ASKER is a native of Southern California. He is presently an Ed. D. candidate at Indiana University and is completing his dissertation. His research project is a study of the impact of financial aid on the persistence of graduate students from selected fields of study in Indiana's public institutions. His business experience is in financial and business system consulting. His higher education related experience is as an analyst at Indiana Education Policy Center and for Indiana University-Purdue University Indianapolis enrollment management office. He has been a research assistant at the education policy center at the University of Dayton. He worked with the facilities department and student taught at the business school at UCLA. He has been a recruiter for West Point and an administrative assistant to a department chair at UC Davis. His education includes a M.Ed. from UC Davis, an M.B.A. from UCLA, and a B. S. from the U.S. Military Academy.

SANDY BAUM is Professor of Economics at Skidmore College. Prior to joining the faculty at Skidmore, Dr. Baum taught at Northeastern University and Wellesley College. She graduated from Bryn Mawr College in 1972 with a major in sociology and received her Ph.D. in economics from Columbia University in 1981. Dr. Baum has written widely on financial aid policy, the distribution of subsidies to college students, merit aid, college savings plans, student debt and other aspects of college finance, as well as *A Primer on Economics for Financial Aid Professionals*. In 1996, she received the NASFAA Golden Quill Award for Outstanding Contributions to the Literature on Student Aid. She serves as consulting economist for the Financial Aid Services and Standards Committee of the College Board's College Scholarship Service and has worked with a variety of other organizations concerned with student aid. She has made numerous presentations on postsecondary education financing to a wide variety of groups.

DAVID W. BRENEMAN, University Professor and Dean of the Curry School of Education at the University of Virginia, is an economist and authority on the finance and economics of higher education. His three decades of experience include service as a professor and subsequently President of Kalamazoo College in Michigan, a think-tank scholar and Senior Fellow in the Economic Studies program at the Brookings Institution, and currently, as Dean of the Curry School of Education. He teaches courses in the Center for the Study of Higher Education. In addition to numerous scholarly articles and book chapters, he is author of *Liberal Arts Colleges: Thriving, Surviving, or Endangered?* (Brookings, 1994) and co-author of *Financing Community Colleges: An Economic Perspective* (Brookings, 1981) and *Public Policy and Private Higher Education* (Brookings, 1978). Recently, the Council of Independent Colleges (CIC) presented Dean Breneman with the Award for Outstanding Service. This award honors Breneman's efforts toward "insuring a robust future for private higher education" and recognizes the numerous contributions he has made to higher education, specifically in the area of financial aspects of private liberal arts colleges.

JAMES L. DOTI is President and Donald Bren Distinguished Professor of Business and Economics at Chapman University. He holds a bachelor's degree in economics from the University of Illinois, Chicago, and master's and doctorate degrees in economics from the University of Chicago, where he was an Edward Hilman Fellow and National Science Foundation Scholar. Dr.

Doti's numerous articles have appeared in academic journals as well as national periodicals such as *The Wall Street Journal* and *The Chronicle of Higher Education*. He co-authored two text-books, *Econometric Analysis—An Applications Approach (1988) and The Practice of Econometrics with EViews (1998)*. In 1991 he co-edited a collection of readings in private enterprise, *The Market Economy— A Reader*, that received the Templeton Honor Award for Scholarly Excellence.

HALIL DUNDAR, Ph.D. in higher education and policy studies, is an Education Economist and Project Manager at the World Bank. Dr. Dundar was previously an Assistant Professor of Educational Policy at the Middle East Technical University in Turkey and Policy Analyst at the University of Minnesota. He has authored or co-authored more than 30 monographs, journal articles and book chapters. His current research interests are in the economics of higher education and evaluation of education in developing countries.

DEBORAH L. GREENE is currently Vice President for Institutional Effectiveness and Planning at the University of Texas Health Science Center in San Antonio. Prior to joining the Health Science Center, Dr. Greene served as the Director of the Division of Medical Education at the Texas Medical Association and Director of the Office of Health Affairs within the Texas Higher Education Coordinating Board. She also served as a legislative policy analyst on higher education for the Texas Senate Education Committee and as a budget analyst for higher education in the Governor's Office of Budget and Planning. She received her doctorate in higher educational administration at The University of Texas at Austin, and her M.S.W. and baccalaureate degrees from the University of Michigan.

SHOUPING HU is Assistant Professor in Educational Administration and Supervision in the College of Education and Human Services at Seton Hall University, South Orange, New Jersey. He received his M.A. degree in Economics in 1998 and Ph.D. degree in Higher Education in 2000, both from Indiana University Bloomington. His current research concentrates on college choice, persistence, financial aid policy, and college student engagement in learning and out-of-class activities. His writings have appeared in *Educational Evaluation and Policy Analysis*, *Journal of Student Financial Aid*, *Journal of College Student Development*, *Journal of Higher Education*, *Research in Higher Education*, and *The Review of Higher Education*.

JAMES C. HEARN is Professor of Higher Education, Chair of the Department of Educational Policy and Administration, and Interim Director of the Postsecondary Education Policy Studies Center at the University of Minnesota. He received his Ph.D. degree from Stanford University and an MBA from the Wharton School at the University of Pennsylvania. Prior to entering his academic career, he worked in policy research on student aid issues for the American College Testing program and for a consulting firm in Washington, DC. His research and teaching focus on policy, finance, and organization in higher education. Professor Hearn's research on college enrollment, educational attainment, and student aid policy has appeared in sociology, economics, and education journals as well as in several books. Recently, he has been examining postsecondary access and related policy issues in Minnesota, P-16 cooperation and planning in Georgia, and the implications of the increasing use of non-tenure-line faculty in research universities.

LUCIE LAPOVSKY is President of Mercy College in New York. She previously served as Vice President for Finance at Goucher College for nine years and prior to that, she worked as

Special Assistant to the President of the University of Maryland at College Park, as Director of Finance and Facilities for the Maryland Higher Education Commission, and as a Fiscal Planner for the Maryland State Department of Budget and Fiscal Planning. She received her B.A. degree from Goucher College, and her M.A. and Ph.D. degrees in Economics from the University of Maryland at College Park. She also attended the Institute for Educational Management at Harvard. Dr. Lapovsky is the author of several articles and has been a frequent speaker on topics ranging from women's leadership to budgeting and resource management in higher education. Her most recent work and speaker presentations have been on tuition discounting. She serves on many professional boards including the Executive Board of the American Council of Education/National Network of Women Leaders and the Tuition Exchange Board, chairs the Institutional Financial Aid Task Force of the National Association of College and University Business Officers, and has served as the Treasurer of Middle States Association of Schools and Colleges.

WILLIAM F. LASHER is Vice Provost for Planning and Assessment at the University of Texas at Austin. He is also professor of educational administration and has served as the director of the UT Austin graduate program in higher education administration. He teaches courses in Higher Education Finance, Higher Education Business Management, Institutional Research and Planning, and Higher Education Legislative Issues. He has also served as Associate Vice President for Budget and Institutional Studies, Director of Institutional Studies, and Associate Dean of the College of Education, all at the UT Austin. He is a Past President of the Association for Institutional Research. He holds a doctorate in higher education from the University of Michigan, a master's degree in college student personnel from Indiana University, and a bachelor's degree in psychology from the University of Rochester.

DARRELL R. LEWIS, Ph.D. in economics, is a Professor of Educational Policy and Administration at the University of Minnesota. Professor Lewis has over 30 years' experience in the employment of economic analysis to examine evaluation and policy questions in the fields of education and disability policy studies. He has authored or co-authored more than 150 books, monographs, journal articles and book chapters and has been a frequent consultant to international, national, state and local agencies in matters of policy, research and evaluation. His current research interests are in the economics of higher education, economic evaluation of education and training, and disability and equity policy studies.

MICHAEL MUMPER is Professor of Political Science and is currently the chair of the department at Ohio University. He holds a Ph.D. from the University of Maryland-College Park in Government and Politics. His area of research specialization is American public policy. In particular his research focuses on government efforts to increase the access and affordability of higher education. He has published articles and reviews in the *Journal of Higher Education*, *The Review of Higher Education*, the *Journal of Education Finance*, the *Journal of Student Financial Aid*, *Urban Education*, *Educational Policy*, *Polity*, and the *Social Science Journal*. His 1996 book, *Removing College Price Barriers: What Government Has Done and Why It Hasn't Worked*, was published by the State University of New York Press as a part of the "Social Context of Education" series.

MICHAEL B. PAULSEN is Professor of Education and Coordinator of Graduate Studies in Higher Education in the Department of Educational Leadership, Counseling and Foundations at the University of New Orleans. He earned his Ph.D. in higher education and economics from the University of Iowa and his M.A. degree in economics from the University of Wisconsin-Milwaukee. His scholarly work in the economics and finance of higher education has been published in both economics and education journals, including *Economics of Education Review, Journal of Education Finance, The Journal of Higher Education, Research in Higher Education, The Review of Higher Education, Educational Evaluation and Policy Analysis*, and other research journals, as well as in his book, *College Choice*. Previously, he held faculty appointments in economics at Coe College and St. Ambrose University and subsequently joined the faculties in higher education at the University of Illinois and the University of Alabama. He is consulting editor for *Research in Higher Education*, associate editor for economics and finance of *Higher Education: Handbook of Theory and Research*, and Chair of the Budget Committee for the Association for the Study of Higher Education.

EDWARD P. ST. JOHN is a Professor in the Department of Educational Leadership and Policy Studies at Indiana University, where he also serves as Director of the Indiana Education Policy Center and Chair of the Higher Education Program. Dr. St. John has also published numerous studies of the impact of student financial aid on college choice and persistence, which have been published in *Research in Higher Education, The Journal of Higher Education* and other research journals. He authored *Prices, Productivity, and Investment* (an ASHE/ERIC Higher Education Report, 1994) and edited *Rethinking Tuition and Student Aid Strategies* (Jossey-Bass, 1995). He is currently working on his latest book, *Refinancing the College Dream*, forthcoming from Johns Hopkins University Press. Previously he has been a professor at the University of Dayton and the University of New Orleans. He also held policy analyst positions with the U. S. Department of Education and the Missouri Department of Education and served as a senior manager in the consulting industry. He holds an Ed. D. from Harvard University and M. Ed. and B. S. degrees from the University of California-Davis.

JOHN C. SMART is Professor of Higher Education at The University of Memphis and formerly was a member of the faculties at the University of Kentucky, Virginia Tech, and the University of Illinois at Chicago. He has served as the editor of *Research in Higher Education* since 1990 and formerly was the editor of *The Review of Higher Education* (1980-86). Professor Smart founded *Higher Education: Handbook of Theory and Research* and has served as editor of the annual volumes since its inception in 1985. He is the recipient of the Distinguished Service Award from the Association for the Study of Higher Education (1993), the Distinguished Career Research Award from the American Educational Research Association (Division J, 1997), and the Sydney Suslow Award from the Association for Institutional Research (1998).

ROBERT K. TOUTKOUSHIAN is the Executive Director of the Office of Policy Analysis for the University System of New Hampshire. He received his Ph.D. in economics from Indiana University in 1991, where he specialized in Finance and Econometrics. Dr. Toutkoushian has published research on the following topics: gender equity for faculty and professional staff in higher education, the determinants of graduate program ratings, an analysis of state appropriations for higher education, the effects of marital status and race/ethnicity on faculty compensation, the use of cost functions for policymaking in higher education, the effects of time allocation on the research productivity of faculty, and an analysis of whether family income and educational attainment affect the initial postsecondary education choices of students in New Hampshire.

RICHARD A. VOORHEES is Associate Vice President for Instruction and Student Services for the Community Colleges of Colorado. His administrative and faculty careers span a variety of institutions including tribal, suburban, and urban community colleges, a research university and a comprehensive four-year institution. His colleagues recently recognized his contributions to community colleges when he was awarded the Practitioners Award by the National Council for Planning and Research. He has served as an academic dean, chief student affairs officer, and campus director of institutional research. Previous work in the area of higher education finance includes a Jossey-Bass sourcebook entitled, *Researching Student Financial Aid*. He also has contributed to the literature of student retention, assessment, and marketing research.

WILLIAM ZUMETA is Professor in the Daniel J. Evans School of Public Affairs and College of Education at the University of Washington. He has also taught at UCLA, the University of British Columbia, and Claremont Graduate University. Professor Zumeta has written extensively on public policy and private higher education, higher education finance and accountability, and policies related to graduate education and the PhD labor market. His work has been sponsored by such agencies as the National Science Foundation, Spencer Foundation, Pew Charitable Trusts, Lilly Endowment, and Alfred P. Sloan Foundation, as well as various national associations and government agencies. He is the author of two books and numerous articles and chapters in the higher education, economics and public policy literatures.

Introduction[1]

Michael B. Paulsen and John C. Smart

We believe that higher education finance is reemerging as a matter of tremendous importance, and as a field of study with the potential to both inform and forearm decision makers as they grapple with the wide range of challenges that characterize the rapidly changing, uncertain and complex environment of the higher education enterprise. However, as we venture into the 21st century, we join others in expressing our impression and concern that federal, state and institutional policies and practices appear to be in a period in which substantial changes in policies and practices are taking place, but without the benefit of a thorough analytic approach and foundation for insightful policy formation, implementation and evaluation. For example, in the Preface to their recent book, *Public and Private Financing of Higher Education*, Callan and Finney (1997), assert that "it would be difficult to identify a public policy area that has undergone as much change with as little public discussion or explicit policy direction as the financing of American higher education in recent years" (p. xi).

It is easy to identify examples of such change. The federal devolution has shifted obligations for various social programs from Washington to state capitols, and thereby has intensified the competition between higher education and other powerful claims on state budgets (Roherty, 1997). As the shares of institutional revenues derived from state appropriations to public institutions and federal grants and contracts to both private and public institutions have decreased (Breneman and Finney, 1997), tuition growth at public and private four-year colleges and universities has outpaced inflation every year since 1980 (College Board, 1999; Lewis, 1989; Paulsen, 2000). The responsibility for financing higher education continues to shift away from government or public sources and toward students and their families; institutions in both private and public sectors continue to derive an expanding share of their resources from tuition revenue paid by students (Kane, 1999; McPherson and Schapiro, 1998). And federal financial aid to students continues its shift away from grants toward loans (Hearn, 1998). Responses of both public and private institutions have included expanded use of institutional aid or tuition discounting to attract students (McPherson and Schapiro, 1998) and expanded efforts to increase private giving (U.S. Department of Education, 1999, Tables 332, 333).

---

[1] We would like to express our appreciation to Jim Hearn for his thoughtful contribution of ideas toward the preparation of this essay.

In an insightful, if somewhat overstated, view of recent developments, Bruce Johnstone (1999) has heightened our awareness of the fundamental nature and extent of recent changes by pointing out that "the fabric of the American 'system' of financial assistance and tuition policy seems to be unraveling" (p. 3). For example, the overarching goals of our financial aid system appear to be shifting from "access" to "affordability" (King, 1999), as evidenced by the substantial increase in the proportion of merit- versus need-based grants to students from both state and institutional sources (Kane, 1999; McPherson and Schapiro, 1998). These shifts in roles, responsibilities and resources are unlikely to moderate. Instead, they are more likely to persist, and perhaps even accelerate. As explained by Kane (1999), "the next fifteen years will offer little respite as demographic forces increase the pressure on higher education budgets with a rebound in the number of college-age youth of all income levels" (p. 3).

Policy analysts Callan and Finney (1997) have also observed that the "respective responsibilities of students, families, colleges and universities, and government have altered significantly, but with little debate and without any public policy consensus" (p. xi). In the absence of careful discussion and debate, the relative shares of educational costs covered by students compared with government or public sources have been altered without adequate attention to, and analysis of, the social benefits and the social rates of return to investment in higher education, or the social efficiency of such a reallocation of our nation's resources (Paulsen, 1996).

Tuition has increased relentlessly, but apparently without adequate attention to the shifting patterns of potential inequities in access or choice in higher education (McPherson and Schapiro, 1998), or to the latest research on how students respond differently to such increases according to income level, race, and type of institution attended (Heller, 1997). And with the apparent aim of enhancing access and choice, loans have come to dominate federal financial aid to students while the purchasing power of Pell grants has been allowed to diminish, even though price-response research indicates that students are significantly more sensitive to the availability of grants than to loans in their enrollment decisions (Heller, 1997).

Moreover, while states have experienced consistent increases in tuition at their public and private institutions, they have not been as consistent in their coordination of tuition and financial aid policies (Griswold and Marine, 1996). As a result, the market-model hypothesis about the high-tuition, high-aid approach to public finance has not been meaningfully tested in states where tuition increases have not been offset by commensurate, need-based increases in state grants to students (Hossler, et al., 1997). Finally, the combination of tuition growth and tighter limits on state budgets has led state agencies to conduct studies of faculty workload (Meyer, 1998) and require that institutions provide adequate educational services with fewer resources (St. John, 1994). However, such actions appear to have been taken with only minimal attention to the underlying economic theories of costs and productivity that can inform such policies and strategies (Hoenack and Collins, 1990).

OVERVIEW OF THE BOOK

The central purpose of this book is to provide a set of rigorous, but accessible and workable, frameworks within which to build strong analytic foundations to better inform the development, implementation and evaluation of policies related to the finance of higher education. There are five distinct parts of the book, each contributing to the purpose in a special way. Part I presents the fundamental facts about where institutions get their funds to cover the costs of educating their students and where students get their funds to pay the out-of-pocket expenses of their college education. Part II provides readers with opportunities to study, learn and apply a range of economic perspectives, theories and models that serve as important and relevant foundations for the study of higher education finance. Part III examines the nature and development of financial policies at the federal and state levels and the special challenges posed by the interplay between rational-empirical perspectives and political-contextual influences in the development, nature, implementation, effectiveness, and evaluation of financial policies. Part IV of this book addresses special topics and issues that are important but rarely receive substantial attention in books on the subject of higher education finance. Finally, Part V provides a critical examination of the field of higher education finance, both synthesizing and critiquing implicit and explicit themes in the book and in the field, and raises challenges for future inquiry, policy analysis and advancement of knowledge in the field.

The chapters in Part I present the most fundamental facts and issues from the perspectives of institutions and students in the finance of higher education. Ultimately, two of the most important sets of financial facts to know about an institution relate to where it gets its funds and how it spends them. And from the perspective of most students and their families, the most important issues relate to how "affordable" college really is and where students get their funds to pay for their college education. Of course, society—either through government or private agencies and individuals—is an important source of funds or "subsidies" for both institutions and students (Winston, 1999).

The first requirement of any substantial analysis of financial policies in higher education is a prior and comprehensive knowledge and understanding of the answers to the two most fundamental and revealing financial questions about the higher education enterprise: "Where does the money come from?" and "Where does the money go?" In Chapter 1, Rob Toutkoushian provides the reader with a comprehensive presentation and analysis of the primary sources of revenues and expenditures for public and private institutions of higher education. Numerous tables and figures serve to thoroughly document and highlight notable trends—from 1975 to 1995—in the sources of revenues and the functional uses of expenditures, illustrating differences in such trends between the private and public sectors. The analysis also features an examination of the relative shares of the expenses an institution incurs in educating its students paid by students and society. An appendix presents clear definitions for all measures of different types of revenues and expenditures examined in the chapter. In combination, these resources provide a rich reference for policy analysts, administrators, researchers and students interested in the financial aspects of the higher education enterprise.

In chapter 2, Sandy Baum examines a wide range of issues related to the affordability of a college education. Written in a very accessible, even conversational style, this chapter begins with an insightful investigation of the meaning of "affordability," presents data on changes in tuition and other costs of college at different types of institutions, and examines where students get funds to pay for college. Changes in the costs of college are related to various indicators of the ability of students and their families to pay; such as trends in family income, saving, and borrowing. Special attention is paid to the types and amounts of financial aid available in the form of loans and grants from federal, state and institutional sources. In addition, this chapter examines a cross-cutting theme regarding the differences in the affordability of college for students from low-, middle-, and upper-income backgrounds.

Higher education is a professional field of study in which inquiry has been well informed by the strong and familiar presence of the many useful concepts and theories drawn from disciplines such as political science, sociology, psychology, history and philosophy. To date, higher education researchers and policy analysts have drawn remarkably less on the concepts and theories of economics, one of the prominent policy sciences. We believe that the study of higher education finance could be substantially enriched by building appropriate concepts and theories from the discipline of economics into the mainstream literature in forms that are more explicit and elaborate. In particular, this "would give higher education scholars a greater range of foundations and perspectives from which to do theoretical and empirical work that would expand our understanding of higher education finance and associated policies" (Paulsen, 2000, p. 40). These perspectives from economics are intended to encourage and inform discussion, debate, and analysis of important issues such as those discussed above, as well as better inform the development, implementation, and evaluation of related financial policies and practices.

Therefore, the chapters in Part II are intended to address this gap in the literature and we view them as foundational to an enriched study of the chapters in Parts I, III and IV of the book. To establish this conceptual and analytic foundation, the chapters in Part II cover the following economic perspectives on higher education finance: theories of investment in human capital (Paulsen, Chapter 3); equity, efficiency and the economics of the public sector (Paulsen, Chapter 4); economic theories of costs and productivity (Lewis and Dundar, Chapter 5); and the marketplace economics of college tuition (Paulsen, Chapter 6). Chapters 3 and 4 were written especially for this volume, while chapters 5 and 6 were previously published in *Higher Education: Handbook of Theory and Research*, in 1999 and 2000, respectively. Even though chapters 5 and 6 were first published very recently, the author of each chapter has written a new epilogue to update, reexamine and elaborate on the themes of their recent analyses in light of the very latest developments in the field.

An additional role of the chapters in Part II is to provide the volume with some of the features of a textbook, rather than only a collection of reviews of the research literature. Toward this end, each chapter provides detailed explanations, examples, and applications—for example, of the analysis of contemporary financial policies in higher education—using the economic concepts and theories to make them more accessible and meaningful for non-economists with interests in higher education finance. Chapter authors have not avoided or downplayed the terminology and jargon of economics. Instead, they have emphasized clarity and thoroughness of explanation, as well as the use of examples and applications to higher education, in presenting many of the most relevant and useful of economic concepts for the study of higher education finance.

We view the nature and development of financial policy as characterized not only by what is straightforward and explicit, or what appears to be rational and empirically supported, but also by what is implicit, indeterminate, and complex. Consistent with this theme, the chapters in *Part III* examine the nature and development of financial policies at the federal and state levels. However, the chapters in Part III also examine the special challenges posed by the ever-present interplay between rational-empirical perspectives and political-contextual-personal influences in the development, nature, implementation, effectiveness, and evaluation of financial policies. In chapter 7, Jim Hearn examines in detail the political history and the palpable paradox of growth in federal student aid programs from 1960 to 1990. Chapters 8 and 9 examine the nature and effects of state-level policies on institutions and students in the public and private sectors, as articulated by Michael Mumper and Bill Zumeta, respectively. These three chapters were previously published in *Higher Education: Handbook of Theory and Research*, in 1993, 1998, and 1997, respectively. Therefore, the authors of each of these chapters have written new epilogues for their chapters that both update and reexamine, with fresh, contemporary perspectives, the themes of their earlier analyses in light of the latest developments in the field.

Part IV includes five chapters that address special topics and issues that are important but rarely receive substantial attention in general books on the subject of higher education finance. In chapter 10, St. John, Asker and Hu articulate the "student choice" construct as a way of expanding our thinking about student decision-making and to provide a framework within which to examine the roles of financial policies in students' college choice and persistence decisions. The student-choice construct serves to focus attention on those student decision-making processes that are responsive to both socio-economic forces such as employment opportunities, and educational trends and policies such as prices and subsidies. Students make decisions in unique, situated contexts, based on their perceptions of opportunities for education and employment, all of which, in combination, lead to diverse individual outcomes of development and attainment.

In chapter 11, Jim Hearn examines issues of equity in access to higher education. In particular, he examines the differences by socioeconomic status in the effects of financial and other policies on access to postsecondary education in terms of both aspirations and participation. This chapter takes the reader to the forefront of thought about equity and access in higher education, asserting that both the meaning of "access" and the appropriate equity-enhancing policies to pursue will have to be reconsidered in light of a series of changes in the form of new kinds of students (e.g., adult learners as consumers), enrollments (e.g., on-line distance enrollment), providers (e.g., profit-oriented virtual universities), faculty (e.g., part-time and virtual faculty), markets (e.g., global and fluid), and outcomes (e.g., practical knowledge and certificates instead of prestigious degrees).

In chapter 12, Breneman, Doti and Lapovsky examine the analytics of tuition discounting as the predominant means by which many private colleges and universities achieve enrollment targets for their freshmen classes. This chapter presents a microeconomic theory of the behavior of private colleges to examine college decision-making behavior in terms of the key relationships between tuition, enrollment, composition of the student body, and tuition discounting practices. The analysis addresses the changing roles of merit-based and need-based institutional aid in achieving enrollment goals. The presentation of recent data on current tuition-discounting practices highlights the similarities and differences between highly selective and less selective private colleges and the changing meaning and importance of the published price relative to the availability of price discounts. This chapter clearly redefines the current boundaries of the field and advances our understanding of tuition discounting in both theory and practice.

The finance of community and technical colleges is often overlooked in research and writing on the finance of higher education. In chapter 13, Rick Voorhees addresses the important and practical issues associated with the finance of such institutions, including the special role of state and local sources of revenue for such institutions and the importance of the tuition charged by such institutions—the tuition which is often viewed as the cost that ultimately enables access to the least-costly or most-affordable postsecondary education alternative. These issues are examined relative to the well-known multifarious mission of such institutions.

In chapter 14, Bill Lasher and Debbi Greene cover the traditional topics about budgeting in higher education, including the budget process, factors that influence budgets, the various types of budgeting (e.g., incremental, formula, program, zero-based, performance, incentive, and cost center budgeting) in the main text of their chapter. Their chapter was previously published in *Higher Education: Handbook of Theory and Research*, in 1993; therefore, the authors have written an extensive new epilogue for their chapter that updates and reexamines the themes of their earlier analyses, but also expands the scope of their chapter in light of the latest developments in the field. In particular, they offer an in-depth analysis of the impact on budgeting practices due to new students, new conceptions of delivery systems, changes in attention to accreditation and accountability, and most notably, the growing and more central importance of performance funding and responsibility center budgeting in higher education.

Finally, in chapter 15 of Part V, St. John and Paulsen critically examine the field of higher education finance, synthesize and critique the overt and covert themes in the previous chapters in the book and in the field, and raise challenges for future inquiry and advancement of knowledge in the field. In addition, this chapter addresses the unique relationship between the pure-hard discipline and policy science of economics and the applied-soft field of higher education finance and policy analysis, as well as the interesting and sustained tension that has evolved between them. The chapter examines the productivity of that tension for the advancement of knowledge in the field of higher education finance.

AUDIENCES FOR THE BOOK

This book is intended to provide a new and substantial resource that will be useful to a variety of groups or audiences who want to become better informed about the economic theories and models, and the federal, state and institutional policies and practices that constitute the primary subject matter and tools of policy analysis in the area of higher education finance. More specifically, we intend our book to serve as a *text* for faculty and students in graduate courses in higher education finance, as a *scholarly foundation* for future research among scholars in the field, and as a *reference and resource* targeted for interested faculty, administrators, business officers, financial aid officials, institutional researchers, and policy analysts at a variety of different types of institutions and agencies at the state, regional and national levels. In other words, we see the audience for the new reader as including faculty and students in the Association for the Study of Higher Education (ASHE) and Division J of the American Educational Research Association (AERA-J), but extending well beyond those groups to audiences comprising members in the national, regional and state (as appropriate) divisions of the Association for Institutional Research (AIR), the National Association of Student Financial Aid Administrators (NASFAA), the National Association of College and University Business Officers (NACUBO), the National Association of State Budget Officers (NASBO), the Society for College and University Planning (SCUP), the State Higher Education Executive Officers (SHEEO), the American Association of State Colleges and Universities (AASCU), the National Association of Independent Colleges and Universities (NAICU), the American Association of Community Colleges (AACC), the National Association of State Universities and Land Grant Colleges (NASULG), the American Association of University Administrators (AAUA), the American Council on Education (ACE), and other groups with interests in the finance of higher education.

ACKNOWLEDGMENTS

It takes many dedicated people to complete a project of this scope, and we recognize that our own contributions to this volume would have been inadequate without the invaluable efforts and support of many others. We are especially grateful to the authors who have written the chapters for this volume. They have labored to produce chapters of the highest quality in terms of both their standards of scholarship and their thorough attention to the very latest work in the field. We believe that this volume has been strengthened by the valuable contributions of economists Dave Breneman, Sandy Baum, Jim Doti, Halil Dundar, Lucie Lapovsky, Darrell Lewis, and Rob Toutkoushian; as well as by the fine scholarly work of a talented set of social scientists and higher education policy analysts, including Debbi Greene, Jim Hearn, Bill Lasher, Michael Mumper, Ed St. John, Rick Voorhees, Bill Zumeta, Shouping Hu, and Erik Asker. We also wish to express our appreciation to quite a list of talented scholars who served as reviewers of earlier versions of the chapters, enhancing the quality of the chapters in the process. We offer a special thanks to Jim Hearn and Ed St. John, each of whom contributed two chapters to this volume, and we would like to express our gratitude for the valuable contributions of Nasrin Fatima, research assistant and doctoral candidate at the University of New Orleans.

Finally, we express our deepest appreciation and gratitude to our immediate family members—Laurey, Emily and Bunty—for their ever-present support and understanding throughout this undertaking and completion of this project.

References

Breneman, D.W., and Finney, J.E. (1997). The changing landscape: Higher education finance in the 1990s. In P.M. Callan and J.E. Finney (eds.), *Public And Private Financing Of Higher Education: Shaping Public Policy For The Future* (pp. 30-59). Phoenix, AZ: The American Council on Education and The Oryx Press.

Callan, P.M., and Finney, J.E. (1997). Preface. In P.M. Callan and J.E. Finney (eds.), *Public And Private Financing Of Higher Education: Shaping Public Policy For The Future* (pp. xi-xiii). Phoenix, AZ: The American Council on Education and The Oryx Press.

College Board. (1999). *Trends In Student Aid: 1989 To 1999*. New York: College Entrance Examination Board.

Griswold, C.P., and Marine, G.M. (1996). Political influences on state policy: Higher-tuition, higher-aid, and the real world. *The Review of Higher Education* 19 (4): 361-389.

Hearn, J.C. (1998). The growing loan orientation in federal financial aid policies: A historical perspective. In R. Fossey and M. Bateman (eds.), *Condemning Students To Debt: College Loans And Public Policy* (pp. 47-75). New York: Teachers College Press.

Heller, D.E. (1997). Student price response in higher education: An update to Leslie and Brinkman. *Journal of Higher Education* 68 (6): 624-659.

Hoenack, S.A., and Collins, E.L. (1990). *The Economics Of American Universities*. Albany: State University of New York Press.

Hossler, D., et al., (1997). State funding for higher education: The Sisyphean task. *Journal of Higher Education* 68 (2): 160-190.

Johnstone, D.B. (1999). Introduction. In J.E. King (ed.). *Financing a College Education: How it Works, How it's Changing*. Phoenix, AZ: The American Council on Education and The Oryx Press.

Kane, T.J. (1999). *The Price of Admission: Rethinking How Americans Pay for College*. Washington, DC: Brookings.

King, J.E. (1999). Conclusion. In J.E. King (ed.). *Financing a College Education: How it Works, How it's Changing*. Phoenix, AZ: The American Council on Education and The Oryx Press.

Lewis, G.L. (1989). Trends in student aid: 1963-64 to 1988-89. *Research in Higher Education* 30 (6): 547-561.

McPherson, M.S., and Schapiro, M.O. (1998). *The Student Aid Game*. Princeton, NJ: Princeton University Press.

Meyer, K.A. (1998). *Faculty Workload Studies: Perspectives, Needs, And Future Directions*. ASHE-ERIC Higher Education Report Volume 26, No. 1. Washington, DC: The George Washington University, Graduate School of Education and Human Development.

Paulsen, M.B. (1996). Higher education and state workforce productivity. *Thought and Action: NEA Higher Education Journal* 12(1): 55-77.

Paulsen, M.B. (2000). Economic perspectives on rising college tuition: A theoretical and empirical analysis. In J.C. Smart (ed.). *Higher Education: Handbook of Theory and Research* Volume XV (pp. 39-104). New York: Agathon Press.

Roherty, B.M. (1997). The price of passive resistance in financing higher education. In P. M. Callan and J. E. Finney (eds.), *Public And Private Financing Of Higher Education: Shaping Public Policy For The Future* (pp. 3-29). Phoenix, AZ: The American Council on Education and The Oryx Press.

St. John, E.P. (1994). *Prices, Productivity, And Investment: Assessing Financial Strategies In Higher Education*, ASHE-ERIC Higher Education Report No. 3. Washington, DC: The George Washington University, School of Education and Human Development.

U.S. Department of Education, National Center for Education Statistics. (1999). *The Digest of Education Statistics 1999*. Washington, DC: U.S. Government Printing Office.

Winston, G.C. (1999). College costs: Who pays and why it matters so. In J.E. King (ed.). *Financing a College Education: How it Works, How it's Changing*. Phoenix, AZ: The American Council on Education and The Oryx Press.

PART I

The Revenues, Expenditures, Costs, and Affordability of Higher Education

Chapter 1

TRENDS IN REVENUES AND EXPENDITURES FOR PUBLIC AND PRIVATE HIGHER EDUCATION[1]

Robert K. Toutkoushian

INTRODUCTION

As the 21st century begins, institutions of higher education find themselves under intense scrutiny and criticism from a variety of stakeholders, including students, parents, legislators, and taxpayers for the level and growth of student charges.[2] To illustrate, the United States Congress created the Higher Education Cost Commission in 1997 to investigate the issues surrounding postsecondary costs and prices, and in 1998 charged the Commission of Education Statistics to conduct a national study of expenditures and tuition and fees. In an interview with the candidates for President of the United States in the year 2000 *(Chronicle of Higher Education,* 2000), four of the five characterized higher education as being "too expensive." Most of the candidates recommended making college more affordable by implementing a variety of saving plans to help students pay for their postsecondary education, although George Bush suggested that "colleges must also do their part to contain the skyrocketing cost of tuition."

It is no secret to most observers that the price of attending college has increased dramatically over time. The College Board (1999) estimates that for 1999-2000 the average

[1] The author would like to thank the following individuals for their helpful comments and suggestions on earlier drafts of this chapter: William Becker, Larry Goldstein at NACUBO, Edward MacKay, Michael Paulsen, and Mark Putnam. All correspondences may be sent to the author at the following address: Myers Financial Center, 27 Concord Rd., Durham, NH 03824 (e-mail: r_toutkoush@usnh.unh.edu).

[2]It is important to distinguish at the outset what is meant by the terms "price" and "cost" in higher education. As used here, costs refer to the expenditures associated with the delivery of instruction, research, and public service, and price is the expense incurred by students and their families to attend college. For the remainder of this chapter, the terms "price" and "student charges" will be used interchangeably, as will the terms "cost" and "expenditure." See the report by the College Board (1999) for a similar description of terms.

sticker price for attending a four-year institution was $15,380 in the private sector and $3,356 for public institutions, and that room, board, and other expenses can often add $7,000 or more to these totals. During the 1980s, tuition and fees rose at two to three times the rate of inflation, and after accounting for the effects of inflation in the 1990s, tuition and fees rose by 51 percent in public institutions and 34 percent in private institutions (College Board, 1999). With regard to ability to pay, the College Board report on pricing also shows that for families in the lowest income quintile, the price of attending a private four-year institution has gone from 91 percent of their income in 1971-72 to over 160 percent of their income in 1999-2000 (Baum, Chapter 2). The price of attending public institutions, as a percentage of family income, also increased substantially, but less dramatically, during the period. Speculation has arisen as to whether this trend has had a negative impact on providing access to higher education. Aggregate statistics, however, seem to suggest that access to higher education has not declined over time. Furthermore, concerns over high tuition may be overstated because over 60 percent of students in four-year institutions are enrolled in colleges and universities with tuition and fees that are less than $5,000 (College Board, 1999), and many students do not pay the full sticker price because of the substantial discounts offered on the prices charged to students through institutional scholarships and grants (Baum, Chapter 2; Breneman, Doti and Lapovsky, Chapter 12).

Concerns about tuition have naturally led to a search for explanations and possible remedies. In response to the Congressional mandate of 1998, for example, the National Center for Education Statistics initiated a request for proposals to conduct a national study of college costs. An excellent review of many of the potential explanations for tuition increases can be found in Paulsen (Chapter 6), who identifies cost-side factors such as falling government appropriations and increasing administrative expenditures, and demand-side factors including the stronger labor market for college graduates. Halstead (1998) attributes rising tuition to four main factors: (1) increased student responsibility to pay for their education, (2) inflation in the prices of goods and services needed to produce educational outcomes, (3) an increase in the resources employed per student, and (4) growth in student aid programs.

Not surprisingly, much of the blame for rising tuition has fallen on the rising cost of providing higher education services. The National Center for Education Statistics (1999, p. 361) reports that between 1969-70 and 1995-96, per-student expenditures have increased fivefold in nominal terms and by 20 percent after taking into account the effects of inflation. Questions have arisen as to why costs have risen faster than inflation and why they often vary dramatically across institutions in both the public and private sectors. At the same time, some college rankings such as those produced by *U.S. News and World Report* reward those institutions having higher per-student expenditure levels with higher rankings relative to their peers. Since a significant portion of normal educational expenditures is subsidized by other revenue sources, student charges may also be influenced by the level of revenues; hence rising prices could be due to the rising costs of providing a postsecondary education, or the falling financial support for subsidizing education, or some combination of the two (Paulsen, Chapter 6).

This chapter is intended to provide the reader with an overview of models, data sources, and financial trends in higher education. Several reviews of revenue and/or expenditure trends for various types of institutions and time periods have appeared in the literature, including Harris (1962), O'Neill (1973), Bowen (1980), Froomkin (1990), Halstead (1991), Blasdell, McPherson, and Schapiro (1993), McPherson and Schapiro (1994), and Winston, Carbone, and Lewis (1998).[3] The data used in this chapter will be primarily drawn from the twenty-year period from 1974-75 through 1994-95. While the federal government has collected financial data on institutions of higher education for over seventy years, the data from the mid-1970s through the mid-1990s are readily available to analysts, and the subcomponents of revenues and expenditures are more consistently defined following the 1974-75 fiscal year.

The chapter begins with a brief discussion of several conceptual models that have been used to describe the behavior of postsecondary institutions, and how they relate to an understanding of financial issues. The major data elements that are available on colleges and universities are then reviewed, followed by an examination of trends in revenues and expenditures for public and private institutions. Particular attention is given to changes in the sources of revenues and expenditures, how they differ between the public and private sectors, and changes in the portion of expenditures that are subsidized by various sources.

The Economic Behavior of Postsecondary Institutions

To review all of the conceptual models that have been suggested to explain the behavior of colleges and universities would merit a chapter in itself, and thus this section will only provide a brief overview of some of the major theories and how they relate to the immediate purpose at hand. The natural starting place for modeling the economic behavior of colleges and universities is the theory of the firm—that is, a collection of economic theories of organizational behavior. There are a number of similarities between postsecondary institutions and for-profit firms that have led some to apply business models to academic institutions. Colleges and universities are similar to firms in that they use inputs or raw materials (e.g., faculty, students, machinery, land) to provide services to customers (e.g., students). Institutions receive revenues from their customers— and others—to pay for the costs of producing these services, and having access to more financial resources presumably allows an institution to purchase more and better inputs or factors of production.

One of the central tenets of the theory of the firm is that, in the long run, the average cost of production can vary with the level of output due to the presence of economies and diseconomies of scale (Lewis and Dundar, Chapter 5). Average cost curves are usually depicted as being "U-shaped." As output initially rises, average costs fall because larger institutions experience the greater efficiencies of large-scale technologies, such as the high

---

[3]O'Neill (1973) and Bowen (1980) focus their attention on financial trends from the 1930s through the late 1960s. In contrast, the studies by McPherson and Schapiro (1994) and Winston, Carbone, and Lewis (1998) compare educational finances for institutions from the mid 1980s to the early and mid 1990s. McPherson and Schapiro (1994) note that there have been few recent attempts to study higher education revenues and expenditures at the national level.

student-faculty ratios available in the mass-class setting; however, the average cost curve will eventually rise as output increases to a level that promotes inefficiencies of coordination and communication associated with additional layers of bureaucracy/administration.

Following this analogy, a number of researchers have examined the relationship between costs and output (usually approximated by enrollments) in an attempt to identify the optimal size of a postsecondary institution and determine if there are economies or diseconomies of scale from changes in the average size of institutions (Hanson, 1964; Maynard, 1971; McLaughlin, et al., 1980; Brinkman, 1981; Cohn, Rhine, and Santos, 1989; deGroot, McMahon, and Volkwein, 1991; Getz, Siegfried, and Zhang, 1991; Nelson and Hevert, 1992; Koshal and Koshal, 1995; Toutkoushian, 1999). These and other studies also considered whether costs per student were affected by factors such as the student/faculty ratio, average faculty salary, type of institution (e.g., Carnegie classification, public vs. private status), and geographic location.[4] It has been observed that the per-student costs are approximately 50 percent higher in private institutions than in public institutions (Winston and Yen, 1995), with only half of this difference being attributed to factors such as faculty salaries, enrollments, and research intensity (Toutkoushian, 1999).

The analogy of a college as a firm, however, has its limitations. Since colleges and universities produce multiple outputs in the areas of teaching, research, and public service, and these outputs are hard to define and properly measure, the notion of cost per unit of output in higher education is elusive at best. A commonly used practice is to simply divide expenditures in designated categories by some measure of enrollments to derive an expenditure per student figure. As noted by Bowen, this is "...an expedient that can be tolerated but not commended." (1980, p.6) The problem with this metric is that since a portion of the expenditures in certain categories may have been incurred for purposes other than teaching, the resulting expenditure per student measure might be biased upward. As an example, the largest single component of the expenditure category for instruction is faculty salaries. In institutions where faculty members spend a significant amount of time on research, some portion of their base salaries are intended to cover costs associated with research activities and thus to attribute all of these salaries to the teaching of students is inaccurate. With few exceptions, however, the expenditure data collected by the federal government are not differentiated by their intended use. Cohn, Rhine, and Santos (1989), deGroot, McMahon, and Volkwein (1991), Toutkoushian (1999), and others address the multi-product nature of postsecondary institutions in their estimation of cost functions, but such approaches by necessity still rely on crude proxies for teaching and research outputs (Lewis and Dundar, Chapter 5). Given the data limitations, analysts have little choice but to follow the convention of reporting expenditurs per student. Nonetheless, analysts need to understand and acknowledge the limitations of this practice.

A second problem with applying the business model to higher education is that in

[4]The literature on institutional costs dates back to Allen (1915; 1917). McNeely (1937) and Kilzer (1937) are among the first to observe differences in per-student expenditures across institutions. The interested reader is directed to surveys by Witmer (1971) and Brinkman (1990) for more information on the history of inquiry on this topic.

the theory of the firm, it is assumed that firms behave as if they were trying to maximize their profits. While most analysts agree that this assumption does not apply to higher education, there is no consensus on what is the appropriate alternative.[5] Bowen (1980), for example, argues that in their never-ending quest for greater prestige, institutions attempt to raise as much money as possible and then spend all that they receive. According to this view, which Bowen refers to as the "revenue theory of cost," expenditures are a function of revenues and will therefore rise indefinitely as long as colleges and universities continue to generate more revenue. An equally compelling case can be made for inverting this model, however, because many institutions in the public sector set tuition rates at levels allowing them to meet budgeted operating expenses. Rather than expenditures being a function of revenues, this would imply that the reverse is true: revenues are a function of expenditures. Brinkman (1990, p.110) argues that "...institutions neither minimize nor maximize costs; instead, they operate within a range of accepted norms for production relationships..."

The type of model assumed for higher education is important because it will have a bearing on our understanding of how prices are set and the possible reasons why they change over time. As noted by Winston, Carbone, and Lewis (1998), profit-seeking entities typically set the price for their goods or service at some level above the cost of production, with the difference being their profit. In this situation, rising costs contribute directly to rising prices, assuming that profit margins are held constant. Since most higher education institutions are not-for-profit entities, it can be seen how the business model has naturally led some observers to focus on rising costs as the only explanation for rising student charges.

Winston, Carbone, and Lewis (1998) introduced a useful framework for examining how prices are set in the postsecondary education market. While they do not offer an alternative model of institutional behavior, they observed that the price charged to students rarely covers all of the costs incurred by the institution, and that institutions rely on subsidies to fully fund their operations. In their formulation, the price equation becomes Price = Cost – Subsidy, where "Subsidy" can be thought of as a catchall category for revenues from non-student sources, such as various levels of government and private individuals.[6] Under this identity, it can be seen that rising tuition rates could be due to either rising costs, or falling subsidies, or a combination of the two forces. Accordingly, both costs and subsidies have a bearing on college prices, and to better understand the changing nature of pricing in higher education, it is necessary to examine both the revenue and expenditure sides of the ledger.

---

[5]A notable exception is offered by Paulsen (Chapter 6), who argues that colleges and universities operate in a monopolistically competitive market and attempt to maximize their discretionary budget. The fact that highly-selective private institutions such as Harvard continue to set prices below their market-clearing levels (as evidenced by the excess demand for places in their freshman classes) is further evidence that even private institutions do not generally behave as profit maximizers.

[6]There is debate within higher education researchers as to whether these subsidies should be viewed as "student subsidies" or "institutional subsidies." Given this debate, Breneman (2000) argues in favor of labeling the subsidy as "non-tuition revenue." The term subsidy is retained here without making any distinction as to whether it should be viewed as a subsidy to students or to institutions.

Primary Sources of Revenue and Expenditure Data

Dating back to the 1930s, the federal government has used survey instruments to collect financial data in various forms from colleges and universities in the United States. The three main surveys that have been used are: (1) the Biennial Survey of Education in the United States; (2) the Higher Education General Information Survey (HEGIS); and (3) the Integrated Postsecondary Education Data Systems (IPEDS). These surveys asked institutions to report financial data on revenues and expenditures in selected categories at the institutional level over a twelve-month period corresponding to their fiscal year. In having "breadth but not depth," the data from these surveys are useful for examining general financial trends across sectors, but not for delving into the finer details of the financial situation at institutions.

The earliest source of financial data is the Biennial Survey of Education in the United States. This survey was first started in 1929-30, and was conducted every other year through 1963-64. Beginning in 1965-66, the federal government implemented the HEGIS as a means of annually collecting financial data at the institutional level. Since its inception, the HEGIS was conducted every year through 1987-88, and is the precursor to the IPEDS. A number of important changes were made in 1974-75 with regard to how revenues and expenditures were classified by the federal government. As a result, it is very difficult to compare current levels in the components of revenues and expenditures with those prior to 1974-75. The HEGIS did not require institutions to break down expenditures into their restricted and unrestricted components, and did not begin to collect data on government grants and contracts until 1974-75.[7]

The HEGIS was replaced in 1988-89 by the IPEDS, which is the current instrument used by the U.S. Department of Education to collect a wide range of data on higher education institutions in the United States. Beginning with the revenue side, the IPEDS collects information on revenues in the following major areas:

- tuition and fees
- appropriations from government sources (federal, state, local)
- grants and contracts from government sources (federal, state, local)
- private gifts, grants, and contracts
- endowment income
- sales and services of educational activities
- auxiliary enterprises
- hospitals
- other sources
- independent operations

More complete descriptions of each category are provided in the Appendix. Revenues in each of these categories are separated into restricted and unrestricted funds. Restricted funds represent the portion of the revenue from each source that can only be used for a specific purpose; in contrast, colleges and universities have full discretion over how they will use unrestricted revenues. The sum of the revenues from all of these categories equals the *cur-*

---

[7]In 1987, the HEGIS expanded the list of revenues that are grouped into the category of hospitals. Prior to 1987, only the revenue derived from the operation of hospitals was included in this category.

rent funds revenues for the institution. Many analysts, however, prefer to focus on only those revenue sources that are typically used to cover the mission-related activities (teaching, research, and service) at the institution. Accordingly, revenues from the sales and services of educational activities, auxiliary enterprises, hospitals, other sources, independent operations, and Pell Grant revenues can be subtracted from current funds revenues to yield what are referred to here as *education and general (E&G) revenues.*

On the expenditure side of the balance sheet, the IPEDS groups institutional expenditures into the following functional categories:

- instruction
- research
- public service
- academic support
- student services
- institutional support
- operations and maintenance of plant
- scholarships and fellowships
- mandatory and non-mandatory transfers
- auxiliary enterprises
- hospitals
- independent operations

These quantities are also defined in more detail in the Appendix. As with revenues, expenditures in each category are divided into unrestricted and restricted components, and beginning with the IPEDS, the amounts of each expenditure category allocated to salaries and wages were also collected. The sum total of all of these expenditure items represents the institution's current funds expenditures. Since expenditures for auxiliary enterprises, hospitals, and independent operations are not directly related to the provision of educational services, they are often subtracted from current funds expenditures, leaving what is known as educational and general (E&G) expenditures. Some analysts advocate going one step further, and subtract expenditures for research and public service from the E&G total in an effort to better isolate expenditures that are more directly related to the teaching mission of institutions. This can be misleading, however, because the resulting expenditure total still includes monies spent on research and public service. Since the subcategory for instruction includes all salaries and wages of faculty, some portion of this salary should be properly attributed to these other functions.

Before proceeding with an analysis of trends in revenues and expenditures, some caveats with these data should be highlighted. The institutional data collected by the IPEDS and its precursors are not without their limitations, especially when used for the purpose of comparisons across institutions. Financial information aggregated at the institution level may mask important differences across institutions in their academic missions, programmatic emphasis, and so on. Variations in accounting practices across institutions could result in the same expenditure item being grouped into different categories. As is true with most survey data, there are instances where data errors exist.

There are other points of contention as well. First, the practice of treating scholarships and fellowships as an expenditure item has been called into question by some who assert that it is more properly defined as a discount from tuition and fee revenue. The consensus among leaders in the field is that despite its label, scholarships and fellowships should be viewed as a revenue discount rather than an expenditure item.[8] Accordingly, two new quantities are defined here. *Net E&G expenditures* are computed as total E&G expenditures minus scholarship and fellowship expenditures. Likewise, *net E&G revenues* are found by subtracting scholarship and fellowship expenditures from gross tuition and fee revenues.

A second concern is that the expenditure categories do not reflect the value, depreciation or replacement cost for plant and equipment. This is an important limitation for analysts charged with trying to measure the true average cost per student, because the costs of making the facilities available are not captured by the IPEDS data. Using economics terminology, the IPEDS financial data typically represent components of variable costs and not fixed costs.

Changes in data collection and accounting practices can also have a bearing on the comparability of the data across institutions and over time. As noted earlier, the National Center for Education Statistics adopted a new classification scheme for financial data beginning in 1974-75. Even more troublesome for analysts interested in studying financial trends in higher education is the fact that starting in 1995, private institutions were no longer required by the Financial Accounting Standards Board to report financial data using the long-established fund accounting conventions used up to that time. This change effectively makes it impossible to compare the financial status of public and private institutions beginning with the 1996-97 fiscal year, as well as examine trends in components of revenues and expenditures for private institutions over time. Similar changes in the reporting requirements for public institutions have been mandated through the General Accounting Standards Board (GASB) and are slated to take effect by 2002. Finally, effective with the 2000-01 academic year, the IPEDS will move from the traditional paper-based collection form to a web-based collection form. As a result of funding problems, some items that have been collected in the areas of revenues and expenditures (such as the distinction between restricted and unrestricted funds) will be discontinued. Taken together, it will be extremely difficult for analysts to merge institutional financial data for the periods prior to and following 1996.

There are a handful of agencies that have facilitated access to institution-level financial data. The WebCASPAR system makes the HEGIS and the IPEDS data available to anyone with access to a web browser.[9] The system is relatively easy to use, but still requires practice and training through an on-line tutorial. John Minter Associates routinely collects the IPEDS data and makes them available to subscribers. The National Center for Education Statistics has developed several user-friendly interfaces for analysts to obtain financial data on institutions. For several years, NCES has produced annual editions in CD-ROM of the Integrated Postsecondary Education Data System

[8]As defined in the IPEDS, the items included under the category scholarships and fellowships include grants and scholarships received from federal, state, and local sources (including Pell Grants), as well as grants and scholarships paid by institutions.

[9]The WebCASPAR system is sponsored by the National Science Foundation, and can be accessed at the following URL: http://caspar.nsf.gov/cgi-bin/WebIC.exe?template=nsf/srs/webcasp/start.wi

and Education Statistics on Disk. In addition, NCES is developing a utility program for their web site that will allow individuals to easily obtain selected financial statistics on different groups of institutions. Finally, Research Associates of Washington and Kent Halstead have collected and assimilated financial data on institutions, and up through 1998 published books on *Higher Education Revenues and Expenditures* and *Inflation Measures for Schools, Colleges & Libraries*.

Trends in Higher Education Revenues and Expenditures

Table 1 provides a general overview of long-term trends from 1959-60 to 1994-95 in the revenues and expenditures for postsecondary institutions in the United States. The first two rows represent total current fund revenues and expenditures for all institutions. The third and fourth rows represent these current fund quantities on a per-student basis, and the following two rows show per-student revenues and expenditures after adjusting for inflation as measured by the Consumer Price Index. Finally, the last row contains information on total postsecondary enrollments for each year. The bottom section of the table reports average annual percentage changes in each of these quantities for the corresponding time periods.

Table 1: Trends in Current Funds Revenues and Expenditures in Higher Education, Selected Years 1959-60 to 1994-95

Category	1959-60	1969-70	1979-80	1989-90	1994-95
Current funds revenues (000's)	$5,785,537	$21,515,242	$58,519,982	$139,635,477	$189,120,570
Current funds expenditures (000's)	$5,601,376	$21,043,113	$56,913,588	$134,655,571	$182,968,610
Current funds revenues per student (current $)	$1,590	$2,688	$5,058	$10,314	$13,245
Current funds expenditures per student (current $)	$1,539	$2,629	$4,919	$9,946	$12,814
Current funds revenues per student (constant $)	$5,246	$6,981	$6,394	$7,971	$8,645
Current funds expenditures per student (constant $)	$5,079	$6,828	$6,219	$7,686	$8,364
Total enrollments	3,639,847	8,004,660	11,569,899	13,538,560	14,278,790

	Average Annual Percentage Changes			
Category	1959-60 to 1969-70	1969-70 to 1979-80	1979-80 to 1989-90	1989-90 to 1994-95
Current funds revenues (000's)	14.0%	10.5%	9.1%	6.3%
Current funds expenditures (000's)	14.2%	10.5%	9.0%	6.3%
Current funds revenues per student (current $)	5.4%	6.5%	7.4%	5.1%
Current funds expenditures per student (current $)	5.5%	6.5%	7.3%	5.2%
Current funds revenues per student (constant $)	2.9%	-0.9%	2.2%	1.6%
Current funds expenditures per student (constant $)	3.0%	-0.9%	2.1%	1.7%
Total enrollments	8.2%	3.8%	1.6%	1.1%

Notes: Current funds and enrollment data were obtained from Digest of Education Statistics 1998, Table 171, p.195. The Consumer Price Index levels were obtained from *Inflation Measure for Schools, Colleges, & Libraries: 1997 Update*, Research Associates of Washington (1982-83=100). Average annual percentage increases are approximated using the formula $i = (F/P)^{1/T} - 1$, where F = value at the end of the time interval, P = value at the beginning of the time interval, and T = number of years within the time interval.

The statistics in Table 1 illustrate the tremendous growth that has occurred in post-secondary education in the United States over this thirty-five year period. As of 1994-95, the current funds revenues of postsecondary institutions totaled nearly $190 billion. In nominal dollar terms, higher education institutions have received double-digit annual increases in current funds revenues throughout the 1960s and 1970s, with smaller but still respectable increases for the 1980s and first half of the 1990s. A large portion of this growth during the 1960s and 1970s was due to increased enrollments, which was most pronounced for the ten-year period between 1959-60 and 1969-70. The fact that current funds expenditure and revenue levels closely follow each other reflects the non-profit nature of most higher education institutions. As discussed earlier in this chapter, whether revenues follow expenditures or vice-versa remains unresolved.

The increases in current funds revenues and expenditures persist even after taking into account the effects of enrollment increases and inflation during this period. On a per-student basis, current funds revenues grew by an average of five to seven percent annually throughout the thirty-five year period shown here. Even in constant dollars, current funds revenues and expenditures per student increased by one to three percent-age points per year above the rate of inflation, with the only exception being the hyper-inflationary period of the 1970s.

Such trends are interesting, but say nothing about the possible sources of growth in revenues and expenditures over time. Similarly, looking only at current funds revenues and expenditures will not reveal what has happened to those revenues and expenditures that are directly related to education and general activities of institutions. These aggre-gates can also mask important differences across institutions within postsecondary edu-cation. In particular, public and private colleges and universities can be dramatically different in their reliance on particular revenue streams (such as state appropriations and private donations), and can also differ in their spending patterns. Clotfelter (1996), for example, attributes much of the differences in recent successes of private and public institutions to their having different degrees of reliance on selected income streams. Likewise, universities that are heavily engaged in research and/or graduate instruction may have different financial profiles than their counterparts who focus relatively more attention on undergraduate instruction.

The next few tables examine in more detail the sources of revenues and expendi-tures for institutions, how they differ between the public and private sectors, and how they have changed over the recent twenty-year period from 1974-75 and 1994-95. The data for these tables were obtained through WebCASPAR, and include all two- and four-year public and private institutions that reported data to NCES through either the HEGIS or the IPEDS in the respective years.[10] Table 2 provides a breakdown of net E&G revenues by source for public and private postsecondary institutions for selected years from 1974-75 through 1994-95. To make the data more comparable across years, Pell Grant revenues have been subtracted from the revenue category "federal appropria-tions" for all years unless otherwise noted. Table 2 also provides calculations of the

---

[10]For the 1994-95 fiscal year, there were 1,816 private institutions and 1,517 public institutions used in the analyses that follow. It should be noted that the institutions included in the data obtained from WebCASPAR may differ from those shown in similar tables produced by NCES.

inflation-adjusted, per-student dollar amounts of net revenue from each source. It should be reiterated that scholarship and fellowship expenditures have been subtracted from the tuition and fee revenues shown here.

Table 2: Breakdown of Net Educational and General Revenues by Source, 1974-75 to 1994-95

Public Institutions:	1974-75	1979-80	1984-85	1989-90	1994-95	Change 1974-75 to 1994-95
Net tuition and fees	13%	13%	16%	18%	21%	7%
Federal appropriations*	3%	3%	3%	3%	2%	-1%
State appropriations	57%	59%	58%	54%	47%	-9%
Local appropriations	6%	4%	4%	4%	5%	-1%
Private gifts, grants, contracts	3%	3%	4%	5%	6%	3%
Endowment income	1%	1%	1%	1%	1%	0%
Government grants & contracts	17%	16%	13%	15%	18%	1%
Total Net E&G Revenues	100%	100%	100%	100%	100%	

Private Institutions:	1974-75	1979-80	1984-85	1989-90	1994-95	Change 1974-75 to 1994-95
Net tuition and fees	47%	49%	53%	53%	55%	8%
Federal appropriations*	1%	1%	1%	1%	1%	0%
State appropriations	2%	2%	2%	1%	1%	-1%
Local appropriations	0%	0%	0%	0%	0%	0%
Private gifts, grants, contracts	16%	15%	16%	15%	15%	-1%
Endowment income	9%	8%	9%	9%	8%	-1%
Government grants & contracts	25%	24%	19%	21%	20%	-4%
Total Net E&G Revenues	100%	100%	100%	100%	100%	

Per-Student Net E&G Revenues by Source (Constant 1995 dollars)

Public Institutions:	1974-75	1979-80	1984-85	1989-90	1994-95	Change 1974-75 to 1994-95
Net tuition and fees	$790	$814	$1,083	$1,257	$1,532	94%
Federal appropriations*	$193	$179	$192	$179	$155	-20%
State appropriations	$3,388	$3,621	$3,900	$3,836	$3,506	3%
Local appropriations	$373	$259	$278	$313	$368	-1%
Private gifts, grants, contracts	$182	$206	$277	$369	$418	129%
Endowment income	$31	$39	$49	$50	$61	94%
Government grants & contracts	$1,003	$979	$890	$1,081	$1,345	34%
Total Net E&G Revenues	$5,961	$6,097	$6,669	$7,086	$7,386	24%

Private Institutions:	1974-75	1979-80	1984-85	1989-90	1994-95	Change 1974-75 to 1994-95
Net tuition and fees	$4,729	$4,840	$5,684	$6,911	$6,850	45%
Federal appropriations*	$109	$122	$118	$106	$73	-33%
State appropriations	$230	$193	$190	$179	$113	-51%
Local appropriations	$1	$1	$1	$2	$1	55%
Private gifts, grants, contracts	$1,635	$1,499	$1,674	$1,919	$1,897	16%
Endowment income	$865	$824	$967	$1,154	$1,016	17%
Government grants & contracts	$2,470	$2,410	$2,071	$2,675	$2,557	4%
Total Net E&G Revenues	$10,039	$9,889	$10,704	$12,945	$12,507	25%

Notes: Data are taken from HEGIS and IPEDS (as reported by WebCASPAR).
*Revenues from Pell Grants have been subtracted from federal appropriations for all years shown here. Scholarship and fellowship expenditures have been subtracted from tuition and fee revenue. Not all column totals are exact because of rounding.

Table 2 illustrates both the significant differences—and similarities—between the public and private sectors in terms of their reliance on various revenue sources to fund their operations. In 1994-95, the largest single source of net revenues for public institutions is clearly state appropriations (47%), followed by net tuition and fee revenue (21%), and government grants and contracts (18%). In the private sector, net tuition and fee revenue accounted for the majority (55%) of net E&G revenues in 1994-95, with government grants and contracts (20%) and private gifts, grants and contracts (15%) being the next largest revenue sources.

Where the public and private sectors are similar is that both have seen a dramatic rise over this twenty-year period in the share of revenues coming from net tuition and fees. A quick glance at the top portion of the table reveals that the rising share of revenues coming from net tuition and fees in the public sector corresponds very closely with the decline in the share of revenues coming from state appropriations, which fell from 58 percent of net E&G revenues in 1984-85 to 47 percent only ten years later (Mumper, Chapter 8). All other major revenue sources appear to have held stable shares of total revenues for the public sector over the period considered here. For private institutions, the rising share of revenues from net tuition and fees can be attributed to the falling share of revenues from government grants and contracts and private gifts, grants and contracts, and smaller share declines in all other E&G revenue sources.

When expressed on a per-student, inflation-adjusted basis, the differences in the revenue environment at public and private institutions become more pronounced. While total revenues per student rose by similar amounts in both sectors (24 percent in public institutions versus 25 percent for private institutions), private institutions received nearly twice the net revenues per student as did public institutions. In the public sector, net tuition and fees per student nearly doubled over this twenty-year period, even after taking into account the effects of inflation. Contrary to the impression that state support for higher education has been falling, it can be seen that the level of state funding has actually kept pace with both enrollment increases and inflation. State funding has not, however, grown at the same rate as overall expenditures. Turning to private institutions, the revenues received from net tuition and fees almost equal the per-student revenues from all sources in the public sector. Private institutions also receive substantially higher revenues per student than public institutions from private sources, endowment income, and government grants and contracts.

Another way of looking at this issue is to group net E&G revenues per student into three categories, according to the source of funds: students, governments, and other sources (includes private gifts, grants, and contracts, plus endowment income). Figures 1 and 2 illustrate how the shares of net E&G revenues in current dollars paid by students, governments, and other sources have changed over this twenty-year period.

Net E&G revenues per-student at private institutions rose by over $9,000 in current dollars during this twenty-year period, and by $5,300 at public institutions for the same years. The bar charts show that while public institutions relied on government sources for over two-thirds of this growth, the share of their revenues coming from government has been falling. Students provided the majority of the revenue growth in the private

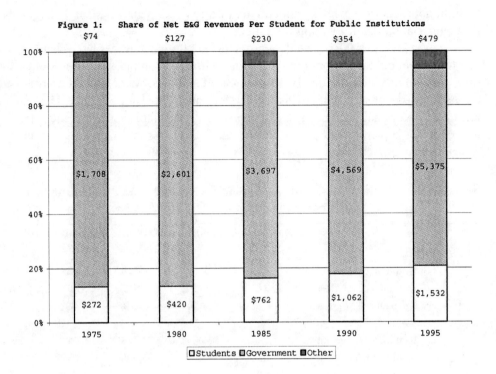

Figure 1: Share of Net E&G Revenues Per Student for Public Institutions

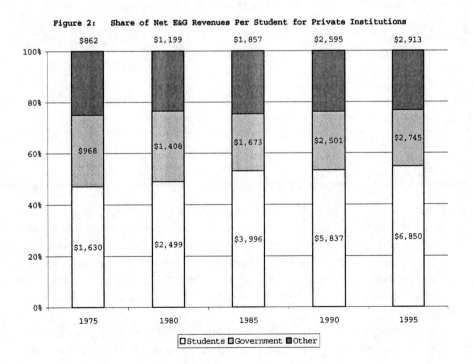

Figure 2: Share of Net E&G Revenues Per Student for Private Institutions

sector. In both sectors, however, students are clearly bearing an increasingly larger share of the financial burden for paying for college.

Table 3 shows how the per-student gross and net tuition and fees have changed from 1975 to 1995 at public and private institutions. Gross tuition per student is simply total tuition and fee revenues divided by the number of students. As noted earlier, net tuition is equal to gross tuition and fees less scholarships and fellowships from state, local, private, and institutional sources. The last four rows in the table represent the difference between average private and public tuition and fees (gross and net) in dollar and percentage terms, respectively.

Table 3: Comparison of Gross and Net Tuition and Fee Revenues Per Student for Public and Private Institutions, 1974-75 to 1994-95

	1974-75	1979-80	1984-85	1989-90	1994-95
Public Institutions:					
Gross tuition per student	$355	$527	$914	$1,285	$1,947
Net tuition per student	$272	$420	$762	$1,062	$1,532
Net as percentage of gross	77%	80%	83%	83%	79%
Private Institutions:					
Gross tuition per student	$1,980	$3,026	$4,882	$7,402	$9,205
Net tuition per student	$1,630	$2,499	$3,996	$5,837	$6,850
Net as percentage of gross	82%	83%	82%	79%	74%
Private/Public Difference in Gross Tuition (in dollars)	$1,625	$2,499	$3,968	$6,117	$7,258
Private/PublicDifference in Net Tuition (in dollars)	$1,358	$2,079	$3,234	$4,775	$5,318
Private/Public Difference in Gross Tuition (in percentages)	458%	474%	434%	476%	373%
Private/Public Difference in Net Tuition (in percentages)	499%	495%	425%	450%	347%

Notes: Net tuition per student equals gross tuition per student minus scholarship and fellowship expenditures from state-local, private, and institutional sources. Both tuition measures include tuition and mandatory fees Scholarship and fellowship totals do not include Pell Grants.

In the public sector, gross and net tuition and fees per student grew at comparable rates over the period from 1974-75 through 1989-90; however, gross tuition outpaced net tuition growth in the public sector during the early 1990s, as evidenced by the smaller share of net to gross tuition and fee revenues. In the private sector, since 1984-85 gross tuition grew at a much faster pace than net tuition, with the net-to-gross ratio falling from 82 percent in 1984-85 to 74 percent in 1994-95. The largest declines in each sector occurred during the early 1990s. These falling shares correspond to the rising levels of institutional financial aid given in the form of grants and scholarships, or "tuition discounting."

A quick comparison of the private and public sectors shows that the dollar gap in the gross price of attending a private versus a public institution has grown considerably between 1975 and 1995, going from \$1,625 in 1974-75 to \$7,258 in 1994-95 (Zumeta, Chapter 9). While the dollar difference in net prices has also increased at an impressive rate during this period, the growth rate in net tuition and fees is smaller than for gross tuition and fees. In particular, note how the private-to-public percentage difference fell dramatically from 1990 to 1995, a period of time when private institutions greatly stepped up their reliance on tuition discounting.

Table 4: Breakdown of Net Educational and General Expenditures by Source, 1974-75 to 1994-95

Public Institutions:	1974-75	1979-80	1984-85	1989-90	1994-95	Change 1974-75 to 1994-95
Instruction	47%	45%	45%	43%	42%	-5%
Research	11%	11%	11%	12%	13%	2%
Public Service	5%	5%	5%	5%	6%	1%
Academic Support	9%	9%	9%	10%	10%	1%
Student Services	5%	6%	6%	6%	6%	1%
Institutional Support	11%	11%	11%	11%	11%	1%
O&M Plant	11%	11%	11%	9%	9%	-2%
Transfers	2%	1%	1%	3%	3%	2%
Total Net E&G Expenditures	100%	100%	100%	100%	100%	

Private Institutions:	1974-75	1979-80	1984-85	1989-90	1994-95	Change 1974-75 to 1994-95
Instruction	42%	41%	41%	39%	40%	-2%
Research	15%	14%	12%	12%	12%	-3%
Public Service	2%	2%	3%	3%	4%	2%
Academic Support	8%	9%	9%	9%	8%	0%
Student Services	6%	6%	7%	7%	8%	2%
Institutional Support	15%	15%	16%	16%	15%	1%
O&M Plant	11%	11%	11%	9%	9%	-2%
Transfers	2%	2%	2%	5%	4%	3%
Total Net E&G Expenditures	100%	100%	100%	100%	100%	

Per-Student Net E&G Expenditures by Source (Constant 1995 dollars)

Public Institutions:	1974-75	1979-80	1984-85	1989-90	1994-95	Change 1974-75 to 1994-95
Instruction	\$2,855	\$2,784	\$3,046	\$3,233	\$3,346	17%
Research	\$662	\$707	\$761	\$933	\$1,046	58%
Public Service	\$300	\$310	\$344	\$408	\$447	49%
Academic Support	\$533	\$581	\$643	\$722	\$754	42%
Student Services	\$326	\$364	\$401	\$442	\$499	53%
Institutional Support	\$638	\$655	\$782	\$830	\$889	39%
O&M Plant	\$645	\$684	\$750	\$699	\$685	6%
Transfers	\$104	\$81	\$75	\$212	\$255	146%
Total Net E&G Expenditures	\$6,062	\$6,166	\$6,802	\$7,479	\$7,921	31%

Private Institutions:	1974-75	1979-80	1984-85	1989-90	1994-95	Change 1974-75 to 1994-95
Instruction	\$4,502	\$4,321	\$4,704	\$5,639	\$5,642	25%
Research	\$1,615	\$1,447	\$1,385	\$1,766	\$1,663	3%
Public Service	\$162	\$221	\$292	\$437	\$524	223%
Academic Support	\$904	\$919	\$1,001	\$1,265	\$1,187	31%
Student Services	\$620	\$667	\$810	\$1,033	\$1,070	72%
Institutional Support	\$1,564	\$1,572	\$1,846	\$2,255	\$2,157	38%
O&M Plant	\$1,162	\$1,169	\$1,248	\$1,339	\$1,251	8%
Transfers	\$162	\$163	\$198	\$706	\$628	288%
Total Net E&G Expenditures	\$10,692	\$10,479	\$11,485	\$14,439	\$14,121	32%

Notes: Net E&G expenditures are defined as total E&G expenditures minus scholarships and fellowships. Source: HEGIS and IPEDS surveys as reported by WebCASPAR. Not all column totals are exact because of rounding.

Turning to expenditures, Table 4 provides a breakdown of net E&G expenditures (E&G expenditures minus scholarships and fellowships) by major expenditure categories, and reports these shares separately for public and private institutions. As in Table 2, these quantities are also expressed in dollars on a per-student, inflation-adjusted basis.

Not surprisingly, instruction comprises the largest share of net E&G expenditures at both public and private institutions, since faculty salary and fringe benefit costs are included in this category and faculty compensation represents the largest single expenditure item for most institutions.[11] The share of total net E&G expenditures for instruction is larger throughout this twenty-year period for public institutions than it is for private institutions. This difference has narrowed considerably over time, however, and can give the misleading impression that public institutions devote more financial resources than private institutions do to instruction-related activities. When expressed on a per-student basis, private institutions on average spend considerably more than public institutions on items in the "instruction" category.

With regard to changes over time, in both the public and private sectors the share of net E&G expenditures devoted to instruction has fallen by five percentage points in the public sector and by two percentage points in the private sector over this twenty-year period. In addition, the percentage of net E&G expenditures devoted to operation and maintenance of the physical plant has declined from 11 percent to 9 percent in each sector. For public institutions, the combined seven percentage point decline in instruction and plant expenditures is offset by small increases in the shares of other items, with the share of expenditures devoted to any other category rising by at most two percentage points. In contrast to the public sector, private institutions experienced a three-percentage-point decline in the share of net E&G expenditures going to research activities. The declining shares of net E&G expenditures for instruction, research, and the physical plant have been made up for by increasing shares of expenditures for public service, academic support, student services, transfers, and institutional support. While scholarships and fellowships are not included in this table, it is worth noting that as a share of all E&G expenditures, scholarships and fellowships increased from 4 percent to 5 percent for public institutions and from 9 percent to 14 percent for private institutions from 1974-75 to 1994-95.

Turning to net E&G expenditures per student, even after taking into account the effects of inflation, net E&G spending per student rose by over 30 percent in each sector. Despite its dropping share of total expenditures, per-student spending on instruction actually increased by 17 percent in public institutions and by 25 percent in private institutions. What is particularly striking is the fact that private institutions spent much more per student than public institutions across all functional areas shown here.

In Table 5, net E&G expenditures for 1974-75 through 1994-95 are shown on a per-student basis for the public and private sectors, along with the portions that are subsidized (all E&G revenue categories except tuition and fees) and the remainder which is

---

[11]For the year 1994-95, for example, 70.7 percent of instructional expenditures in public institutions and 65.5 percent of instructional expenditures in private institutions were due to salaries (not including benefits). Source: WebCASPAR data from NCES.

referred to here as unsubsidized. The unsubsidized portions of E&G expenditures are thus the same as the net tuition and fees per student shown in Table 3. The top half of the table reports these quantities in current (non inflation-adjusted) dollars, whereas the bottom half of the table expresses the same per-student totals in constant (1995) dollars. The last column calculates the annual average percentage increases in each of these three quantities.

Table 5: Changes in the Share of Net E&G Expenditures Per Student Subsidized by Other Sources, 1974-75 to 1994-95

	Current Dollars					Average Annual
Public Institutions:	1974-75	1979-80	1984-85	1989-90	1994-95	% Growth
Unsubsidized net E&G expenditures/student	$272	$420	$762	$1,062	$1,532	9.0%
Subsidized net E&G expenditures/student	$1,817	$2,764	$4,020	$5,255	$6,389	6.5%
Net E&G expenditures/student	$2,089	$3,184	$4,782	$6,317	$7,921	6.9%
% subsidized net E&G expenditures/student	87%	87%	84%	83%	81%	
Private Institutions:						
Unsubsidized net E&G expenditures/student	$1,630	$2,499	$3,996	$5,837	$6,850	7.4%
Subsidized net E&G expenditures/student	$2,055	$2,911	$4,078	$6,359	$7,271	6.5%
Net E&G expenditures/student	$3,685	$5,410	$8,074	$12,196	$14,121	6.9%
% subsidized net E&G expenditures/student	56%	54%	51%	52%	51%	

	Constant Dollars (1982-83=100)					Average Annual
Public Institutions:	1974-75	1979-80	1984-85	1989-90	1994-95	% Growth
Unsubsidized net E&G expenditures/student	$515	$531	$708	$821	$1,000	3.4%
Subsidized net E&G expenditures/student	$3,442	$3,494	$3,732	$4,061	$4,170	1.0%
Net E&G expenditures/student	$3,957	$4,025	$4,440	$4,882	$5,170	1.3%
Private Institutions:						
Unsubsidized net E&G expenditures/student	$3,087	$3,159	$3,710	$4,511	$4,471	1.9%
Subsidized net E&G expenditures/student	$3,892	$3,681	$3,787	$4,914	$4,746	1.0%
Net E&G expenditures/student	$6,979	$6,840	$7,497	$9,425	$9,217	1.4%

Notes: Unsubsidized net E&G expenditures/student are defined as net tuition and fees per student. Net E&G expenditures per student equal E&G expenditures per student less scholarships and fellowships. Subsidized net E&G expenditures represents the portion of net E&G expenditures not covered by net student charges, including the discrepancy between net E&G revenues per student and net E&G expenditures per student. Sources: expenditure and revenue data are taken from HEGIS and IPEDS surveys as reported by WebCASPAR. The Consumer Price Index levels were obtained from Inflation Measures for Schools, Colleges, & Libraries: 1997 Updates, Research Associates of Washington (1982-83=100). Average annual percentage increases are approximated using the formula $I = (F/P)^{1/T}-1$, where F = value at the end of the time interval, P = value at the beginning of the time interval, and T = number of years within the time interval.

As can be seen, the portions of net E&G expenditures that are subsidized by various parties have diminished considerably in both the public and private sectors. Subsidies now cover over 80 percent of the net E&G costs per student in public colleges and universities, and slightly more than half of the cost of education in private institutions. After taking into account the effects of inflation, the real unsubsidized portion of net E&G expenditures has grown by 3 percent per year in public institutions and by 2 percent per year in private institutions. In each sector, net E&G expenditures per student exceeded inflation by only 1 percent per year, and the growth in subsidies per student over time exceeded the rate of inflation by one percentage point per year. Taken together, these data reveal that the rising unsubsidized share of college expenses is due to both expenditures that have risen faster than inflation, and subsidies that have not kept pace with expenditures.

In order to get a better understanding of how the finances differ between public and private institutions, Table 6 combines the net E&G revenue and expenditure totals for major categories on a per-student basis reported earlier for the 1994-95 fiscal year, and highlights the private-to-public ratio for each functional area.

Table 6: Comparison of the Per-Student Net Education and General Revenues and Expenditures for Public and Private Institutions, 1994-95

Revenue Category	*Public*	*Private*	*Ratio: Private to Public*
Net tuition and fees	$1,532	$6,850	447%
Government support	$4,029	$188	5%
Private gifts, grants, contracts	$418	$1,897	453%
Endowment income	$61	$1,016	1663%
Govt. grants & contracts	$1,345	$2,557	190%
Net E&G Revenues Per Student	$7,386	$12,507	169%

Expenditure Category	*Public*	*Private*	*Ratio: Private to Public*
Instruction	$3,346	$5,642	169%
Research	$1,046	$1,663	159%
Public service	$447	$524	117%
Academic support	$754	$1,187	157%
Student services	$499	$1,070	215%
Institutional support	$889	$2,157	243%
O&M plant	$685	$1,251	182%
Transfers	$255	$628	246%
Net E&G Expenditures Per Student	$7,921	$14,121	178%

Notes: Pell Grants have been subtracted from Scholarship and Fellowship expenditures. Source: IPEDS Finance Survey FY95, as reported by WebCASPAR. Not all column totals are exact because of rounding.

The top half of Table 6 reveals dramatic differences in the funding patterns for public and private institutions. Private institutions receive significantly higher revenues per student than public institutions in the areas of endowment income, tuition and fees, and private gifts, grants and contracts. At the other extreme, per-student government appropriations at private institutions are only 5 percent of the per-student total at public institutions. Therefore, the government provides most of the subsidy in the public sector, whereas both the government and private sources contribute to the subsidy at private institutions.

With regard to expenditures, it can be seen that private institutions spend significantly more than public institutions on a per-student basis across most expenditure categories, with the largest percentage difference being for transfers and institutional support. Therefore, while the shares of net E&G expenditures devoted to instruction and research are slightly lower at private institutions than they are at public institutions, when expressed on a per-student basis private institutions spend more per student than public institutions in these areas.

Another important way in which finances of institutions can differ is with regard to mission. In particular, research activities are viewed as being more costly than teaching activities for institutions, so it might be expected that institutions where research is a major component of faculty activity would have higher levels of expenditures and revenues per student. At the same time, there may be some cost savings from the joint production of teaching and research if graduate students are used to teach undergraduate students. Table 7 combines information from selected NCES tables to provide a snapshot of how revenues and expenditures vary not only between the public and private sectors, but also between universities and four-year colleges.[12] The first four rows of the table contain data on per-student E&G expenditures by institution type. The second portion of the table concentrates on gross student charges. It should be noted that student charges focus on the average "sticker price" charged to students, whereas previous tables reported tuition and fee income collected by students after accounting for scholarships and fellowships. The third portion of the table provides information on the ratio of student charges to E&G expenditures. Finally, the bottom rows on the table show the private to public ratios of selected statistics for different types of institutions. The figures reported in Tables 7 and 8 will differ from those in earlier tables because they rely on gross and not net E&G expenditures, and thus include scholarship and fellowship expenditures, and the group of institutions included in Tables 7 and 8 may differ slightly from those used earlier since this information was compiled by NCES.

Beginning with E&G expenditures per student, it can be seen that the per-student spending levels at private and public four-year colleges are very comparable to each other—$11,478 in privates and $10,128 in publics as of 1994-95—with most of the difference emerging during the 1985-95 period. At the same time, the ratio of per-student expenditures at private relative to public universities has risen from 149 percent in 1974-75 to 199 percent in 1994-95. Surprisingly, the expenditures per student at public universities are very similar to the per-student expenditure levels at public four-year colleges. This result is important because it suggests that the costs of maintaining research programs in and of themselves do not lead to higher per-student expenditures at universities versus four-year colleges. The data show that the perceived cost differences between private versus public and research versus teaching institutions are primarily due to unusually high expenditure levels at private universities. This may suggest that public research universities have been more successful than their private counterparts at achieving cost savings from using graduate students as instructors.

With regard to tuition and fees, the gross student charges in the private sector tend to be four to five times as high as in the public sector. University student charges average

---

[12]Since this table relies on existing NCES tables, it is not apparent how to derive a measure of net E&G expenditures per student from the data. Therefore, Tables 7 and 8 will rely on statistics for gross tuition and total E&G expenditure, rather than net tuition and net E&G expenditures.

Table 7: Breakdown of Education and General Expenditures and Student Charges by Sector and Type of Institution, 1974-75 to 1994-95

Category	1974-75	1979-80	1984-85	1989-90	1994-95
E&G Expenditures/Student:					
Public University	$3,150	$4,749	$7,068	$9,448	$11,824
Public Four-Year College	$2,827	$4,352	$6,441	$8,288	$10,128
Private University	$4,686	$7,153	$11,670	$17,446	$23,564
Private Four-Year College	$2,947	$4,210	$6,559	$9,390	$11,478
Gross Student Charges:					
Public University	$599	$840	$1,386	$2,035	$2,977
Public Four-Year College	$448	$662	$1,117	$1,608	$2,499
Private University	$2,614	$3,811	$6,843	$10,348	$14,537
Private Four-Year College	$1,954	$3,020	$5,135	$7,778	$10,653
Ratio of Student Charges to E&G Expenditures:					
Public University	19%	18%	20%	22%	25%
Public Four-Year College	16%	15%	17%	19%	25%
Private University	56%	53%	59%	59%	62%
Private Four-Year College	66%	72%	78%	83%	93%
Ratio of Private to Public:					
E&G Expenditures (University)	149%	151%	165%	185%	199%
E&G Expenditures (Four-Year College)	104%	97%	102%	113%	113%
Gross Student Charges (University)	436%	454%	494%	509%	488%
Gross Student Charges (Four-Year College)	436%	456%	460%	484%	426%

Notes: E&G expenditures per student are taken from Inflation Measures for Schools, Colleges, & Libraries: 1997 Update (Table 2-A, p.14-15). Gross student charges are taken from Table 311 in the Digest of Education Statistics 1998, pp. 334-335.

about 40 percent higher than at four-year colleges in the private sector, and are about 20 percent higher in the public sector. If the subsidy per student is approximated by the share of E&G expenditures per student *not* covered by gross student charges, it can be seen that subsidies have fallen in both the public and private sectors, most notably for private four-year colleges (34 percent in 1975 and 7 percent in 1995).[13] In fact, the dollar subsidy per student (E&G expenditures/student minus gross student charges) has actually fallen by 50 percent for private four-year colleges during the period from 1990 to 1995, going from $9,390 - $7,778 = $1,612 in 1989-90 to $11,478 - $10,653 = $825 in 1994-95, while the dollar subsidy per student has risen in the other three groups for the same period.

---

[13]This definition of subsidy differs from that used earlier in this paper and suggested by Winston and others, because both gross tuition and fees and E&G expenditures per student include scholarships and fellowships. The data provided in the NCES tables do not allow for these quantities to be directly adjusted so that they are more comparable to previous figures.

This trend can also be seen in Table 8, where the per-student E&G expenditures for each type of institution are broken down into their subsidized and unsubsidized portions, and reported in both current and constant dollars. The figures reported in Table 8 differ from those in Table 5 because the subsidized portion of E&G expenditures is approximated by gross student charges rather than net tuition and fee revenue.

Table 8: E&G Expenditures Per Student Subsidized by Other Sources by Type of Institution, 1974-75 to 1994-95

	Current Dollars					Average Annual % Growth
	1974-75	1979-80	1984-85	1989-90	1994-95	
Public Universities:						
Unsubsidized E&G expenditures/student	$599	$840	$1,386	$2,035	$2,977	8.3%
Subsidized E&G expenditures/student	$2,551	$3,909	$5,682	$7,413	$8,847	6.4%
E&G expenditures/student	$3,150	$4,749	$7,068	$9,448	$11,824	6.8%
% subsidized E&G expenditures/student	81%	82%	80%	78%	75%	
Public Four-Year Colleges:						
Unsubsidized E&G expenditures/student	$448	$662	$1,117	$1,608	$2,499	9.0%
Subsidized E&G expenditures/student	$2,379	$3,690	$5,324	$6,680	$7,629	6.0%
E&G expenditures/student	$2,827	$4,352	$6,441	$8,288	$10,128	6.6%
% subsidized E&G expenditures/student	84%	85%	83%	81%	75%	
Private Universities:						
Unsubsidized E&G expenditures/student	$2,614	$3,811	$6,843	$10,348	$14,537	9.0%
Subsidized E&G expenditures/student	$2,072	$3,342	$4,827	$7,098	$9,027	7.6%
E&G expenditures/student	$4,686	$7,153	$11,670	$17,446	$23,564	8.4%
% subsidized E&G expenditures/student	44%	47%	41%	41%	38%	
Private Four-Year Colleges:						
Unsubsidized E&G expenditures/student	$1,954	$3,020	$5,135	$7,778	$10,653	8.8%
Subsidized E&G expenditures/student	$993	$1,190	$1,424	$1,612	$825	-0.9%
E&G expenditures/student	$2,947	$4,210	$6,559	$9,390	$11,478	7.0%
% subsidized E&G expenditures/student	34%	28%	22%	17%	7%	
	Constant Dollars (1982-83=100)					Average Annual % Growth
	1974-75	1979-80	1984-85	1989-90	1994-95	
Public Universities:						
Unsubsidized E&G expenditures/student	$1,134	$1,062	$1,287	$1,573	$1,943	2.7%
Subsidized E&G expenditures/student	$4,831	$4,942	$5,276	$5,729	$5,775	0.9%
E&G expenditures/student	$5,965	$6,004	$6,563	$7,302	$7,718	1.3%
Public Four-Year Colleges:						
Unsubsidized E&G expenditures/student	$848	$837	$1,037	$1,243	$1,631	3.3%
Subsidized E&G expenditures/student	$4,506	$4,665	$4,943	$5,162	$4,980	0.5%
E&G expenditures/student	$5,354	$5,502	$5,980	$6,405	$6,611	1.1%
Private Universities:						
Unsubsidized E&G expenditures/student	$4,951	$4,818	$6,354	$7,997	$9,489	3.3%
Subsidized E&G expenditures/student	$3,924	$4,225	$4,482	$5,485	$5,892	2.1%
E&G expenditures/student	$8,875	$9,043	$10,836	$13,482	$15,381	2.8%
Private Four-Year Colleges:						
Unsubsidized E&G expenditures/student	$3,701	$3,818	$4,768	$6,011	$6,954	3.2%
Subsidized E&G expenditures/student	$1,881	$1,504	$1,322	$1,246	$539	-6.1%
E&G expenditures/student	$5,581	$5,322	$6,090	$7,257	$7,493	1.5%

Notes: E&G expenditures per student are taken from Inflation Measures for Schools, Colleges, & Libraries: 1997 Update (Table 2-A, p.14-15). Gross student charges are taken from Table 311 in the Digest of Education Statistics 1998, p.334-335. Unsubsidized E&G expenditures are defined as gross student charges, and subsidized E&G expenditures = total E&G expenditures minus unsubsidized E&G expenditures. Average annual percentage increases are approximated using the formula $I=(F/P)^{1/T}-1$, where F = value at the end of the time interval, P = value at the beginning of the time interval, and T = number of years within the time interval.

Interestingly, the subsidized shares of E&G expenditures at public universities and four-year colleges are very comparable to each other, whereas universities in the private sector received considerably larger subsidies than private four-year colleges. In the bottom half of the table, it is shown that the per-student subsidies in the public sector kept pace with inflation, as evidenced by average annual growth rates between zero and one percent, but did not keep pace with expenditures, which experienced average annual growth rates of more than one percent. In the private sector, however, per-student subsidies at private universities exceeded the rate of inflation by two percentage points annually, but fell in real terms by six percentage points annually for private four-year colleges.

SUMMARY

In this chapter, I have reviewed the major sources of financial information available on colleges and universities in the United States, and explored how revenues and expenditures have changed over time for these institutions. The results clearly show that the cost of providing higher education services has outpaced the rate of inflation for the past twenty years. This fact alone, however, is not sufficient to conclude that the cost increases of the past twenty years are "excessive." It could be that the nature of the education production function is such that the cost of providing educational services should have risen at a rate greater than for the economy as a whole. Likewise, cost increases could have been accompanied by increases in the quality of research, teaching, and public service outputs. The fact that institutions have been successful in finding revenues from various sources to cover these expenditures suggests that students and subsidizers still find higher education to be worthy of financial support.

The data also reveal interesting differences in expenditures by institution type. Perhaps contrary to conventional wisdom, the aggregate differences in expenditures per student between universities and four-year colleges are not due to research activities being more expensive to finance than teaching activities; rather, these differences are driven by the very high expenditure levels at private universities. These results argue for more in-depth analysis on the finances and operations of private universities to learn why they differ from other institutions.

Turning to prices, the results presented here show that rising educational prices have been due to *both* rising costs of education and falling subsidies from government and private sources. The problem of falling relative subsidies is perhaps greatest for the private four-year colleges, where students are now required to nearly cover the entire cost of their education. The relevant question becomes whether these increases in the price of attendance have led to reductions in access to higher education, and/or inappropriate restrictions in student choice. In the aggregate, it is hard to make the argument that price increases have significantly reduced access to higher education. Data from the NCES (1999) show that the proportion of high school graduates going directly to college has increased from 51 percent in 1975 to 62 percent in 1995. Furthermore, enrollments over this period increased by 26 percent for public institutions and 35 percent for private institutions, showing that there has not been a great migration from one sector to the other perhaps due to price. There is still the possibility, however, that students from lower-income families are being increasingly priced out of many private institutions, and that these demographic changes might be hidden in the aggregate totals. To the extent that the returns on education for attending a selective private institutions may be higher than for other institutions, determining if there is appropriate access to these institutions for students from lower-income families becomes an issue worthy of future -—and continued—study.

What are some of the short-term prospects and issues for higher education revenues, expenditures, and prices? With regard to expenditures, several forces may converge to lead to even greater growth in expenditures in the near future. Agencies such as the NCES predict that postsecondary institutions should see unprecedented levels of demand through the year 2010 as the children of the baby boomer generation enter postsecondary system. Likewise, many institutions are having to make significant investments in their technology infrastructure, and/or have large levels of deferred maintenance. On a per-student basis, however, the expenditure growth may not be quite as dramatic due to the fact that the marginal costs of servicing the additional projected students will likely be lower than the average costs. This depends, of course, on the extent to which institutions choose to accommodate those additional students who wish to enroll rather than tighten admissions standards to hold enrollments at their present levels.

On the revenue side, the unprecedented bull market of the late 1990s may benefit postsecondary institutions in the near term as states, realizing higher tax revenues from capital gains, may pass some portion along to higher education. Furthermore the demand for state funding from the K-12 sector should decrease as the children of the baby boomers leave K-12 grades for postsecondary education. The rising stock market has also contributed to robust growth in the endowments at many institutions. Institutions in both the public and private sectors have become more aggressive at seeking out private donations to help subsidize the cost of education services. Institutions may see higher future levels of bequeaths from the parents of baby boomers, and ultimately the baby boomers themselves. Taken together, it seems likely that the past expenditure and revenue trends will continue into the next decade.

Finally, pending changes in financial reporting for the public sector pose further difficulties for analysts who would want to examine similar financial trends in future years. The Government Accounting Standards Board has mandated that beginning with the 2001-02 fiscal year, public colleges and universities will change their reporting practices from the current fund accounting methodology to an approach very similar to that used by private institutions. While this will help to make public and private financial data more comparable to each other in future years, it will have a detrimental effect on the ability of researchers to determine if and how the financial picture of public institutions is changing over the long term.

References

Allen, W. (1915). *Self-Surveys by Colleges and Universities.* Yonkers-on-Hudson, New York: World.

Allen, W. *et al.* (1917). *Report Upon the Survey of the University of Wisconsin, Findings of the Board of Public Affairs and its Report to the Legislature.* Madison, WI: The Board of Public Affairs.

Blasdell, S., McPherson, M., and Schapiro, M. (1993). Trends in revenues and expenditures in U.S. higher education: Where does the money come from? Where does it go? In M. McPherson, M. Schapiro, and G. Winston (eds.), *Paying the Piper: Productivity, Incentives, and Financing in U.S. Higher Educa-*

tion. Ann Arbor: The University of Michigan Press.

Bowen, H. (1980). *The Costs of Higher Education*. San Francisco: Jossey-Bass.

Breneman, D. (2000). An essay on college costs. Unpublished paper, Curry School of Education, University of Virginia. Presented at the NCES Meeting on College Costs, August 2-3, Washington, DC.

Brinkman, P. (1981). Factors affecting instructional costs at major research universities. *Journal of Higher Education* 52: 265-279.

Brinkman, P. (1990). Higher education cost functions. In S. Hoenack and E. Collins (eds.), *The Economics of American Universities: Management, Operations, and Fiscal Environment*. New York: State University of New York Press.

Chronicle of Higher Education (2000). Q&A: The candidates on college issues. *Chronicle of Higher Education* February 25: A30-A38.

Clotfelter, C. (1996). The changing revenues of universities: A pilot application. Unpublished working paper. Duke University and NBER.

Cohn, E., Rhine, S., and Santos, M. (1989). Institutions of higher education as multi-product firms: Economies of scale and scope. *The Review of Economics and Statistics* 71: 284-290.

College Board (1999). *Trends in College Pricing 1999*. New York: College Entrance Examination Board.

deGroot, H., McMahon, W., and Volkwein, J. (1991). The cost structure of American research universities. *The Review of Economics and Statistics* 73: 424-431.

Froomkin, J. (1990). The impacts of changing levels of financial resources on the structure of colleges and universities. In S. Hoenack and E. Collins (eds.), *The Economics of American Universities*. Buffalo: State University of New York Press.

Getz, M., Siegfried, J., and Zhang, H. (1991). Estimating economies of scale in higher education. *Economics Letters* 37: 203-208.

Halstead, K. (1991). *Higher Education Revenues & Expenditures: A Study of Institutional Costs*. Washington, DC: Research Associates of Washington.

Halstead, K. (1997). *Inflation Measures for Schools, Colleges, & Libraries: 1997 Update*. Arlington, VA: Research Associates of Washington.

Halstead, K. (1998). *Tuition Fact Book 1998: A Compendium of Data and Analyses*. Arlington, VA: Research Associates of Washington.

Hanson, N. (1964). Economy of scale as a cost factor in financing public schools. *National Tax Journal* 17: 92-95.

Harris, S. (1962). *Higher Education: Resources and Finance*. New York: McGraw-Hill Book Company, Inc.

Kilzer, L. (1937). How local public junior colleges are financed. *School Record* 45: 686-694.

Koshal, R. and Koshal, M. (1995). Quality and economies of scale in higher education. *Applied Economics* 27: 773-778.

Maynard, J. (1971). *Some Microeconomics of Higher Education: Economies of Scale*. Lincoln, NE: University of Nebraska Press.

McLaughlin, G., Montgomery, J., Smith, A., Mahan, B., and Broomall, L. (1980). Size and efficiency. *Research in Higher Education* 12: 53-66.

McNeely, J. (1937). *University Unit Costs*. Bulletin No. 21. Washington, DC: United States Office of Education.

McPherson, M., and Schapiro, M. (1994). Expenditures and revenues in American higher education. Unpublished discussion paper DP-27, Williams Project on the Economics of Higher Education. Williamstown, MA: Williams College.

National Center for Education Statistics (1999). *Digest of Education Statistics 1998*, NCES 1999-036, by T.D. Snyder. Washington, DC: U.S. Department of Education.

Nelson, R. and Hevert, K. (1992). Effect of class size on economies of scale and marginal costs in higher education. *Applied Economics* 24: 473-482.

O'Neill, J. (1973). *Sources of Funds to Colleges and Universities*. Carnegie Commission on Higher Education.

Paulsen, M. (2000). Economic perspectives on rising college tuition. In *Higher Education: Handbook of Theory and Research*, Vol. XV. New York: Agathon Press.

Toutkoushian, R. (1999). The value of cost functions for policymaking and institutional research. *Research in Higher Education* 40: 1-16.

Winston, G., and Yen, I. (1995). Costs, prices, subsidies, and aid in U.S. higher education. Unpublished discussion paper DP-32, Williams Project on the Economics of Higher Education. Williamstown, MA: Williams College.

Winston, G. (1998). A guide to measuring college costs. Unpublished discussion paper DP-46, Williams Project on the Economics of Higher Education. Williamstown, MA: Williams College.

Winston, G., Carbone, J., and Lewis, E. (1998). What's been happening to higher education? Facts, trends, and data. Unpublished discussion paper DP-47, Williams Project on the Economics of Higher Education. Williamstown, MA: Williams College.

Witmer, D. (1971). Cost studies in higher education. *Review of Educational Research* 42: 99-127.Appendix

APPENDIX
IPEDS Revenue and Expenditure Data Definitions

Revenue Categories

Tuition and Fees. Revenues from student payments for educational activities. Includes the gross receipts from tuition and mandatory fees, assuming that all students pay the full sticker price charged by the institution. Does not include student charges for items such as room and board, educational supplies, etc. [IPEDS Finance Survey, Part A, line 01].

Federal Appropriations. Revenues appropriated directly to institutions from the federal government. Includes federal appropriations made through state channels [IPEDS Finance Survey, Part A, line 02].

State Appropriations. Revenues appropriated directly to institutions through acts of a state legislative body. Does not include state grants and contracts [IPEDS Finance Survey, Part A, line 04].

Local Appropriations. Revenues appropriated directly to institutions from local governments [IPEDS Finance Survey, Part A, line 05].

Federal Grants & Contracts. Grant and contract revenues from the federal government. Pell Grant revenues have been subtracted from the total reported to IPEDS. The federal total does not include FDSL loans [IPEDS Finance Survey, Part A, line 06 minus IPEDS Finance Survey, Part E, line 01].

State Grants & Contracts. Grant and contract revenues from state governments [IPEDS Finance Survey, Part A, line 07].

Local Grants & Contracts. Grant and contract revenues from local governments [IPEDS Finance Survey, Part A, line 08].

Private Gifts, Grants, & Contracts. Revenues received from private donors for activities relating to the teaching, research, and service missions of the institution. Does not include endowment income [IPEDS Finance Survey, Part A, line 09].

Endowment Income. Revenues earned from the appreciation of the institution=s endowment. [IPEDS Finance Survey, Part A, line 10].

Sales and Services of Educational Activities. Revenues received from other education activities [IPEDS Finance Survey, Part A, line 11].

Auxiliary Enterprises. Revenues received from the operation of auxiliaries [IPEDS Finance Survey, Part A, line 12].

Hospitals. Revenues received from the operation of university hospitals [IPEDS Finance Survey, Part A, line 13].

Independent Operations. Revenues received from the operation of independent entities within colleges and universities [IPEDS Finance Survey, Part A, line 14].

Other Sources. Revenues received from other sources not shown here [IPEDS Finance Survey, Part A, line 15].

Education and General (E&G) Revenues. Revenues that are targeted towards the teaching, research, and public service missions of the institution. Includes revenues from the following categories: tuition and fees, federal appropriations, state appropriations, local appropriations, federal grants and contracts (less Pell Grants), state grants and contracts, local grants and contracts, and private gifts, grants and contracts.

Net Tuition and Fees. Defined here as tuition and fee revenues minus scholarship and fellowship expenditures.

Net E&G Revenues. Defined here as E&G revenues minus scholarship and fellowship expenditures.

Current Funds Revenues. E&G revenues, plus endowment income, sales and services of educational activities, auxiliary enterprises, hospitals, independent operations, other sources, and Pell Grants [IPEDS Finance Survey, Part A, line 16].

Expenditure Categories

Instruction. Includes expenditures on the general instructional activities within academic divisions of the institution. Includes faculty salaries, teaching supplies, as well as expenditures for departmental research and public service activities that are not separately budgeted [IPEDS Finance Survey, Part B, line 01].

Research. Expenditures on activities at the institution that are primarily research in nature, and funded from either an external agency or an internal unit exclusively for research. Does not include the portion of salaries paid to instructional faculty for their time spent on research activities [IPEDS Finance Survey, Part B, line 02].

Public Service. Expenditures on the separately budgeted public service activities of the institution. Includes projects for community service, cooperative extension, etc. [IPEDS Finance Survey, Part B, line 03].

Academic Support. Includes expenditures on activities that support the teaching,

/Trends in Revenues and Expenditures for Public and Private Universities*

research, and service functions of institutions. Includes expenditures on the library, academic computing, academic (but not general) administration, curriculum development, etc. [IPEDS Finance Survey, Part B, line 04].

Student Services. Expenditures on services designed to contribute to the support of students. Includes items such as admissions, recruitment, counseling, student activities, etc. [IPEDS Finance Survey, Part B, line 06].

Institutional Support. Expenditures on items that facilitate the operational functioning of the institution on a daily basis. Includes items such as general administration, legal counsel, administrative computing, etc. [IPEDS Finance Survey, Part B, line 07].

Operation and Maintenance of Plant. Expenditures on items that relate to repairs and renovations of the physical plant, plus daily upkeep of facilities. Typically does not include the cost of acquiring/building new facilities [IPEDS Finance Survey, Part B, line 08].

Scholarships & Fellowships. Financial aid in the form of scholarships and fellowships given to students. Includes scholarships and fellowships from the federal government, state government, local government, private sources, and institutional sources. The totals shown here do not include federal Pell Grants [IPEDS Finance Survey, Part E, line 07 minus line 01].

Mandatory and Nonmandatory Transfers. Transfers of funds between entities. Includes items such as campus contributions to system operations, etc. [IPEDS Finance Survey, Part B, lines 10 and 11].

Auxiliary Enterprises. Expenditures for activities that are not central to the institution's mission of teaching, research, and public service. Includes items such as dining halls, dormitories, etc. [IPEDS Finance Survey, Part B, line 13].

Hospitals. Expenditures for all activities dealing with the operation of hospitals [IPEDS Finance Survey, Part B, line 16].

Independent Operations. Expenditures for enterprises at the institutions that function as independent units. Includes items such as campus bookstores, etc. [IPEDS Finance Survey, Part B, line 19]

Education and General (E&G) Expenditures. The sum of expenditures for the following categories: instruction, research, public service, academic support, student services, institutional support, operation and maintenance of plant, scholarships and fellowships (minus Pell Grants), and transfers [IPEDS Finance Survey, Part B, line 12, minus IPEDS Finance Survey, Part E, line 01].

Net Education and General Expenditures. Defined here as E&G expenditures minus scholarship and fellowship expenditures [IPEDS Finance Survey, Part B, line 12 minus line 09].

Unsubsidized Net E&G Expenditures. Defined here as tuition and fee revenues minus scholarship and fellowship expenditures.

Subsidized Net E&G Expenditures. Defined here as net E&G expenditures minus unsubsidized net E&G expenditures. Includes the discrepancy between net E&G revenues and net E&G expenditures.

Current Funds Expenditures. E&G expenditures plus expenditures for auxiliary enterprises, hospitals, independent operations, and Pell Grant expenditures [IPEDS Finance Survey, Part B, line 22]

Chapter 2

COLLEGE EDUCATION: WHO CAN AFFORD IT?

Sandy Baum

The popular press is full of articles about the rising cost of college, the struggle of middle-class families to finance their children's education, and questions about the value of a high-priced education. In 1985, 63 percent of college freshmen had concerns about financing their education and 13 percent described themselves as having major concerns. A decade later, 70 percent were concerned and 18 percent had major concerns (Miller, 1997). Although they are sympathetic to this perceived problem, many educators and policy analysts are critical of the shifting focus away from the accessibility of higher education for low-income students towards affordability for middle-income students. The real social problem is the fact that the probability that high school graduates will go on to college declines dramatically with family income.

There is no doubt that the price of college has risen relative to the prices of other goods and services and that college tuition takes a bigger bite out of the typical family budget than it did a generation ago. What has not changed is that college is expensive but affordable for many Americans, while effectively out of reach for many others.

What Is Affordability?

Before reviewing the basic facts about trends in college costs, it will be useful to frame the question of affordability more completely. How might we define what is affordable for a family and what is not?   According to Webster's, to afford means "to be able to bear expenses, or the price of, without serious inconvenience" (Webster's, 1983). The word "inconvenience" is obviously open to interpretation. If something has a price tag that exceeds the level of a family's total resources, it could be unaffordable. We would all agree that a family with an income of $30,000 a year and no assets cannot afford a Rolls Royce. But can they afford a $50,000 home? Probably—if they have access to credit. And few of us would jump to oppose such an investment. We would, on the other hand, likely try to convince this family that they cannot afford a $5,000 vacation cruise.

A brief look at the way many economists analyze consumer options can be instructive here. All consumers have choices about what to buy. They also have budget constraints that limit their options. The budget constraint depends both on the resources available to them and on the prices of the goods and services among which they are choosing. In the simplest type of example, suppose Sarah has $100 to spend in a market that offers pizzas for $10 and shoes for $20. She can choose to buy ten pizzas, five pairs of shoes, or some combination of pizzas and shoes that adds up to $100. Different individuals would choose different consumption bundles, depending on their preferences. A fundamental idea here is that consumers get more satisfaction if they have more stuff, but more and more of the same item is likely to add to their satisfaction at a diminishing rate. Most of us would rather have some pizza and some shoes, rather than put all of our money in one place.

What does this example tell us about affordability? Sarah cannot afford five pizzas and five pairs of shoes—unless she can borrow money for her purchases. But can she afford ten pizzas? Sure—as long as she is willing to wear her old shoes. Clearly, affordability is not an absolute concept.

Can this simple story help us to understand college affordability? If we look only at annual income and the price tag on a typical college education, we will find that for many families college seems absolutely unaffordable. But given the availability of education loans for both parents and students, for most families the issue is what other goods and services they will have to sacrifice in order to pay for college. There are several mitigating factors affecting the necessary sacrifices. Many students do not actually pay the price on the sticker—they receive some form of discount in the form of financial aid. In addition, many families have assets. They may have other ideas about the purpose of these assets, but they have a choice about devoting some of this wealth to paying for education. Moreover, borrowing to finance college is much more like borrowing to buy a house than it is like borrowing to pay for a vacation, since a college education is an investment, with the benefits enjoyed over a lifetime.

In other words, in order to understand college affordability it is not enough to understand trends in college prices, the prices of other goods and services, and family incomes. We must also understand the discounts available on college prices, the preferences of students and families, and the saving and borrowing options available to pay for college. Another issue is that the discussion of college prices and of family incomes must include more than just averages. In addition to the fact that the variation in prices is significant, the dispersion in incomes has increased dramatically in recent decades. As a result, circumstances have changed in very different ways for different types of households. Let us begin with the basic facts about prices and incomes.

College Prices and Family Incomes

On average, the cost of attending college has increased much more rapidly in recent years than have either the prices of other goods and services or family incomes. Between 1971-72 and 1999-2000, tuition at public two-year institutions rose from $192 to $1,627 in current dollars and from $775 to $1,627 in inflation-adjusted 1999 dollar— a real increase of 110%. (See Table 1.) Although its starting point was much higher, private four-year college and university tuition rose at about the same rate over this 28-year period, from $1,820 to $15,380 in current dollars. For public four-year institutions, the rate of increase was even more rapid—121 percent in real terms, with the 1999-2000 average being $3,356 (College Board, 1999a).

Table 1. Average Tuition and Fees in Current and Constant Dollars: 1971-72 to 1999-00

	Public Two-Year		Public Four-Year		Private Four-Year	
	Current $$	Constant $$	Current $$	Constant $$	Current $$	Constant $$
1971-72	$192	$775	$376	$1,519	$1,820	$7,351
1978-79	$327	$793	$688	$1,669	$2,958	$7,177
1985-86	$659	$1,007	$1,242	$1,897	$5,418	$8,275
1992-93	$1,292	$1,507	$2,315	$2,700	$10,498	$12,242
1999-00	$1,627	$1,627	$3,356	$3,356	$15,380	$15,380
Growth Rates						
1971-78	+70%	+2%	+83%	+10%	+63%	-2%
1978-85	+102%	+27%	+81%	+14%	+83%	+15%
1985-92	+96%	+50%	+86%	+42%	+94%	+48%
1992-99	+26%	+8%	+45%	+24%	+47%	+26%
1971-99	+747%	$110%	+793%	+121%	+745%	+109%

Source: *Trends in College Pricing*, The College Board, 1999, p.7

As Table 1 indicates, tuition growth in the middle and late 1990s was considerably slower than it had been in the late 1980s. Public four-year tuition and fees, for example, rose 42 percent between 1985 and 1992, after adjusting for inflation. The increase between 1992 and 1999, in contrast, was only 24 percent. Because tuition and fees grew more rapidly in all sectors than did room and board, the real growth in the total cost of attendance in the last decade has been significantly lower than the figures in Table 1 might suggest—13 percent at two-year public institutions, 31 percent at four-year publics, and 29 percent at four-year private colleges and universities (College Board, 1999a, p. 9).

These changes in the "sticker price" of college are notable, but must be interpreted with caution. Different people face very different college costs. Aside from the differences across institutional types, there are significant regional differences. In the Southwest, the average 1999-2000 tuition and fees at four-year publics was only $2,536, compared with $4,727 in New England. Four-year privates averaged $11,275 and $20,171 respectively in these regions. Moreover, the variation in tuition levels within institutional type and within regions is significant. More than half of students at four-year schools pay less than $4,000 in tuition and fees, while 7 percent pay $20,000 or more (College Board, 1999a, p.1).

Over the last three decades median family income has risen much more slowly than college tuition—from $9,867 in 1970 to $44,568 in 1997. This constitutes a real increase of about 16 percent, compared with an increase of over 100 percent in the sticker price of college (U.S. Census Bureau, 1999, Table 750). In 1971-72, the average tuition and fees for a private four-year college constituted about 18 percent of median family income and public four-year colleges averaged less than 4 percent of median income. By 1985, these figures were not much higher—about 20 percent and just over 4 percent. But by 1997, they were 31 percent and 7 percent. In light of these figures, the increasing concern about the affordability of higher education is hardly surprising.

Because of the uneven growth in incomes among different groups, rising college costs have affected affordability differently for those at different places in the income distribution. In 1970, the top 5 percent of families in the U.S. had 16 percent of total family income. By 1997, this group (with incomes above $137,000) had 21 percent of total income. Both low- and middle-income families suffered in relative terms, with the share of the bottom 20 percent falling from 5.4 percent to 4.6 percent between 1970 and 1997, and the share of the middle 20 percent declining from 18 percent to 15 percent. Defining the middle more broadly, the share of the middle 60 percent of families also fell over this time period (U.S. Census Bureau, 1999, Table 751). This change helps to explain the strain middle-income families are feeling.

The increase in inequality in the 1980s and 1990s has been widely documented and is reflected in almost any measure of income. Among males, annual earnings for the bottom 20 percent fell about 19 percent between 1979 and 1996, while the top 10 percent enjoyed an increase of over 10 percent. The lowest earners among full-time working women saw their earnings rise by 8 percent over this period, but the top fifth earned 40 percent more in 1996 than in 1979 (Burtless, 1999).

As a result of these disparities, the cost of college attendance grew much more relative to the resources of low-income families than high-income families. Table 2 shows average cost of attendance at public and private four-year colleges as a percentage of income in the lowest, middle and highest fifth of families from 1971 to 1999. For those near the top of the income distribution, the sticker price of college has not become less affordable in any meaningful sense. The average cost of attendance at private four-year colleges has ranged between 12 percent and 15 percent of income over the entire 30-year period for the top fifth of families. The less affluent have been less fortunate in this regard. The share of average families' income required to pay this entire bill has gone from 27-29 percent in the 1970s and early 1980s to 44 percent in 1999-2000. For the lowest-income families, the jump was from 91 percent in 1971 and 84 percent in 1976, to 162 percent in 1999-2000.

Table 2. Cost of Attendance Relative to Family Incomes

	Public Four-Year			Private Four-Year		
	Low Income	Middle Income	High Income	Low Income	Middle Income	High Income
1971-72	42%	13%	6%	91%	29%	12%
1976-77	41%	13%	6%	84%	27%	12%
1981-82	42%	13%	5%	93%	28%	12%
1986-87	48%	13%	5%	106%	29%	11%
1991-92	56%	15%	6%	148%	40%	15%
1996-97	63%	17%	6%	160%	43%	14%
1999-00	61%	17%	5%	162%	44%	14%

Source: The College Board, *Trends in College Pricing, 1999*, p.15

These numbers do not give a complete picture of what is really required, since many students to not pay the sticker price, but benefit from student aid. As discussed below, the distribution of student aid dollars has also changed over time, again working against those at the bottom of the income distribution.

Price Discounts

Virtually all students are subsidized in college because even the full sticker price is considerably less than the actual cost of education. At public colleges and universities, taxpayers foot a significant portion of the bill. In the private sector, private donors subsidize students through income from endowments and annual giving. Beyond these general subsidies, many students receive direct student aid in the form of grants, loans and work subsidies from the federal government, state governments and institutional funds. On average, students and their families pay about two-thirds of the gross tuition charge (McPherson and Schapiro, 1997). Two-thirds of the students enrolled full-time in public institutions and 80 percent of those at private colleges and universities receive some form of student aid.

In 1998-99, over $64 billion in aid was awarded to students. Although over half of these dollars were in the form of federal loans, students also received about $8 billion in federal grant aid, $3.5 billion in state grants, and over $12 billion in institutional and other grants.

As shown in Tables 3 and 4, the composition of student aid has changed over time, with available loan dollars growing much more rapidly than grants. As Table 3 reveals, federal need-based grant aid has grown in real terms during both of the last two decades, although it did not keep up with inflation during the mid-1990s. Federal grants directed at veterans and other groups have, however, been dramatically reduced. In contrast, federal loans have become much more widely available, with a dramatic increase in 1980 and more recently, the introduction of non-need-based unsubsidized federal loans. Hidden in the table is the 38% increase in loan dollars between 1992 and 1993, which resulted from the introduction of this new program. This policy change, which increased access to liquidity for middle- and upper-income students without affecting access to grants, explains the leap in the share of loans in total aid between 1992 and 1994. (See Table 4).

The expansion of federal loan programs has significantly increased the loan/grant ratio of student aid, but it is important to realize that grant aid has also grown, with relatively small real growth in federal grants supplemented by rapid growth in state grant programs (Mumper, Chapter 9) and particularly in the grants awarded by institutions to their students (See Table 3).

Almost 4 million students receive grants from the largest federal program, the Pell grant program. After adjusting for inflation, grant aid rose 63 percent between 1988 and 1998 and now averages about $2500 per full-time-equivalent student. Total aid, including loans, averages over $6,000 per student. In other words, changes in the sticker price of college do not give a realistic picture of the actual amount people pay because of the very significant role of financial aid (College Board, 1999b).

Despite the sizable subsidies received by college students, they and their families pay a significantly higher percentage of the cost of their education now than they did 30 years ago. Because state funding for higher education has suffered from tight budgets

Table 3. Trends in Sources of Aid

	Millions of 1998-99 Dollars					% change	
	1977-78	1982-83	1987-88	1992-93	1997-98	1977-1987	1987-1997
Pell Grants	$4,001	$4,054	$5,328	$7,124	$6,435	+33%	+21%
Supplemental Educational Opportunity Grants	$656	$590	$585	$669	$593	-11%	+1%
Leveraging Educ. Assist. Partnerships (LEAP)/ State Student Incentive Grants (SSIG)	$157	$124	$107	$82	$51	-32%	-52%
Total Federal Need-Based Grants	**$4,814**	**$4,768**	**$6,020**	**$7,875**	**$7,079**	**+25%**	**+18%**
Perkins Loans	$1,614	$1,000	$1,143	$1,029	$1,079	-29%	-6%
Income-Contingent Loans	-	-	$7	-		-	-
Unsubsidized Ford Direct Loans	-	-	-		$3,732	-	-
Subsidized Ford Direct Loans	-	-	-		$6,185	-	-
Direct Parent Loans for Undergraduate Students (PLUS)	-	-	-		$1,109	-	-
Family Education/Stafford Unsubsidized Loans	-	-	-	$372	$8,077	-	-
Family Education/Stafford Subsidized Loans	$4,559	$11,215	$16,157	$12,616	$12,089	+254%	-12%
Family Education Parent Loans for Undergraduate Students (PLUS)				$1,475	$2,084		
Family Education Supplemental Loans for Students (SLS)				$2,739	-		
Total Federal Loans	**$6,173**	**$12,215**	**$18,231**	**$17,202**	**$34,356**	**+195%**	**+88%**
Federal Work-Study	**$1,231**	**$1,030**	**$901**	**$900**	**$921**	**-27%**	**+2%**
Veterans, Military and Other Directed Aid	**$11,284**	**$4,439**	**$2,131**	**$2,311**	**$2,317**	**-81%**	**+9%**
Total Federal Aid	**$23,503**	**$22,451**	**$26,359**	**$29,322**	**$44,674**	**+12%**	**+69%**
State Grant Programs	$1,777	$1,685	$2,133	$2,452	$3,374	+20%	+58%
State Loans	NA	NA	NA	NA	$359	-	-
Private Loans	NA	NA	NA	NA	$1,597	-	-
Institutional and Other Grants	$3,223	$3,282	$5,404	$8,179	$11,389	+68%	+111%
Total Federal, State and Institutional Aid	**$28,503**	**$27,418**	**$33,897**	**$39,953**	**$61,392**	**+19%**	**+81%**

Source: The College Board, Trends in Student Aid, 1999

and the pressures of expenditures on corrections and health care, tuition provided about a quarter of total revenues at public institutions in the early 1990s, compared with just 13 percent in 1960. Tuition plays a larger role for private colleges and universities and rose from 43 percent to 54 percent of revenues in this sector over the same period. Compounding the problem for families, their share of total tuition costs also increased over this period, from a quarter to over a third. It is noteworthy that these trends did not raise family responsibilities to record high levels, but returned the share of total institutional

Table 4. Trends in Pell Grants and Stafford Loans

	1988-89	*1990-91*	*1992-93*	*1994-95*	*1996-97*	*1998-99*
PELL GRANTS						
AVERAGE 1998-99	$1,898	$1,779	$1,705	$1,642	$1,661	$1,869
% public 4-yr cost	43%	36%	29%	25%	23%	24%
% private 4-yr cost	17%	13%	11%	10%	9%	9%
MAXIMUM 1998-99 $	$3,049	$2,896	$2,797	$2,535	$2,576	$3,000
% public 4-yr cost	69%	58%	48%	39%	36%	39%
% private 4-yr cost	27%	21%	19%	15%	14%	15%
STAFFORD LOANS						
AVERAGE SUB 1998-99 $	$3,486	$3,329	$3,249	$3,708	$3,608	$3,499
% public 4-yr cost	78%	67%	56%	57%	51%	45%
% private 4-yr cost	31%	25%	22%	22%	20%	17%
AVERAGE UNSUB 1998-99 $	-	-	$2,483	$3,886	$3,783	$3,886
% public 4-yr cost	-	-	43%	60%	53%	50%
% private 4-yr cost	-	-	16%	23%	21%	19%
GRANTS/ TOTAL AID	46%	49%	51%	42%	39%	40%
LOANS/ TOTAL AID	52%	48%	47%	56%	60%	58

Source: The College Board, Trends in Student Aid, 1999

revenues provided by families to the level it had been in 1950, before post-War college subsidies became established (McPherson and Schapiro, 1998).

As mentioned above, the patterns in the distribution of student aid are changing. Institutions, as well as states and the federal government, are targeting a lower portion of their subsidies at the lowest-income students. Colleges are using more of their financial aid funds to attract desirable students and to compete with other institutions and are focusing less on increasing access for those who cannot afford to pay (Breneman, Doti and Lapovsky, Chapter 12). More than a quarter of the $10 billion of institutional aid is now non-need based and fewer and fewer schools are able to accept candidates without regard to financial circumstances and meet the documented need of all students (McPherson and Schapiro, 1998). Students with the highest levels of need are likely to lose out in this competitive environment.

State government spending on merit-based aid for college was 19 percent higher in 1998-99 than a year earlier, and 47 percent higher than two years earlier. It now constitutes almost 20 percent of state scholarship aid (McPherson and Schapiro, 1997). Federal aid policies are also more tilted towards the middle-class than they were a decade ago. Unlike the long-standing program of direct federal grants to students, the recently implemented non-refundable tax credits for college costs give subsidies only to those whose income is sufficiently high for them to owe federal taxes. The anti-poor character of the policy is reinforced by the fact that only out-of-pocket tuition expenditures count, so students receiving grant aid at low-cost colleges are not eligible.

The changing distribution of financial aid exacerbates the problem created by the increasing inequality in the distribution of income. Not only has the sticker price of college grown more relative to lower than to higher incomes, but the net prices being paid by families at different income levels are converging. In 1986, low-income families paid about 19 percent of the amount high-income families had to pay for private four-year colleges. Middle-income families paid about 55 percent. By 1992, those ratios had increased to 31 percent and 66 percent respectively of the amounts paid by high-income students (McPherson and Schapiro, 1998, calculated from Table 4). The college affordability problem has clearly grown most for those least able to address it.

Preferences and Priorities

Probably because of the increasing differential between the earnings of college graduates and people with only high school degrees, interest in attaining higher education has intensified despite the price tag. Surveys indicate that in 1990, more than half of even the lowest performing students were advised to attend college. About 80 percent of students reported that their parents encouraged them to do so, compared with about 60 percent ten years earlier. Almost all high school completers in 1992 reported that they planned to continue their education at some point (Choy, 1998).

However, willingness to sacrifice in order to finance higher education has not grown commensurately. Rather, the sense of entitlement, particularly among middle- and upper-middle-income students and families has increased the tension surrounding financing college. An expectation that someone else will pay a substantial proportion of the bill has been fostered by the growing visibility of financial aid and publicity surrounding the susceptibility to bargaining among colleges competing for students. In an era when a sense of entitlement is widespread and when all except the wealthiest Americans perceive their real incomes stagnating, almost everyone thinks they need and deserve as much assistance as anyone else in financing college. Many financial aid professionals report that when families are asked how much they can contribute to their children's costs of attendance, low-income families are generally willing to stretch, but more affluent families are likely to offer quite limited amounts. They want a good education for their children, but are reluctant to make any significant sacrifices.

Part of the middle-income squeeze is the very real change in the price of higher education, and private higher education in particular, relative to family income. But the strength of the negative public reaction toward higher education pricing is more readily understood if we also acknowledge changes in attitudes and priorities. Their relative income decline doesn't mean that middle-income families can buy fewer goods and services than they could a decade ago. Purchasing power for average families did stagnate in the 1980s, but it was about 3 percent higher in 1991 than it had been in 1980. These families have not been able to increase their consumption as much as they would like to, or as much as wealthy families have been able to. Families who choose to purchase higher education have to make increasingly difficult choices about how to allocate their limited resources. The prevalence of new and exciting ways to spend money—computers, VCRs, compact disc players, expensive sneakers—may make paying for college feel like a bigger sacrifice. But the reality remains that there are more dollars left over for discretionary spending than there were a generation ago.

The questions raised here about willingness to pay for college arise from increased attention both in the media and in Congress to public concerns about the price of higher education, from experiences of campus administrators with reluctant families, and from a variety of indicators that students are becoming increasingly responsive to price differentials among colleges. However, the reality that even in the face of rapidly rising tuition levels, college enrollment rates have continued to increase suggests that the demand for higher education has not weakened.

Fifteen million students were enrolled in postsecondary institutions in the fall of 1997—about 9 million of them in four-year colleges and universities. That number is up 29 percent, from under 12 million in 1979-80. This increase came over a time period when the population between the ages of 20 and 24 declined by about 17 percent (U.S. Census Bureau, 1999, Table 14 and National Center for Education Statistics, 1999, Tables 173 and 174). Part of the explanation for this phenomenon is a dramatic rise in the enrollment of people 30 and older in the late 1980s, but enrollment rates among those of traditional college age also increased measurably. As Table 5 indicates, the proportion of 16- to 24-year-olds continuing their education immediately after high school rose significantly during the 1980s and 1990s. Enrollment rates grew particularly rapidly during periods of rapid increases in tuition levels.

It is not difficult to explain this enrollment trend, even in the face of the rise in tuition relative to income levels and increasing reluctance to sacrifice other goods and services in the interest of education. The real price of going to college is not just a function of the amount paid, but also of the return to the investment (Paulsen, Chapter 3). The earnings of college graduates relative to those of high school graduates increased quite dramatically during the 1980s. In 1998, full-time workers with a college degree or higher earned almost twice as much as high school graduates, while those with some college earned about 20 percent more (U.S. Census Bureau, 1999, Table 266). Calculation of the present value of the future earnings differentials over the lifetime of male workers (accounting for the reduced value of earnings premiums in the future) suggests that between 1980 and 1992, the value of future earnings differentials between high school and some college for men increased about 116 percent (Kane, 1999, p.116). In other words, the cost of not going to college has skyrocketed.

Table 5. College Enrollment Rates of High School Graduates
(16-24 year-olds who graduated during the preceding 12 months)

	Total	Male	Female
1960	45%	54%	38%
1965	51%	57%	45%
1970	52%	55%	49%
1975	51%	53%	49%
1980	49%	47%	52%
1985	58%	59%	57%
1990	60%	58%	62%
1995	62%	63%	61%
1998	66%	62%	69%

Source: *The Condition of Education, 1999*, Table 187

It may be misleading to suggest that young people make careful calculations of the expected financial return to their education. But the reality of declining wages for male high school graduates and increased demand for well-trained workers in the high-tech economy has clearly influenced the decision-making process. The real sacrifice in terms of material well-being comes not with financing college, but with living on the earnings available to non-college graduates.

Affordability is a subjective phenomenon. It depends on not only on the out-of-pocket costs, but also on perceptions of the cost of college and on potential earnings both during college years and throughout life. Many families who could easily pay for private college if they limited themselves to basic necessities quite reasonably do not consider college affordable. The debate is not really over how many dollars there are, but how much consumption of other goods and services families should have to sacrifice in order to finance higher education. While for the students themselves, the long-term financial choice may be clear, for families sacrificing in the interest of young people, and for young people with short time horizons, the current price tag on college education may be a significant barrier.

Saving and Borrowing

As the discussion of available financial aid resources indicates, borrowing has become an established means of financing higher education. Serious concerns have been raised about whether students are accumulating unacceptable amounts of debt, but the evidence suggests that this is not generally the case. While some students do borrow more than they can reasonably be expected to pay back, average debt levels, particularly among undergraduate borrowers, are quite manageable. The availability of credit appears to have significantly increased access to college without—at least so far—

becoming excessive. In one recent empirical study, median undergraduate debt for students who ended their studies between 1993 and 1995 was $9,500 (with a mean of $11,400) and while 17 percent had monthly payments exceeding 20 percent of their current incomes, over half used less than 10 percent of their incomes to repay their loans (Baum and Saunders, 1998).

Aside from the pragmatic reality that the combination of existing family resources and available grant aid is not likely to be sufficient to cover the cost of attendance for most students in the foreseeable future, borrowing is a perfectly sensible strategy. No one expects to be able to pay cash when they start a business or buy a house. They expect to borrow and pay over time—as they enjoy the profits from the business and the consumption value of the house. College graduates earn higher wages throughout their lives than high school graduates do. Spending a fraction of their earnings premium on repaying debt does not negate the financial benefit of higher education.

A more important concern about the shifting emphasis from grants to loans is the question of whether certain groups of students are likely to be particularly reluctant to incur debt and therefore not to enroll in college. This phenomenon is difficult to document, but it is not unreasonable to believe that young people from low-income families who would be first-generation college students may be less likely to undertake the investment. So while loans clearly increase the affordability of college, they almost certainly have less impact on access than grant aid would have.

Loans and grants serve somewhat different purposes, although both increase affordability. Grants help to solve the long-run problem of inadequate resources. Loans solve temporary liquidity problems. To some extent, family financial circumstances when students are applying to college are a good indicator of long-term needs. Those from low-income families are less likely to get financial assistance from their families when it is time to buy a house or to get bequests. They are more likely to contribute part of their earnings to their families' support. Moreover, they and their families are not in a position to make different choices in order to finance college—they simply lack the resources.

That said, the reality is that education and occupational choice are better predictors of future earnings than parental income is. Many students who could not attend college without assistance will end up near the top of the income distribution. A significant number of those whose families are more affluent will enter low-paying occupations and may have trouble paying off their student loans. In other words, there is a strong argument to be made for making some component of the student aid subsidy dependent on future income rather than current family income. This is another argument for partial reliance on loans. Grants can only be allocated on the basis of current financial circumstances, while loan repayment requirements can be based on future earnings.

Given the high cost of higher education relative to family incomes, the inadequacy of grant resources, and the limits to reasonable debt levels, encouraging saving for college is a critical part of keeping college affordable. The personal savings rate has declined dramatically during the 1990s, from 5.3 percent of disposable personal income in 1990 and 6.2 percent in 1992 to 2.1 percent in 1997 and a startling 0.5 percent in 1998 (U.S. Census Bureau, 1999, Table 730). However, the bottom 60 percent of households find themselves spending more than they earn, while the upper 40 percent save at higher rates than the averages suggest. According to the Consumer Expenditure Survey, in 1998, households in the fourth quintile of the income distribution, averaging about $50,000 of income, saved 5 percent of their incomes. Higher income earners saved considerably more (U.S. Department of Commerce, 1998, Table 1).

Some controversy has emerged over the advisability of saving for college because of the reliance of the financial aid formula on a combination of income and assets. The argument is that because families with higher assets are expected to make larger contributions to their children's education, accumulating assets may be self-defeating. Almost all 50 states now have some sort of state-sponsored college saving plan and over a million accounts have been opened under these plans. The need analysis treatment of prepaid tuition plans, which is the form taken by most of the current state savings plan dollars, is particularly harsh and often decreases aid dollar for dollar. However, under the current aid formulas, the maximum added contribution expected from $1,000 of parental assets in any other form is $56. Families who have saved for college will have a much easier time coming up with their expected contributions from income than will those who have been less thrifty. The realities of compound interest will make their long-term sacrifice less than that required of families who fail to save.

Public policies designed to encourage saving are clearly advisable—as long as they do not transfer significant subsidy dollars from low-income families without the ability to save to middle- and upper-income families who might save even without incentives in place.

Access vs. Affordability

The evidence presented in this chapter suggests that while the strain on typical family budgets generated by college tuition rates that have risen dramatically in recent years is quite real, college remains affordable for most middle- and upper-income families and students. The availability of public subsidies significantly lowers the cost to students. Guaranteed loan programs provide needed liquidity. Nonetheless, there are strong indications that financial constraints remain a significant barrier to educational opportunities for people from low-income families (Hearn, Chapter 11). The fact that low-income students are much more sensitive to tuition increases than higher-income students is well-documented. Most recently, Tom Kane's careful analysis confirms the idea that increases in both two-year and four-year tuition levels have a significantly larger effect on enrollment rates at lower income levels. He concludes that low-income students act as though they lack access to capital. It is unclear whether they are simply afraid to borrow, whether they have difficulty navigating the complex student aid application process, or whether they lack adequate information. What is clear is that even at the highest ability levels, low-income students are much less likely than others to participate in higher education (Kane, 1999).

Among 1992 high school graduates, the average person from the highest 20 percent of the income distribution was 34 percentage points more likely than the average person from the lowest quintile to go to college. Controlling for differences in test scores reduces this differential, but it remains 21 percentage points. Among students who scored in the top 25 percent of test takers, 94 percent enrolled in college. However, those at the top of the income distribution were still 14 percentage points more likely than those at the bottom with the same high test scores to go to college (Kane, 1999, pp.98+). Similar results emerge if class rank is used to identify high-ability students.

This income-based gap in enrollment rates is even more disturbing because it has increased over time. The difference in enrollment rates between students from the lowest income quartile and those from the other three quartiles grew by 12 percentage points between 1980 and 1993 (Kane, 1995, p.6). Similarly, the 1976 enrollment rate of 49 percent for white high school graduates rose to 64 percent by 1994, while at the same time, the rate for blacks went only from 42 percent to 51 percent (McPherson and Schapiro, 1998, p. 38).

Among those who do continue their education after high school, institutional choice also appears to be much more price-sensitive among lower-income students. Over half of the wealthiest students enroll in private, non-profit colleges and universities, while only about 20 percent of lower- and lower-middle income students make this choice. On the other hand, almost half of the college students from low-income families are at two-year public institutions, while a third of middle-income students and fewer than 10 percent of those from the most affluent families attend these schools (McPherson and Schapiro, 1998, p. 44).

Part of the explanation for these different enrollment factors is that the difference in relative net prices of the sectors varies quite a bit by family income levels. At the lowest income levels, grant aid is adequate to cover the cost of tuition at the average two-year public college. Up to incomes of about $30,000, the net price of a two-year college is only about 10 percent that of a four-year public, and the net price of a public four-year college is only about 15 percent that of a four-year private. The difference in net price is, in proportionate terms, considerably less for middle- and upper-income students, who receive less need-based aid—and who tend to choose higher cost institutions within sectors (Kane, 1999, p.35).

Higher education is a big investment. It is expensive and requires considerable time, energy and effort in order to be successful. Still, it yields very high returns and college enrollment rates are at an all-time high, despite the high price tag. But the unfortunate reality is that while low-cost options are available, there is evidence that financial constraints play a significant role in limiting the educational opportunities of low-income people.

Increasing access for academically prepared low-income students should be the first priority. For those with average or even above-average resource levels, paying for college and university is frequently a stretch. It requires considerable sacrifice, at least in the short run. The rising price tag, lagging income for all but the wealthiest Americans, and a system of subsidies that is complicated, sometimes misdirected, and unable to keep up with tuition increases all contribute to the fear that college may soon be out of reach for many. Still, the existence of a variety of institutional choices, financial aid in the form of both grants and loans, and the high rate of return to education make college not only affordable, but the only promising path to a secure financial future for most people. Continued vigilance and renewed efforts in both the public policy arena and on college campuses are required to keep higher education widely accessible. But students and their families must also be willing to take responsibility for financing this investment if college is to remain affordable.

References

Baum, S., and Saunders, D. (1998). *Life After Debt: Results of the National Student Loan Survey.* Braintree: Nellie Mae.

Burtless, G. (1999). Effects of growing wage disparities and changing family composition on the U.S. income distribution. \

Brookings Institution. Center on Social and Economic Dynamics, Working Paper No. 4.

Choy, S. (1998). College access and affordability. National Center for Education Statistics. Nces.ed.gov/pubs98/condition98/c98005/html.

College Board (1999a). *Trends in College Pricing.* Washington, DC: The College Board.

College Board (1999b). *Trends in Student Aid.* Washington, DC: The College Board.

Kane, T. (1995). Rising public college tuition and college entry: how well do public subsidies promote access to college? National Bureau of Economic Research Working Paper No.5164. July.

Kane, T. (1999). *The Price of Admission: Rethinking How Americans Pay for College.* Washington, DC: Brookings.

McPherson, M., and Schapiro, M. (1997). Financing undergraduate education, *National Tax Journal* 50(3): 557-572.

McPherson, M., and Schapiro, M. (1998). *The Student Aid Game: Meeting Need and Rewarding Talent in American Higher Education.* Princeton: Princeton University Press.

Miller, E. (1997). Parents' views on the value of a college education and how they will pay for it. *Journal of Student Financial Aid* 27(1):7-20.

National Center for Education Statistics (1999). *The Condition of Education: 1999.* U.S. Department of Education.

U.S. Census Bureau (1999). *Statistical Abstract of the United States: 1999.* U.S. Department of Commerce.

U.S. Department of Commerce (1998). *Consumer Expenditure Survey,* 1998.

Webster's (1983). *New Universal Unabridged Dictionary* New York: Simon and Schuster.

PART II
Economic Theories and the Finance of Higher Education

Chapter 3

THE ECONOMICS OF HUMAN CAPITAL AND INVESTMENT IN HIGHER EDUCATION[1]

Michael B. Paulsen

A variety of economic concepts, theories, and models have been useful in the study of the finance of higher education (Cohn and Geske, 1990; Leslie and Brinkman, 1988; Paulsen, 1998). Most of these tools of analysis have been drawn from the broad theoretical framework of microeconomics. For example, the economics of the public sector is an applied field of microeconomics that has been useful in the study of the role of government in the finance of higher education; and the economics of human capital is one theoretical approach drawn from another applied field of microeconomics (labor economics) that has been useful in the study of the effects of financial and non-financial factors on students' college-going behavior. The purpose of this chapter is to introduce, explain, and illustrate the use of selected concepts and models from the economics of human capital that have proven to be useful in analyzing and understanding the finance of higher education. The next chapter (Paulsen, chapter 4) will address the nature, role and application of the economics of the public sector in the finance of higher education. And the final two chapters in this part of the book will present and apply general concepts from microeconomics—especially from the theories of demand, price, costs and production—that have helped enhance our understanding about costs and productivity (Lewis and Dundar, chapter 5) and rising college tuition (Paulsen, chapter 6) in higher education.

THE CONCEPT OF HUMAN CAPITAL AND THE INDIVIDUAL INVESTMENT DECISION

This section presents a model of rational decision-making first proposed by the pioneers of human capital theory in the late 1950s and early 1960s (Kiker, 1971a). Although the explanations and illustrations presented in this section add to our understanding of how students make their college-going decisions, they certainly do *not* tell the whole story. Therefore,

---

[1]I would like to thank Sandy Baum and Rob Toutkoushian for their helpful comments on an earlier draft of this chapter.

subsequent sections of this chapter and the next chapter (Paulsen, chapter 4) examine the ways in which human capital theorists, along with many other economists and social scientists from other disciplines, have elaborated, expanded, adapted, and improved upon this original rational decision-making model to further enhance our understanding of the roles of a variety of tangible *and* intangible factors, and the many other important complexities, that characterize the decision-making behavior of students considering an investment in higher education.

Students make a series of choices that are manifested in their college-going behavior (St. John, 1994; St. John, Asker and Hu, Chapter 10). They choose whether or not to attend college (an access decision), which college to attend (a college-choice decision), and whether or not to re-enroll each semester and year (a persistence decision). Human capital theorists view these choices as the results of students' decisions to make investments in higher education—a form of human capital (G. Becker, 1993; Hansen, 1971; Kiker, 1971b; Mincer, 1993a, 1993b; Schultz, 1961; Weisbrod, 1968). *Human capital* can be defined as the productive capacities—knowledge, understandings, talents, and skills—possessed by an individual or society; and *investment in human capital* refers to expenditures on education, health and other activities that augment these productive capacities (Arai, 1998; Johnes, 1993; Paulsen and Peseau, 1989; Schultz, 1961; Thurow, 1970; Woodhall, 1995). Investment in human capital is attractive to both individual and government investors. The greater productivity of individual workers is related to increases in their lifetime earnings, and by expanding the productive capacities of the workforce, investments in human capital are also positively related to increases in the general levels of local, state, regional and national output and income (Denison, 1962, 1984; Leslie and Brinkman, 1988; Paulsen, 1996a, 1996b; Pencavel, 1993; Psacharopoulos, 1973).[2]

A central assumption of the model of rational investment decision making proposed by human capital theorists is that in order to make sensible investment decisions, individual students *implicitly* calculate whether or not a college education is worthwhile by comparing the expected benefits with the expected costs associated with an investment

---

[2]Human capital theory has served as a useful component of the field of economics of education for the past forty years. There has been consistent empirical support for its various components, and it has helped explain a range of economic phenomena related to educational decision-making. Nevertheless, a number of important competing (or complementary) hypotheses and perspectives have been presented in response to human capital theory's central proposition that education increases one's productivity, which in turn, leads to greater earnings. These include the screening hypothesis (e.g., Spence, 1973), the job competition model (e.g., Thurow, 1975), the dual labor market hypothesis (e.g. Doeringer and Piore, 1971), and the social class approach (e.g., Bowles and Gintis, 1976). Each of these theories has helped draw our attention to important practical and realistic aspects of the relation between educational attainment and earnings, and it is important to continue to examine these hypotheses in conjunction with human capital theory. In subsequent sections, this chapter does examine the effect of social class, or more particularly, the socioeconomic background of a student, on the nature of her or his college-going behavior. However, a thorough examination of all of these perspectives is beyond the scope of this chapter. Therefore, the interested reader may wish to consult Cohn and Geske's (1990) review and analysis of these different views, as well as their references to the additional literature that examines these approaches in more detail.

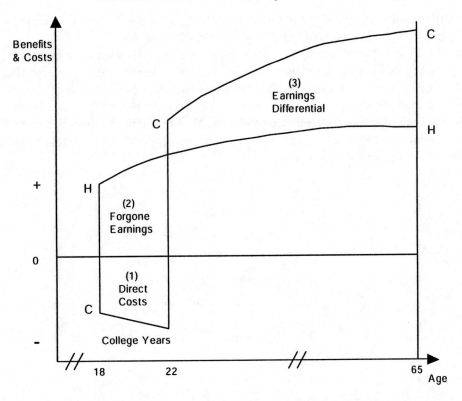

Figure 1. Benefits, Costs, and Investment in Higher Education

in a college education. The primary benefits and costs students consider and compare in this model of a higher education investment decision are illustrated in Figure 1 (Arai, 1998; Carnoy, 1995c; Douglas, 1977; Kaufman, 1994; McConnell and Brue, 1995; McMahon and Wagner, 1982). More particularly, Figure 1 portrays the central monetary factors considered by a high school graduate of traditional college-going age who considers an investment in a college education. The HH line illustrates the expected earnings of a student who decides to enter the labor force and take a full-time job right after high school instead of pursuing a college education. The CCC line illustrates the expected benefits and costs of a student who elects to attend college full-time right after high school instead of entering the labor force and seeking a full-time job. Area (1)— right below the horizontal line labeled "0" on the vertical axis—represents the out-of-pocket or *direct costs* a student faces when attending college (e.g., tuition, fees, books). Area (2)—above the "0" line but below the HH line—represents the *indirect costs* of college, corresponding to the earnings forgone by students who do not work while they attend college (i.e., the earnings they could have received with their high school diplomas if they had entered the labor force instead of attending college right after high school). Area (3) represents the widening vertical difference between the CCC and HH lines over the 43-year work life of a college graduate from age 22 to 65. This area shows the earnings differential between college and high-school graduates over a lifetime. The earnings differential corresponds to the incremental or additional income of a college graduate compared to a high school graduate from age 22 to age 65.

Figure 2 portrays a similar combination of benefits and costs considered by potential students when making an investment decision. However, Figure 2 elaborates on the factors presented in Figure 1 by showing how area (1) (the direct costs of college) would be reduced for students who receive subsidies (e.g., grants, loans) that might offset some of the direct costs of college attendance; and area (2) (the indirect costs of college) would be reduced for students who earn income from part-time employment that might offset some of the indirect costs of attendance.[3]

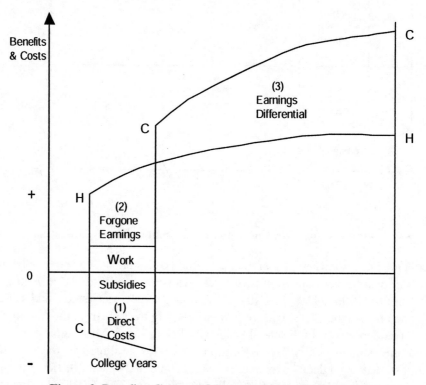

Figure 2. Benefits, Costs, and Investment: An Elaboration

Both benefits and costs occur over time; therefore, benefits to be received and costs to be incurred in the future must be adjusted using an appropriate discount rate—an appropriate market rate of interest (i)—to determine their present value. Assuming a four-year period of investment in college, the present discounted value of the earnings differential—which begins in the fifth year, one year after the investment period—between college and high school graduates ($E_{it}^C - E_{it}^H$) is determined as follows:

(Equation 1)

$$PDV^{C-H} = \sum_{t=5}^{T} \frac{E_{it}^C - E_{it}^H}{(1+i)^t} = \frac{E_{i5}^C - E_{i5}^H}{(1+i)^5} + \frac{E_{i6}^C - E_{i6}^H}{(1+i)^6} + \dots + \frac{E_{iT}^C - E_{iT}^H}{(1+i)^T}$$

The direct costs of college attendance include outlays for tuition, fees and books (C_t), net of any subsidies, such as scholarships, grants, loans that help offset out-of-pocket expenses ($-S_t$). The indirect costs of college attendance include the earnings forgone by students while attending college (E_{it}^H), net of any earnings due to part-time work while attending that help offset some of the income that would otherwise be forgone (E_{it}^{PT}). The present discounted values of the direct (DC) and indirect costs (IC) of college—which are incurred during the four-year investment period—are calculated using Equations 2 and 3, respectively, as follows:

$$PDV^{DC} = \sum_{t=1}^{4} \frac{C_t - S_t}{(1+i)^t} = \frac{C_1 - S_1}{(1+i)^1} + \frac{C_2 - S_2}{(1+i)^2} + \dots + \frac{C_4 - S_4}{(1+i)^4} \qquad \text{(Equation 2)}$$

$$PDV^{IC} = \sum_{t=1}^{4} \frac{E_{it}^H - E_{it}^{PT}}{(1+i)^t} = \frac{E_{i1}^H - E_{i1}^{PT}}{(1+i)^1} + \frac{E_{i2}^H - E_{i2}^{PT}}{(1+i)^2} + \dots + \frac{E_{i4}^H - E_{i4}^{PT}}{(1+i)^4} \qquad \text{(Equation 3)}$$

Based on the present-value criterion, the investment in higher education would be worthwhile if the present discounted value (PDV) of the benefits (earnings differential) were greater than the present discounted values of the direct and indirect costs of the investment, as illustrated in the equation below.

$$\sum_{t=5}^{T} \frac{E_{it}^C - E_{it}^H}{(1+i)^t} > \sum_{t=1}^{4} \frac{C_t - S_t}{(1+i)^t} + \sum_{t=1}^{4} \frac{E_{it}^H - E_{it}^{PT}}{(1+i)^t} \qquad \text{(Equation 4)}$$

This result is equivalent to that produced by the internal rate-of-return criterion. The internal rate of return is the discount rate (r) that equates the present discounted values of the benefits (the earnings differential) and the costs (both direct and indirect costs, net of subsidies and part-time work) associated with the investment, as illustrated in the equation below.

$$\qquad \text{(Equation 5)}$$

$$\sum_{t=5}^{T} \frac{E_{it}^C - E_{it}^H}{(1+r)^t} = \sum_{t=1}^{4} \frac{C_t - S_t}{(1+r)^t} + \sum_{t=1}^{4} \frac{E_{it}^H - E_{it}^{PT}}{(1+r)^t}$$

In general, the investment would be worthwhile when the internal rate of return on

---

[3]Figures 1 and 2 portray the nature and relations between the benefits and costs bearing on the investment decision of an individual considering the traditional attendance pattern of a high school senior of traditional college-going age. The figure is drawn based on the assumption of full-time attendance at a four-year college, an expectation of graduation in four years, and plans to either not work, or only work part-time, during those four years. However, this figure could easily be modified to represent various benefit-cost scenarios that would meaningfully portray the decision-making behavior of students of non-traditional age, those anticipating enrolling or re-enrolling in a community college (academic or vocational) or graduate school program, those planning to work full time while attending college, those expecting to complete their postsecondary experience over a period of time in excess of four years, and those planning to stop out or drop out before receiving a certificate or degree. The logic of the analysis would be similar regarding the weighing of costs and benefits relevant to each of these other scenarios.

the investment (r) exceeds the market rate of interest (i) (Arai, 1998; Carnoy, 1995c; Cohn and Geske, 1990; Johnes, 1993; Leslie and Brinkman, 1988; Paulsen, 1998; Perlman, 1973; Psacharopoulos, 1973).

The "principle of marginalism" in microeconomics provides a useful framework for expressing this investment criterion (Apgar and Brown, 1987). According to this principle, the additional benefits that accrue to the investor due to a one-unit increase in an investment—in this case, a college education—are defined as the "marginal" benefits (MB) of the investment. Similarly, the additional costs that are incurred by the investor are defined as the "marginal" costs (MC) of the investment. The internal rate of return (r) and the market rate of interest (i) express MB and MC, respectively, in terms of rates or percentages. The internal rate of return (r) indicates the percentage yield a college graduate would gain from the investment in a college education, and the market rate of interest (i) corresponds to either the rate at which interest income could have been earned if the individual's funds had not been spent on college or the rate at which interest costs would have to be paid to acquire the funds necessary to make the college investment. In summary, an investment in a college education would be worthwhile if the marginal benefits exceeded the marginal costs associated with the investment, that is, if $r > i$, or equivalently, if MB > MC (Arai, 1998; Johnes, 1993).[4]

The human capital model has a considerable amount of explanatory power when it comes to predicting the effects of changes in monetary benefits and costs on student enrollment behavior. However, the relative magnitudes of these monetary benefits and costs may vary substantially across individuals due to differences in other factors that are often non-monetary, less tangible, and more difficult to assess or estimate, plan for or control, and more difficult to influence through public policy. Examples of such factors include differences in socioeconomic status and background, academic ability, access to information about postsecondary opportunities, financial opportunities in the credit markets, employment opportunities in the job markets, discriminatory practices in the credit or job markets or at institutions of higher education, and early home and school environments. The important effects of these factors on students' college-going behavior has drawn attention to some of the practical limitations of the simple model of rational decision making proposed by the pioneers of human capital theory. Subsequent sections of this chapter and the next chapter examine the efforts of economists and other social scientists to elaborate on the original model of human capital in ways that provide a more complete portrayal and help us develop a fuller understanding of college-going behavior.

The monetary components of benefits and costs, and the relations among them—as presented in Figures 1 and 2 and Equations 1-5—point to a set of generalizations about the

---

[4]MB is defined here as the internal rate of return (r) associated with each additional unit of investment in higher education. As can be seen in the equations above, the rate of return (r) is based on, and affected by, the amounts of both benefits and costs associated with an investment in higher education. For example, the internal rate of return in Equation 5 is the expected net economic payoff to an investment in higher education, and can be defined as the "value of the (discounted lifetime) gains due to an individual's education expressed as a percentage of the (discounted) costs to the individual of acquiring that education" (Johnes, 1993, p. 28). Therefore, marginal benefits, in this instance, means the student's gain in benefits, net of costs of attendance, associated with an investment in higher education.

effects of a range of financial factors on students' decisions to invest in higher education (Ehrenberg and Smith, 1982; Kaufman, 1986, 1994; McConnell and Brue, 1995; McMahon and Wagner, 1982). Each of the following generalizations has been widely and consistently supported by both extensive research and common experience. All else equal, the rate of return to investment in college education—and therefore, the likelihood that a student will enroll (or re-enroll) in a postsecondary institution—will be higher:

- the greater the magnitude of the earnings differential between college and high school graduates. The responsiveness of student enrollment to variations in the college-high school earnings differential has been documented in many studies (see for example, Freeman, 1976; Murphy and Welch, 1992; Paulsen and Pogue, 1988; Wish and Hamilton, 1980). The most dramatic example was observed before, during and after the recession in the job market for college graduates in the 1970s (Freeman, 1975; Rumberger, 1984).

- the lower the direct costs of college, such as tuition, fees, books and living costs. Most studies of enrollment demand or individual student access, choice and persistence have consistently found student enrollment to be inversely related to the direct or out-of-pocket costs of college (W. Becker, 1990; Jackson and Weathersby, 1975; Heller, 1997; Hossler, et al., 1989; Kane, 1999c; Leslie and Brinkman, 1988; Manski and Wise, 1983; McPherson, 1978; McPherson and Schapiro, 1991; Paulsen, 1990).

- the higher the subsidies, such as scholarships, grants or loans, that help students offset the direct costs of college. Research has shown that student aid affects student decisions regarding access, choice and persistence in college (Leslie and Brinkman, 1988; St. John, 2000); although the effects may differ across different types (e.g., choice and persistence) of enrollment decisions (see for example, Paulsen and St. John, 1997, in press), and students tend to be more responsive to some types of subsidies than to others—in particular, research indicates that students are more responsive to grants than to loans in their enrollment decisions (Heller, 1997).

- the lower the earnings forgone by students while attending college, a condition that occurs when the general economy is in a recession (e.g., overall unemployment rates rise) or when students elect to work part-time while attending college. In general, enrollment growth is greatest when the general economy moves into a recession, because the opportunity cost (earnings forgone) decreases for students attending college, thereby increasing their perceived rate of return and the likelihood of the enrollment (Hoenack and Weiler, 1979; Kane, 1995, 1999c; Rouse, 1994).

- the less present-oriented the student; that is, everyone discounts the value of a dollar in the future compared with its value in the present, but some students—perhaps due to the pressing current needs of lower-income households—discount the value of a future dollar at rates (i) much higher than those of others, and therefore, might hesitate to spend today's "certain" dollars on an education that offers only a "possibility" of more dollars in the future (McConnell and Brue, 1995; Thurow, 1970).

- the higher the earnings differential associated with a student's intended major field of study—that is, the earnings differential between college and high school graduates is especially high for engineering and business graduates, compared with graduates in the humanities and arts. Students' choices of major fields of study—along with their propensities to attend college—have been consistently responsive to differential returns available in different fields (Fiorito and Dauffenbach, 1982; Freeman, 1971, 1976; Paulsen and Pogue, 1988).

Adolescent Econometricians?

The individual's decision to make an investment in higher education is essentially an exercise in making an important life-influencing decision in the face of uncertainty (Hanushek, 1993). Although the college-going decision is not a purely financial one, a fundamental tenet of human capital theory—particularly in the study of college-going behavior—is that students choose whether or not to attend college, which college to attend, whether or not to re-enroll each term, and what field in which to major, based in part on their perceptions of the returns (earnings differentials) related to their investment. Although economists do *not* assume students actually calculate internal rates of return on investment—that is, as Manski asserts, many are only "adolescent econometricians" (1993, p. 43)—economists do assume that students compare their expected benefits and costs and choose the best available postsecondary investment option. And they view students as making informal comparisons between their perceived benefits and costs with sufficient care that the more formal rate-of-return criterion offers a reasonable approximation of the investment decision-making process (Arai, 1998).

These assumptions raise the important question of just how accurate current and potential college students are in their perceptions of the future earnings associated with the investments they are contemplating or have begun to make (Freeman, 1971). Fortunately, a number of recent studies have been conducted to explore answers to this question (Betts, 1996; Blau and Ferber, 1991; Dominitz and Manski, 1996; Smith and Powell, 1990). Dominitz and Manski (1996) surveyed male and female high school and college students regarding their perceptions of the earnings of college and high school graduates. There was very little variation in the perceptions between groups, but substantial variation in perceptions within groups. However, male respondents' median perceptions of the median earnings of males, and female respondents' median perceptions of the median earnings of females who worked full-time, year-round, showed a high degree of accuracy. Smith and Powell (1990) found college students' perceptions of earnings of college graduates relative to high school graduates to be reasonably accurate, although male respondents tended to overestimate or "self-enhance" their own expected earnings.

Finally, Betts (1996) found that college students' (freshmen through seniors) average estimates of the ratio of earnings of college relative to high school graduates, between 25 and 34 years of age in 1990, were quite accurate, with estimates of 57.8 percent compared with an actual ratio of 50.9 percent. Students' errors were even smaller when their estimates pertained to their major field of study or interest, and students' accuracy improved each year, although the difference was statistically significant only between the freshman and senior years. Another important finding was that lower-income students had much larger errors of estimation; in particular, they substantially underestimated the earnings of college graduates. This is disturbing, with substantial implications regarding the inequity with which information about postsecondary opportunities and outcomes is distributed, and the need for more effective public policies to disseminate such information, such as the statewide efforts associated with the Indiana Postsecondary Encouragement Experiment (Hossler and Schmit, 1995).[5] Betts offered several possible explanations: first, "higher family income itself buys better information;" second, "since lower income is often associated with retirement or families in which only one parent works, it may be that a working parent provides a child with a valuable window into the workplace;" and third, "children from poorer neighborhoods may underestimate the returns to college due to a lack of information" (Betts, 1996, p. 43).[6] Betts concluded his study with the following statement:

> [T]aken as a whole, the above findings strongly support the assumption made by human capital theory that workers acquire information about earnings by level of education in order to choose their optimal level of education. Information is not perfect, but a process of learning over time is clearly discernible" (p. 50).

The findings of these studies are also consistent with, and supportive of, the findings of Freeman (1971) about the accuracy of student estimates of both their future and forgone earnings. In combination, the results of these studies indicate that many of the "adolescent econometricians" who constitute a substantial portion of the potential and current pool of college students appear to be reasonably careful and accurate in their acquisition of information about earnings differentials. Indeed, they may, in their informal way, acquire information that is adequate to make more or less economically rational college-going decisions.[7]

PRIVATE RETURNS TO INVESTMENT IN BACCALAUREATE-LEVEL HIGHER EDUCATION

The most straightforward and accessible means by which to assess the private returns[8] to investment in higher education is to calculate the earnings differential between col-

---

[5]This statewide initiative is based primarily on contact with high school students and their families and, even more centrally, on an innovative and expansive effort to disseminate information about postsecondary opportunities in the state of Indiana. For more information about this impressive and largely successful program—they report increases in college participation rates across income levels and across racial and ethnic groups—see Hossler and Schmit (1995) and Hossler, et al. (1999), and other publications cited therein.

[6]From a sociological perspective, these observations may also be based, in part, on differences in one's access to different forms of cultural capital, such as knowing people who went to college who have "insider" information about postsecondary opportunities; or because of class-based differences in students' habiti that encourage some to be more aware of and open to information about the college option and others more aware of and open to the work option after high school (Bourdieu and Passeron, 1990; McDonough, 1997).

[7]Clearly, human capital theory would benefit from a deeper understanding of both students' expectations and their process of expectation formation; and a better understanding would assist policy-makers in intervening to improve the equity and accuracy with which information is disseminated. However, as Manski (1993) explains, "progress is possible only if economists become more willing to entertain the use of subjective data in empirical analysis. Decisions under uncertainty reflect the interplay of preferences, expectations, and opportunities....[The] problem can be solved if choice data are combined with interpretable subjective data on expectations and/or preferences" (p. 55).

[8]See Paulsen, Chapter 4, in this volume for an examination of the literature related to the *social* returns to investment in higher education.

lege and high school graduates (W. Becker, 1992; Paulsen, 1998). The long-term trend in this differential has been upward, with some notable cyclical periods. The cyclical swings in the job market are most evident in the starting salaries of recent graduates (Freeman, 1976; Paulsen and Pogue, 1988). Considering all fields and years of work experience, Murphy and Welch (1989, 1992) reported that earnings of college graduates have exceeded those of high school graduates by substantial margins: 47 percent in 1963, 61 percent in 1971, and 48 percent during the late 1970s—a period characterized by a downturn in the job market for college graduates, due to large increases in the supply of college-educated workers, combined with stagnant growth in the demand for college-educated workers (see e.g., Freeman, 1976; Rumberger, 1984). And when the long-term trend of growth re-established itself in the 1980s, the differential reached 67 percent (Murphy and Welch, 1992). In addition, more or less parallel patterns for earnings differentials or premiums were observed for men and women, blacks and whites (W. Becker, 1992; Murphy and Welch, 1992).

Furthermore, from the early 1960s to the late 1980s, graduation rates for white males exhibited a close and consistent three-year lagged response to the college-high school earnings differential (Murphy and Welch, 1992). However, Murphy and Welch (1992) explain that the close relation between graduation rates and the earnings premium for college graduates has not held as consistently for women or blacks, due to structural differences in the labor supply behavior. In the mid-1960s, women completed only about one-third of the bachelor's degrees conferred; however, in the 1970s, women—many of non-traditional age—began to attend college in increasing numbers, and as a result, their graduation rates did not decline in step with the diminishing college earnings premium. But this does not explain the supply behavior of blacks. Even though their graduation rates were relatively consistent with fluctuations in the earnings premiums in the 1960s and 1970s, when those earnings premiums grew more rapidly in the 1980s, their participation and graduation rates did not follow suit. McPherson and Schapiro (1998) have addressed this apparent inconsistency in terms of differential responses to the changing affordability of a college education in the 1980s. Tuition increased rapidly during the 1980s and simultaneously, the purchasing power of need-based grant aid for lower-income students decreased, thereby reducing the affordability of college. Lower-income students—who are disproportionately represented among minority groups—are much more tuition-sensitive than higher-income students in their enrollment behavior. In other words, even though rapidly growing earnings premiums may have been adequate to offset the rapid increases in tuition among middle- and upper-income students, the incentive appears to have been inadequate to offset the negative enrollment effect of decreases in the affordability of college for some lower-income and minority students.

More recent data on the earnings differential between college and high school graduates is now available. Based on average incomes of college and high school graduates (in place of the average wages used by Murphy and Welch, 1989, 1992), at the end of the decade characterized by recession in the college job market—1979—college graduates earned 55 percent more than high school graduates. This earnings differential grew to 60 percent in 1980, 69 percent in 1985, 75 percent in

1990, and has remained relatively stable at this robust level through the 1990s, at 73 percent in 1995 and 77 percent in 1997 (The College Board, 1999a, p. 20).

The earnings differential is less sophisticated as an estimate of the private returns to investment than calculations of internal rates of return (Arai, 1998; Leslie and Brinkman, 1988). For example, costs of college attendance are not considered, and there are no controls for differences between college and high school graduates in terms of ability or motivation, parents' education, income, occupation, and marital status, as well as work experience. However, the earnings differential is relatively simple to compute and communicates a substantial amount of information about the college job market to potential students in an efficient manner (W. Becker, 1992; Paulsen, 1998).[9]

A number of researchers have extended the study of returns to the search for differential returns for college study in different major fields (Berger, 1992; Grubb, 1996; McMahon and Wagner, 1982). For the past twenty years or so, findings in this area have been very consistent in ranking the earnings premiums related to different major fields, in spite of a wide variety of approaches to estimating the returns by major. In general, researchers have found that students who major in engineering, computers, and business experience the highest returns, while students majoring in the traditional areas of liberal arts, humanities and education are well behind, both in their starting salaries and in the rates of growth in their incomes over their careers.

Economists estimate private internal rates of return and compare them with interest rates on alternative investments as one approximation of the student's enrollment decision-making process (G. Becker, 1993; Cohn and Geske, 1990; Johnes, 1993; Perlman, 1973; Psacharopoulos, 1973). The calculation of private rates of return considers only the private benefits affecting the individual student directly—the after-tax earnings differential—and the private costs, that is, the direct costs and earnings forgone. Based on a meta-analysis of many internal rate-of-return studies, Leslie and Brinkman (1988) reported average private rates of return between 11.8 and 13.4 percent; these rates are attractive in comparison with average market interest rates on alternative financial assets. Other literature reviews have reported average rates of returns from 9 to 14 percent (Douglass, 1977), 9.6 to 14.8 percent (Perlman, 1973), and 10 to 15 percent (Cohn and Geske, 1990), the ranges of which bracket Leslie and Brinkman's findings. Finally, in order to obtain estimates that would be relatively insensitive to fluctuations in the college job market, McMahon and Wagner (1982) estimated internal rates of return using later points or periods in the age-earnings profile, unlike others who have often included earnings of more recent graduates in their

---

[9]Psacharopoulos (1981, p. 325) has designed a "short-cut method" or formula for transforming data on earnings differentials into approximations of rates of return. However, this formula is expressed in an equivalent, but simpler form, by Cohn and Geske (1990, p. 110). The brief version of the equation is as follows:

$$= (0.25)\left[\left(\frac{\overline{Y_C}}{\overline{Y_H}}\right) - 1\right]$$ where Y_C and Y_H are the average earnings of workers that have completed the educational level that is signified by the subscript, in this case "C" for college graduate and "H" for high school graduate.

calculations. Their estimates of what they call the "long-run" private rate of return to investment in college were 13 to 14 percent, quite consistent with, and lending credence to, the estimates from other studies.

Another method for estimating returns to education is based on the estimation of Mincerian earnings functions (Arai, 1998; Carnoy, 1995c; Johnes, 1993; Mincer, 1974, 1993a). These functions typically provide estimates of the increment in earnings—in dollars or percentage change—per one-unit change in postsecondary education. A unit of such education could be one year or a number of years, such as two or four, that correspond to the average time to complete a degree or certificate. An advantage of Mincerian earnings functions is that they require both less data and less computation than internal rate of return studies (Arai, 1998). However, a disadvantage is that they do not consider the direct costs of college attendance, and therefore, "cannot analyze how changes in tuition and fees affect the rate of return" (p. 38). Recent efforts in this area use rather sophisticated controls for "other" non-education factors that may influence one's earnings, such as a student's family background, income, work experience or ability. Recent estimates have found that one year of academic credits at a four-year college increases annual earnings from 6 to 9 percent (Kane and Rouse, 1995; Monk-Turner, 1994). Of particular interest, in terms of the nature and degree of control for other factors, are the recent studies of identical twins in the U.S. and Australia. For example, Ashenfelter and Krueger (1994) observed 12 to 16 percent increases in earnings due to a single additional year of education. Updating this study, using three additional years of twins data, Rouse (1999) found per-year increases of 10 percent. Findings for similar studies with Australian twins have been comparable (Miller et al., 1995). Because the "twins" studies appear to offer quite comprehensive controls, the estimated magnitudes of the effect of one additional year of college may offer a promising note of support for human capital theory, as well as for the wisdom of private investment in higher education.

RETURNS TO INVESTMENT IN SUB-BACCALAUREATE POSTSECONDARY EDUCATION

The returns to investment in sub-baccalaureate postsecondary education have been studied at some length during the past ten years (Grubb, 1995, 1996; Kane and Rouse, 1995; Lanaan, 1998; Leigh and Gill, 1997; Lewis et al., 1993; Monk-Turner, 1994; Sanchez and Lanaan, 1998). Prior to that, estimates of such returns had been rare, even though more than one-half of all first-time, first-year enrollments are in two-year colleges (Cohen and Brawer, 1996). Community colleges serve a wide range of needs for a diverse group of students (Kane and Rouse, 1999; Rouse, 1994). A large portion of their students work while attending, are from lower-income groups, are from minority groups, are local and geographically bound, attend part time, are of nontraditional age, are underprepared and require developmental coursework. Many of their students pursue associate degrees in academic or vocational areas, vocational or occupational certificates, while others participate in a limitless array of continuing education and community service programs. Furthermore, persistence to program completion is not necessarily a valued goal of many community college students; often they are non-completers for constructive or understandable reasons. Some are experimenting with post-secondary opportunities, seeking to meet self-development needs, stopping out to work or reconsider their options, preparing for transfer to a four-year institution, pursuing goals related to workforce and skill development, or other educational goals related to their transition from welfare to work. Therefore, accurate information about the returns to investment in sub-baccalaureate postsecondary education—both for credentials and program completion, as well as for credits without program completion—are both problematic and very important.

Kane and Rouse (1999) have provided an excellent review of a set of recent studies that have estimated Mincerian-like earnings functions using substantial controls for a wide range of student and family background factors. First, the average student attending a community college, without completing a degree or certificate, and never having attended a four-year institution, earned between 9 and 13 percent more than high school graduates with similar background characteristics (Kane and Rouse, 1995; Leigh and Gill, 1997). Second, for community college students, on average, one-year of credit—independent of earning a degree—increased earnings by 5 to 8 percent (Grubb, 1995, 1996; Kane and Rouse, 1995; Monk-Turner, 1994), an increase comparable to that for one year of four-year college credit. Finally, a study of adults' yearly earnings five years after their expected date of high school graduation revealed a substantial and significant earnings differential between those who had completed at least six months of any type of vocational postsecondary education at two-year institutions and those who had completed only high school (Lewis, et al., 1993). Of particular importance, the study found that the earnings differential was greatest for two groups: women and low-income students. These findings regarding returns to investment in sub-baccalaureate postsecondary education make for welcome news for students and staff at community colleges. Because of the short-term time limits on training opportunities associated with welfare-to-work or workforce requirements, these substantial incremental earnings for completing credits without credentials seem particularly promising.

What is often referred to as the "sheepskin" effect—that is, incremental earnings due to completion of a degree, above and beyond that due to completion of credits alone—may well be present, but may not be very large (Kane and Rouse, 1999). Estimates of the sheepskin or credential effect range from 15 to 27 percent increases in earnings; but community college credit, without credentials, yields earnings increases of 5 to 8 percent per year, which corresponds to 10 to 16 percent for two years. This would appear to leave room for a sheepskin effect; however, further analysis has demonstrated that about one-third of the estimated earnings differential may be due to an attractive return to the associate's degree in nursing (Kane and Rouse, 1999, p. 76).[10] More research is clearly needed in this under-investigated, but quite important area.

---

[10]One reviewer of an earlier version of this chapter pointed out that evidence of a sheepskin effect may also reflect the fact that many jobs have minimum degree requirements; and furthermore, not finishing a degree program might send a negative signal to some employers.

THE DEMAND FOR AND SUPPLY OF HUMAN CAPITAL: UNDERSTANDING INDIVIDUAL AND GROUP DIFFERENCES IN INVESTMENT IN HIGHER EDUCATION

Gary Becker (1975, 1993) developed a model of the demand for and supply of human capital that has proven to be very useful in explaining the differences between the amounts of higher education in which various individuals and groups invest. Variations across individuals and groups in their investments are attributable to differences in the determinants of the demand for human capital and the supply of funds to invest in human capital—that is, the market for human capital. A number of economists have offered thorough presentations and explanations of this model and elaborated on its meaning and usefulness (Arai, 1998; G. Becker, 1975, 1993; Kaufman, 1986, 1994; McConnell and Brue, 1995; Mincer, 1993b; Psacharopoulos, 1973). The fundamental relations between demand- and supply-side factors and the amount invested in higher education that constitute the primary features of the model have received substantial empirical support from a variety of previous studies. In addition to the specific research cited in each subsection of this chapter, one of the most comprehensive tests, and formal estimations of the parameters of the demand for, and supply of, human capital curves— as applied to investment in higher education—was conducted by McMahon (1991). He used three-stage least squares for simultaneous estimation of demand and supply functions in the market for human capital. His research identified both demand- and supply-side determinants of the amount invested in higher education that provide substantial and consistent empirical support for the theoretical perspectives and elements of Becker's model of the market for human capital.

This section of the chapter presents, explains and illustrates the nature, meaning and usefulness of, as well as the research-based support for, the fundamental elements of the conceptual framework of the model. Separate subsections examine the derivations of the demand for human capital and supply of funds to invest in human capital, demand- and supply-side determinants of investment in human capital (higher education); the nature of, and changes in, the equilibrium level of investment in the market for human capital; and the effects of public policy on the investment behavior of students interested in higher education.

The Demand for Human Capital

The first step in deriving the demand for human capital involves examining the relation between the internal rate of return (r) and the amount invested in human capital ($). As noted above, the internal rate of return indicates the marginal benefit (MB) due to a one-unit increase in the amount invested in human capital. Figure 3 presents an individual's marginal-benefit or MB-curve for human capital. The amount invested ($) in human capital (higher education) is measured along the horizontal axis and the rate of return (r) is measured along the vertical axis. The MB-curve essentially shows the rate of return for each dollar spent on higher education. That is, the MB or rate of return for the last dollar spent of the amount $0\$_2$ is r_3, which is at point A on the MB-curve. For the last dollar spent out of the amount $0\$_3$, the MB or rate of return is r_2 (at point B on the MB curve), and so forth.

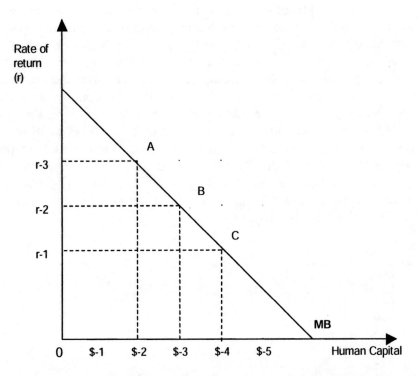

Figure 3. Rate of Return and Investment in Human Capital

There are several reasons that the MB-curve is downward-sloping. First, as additional units of human capital (higher education) are added to a student's limited time and physical and mental capacities, the marginal benefits (r) of successive units invested would remain positive but would decline because a student's productivity and earnings would increase at a diminishing rate (G. Becker, 1993). Second, for each additional year of higher education, the number of years the student has left to reap the benefits of the earnings differential from the investment decreases (see Figures 1 and 2). Third, as the amount invested in higher education increases, a student's forgone earnings rise, because the student could leave college and obtain a higher-paying job after each additional year of college. Fourth, as a student invests in additional years of education, tuition and other direct costs of college increase. In combination, these four factors mean that the marginal benefit (MB) of investment in higher education—while remaining high—decreases with each equal additional amount invested.

If the rate of return or MB becomes smaller for each additional unit of higher education invested, why would a student wish to invest in more human capital and how is the optimal amount of investment determined? These questions are answered in the next step of the derivation of the demand curve for human capital. This step depends on the application of the criterion for optimum investment in human capital explained above. It would be worthwhile for a student to continue to invest in additional units of human capital (higher education) as long as the marginal benefit (MB) exceeds the marginal cost (MC) for the last unit of the investment—that is, as long as MB > MC, or equivalently, r > i. While the MB of investment in an additional unit is represented by the rate of return (r), the MC corresponds to the market rate of interest or interest cost (i) of the additional funds required to make the investment. For each additional unit of investment considered, the MB would be compared to the MC, and investment would continue until MB = MC for the last unit (dollar) invested. The amount of investment in human capital that corresponds to the point where MB = MC would be the optimum amount.

When this investment rule or criterion is applied to the MB-curve for different possible levels of the market rate of interest (i)—that is, the MC of funds to invest—the MB-curve is then redefined as the demand curve for human capital. Each point (A, B, C) along the MB-curve in Figure 3 indicated the corresponding rate of return (r) for the last dollar of each amount of investment ($) on the horizontal axis. For example, for each amount invested up to $-2, the rate of return was equal to or greater than r-3, as illustrated by point A on the MB-curve.

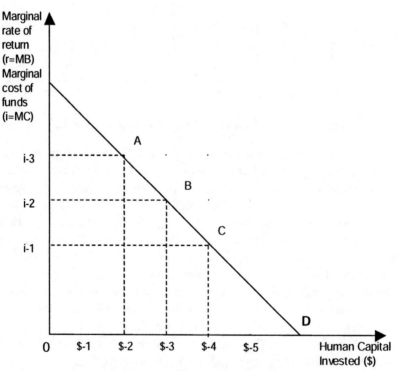

Figure 4. The Demand for New Capital

Figure 4 applies the MB ≥ MC criterion to identify the optimum amount of investment for several different levels of the marginal interest cost of funds (MC). When MC = i-3, MB exceeds MC for all amounts invested up to $-2, where MB = MC and r = i at point A on the demand curve. However, if an individual were to be able to obtain funds to invest at a MC equal to i-2, MB would exceed MC for all amounts invested up to $-3, where MB once again equals MC and r = i, at point B on the demand curve. Essentially, each level of the marginal interest cost of funds (i=MC) represents the financial "price" of funds to invest in an additional unit of human capital. Together, the information on the financial prices (i=MC) on the vertical axis and the corresponding optimal amounts of investment on the horizontal axis constitute the price-quantity relationship that microeconomists define as a demand curve; in this case, it is the demand for human capital (McConnell and Brue, 1995; Kaufman, 1994).

The Supply of Funds for Investment in Human Capital

Figure 5 illustrates the supply curve of funds to invest in human capital—that is, higher education—for a representative individual. It shows the various sources of funds that will be available in limited quantities to this student, arranged according to the interest cost or marginal cost of funds for each source of funds. The amount available for investment in human capital ($) is measured along the horizontal axis and the marginal cost of funds (i) for each amount invested is measured along the vertical axis. On the supply side of the market for human capital, there are many different sources and types of funds, with some that are available at a lower marginal or interest cost than others. Although some funds are available from cheaper sources than others, the amount of low-cost funds available is lim-

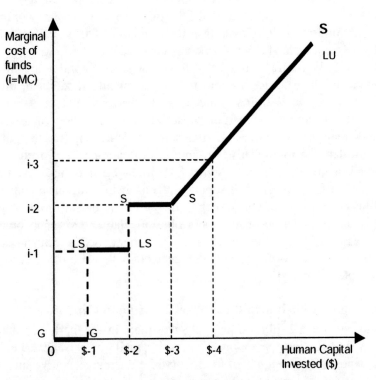

Figure 5. The Supply of Funds for Investment in Human Capital

ited. Therefore, an individual requiring funds to invest in human capital will use as much of the cheapest source as is available and then will have to move on to funds from more expensive sources. It is the increasing marginal or interest costs of the additional funds available for an individual to finance college investment that is responsible for the upward slope of the supply curve of funds portrayed in Figure 5.

The first segment of the supply of funds curve, GG, corresponds to the amount, $0\$_1$, that would be available at zero (0) marginal cost. This represents the amount of funds from gifts or grants from family, government or foundation available to this student. Only a small percentage of students would be able to acquire all their needed funds from this zero-cost gift-or-grant source. Pell grants, scholarships, and other such sources of funds are limited and must be rationed among eligible students. Parental gifts sufficient to cover all costs of college are available to only a small percentage of the population of potential student investors. The next cheapest source of funds would be from guaranteed or subsidized student loans (subsidized Stafford loans), which are available to the student at a marginal cost of i_1, represented along the portion of the supply curve labeled LSLS. The funds available through subsidized loans would provide for an additional $\$_1\$_2$ amount of funds, for a total of $0\$_2$ supplied. For additional funds, the next cheapest source would be from the student's own earnings or savings, for which there would be a marginal cost equal to i_2. This marginal cost would be equal to the rate of interest (i_2) at which the student forgoes the opportunity to earn interest income from the best available alternative investment of the funds. This portion of the supply curve, based on funds saved from one's own income, is labeled SS. Funds from this source will make an additional $\$_2\$_3$ of funds available, making a total amount of $0\$_3$ available, based on all sources of funds available at below-market or low-market interest rates.

For students who desire more than $\$_3$ funds for investment, but are either ineligible for, unable or unwilling to acquire, or unaware or misinformed about, the funds from cheaper alternatives; *unsubsidized* educational loans are available at various increasingly higher rates of interest or marginal cost (e.g., i_3)—from government, institutional, business and other private sources—so that some students may find that funds in excess of $0\$_3$ are available to them. This last, and upward-sloping, part of the supply curve, based on funds available at various higher rates in the open, competitive financial market, is labeled SLU—representing supplies of unsubsidized educational loans. Need-based, public student-aid programs, such as the Pell grant or Stafford loan programs are intended to make more low-cost sources of funds available to lower-income students, in order to increase their opportunities to invest in higher education. Such issues of public policy are discussed below in this and other chapters in this volume (e.g., Baum, chapter 2; Hearn, chapters 7 and 11).

Understanding Equilibrium in the Market for Human Capital

Figure 6 presents the equilibrium level of investment in the market for human capital. Both the demand for and the supply of human capital are presented. For ease of diagrammatic exposition, the supply of funds curve for the representative student in the figure is presented as a continuous, upward-sloping line, which is consistent with the general pattern illustrated in Figure 5 in the previous section. In Figure 6, the equilibrium and optimum amount invested can be identified by applying the investment criteria represented earlier in Figures 1 and 2, Equations 1 through 5, and the general MB $\geq$ MC criterion. In other words, a student's investment in human capital would be worthwhile as long as the MB or rate of return (r) exceeded the MC or interest cost of funds (i). In Figure 6, this would be the case for all amounts invested until demand D1 intersects supply S1 at point A, where MB = MC or equivalently, $r_2 = i_2$, for the last dollar of the total equilibrium amount of 0$\$_3$ invested.

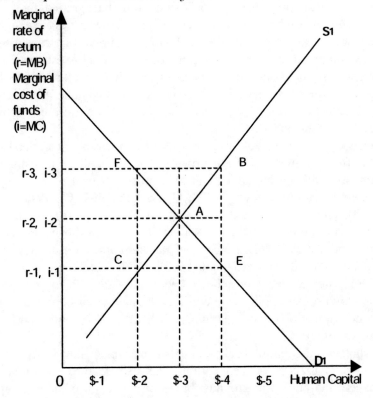

Figure 6. Equilibrium Level of Human Capital Investment

As illustrated in Figure 6, as additional amounts (\$) are invested in human capital, the MB decreases along the demand curve and the MC increases along the supply curve. For any amount invested between 0 and \$-3, MB > MC. For any amount invested that is greater than \$-3, MC > MB. Therefore, the optimum amount is at point A where MB = MC for the last dollar invested.

Differences in Demand and Investment in Higher Education

In his original model, G. Becker (1975, 1993) proposed that an individual student's demand curves for human capital would differ due to differences in students in their opportunities to benefit from investment in higher education. The key point here is that the college-going decision is *not* a purely financial one. A student's decision-making process is not so straightforward as implied in the simple form of the rational decision-making process assumed to underlie the original human capital investment model. Potential students do *not* simply access readily available information on an easily identifiable set of monetary benefits and costs that will result from a student's investment in college. In fact, the relative magnitudes of the monetary benefits and costs of college vary substantially from one individual to another. Each student makes a decision in a unique context that is shaped by the individual's own background, experiences, and environment.

An individual's academic ability, socioeconomic and family background, the quality of pre-college and college-level schooling, and discriminatory experiences are examples of features of a student's background, experiences and environment that can result in individual differences and inequalities in the marginal benefits of an investment in college. Because differences in these and other aspects of each individual's unique decision-making context result in individual differences in the marginal benefits of college investment, these differences manifest themselves in the form of different demand curves in the market for human capital.[11]

The idea that a student's academic ability, and its various measures, correlates, and determinants, would affect earnings—a major private benefit of college investment—has been widely supported among human capital economists, as well as sociologists, based on strong theoretical grounds (Arai, 1998; G. Becker, 1993; Cipillone, 1995; Cohn and Geske, 1990; Thurow, 1970) and consistent empirical support (Alwin, 1976; Griliches, 1977; Jencks and Phillips, 1999; Johnson and Neal, 1998; Leslie and Brinkman, 1988; Taubman and Wales, 1974). Reviews of the literature on estimates of the portion of incremental earnings that is attributable to ability-related factors, independent of education, have computed averages of about 20 percent. Many economists believe this estimate to be too high because it does not consider the interactions between ability and education in the determination of one's earnings (Griliches, 1977; Leslie and Brinkman, 1988; Psacharopoulos, 1975).

Similarly, the hypothesis that family background—such as parents' education, occupation and income—would affect subsequent earnings has also received consistent support on both theoretical and empirical grounds, based on the work of human capital economists, as well as sociologists and other scholars (Alwin, 1976; G. Becker, 1993; Behrman, et. al., 1992; Jencks, 1972, 1979; Korenman and Winship, 2000; Sewell and Hauser, 1976). Family background variables have been found to influence one's future earnings both directly and indirectly through mediating variables.[12]

As a result of these theoretical and empirical developments, in recent years, economists have consistently estimated earnings functions and rates of return to investments in higher education using controls for a wide range of factors in addition to education and experience, including ability and other student and family background characteris-

---

[11]Some aspects of an individual student's background, experiences and environment can also influence the supply curve of funds that the student faces. The funds available for potential students at lower versus higher interest costs are determined primarily by family income and wealth (G. Becker, 1993; McMahon, 1991; Mincer, 1993b). This important source of individual differences and inequalities in the marginal costs of investment in college is addressed in more detail below.

tics that may be related to one's subsequent earnings (Ashenfelter and Krueger, 1994; Grubb, 1995, 1996; Kane and Rouse, 1995; Leigh and Gill, 1997; Monk-Turner, 1994; Rouse, 1999).

Economists' research on how an individual's family background may either expand or constrain a student's future educational attainment and earnings—that is, the marginal benefits that accrue to an individual investing in a college education—is similar to the theoretical and empirical work of sociologists associated with the constructs of habitus and cultural capital (Bourdieu, 1977a, 1977b; Bourdieu and Passeron, 1990; McDonough, 1997, 1998; Swartz, 1997). *Habitus* refers to the enduring, internal system of attitudes, beliefs, actions and fundamental values, acquired from the immediate family, school, and community environments of the student. *Cultural capital* refers to the kinds of symbolic wealth transmitted from middle- and upper-income parents to their children to sustain family status across generations (McDonough, 1997). Examples include familiarity with and access to the forms of communication, school-related information, social networks, and educational credentials of dominant groups (Bourdieu, 1977a, 1977b; Bourdieu and Passeron, 1990; McDonough, 1997, 1998; Swartz, 1997). Students' social class, and related cultural capital and habiti, consistently frame, structure, and constrain their patterns of college-going decision-making (Bourdieu, 1977a, 1977b; McDonough, 1997, 1998; Paulsen and St. John, in press). Recent research has also indicated that models of investment in higher education based on human capital theory may have greater explanatory power when they include explicit measures of habitus, social and cultural capital (Hurtado, et al., 1997; Perna, 2000).[13]

In his model of the market for human capital, G. Becker (1975, 1993) considered the effects of still other important factors that could result in individual differences and

---

[12]It is noteworthy that G. Becker also used theoretical and empirical evidence to demonstrate that indeed ability and family background factors were correlated with earnings; however, he expressed concern that researchers, in their best efforts to use advanced measurement and statistical techniques to accurately estimate the effect of education on earnings, independent of all background and related factors, would neglect the centrality of education's *interaction* with such factors (e.g., academic ability) in its production of human capital:

> In general, when [using] multiple regression or some other technique to obtain the effect of education on earnings, one must be careful not to go too far. For education has little direct effect on earnings; it operates primarily indirectly through the effect on knowledge and skills. Consequently, by [controlling] for enough measures of knowledge and skill, such as occupation or ability to communicate, one can eliminate the entire true effect of education on earnings" (1975, p. 164, 1993, p. 178).

In addition, Mincer's (1993a) analysis of this issue and his review of the broader literature support Becker's concern and assertion. He offers a related perspective or rationale as to the nature of the role of background factors. "The economic analysis of human capital investment decisions suggests that the effects of background variables are *indirect* by influencing the accumulation of human capital. Since the latter is commonly measured only crudely by years of schooling and by years of work experience, the relatively small direct (net) effects of background variables that remain might well disappear with the introduction of more-refined measures of human capital" (1993a, p. 93).

[13]A thorough examination of these important contributions of educational sociologists to our understanding of the nature and complexity of college-going behavior is beyond the scope of this chapter. Therefore, interested readers are encouraged to consult the various references cited in the text for a more detailed look at this expanding and vibrant literature.

inequalities in the marginal benefits of an investment in college, and therefore, different demand curves between individuals. Most noteworthy among these other factors was the effect of discrimination.[14] G. Becker emphasized discrimination against women and people of color in the labor market in his presentation of the market for human capital, but the model is readily applicable to the study of other individuals and groups who experience various forms of discrimination.

In spite of the impressive ratios of the earnings of college relative to high-school graduates, among college graduates, the absolute dollar amount of earnings and employment rates are lower for women and people of color than for white males (Carnoy, 1995b; Ferber, 1995; National Center for Educational Statistics, 1997, Table 33-1, pp. 281-282; National Center for Educational Statistics, 1999, Tables 385, 386, pp. 435-436). Women, blacks and Latinos have all experienced steady reductions in earnings-based discrimination, yet substantial earnings differences remain. Analysts have been able to explain a substantial portion of these changes in terms of concepts and models from labor economics and human capital (Card and Krueger, 1992b; Smith and Welch, 1989); however, one of these explanations is that public policies guiding direct government intervention in the labor market (e.g., affirmative action) have been a positive contributing factor in the reduction of discriminatory practices (Card and Krueger, 1993; Carnoy, 1995b).

G. Becker (1993) proposed that because of the substantial correlations between earnings and race, ethnicity, and gender, discrimination in the labor market was highly likely to be another basis for individual differences and inequalities in the marginal benefits accruing to individuals who invest in higher education. These differences in marginal benefits because of discrimination would, in turn, manifest themselves in the form of different demand curves in the market for human capital.

Economists have also been successful in their investigations of the effects of "school quality" on the subsequent earnings of its graduates during their adult, working years. These studies have demonstrated that the quality of both pre-college and college-level schooling is significantly and directly related to subsequent earnings of graduates (Behrman, et al., 1996; Card and Krueger, 1992a; James and Alsalam, 1993; James, et al., 1989; Rumberger and Thomas, 1993). Therefore, this factor serves as another fundamental source of variation and inequalities in the marginal benefits accruing to individuals who invest in higher education.

Measures of school quality, such as pupil-teacher ratio, length of school term, and relative teacher pay, for pre-college schooling, and selectivity, prestige and expenditures per student for college-level schooling, have been found to have significant and direct positive effects on students' future earnings and private returns to investment in education, as well as indirect effects on earnings through their interactions with other student

---

[14]The reader may wish to consult G. Becker's treatise, *The Economics of Discrimination* (1971), for a formal and more comprehensive treatment of this subject; or to examine Carnoy (1995b), to learn more about the contemporary views and interpretations of the facts, theories and research on this issue, particularly regarding earnings and discrimination between racial and ethnic groups. In order to examine some of the parallels, as well as differences in gender-based earnings differences, accessible surveys of the literature would include Ferber (1995) and Strober (1995).

and institutional characteristics. For example, researchers have found that quality of pre-college schooling—measured as the average family income of students attending the school—has indirect effects on earnings through its direct effects on students' scholastic achievement (Behrman, et al., 1992). The investigators reported and interpreted their findings as follows:

> Length of the school year is not significant, but students from schools with more affluent clienteles do better on the tests. This may reflect peer effects in learning (given that more affluent students generally have higher achievement), differences in the resources available to schools with wealthier and poorer students, or other effects associated with the neighborhoods where students reside" (p. 9).

In summary, the higher the quality of school that a student attends the greater will be the student's future academic achievement, educational attainment, and earnings. In terms of the market for human capital, this would be yet another source of variation and inequalities in students' marginal benefits from college and would manifest itself in different demand curves.

Figure 7 presents three different demand for human capital curves: D1, which corresponds to the moderate level of demand portrayed in Figure 6; D2, which illustrates a higher marginal benefit (MB) or rate of return for each level of investment ($) along the horizontal axis, when compared to D1; and D3, which illustrates a lower MB or rate of

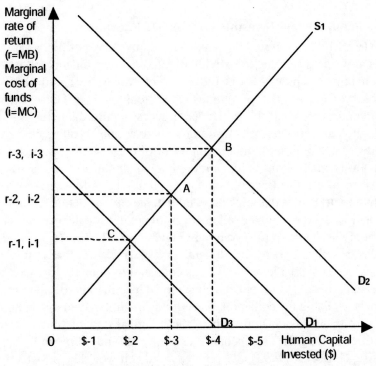

Figure 7. Difference in Demand and Investment in Higher Education

return for each level of investment. Based on Becker's model, D2 would be the demand for human capital for a student who anticipates a high level of marginal benefits from a college investment, due to particular *advantages* on one or more of several factors—academic ability (e.g., high scholastic achievement test scores), family background (e.g., an advanced level of parental education), positive discrimination (e.g., more job offers and/or higher starting salaries upon graduation), or a high quality of pre-college and college-level schooling experience. Alternatively, D3 would be the demand curve for a student who anticipates lower levels of marginal benefits from a college investment due to relative *disadvantages* on one or more of these several factors.

Figure 7 illustrates how these two students' different sets of expected marginal benefits—as evidenced by the relative positions of their respective demand curves—would lead them to different decisions regarding their perceived optimum levels of investment in higher education. These optimum amounts can be readily identified using the general MB $\geq$ MC criterion. For the student with demand curve D2, MB = MC at point B and $\$_4$ would be the optimum level of investment. For the student on demand curve D3, MB = MC at point C and $\$_2$ would be the optimum level investment. For these two students, the difference in their optimum investments would equal $\$_4 - \$_2$. Clearly, the student with demand curve D2 would find a much larger investment to be worthwhile than the student with demand curve D3. The substantial difference in investment is due to differences in the expected marginal benefits of the two students. Relative to the student on demand curve D3, the student on D2 is apparently *advantaged* in terms of academic ability, family background, discrimination, quality of schooling experience, or other factors.

Differences in Supply and Investment in Higher Education

G. Becker (1975, 1993) proposed that students' supply curves of funds for investment in human capital would differ due to individual differences in students' access to funds for investment in human capital—that is, the degree of availability and the cost of funds for investment as well as overall opportunities in the credit markets. One of the most important and influential determinants of a student's access to affordable funds—and postsecondary educational opportunities—is family income and wealth, the latter being an unequally distributed and influential component of one's socioeconomic status. A student with high-income parents is much more likely than those at lower income levels to be in a position to acquire financial capital at an attractive low or zero cost of funds. There are two central ways that high parental income can make this possible: first, a gift from a parent to a child that covers all the costs of college attendance coincides with the GG segment of the supply of funds curve in Figure 5 (p. 71); this segment represents the funds available at zero cost to the student. The other way is that family wealth (real assets) can be made available or pledged as collateral to obtain a low-interest loan, that is, in the general, private, unsubsidized educational loan market. Because of the substantial real assets available for collateral, these funds might be available at an interest cost comparable to, or not much higher than, the marginal cost of funds from subsidized loans, identified as the LSLS segment of the supply of funds curve in Figure 5.

Of course, G. Becker (1993) also pointed out that it would be possible for federal or state student aid programs, that provide subsidies to students based on need or merit, to

contribute to a more favorable supply of funds for some students. Under optimal circumstances—that is, adequate funding relative to college costs and equal distribution of
full and accurate information about availability, eligibility, and application for such
aid—this would be true, and for some students it has surely increased their supply of
funds curves as expected.

However, neither the availability of such subsidies (grants and loans), nor a student's eligibility for them, will necessarily always lead to the increase in access to
higher education intended from such need-based aid programs (Hearn, chapters 7 and
11). There are a number of reasons that a supply of funds curve for a financially needy
student may not increase, even when more aid is actually available. First, this would be
the case if a substantial portion of an increase in need-based aid were to go to middle-
income students with less financial need than low-income students. In addition, low-
income and first-generation students are more likely than others to lack accurate information and even be unaware of either student aid programs or their eligibility for aid.
Such students are also more likely to lack an understanding of how to successfully navigate the cumbersome, and often inefficient, process of applying for aid (Ikenberry and
Hartle, 1998; Kane, 1995, 1999c; King, 1999; Levine and Nidiffer, 1996; Mumper,
1996; Orfield, 1992). One of these views is expressed by Kane (1999c) as follows:

> [L]ow-income families' lack of information about financial aid programs blunts their
> impact. Students can read about tuition hikes in the local newspapers, but they may invest
> the time to learn about the availability of financial aid only if they are fairly committed to
> attending college (pp. 119-120).

Finally, in spite of expansion in the volume of federal student aid programs (Baum,
chapter 2; College Board, 1999b; Hearn, chapter 7), in an era of rapidly rising sticker
prices (Toutkoushian, chapter 1; Paulsen, chapter 6), those potential students with the
greatest financial need may also be more likely to perceive or assume available aid to be
inadequate, and recent research has suggested that such an assumption may be a reasonable judgment for low-income individuals (Paulsen and St. John, in press; St. John,
2000).

When access to funds for investment differs between students, the result will be different supply of funds curves (see Figure 8) that illustrate differences in the marginal
cost (MC) or interest rate (i) at which various amounts of funds would be available.
Those students with an advantaged socioeconomic status—for example, those from
families with high levels of income and wealth—would be more likely to face supply of
funds curves that portray the availability of large amounts of funds at relatively low
interest rates or marginal cost, while students from families with less income and wealth
would tend to face supply curves that portray higher marginal costs of funds for each
amount supplied.

Figure 8 presents three different supply of funds curves: S1, which corresponds to
the moderate level of MC of funds for each amount supplied portrayed in Figure 7; S2,
which illustrates a much lower MC or interest rate (i) for each amount of funds supplied
($) along the horizontal axis, when compared to S1; and S3, which illustrates a much
higher MC for each amount of funds supplied. Based on Becker's model, S2 would rep-

resent a supply of funds curve for a student who finds various amounts of funds supplied to be available at relatively low levels of MC, which could occur because the student's family income and wealth are high. Alternatively, S3 would illustrate the supply of funds curve for a student who faces higher MC for various amounts of funds supplied, which could occur because a student's family has relatively low income and wealth.

Figure 8 illustrates how these two students' different sets of expected marginal costs

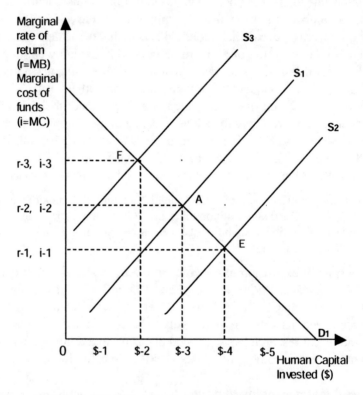

Figure 8. Differences in Supply and Investment in Higher Education

of funds—as evidenced by the relative positions of their respective supply of funds curves—would lead them to different decisions regarding their perceived optimum levels of investment in higher education. These optimum amounts can be readily identified using the general MB ≥ MC criterion. For the student with supply curve S2, MB = MC at point E and $4 would be the optimum level of investment. For the student on supply curve S3, MB = MC at point F and $2 would be the optimum level investment. For these two students, the difference in their optimum investments would equal $4 – $2. Clearly, the student facing supply of funds curve S2 will invest substantially more than the student facing supply curve S3. The substantial difference in amount invested is due to differences between the two students in their access to funds in the market for human capital. In this case, relative to the student facing supply curve S3, the student facing supply curve S2 has a relative, and substantial, advantage in terms of family income and wealth, which, for the reasons described above, typically leads to the availability of more funds at lower marginal costs.

Differences in Demand, Supply and Investment in Higher Education

As illustrated above, both demand-side and supply-side factors influence a student's optimum amount invested in human capital. Figure 9 combines the multiple demand curves of Figure 7 with the multiple supply curves of Figure 8 to illustrate the potential differences in investments in higher education among students in different circumstances. Points G and H correspond to the highest ($\$_5$) and lowest ($\$_1$) amounts that individuals would invest, given all possible combinations of demand and supply curves presented in Figure 9. A student investing $\$_5$ at point G would be on demand curve D2 and face supply of funds curve S2, while a student investing $\$_1$ at point H would be on demand curve D3 and face supply curve S3. The substantial difference in investment between students at point G and H ($\$_5 - \$_1$) is due to differences in both the marginal benefits (demand) and marginal costs of funds (supply) expected by the two students. Relative to the student on demand curve D3, the student on D2 is apparently *advantaged* in terms of either academic ability, family background, discrimination, quality of schooling experience, or other factors that could lead to an expectation of greater marginal benefits due to investment in college. Relative to the student facing supply of

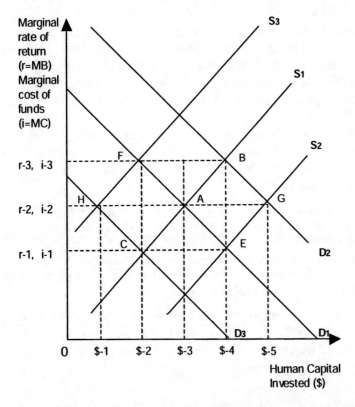

Figure 9. Differences in Demand, Supply, and Investment in Higher Education

funds curve S3, the student facing S2 is apparently *advantaged* in terms of family income and wealth or other factors that could lead to an expectation of lower marginal costs of funds for investment in college.[15]

An important focus of concern here is the well-being of the individual student at point H who identifies such a very small amount of investment in higher education as optimum—an amount that could, in fact, under even less favorable circumstances, have been zero. And this same focus of concern would naturally apply to all other students or "potential" students who find themselves in the same or similar circumstances. Furthermore, society in general is likely to miss out on the tangible and intangible social or public benefits that could potentially be distributed across the population if students such as this one had the same opportunities to realistically expect marginal benefits and costs similar to those available to the most advantaged of students like the one optimizing investment at point G (Paulsen, chapter 4).

Public Policies, Demand, Supply and Investment in Higher Education.

There is a range of public policies that could, individually or in combination, work through the demand and supply sides of the market for human capital to move the student at point H—a position of disadvantage in Figure 9—toward the more-advantaged position of the student at point G. In G. Becker's model of the market for human capital, increases in demand result from increases in students' expectations about the marginal benefits from investment in higher education. A variety of demand-side policies have been recommended that would tend to increase expectations of marginal benefits, shift a student's demand curve for human capital to the right, and therefore, increase their investment in higher education. Several of these policies are briefly considered here as illustrations of potential ways to stimulate a rightward shift in the demand for investment in higher education among members of various groups of current and potential students.

First, higher education scholars and analysts have come to realize that, in spite of its importance, by itself, "financial aid is not enough" to stimulate adequate investment in higher education, especially for low-income and first-generation students. Gladieux and Swail (1999) explain this as follows:

> Enrollment and success in higher education are clearly influenced by many factors: prior schooling and academic achievement, the rigor and pattern of courses taken in secondary school, family and cultural attitudes, motivation, and awareness of opportunities—not just ability to pay, which has been the primary emphasis of federal [student aid] policy. For low-income students, removing financial barriers is critical, but so are many things starting much earlier both in life and in the educational pipeline (p. 184).

These and other higher education scholars recommend that our society expand its investment in mentoring and other early intervention programs—such as the TRIO programs, the best-known of which is the Upward Bound program, initialized in the Eco-

---

[15]This model can also be used to illustrate and explain the unequal distribution of earnings and income, including both the dispersion and skewness of this distribution (Mincer 1993a, 1993b).

nomic Opportunity Act of 1964—that have the potential to influence the nature and importance of college-going aspirations in a student's early home and school environments (Fenske, et al., 1997; Gladieux and Swail, 1999; Levine and Nidiffer, 1996).

In order for students to anticipate higher marginal benefits from investment in college, and to be more productive in achieving future gains in incremental earnings, they need—among other things—an accurate view of the value of the opportunities provided by higher education; an adequate level of academic preparation and academic achievement sufficient for expectations of success in college-level studies; and adequate financial and academic support for college attendance. The TRIO programs have been successful in helping low-income and first-generation college students by using a general approach that helps address these issues. "Initially, promising students are identified (Talent Search), then prepared for the rigors of college-level academic work (Upward Bound), offered information on academic and financial aid opportunities (Educational Opportunity Centers), and, finally, as college students, offered tutoring and support (Student Support Services)" (Fenske, et al., 1997, p. 43). However, in order to shift the demand curve for human capital to the right for low-income and first-generation college students, increased funding of these and other mentoring and early intervention programs would be necessary.

> The challenge for public policy is to leverage such programs that work to a vastly larger scale. Upward Bound, Talent Search, and other so-called TRIO programs...are estimated to serve less than 10 percent of the eligible student population. Further, only a small portion of TRIO services is dedicated to intervening with kids and their families during middle school or earlier (Gladieux and Swail, 1999, p. 191).

Second, a number of policy analysts have expressed concern about the emergence of a more hostile environment for our longstanding affirmative action policies and recommend that we retain, improve, or re-instate such anti-discrimination measures in college admissions and the job market (Kane, 1998; Karabel, 1998; Orfield, 1998). A number of economists have argued on both theoretical and empirical grounds that demand-side factors, such as "legal and direct employment intervention by government," have been instrumental in the persistent pattern of reduction in discriminatory differences in earnings and other opportunities among women and people of color relative to white males in the second half of the twentieth century (Carnoy, 1995b, p. 239). In terms of G. Becker's (1993) model of the market for human capital, such reductions in earnings gaps over the years would have served to shift an individual's demand curve for human capital to the right, thereby stimulating greater investment in higher education. Within the context of the re-affirmation of the Equal Protection clause of the Fourteenth Amendment, *Brown v. Board of Education*, the Civil Rights Act of 1964, the Economic Opportunity Act of 1964, and the evolving Title III and IV programs under the Higher Education Act, *Regents of the University of California v. Bakke* "enabled colleges wanting to maintain a significant minority presence to do so even as [existing] anti-poverty programs were dismantled in the 1980s, and in spite of continuing large gaps in the preparation of minority students" (Orfield, 1998, p. 2). Nevertheless, because of SP-1 and Proposition 209 in California and Hopwood v. Texas, affirmative action as a more-or-less uniform national policy is imperiled. A number of policy analysts argue that color-blind, and even class-conscious, admissions would threaten, and even potentially reverse, the advances in inclusion and diversity on American campuses achieved over the past forty years (Kane, 1998; Karabel, 1998).[16]

Finally, research on the positive effects of the quality of pre-college and college-level schooling on the subsequent earnings of graduates offers some other potential ways to increase students' expected marginal benefits from college—such as greater incremental earnings—and increase their demand for human capital. A number of recent studies have found that various measures of pre-college school quality—such as pupil-teacher-ratio, teacher pay, school expenditures, length of school term, teacher education, and achievement test scores—-are significantly related to students' subsequent earnings or returns to education (Altonji and Dunn, 1996; Card and Krueger, 1992a, 1992b; Carnoy, 1995a; Grogger, 1996; Maxwell, 1994). Of particular importance are the findings of some of these studies that differences in school quality variables explain a substantial portion of black-white wage or earnings differentials (Card and Krueger, 1992b; Maxwell, 1994). Based on the specific measures of school quality used in these studies, it is apparent that differences in school resources and the academic skills students learn are especially important in explaining differences in subsequent gains in earnings. Therefore, policies that increase school resources and effectiveness in the development of academic skills might increase the marginal benefits of college and likelihood of further investment in higher education. Commenting on both the findings of her own study and the general literature on the black-white earnings gap, Maxwell (1994) explains the importance of such policies in the following way.

> In particular, since black high school students are less likely to go on to college than are white high school students of comparable ability, efforts should be made to ease the transition from high school to college for black students. Perhaps the residential segregation that blacks face or the relative poverty of the high schools they attend prevents them from gaining the information necessary to make this transition....The educational isolation of blacks leads to inadequate preparation in basic skills, which makes it difficult for them to continue their education and to receive high wages in a labor market that values skills highly. Improving education quality for blacks...is perhaps the most direct way to give them a chance to improve their basic sills and increase their earnings (p. 261).

In addition, a number of recent studies have found that various measures of college quality or a high-quality college experience—such as institutional selectivity, private versus public institutions, Eastern versus other regional institutions, high-paying majors (e.g., engineering, business, science/math), course work in mathematics, longer time in college, and college performance (GPA)—are significantly related to students' subsequent earnings or returns to investment in a college education (Behrman, et. al., 1996;

---

[16]A thorough examination of this complex and very important issue—that is, the effects of dismantling the long-standing practices of affirmative action in admission on access and diversity in higher education institutions—is beyond the scope of this chapter. For a thoughtful analysis, from a variety of perspectives, see Orfield and Miller's (1998) edited volume, *Chilling Admissions: The Affirmative Action Crisis and the Search for Alternatives.*

Brewer, Eide and Ehrenberg, 1999; Gillmore, 1990; James and Alsalam, 1993; James, et al., 1989; Loury and Garman, 1995; Rumberger and Thomas, 1993).[17]

Research on measures of a high-quality college experience suggests that marginal benefits (rates of return), and therefore, student demand for human capital, might be greater for some students if they received detailed advice and accurate information regarding the trends in salary differentials between graduates of different colleges, the most financially profitable fields in which they might major, and the important role and influence of academic achievement or GPA when it comes to determining one's future earnings.

In G. Becker's model of the market for human capital, increases in supply—like those that would help move a student from point G to point H on Figure 9—result from increases in students' access to funds and decreases in the marginal costs of funds to finance investments in higher education. However, these factors depend, in turn, on a student's awareness of, information about, and eligibility for such funds. And the primary determinants of the position of a student's supply of funds curve are the income and wealth of a student's family and the availability of subsidies to students (e.g., grants, loans) from public or private sources. It is not difficult to understand that the primary determinants of one's financial opportunities in the market for human capital depend on either family income and wealth or public subsidization.

> Thus one needs no complicated framework of family decision-making to explain the differences in college attendance by family income. Higher-income parents subsidize the costs of college more heavily than low-income parents....Even if the hopes and dreams of 18-year-olds were similar regardless of the income of their parents and even if they were all similarly averse to postponing gratification regardless of their parents' incomes, differences in college enrollment rates between high- and low-income youth could be explained simply by referring to the choices their parents are able to create for them by more heavily subsidizing college attendance....Although young people from high-income families may be able to secure financing from their parents, those from low-income families cannot. To remedy this

---

[17]The issue of whether or not the high price of attendance at an elite private institution is worth the investment, in terms of future earnings, is certainly not resolved. Although the balance of evidence has demonstrated that graduates of the most selective or elite institutions earn higher future incomes than graduates of less-selective institutions, new studies continue to be conducted in an ongoing effort to improve the methods used to frame investigations about this cost-benefit issue. In particular, Dale and Krueger's (1999) recent paper, published as part of the Working Paper Series of the National Bureau of Economic Research has attracted a good deal of attention. They studied the incomes of students who had all been accepted to the most highly selective institutions in the country. But they compared the incomes of those who actually attended those highly selective institutions with those who elected to attend a less-selective institution instead. As a result, they found nearly equal average earnings between graduates in the two groups (in fact, earnings among those attending the less-selective institutions was slightly higher: $77,700 versus $76,800). However, the study has already been criticized for not comparing graduates of the highly selective institutions with those who attended institutions that were truly less-selective. For example, while their highly selective group included Harvard, what they referred to as their less-selective group included Tulane University and University of North Carolina-Chapel Hill. Most potential students, their parents, faculty, and administrators and counselors would view these as among the highly selective institutions. A stronger comparison would examine differences in earnings between graduates of the highly selective and graduates of institutions that were clearly, and more realistically, in the less-selective category (Gose, 2000).

market imperfection, societies have invented a variety of mechanisms--direct subsidies to institutions, means-tested voucher programs for low-income students, federally guaranteed loan programs--for channeling the resources to students and families when it comes time to invest in college (Kane, 1999c, p. 91, 125).

A variety of supply-side policies have been recommended that would tend to decrease the marginal cost of funds, shift a student's supply curve for human capital to the right, and therefore, increase their investment in higher education. Several of these policies are briefly considered here as illustrations of potential ways to stimulate a rightward shift in the supply of funds for investment in higher education among members of various groups of current and potential students.

Supply-side policies that have been recommended would primarily emphasize increasing the availability of funds and information about them. In general, the availability of funds would be enhanced by increasing and then maintaining the need-based portion of federal and state student aid—not at the expense of merit-based aid, but to promote proportional gains in need-based aid—and providing incentives for institutions to do the same. McPherson and Schapiro (1998) argue that tax incentives in place of direct expenditures as a new foundation for federal student aid would not meet this criterion. Such plans would be much harder to target on the most needy students and families, and the neediest families would be less likely to benefit from tax incentives than from Pell grants.

In 1991, McPherson and Schapiro proposed to "federalize" the way that higher education is financed for the lower-income students. Under their proposal, all federal aid would be combined into one federal grant program. Unsubsidized guaranteed loans would be accessible to students from all income backgrounds. The maximum federal grant would be similar in amount to a public community college's institutional cost of "providing" one year of education (Voorhees, chapter 13), minus a student contribution from work or loans that would be very small for the lowest-income students and rise modestly for less-needy students. The maximum award would not exceed a student's net cost of attending a particular institution. This would shift more of the burden of financing higher education for the needy to the federal government. The larger federal grants would provide incentives for states and public institutions to raise tuitions to capture a substantial portion of the revenues from the new federal grant program. Among private institutions, there would be a similar result as federal grant revenues replaced the tuition discounts that institutions were previously providing to their lower-income students.

In 1998, McPherson and Schapiro offered another perspective on the substantial role and responsibility they see for the federal government in financing the education of lower-income students. They proposed that instead of increasing the amount funded for the existing Pell grant program, a new federal grant program—with quite a different incentive structure—be "piggybacked" on top of the program. These means-tested "access" grants would include an eligibility requirement for institutional participation. In order for an institution's students to be eligible to receive the new grants, a school would have to "demonstrate that it met at least 90 percent of the financial need of all full-time, dependent undergraduate students from families with incomes below $40,000 per year" (p. 89). Federal formulas would be used to calculate need, which would be met with grants, loans and work. This proposal would help guarantee that private institutions were targeting substantial financial aid for the most needy students; and the proposal would require that public institutions respond in one of two ways. States could elect to subsidize institutions and keep tuition sufficiently low for all students so that the financial needs of even the neediest students were met. Or states could increase tuition and use the additional tuition revenue to provide substantial grants to low-income students.

A lack of awareness about available aid or one's eligibility for it, or a "lack of understanding of how to apply for student financial aid may be the obstacle" (p. 127) that stands in the way of the "effective" provision of adequate supply-side "opportunities" in the market for human capital (Kane, 1999c). However, a lack of awareness or understanding about the availability of, eligibility or application for, financial aid could be effectively addressed by planning and implementing more programs like the successful Indiana College Placement and Assessment Center—ICPAC (Hossler and Schmit, 1995). The ICPAC program surveys a large number of high school students and their parents about postsecondary aspirations and plans and identifies student and parental concerns; disseminates a wide range of information about college and career opportunities, to assist and support them in their planning, and maintains an information hotline for parents, students, and counselors. Eventually, financial issues became a central focus of their programmatic efforts.

> It also became clear through the research that financial aid continued to be a concern for parents, even into the senior year in high school. Most students reported that financing college was the responsibility of their parents, at the same time, the parents consistently reported being very concerned about this issue. These results helped ICPAC design an information series focused on financing education and describing the financial aid process (pp. 35-36).

Remarkably, over an initial four-year period, ICPAC increased the college participation rate of high school graduates in the state from 41.6 to 49.6 percent.

Finally, Kane (1999a, 1999b, 1999c) has proposed a number of changes in the way the federal government provides subsidies to students (student aid), especially to finance the college investments of lower-income students. These are presented briefly here as illustrations of policies that could promote more investment in higher education.

- Dedicate federal funds to promote equitable marketing and distribution of information about financial aid programs, including training to educate and assist students in preparing to apply for all funds for which they are eligible, and the provision of a simpler process for applying for aid.
- Pell grant funding should be front-loaded, that is, the whole amount for which students are eligible should be shifted into the first two years, which, even without increased overall funding, would increase the maximum award substantially, and better target aid for those lower-income students who are truly at the margin between attendance and non-attendance.[18]
- Reinstate the earlier progressivity constraints—which have been eroded over time—associated with the EFC (expected family contribution) portion of the fed-

eral aid formula to re-target the aid at the low-income student.

- Increase the limits of borrowing in existing student loan programs and extend the eligibility to part-time students.
- Establish an effective income-contingent loan program—which would have provisions somewhat different than the income-contingent option in current direct-lending programs—that would be based on forward-looking means testing and include appropriate loan forgiveness provisions.

CONCLUSION

This chapter has used human capital theory as an overarching theoretical context and has presented, explained, and illustrated the use of selected concepts and models from the economic theory of human capital that are effective in analyzing and understanding student decision-making in the market for higher education. In addition, this chapter has presented a representative view of the literature on the theory and research that supports the economic concepts of human capital theory examined, and has provided examples, using a diagrammatic exposition, of how selected concepts and models from the economics of human capital can be used to examine and explain how financial and other factors influence students' college-going behavior.

Concepts and models presented in some detail include the types of monetary benefits and costs bearing on a student's decision to invest in college, the accuracy of high school and college students in their estimation of the benefits of a college education, the study of private returns to baccalaureate and sub-baccalaureate investments, the model of the market for investment in human capital, and the MB = MC criterion for optimal investment. Particular emphasis was given to how differences in demand-side factors— such as an individual's academic ability, socioeconomic and family background, the quality of pre-college and college-level schooling, and discriminatory experiences—and supply-side factors—such as a student's family income and wealth, the availability of financial aid, and the accessibility and accuracy of information about financial aid and how to acquire it—can affect the amount a student invests in higher education.

The chapter also examined a variety of recent public-policy proposals that might have some potential to influence the demand or supply side of the market for human capital in ways that could expand student investment in higher education—and in particular, move a student from a disadvantaged to an advantaged position in the market for investment in human capital.

Chapter four presents and examines in some detail the nature, role and application of public sector economics in the finance of higher education. Then, chapters five and six will present and apply selected concepts from microeconomics—especially from the theories of demand, price, costs and production—that help deepen our understanding of such issues as rising college tuition and concerns about costs and productivity in higher education.

---

[18]It should be noted that front-loading of Pell grants is controversial. For example, even though front-loading may have a favorable effect on access, the potential negative effects on students' subsequent persistence decisions could constitute a substantial source of concern.

References

Altonji, J.G., and Dunn, T.A. (1996). Using siblings to estimate the effect of school quality on wages. *Review of Economics and Statistics* 78(4): 665-671.

Alwin, D.F., (1976). Socioeconomic background, colleges, and post-collegiate achievements. In W.H. Sewell, R.M. Hauser, and D.L. Featherman (eds.), *Schooling and Achievement in American Society.* New York: Academic Press.

Apgar, W.C., and Brown, H.J. (1987). *Microeconomics and Public Policy.* Glenview, IL: Scott, Foresman, and Company.

Arai, K. (1998). *The Economics of Education: An analysis of College-Going Behavior.* New York: Springer-Verlag.

Ashenfelter, O., and Krueger, A. (1994). Estimating the returns to schooling using a new sample of twins. *American Economic Review* 84: 1157–1173.

Becker, W.E., (1990). The demand for higher education. In S.A. Hoenack and E.L. Collins (eds.), *The Economics of American Universities.* Albany: State University of New York Press.

Becker, W.E. (1992). Why go to college? The value of an investment in higher education. In W.E. Becker and D.R. Lewis (eds.), *The Economics of American Higher Education.* Boston, MA: Kluwer Academic Publishers.

Becker, G.S. (1971). *The Economics of Discrimination* (2nd ed.). Chicago: University of Chicago Press.

Becker, G.S. (1975). *Human Capital: A Theoretical and Empirical Analysis with Special Reference to Education* (2nd ed). New York: Columbia University Press.

Becker, G.S. (1993). *Human Capital: A Theoretical and Empirical Analysis with Special Reference to Education* (3rd ed). Chicago: The University of Chicago Press.

Behrman, J.R., Constantine, J., Kletzer, L., McPherson, M., and Schapiro, M.O. (1996). *The Impact Of College Quality On Wages: Are There Differences Among Demographic Groups?* Discussion Paper Series No. 38. Williamstown, MA: Williams Project on the Economics of Higher Education.

Behrman, J.R., Kletzer, L.G., McPherson, M.S., and Schapiro, M.O. (1992). *The College Investment Decision: Direct and Indirect Effects of Family Background on Choice of Postsecondary Enrollment and Quality.* Discussion Paper Series No. 18. Williamstown, MA: Williams Project on the Economics of Higher Education.

Berger, M.C. (1992). Private returns to specific college majors. In W.E. Becker and D.R. Lewis (1992). *The Economic of American Higher Education.* Boston, MA: Kluwer Academic Publishers.

Betts, J.R. (1996). What do students know about wages? Evidence from a survey of undergraduates. *Journal of Human Resources* 31(1): 27-56.

Blau, F.D., and Ferber, M.A. (1991). Career plans and expectations of young women and men: The earnings gap and labor force participation. *Journal of Human Resources.* 26(4): 581-607.

Bourdieu, P. (1977a). Cultural reproduction and social reproduction. In J. Karabel and A. H. Halsey (eds.), *Power and Ideology in Education* (pp. 487-511). New York: Oxford University Press.

Bourdieu, P. (1977b). *Outline of a Theory of Practice.* Cambridge, UK: University Press.

Bourdieu, P., and Passeron, J-C. (1990). *Reproduction in Education, Society, and Culture.* Beverly Hills, CA: Sage.

Bowles, S., and Gintis, H. (1976). *Schooling in Capitalist America: Educational Reform and the Contradictions of Economic Life.* New York: Basic Books.

Brewer, D.J., Eide, E., and Ehrenberg, R.G. (1996). Does it pay to attend an elite private college? Cross cohort evidence on the effects of college quality on earnings. Working Paper No. 5613, Cambridge, MA: National Bureau of Economic Research.

Card, D., and Krueger, A. (1992a). Does school quality matter? Returns to education and the characteristics of public schools in the United States. *Journal of Political* Economy 100(1): 1-40.

Card, D., and Krueger, A. (1992b). School quality and black/white relative earnings: A direct assessment. *Quarterly Journal of Economics* 107(1): 151-200.

Card, D., and Krueger, A. (1993). Trends in relative black-white earnings revisited. *American Economic Review* 83(2): 85-91.

Carnoy, M. (1995a). Benefits of improving the quality of education. In M. Carnoy (ed.), *International Encyclopedia of Economics of Education* (2nd ed.). Tarrytown, NY: Elsevier.

Carnoy, M. (1995b). Race earnings differentials. In M. Carnoy (ed.), *International Encyclopedia of Eco-*

nomics of Education (2nd ed.). Tarrytown, NY: Elsevier.

Carnoy, M. (1995c). Rates of return to education. In M. Carnoy (ed.), *International Encyclopedia of Economics of Education* (2nd ed.). Tarrytown, NY: Elsevier.

Cipillone, P. (1995). Education and earnings. In M. Carnoy (ed.), *International Encyclopedia of Economics of Education* (2nd ed.). Tarrytown, NY: Elsevier.

Cohen, A.M., and Brawer, F.B. (1996). *The American Community College* (3rd ed.). San Francisco: Jossey-Bass.

Cohn, E., and Geske, T. (1990). *The Economics of Education* (3rd ed). New York: Pergamon Press.

College Board, (1999a). *Trends in College Pricing.* Washington, DC: The College Board.

College Board, (1999b). *Trends in Student Aid.* Washington, DC: The College Board.

Dale, S.B., and Krueger, A.B. (1999). *Estimating The Payoff To Attending A More Selective College: An Application Of Selection And Unobservables.* Cambridge, MA: National Bureau of Economic Research Working Paper No. W7322.

Dominitz, J., and Manski, C.F. (1996). Eliciting student expectations of the returns to schooling. *Journal of Human Resources* 31(1): 1-26.

Denison, E.F. (1962). *The Sources of Economic Growth in the United States.* New York: Committee for Economic Development.

Denison, E.F. (1984). Accounting for slower economic growth: An update. In J.W. Kendrick (ed.), *International Comparisons of Productivity and Causes of the Slowdown.* Cambridge, MA: Ballinger.

Doeringer, P.B., and Piore, M.J. (1971). *Internal Labor Markets and Manpower Analysis.* Lexington, MA: D. C. Heath.

Douglass, G.K. (1977). Economic returns on investments in higher education. In H.R. Bowen, *Investment in Learning: The Individual and Social Value of American Higher Education.* San Francisco: Jossey-Bass.

Ehrenberg, R.G., and Smith, R.S. (1982). *Modern Labor Economics: Theory and Public Policy.* Glenview, IL: Scott, Foresman and Co.

Fenske, R.H., Geranios, C.A, Keller, J.E., and Moore, D.E. (1997). *Early Intervention Programs: Opening the Door to Higher Education.* ASHE-ERIC Higher Education Report No. 6. Washington, DC: The George Washington University.

Ferber, M.A. (1995). Gender differences in earnings. In M. Carnoy (ed.), *International Encyclopedia of Economics of Education* (2nd ed.). Tarrytown, NY: Elsevier.

Fiorito, J., and Dauffenbach, R.C. (1982). Market and non-market influences on curriculum choice by college students. *Industrial and Labor Relations Review* 36(1): 88-103.

Freeman, R.B. (1971). *The Market for College-Trained Manpower: A Study in the Economics of Career Choice.* Cambridge, MA: Harvard University Press.

Freeman, R.B. (1975). Overinvestment in college training? *Journal of Human Resources* 10(3): 287-311.

Freeman, R.B. (1976). *The Overeducated American.* New York: Academic Press.

Gillmore, J.L. (1990). *Price and Quality in Higher Education.* Washington, DC: U.S. Government Printing Office.

Gladieux, L.E., and Swail, W.S. (1999). Financial aid is not enough: Improving the odds for minority and low-income students. In J. King (ed.), *Financing a College Education: How it Works, How it's Changing.* Phoenix, AZ: Oryx Press and ACE.

Gose, B. (2000). Measuring the value of an Ivy degree: New study questions the economic benefit of attending elite institutions. *The Chronicle of Higher Education* January 14: A52.

Griliches, Z. (1977). Estimating the returns to schooling: Some econometric problems. *Econometrica* 45: 1-22.

Grogger, J. (1996). School expenditures and post-schooling earnings: Evidence from High School and Beyond. *Review of Economics and Statistics* 78(4): 628-637.

Grubb, W.N. (1995). Postsecondary education and the sub-baccalaureate labor market: Corrections and extensions. *Economics of Education Review* 14(3): 285-299.

Grubb, W.N. (1996). *Working in the Middle: Strengthening Education and Training for the Mid-Skilled Labor Force.* San Francisco: Jossey-Bass.

Hansen, W.L. (1971). Total and private rates of return to investment in schooling. In B.F. Kiker (ed.), *Investment in Human Capital.* Columbia, SC: University of South Carolina Press.

Hanushek, E.A. (1993). Comment. In C.T. Clotfelter and M. Rothschild (eds.), *Studies of Supply and Demand in Higher Education*. Chicago: University of Chicago Press.

Heller, D.E. (1997). Student price response in higher education: An update to Leslie and Brinkman. *Journal of Higher Education* 68(6): 624-659.

Hoenack, S.A., and Weiler, W.C. (1979). The demand for higher education and institutional enrollment forecasting. *Economic Inquiry* 17: 89-113.

Hossler, D., Braxton, J., and Coopersmith, G. (1989). Understanding student college choice. In J. Smart (ed.), *Higher Education: Handbook of Theory and Research Volume 4*. New York: Agathon Press.

Hossler, D., and Schmit, J. (1995). The Indiana Postsecondary-Encouragement Experiment. In E.P. St. John (ed.), *Rethinking Tuition and Student Aid Strategies*. New Directions for Higher Education No. 89. San Francisco: Jossey-Bass.

Hossler, D., Schmit, J., and Vesper, N. (1999). *Going to College: How social, Economic, and Educational Factors Influence the Decisions Students Make*. Baltimore, MD: The Johns Hopkins University Press.

Hurtado, S., Inkelas, K.K., Briggs, C., and Rhee, B-S. (1997). Differences in college access and choice among racial/ethnic groups: Identifying continuing barriers. *Research in Higher Education* 38(1): 43-75.

Ikenberry, S.O., and Hartle, T.W. (1998). *Too Little Knowledge Is a Dangerous Thing: What the Public Thinks and Knows about Paying for College*. Washington, DC: American Council on Education.

Jackson, G.A., and Weathersby, G.B. (1975). Individual demand for higher education: A review and analysis of recent empirical studies. *Journal of Higher Education* 46(6): 623-652.

James, E., and Alsalam, N. (1993). College choice, academic achievement and future earnings. In E.P. Hoffman, (ed.), *Essays on the Economics of Education*. Kalamazoo, MI: W.E. Upjohn Institute for Employment Research.

James, E., Alsalam, N., Conaty, J.C., and To, D-L. (1989). College quality and future earnings: Where should you send your child to college? *American Economic Review* 79: 247-252.

Jencks, C., (1972). *Inequality: A Reassessment of the Effect of Family and Schools in America*. New York: Basic Books.

Jencks, C., (1979). *Who Gets Ahead? The Determinants of Economic Success in America*. New York: Basic Books.

Jencks, C., and Phillips, M. (1999). Aptitude or achievement: Why do test scores predict education attainment and earnings? In S.E. Mayer and P.E. Peterson (eds.), *Earning and Learning: How Schools Matter*. Washington, DC: Brookings Institution Press.

Johnes, G. (1993). *The Economics of Education*. New York: St. Martin's Press.

Johnson, W.R., and Neal, D. (1998). Basic skills and the black-white earnings gap. In C. Jencks and M. Phillips (eds.), *The Black-White Test Score Gap*. Washington, DC: Brookings Institution Press.

Kane, T.J. (1995). *Rising Public College Tuition and College Entry: How Well Do Public Subsidies Promote Access to College?* Cambridge, MA: National Bureau of Economic Research Working Paper No. 5164.

Kane, T.J. (1998). Misconceptions in the debate over affirmative action in college admissions. In G. Orfield, and E. Miller (eds.), *Chilling Admissions: The Affirmative Action Crisis and the Search for Alternatives*. Cambridge, MA: Harvard University Publishing Group.

Kane, T.J. (1999a). Reforming public subsidies for higher education. In M. H. Kosters (ed.), *Financing College Tuition: Government Policies and Educational Priorities*. Washington, DC: American Enterprise Institute.

Kane, T.J. (1999b). Student aid after tax reform: Risks and opportunities. In J. King (ed.), *Financing a College Education: How it Works, How it's Changing*. Phoenix, AZ: Oryx Press and ACE.

Kane, T.J. (1999c). *The Price of Admission: Rethinking How Americans Pay for College*. Washington, DC: The Brookings Institution.

Kane, T.J., and Rouse, C.E. (1995). Labor-market returns to two- and four-year college. *American Economic Review* 85(3): 600-614.

Kane, T.J., and Rouse, C.E. (1999). The community college: Educating students at the margin between college and work. *Journal of Economic Perspectives* 13(1): 63-84.

Karabel, J. (1998). No alternative: The effects of color-blind admissions in California. In G. Orfield, and E. Miller (eds.), *Chilling Admissions: The Affirmative Action Crisis and the Search for Alternatives*. Cambridge, MA: Harvard University Publishing Group.

Kaufman, B.E. (1986). *The Economics of Labor Markets and Labor Relations.* New York: The Dryden Press.

Kaufman, B.E. (1994). *The Economics of Labor Markets* (4th ed.). New York: The Dryden Press.

Kiker, B.F. (ed.), (1971a). *Investment in Human Capital.* Columbia, SC: University of South Carolina Press.

Kiker, B.F. (1971b). The historical roots of the concept of human capital. In B.F. Kiker (ed.), *Investment in Human Capital.* Columbia, SC: University of South Carolina Press.

King, J.E. (1999). Conclusion. In J. King (ed.), *Financing a College Education: How It Works, How It's Changing.* New York: The American Council on Education and Oryx Press.

Korenman, S., and Winship, C. (2000). A reanalysis of *The Bell Curve*: Intelligence, family background and schooling. In K. Arrow, S. Bowles, and S. Durlauf (eds.). *Meritocracy and Economic Inequality.* Princeton, NJ: Princeton University Press.

Lanaan, F.S. (1998). Descriptive analysis of students' post-college earnings from California community colleges. In J.R. Sanchez, and F.S. Lanaan (1998) (eds.). *Determining the Economic Benefits of Attending Community College.* New Directions for Community Colleges No. 104. San Francisco: Jossey-Bass.

Leigh, D.E., and Gill, A.M. (1997). Labor market returns to community colleges: Evidence for returning adults. *Journal of Human Resources* 32(2): 334-353.

Leslie, L.L., and Brinkman, P.T. (1988). *The Economic Value of Higher Education.* New York: ACE/Macmillan.

Levine, A., and Nidiffer, J. (1996). *Beating the Odds: How the Poor Get to College.* San Francisco: Jossey-Bass.

Lewis, D.R., Hearn, J.C., and Zilbert, E.E. (1993). Efficiency and equity effects of vocationally focused postsecondary education. *Sociology of Education* 66: 188-205.

Loury, L.D., and Garman, D. (1995). College selectivity and earnings. *Journal of Labor Economics* 13(2): 289-308.

Manski, C.F. (1993). Adolescent econometricians: How do youth infer the returns to schooling? In C.T. Clotfelter and M. Rothschild (eds.), *Studies of Supply and Demand in Higher Education.* Chicago: University of Chicago Press.

Manski, C.F., and Wise, D.A. (1983). *College Choice in America.* Cambridge, MA: Harvard University Press.

Maxwell, N.L. (1994). The effect on black-white wage differences of differences in the quantity and quality of education. *Industrial and Labor Relations Review* 47(2): 249-264.

McConnell, C.R., and Brue, S.L. (1995). *Contemporary Labor Economics* (4th ed.). New York: McGraw-Hill.

McDonough, P.M. (1997). *Choosing Colleges: How Social Class and Schools Structure Opportunity.* Albany: State University of New York Press.

McDonough, P. M. (1998). Structuring college opportunities: A cross-case analysis or organizational cultures, climates, and habiti. In C.A. Torres and T. R. Mitchell (eds.), *Sociology of Education: Emerging Perspectives.* (pp. 181-210). Albany: State University of New York Press.

McMahon, W.W. (1991). Improving higher education through increased efficiency. In D.H. Finifter, R.G Baldwin, J.R. Thelin (eds.), *The Uneasy Public Policy Triangle in Higher Education: Quality, Diversity, and Budgetary Efficiency.* New York: ACE/Macmillan.

McMahon, W.W., and Wagner, A.P. (1982). The monetary returns to education as partial social efficiency criteria. In W.W. McMahon and T.G. Geske (eds.), *Financing Education: Overcoming Inefficiency and Inequity.* Urbana, IL: University of Illinois Press.

McPherson, M.S. (1978). The demand for higher education. In D.W. Breneman and C.E. Finn (eds.), *Public Policy and Private Higher Education.* Washington, DC: The Brookings Institution.

McPherson, M.S., and Schapiro, M.O. (1991). *Keeping College Affordable: Government and Educational Opportunity.* Washington, DC: The Brookings Institution.

McPherson, M.S., and Schapiro, M.O. (1998). *The Student Aid Game: Meeting Need and Rewarding Talent in American Higher Education.* Princeton, NJ: Princeton University Press.

Miller, P., Mulvey, C., and Martin, N. (1995). What do twins studies reveal about the economic returns to education? A comparison of Australian and U.S. findings. *American Economic Review.* 85(3): 586-599.

Mincer, J. (1974). *Schooling, Experience and Earnings.* New York: National Bureau of Economic

Research.

Mincer, J. (1993a). Human capital and earnings. In J. Mincer (ed.), *Studies in Human Capital: Collected Essays of Jacob Mincer*. Brookfield, VT: Edward Elgar.

Mincer, J. (1993b). The distribution of labor incomes: A survey. In J. Mincer (ed.), *Studies in Human Capital: Collected Essays of Jacob Mincer*. Brookfield, VT: Edward Elgar.

Monk-Turner, E. (1994). Economic returns to community and four-year college education. *Journal of Socio-Economics* 23(4): 441-447.

Mumper, M. (1996). *Removing College Price Barriers*. Albany, NY: State University of New York Press.

Murphy, K.M., and Welch, F. (1989). Wage premiums for college graduates: Recent growth and possible explanations. *Educational Researcher* 18(4): 17-26.

Murphy, K.M., and Welch, F. (1992). The structure of wages. *Quarterly Journal of Economics* 107(1): 285-326.

National Center for Education Statistics. (1997). *The Condition of Education*. Washington, DC: U.S. Department of Education.

National Center for Education Statistics. (1999). *Digest of Education Statistics*. Washington, DC: U.S. Department of Education.

Orfield, G. (1992). Money, equity, and college access. *Harvard Educational Review* 62(3): 337-372.

Orfield, G. (1998). Campus resegregation and its alternatives. In G. Orfield, and E. Miller (eds.), *Chilling Admissions: The Affirmative Action Crisis and the Search for Alternatives*. Cambridge, MA: Harvard University Publishing Group.

Orfield, G., and Miller, E. (1998). (eds.), *Chilling Admissions: The Affirmative Action Crisis and the Search for Alternatives*. Cambridge, MA: Harvard University Publishing Group.

Paulsen, M.B. (1990). *College Choice: Understanding Student Enrollment Behavior.* ASHE-ERIC Higher Education Report No. 6. Washington, DC: The George Washington University.

Paulsen, M.B. (1996a). Higher education and productivity: An afterword. *Thought and Action: NEA Higher Education Journal* 12(2): 135-139.

Paulsen, M.B. (1996b). Higher education and state workforce productivity. *Thought and Action: NEA Higher Education Journal* 12(1): 55-77.

Paulsen, M.B. (1998). Recent research on the economics of attending college: Returns on investment and responsiveness to price. *Research in Higher Education* 39(4): 471-489.

Paulsen, M.B., and Peseau, B.A. (1989). Ten essential economic concepts every administrator should know. *Journal for Higher Education Management* 5(1): 9-17.

Paulsen, M.B., and Pogue, T.F. (1988). Higher education enrollment: The interaction of labor market conditions, curriculum and selectivity. *Economics of Education Review* 7(3): 275-290.

Paulsen, M.B., and St. John, E.P. (1997). The financial nexus between college choice and persistence. In R. Voorhees (ed.), *Researching Student Financial Aid*. New Directions for Institutional Research No. 95. San Francisco: Jossey-Bass.

Paulsen, M.B., and St. John, E.P. (in press). Social class and college costs: Examining the financial nexus between college choice and persistence. *The Journal of Higher Education* 73.

Pencavel, J. (1993). Higher education, economic growth, and earnings. In W.E. Becker and D.R. Lewis (eds.), *The Economics of American Higher Education*. Boston, MA: Kluwer Academic Publishers.

Perlman, R. (1973). *The Economics of Education*. New york: McGraw-Hill.

Perna, L.W. (2000). Differences in the decision to attend college among African Americans, Hispanics, and whites. *The Journal of Higher Education* 71(2): 117-141.

Psacharopoulos, G. (1973). *Returns to Education: An International Comparison*. Amsterdam: Elsevier-Jossey-Bass.

Psacharopoulos, G. (1975). *Earnings and Education in OECD Countries*. Paris: OECD.

Psacharopoulos, G. (1981). Returns to education: An updated international comparison. *Comparative Education* 17(3): 321-341.

Rouse, C.E. (1994). What to do after high school: The two-year versus four-year college decision. In R.G. Ehrenberg (ed.), *Choices and Consequences: Contemporary Policy Issues in Education*. Ithaca, NY: ILR Press.

Rouse, C.E. (1999). Further estimates of the economic return to schooling from a new sample of twins. *Economics of Education Review* 18: 149-157.

Rumberger, R.W. (1984). The changing economic benefits of college graduates. *Economics of Education Review* 3: 3-11.

Rumberger, R.W., and Thomas, S.L. (1993). The economic returns to college major, quality and performance: A multi-level analysis of recent graduates. *Economics of Education Review* 12(1): 1-19.

Sanchez, J.R., and Lanaan, F.S. (1998) (eds.). *Determining the Economic Benefits of Attending Community College*. New Directions for Community Colleges No. 104. San Francisco: Jossey-Bass.

Schultz, T.W. (1961). Investment in human capital. *American Economic Review* 51: 1035-1039.

Sewell, W.H., and Hauser, R.M. (1976). Causes and consequences of higher education: Models of the status attainment process. In W.H. Sewell, R.M. Hauser, and D.L. Featherman (eds.), *Schooling and Achievement in American Society*. New York: Academic Press.

Smith, J., and Welch, F. (1989). Black economic progress after Myrdal. *Journal of Economic Literature* 27(2): 519-564.

Strober, M.H. (1995). Gender and occupational segregation. In M. Carnoy (ed.), *International Encyclopedia of Economics of Education* (2nd ed.). Tarrytown, NY: Elsevier.

Smith, H.L., and Powell, B. (1990). Great expectations: Variations in income expectations among college seniors. *Sociology of Education*. 63: 194-207.

Spence, D. (1973). Job market signaling. *Quarterly Journal of Economics* 87: 355-374.

St. John, E.P. (1994). *Prices, Productivity, and Investment: Assessing Financial Strategies in Higher Education*. ASHE-ERIC Higher Education Report No. 3. Washington, DC: The George Washington University, School of Education and Human Development.

St. John, E.P. (2000). The impact of student aid on recruitment and retention: What the research indicates. In M.D. Coomes (ed.), *The Role Student Aid Plays in Enrollment Management*. New Directions for Student Services No. 89. San Francisco: Jossey-Bass.

Swartz, D. (1997). *Culture and Power: The Sociology of Pierre Bourdieu*. Chicago: University of Chicago Press.

Taubman, P., and Wales, T. (1974). *Higher Education and Earnings: College as an Investment and a Screening Device*. New York: McGraw-Hill.

Thurow, L. (1970). *Investment in Human Capital*. Belmont, CA: Wadsworth.

Thurow, L.C. (1975). *Generating Inequality: Mechanisms of Distribution in the U.S. Economy*. New York: Basic Books.

Weisbrod, B.A. (1968). External effects of investment in education. In M. Blaug (ed.), *Economics of Education I*. Baltimore, MD: Penguin Books.

Wish, J.R., and Hamilton, W.D. (1980). Replicating Freeman's recursive adjustment model of demand for higher education. *Research in Higher Education* 12(1): 83-95.

Woodhall, M. (1995). Human capital concepts. In M. Carnoy (ed.), *International Encyclopedia of Economics of Education* (2nd ed.). Tarrytown, NY: Elsevier.

Chapter 4

THE ECONOMICS OF THE PUBLIC SECTOR:
The Nature and Role of Public Policy in the Finance of Higher Education[1]

Michael B. Paulsen

The American economy is a mixed system; that is, it has a private sector and a public sector, and there are many situations in which the government (federal, state or local) has good reason to intervene to influence the structure of incentives that guide the marketplace. There are three primary "economic" functions of the government: the efficient "allocation" of resources in the provision of goods and services in the economy, the equitable "distribution" of the costs and benefits of economic activity, and the "stabilization" of production, employment and prices in the economy (Musgrave and Musgrave, 1973, 1984). Public sector economics is primarily concerned with the study of government activity in its performance of the first two of these functions: allocation and distribution (Stiglitz, 2000). The purpose of this chapter is to introduce, explain, and illustrate the use of selected concepts and models from the economics of the public sector that have proven to be particularly effective in analyzing and understanding the finance of higher education. The economics of the public sector can be defined as "the study of how government policy, especially tax and expenditure policy, affects the economy and thereby the welfare of its citizens" (Browning and Browning, 1994, p. 1).

The primary tools of the public sector economist are dedicated to the analysis of government policies, including those related to the finance of higher education. An efficient allocation of resources between higher education and other uses depends on the relations between the marginal benefits and marginal costs associated with additional expenditures on higher education (Bowen, 1980). In order to ensure an efficient allocation of resources, increases in resources or expenditures on higher education should con-

---

[1]I would like to thank Sandy Baum and Rob Toutkoushian for their helpful comments on earlier drafts of this chapter.

tinue as long as the marginal benefit of the last increment of expenditure exceeds its marginal cost. When the two become equal, total benefits exceed total costs by the greatest possible amount and resources have been efficiently allocated between higher education and other uses (Bowen, 1980; Hoenack, 1982). However, when the competitive economic system fails to allocate resources efficiently or distribute benefits and costs equitably, public policies are designed to improve the effectiveness of the relevant markets.

The two primary criteria used by economists to evaluate public policies for application in such instances are *efficiency* and *equity*.[2,3] Economists' view of "efficiency" does not focus narrowly on institutional budget cuts or increases in faculty workloads and student-faculty ratios. In fact, these factors may not result in increases in "economic" efficiency. Rather, the concept of economic efficiency is much broader. It is quite possible, for example, for a university or a statewide higher education system to improve its economic efficiency by increasing its expenditures (i.e., expanding its budget) and simultaneously increasing its effectiveness in producing valued learning outcomes by a greater amount (McMahon, 1991b). An economic or *Pareto* "efficient allocation of resources is one in which it is impossible, through any change in resource allocation, to make some person or persons better off without making someone else worse off" (Browning and Browning, 1994, p. 11).

Equity, as a criterion for policy evaluation, refers to the effects of a public policy on the fairness of the distribution of benefits and costs in society; that is, whether or not a public policy has generated a more just, fair, or equitable distribution of income. Public policies related to expenditure and taxation can be assessed in terms of two perspectives on equity: horizontal equity and vertical equity (Baum, 1996). The principle of horizontal equity requires that individuals in like circumstances should be treated in a like manner by public expenditure and taxation policies. The principle of vertical equity requires that individuals in dissimilar circumstances should be treated in appropriately dissimilar ways when applying public expenditure and taxation policies.

> The personal income tax provides a good example for examining issues of horizontal and vertical equity. Horizontal equity requires that people with equal incomes should pay equal amounts of tax…[and that] those with higher incomes pay a higher percentage of their income in tax than do those with lower incomes, because there is a general sense that this constitutes appropriately different treatment of people in different circumstances (Baum, 1996, pp. 23-24).

---

[2]It has been common to refer to efficiency and equity as competing or contradictory criteria involving a necessary tradeoff (e.g., Okun, 1975). However, as explained below, simultaneous increases in both equity and efficiency are possible (McMahon, 1982), and society's desire for a more equitable distribution of income and opportunities can be viewed as an externality that requires government intervention to produce a socially efficient redistribution (e.g., Boadway, 1979). This issue is addressed at some length below.

[3]A comprehensive and elaborate treatment of the concepts of efficiency and equity, with special reference to education, is provided in McMahon (1982). Although his extensive analysis is beyond the scope of this chapter, it is a highly instructive examination of these central concepts and their relationships in allocation and distributional decision-making in education.

McMahon (1982) defines equity in a way that is especially appropriate and meaningful for application to education.

> Equity is defined as involving a redistribution of resources (or of costs) designed to achieve the community's philosophical and ethical standards of fairness (p. 16).

> [It] deals with a different question—the question of the justice with which the benefits of education, or taxation or other burdens, are distributed. The achievement of equity is defined in the purest sense as concerned with the redistribution of resources where some gain and some lose. If all possible improvements in efficiency have been made so that there are no untapped resources available, and if justice in the initial distribution has not been achieved, to improve equity would require a redistribution of the educational benefits (or tax burdens). This process makes some better off, but some worse off, albeit in the interest of greater distributive justice (p. 4).

In an imagined world of free markets and perfect competition, and one in which the initial distributions of income and opportunities are just, the competitive private-market system will allocate resources in such a way that a Pareto-efficient solution will occur. However, there are many common instances in which the market system is not perfectly competitive and it does not automatically produce Pareto-efficient resource allocations, nor does it create or result in an equitable distribution of benefits and costs. The market system fails to generate an economically efficient allocation of resources in the presence of externalities, public or quasi-public goods, or imperfect markets. When these "market failures" occur, a public policy intervention by government is necessary to correct the misallocations that result. Similarly, public policies are needed when either merit goods are present or a redistribution of income and opportunities is necessary to bring about a more just distribution (Stiglitz, 2000).[4] Every one of these circumstances calls for government intervention with appropriate public policy. Therefore, the next section of this chapter defines and examines each of these "market failures" and other justifications for government intervention in some detail, with an eye toward their implications for higher education.

The economics of the public sector is highly relevant to the study of the finance of higher education because the market for investment in higher education (Paulsen, Chapter 3) and the market for enrollment places in colleges and universities or units of higher education (examined below) are arenas in which federal, state, or local governments are actively involved. Furthermore, market failures, unjust distributions and merit goods are all characteristic of, and relevant to, the markets for human capital and enrollment places in higher education.

---

[4]As explained in a later section, even though equity arguments—that is, the declared need to move toward a more equitable distribution of opportunities in higher education—are commonly used to justify government subsidies to students and institutions, the distribution of income or other benefits can, in and of itself, be viewed as a quasi-public good creating externalities, in which case another strong justification for public support for higher education can be justified in terms of the "market failures" arguments (see e.g., Boadway, 1979; Hochman and Rogers, 1969; Musgrave and Musgrave, 1973, 1984; Thurow, 1971).

THE ROLE OF GOVERNMENT IN HIGHER EDUCATION

Some of the primary justifications for government intervention or assistance with incentives to impact the behavior of market participants are based on the existence of "market failures," broadly defined as situations in which the market mechanism fails to allocate resources efficiently and equitably (Apgar and Brown, 1987; Boadway, 1979; Browning and Browning, 1983, 1994; Musgrave and Musgrave, 1973, 1984; Stiglitz, 2000). Economists who study investment in higher education have developed a comprehensive set of reasons for government involvement in the market for higher education (Bowen, 1977, 1980; Breneman and Nelson, 1981; Cohn and Geske, 1990; Geske and Cohn, 1998; Kane, 1999c; McMahon, 1991a, 1991b, 1991c; McPherson and Schapiro, 1991; Paulsen, 1996b, 1998; Thurow, 1970). These reasons are based on the socially efficient allocation of resources to investment in higher education and the equitable distribution of access, benefits, and costs related to participation in postsecondary education. Behrman, Crawford and Stacey (1997) express the bases for "policy interventions" in the following way:

> The basic rationales for policy interventions are concerns about the efficiency of economic behavior and the equity of the distribution of income and other benefits. It is desirable to achieve distributional aims as efficiently as possible because there often are tradeoffs between distributional and efficiency goals....That education may have some strong positive social benefits is *not* in itself an efficiency reason for policy intervention and support. In addition, there must be a presumption of "market failures," in the sense that the total effects differ from the private effects, and...such "market failures" are thought to arise possibly because of imperfect capital and insurance markets (e.g., difficulties in obtaining financing for educational investments and in pooling risks), information problems, and the public goods or external aspects of education (e.g., effects on persons other than the individual being educated that are transferred other than through markets) (p. 251).

Each of the individual bases for policy interventions by government that have been presented consistently by public-sector and educational economists are considered in this section as they relate to the market for higher education.

Higher Education Creates External or Public Benefits.

The individual student investing in higher education naturally considers only the private benefits of the investment—that is, those benefits that accrue to, and can be internalized by, the individual student alone. But this individual's investment is also likely to create additional benefits that accrue to persons other than this investor (Bowen, 1977). Such benefits are "external" to the investing individual and other persons cannot be excluded from experiencing these benefits (Paulsen and Peseau, 1989). External benefits are sometimes referred to as public benefits. Many examples of external or public benefits of higher education have been identified (Bowen, 1977; Carnegie Commission on Higher Education, 1973; Douglass, 1977; Pascarella and Terenzini, 1991; Salmon and Fagnano, 1995; Schultz, 1963; Weisbrod, 1968; Wolfe, 1995).

First, there are many non-monetary benefits of higher education that have a public or external component. Of course, the measurement of non-monetary benefits is clearly problematic (Behrman, 1997). Nevertheless, there are some non-monetary external benefits that have been empirically related to investments in higher education: receptivity, inclination, and adaptability to change; the development of political attitudes in support of public programs; increased awareness and involvement in political affairs; greater involvement in public service and volunteer work; increased charitable giving, lower unemployment, a reduction in criminal activities; improved health for both educated parents and their children, and lower public expenditures for welfare and Medicaid (Bowen, 1977; Haveman and Wolfe, 1984; Michael, 1982; Wolfe, 1995).

However, there are also some kinds of public or external benefits that are somewhat easier to quantify, albeit most often for purposes of estimation, at best, rather than for precise measurement. Leslie and Brinkman (1988) assert that there are three primary ways to quantitatively assess the social or public benefits of higher education: computing social rates of return, estimating the contribution of higher education to economic growth, and the economic impacts of postsecondary institutions on local communities. The role of social rates of return is discussed in the next section, but economic impact studies and the effect of higher education on economic growth are discussed briefly here. Most economic impact studies of colleges and universities have used the traditional methodology of Caffrey and Isaacs, (1971). A review of research on the impact of higher education on economic activity in local and regional economies indicated that, on average, an additional $1.8 million of business spending and 53 additional jobs were generated from each $1 million of spending from a four-year college budget (Leslie and Slaughter, 1992). These findings are very consistent with those of Leslie and Brinkman (1988), who reported that for each $1 million in a public college's budget, on average, about 59 jobs are created and about $1.5 to $1.6 million of business volume was generated in the local economy.

The public or external benefit aspects of the contribution of investments in higher education to growth in output, income and productivity have been the most widely studied of the potentially quantifiable types of external benefits of higher education (Wolfe, 1995). However, it is important to note that in order for the contribution of higher education to growth in national income and productivity to yield an external benefit, the contribution must be above and beyond the increases in earnings that would accrue to the college-educated workers themselves (Baumol, et al., 1989). In other words, if the investment in higher education "were also to result in increases in productivity that added to *everyone's* income…going beyond the private returns to the recipients of the enhanced education," an unambiguous public or external benefit would be present (p. 200). Economists have been clear and consistent in their explanations and demonstrations of why they are confident that such external benefits do indeed occur.

> The education of one worker may have favorable external effects on the productivity of others. Where production involves the cooperative efforts of workers, flexibility and adaptability of one worker will redound to the advantage of others. Productivity of each member of the group influences the productivity of each other member (Weisbrod, 1968, p. 176).

> [To] argue that there are no externalities, one would have to accept the unlikely idea that the entire increase in productivity resulting from higher education is reflected in wages. In fact, better educated students are more likely to engage in professional activities with significant

social benefits not fully compensated by the market. Even when high productivity levels are accompanied by commensurate individual financial rewards, the rest of society benefits from innovations and contributions. We are all affected not only by the level and quality of our own education but also by that of those around us, who can communicate and work more effectively if they are well-educated (Baum, 1995, p. 2).

In brief, when a student graduates from college, "his or her increased productivity could result in the greater productivity of coworkers, employees, and employers" (Geske and Cohn, 1998, p. 20). Assuming workers are paid in accordance with their productivity—the conventional marginal product theory of wages in microeconomics—this individual college graduate would not be paid extra wages for every increase in the productivity of other workers that occurs due to this worker's investment in higher education. Instead, the incomes of the other workers would rise as they are paid in accordance with their now-higher productivity, which in turn, would be due to the external benefits arising from their college-educated co-worker's investment in higher education. This externality would, in turn, multiply or snowball as other co-workers invested in higher education, increased their productivities and individual incomes, and finally, contributed—by way of external benefits—to increases in the productivities and higher incomes of their co-workers.

Based on their review of research on education and economic growth, Leslie and Brinkman (1988) found that investments in education account for about 15 to 20 percent of our economic growth, with about one-fourth of that amount directly attributable to investments in higher education. Pencavel (1993) found that 14.6 percent of American economic growth between 1973 and 1984 was attributable to investment in higher education. And, examining education's contribution from another perspective, Leslie and Brinkman (1988) found that from 20 to 40 percent of economic growth could be attributed to higher education's role in the advancement and application of knowledge. Finally, in a recent study, Paulsen (1996a, 1996b) found that for each one-percentage-point increase in the share of a state's high school graduates who had college degrees, the subsequent growth in the state's workforce productivity (output and income per worker) increased by 1.2 percent.

Unfortunately, society's preferences for these public or external benefits will not be revealed in the marketplace without government intervention. Because these external benefits are so diffused across the general population, individual student investors cannot capture these external benefits for themselves. Therefore they do not consider them in making their investment decisions. Because they will underestimate the returns or benefits from their investments, students will invest less than a socially optimum amount in higher education. This "underinvestment" in higher education calls for public policy in the form of subsidies to students or institutions. As examined in more detail in a subsequent section, these subsidies make it possible to effectively "internalize" these external benefits. In effect, appropriate policies create incentives for individual investors so that they will behave in a way that resembles how they would behave if they actually did consider external benefits in their investment decisions.

The Social Rate of Return to Investment in Higher Education Is Attractive Relative to Rates of Return on Alternative Investments

The computation of social rates of return to investment in higher education is generally similar to the computation of private rates. Referring to the portrayal of the components of such computations in Figures 1 and 2 of Chapter 3 (pages 57 and 58 in this volume), the few necessary changes would be to set the earnings differential equal to pretax, rather than after-tax earnings, so that it will represent benefits that accrue to society in general (e.g., tax revenue can be used by government to finance other expenditures for society's benefit); include all costs to society, which means adding subsidies (e.g., grants or scholarships) to other direct (e.g., tuition) and indirect (earnings forgone) costs; and to the extent they can be quantified, adding non-monetary public benefits on top of the area corresponding to the earnings differential (McMahon and Wagner, 1982). Among the recent estimates of social rates of return to higher education, McMahon and Wagner (1982) calculated rates of over 13 percent; McMahon (1991c) computed rates that were in the 12 to 13 percent range by the late 1980s; and Leslie and Brinkman's (1988) meta-analysis yielded a median rate of 12.5 percent. There is substantial consistency among these estimates and they compare quite favorably with average rates of interest on alternative financial assets (McMahon, 1991c; McMahon and Wagner, 1982). Social rates of return that exceed rates on alternative investments (e.g., physical capital or housing) indicate an underinvestment in higher education (McMahon, 1991c).[5]

Higher Education Has Some of the Characteristics of a Pure Public Good

Higher education is not a pure public good, but it possesses some of the characteristics of such a good; therefore it would be appropriately classified as what economists have come to call an impure, quasi-public or even a "publicly provided private good" (Breneman and Nelson, 1981; Stiglitz, 2000). The best-known example of a pure public good is national defense. It is a "pure" public good because it illustrates the extreme example of the two primary characteristics of public goods: non-exclusion from benefits and non-rivalry in consumption of benefits. Non-rivalry means that one person's "consumption" of national defense does not keep others from consuming it too. Non-exclusion means that there is no feasible way to exclude or deprive anyone from the benefits of national defense whether or not they provide any financial support for it (i.e., pay taxes).

Higher education has these characteristics to a limited extent because it creates external benefits. In fact public goods can be viewed as a case of externalities in the extreme (Stiglitz, 2000). For example, if a state invests in the higher education of its citizens, and thereby increases the overall productivity of its workforce—that is,

---

[5]Furthermore, any indicators of underinvestment in higher education based on social rates of return to investment in higher education relative to alternatives—such as investment in other financial assets, physical capital and housing—are likely to understate the magnitude of underinvestment in college. One of the primary reasons for this is the substantially greater non-monetary benefits that are likely to be associated with investment in higher education compared with alternative investments.

increases in output and income per worker in the general economy that extend beyond just the incremental earnings of those who invested in college—an external benefit has been created; that is, many participants in the state's economy would benefit from the more productive workforce (see, e.g., Paulsen, 1996a, 1996b). Many citizens in the state would benefit from this externality, whether or not they attended college themselves. It would also be nearly impossible to exclude most citizens from benefiting in some way from the statewide gains associated with a more productive workforce. But society's preferences for these external benefits would not be revealed in the market without government intervention. Just as with the discussion of external benefits above, individual students who are deciding how much to invest in higher education will not consider these public benefits, and will therefore, underinvest in higher education. Again, public policy intervention would be called for to promote a more socially efficient allocation of resources to higher education in the state.

Investment in Higher Education Takes Place in the Context of Imperfect Capital Markets

In the market for funds to invest in human capital, there are imperfections that are inherent due to the circumstances under which funds might be acquired (Arai, 1998; Thurow, 1970).[6] Therefore, in the absence of government policy intervention, there are substantial limits on the availability of funds. Some of the primary reasons for this are that the future earnings capacities of student investors in human capital cannot be offered as collateral—at least not in the same sense that a family house or a private business can be and are regularly offered as collateral—for a loan; human capital is embodied in a person and therefore, certainly cannot be sold; it cannot be repossessed; and it is a highly illiquid asset (G. Becker, 1993; Kane, 1999c; McPherson and Schapiro, 1991; Thurow, 1970).[7] Again, in the absence of government guarantees, subsidies or insurance provisions, these circumstances make an educational loan a risky undertaking for lending institutions (Thurow, 1970). In fact, lenders face such uncertainty that they do not even know the potential return on their investment; that is, how much human capital the lending institution's financial investment will create. Because of the uncertainty and risk experienced by the lender, extra premiums would be added onto market lending rates.

---

[6]Much of the material in this section is drawn from Lester Thurow's (1970) analysis of the imperfections and information problems that plague markets for human capital. See especially Chapter 5: Individual Investment Decisions.

[7]One way to address some of the problematic imperfections in the human capital market is through the use of various forms of an income-contingent loan repayment program. Suggested quite some time ago by Friedman (1962), its merits and limitations continue to be examined and debated (see e.g., Kane, 1999a, 1999c; McPherson and Schapiro, 1991). However, this conversation has expanded because a living laboratory is now available for studying its feasibility and effectiveness. One form of the income-contingent loan approach was initiated as an option in the direct loan program under the Student Loan Reform Act of 1993. Specifically, at the time of repayment, students were given the opportunity of choosing between a traditional repayment plan or an income-sensitive plan. See Kane (1999b) for a set of recommendations and an analysis of the pros and cons of this "forward-looking means-testing" (pp. 146-148).

Unfortunately, there are other sources of imperfections and inequities in the market for funds to invest in higher education that result in substantial individual differences in access to funds for investment (Kane, 1999c; Paulsen, Chapter 3). For example, an important determinant of a student's access to funds in the market for human capital is family income and wealth, which are unequally distributed among students and their families. A student with high-income parents is much more likely than those from lower-income backgrounds to be in a position to acquire financial capital for college investment. Among students from higher-income backgrounds, family wealth (real assets) can be pledged as collateral to obtain a low-interest loan in the general, private, unsubsidized educational loan market. Finally, based on the principles illustrated in Figures 1 and 2 and Equations 1-5 in Chapter 3, younger students—those of traditional college-going age—are likely to have the longest period of productive earning years; however, such students often do not have collateral or even a credit rating at that age (Thurow, 1970). In combination, these market imperfections will lead to an underallocation of resources to investment in higher education, unless appropriate policy interventions take place.

The Equitable Distribution of Human Capital in the Market Depends on the Degree to Which the Current Distribution of Income Is Equitable

The problems that result from market imperfections discussed in the previous section constitute much more substantial barriers for low-income than for high-income students and their families (Geske and Cohn, 1998; Kane, 1999a, 1999c; McPherson and Schapiro, 1991; Mumper, 1996; Thurow, 1970). Geske and Cohn (1998) make the central argument as follows:

> Perhaps a more compelling argument in favor of government support of higher education is that unsubsidized, private higher education would be open almost exclusively to high-income families, denying higher education to the lower-income masses. There are two arguments here. First, if financial markets make it difficult—frequently impossible—for low-income families to borrow for higher education without government interference, then even if *all* of the benefits of higher education can be captured by the students and their families, still a large number of students would not enroll, simply because they lack the necessary funds. Ignoring egalitarian arguments, such a situation is *inefficient*, because some human resources are not being developed to their full potential. This situation would call for government action, most notably some form of a government-guaranteed (perhaps subsidized) student loan program (pp. 20-21).

The severity of the market imperfections as barriers to investment in higher education is related to differences in how willing low- versus high-income families are to forgo income and spending today in order to borrow funds and invest in possible higher income in the future. In general, the value of a dollar today compared with a dollar in the future—typically referred to as one's time preference—increases as family income decreases (Thurow, 1970). Among low-income families the value of current income is very high because of the immediate need of income to pay bills and survive right now. Low-income families face a budget constraint that is much more severe than that of higher-income families. Thurow explains the disturbing, albeit likely, outcomes of this scenario for the participation of low-income students and families in the market for human capital and investment in higher education.[8]

> The poor may know that the discounted benefits of more human capital exceed the discounted costs of acquiring human capital at prevailing market interest rates, but they may still be unable to acquire more human capital. They simply cannot command investment resources. The result is less human investment by those with low incomes, and thus a vicious circle of poverty (p. 79).

In the absence of substantial public policy interventions that effectively address the distributional inequities that render the market for human capital inefficient and unfair, underinvestment in higher education would, in all likelihood, continue to be substantial.

Society May Prefer a More Equal Distribution of Income, and Access to Higher Education Is a Means Toward That End

A redistribution of income—that is, toward a more equal distribution of income—has all the characteristics of an externality and of a pure public good, including non-excludability and non-rivalry (Boadway, 1979; Hochman and Rogers, 1969; Stiglitz, 2000; Thurow, 1971).[9] Therefore, if society's well-being can be improved through a more

---

[8]Readers may note that this issue of the harsher effects of "market imperfections" on low-income families is clearly related to, and can also be examined in terms of, G. Becker's (1993) model of the market for human capital, as presented and discussed in Paulsen (Chapter 3). Becker acknowledged another way (not explicitly addressed in Chapter 3 of this volume) in which a student's opportunities or access to funds (i.e., the supply of funds curve)—and the attendant investment in higher education—may vary by family income and wealth. Potentially, this perspective is neither strictly a supply side or demand-side phenomenon in the market for human capital. Because it has implications for shifts in both demand and supply, this complication is introduced in this footnote and left for the interested reader to explore in greater depth (see G. Becker, 1975, 1993; Kaufman, 1986, 1994; McConnell and Brue, 1995; Mincer, 1993b; and Thurow, 1970; for additional study). This view has to do with how the student and family value current income relative to income earned in the future. Expressed in the technical terms introduced in Chapter 3, the present value of a dollar in the future is worth much less to a lower-income than to a higher-income person (Thurow, 1970). The reason is that because of their immediate dependence on current income for survival, low-income households essentially use a much higher rate of interest to discount future earnings and assign them a present value. Because of their rational decision not to set aside a portion of their limited current income for spending on education and their inability to use current income or nonexistent wealth or assets as collateral for a loan, they are less likely than middle- or upper-income families to either save or borrow to invest in higher education. Although time preference can directly affect the supply of funds for investment in higher education, it can also directly affect the demand curve, because families with different time preferences would use different interest rates to discount future earnings, thereby perceiving different rates of return to investment. Different sets of rates of return are manifested in different demand curves in Becker's model of the market for investment in human capital. Whether viewed as a demand- or supply-side influence, however, differences in time preferences will frequently lead to more advantaged positions for high-income compared with low-income families in the market for human capital. This result is due, in large part, to an unequal distribution of income. And because of the unequal distribution of income, there will be substantial dispersion in levels of investment in higher education corresponding to the unequal income distribution. Finally, the ensuing expansion in the distribution of opportunities for higher education will, in turn, perpetuate or even widen the unequal distribution of income. It may be viewed as one way of conceptualizing the vicious circle of poverty.

equal distribution of income, public policy intervention—such as taxes, transfers, and subsidies—would be required in order to correct for the existing market failures implicated in the matter of distributional equity (Hochman and Rogers, 1969; Stiglitz, 2000; Thurow, 1971). Variation in educational attainment is correlated with dispersion in the distribution of income (e.g., G. Becker, 1993; Mincer, 1993a, 1993b). And even though a redistribution of income—that is, one that would make everyone better off—could be achieved through direct transfer payments to low-income households, that is probably not the most efficient approach (Thurow, 1970). Whereas transfer payments would have to be made every year to maintain a new distribution of income, subsidies that are effective in promoting investments in human capital by lower-income individuals would have to be made only once to create and maintain a more equal distribution of income in the future. In fact, investment in human capital (higher education) is the more efficient approach not only because fewer resources would be required, but also because the investments in human capital would generate new private and public benefits, including externalities valued by society.

Society May View Higher Education as a Merit Good

One remaining argument and rationale for the involvement of government in the market for investment in human capital, such as higher education, is that society might view higher education as meritorious or as a "merit good" (Musgrave and Musgrave, 1973, 1984; Stiglitz, 2000; Thurow, 1970). In brief, this means that policy-makers view individual's expenditures on certain goods (e.g., education and health) as meritorious and expenditures on others as deleterious (e.g., alcohol and cigarettes). As a result, society uses subsidies to encourage spending on meritorious goods and taxes to discourage spending on undesirable goods. This clearly involves paternalistic interference with the revealed preferences of individuals and the imposition of the preferences of a policy-making body (Browning and Browning, 1994). However, the underlying philosophical argument is based on the view that sometimes people lack adequate information about the benefits from acquisition of more of a merit good, the extent to which they deserve greater access to it, the rights or opportunities they might have to acquire it, or their future preferences for it after learning from experience with it (Baum, 1996; Musgrave and Musgrave, 1973; Thurow, 1970). When encouraged to

---

[9]Technically, this view is based on the assumption of interdependent utility functions (e.g., see Boadway, 1979; Hochman and Rogers, 1969; Thurow, 1971 for a more complete explanation). In brief, this means that the well-being or satisfaction of one individual or group depends not only on her or their own income and consumption, but on the income and consumption of others as well. In particular, if members of the high-income class gain more satisfaction from an increment in the income of members of the low-income class than from a similar increment in their own incomes, then both groups could be made better off overall as a result of a transfer of income from the higher to the lower income groups. Presumably, in the case of higher education, this would occur as a result of sufficient and effective subsidies that stimulate more investment in higher education—which will lead to higher incomes—among students from lower-income families. See Browning and Browning (1983, pp. 224-226) for a clear demonstration of the meaning and impact of the assumption of interdependent utility functions using indifference curves and budget constraints to analyze the optimizing behavior of higher- and lower-income groups.

spend some or more of one's resources and time on investments in merit goods, like higher education, the experience—for example, of participation in college—provides the individual with new information and opportunities to learn about the "merits" (benefits) of investments in higher education. Presumably, due to this "learning" about the benefits that will accrue to the individual who attends college will help this student—as well as his or her friends and family members—to make more informed decisions about investments in higher education in the future, which may, in turn, lead to additional public benefits as well.[10]

PUBLIC POLICY INTERVENTIONS: APPLICATIONS IN THE MARKET FOR HIGHER EDUCATION

Two of the most common instances of market failure in the provision of higher education occur in the presence of externalities and quasi-public goods. In either of these situations, the private market mechanism fails to produce an optimum allocation of resources to investment in higher education. In the absence of a government (federal, state, or local, as appropriate) public policy intervention, there will be an underallocation of resources to higher education.

Identifying the Optimum Allocation of Resources to Higher Education in the Presence of Externalities and Quasi-Public Goods

The allocation of resources between higher education and alternative uses depends, in part, on the enrollment behavior of college-bound students and the various ways in which student characteristics, institutional characteristics and public policies affect the propensities of these individual students to invest in higher education. As explained in a previous section, the decisions of individual students to invest in higher education lead to attractive private benefits, but also generate a variety of monetary and non-monetary public benefits. These public benefits are external to the individual's investment decision, are diffused across the general population, and accrue to society. Individual student investors cannot capture or internalize these benefits for themselves. Therefore the individual student naturally considers only the private benefits of the investment. As a result, society's preferences for the public benefits from the investments of individual students will not be revealed in the amounts invested in the market for human capital without government intervention. In the absence of appropriate public policies, the aggregation of the levels of private demand for units (e.g., years or credit hours) of higher education—based on the horizontal summation of units demanded by individual students at existing tuition prices—will understate the demand of society for higher education, and individual students, in combination, will invest less than a socially optimum amount in higher education.

It is possible to theoretically identify the optimal allocation of resources invested in

---

[10]For a clear and straightforward explanation of this concept, see the classic treatment by Musgrave and Musgrave (1973, pp. 80-81).

higher education.[11] This is typically accomplished by postulating a private demand, a public demand for external benefits—which expresses the value that society would place on externalities associated with the private demand—and a social demand equal to the vertical summation of the private demand and the public demand for externalities (see e.g., Browning and Browning, 1983, 1994; Musgrave and Musgrave, 1973, 1984; Wolfe, 1995). Figure 1 illustrates this approach, and represents the market for higher education based on the four-year public colleges and universities in a given state. This model follows the lead of many previous economic analyses of higher education markets—both theoretical and empirical (see e.g., Baum, 1996; Clotfelter, 1991; Heller, 1999; Paulsen and Pogue, 1988; Rothschild and White, 1995)—by assuming students face a perfectly elastic or horizontal supply curve. It is assumed that demand intersects supply at a point that is less than institutional capacity (Baum, 1996; Clotfelter, 1991; Paulsen and Pogue, 1988), and "public institutions will accommodate any and all students who wish to enroll (and meet the minimum admissions requirements)" (Heller, 1999, p. 72). The horizontal supply curve corresponds to the level of tuition, assumed to be more-or-less equal across a state's public four-year institutions, and the tuition is assumed to have been set at a level necessary to cover costs per student, adjusted for subsidies from public and private sources (Paulsen, Chapter 6; Winston, 1999a, 1999b).

Figure 1 shows the downward-sloping private demand for higher education (D_p). For a given number of units of higher education demanded, the height of the private demand curve indicates the value individuals place on the consumption of that unit—that is, the marginal benefit of that unit—which, for private demand, is the same as the price (tuition) students are willing to pay per unit of higher education. The supply curve of higher education is indicated by S_1, which appears as a horizontal line, for the reasons given above. The equilibrium number of units of higher education would be H_1, corresponding to the intersection of private demand, D_p, and market supply, S_1, at point A_1 above. In equilibrium, for the students whose preferences for higher education are represented along the private demand curve, the tuition they are willing to pay for the last unit of higher education—that is, the marginal benefit of the last unit—is equal to $5. Of course, individual student investors disregard public benefits or externalities in their investment decision-making.

However, the effect of the presence of external benefits from higher education is

---

[11]The optimal allocation of resources to the market for higher education is said to be "theoretically" identifiable. The reason it is only theoretically, and not practically, identifiable is because members of society in a given state do not reveal the actual dollar values they place on marginal units of the public benefits or externalities that they enjoy due to the college attendance of others (see for example, Browning and Browning, 1983, 1994). However, it is only the exact value of the marginal benefit of a unit of the externality that we do not know—that is, short of surveying the state's population (which would still yield questionable estimates). Even if the exact values must be estimated, if positive externalities (public benefits) are created by students' college attendance, then there will be an underallocation of resources to the market for higher education, just as the diagrammatic exposition in this section illustrates. Neither the general conclusion about underinvestment nor the nature and direction of the effects of appropriate public policies are dependent on knowing the exact values of the public benefits to society. In any event, in the case of market failure, such as with external benefits, it is ultimately the political process that must work to promote efficient allocation of resources between higher education and other uses.

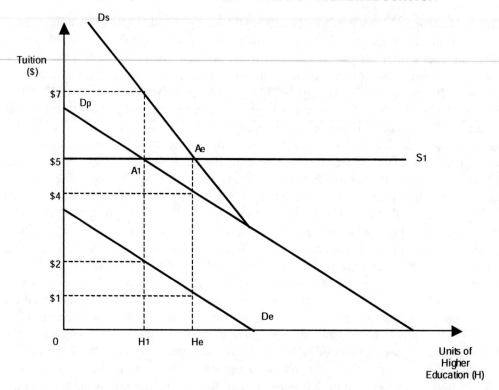

Figure 1. Identifying Optimal Allocation of Resources to Higher Education in the Case of Externalities

clearly illustrated in Figure 1. The demand for the external or public benefits generated from higher education is shown as D_e. The height of this curve represents the values or marginal benefits of various units of higher education to people other than current students. The demand for external benefits is determined by vertical summation of all beneficiaries in the state, other than the immediate consumers of higher education—the students.[12] Finally, society's demand for higher education, D_s, is determined by vertical summation of private demand, D_p, and public demand for external benefits, D_e.[13] The optimum level of resource allocation to the market for higher education—given the presence of external benefits due to student consumption of higher education—is deter-

---

[12]The summation of demand curves must be vertical in this instance, because of the non-rival nature of public consumption of external benefits. Non-rival consumption—as explained in a previous section—means that the consumption of the external benefits by one person does not diminish the quantity that can be consumed by other persons (e.g., see Apgar and Brown, 1987; Boadway, 1979).

[13]This vertical summation can be checked graphically in Figure 1. For H_1 units, the marginal benefit for students is read off the private demand curve, D_p, to equal a tuition of $5; while the marginal benefit for consumers other than the students—the general population of the state—is read off the curve of the public demand for external benefits, D_e, to equal a tuition of $2. Together, for H_1 units, the marginal benefit of $5 from private demand and the marginal benefit of $2 from public demand must sum to the marginal benefit or tuition corresponding to H_1 units on society's demand, D_s, which equals, as it should, $7.

mined where the supply of higher education, S_1, intersects society's demand, D_s. This occurs at point A_e, and corresponds to H_e units of higher education supplied. As Hoenack (1982) explains, "benefits others might receive from a student's education thus tend to reduce students' demands for higher education below socially desirable levels" (p. 409). In this way, the model in Figure 1 demonstrates the underallocation of resources and underinvestment in higher education ($H_e - H_1$) that results when external benefits accompany the consumption of higher education—in this case in a statewide market. Geske and Cohn (1998) recently summarized the efficiency implications of external benefits in the market for higher education in the following way:

> These are benefits that are created by higher education, but which are not captured by the student or his or her family. An educated individual, for example, may be more civic-minded, and his or her increased productivity could result in the greater productivity of coworkers, employees, and employers....A likely result is that the private demand for higher education will be less than the social demand. With the process left to the private market, underenrollment would result....The foregoing provides a rationale for government intervention, in the form of subsidies to individuals, institutions, or both, operation or control of IHEs, or both (p. 20).

Public Policy to Promote the Optimum Allocation of Resources to Higher Education in the Presence of External Benefits: Subsidies for Institutions and Students.

There are two primary types of subsidies that can promote a more efficient allocation and use of resources in higher education: subsidies to institutions and subsidies to students. Figure 2 illustrates the same situation portrayed above in Figure 1; that is, the market for higher education at public four-year colleges and universities in a given state. Private demand and supply intersect at point A_1, which corresponds to H_1 units of higher education. This is below the optimal allocation of resources to higher education by an amount equal to $H_e - H_1$; therefore, this amount illustrates the underinvestment in higher education. One type of public policy that can provide effective incentives for participants in the market to expand both the provision of, and demand for, units of higher education is the long-standing practice of subsidizing institutions of higher education with state appropriations. An appropriate increase in state appropriations covers an increasing portion of costs per student, making it possible for the public institutions to charge a lower tuition and still cover the remainder of their costs per student. All else equal, the supply curve would shift downward from S_1 to S_2, the new supply curve would intersect private demand, D_p, at point A_e, which corresponds to the optimum level of allocation of resources to, and investment in, higher education, H_e. The amount of the appropriate subsidy in this case is equal to the $1 downward shift in the supply curve. Clearly, this is a supply-side subsidy, but the subsidy stimulates an increase in the investment in higher education by students along their private demand curve from H_1 to H_e units. Note that it is only the students themselves who respond to the lower tuition price by investing more; however, the additional private investment leads to the optimum level desired by society. (See Toutkoushian, Chapter 1, in this volume for a report of recent trends in state appropriations and tuition

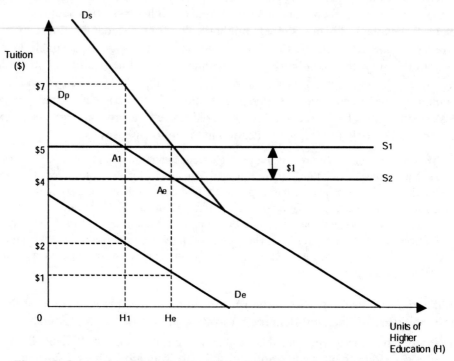

**Figure 2. Promoting Optimal Allocation of Resources to Higher Education
Using Subsidies to Instituituons**

costs, and see Paulsen, Chapter 6, for an examination of how changes in the proportion of an institution's expenses covered by appropriations affect tuition and enrollment).

This same outcome can be achieved through direct subsidies to the students who are investing. Figure 3 illustrates this situation. Once again, the private equilibrium—in the absence of public policy or subsidy—will occur where private demand, D_p, intersects supply S_1 at point A_1, corresponding to H_1 units of higher education demanded and supplied. This represents an underinvestment equal to $H_1 - H_e$ units. As illustrated in Figure 3, a subsidy to students of \$1 would increase the tuition students are willing to pay by that same amount. As a result, the private demand by investing students, D_p, would shift upward to D'_p. This new private demand now intersects the supply curve, S_1, at point A_e, which corresponds to the optimum number of units of higher education demanded and supplied—H_e, which eliminates the previous underinvestment in higher education. Clearly, this is a demand-side policy intervention. Examples of policies that could operate in this way would be expanded funding for, or front-loading of, Pell grant awards; or because Figures 1-3 portray a statewide market model, increases in state grant awards (Mumper, Chapter 8), based on need or merit, as appropriate in terms of efficiency and equity considerations (see e.g., Kane, 1999a, 1999b, 1999c; McPherson and Schapiro, 1991, 1998a, 1998b; Mumper, 1996).

Increases in funding of need-tested subsidies, such as Pell or state grant programs, are targeted at low-income students. However, in the absence of such subsidies, more

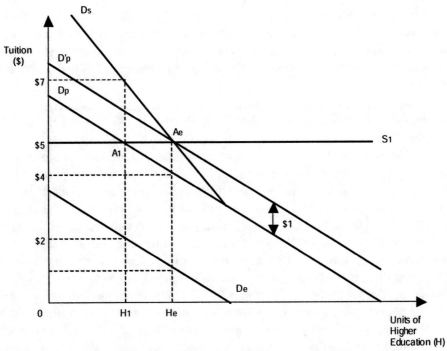

**Figure 3. Promoting Optimal Allocation of Resources to Higher Education
Using Subsidies to Students**

low-income students are likely to be excluded from higher education. The exclusion of low-income students can be problematic on both efficiency and equity grounds. This would be economically inefficient because a substantial portion of our nation's human resources would not be developed to the greatest extent possible (Geske and Cohn, 1998). In terms of equity, the lack of equal opportunities to invest in higher education will tend to promote a more unequal distribution of income (G. Becker, 1993; Kaufman, 1986, 1994; Mincer 1993b).

Recent proposals regarding the expansion, restructuring,[14] and retargeting of

---

[14]Among recent proposals for the restructuring of awards from the Pell grant program, front-loading—that is, applying all or most of the Pell grant amounts for which a student is eligible to the first two years of college—has been criticized; in particular, because of the anticipation of negative effects on students' enrollment decisions at the time of subsequent persistence decisions after the front-loaded funds have exhausted a students' eligibility for Pell grant aid. Although these anticipated consequences are based on extant theory rather than empirical evidence, this is clearly a plausible and worrisome scenario. At this time, it is difficult to foretell whether such potential negative effects on persistence-related enrollment decisions would be less than, equal to, or greater than the expected first-time-enrollment-enhancing effects anticipated by the proponents of front-loading. Because of these potentially conflicting outcomes, it is difficult to assess the effectiveness of front-loading in terms of either equity or efficiency criteria. Nevertheless, those who wish to seriously consider front-loading as a means for enhancing equity and efficiency will certainly need to address the probability of its negative consequences related to student persistence decisions.

awards from the Pell grant program (Kane, 1999a, 1999b, 1999c; McPherson and Schapiro, 1991, 1998a, 1998b) would appear to be among the appropriate kinds of subsidies to low-income students to effectively address and correct for market failures—and promote a Pareto-optimal reallocation of resources to higher education—due to the public good or external benefits that arise from society's preferences for a more equitable distribution of income.[15]

Who Should Pay for Higher Education? Applying Efficiency- and Equity-related Principles

Who should pay for higher education? Of course, there are as many possible answers to this question as there are people interested in the question.[16] However, public sector economics provides efficiency- and equity-based principles to guide deliberation and decision-making among policy-makers in the face of this persistent challenge. A useful efficiency-based principle is the benefits-received approach (Browning and Browning, 1983, 1994). This principle is useful in higher education, where there are both private (internal) and public (external) benefits from investment. Private benefits accrue only to the individual student investor, while public benefits are external to the confines of a private market transaction and are diffused across the general population. For a state deciding how to assign payment for higher education, the typical tradeoff is between user charges (tuition) for students and taxes or philanthropic gifts from the general population (society). The relative share of the cost should be consistent with the relative share of benefits received by students and society. In brief, the benefits-received principle states that individuals should be charged or taxed in accordance with the marginal benefits they receive from investment in the activity (Browning and Browning, 1983, 1994; Musgrave and Musgrave, 1973, 1984).

For students, efforts should be made to set tuition equal to the marginal value that students assign to the private benefits they internalize. For society, the taxes collected, and private giving requested, from the general population should be in proportion to the marginal value society assigns to the external benefits they enjoy. In general, the attainment of economic efficiency requires that prices be established and resources allocated according to the rule that the marginal "opportunity" cost of

---

[15]An interesting perspective on the equity issue was recently reported by NCES. Among college-qualified students from the class of 1992, the participation rates for low- middle- and high-income groups were 52, 62, and 83 percent, respectively—a familiar pattern consistent with the long-standing inverse relation between college attendance and income. However, "among those who are college-qualified and take the steps necessary for admission [took a college admissions test and applied for admission to a 4-year institution], low-income students are just as likely as middle-income students to enroll in a 4-year institution" (NCES, 2000, top of p. 48) The equity issues raised in this section of the chapter are very central to the study of higher education finance and critical to the formulation and implementation of effective public policies. For a current, thorough, and even-handed examination of available evidence on the extent to which student aid programs are increasing the higher education participation of students from low-income backgrounds, see Hearn (Chapter 11) in this volume.

[16]For two rather stark and conflicting views, see Bowen (1977) and Friedman (1962).

every investment or expenditure on higher education equal its marginal benefit to society.[17] If the marginal opportunity cost of additional resources allocated to higher education is such that if the resources were allocated to another purpose, the total benefits to society would increase, then economic efficiency has not been achieved (Hoenack, 1982).

A useful equity-based principle is the ability-to-pay approach (Browning and Browning, 1983, 1994; Musgrave and Musgrave, 1973, 1984). This principle is the fundamental criterion of justice in the distribution of burdens in the economy. One of the simpler, though not necessarily the most accurate, way to assess people's ability to pay is in terms of their income.[18] The ability-to-pay principle guides policy-makers in the distribution of taxes, costs and other burdens in a fair way. The principles of horizontal and vertical equity help clarify the meaning of the ability-to-pay principle. The principle of horizontal equity states that persons with similar abilities to pay should be asked to bear similar burdens, while the principle of vertical equity states that those with dissimilar abilities to pay should bear appropriately different shares of the total burdens to be distributed (Browning and Browning, 1994).

The application of both principles is, of course, much easier said than done; nevertheless, their implications are clear enough. Given the investment costs of a unit of higher education, the benefits-received principle recommends that students and society should pay—in tuition, taxes or donations—portions of the investment cost that correspond as closely as possible to their respective shares of the total benefits from the investment. However, a critical factor in this assignment of burdens is the judgment about the shares of private benefits received by students compared with public benefits received by society. This matter has long been a bone of contention among analysts (e.g., see Stampen, 1980), and of course, in the case of benefits that are not distributed directly through a private market mechanism (e.g., external benefits of higher education), a precise estimate of the relative shares still appears to remain well beyond the methodological grasp of social science (Pechman, 1970).

One useful way to study the matter is to examine estimates of the shares of the educational and general expenditures of institutions that are covered from tuition revenue—the student's share—or other sources of revenue that serve as subsidies to the institution—that is, society's share. Several researchers have attempted to estimate the relative shares of educational costs paid by students with tuition or by society through their contributions to non-tuition sources of revenue (Halstead, 1974; Toutkoushian, Chapter 1; Winston, 1999a).

---

[17]The economist's term, "opportunity cost," is sometimes casually defined as whatever you gave up to get what you got. It refers to "the value of all things which must be given up in order to obtain something else of value" (Paulsen and Peseau, 1989, pp. 10-11). In this instance, the term is being used to refer to the value to society of the forgone opportunities to have allocated and used these "higher education" resources elsewhere—that is, in the service of another activity of value to society, such as reduction of crime or improvement of the environment.

[18]When alternative measures—such as income and wealth—are considered, it gets more complicated, but also tends to be more accurate, depending upon the purpose of the assessment.

Table 1 compares the shares of educational costs paid by students and society based on Halstead's, Winston's and Toutkoushian's calculations.[19] Using data on student and institutional expenditures on higher education at four-year colleges and universities for 1970-71, Halstead (1974) calculated the net tuition (tuition and fees less individually targeted grants) paid by students and the per-student expenditures by institutions on the education of their students. The figures in Table 1 are based on net tuition (what students paid) and revenues from all other sources (what society paid) as a percentage of per-student institutional education expenditures. Based on Halstead's work, for public institutions, students' net tuition and fees was only 13 percent of institutional educational expenditures, while society—through government, endowment income, private gifts, and grants to students—provided subsidies that accounted for the remaining 87 percent. For private institutions, which had higher educational expenditures, but much higher tuition, the parallel figures were 52 and 48 percent, respectively for students' and society's shares.

Table 1. Estimates of the Shares of Educational Costs Paid by Students and Society, 1970-71, 1974-75 and 1994-95

	Public 1970-71	Public 1974-75	Public 1994-95	Public 1994-95	Private 1970-71	Private 1974-75	Private 1994-95	Private 1994-95
Student Share %	13.0	13.0	19.3	12.4	52.0	44.2	48.5	45.9
Society Share %	87.0	87.0	80.7	87.6	48.0	55.8	51.5	54.1
	Halstead 4-yr only	Toutkoushian 4-yr and 2-yr		Winston 4yr/2yr	Halstead 4-yr only	Toutkoushian 4-yr and 2-yr		Winston 4yr/2yr

Using IPEDS data for 1994-95 on 2,739 two-year and four-year institutions, Winston (1999a; Winston and Yen, 1995) calculated net tuition as a percentage of a measure of educational spending similar, but not identical to, that used by Halstead. He reported that net tuition and fees, as a percentage of per-student educational spending was 12.4 percent for public institutions and 45.9 percent for private institutions. The shares paid by society—attributable to what he called the "student subsidy" from government and philanthropic sources—were 87.6 and 54.1 percent, respectively for public and private institutions.[20]

---

[19]These researchers used different samples of institutions, data for different years, and similar—though not identical—definitions of the institution's cost of educating a student. Given these differences, their estimates of the shares of educational costs paid by students and society show an impressive degree of similarity. The interested reader should consult the following individual references for more details about similarities and differences in their data and methodologies (Halstead, 1974; Toutkoushian, Chapter 1; Winston, 1999a; Winston and Yen, 1995).

[20]I used data from Table 2.1 on p. 35 of Winston (1999a) to calculate these latter percentages. For each sector, public and private in turn, the value of "subsidy" in column (3) was divided by the value of "educational spending" in column (4), to obtain the percentages of educational spending attributable to societal sources—both government and philanthropic.

Using IPEDS data for 1974-75 and 1994-95 on 3,324 two-year and four-year institutions, Toutkoushian (Chapter 1) calculated net tuition as a percentage of a measure of
educational spending similar, but not identical to, those used by Winston and Halstead.
He found that in 1974-75, net tuition and fees, as a percentage of per-student educational spending at public and private institutions were 13 and 44.2 percent, respectively;
and the corresponding percentages for society were 87 and 55.8 percent. For 1994-95,
the student shares for public and private institutions were 19.3 and 48.5 percent, respectively; and the corresponding shares paid by society were 80.7 and 51.5 percent of educational spending.

Finally, the shares of educational costs paid by students and society have changed
over the past two decades, as illustrated in Table 1. Because Toutkoushian (Chapter 1)
uses the most comprehensive set of institutions and a consistent method for making estimates for both 1974-75 and 1994-95, his results would appear to provide the best indication of changes or trends in these shares over time. Between 1974-75 and 1994-95, the
percentage of educational costs paid by students rose from 13 to 19.3 percent, respectively, at public institutions, and from 44.2 to 48.5 percent, respectively, at private institutions. The corresponding percentages of educational costs paid by society decreased
from 87 to 80.7 percent at public institutions and from 55.8 to 51.5 percent at private
institutions.

For some, the estimated shares of educational costs actually paid by students, especially in the public sector, may appear remarkable for how very small they are (13.0,
12.4, and 19.3 percent), in comparison with the shares borne by society (87.0, 87.6 and
80.7 percent). However, these calculations may distort the shares of costs paid in one
very important respect. The largest part of the costs of a college education is indirect and
comprises the student's forgone earnings, rather than direct and comprising out-of-
pocket expenses such as tuition and fees. This is an important issue, and can provide a
different perspective when it comes to interpreting the shares as estimated and reported
in Table 1.

Economists have estimated that for a full-time student who does not work, forgone earnings account for two-thirds to three-fourths of the overall costs of college
attendance (G. Becker, 1993; Halstead, 1974). Nevertheless, policy-makers at all
levels appear to have held persistently to the long-standing consensus that the student should bear the full amount of these "indirect (forgone earnings) costs" of college. In this instance, the student is the one who elects to give up the "opportunity"
to earn income in order to apply his or her full attention to college study. However,
Halstead (1974) draws our attention to the important equity issues implicit (perhaps
even hidden) in this rarely questioned policy, by explaining that "Poor youths who
are needed at home, either to work to support the family, or to care for younger children, elderly parents, etc., should be entitled to receive a subsidy to compensate
them for earnings forgone while attending college" (p. 553). Whether or not students from low-income families need or deserve such a subsidy is a matter for
debate among policy analysts, but recent research has supported Halstead's
expressed concerns about the potentially strong incentives that forgone income
might pose among low-income students when it comes to a college attendance deci-

sion (Mbadugha, 2000; Paulsen and St. John, in press).[21] In any event, the key idea here is that because of the dominant size and role of forgone earnings in the cost of college, among students engaged in traditional college-going behavior, most, including those in the public sector, still bear the majority of the total costs of their college education.

For many years, higher education scholars, policy analysts, and decision-makers have asked: Who benefits? Who pays? and Who should pay? for higher education in America. They have also suggested considering the implications of alternative policies for efficiency in the allocation of our nations resources between higher education and alternative uses, and equity in the distribution of the benefits and costs associated with higher education. Nevertheless, two relatively distinct and contrasting sets of conclusions and accompanying rationales have emerged in the literature. More particularly, two different, distinguishable sets of conclusions have been reached regarding the relative shares of the benefits of higher education accruing to students and society, and two quite different approaches have been advanced regarding how to enhance equity of access to higher education according to ability to pay (Bowen, 1971; Carnegie Commission, 1973; Friedman, 1962; Gladieux and Wolanin, 1976; Halstead, 1974; Hansen, 1983; Hansen and Weisbrod, 1969; Johnstone, 1999; McPherson and Schapiro, 1991; Orwig, 1971; Pechman, 1970; Nelson, 1978; Stampen, 1980; Windham, 1976). Of course, these two approaches are easily recognizable and manifest themselves in some of the noteworthy differences in the two sectors—public and private—that constitute our long-standing dual system of higher education.

Discussion has largely centered on the low-tuition approach of the public sector versus the high-tuition approach of the private sector (e.g., see Halstead, 1974; McPherson, 1978; Stampen, 1980). Supporters of the high-tuition approach believe that students reap a large share of the benefits of investment in higher education, and therefore, should be asked to pay a substantial share of educational costs in the form of tuition (Stampen, 1980).[22] The estimates of shares paid reported in Table 1 clearly indicate that students at private colleges do pay a much larger share (nearly 50 percent) of their educational costs through higher tuition, in comparison with students in the public sector. The preferences of high-tuition proponents are quite consistent with their beliefs about the large relative share of benefits received by students versus society from investment in higher education (Halstead, 1974). Given their beliefs, the setting of higher tuition is also consistent with appli-

---

[21]For example, recent research on the relations among college costs, social class and student college choice and persistence behavior, found that women in the lowest income group were less likely than men to persist (Paulsen and St. John, in press). During an era when women are attending and persisting at such impressive rates, this finding led the authors to suggest that "the opportunities to increase income due to only 'some' postsecondary education, coupled with the demands of supporting a family—due to the prevalence of single-female-parent households among low-income families—might function, in combination, to motivate low-income women to be less likely than men to maintain continuous enrollment" (p. 24). Furthermore, in a recent study of persistence among community college students, those whose mothers had less than a high school education were less likely than others to persist, perhaps because they "had many other life challenges and responsibilities, so that it was not possible for them to maintain college attendance as a high priority" (Mbadugha, 2000, p. 248). These researchers are clearly thinking about opportunity costs (forgone income) as an important factor in students' decisions about whether or not to attend college—and both findings are clearly based on the experiences of students from disadvantaged socioeconomic backgrounds.

cation of the benefits-received principle of efficiency in pricing for economic efficiency.

Proponents of high tuition have also been concerned about equity with respect to access to higher education and subsequently to the higher earnings and occupational status that result. Their approach to promoting equity has been based primarily on the practice of targeting institutional grants to low-income students (McPherson, 1978)—a clear application of the ability-to-pay principle, and this practice has expanded greatly in the past decade (Breneman, Doti and Lapovsky, Chapter 12; Zumeta, Chapter 9).[23] Subsidies to students from society come largely in the form of philanthropic or "donative" income for private colleges (Winston, 1999a, 1999b).

Supporters of the low-tuition approach believe that there are substantial external benefits to society due to individual students' decisions to invest in higher education, and therefore, society should be asked to pay a substantial share of educational costs in the form of taxes, which will be used to provide institutional subsidies that permit public institutions to set tuition low and still cover the remainder of their educational costs (Halstead, 1974; Stampen, 1980). The estimates of shares paid made by Halstead (1974), Toutkoushian (Chapter 1) and Winston (1999a) clearly indicate that society does bear the burden of a much larger share (over 80 percent) of educational costs, primarily through taxes, in comparison with students in the private sector. The determination of proponents of the low-tuition approach to keep tuitions low is quite consistent with their beliefs about the large relative share of external benefits that are diffused across the general population (society) compared with the internalized benefits of student investors (Halstead, 1974). Given their beliefs, keeping tuition low for all students is consistent with application of the benefits-received principle of efficiency in pricing for economic efficiency.

Proponents of low tuition have addressed issues of equity with respect to access to higher education. They believe that equity is enhanced for several reasons. First, because students are much more responsive to the widely publicized increases in tuition than they are to financial aid—which they may not even know is available—low tuition for all promotes equal access and increases in enrollment across all income groups (Mumper, 1996). And they also expect this approach will enhance equity because revenues for tuition subsidies are raised through our progressive tax system (Halstead, 1974).[24] In addition, they recommend that the low tuition be supplemented by need-

---

[22]In 1973, the Carnegie Commission on Higher Education published its widely read report, *Higher Education: Who Pays? Who Benefits? Who Should Pay?*, in which it recommended "the gradual increase of tuition charges in public institutions over the next decade or so toward one-third of the cost of education, with a corresponding increase in student aid based upon need" (p. 117). Increasing tuition from 13 to 33 percent of the total costs of a student's education would have increased the student's share of the cost or burden by 254 percent! Of course, tuition has increased dramatically over the past 25 years or more, but so has institutional spending to educate a student (e.g., see Paulsen, Chapter 6; Toutkoushian, Chapter 1).

[23]See McPherson and Schapiro (1998a) for an up-to-date examination of the issues and implications of the fact that a growing share of institutional aid is based on merit rather than need.

[24]It is important to remember here that many of our states rely heavily on regressive features of their state's tax structure to raise revenues for many of state and local government expenditures. In other words, even if a substantial share of revenues used for tuition subsidies are raised through progressive aspects of a state's tax structure, this certainly does not make a state's overall tax-expenditure system "progressive" in nature.

based aid to address other unmet needs of low-income students (Stampen, 1980). Each of these arguments is quite consistent with the ability-to-pay principle.

Just as there are strong arguments *for* both positions, there are compelling arguments *against* each approach as well—and the arguments are based on the same efficiency- and equity-based principles. Proponents of high tuition argue that low-tuition is economically inefficient because a good portion of the students subsidized wouldn't have needed the subsidy to encourage them to attend, and therefore, the resources used to subsidize the well-to-do could have been used for an alternative activity that would yield a higher benefit to society (Hearn and Longanecker, 1985). By setting the same low tuition for all students, they would be committing Hoenack's (1982) "second error" in their efforts to assign selective subsidies in an efficient manner.

> The second error is subsidizing students who would attend without the subsidy when there is no specific intent to transfer income to them. This error results in forgone opportunities for increasing other enrollments or for using the resources to achieve other goals (p. 411).

Proponents of high tuition also argue that the low-tuition approach is also inequitable "because the benefits of the public subsidy [flow] disproportionately to students from middle- and upper-income families" (Stampen, 1980, p. 19).

On the other hand, proponents of low tuition argue that those who propose to simultaneously set tuition high and target grants to low-income students are counting on the validity of a very important assumption that low-income students will be equally responsive—dollar for dollar—to equal, but opposite, changes in tuition and institutional grants (Hearn and Longanecker, 1985). However, based on a review of the recent research, Heller (1997) found no evidence that this is the case.

> If one assumes that financial aid is nothing more than a discount to the posted tuition price, then students should react similarly to the same-sized increase in financial aid or cut in tuition, because both would result in the same net cost to the student. Unfortunately for policy-makers, this does not appear to be the case. (p. 631).

Therefore, even if increases in tuition are accompanied by equal increases in financial aid, low-income students may respond more to the change in tuition than to the change in aid—if not because of different price-responsiveness, then perhaps because of a lack of information about the availability of additional financial aid to them (Kane, 1999c; Mumper, 1996). If they respond more to tuition than aid changes, then enrollment will decrease among low-income students; that is, the targeting of the subsidy will not have been effective. The result would be an underinvestment in higher education among low-income students. This would be a clear instance of commission of Hoenack's (1982) "first error" in their efforts to assign selective subsidies in an efficient manner.

> The first error is not directing subsidies specifically to those categories of enrollments whose demand is lowest in relation to the socially desirable level. While enrollments from other groups may be increased when subsidies are not directed to these low-demand groups, the subsidy's purpose will not be achieved (p. 411).

Furthermore, if this underinvestment occurs among low-income students, then there is also a serious inequity issue as well, because students from the most disadvantaged backgrounds will miss out on their best opportunity for higher incomes, occupational status and social mobility that follow investments in higher education (Levin, 1979).

STUDENT RESPONSIVENESS TO PRICES AND SUBSIDIES: THE EFFECTS OF PUBLIC POLICY INTERVENTIONS IN THE MARKET FOR HIGHER EDUCATION

The economic theory of human capital asserts that students weigh their perceptions of costs and benefits associated with college attendance in order to make the wisest decision about enrollment (G. Becker, 1993; Johnes, 1993; Mincer, 1993a; Paulsen, Chapter 3; Paulsen and Peseau, 1989; Perlman, 1973; Schultz, 1961, 1963). In order to make their final decision, they compare expected returns on investments in higher education with returns available from alternative investments (McMahon, 1991c). Recent research has demonstrated that, in their college-going investment decisions, students are considerably more "responsive" or sensitive to changes in the costs of higher education than they are to changes in the benefits or returns (Kane, 1999c; Leslie and Brinkman, 1988).[25] [26] This has been good news for policy-makers who have adopted changes in tuition and financial aid as the policy instruments of choice—that is, sources of subsidies—in efforts to promote efficiency in the allocation of society's resources and equity in access, choice and persistence in higher education for students (Paulsen, 1998).

Between 1980 and the mid-to-late 1990s, an extraordinary confluence of events and circumstances (reduced affordability), and correlates or consequences (a lack of socially desired changes in student enrollment rates) has occurred—heightening the concerns,

---

[25]Estimates of student responsiveness to college costs originally came from the student demand studies—that is, studies of the determinants of students' demand for enrollment places at colleges and universities. Examples of such studies include Freeman (1976), Hoenack and Weiler (1979), Manski and Wise, (1983), Paulsen and Pogue, (1988); and thorough reviews of that extensive literature include those by W. Becker (1990), McPherson (1978), Paulsen (1990), and Weiler (1984).

[26]The expression "student price response" is not a term from the jargon of economics; rather it is a term that has evolved in the literature on the economics and finance of higher education (Heller, 1997; Jackson and Weathersby, 1975; Leslie and Brinkman, 1988; McPherson, 1978). Presumably, it is a product of the interactions between policy-oriented economists and educationists. In any event, the specific measure called the "student price response coefficient" or SPRC refers to the percentage change in enrollment per $100 change in a price or a subsidy. Sometimes they are expressed in terms of percentage changes in enrollment per $1000 change in tuition—which yields an SPRC 10 times as large. The term from economics that has a similar—but not identical—meaning is "elasticity". The price elasticity of demand can be formally defined as "the proportionate rate of change of [enrollment] divided by the proportionate rate of change of [tuition]" (Henderson and Quandt, 1971, p. 27), or more simply, as the percentage change in enrollment divided by the percentage change in price (Paulsen and Peseau, 1989). For those who prefer elasticities over SPRC measurements of price effects, in most instances, SPRCs can be readily converted into elasticities. If a given study reports an SPRC for tuition of -1.5, they are stating that a $100 increment in tuition is associated with a 1.5 percent decrease in enrollment. The $100 increment needs to be translated into a percentage change in tuition. Researchers typically use either the mean or median tuition for a given sample for this purpose. Dividing $100 by the mean or median sample tuition converts the $100 into a percentage change in the average tuition for that sample (see Rouse, 1994, for a good explanation of when and how to make additional adjustments for changes in the purchasing power of average tuition at different points in time to promote meaningful comparisons between results of different studies).

and expanding the diversity of views, about matters of economic efficiency and equity in the market for higher education among educational economists and leaders and policy-makers in the higher education community. The following items have been documented for the period from 1980 to the mid-to-late 1990s:

- The percentage of total revenue for public institutions attributable to state appropriations—a prominent subsidy to public institutions—decreased substantially from 44 percent in 1980 to only 32.5 percent in 1995-96. Simultaneously, tuition as a percentage of revenue increased substantially from 12.9 percent in 1980 to 18.8 percent in 1995-96 (NCES, 1999, Table 332, p. 359).
- Increases in tuition at four-year colleges and universities have exceeded the rate of inflation every year (College Board, 1999a, 1999b).
- Increases in the average amounts of Pell grant awards, subsidized Stafford loans, and state grants, as well as growth in median family income, have all failed by a wide margin to keep pace with the rate of increase in tuition (College Board, 1999a, 1999b; Gillespie and Carlson, 1983; Mumper, 1996).
- Between 1980 and 1998, loans as a share of total student aid have grown from 41 to 58 percent, while grants have fallen from 56 to 40 percent (College Board, 1999a, 1999b; Gillespie and Carlson, 1983).
- The percentage of high school completers who attended college the year after graduation were higher for whites than for blacks or Hispanics in both 1980 and in 1997; however, the gaps in these participation rates widened during the interval (NCES, 2000, Table 32-1, p. 149).
- The percentage of high school completers aged 25-29 who completed some college and the percentage of those with a college degree were higher for whites than for blacks or Hispanics in both 1980 and in 1997; however, the gaps in these participation rates also widened during the interval (NCES, 2000, Table 38-2, p. 155; Table 38-3, p. 156).
- The percentage of high school completers who attended college the year after graduation were higher for high- and middle-income than for low-income students in both 1980 and 1997; and the gaps in these participation rates remained virtually unchanged during the interval (NCES, 2000, Table 32-1, p. 149).
- The distribution of enrollment rates among students from different income groups changed substantially across institutional type between 1980 and 1994 (McPherson and Schapiro, 1998a). Most striking of all was the increasing concentration of low-income students—who are already disproportionately represented at our most affordable (community) colleges—at public two-year colleges. This was also accompanied by a rather substantial middle- and upper-income "flight" from community colleges (McPherson and Schapiro, 1998a, p. 46).

In light of the above profile of changes in the affordability of college since 1980 (Baum, Chapter 2), all of the changes (itemized above) in student enrollment rates and patterns between 1980 and the mid-to-late 1990s have meaningful interpretations. First of all, the rapid increase in tuition, in excess of the general rate of inflation, was apparently accelerated by the decreasing percentage of institutional revenues available to public colleges from state appropriations over the interval (Paulsen, 1991, Chapter 6). However, the construction of meaningful interpretations for each of the reported changes or patterns in student enrollment rates (above) depends on the ways in which student responsiveness to prices (tuition) and subsidies (aid) vary according to student characteristics, institutional characteristics and type of aid. In the latest of a series of comprehensive reviews of the literature on student responsiveness to prices and subsidies in their enrollment behavior (e.g., Jackson and Weathersby, 1975; Leslie and Brinkman, 1988; McPherson, 1978), Heller (1997) has reported the following findings:

- Students continue to be quite sensitive to increases in tuition in their enrollment behavior.
- Students are responsive to financial aid in their enrollment, but they are more responsive to increases in grants than loans.
- Lower-income students are more responsive than middle- or upper-income students to changes in both tuition and aid.
- Minority students—especially black students—are more responsive than white students to changes in tuition and aid.
- Students at community colleges are more responsive to changes in tuition and aid than those attending four-year institutions.

Other researchers have found that students' price responsiveness differs according to still other student characteristics (Hippensteel, St. John, and Starkey, 1996; Mbadugha, 2000; Paulsen and St. John, 1997, in press; St. John, 2000; St. John, Paulsen and Starkey, 1996; St. John and Starkey, 1994, 1995; Starkey, 1994):

- Students are responsive to changes in both tuition and aid in their persistence as well as their initial enrollment decisions.
- Lower-income students are more responsive than middle- or upper-income students to tuition and aid in their persistence decisions.
- Students attending community colleges are more responsive to tuition and aid than those attending other types of institutions.
- Students attending part-time are much more sensitive to changes in prices and subsidies than full-time students.
- Students of non-traditional age are more responsive to tuition and aid than those of traditional age.
- Students may respond negatively to increases in aid when aid is inadequate to cover their costs of attendance as reflected in their unmet need.

Armed with these research findings about student responsiveness to prices and subsidies, interpreting students' enrollment behavior between 1980 and the late 1990s can be more meaningful. During these years, as tuition was rising rapidly and the purchasing power of aid and income were trailing by a considerable margin, the cost of college attendance was increasing—that is, the affordability of a college education was decreasing. Research has demonstrated that rising tuition, slower growth in aid, and a dramatic shift from grant to loan aid, affect individuals and groups of students differently. For low-income students—who are very sensitive to prices and subsidies, and more sensitive to increases in grant than loan aid—it is not surprising that, in spite of the increases in aid during these years, the gaps in their enrollment rates, compared with higher-income students, did not narrow. Even though this finding is not surprising, it is certainly disturbing and contrary to the espoused goals of programs to subsidize institutions and students.

The increasing gap in the enrollment rates of white and black students is quite understandable. Black students are more sensitive than whites to changes in prices and subsidies—and are also more likely to have lower incomes than white students. Therefore the widening gap in their enrollment rates is not an unexpected finding; nevertheless, it is a very troubling result, and it, too, clearly stands in stark contradiction to the espoused goals of using subsidies to institutions and subsidies to encourage greater enrollment rates among minorities and disadvantaged groups.

The increasing concentration of low-income students at community colleges is also understandable because these institutions provide postsecondary education at by far the lowest level of tuition compared with any other type of institution of higher education (College Board, 1999b). Community colleges are truly our nation's "access" institutions (Halstead, 1996). However, what is most disturbing about the growing concentration of low-income students at community colleges is that between 1980 and 1999, tuition at public two-year colleges themselves increased from an average of $391 in 1980 to $1,627 in 1999; and even after adjustment for inflation, from $750 to $1,627 (College Board, 1999a). The concern here is based on the research that tells us that community college students are more sensitive to tuition increases than students attending any other kind of college or university (Heller, 1997; Mbadugha, 2000). In all likelihood this high level of responsiveness is due to the fact that virtually all of the student characteristics that are positively related to greater price sensitivity are disproportionately represented among community college students—for example, students from low-income backgrounds, from minority groups (especially black and Hispanic), students of non-traditional age, and part-time attenders (Mbadugha, 2000).

Figure 4 portrays the demand for, and supply of, enrollment places at one of the four-year public colleges and universities in a given state. In some ways like the approach taken in Figure 1, this model follows the lead of previous economic analyses of higher education markets (see e.g., Baum, 1996; Clotfelter, 1991; Heller, 1999; Kane, 1995; Paulsen and Pogue, 1988; Rothschild and White, 1995), by assuming students face a perfectly elastic or horizontal supply curve. The horizontal supply curve corresponds to this particular public institution's level of tuition, which is assumed to have been set at a level necessary to cover costs per student, adjusted for subsidies from public and private sources. The upward shift in the supply curve in Figure 4 is due to a combination of slow increases in state appropriations (institutional subsidies), coupled with much faster increases in the institution's educational costs. The result is that the portion of the cost of educating a student that is being covered by state appropriation subsidies is getting smaller and therefore, the institution—and probably others like it in the state system—must raise their tuition charges in order to bring in enough revenue to cover all their costs (Paulsen, Chapter 6).

Figure 4a shows the demand for enrollment places at this institution by higher-

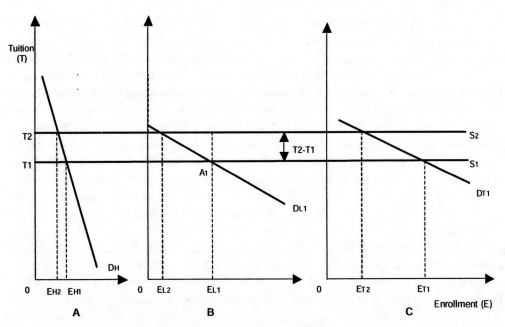

Figure 4. Differential Student Price Response:
Changes in Tuition, Institutional Subsidy, and Enrollment

income students who have a relatively low level of responsiveness to price (tuition) changes (D_H). At the initial level of tuition (T_1), the number of higher-income students who want to enroll is E_{H1}. The negative or downward slope of the demand curve indicates that as tuition rises, fewer students would wish to enroll, all else unchanged. What is especially noteworthy about Figure 4a is that when the institution's supply of enrollment places shifts upward (from S_1 to S_2)—which means that enrollment places are being offered at a higher price than before (T_2)—there is only a small decrease in the number of students who wish to enroll (from E_{H1} to E_{H2}).

Figure 4b tells a somewhat different story. It shows the demand for enrollment places at this institution by lower-income students who have a relatively high level of responsiveness to tuition changes (D_L). At the initial level of tuition (T_1), the number of low-income students who want to enroll is E_{L1}. However, what is different about Figure 4b is that when the institution's supply of enrollment places shifts upward (from S_1 to S_2)—which means that enrollment places are being offered at a higher price than before (T_2)—there is quite a large decrease in the number of students who wish to enroll (from E_{L1} to E_{L2}). Of course, this happens because these low-income students are very responsive to tuition changes in their enrollment behavior.

Figure 4c is basically a summary of what has happened in Figures 4a and 4b so far. The demand curve is the horizontal summation of the numbers of students that want to enroll at each possible tuition from the two income groups represented in Figures 4a and 4b—that is, $E_T = E_H + E_L$. The enrollment demand curve in Figure 4a is very steep because the high-income students are relatively unresponsive to tuition changes. On the other hand, the demand curve in Figure 4b is much flatter, because the low-income students are highly responsive to tuition changes.

Figure 4 illustrates that, as state appropriations wane and tuition is raised, the result is a large negative enrollment effect on the low-income students. This change generates problems on both efficiency and equity grounds. The fundamental justification for the subsidies is that due to external benefits to society that accompany student investment in higher education, there would be an underallocation of resources to higher education in the state if the private market prices were allowed to prevail. The students whose demand is likely to be the lowest in the absence of subsidies are the low-income students. Efficient subsidies must be sufficient and appropriately targeted or directed at those subgroups of students "whose demand is lowest in relation to the socially desirable level" (Hoenack, 1982, p. 411). Rates of participation in higher education have been consistently and substantially lower for low- compared with high-income students (NCES, 2000). Yes, the low-income students are clearly the selectively targeted groups for the subsidies. Furthermore, there is the clear element of inequity in this set of circumstances. The group of students that was already the most marginalized and excluded relative to other groups is this low-income group. They already had the lowest participation rates of all groups, and now this tuition increase has worsened what was already an inequitable distribution of opportunities for investment in a college education.

There are two fundamental forms (with variations) of subsidization that might potentially help reverse this process that has generated inefficiency and inequity: either sufficiently increase the subsidies to the university through state appropriations so they can reduce tuition enough to encourage a desired level of investment from the low-income students (E_{L1}), or permit tuition increases and directly subsidize the students with grants to offset each tuition increase. Both might serve as potential approaches to reversing the trend toward inefficiency and inequity.

The first option can be illustrated by a reexamination of Figure 4. Adequate increases in appropriations would require that they exceed the rate of growth in the institution's educational costs; but if this can be accomplished, then an institutional subsidy could lead to a downward shift in supply (from S_2 down to S_1), which in turn, would stimulate the desired large positive enrollment effect for low-income students (from E_{L2} up to E_{L1}), improving both economic efficiency and distributional equity.

The other approach is to directly subsidize the low-income students with grants that would exactly offset the tuition increase and increase the number that are willing *and* able to enroll to E_{L1}. This is illustrated in Figure 5, which has three parts much like Figure 4. Assuming that the upward shift in supply (from S_1 to S_2) is sustained, along with its accompanying tuition increase like in Figure 4 (from T_1 to T_2), the stimulation of the desired increase in enrollment places demanded by low-income students would call for a change in demand. By giving the low-income students tuition-offsetting grants, their incomes or purchasing power would be increased.

The tuition charge that each number of possible enrolled students would be willing and able to pay would be increased by the exact amount of the tuition-offsetting grant—this is measured by vertical amount $[A_2 - A_1]$ dollars in Figure 5b. After demand shifts from D_{L1} up to D_{L2}, it will intersect supply curve S_2 at point A_2, where the enrollment

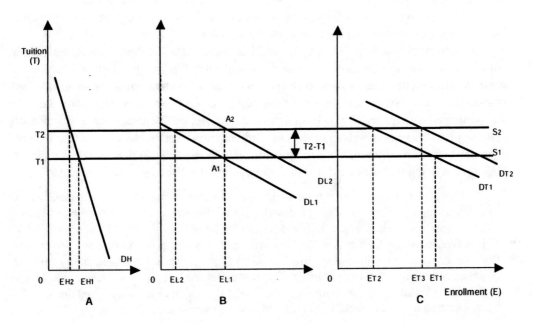

Figure 5. Differential Student Price Response:
Changes in Tuition, Student Subsidy, and Enrollment

demand of low-income students would be at amount E_{L1}. This whole process is once again summarized in Figure 5c. Of course, because the subsidies (grants) are given only to the low-income students, the increase in demand in Figure 5c will be somewhat less than it is in Figure 5b for low-income students, and its rightward shift will only bring enrollment back to E_{T3} instead of all the way back up to E_{T1}. This is because the high-income students—having received no grants—retain their enrollment demand at E_{H2}, corresponding to the higher tuition of T_2.

The two types of subsidization that Figures 4 and 5 demonstrate are, of course, precisely those that correspond to the low-tuition, low-aid and the high-tuition, high-aid approaches discussed at length in an earlier section, with an emphasis on the efficiency and equity arguments for both approaches. The models in Figures 4 and 5 are tools for analysis of the means and the effects of these two approaches toward subsidization in pursuit of greater efficiency and equity. Of course, which approach is truly better still appears to be well-classified as a perennial argument.[27] It should be noted that one of

---

[27]For example, an insightful reviewer of an earlier version of this chapter pointed out that it might be possible that the enrollment rates of high-income students are too high, or would be too high, under a low-tuition scenario, especially from the standpoint of economic efficiency as explained earlier in this chapter. In particular, it seems very likely that there would be greater externalities or social benefits from increased enrollment among low-income than high-income students. In terms of this argument, the direct subsidization of low-income students (with no additional subsidies for high-income students) that characterizes the second of the two approaches discussed above would appear to be more socially or economically efficient.

the central points of this section of the chapter has been to demonstrate that the manner and the extent to which these two approaches to subsidization work are very dependent on the differential price responsiveness of students with different characteristics such as low- versus high-income backgrounds, as illustrated above.

An important and highly relevant question, especially for determining whether or not the high-tuition, high-aid approach could truly be effective is whether low-income students are equally responsive to dollar-for-dollar offsetting changes in tuition and grants. Unfortunately, the results from the latest research on this question continue to be inconclusive (see Heller, 1997). In their excellent book on the financing of community colleges, Breneman and Nelson (1981) are bold enough to state clearly what they would consider to be the better of the two subsidization approaches—that is, LT/LA or HT/HA—given that a particular answer to the question posed above evolves in time:

> The day that students view net tuition—not posted tuition—as the relevant financial barrier to attending a [college] will be the day that tuition below the level dictated by efficiency considerations (including public benefits) can no longer be justified. In this ideal world, however, the student aid system could provide all the access necessary for low-income students, stripping low tuition of its justification on equity grounds. Moreover, equity considerations alone might favor the higher tuition/higher aid strategy; it could be possible to offer enough financial aid to very poor students—perhaps even up to full need—that the probability of attending college would be equalized across income classes (p. 109).

During the past two decades—a period of unprecedented tuition growth—the arguments in favor of the high-tuition, high-aid approach (or "market model" strategy) have been clearly rearticulated for application at public sector institutions (Hearn and Longanecker, 1985). Unfortunately, out of the many states that have raised tuition during the interval, most such increases have not been accompanied by offsetting grants to high-need, low-income students; which means that a high-tuition, low-aid scenario has too often been the "unintended" outcome—an outcome that threatens both efficiency and equity regarding resource allocation and access to higher education. Hossler, et al. (1997) observed that the "rhetoric of the market model is being used as a justification for reduced state appropriations to public institutions and increased tuition levels in the public sector, but public policymakers have ignored the other part of the market model equation—higher levels of state financial aid" (p. 182) (see Chapter 8 in this volume, "State Efforts to Keep Public Colleges Affordable in the Face of Fiscal Stress," an empirical and thoughtful look at states' experiences with various tuition and aid strategies). Griswold and Marine (1996) conducted case studies of several states' efforts to develop more coordinated tuition-aid strategies. Based on their findings, they offer political advice and point out that one "of the challenges facing supporters of such programs is garnering support for a program which seems to aid groups with less political clout at the expense of those with more power and who are more likely to vote" (p. 384). One state—Minnesota—has had some noteworthy success in keeping enrollment rates stable across all income levels. Apparently, the "Minnesota Experiment" is one to learn from (Hearn and Anderson, 1995).

Finally, the market-model or high-tuition, high-aid strategy has been expanded substantially among private sector institutions during the 1990s (Breneman, 1994; National

Association of College and University Business Officers, 1999). Their approach is quite different from the public-sector approaches described, illustrated and assessed in this chapter. This important topic will not be addressed in this chapter because Chapter 12 in this volume presents a state-of-the-art theoretical and empirical examination of the private colleges' approach to the high-tuition, high-aid strategy—one that is based on extensive tuition-discounting practices (also see Chapter 6 in this volume for an application of a model of the perfect, price-discriminating, monopolistically competitive private college engaged in tuition-discounting behavior).

CONCLUSION

This chapter has presented, explained, and illustrated the use of selected concepts and models from the economics of the public sector that are effective in analyzing and understanding the finance of higher education. In addition, this chapter has presented a representative view of the literature on the theory and research that supports the public-sector economic concepts and models examined, and has provided examples, using a diagrammatic exposition, of how selected concepts and models from public sector economics can be used to plan, implement and assess the effects of various public policies related to the efficient allocation of resources and equitable distribution of benefits and costs in pursuit of an effective set of policies for the finance of higher education.

Concepts and models presented in some detail include the nature of the allocation and distribution functions of the public sector of the economy; the concepts of economic (Pareto) efficiency and equity, which are central to an examination of the nature and impact of various public policies used by the government to perform its allocation and distribution functions; the basic rationales for government intervention in the application of public policies to influence the behavior of demanders or suppliers in the market place (e.g., externalities, quasi-public goods, social rates of return, and market imperfections)—each presented using examples from higher education; models and effective approaches for identifying the optimum level of investment in higher education in the case of external benefits; public policy interventions—subsidies to institutions and students—to promote the optimum level of investment in higher education; the role of differential responsiveness to changes in prices and subsidies in the application of public policies in the market for enrollment places in higher education; and analysis of the perennial questions of who should pay and of pricing higher education according to benefits-received and ability-to-pay principles.

Chapters 5 and 6 present and apply microeconomic concepts and theories—such as price and demand theory, cost and production theory—that are particularly effective in deepening our understanding of current issues like increasing educational costs and tuition, and slow growth in productivity in higher education.

References

Apgar, W.C., and Brown, H.J. (1987). *Microeconomics and Public Policy*. Glenview, IL: Scott, Foresman, and Company.

Arai, K. (1998). *The Economics of Education: An Analysis of College-Going Behavior*. New York: Springer-Verlag.

Ashenfelter, O., and Krueger, A. (1994). Estimating the returns to schooling using a new sample of twins. *American Economic Review* 84: 1157–1173.

Baum, S. (1995). The federal role in financing higher education: An economic perspective. Paper presented at the National Conference on the Best Ways for the Federal Government to Help Students and Families Finance Postsecondary Education. Charleston, South Carolina, October.

Baum, S. (1996). *A Primer on Economics for Financial Aid Professionals.* Washington, DC: National Association of Student Financial Aid Administrators.

Baumol, W.J., Blackman, S.A.B., and Wolff, E.N. (1989). *Productivity and American Leadership: The Long View.* Cambridge, MA: the MIT Press.

Becker, G.S. (1975). *Human Capital: A Theoretical and Empirical Analysis with Special Reference to Education* (2nd ed). New York: Columbia University Press.

Becker, G.S. (1993). *Human Capital: A Theoretical and Empirical Analysis with Special Reference to Education* (3rd ed). Chicago: The University of Chicago Press.

Becker, W. E., (1990). The demand for higher education. In S.A. Hoenack and E.L. Collins (eds.), *The Economics of American Universities.* Albany: State University of New York Press.

Behrman, J.R. (1997). Conceptual and measurement issues. In J. Behrman and N. Stacey (eds.), *The Social Benefits of Higher Education.* Ann Arbor, MI: University of Michigan Press.

Behrman, J.R., Crawford, D.L., and Stacey, N., (1997). Conclusion. In J. Behrman and N. Stacey (eds.), *The Social Benefits of Higher Education.* Ann Arbor, MI: University of Michigan Press.

Berger, M.C. (1992). Private returns to specific college majors. In W.E. Becker and D.R. Lewis (1992). *The Economic of American Higher Education.* Boston, MA: Kluwer Academic Publishers.

Betts, J.R. (1996). What do students know about wages? Evidence from a survey of undergraduates. *Journal of Human Resources* 31(1): 27-56.

Blau, F.D., and Ferber, M.A. (1991). Career plans and expectations of young women and men: The earnings gap and labor force participation. *Journal of Human Resources* 26(4): 581-607.

Boadway, R.W. (1979). *Public Sector Economics.* Cambridge, MA: Winthrop Publishers.

Bowen, H.R. (1971). Who pays the higher education bill? In M.D. Orwig (ed.), *Financing Higher Education: Alternatives for the Federal Government.* Iowa City, IA: ACT.

Bowen, H.R. (1977). *Investment in Learning: The Individual and Social Value of American Higher Education.* San Francisco: Jossey-Bass.

Bowen, H.R. (1980). *The Costs of Higher Education.* San Francisco: Jossey-Bass.

Bowles, S., and Gintis, H. (1976). *Schooling in Capitalist America: Educational Reform and the Contradictions of Economic Life.* New York: Basic Books.

Breneman, D.W. (1994). *Liberal Arts Colleges: Thriving, surviving, or endangered?* Washington, DC: The Brookings Institution.

Breneman, D.W., and Nelson, S.C. (1981). *Financing Community Colleges: An Economic Perspective.* Washington, DC: The Brookings Institution.

Browning, E.K., and Browning, J.M. (1983). *Public Finance and the Price System.* New York: Macmillan.

Browning, E.K., and Browning, J.M. (1994). *Public Finance and the Price System.* Englewood Cliffs: Prentice-Hall.

Caffrey, J., and Isaacs, H. (1971). *Estimating the Impact of a College or University on the Local Economy.* Washington, DC: American Council on Education.

Carnegie Commission on Higher Education. (1973). *Higher Education: Who Pays? Who Benefits? Who Should Pay?* New York: McGraw-Hill.

Clotfelter, C.T. (1991). Demand for undergraduate education. In C.T. Clotfelter, R.G. Ehrenberg, M. Getz, and J.J. Siegfried (eds.), *Economic Challenges in Higher Education.* Chicago: The University of Chicago Press.

College Board, (1999a). *Trends in College Pricing.* Washington, DC: The College Board.

College Board, (1999b). *Trends in Student Aid.* Washington, DC: The College Board.

Cohn, E., and Geske, T.G. (1990). *The Economics of Education* (3rd ed.). New York: Pergamon Press.

Douglass, G.K. (1977). Economic returns on investments in higher education. In H.R. Bowen, *Investment in Learning: The Individual and Social Value of American Higher Education.* San Francisco: Jossey-Bass.

Freeman, R.B. (1971). *The Market for College-Trained Manpower: A Study in the Economics of Career*

Choice. Cambridge, MA: Harvard University Press.

Freeman, R.B. (1976). *The Overeducated American*. New York: Academic Press.

Friedman, M. (1962). *Capitalism and Freedom*. Chicago: Univeristy of Chicago Press.

Geske, T.G., and Cohn, E. (1998). Why is a high school diploma no longer enough? The economic and social benefits of higher education. In R. Fossey and M. Bateman (eds.), *Condemning Students to Debt: College Loans and Public Policy*. New York: Teachers College Press.

Gillespie, D.A., and Carlson, N. (1983). *Trends in Student Aid: 1963 to 1983*. Washington, DC: The College Board.

Gladieux, L.E., and Wolanin, T.R. (1976). *Congress and the Colleges*. Lexington, MA: Lexington Books.

Griswold, C.P., and Marine, G.M. (1996). Political influences on state policy: Higher-tuition, higher-aid, and the real world. *The Review of Higher Education* 19(4): 361-389.

Halstead, D.K. (1974). *Statewide Planning in Higher Education*. Washington, DC: U.S. Government Printing Office.

Halstead, D.K. (1996). *Higher Education Report Card 1995*. Washington, DC: Research Associates.

Hansen, W.L. (1983). The impact of student financial aid on access. In J. Froomkin (ed.), *The Crisis in Higher Educaiton*. New York: Academy of Political Science.

Hansen, W.L., and Weisbrod, B.R. (1969).*Benefits, Costs, and Finance of Public Higher Education*. Chicago: Markham Publishing.

Haveman, R.H., and Wolfe, B.L. (1984). Schooling and economic well-being: The role of nonmarket effects. *Journal of Human Resources* 19(3): 377-407.

Hearn, J.C., and Anderson, M.S. (1995). The Minnesota financing experiment. In E.P. St. John (ed.), *Rethinking Tuition and Student Aid Strategies*. New Directions for Higher Education No. 89. San Francisco: Jossey-Bass.

Hearn, J.C., and Longanecker, D. (1985). Enrollment effects of alternative postsecondary pricing policies. *Journal of Higher Education* 56(5): 485-508.

Heller, D.E. (1997). Student price response in higher education: An update to Leslie and Brinkman. *Journal of Higher Education* 68(6): 624-659.

Heller, D.E. (1999). The effects of tuition and state financial aid on public college enrollment. *The Review of Higher Education* 23(1): 65-89.

Henderson, J.M., and Quandt, R.E. (1971). *Microeconomic Theory: A Mathematical Approach*. New York: McGraw-Hill.

Hippensteel, D.G., St. John, E.P., and Starkey, J.B. (1996). Influence of tuition and student aid on within-year persistence by adults in two-year colleges. *Community College Journal of Research and Practice* 20: 233-242.

Hochman, H.M., and Rogers, J.D. (1969). Pareto optimal redistribution. *American Economic Review* 59: 542-557.

Hoenack, S.A. (1982). Pricing and efficiency in higher education. *Journal of Higher Education* 53(4): 403-418.

Hoenack, S.A., and Weiler, W.C. (1979). The demand for higher education and institutional enrollment forecasting. *Economic Inquiry* 17: 89-113.

Hossler, D., Lund, J.P., Ramin, J., Westfall, S., and Irish, S. (1997). State funding for higher education: The Sisyphean task. *The Journal of Higher Education* 68(2): 160-190.

Jackson, G.A., and Weathersby, G.B. (1975). Individual demand for higher education: A review and analysis of recent empirical studies. *Journal of Higher Education* 46(6): 623-652.

Johnes, G. (1993). *The Economics of Education*. New York: St. Martin's Press.

Johnstone, D.B. (1999). Financing higher education: Who should pay? In P.G. Altbach, R.O. Berdahl, and P.J. Gumport. *American Higher Education in the Twenty-first Century: Social, Political, and Economic Challenges*. Baltimore, MD: The Johns Hopkins University Press.

Kane, T.J. (1995). *Rising Public College Tuition and College Entry: How Well Do Public Subsidies Promote Access to College?* Cambridge, MA: National Bureau of Economic Research Working Paper No. 5164.

Kane, T.J. (1999a). Reforming public subsidies for higher education. In M.H. Kosters (ed.), *Financing College Tuition: Government Policies and Educational Priorities*. Washington, DC: American Enterprise Institute.

Kane, T.J. (1999b). Student aid after tax reform: Risks and opportunities. In J. King (ed.), *Financing a Col-

lege Education: How it Works, How it's Changing. Phoenix, AZ: Oryx Press and ACE.

Kane, T.J. (1999c). *The Price of Admission: Rethinking How Americans Pay for College*. Washington, DC: The Brookings Institution.

Kaufman, B.E. (1986). *The Economics of Labor Markets and Labor Relations*. New York: The Dryden Press.

Kaufman, B.E. (1994). *The Economics of Labor Markets* (4th ed.). New York: The Dryden Press.

Leslie, L.L., and Brinkman, P.T. (1988). *The Economic Value of Higher Education*. New York: ACE/Macmillan.

Leslie, L.L., and Slaughter, S.A. (1992). Higher education and regional economic development. In W.E. Becker and D.R. Lewis (eds.), *The Economics of American Higher Education*. Boston, MA: Kluwer Academic Publishers.

Levin, H. M., (1979). What are the returns on a college education? In J.W. Peltason and M.V. Messengale (eds.), *Students and Their Institutions: A Changing Relationship*. Washington, DC: American Council on Education.

Lewis, D.R., Hearn, J.C., and Zilbert, E.E. (1993). Efficiency and equity effects of vocationally focused postsecondary education. *Sociology of Education* 66: 188-205.

Manski, C.F., and Wise, D.A. (1983). *College Choice in America*. Cambridge, MA: Harvard University Press.

Mbadugha, L.N.A. (2000). The financial nexus between college choice and persistence for community college students: A financial impact model. Unpublished doctoral dissertation, University of New Orleans.

McConnell, C.R., and Brue, S.L. (1995). *Contemporary Labor Economics* (4th ed.). New York: McGraw-Hill.

McMahon, W.W. (1982). Efficiency and equity criteria for educational budgeting and finance. In W.W. McMahon and T.G. Geske (eds.), *Financing Education: Overcoming Inefficiency and Inequity*. Urbana, IL: University of Illinois Press.

McMahon, W.W. (1991a). Improving higher education through increased efficiency. In D.H. Finifter, R.G Baldwin, J.R. Thelin (eds.), *The Uneasy Public Policy Triangle in Higher Education: Quality, Diversity, and Budgetary Efficiency*. New York: ACE/Macmillan.

McMahon, W.W. (1991b). Efficiency and equity criteria for educational budgeting and finance. In W.W. McMahon and T.G. Geske (eds.), *Financing Education: Overcoming Inefficiency and Inequity*. Urbana, IL: University of Illinois Press.

McMahon, W.W. (1991c). Relative returns to human and physical capital in the U.S. and efficient investment strategies. *Economics of Education Review* 10(4): 283-296.

McMahon, W.W., and Wagner, A.P. (1982). The monetary returns to education as partial social efficiency criteria. In W.W. McMahon and T.G. Geske (eds.), *Financing Education: Overcoming Inefficiency and Inequity*. Urbana, IL: University of Illinois Press.

McPherson, M.S. (1978). The demand for higher education. In D.W. Breneman and C.E. Finn (eds.), *Public Policy and Private Higher Education*. Washington, DC: The Brookings Institution.

McPherson, M.S., and Schapiro, M.O. (1991). *Keeping College Affordable: Government and Educational Opportunity*. Washington, DC: The Brookings Institution.

McPherson, M.S., and Schapiro, M.O. (1998a). *The Student Aid Game: Meeting Need and Rewarding Talent in American Higher Education*. Princeton, NJ: Princeton University Press.

McPherson, M.S., and Schapiro, M.O. (1998b). Priorities for federal student aid policy: Looking beyond Pell grants. In L.E. Gladieux, B. Astor, and W.S. Swail (eds.), *Memory, Reason, Imagination: A Quarter Century of Pell Grants*. New York: The College Board.

Michael, R.T. (1982). Measuring non-monetary benefits of education: A survey. In W.W. McMahon and T.G. Geske (eds.), *Financing Education: Overcoming Inefficiency and Inequity*. Urbana, IL: University of Illinois Press.

Mincer, J. (1993a). Human capital and earnings. In J. Mincer (ed.), *Studies in Human Capital: Collected Essays of Jacob Mincer*. Brookfield, VT: Edward Elgar.

Mincer, J. (1993b). The distribution of labor incomes: A survey. In J. Mincer (ed.), *Studies in Human Capital: Collected Essays of Jacob Mincer*. Brookfield, VT: Edward Elgar.

Mumper, M. (1996). *Removing College Price Barriers*. Albany, NY: State University of New York Press.

Musgrave, R.S., and Musgrave, P.B. (1973). *Public Finance in Theory and Practice*. New York: McGraw-

Hill.

Musgrave, and Musgrave, (1984). *Public Finance in Theory and Practice* (4th ed), New York: McGraw-Hill.

National Association of College and University Business Officers. (1999). *1999 NACUBO Tuition Discounting Survey*. Washington, DC: National Association of College and University Business Officers.

National Center for Education Statistics. (1999). *Digest of Education Statistics*. Washington, DC: U.S. Department of Education.

National Center for Education Statistics. (2000). *The Condition of Education*. Washington, DC: U.S. Department of Education.

Nelson, S.C., (1978). *The Equity of Public Subsidies for Higher Education: Some Thoughts on the Literature*. Papers in Education Finance No. 5. Denver, CO: Education Finance Center, Education Commission of the States.

Okun, A.M. (1975). *Equality and Efficiency: The Big Tradeoff*. Washington, DC: The Brookings Institution.

Orwig, M.D. (1971). (ed.), *Financing Higher Education: Alternatives for the Federal Government*. Iowa City, IA: ACT.

Pascarella, E.T., and Terenzini, P.T. (1991). *How College Affects Students*. San Francisco: Jossey-Bass.

Paulsen, M.B. (1990). *College Choice: Understanding Student Enrollment Behavior*. ASHE-ERIC Higher Education Report No. 6. Washington, DC: The George Washington University.

Paulsen, M.B. (1991). College tuition: Demand and supply determinants from 1960 to 1986. *The Review of Higher Education* 14(3): 339-358.

Paulsen, M.B. (1996a). Higher education and productivity: An afterword. *Thought and Action: NEA Higher Education Journal* 12(2): 135-139.

Paulsen, M.B. (1996b). Higher education and state workforce productivity. *Thought and Action: NEA Higher Education Journal* 12(1): 55-77.

Paulsen, M.B. (1998). Recent research on the economics of attending college: Returns on investment and responsiveness to price. *Research in Higher Education* 39(4): 471-489.

Paulsen, M.B., and Peseau, B.A. (1989). Ten essential economic concepts every administrator should know. *Journal for Higher Education Management* 5(1): 9-17.

Paulsen, M.B., and Pogue, T.F. (1988). Higher education enrollment: The interaction of labor market conditions, curriculum and selectivity. *Economics of Education Review* 7(3): 275-290.

Paulsen, M.B., and St. John, E.P. (1997). The financial nexus between college choice and persistence. In R. Voorhees (ed.), *Researching Student Financial Aid*. New Directions for Institutional Research No. 95. San Francisco: Jossey-Bass.

Paulsen, M.B., and St. John, E.P. (in press). Social class and college costs: Examining the financial nexus between college choice and persistence. *The Journal of Higher Education* 73.

Pechman, J.A. (1970). The distributional effects of public higher education in California. *Journal of Human Resources* 5: 361-370.

Pencavel, J. (1993). Higher education, economic growth, and earnings. In W.E. Becker and D.R. Lewis (eds.), *The Economics of American Higher Education*. Boston, MA: Kluwer Academic Publishers.

Perlman, R. (1973). *The Economics of Education*. New york: McGraw-Hill.

Rothschild, M., and White, L.J. (1995). The analytics of the pricing of higher education and other services in which the customers are inputs. *Journal of Political Economy* 103(3): 573-586.

Rouse, C.E. (1994). What to do after high school: The two-year versus four-year college decision. In R.G. Ehrenberg (ed.), *Choices and Consequences: Contemporary Policy Issues in Education*. Ithaca, NY: ILR Press.

Salmon, L.C., and Fagnano, C.L. (1995). Benefits of education. In M. Carnoy (ed.), *International Encyclopedia of Economics of Education* (2nd ed.). Tarrytown, NY: Elsevier.

Schultz, T.W. (1961). Investment in human capital. *American Economic Review* 51: 1035-1039.

Schultz, T.W. (1963). *The Economic Value of Education*. New York: Columbia University Press.

Smith, H.L., and Powell, B. (1990). Great expectations: Variations in income expectations among college seniors. *Sociology of Education*. 63: 194-207.

St. John, E.P. (1994). *Prices, Productivity, and Investment: Assessing Financial Strategies in Higher Education*. ASHE-ERIC Higher Education Report No. 3. Washington, DC: The George Washington University, School of Education and Human Development.

St. John, E.P. (2000). The impact of student aid on recruitment and retention: What the research indicates. In M.D. Coomes (ed.), *The Role Student Aid Plays in Enrollment Management.* New Directions for Student Services No. 89. San Francisco: Jossey-Bass.

St. John, E.P., Paulsen, M.B., and Starkey, J.B. (1996). The nexus between college choice and persistence. *Research in Higher Education* 37(2): 175-220.

St. John, E.P., and Starkey, J.B. (1994). The influence of costs on persistence by traditional college-age students in community colleges. *Community College Journal of Research and Practice* 18:201-213.

St. John, E.P., and Starkey, J.B. (1995). An alternative to net price: Assessing the influence of prices and subsidies on within-year persistence. *Journal of Higher Education* 66(2): 154-186.

Stampen, J. (1980). *The Financing of Public Higher Education: Low Tuition, Student Aid, and the Federal Government.* ASHE-ERIC Higher Education Report No. 9. Washington, DC: The George Washington University.

Starkey, J.B. (1994). The influence of prices and price subsidies on the within-year persistence by part-time undergraduate students: A sequential analysis. Unpublished doctoral dissertation, University of New Orleans.

Stiglitz, J.E. (2000). *Economics of the Public Sector* (3rd ed.). New York: W.W. Norton.

Thurow, L. (1970). *Investment in Human Capital.* Belmont, CA: Wadsworth.

Thurow, L.C. (1971). The income distribution as a pure public good. *Quarterly Journal of Economics* 85: 327-336.

Weiler, W.C. (1984). Using enrollment demand models in institutional pricing decisions. In L.L. Litten (ed.), *Issues in Pricing Undergraduate Education.* New Directions for Institutional Research No. 42. San Francisco: Jossey-Bass.

Weisbrod, B.A. (1968). External effects of investment in education. In M. Blaug (ed.), *Economics of Education I.* Baltimore, MD: Penguin Books.

Windham, D.M., (1976). Social benefits and the subsidization of higher education: A critique. *Higher Education* 5: 237-252.

Winston, G.C. (1999a). College costs: Who pays and why it matters so. In J. King (ed.), *Financing a College Education: How it Works, How it's Changing.* Phoenix, AZ: Oryx Press and ACE.

Winston, G.C. (1999b). Subsidies, hierarchy and peers: The awkward economics of higher education. *Journal of Economic Perspectives.* 13(1): 13-36.

Winston, G.C., and Yen, I.C. (1995). *Costs, Prices, Subsidies, and Aid in U.S. Higher Education.* Discussion Paper Series No. 32. Williamstown, MA: Williams Project on the Economics of Higher Education.

Wolfe, B.L. (1995). External benefits of education. In M. Carnoy (ed.), *International Encyclopedia of Economics of Education* (2nd ed.). Tarrytown, NY: Elsevier.

Chapter 5

COSTS AND PRODUCTIVITY IN HIGHER EDUCATION:
Theory, Evidence, and Policy Implications[1]

Darrell R. Lewis and Halil Dundar

Cost issues in higher education have received considerable attention in the literature of higher education over the past three decades. Since the early 1970s, numerous studies (e.g., Witmer, 1972; Allen and Brinkman, 1984; Brinkman and Leslie, 1987; Tsang, 1989; Schapiro, 1993; Brinkman, 1990; St. John, 1994; Olson, 1996) have provided extensive reviews of the literature on the subject. Studies examining institutional costs to analyze internal efficiency have used various frameworks and methods. These studies have examined a large number of concepts (e.g., unit costs, expenditures by function, the structures of costs, and economies of scale and scope) in order to better understand the use of resources in higher education to produce certain outputs. The majority of the studies have examined instructional costs. Typically, they were interested in the following types of questions: How much does it cost to educate each student? Are there any significant variations in the cost of educating students across institutions or within institutions? How much was spent by function (e.g., instruction, research, administration, outreach services, and various forms of infrastructure support)? Have there been significant changes over time in per student costs or expenditures by function (i.e., trend analyses). Are there economies of scale and scope?

Several critical concerns about higher education provided increasing impetus for examining the issues of costs and institutional productivity: Perceived declines in quality, concerns about institutional inefficiency and declining productivity, and concerns about rising costs and affordability have all arisen (see, for example, Clotfelter et al., 1991; McPherson and Winston., 1993; Graham et al., 1995). Partly as a result of such concerns, public resources allocated to higher education have come under greater scrutiny. The quality of institutions and their utilization of resources have become particular matters of

---

[1]This chapter was originally published in Volume XIV of *Higher Education: Handbook of Theory and Research,* © 1999 by Agathon Press. It has been updated with an Epilogue written especially for this volume.

increasing public debate and scrutiny. These moves towards greater accountability and productivity have resulted in a growing interest for examining the performance and productivity of higher education institutions as well as for the use of performance indicators for higher education to improve accountability (i.e., to monitor the "public investment") and improve internal efficiency.

While there are already several extensive reviews of the related literature, we believe that this chapter will contribute to the literature by (1) providing an extensive review of the literature within a framework of internal efficiency; (2) updating the literature, especially by focusing on the joint production of several outputs of higher education institutions; and (3) identifying a number of policy recommendations from the past studies which are useful for both public policy and institutional decision making. As the title of the chapter suggests, we attempt to provide a broader view of costs and productivity issues in higher education by integrating the three important dimensions of cost studies in the field (i.e., theory, empirical evidence, and policy recommendations).

The purpose of this chapter is to review and synthesize the literature on the costs and productivity in higher education. Although it is concerned with both colleges and universities, it does give particular focus to research universities. The chapter directly examines several questions: (1) What are the average and marginal costs of different outputs? (2) Are there ray and product-specific economies of scale? (3) Are there complementarities and economies of scope among various outputs of higher education (e.g., undergraduate, masters, and doctoral teaching, and faculty research) through their joint production? (4) Does the type of production (e.g., social science or engineering) influence costs and efficiency? If so, do academic units vary in their economies of scale, scope, and marginal costs? (5) What are the optimum levels and mix of outputs? (6) How does the quality of a department and its product(s) affect its costs?

The chapter is divided into five sections. The first section gives overview to the costs of higher education, and presents a summary of some related concepts and approaches for examining the costs of such institutions. The second section presents the cost behavior of higher education institutions with a particular focus on their multiproduct nature. A third section presents the conceptual foundation for examining these multiproduct cost concepts. A fourth section reviews findings from empirical studies that have examined these costs. Particular attention is paid to estimates and analyses of scale and scope economies. The final section provides policy recommendations for institutional administrators and public policy makers and suggests directions for future research.

COST ANALYSIS IN HIGHER EDUCATION

In this section we give overview to the costs of higher education, identify methods to analyze these costs, and discuss prospective uses of such cost studies.

Description of the Costs

What is cost in higher education? Adams, Hankins, and Schroder (1978) argued that the definition of cost varies with one's perspective and purposes. There are different variations of costs, each of which has a different definition of cost. They categorized costs in higher education into three perspectives: Financial accounting (reporting), cost accounting (managerial), and economic accounting (theoretical and analytical). They noted that "financial accounting" is concerned with recording, classifying, summarizing, and analyzing financial data. "Cost is defined as the amount or equivalent paid or charged for something of value" (p.13). They reported that "cost accounting" is concerned with accumulating, classifying, summarizing, interpreting, and reporting the cost of personnel compensation, goods and services, and other expenses incurred. The cost accounting process is designed to assign or allocate costs to particular outputs in a given period. The costs derived may be actual costs or may be other costs such as replacement, projected, and imputed costs. Their definition of costs in economics can be examined from a macro (i.e., societal), micro (i.e., institutional), or individual (i.e., student) perspective. The macro definition of costs typically considers society as a whole and includes all costs spent for higher education to produce all the outcomes and outputs. Typically, it includes institutional expenditures, individual "out of pocket" costs, opportunity costs, and other societal costs. On the other hand, the micro definition of costs focuses on the activities of a particular institution or organization. An institutional perspective includes all the expenditures spent by the institution to produce all the outcomes and outputs. This perspective does not include opportunity costs and student expenditures for higher education. A student perspective includes all the client or individual costs for receiving higher education. This includes all the tuition and fees, expenditures due to attending college (books, transportation, etc.), and opportunity costs (Adams, Hankins, and Schroder, 1978, p.13).

This chapter will largely focus upon institutional costs. From an institutional perspective, the costs of colleges and universities include all the payments necessary to acquire the resources needed to operate the institution. In examining the costs of higher education institutions, much of our focus will be on the use of institutional resources for the production of a set of outputs.

The financial data for examining the costs of higher education usually come from the financial records of an institution. Thus, it is relatively easy to estimate the total annual spending for the operation of a college or university. Traditionally, the focus has been upon institutional expenditures for instruction, although sometimes expenditures for departmental research and/or sponsored research expenditures have been reported separately. Limited attention has been given to the costs of research and public service and outreach activities largely due to the difficulty in measuring outputs pertinent to these functions. This encourages most studies to examine instructional expenditures from the perspective of financial accounting and deals mainly with recorded costs. As a result, most studies examining institutional costs have excluded the costs resulting from the loss of taxes, other imputed costs of colleges and universities facilities related to exemptions, student opportunity costs, and student out-of-packet costs for books and living expenses (Adams, Hankins, and Schroder, 1978; Bowen, 1981).

In this chapter we also view cost as the amount or equivalent spent to produce specific amounts of outputs. And we expressly recognize that a research university produces multiple outputs in the realms of teaching/learning, research, and service/outreach. The chapter focuses on all institutional expenditures for the production of outputs in these three functional areas.

Costs also can be identified according to an objective. A cost objective can be defined according to the entity to which the cost is related. Adams, Hankins, and Schroeder (1978) identified the following types of cost objectives:

a) Specific categories of input: Inputs used in higher education include faculty/staff (e.g., wages, fringe benefits, travel, fuel), student full-time equivalent enrollment (i.e., students? time), library, laboratory, computing, and other resources used to produce teaching/learning, research, and service outputs.

b) Specific categories of outputs: Some specific output measures include student credit hours, number of full-time equivalent students, number of graduates, and number of research publications. Very few specific service and outreach outputs have been used in past studies. Outputs in these categories are often produced jointly and it is difficult to determine the amount of resources spent to produce them.

c) Activity-based cost categories: Costs can also be classified according to activity or function such as direct instruction, research, administration (e.g., central, registration, admission), student services, and building maintenance.

d) Unit-based cost categories: Costs can be classified according to organizational units (e.g., departments, colleges, and the entire institution).

e) Costs based on assignability: Costs also can be defined in terms of their assignability—i.e., as direct, indirect, and full. Direct costs can be described as the cost that is readily assignable to a specific organizational unit (or other cost objective); indirect cost is the cost of one organizational unit (or other cost objective) that is attributed or allocated to another organizational unit (or other cost objective) because of a supporting relationship; full cost is the sum of the direct costs of an organizational unit (or other cost objective) plus the allocated cost of the unit supporting it.

f) Costs based on changes in the level of activity: Costs can be defined according to changes in the activity level—i.e., fixed or variable. Fixed cost is the resource cost which does not vary with the activity level (volume of output) of the category of cost being considered. Variable cost is the resource cost that varies directly with the level of activity (e.g., numbers of students or volumes of output) of the category of cost being considered.

Costs can also be described by the relationship of the cost to the activity level of the cost objective—i.e., total, average or marginal. Total cost is the cost that is the sum of all costs that are related to a particular objective. Average cost is derived by dividing the total cost corresponding to the cost objective by the number of units associated with the cost objective. Marginal (incremental) cost is the cost associated with a specific change (increase or decrease) of a cost objective.

(g) Costs based on impact within a fiscal period: Cost can also be examined by its impact on a fiscal period. Operating (i.e., recurrent) cost is a cost that has its impact within a current fiscal period. Capital cost is a cost that has impact affects throughout several fiscal periods.

This chapter is mainly concerned about the cost behavior of colleges and universities and we examine institutional expenditures for instruction and research. Instructional expenditures include both direct expenditures for instruction and indirect expenditures for student services. Similarly, research includes both sponsored funding and departmental research. Although instructional costs are closely related to auxiliary enterprises, teaching hospitals, student financial aid and capitalization of facilities, our purpose is to focus on annualized institutional expenditures as they relate directly to instruction and research. Our goal is to compare costs within and among institutions and identify some of the issues relating to the development of greater internal efficiency.

Determinants of the Costs of Higher Education

Over the past half century a large number of studies examining the costs of higher education have found substantial differences in per unit costs between institutions. Moreover, since the early 1980s there has been a growing concern about the rising costs of higher education. In this subsection we summarize the major factors that likely determine most cost differences among higher education institutions and that likely have contributed to the escalation of costs in higher education. It is important to note that others have likewise provided summaries and anthologies on the perceived increasing costs in higher education. Olson (1996), for example, in a previous chapter in this Handbook series has reported on the organizational pathologies that have likely contributed to such costs as they were originally reported by Getz and Siegfried (1991), Gumport and Pusser (1995), Leslie and Rhoades (1995), Massy (1991), and Massy and Wilger, (1995).

Bowen (1981), in his classic book on the costs of higher education, has noted that some cost variations could be explained by differences in mission, location, size, or institutional quality. In fact, he argued, cost differences resulting from such diversity could be justified and viewed as beneficial since they may foster innovation in higher education. However, in his early study Bowen also found large differences in costs per student among institutions which were actually homogeneous with respect to their mission, size, or institutional quality. When seemingly similar institutions are producing substantially similar outputs and these outputs have greatly different unit costs, then decision and policymakers should appropriately ask why these costs have such wide variation. Such findings also result in a growing demand for greater internal efficiency and accountability in higher education.

In the long run, total costs will be determined by the societal and political decisions that reflect the combined influences of the public who control the flow of funds to higher education. Three related decisions are made by society: The total amount to be spent on higher education, the number of units of services to be provided, and the level of quality. Most of the differences found within the total costs of higher education between states and countries can be attributed to such value driven attributes of costs. In the short run, however, the use and deployment of resources within institutions become very critical for determining costs.

Almost all studies examining the costs of higher education have found that there are considerable variations among higher education institutions with respect to costs per student or costs per research output. Bowen (1981), for example, found an enormous cost differential per student-credit hour among institutions, including those whom appear to be quite comparable institutions. What are the possible explanations for these variations in the costs of higher education across institutions? According to Bowen, at least in the short run the primary factor affecting an institution's expenditure is its revenue. In other words, Bowen posits that the educational expenditures of an institution are largely determined by the amount of available revenue. Each institution raises all the money it can and then it spends all that it raises in order to maximize its prestige and quality. Bowen described this notion and behavior as the "revenue theory of costs." While it has been generally conceded that the role of revenues has likely contributed to changes in costs in higher education institutions, many other observers have argued that there are certainly other factors which can and do determine costs and prospective internal efficiencies within institutions.

The most important other factors explaining differences in unit costs between institutions are size of academic programs, types of academic programs, and types of outputs (e.g., undergraduate, graduate, research, and outreach). Recent studies, for example, have demonstrated the powerful effects of all three of these factors on the costs of higher education. Increasing rates of personnel compensation and socially imposed costs have also been noted as important determinants of the costs of higher education. Moreover, institutional attempts to enhance the quality of their services and outputs (i.e., by lowering the ratio of faculty to students, or by improving materials, facilities and equipment) are likely to increase costs.

Uses of Cost Studies in Higher Education

Cost studies with a particular attention to unit costs and expenditures by functions have received a great deal of attention from policy makers and institutional administrators over the past thirty years. How much do higher education institutions spend to educate students, to produce research products, and to serve the public? Why are there differences among institutions? How much should it cost? How can we spend the resources to increase efficiency within the system? Could we produce the same level output with less money? Or should we produce more output with the same level of money? These are some of the fundamental internal efficiency and productivity questions being confronted by governing boards and administrators. There is a growing body of literature examining costs and productivity issues in higher education which often do suggest considerable inefficiencies within the system.

A better understanding of the relationships between costs and outputs is essential to improving the internal efficiency in higher education. Since the limited operation of market forces does not provide sufficient incentives for efficient resource allocation and rational decision making in higher education, some knowledge about the costs of producing the various levels and mixes of outputs is essential for planning and improving internal efficiency (Verry, 1987). The purpose of cost studies in higher education is to provide the data and information necessary for policy makers and institutional administrators to make more informed and rational decisions. The basic underlying process in all cost and internal efficiency studies is to measure certain costs and then to compare these costs with something. And there are a wide variety of types of comparisons and cost analysis methods that can be used for these purposes in higher education.

Methods of Cost An\alysis

Despite the substantial interest in examining the costs of higher education, the question has often become *how* such costs can be analyzed rather than how such costs are identified and measured. Frequently, cost measurement problems have arisen and, as discussed later in this chapter, attempts to analyze the costs of higher education have often resulted in failure due to substantial measurement problems of outputs and their joint production. In addition, study results are often different due to the notion of time, wherein the data can be presented over time (i.e., by trend analysis) or by institutional and inter-institutional cost comparisons (Adams, Hankins, and Schroeder, 1978). But even the analytical methods examining the costs of higher education have come under strong criticism. Since many of our review findings were based on studies using a wide variety of cost methods, we need to first provide an overview of their analytical methods.

There are several major methods of cost analysis. The first form is "composition analysis" and this is simply the sub-categorization of aggregate costs. This type of analysis breaks down aggregate cost into its component parts to gain a better understanding of overall total costs. This breakdown can be shown in terms of dollars or as percentages of the total (e.g., expenditures by functions). For example, Bowen (1981) found that expenditures for administration and research rose more than expenditures for instruction between 1930 and 1980. He also found that scholarship and fellowship expenditures also rose a great deal during this period. This type of analysis is useful to examine trends in the allocation of resources among various functions of higher education; yet, it is limited when there are substantial amounts of joint production taking place. Second, overall institutional expenditures can be examined as "comparisons over time" (i.e., whether there is an overall increase or decline in the costs of higher education over time) or relative to other sectors in the economy (e.g., K-12, health, transportation).

A third method is "relational analysis." Here the determination is of the functional relationship between cost and independent variable(s). The independent variable also can be time. This form of analysis is called "trend analysis.". Another form of relational analysis is to show cost variation with changes in the volume of operations. Volume is a measure of the output(s) of the higher education process. A major problem with this type of analysis is in the measurement of output.

There are a wide variety of ways to examine relationships between costs and outcomes. Perhaps the most common in higher education has been *unit cost analysis* which indicates costs per unit of something. Here, costs indicate the total cost of producing a specific output (usually per full-time equivalent student or per student credit hour). Traditionally, cost per unit is computed simply by adding up total institutional expenditures for all purposes and dividing by the number of full-time equivalent students or student credit hours. This is called cost per student or cost per student credit hour. A common way to examine relationships between cost and its outcomes in higher education has been to estimate a cost function and compute average and marginal costs. Despite their widespread use in higher education, unit cost studies have been criticized because of their difficulty in identifying all the outputs of higher education and the multiproduct nature of higher education production. Therefore, an increasing number of studies have employed econometric models to estimate costs from actual data and then determine the existence of scale and scope economies. A second form is by direct comparison, such as comparisons of actual costs with budgeted costs or standard costs; comparisons between or among the costs of organizational units; comparisons between or among the costs of outcome categories (e.g., different degree programs); and direct cost comparisons between or among the costs of specific decision alternatives (Adams, Hankins, and Schroeder, , 1978, p. 24).

Estimating instructional costs has been particularly difficult because of the use of resources in joint production. Traditionally, most unit cost studies have included all expenditures for instruction and departmental research while estimating costs per student. Bowen (1981), for example, found that only one third of all institutional expenditures are spent directly for instruction and departmental research. However, when student services, scholarships and fellowships, prorated shares of academic support, and operations and maintenance of plant are included, the percentage that may be allocated to the instruction of students was almost 60 percent of total expenditures.

Cost Functions in Higher Education

Cost functions have been an important topic in many empirical studies in economics since the turn of the century. These types of studies have provided important information in many sectors of the economy about decision making with respect to resource allocation and improving efficiency. Although estimating cost functions in higher education has been quite limited until only recently (Smith, 1978), concerns about increasing efficiency during the 1970s and 1980s generated numerous such studies.

By and large, there was one main problem in almost all of these early studies. Most of the studies simply assumed that production could be characterized by a single homogeneous output, and in most uses it was assumed to be instruction and was measured by either full-time equivalent students or student credit hours. Indeed, this limited attention to the multiproduct nature of higher education was not due to any lack of interest on the part of economists or higher education analysts in multiproduct cost functions. Rather, as Maynard (1971) noted more than two decades ago, numerous methodological and data problems had been important obstacles to further research in industry and business, as well as in non-profit organizations such as higher education. The lack of appropriate econometric models for explaining the nature of multiproduct firms was the foremost problem that prevented the analysis of all multiproduct firms, including those in higher education (Friedlaender et al., 1983).

Fortunately, recent developments in the economics literature relative to the theory of industrial organizations that deal explicitly with a variety of outputs, prices and production processes now permit an endogenous determination of the cost structures of multiproduct firms (Bailey, 1988). Over the past decade, an outpouring of empirical studies using multiproduct cost concepts have provided insights into the cost behavior and technology of multiproduct firms in a wide range of industries, including banking, transportation, telecommunication, petroleum, and hospitals, among others (see Baumol et al., 1988; Shoesmith, 1988; Wang Chiang and Friedlaender, 1985). Although it is still limited, a growing body of literature has begun to analyze the cost structures of higher education institutions using multiproduct cost concepts here in the United States (e.g., Cohn et al., 1989; Nelson and Heverth, 1993; de Groot et al., 1991; Dundar and Lewis, 1995), as well as in a diverse number of other countries such as the United Kingdom (Johnes, 1994), Australia (Lloyd et al., 1993), and Turkey (Lewis and Dundar, 1995).

Two recent studies on the multiproduct nature of costs of higher education by Cohn et al. (1989) and de Groot et al. (1991) used institutions as the unit of analysis for their cost functions. On the other hand, previous cost studies in higher education found that costs differ across academic departments and disciplines in relation to outputs (e.g., Carlson, 1972; Berg and Hoenack, 1987). Carlson (1972), for example, reported that there exists extreme variation in general educational expenditures per student even within relatively homogeneous groups of institutions. Thus, the most important problem seems to be that different production technologies among academic disciplines may generate problems in analyzing departmental cost functions. For instance, results may be misleading if a single cost function is estimated for both chemistry and English departments because they have quite dissimilar production functions. Since aggregating institutional outputs may often yield unreliable conclusions concerning the costs of outputs and the existence of economies of scale and scope in higher education, Tierney (1980) has recommended that separate analyses ought to be conducted for each academic department.

Recently, adopting such a methodology, Nelson and Heverth (1992) examined the marginal costs of teaching outputs and the existence of economies of scale and scope in higher education utilizing data from a single research university. However, this study has limited generalizability since it represents only the cost behavior in a single university. To overcome this limitation, data from departments within a homogeneous group of institutions must be used.

The literature on cost functions in higher education over the past two decades has yielded substantial insights regarding scale economies and the costs of instruction. Although several earlier studies (Butter, 1967; Sengupta, 1975; Southwick, 1969; Carlson, 1972; Verry and Davies, 1976; Verry and Layard, 1975; Bear, 1974; Brinkman, 1981; James, 1978) recognized the fact that higher education institutions, particularly universities, are multiproduct firms, there was mixed evidence on the existence of scale economies and little evidence on the presence of scope economies. Brinkman (1990) underlined the importance of such evidence before arriving at any definitive conclusions because to date only a few studies have analyzed the costs of higher education by employing multiproduct cost function techniques.

The lack of studies employing these new techniques presented several obstacles to our understanding the cost structures of higher education institutions. Despite ample evidence regarding scale economies, particularly in two- and four-year colleges, a major limitation of most early studies was that they used only single-output cost functions. As Cohn et al. (1989) have suggested, in the case of the multiproduct nature of most higher education institutions, the results of most single or aggregated output cost functions studies should be read "at best tentative, and at worst, wholly misleading" (p. 289). James (1978) also argued that "the failure in previous studies to adjust correctly for the substantial allocation to research and graduate training has apparently meant that undergraduate costs have been overstated, the social rates of return to undergraduate... [study and] estimates of productivity growth through time have been understated" (p. 184). Despite the substantial body of literature on economies of scale and recognition of the multiproduct nature of higher education institutions, almost all studies have fallen short of a rigorous analysis of scale and scope economies.

COST BEHAVIOR OF INSTITUTIONS IN HIGHER EDUCATION

Although a number of studies have examined the relationship between costs and outputs, it is difficult to generalize from the findings of these studies because of their mixed results. Even though there is little debate on the question of the multiplicity of outputs in higher education, there has been a continuing controversy as to whether or not higher education institutions can be analyzed as industrial organizations with respect to the cost structure and the existence of economies of scale and scope in their operations (Cohn and Geske, 1991).

The argument is rooted in the limited and problematic availability of data regarding outputs of higher education. Hopkins (1990), for example, argued that "there is no reason to believe that the educational enterprise has been operating on their [most] efficient production possibilities; and there are many reasons to believe that it has not. This means that, even if we were able to specify the true and complete functional form, we would still be unable to estimate the true coefficients of the model from any existing set of data" (p. 13). The nature of the production process and outputs of higher education institutions, particularly research institutions, limits the applied research that attempts to analyze the existence of scale and scope economies and to estimate the costs of outputs in higher education. Nonetheless, as Dolan and his colleagues (1993) have argued, in the case of a production function for higher education a number of proxies for teaching and research outputs can be utilized to examine cost structures. The following subsections present a theoretical framework for the cost behavior of higher education institutions, with a particular focus on describing the nature of multiproduction of higher education institutions; they discuss the costs and sources of multiproduct economies in higher education.

Production and Costs in Higher Education

Higher education institutions, like industrial firms, transform a number of inputs into products through a production process. The main differences of this production process in higher education are that institutions, particularly American research universities, produce a wide variety of qualitatively different outputs and they do this jointly with many of the same resources (Getz and Siegfried, 1993). Thus, it is critical to carefully describe the outputs, inputs, transformation process, and multiproduct nature of higher education institutions in order to analyze their cost behavior.

Outputs

The mission and goal statements of most American research institutions specify instruction, research and public service. The output measures of universities are, in turn, related to their three-part mission of higher education. This suggests that American research universities, at both the institutional and departmental levels, typically represent multiproduct firms with multiple outputs when they are compared with universities in other countries where research activities are often separated from instructional activities (Massy, 1990).

Despite these clear-cut definitions or domains of production of higher education institutions, there is no cost study that explicitly defines and measures the full range of products of higher education institutions. Typically, a college or university transforms a number of inputs into a wide range of outcomes. Although it is often easy to identify the inputs and outputs of higher education, it is extremely difficult to quantify their precise measures because of the intangible features of many of these inputs and outputs. To illustrate this difficulty, Hopkins and Massy (1981) have identified both the tangible and intangible inputs and outputs of higher education in Table 1.

TABLE 1. Identification of Inputs and Outputs of Higher Education

Tangible	*Intangible*
Inputs	
New students matriculating	Quality and diversity of matriculating students
Faculty time and effort	Quality of effort put forth by faculty
Student time and effort	Quality of effort put forth by students
Staff time and effort	Quality of effort put forth by staff
Building and equipment	Quality, age, style of buildings and equipment
Library holdings and acquisitions	Quality of library holdings and acquisitions
Endowments	
Outputs	
Student enrollment in courses	Quality of education obtained
Degrees awarded	Quality of education obtained
Research awards, articles, and citations	Quality and quantity of research performed
Services rendered to the general public	Quality of services rendered
	Goodwill
	Reputation
Source: Adapted from Hopkins, D., and Massy, W. F. (1981). *Planning Models for Colleges and Universities.* Palo Alto, CA: Stanford University Press.	

It is fairly obvious from such an identification of the inputs and outputs of higher education that we still lack appropriate measures for many tangible and almost all intangible aspects of both inputs and outputs. The lack of appropriate measures for the quality of outputs is one important reason why estimates of production and cost functions in higher education have not been well developed. Some cost studies do not even take into account the quality of instruction, research, and service outputs as a separate output, and most empirical studies have focused only on the quantifiable measures of teaching output.

Production and outputs of instruction. All postsecondary institutions have a major responsibility for transmitting existing knowledge to their students—i.e., the teaching or instruction function of higher education. The expected output may be measured by the amount of knowledge learned in different levels and departments. Although a value-added approach to measuring changes in the stock of knowledge seems to be most appropriate, no study in the literature has used such a measure to estimate the costs of teaching output because of the difficulty of devising a standardized test that could be used to measure knowledge gained in different areas of specialization (Nelson and Heverth, 1992). Rather, the most common way to measure the output of teaching has been to use proxies. The number of students is used as the most common proxy for instructional output (e.g., Maynard, 1971; Tierney, 1980; Verry and Davies, 1976; Lewis and Dundar, 1995). The number of student credit hours has been the second most common measure used to estimate the costs of instruction (e.g., Nelson and Heverth, 1992; Dundar and Lewis, 1995). The number of graduates has also been used as a proxy for teaching outputs (Verry and Davies, 1976; de Groot et al., 1991). It is clear that all these variables ignore quality differentials across producing units (e.g., institutions, departments).

While acknowledging the intangible qualities of teaching output, some studies have either estimated separate cost functions for different production units (e.g., Cohn et al., 1989), or else used an index for the quality of the output (e.g., Carlson, 1972; Tierney, 1980; de Groot et al., 1991). In the first case, studies attempt to examine a homogeneous set of institutions with similar production technology. For example, it is often accepted that private higher education institutions have different production technologies when compared with public higher education. If both sectors are merged into one data set, the question arises about whether an analysis of public and private higher education together would provide accurate information regarding costs. Since the answer is largely unknown, the standard methodology has been to analyze private and public higher education as separate production units. In the second case, although the quality of outputs is not directly measured, a quality variable, usually represented by a reputational rating of the institution or department, is used to test the impact of quality on costs. Recently, Dundar and Lewis (1995) employed both approaches in estimating departmental cost functions. They focused on a set of relatively homogeneous public research universities and used reputational ratings of doctoral programs as a proxy for departmental quality in order to control for variation in quality among departments.

Outputs of research. A major characteristic of post-war universities in the United States is their increasing emphasis on research. Universities allocate a material amount of their recurring human and physical resources for the production of research. Besides departmental research, which is largely seen as complementary to the teaching function of the traditional university, externally sponsored organized research also has become a large enterprise for many research universities. Departmental research is viewed as the ordinary research that many faculty pursue as part of their regular work and appointment. Organized (i.e., externally sponsored) research, on the other hand, is separately funded and budgeted.

While such a distinction is necessary, the lines between the two types of research activities are often not as clear as most policy makers would like to see. In fact, several critics have pointed out that this is one of the major reasons for increasing costs in higher education. While the proportion of resources devoted to teaching and instruction has been declining over recent decades, the proportion of institutional resources devoted to research has been increasing. Thus, any cost study examining internal efficiency within universities in general, and in research universities in particular, *must* take into account the inputs and outcomes of research production. While few would disagree with such a statement, many would disagree with how to measure such activities.

Research output of higher education includes creating and discovering new knowledge and disseminating this new knowledge. Although a research mission is not solely confined to major research universities, a clear majority of all research within higher education is done in these institutions. Although creating new knowledge is a major function of the research, the research output of universities has been difficult to reliably measure and has rarely been reported. Two major problems are associated with the quantification of the costs of research outputs. First, as James (1978) pointed out almost two decades ago, we still lack even a crude quantity index that relates to such matters as numbers of articles and books, conference presentations, and the like for most disciplines. And second, we also lack a reasonable quality index. Although citation analyses have been used as proxies for quality and quantity of research output, there has been no cost study that used citations as a proxy for research output. The best available studies to date on research productivity are by Jones et al. (1982) and Goldberger et al. (1995) as they examine the reputational qualities of graduate programs, but even these studies have failed to account for all the research output for given departments. These studies provide measures such as the number of published journal articles and of citations attributed to program faculty.

Studies examining the costs of higher education treat research output in various ways. Four approaches are often used as proxies for research output. First, the number of articles, and/or books published is used as a proxy for research output (Verry and Layard, 1975; Verry and Davies, 1976; de Groot et al., 1991; Dundar and Lewis, 1995; Lewis and Dundar, 1995). Second, other studies have argued that the amount of research grants that universities receive from the federal government or other agencies can be used to measure their research productivity (Brinkman, 1981; Cohn et al., 1989). Third, other studies view research as a separate output, but measure it in terms of input variables. For example, hours spent (i.e., effort) by staff on personal research has been used a proxy for the research output of universities. Studies by Verry and Davies (1976) and Verry and Layard (1975) on the costs of British universities, and James (1978) and Nelson and Heverth (1992) on the costs of higher education in the United States all employed the research hours spent by faculty in their cost functions. Since this is an input for the production of research output, they justified its use as part of an attempt to obtain meaningful estimates of the marginal cost of teaching, rather than research outputs. Finally, citation indexes may be used to create a proxy for the research output of each department or institution. Perhaps because of the well documented problems with using citation indexes (see Johnes, 1988) they have never been used. Nevertheless, we are still at a very early stage in measuring, at least in crude terms, the quantity and quality of research output. But the availability of computerized data bases can provide further incentives to measure the quantify and quality of research output.

Productivity and outputs of service. In addition to the largely known instructional and research products of research universities, most such institutions also have products in the area of public service and outreach. Public service is particularly important for public research universities since most are expected to transfer knowledge to others outside of the institutions. Ideally, we would like to have some index or proxy of the public service produced by our higher education institutions, but these data are not yet available. As a consequence, almost all studies have examined only the teaching and research outputs of higher education, ignoring public service and outreach almost completely.

For purposes of estimating the costs of outputs, it is imperative to identify and measure both the quantity and quality of all outputs in higher education. Yet, most studies have concentrated on only the teaching and research outputs by using proxies, such as the number of students as proxy for instruction and the number of publications as proxy for research. All cost studies to date have ignored public service and outreach activities and the more intangible functions such as the preservation of knowledge. Rarely have cost studies addressed the quality of the products of higher education institutions. If the quality of higher education programs differ from one institution to another, then ignoring the quality of such outputs will provide inaccurate pictures. Although many studies acknowledge these problems, most end up only using the number of undergraduate and graduate students as proxies for instruction and the number of publications as proxies for research.

Inputs

The most important resource used in higher education is human resources. If we consider academic departments as the principal units of production in higher education, each department can be viewed as maintaining a minimal administrative unit (e.g., chairperson, administrative secretary, and other support staff, and the like) along with instructional and research resources (e.g., faculty, teaching, and research assistants) and support equipment (e.g., office equipment, computers, and the like).

Clearly, the most important human resource of a university is its faculty. The cost of faculty resources is determined not only by the number of staff employed but also by their qualifications (i.e., education), status (i.e., full-time versus part-time), age, rank, productivity (e.g., merit-based salary increases), and competitive salaries (i.e., relative to salaries of a similar profession in the market). Non-faculty staff also have become an important input during the past several decades. An increase in their number has greatly affected costs in higher education (Massy and Wilger, 1992).

It should also be emphasized that graduate students, particularly at the advanced levels, are also an important source of teaching and research inputs in research universities. As we will discuss below, the duality of graduate students as outputs and inputs makes it difficult to estimate the costs of graduate students because their costs also depend on their utilization as inputs. The most common approach for measuring teaching output has been to use full-time equivalent enrollments. Often full-time equivalent enrollments are divided into undergraduate (and sometimes between upper and lower levels) and graduate enrollments to indicate two (and sometimes three) types of enrollment, based on the assumption that undergraduate and graduate education have different inputs. A problem with this type of approach is that the effect of enrollment increases at the graduate level is assumed to be homogeneous. In reality, the likely impact of additional students in graduate programs also depends on the quality, level, and use of graduate students, because higher-quality graduate students working as research assistants and teaching assistants might increase research and teaching outputs. If it is assumed that because doctoral students are more qualified and thus more likely to be employed as research or teaching assistants than master level students, the costs of the two products might be different. In addition, the costs of graduate students might differ substantially across departments according to their utilization as an input for the production of other teaching and research outputs. Although differential costs of each level (including graduate levels) and field have been routinely addressed in recent economics of higher education literature (e.g., Hoenack and Weiler, 1975; Berg and Hoenack, 1987; Smith, 1978) independent of cost functions, only two multiproduct cost function studies have examined and used such factors to estimate costs in higher education (Lewis and Dundar, 1995; Dundar and Lewis, 1995).

Although some studies estimate that 70-80 percent of institutional costs are related to departmental expenditures (Tierney, 1980), there also are the joint uses of various inputs that some or all departments share. In fact, most studies have found that both scale and scope economies arise from the use of these joint central costs—i.e., central administration, plant operation and maintenance, libraries, and the like (Nelson and Heverth, 1992).

The actual deployment of institutional resources also materially affect costs. The allocation of personnel to either instruction or to administration or other forms of infrastructure support can greatly influence costs. Class size, for example, is a significant variable affecting the costs of higher education and results in important ways from such allocations. Logically, as average class size gets smaller, the costs of higher education increase.

Although this brief description of inputs covers most of the measurable inputs of higher education production, the problem with this description is that it misses several important resource inputs. For example, the time of students and the quality of students are usually not included in most cost studies, suggesting that they do not have any effect on the costs of departmental production. In contrast with such an assumption, a number of researchers have argued that the quality and time of students affect both the productivity of teaching and research (e.g., Hoenack et al., 1986).

The Multiproduct Nature of Higher Education

While in a single output production the cost of output depends on the level of production of that output, in the case of multiproduction the costs of outputs depend on both the level and the mix of products. This important distinction can be illustrated by considering a simple single-output product case. Assume, for example, that an academic department produces *only* undergraduate students (y_1). In the case of an increase in y_1, average costs (*AC*) and marginal costs (*MC*) will change according to the level of output, holding the quality and prices of inputs constant.

Figure 1 illustrates the situation for a single-product case. Although the true cost functions of higher education institutions are still not exactly known, the simplified model of Figure 1 indicates typical long-run average and marginal cost curves and the most efficient production level that will be at y_1^*, where *AC* and *MC* are equal to each other. Economies of scale will be present between the range of $0y_1^*$, where an increase in output level results in a decline of both *AC* and *MC*, but *MC* is still lower than *AC*. However, for production levels above y_1^*, *MC* is greater than *AC*, suggesting that an increase

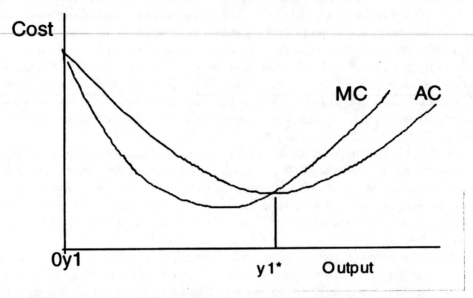

Figure 1. Average and Marginal Cost Curves in Single-Output Production

in production level will likely result in diseconomies of scale. Thus, the main determinant of the presence of economies of scale in the case of a single output is the level of output (see Halstead, 1991).

However, most educational organizations do not have such simple cost behavior and representative cost curves with prospective economies of scale. The major problem comes from the fact that higher education institutions produce multiple outputs as do most other multiproduct firms utilizing a number of sharable inputs. In a multiproduct case, the costs of outputs not only depend on the level of outputs but also depend on the mix of outputs, suggesting a change in the level of one output affects the costs of the other outputs.

Two important policy questions in higher education are whether the costs of instruction increase by instructional level and whether they differ across academic programs. The literature on the costs of higher education has reported important findings on these two questions. First, in general, the costs of instruction rise by level of academic programs. Nelson and Heverth (1992) summarized these findings by stating that "graduate students are generally considered to be more expensive to educate than undergraduates, and upper level undergraduates are thought to be more expensive" than lower level undergraduates, despite the existence of a wide range of variations in the estimated magnitude of costs. Second, the costs of outputs do indeed vary across academic programs. For instance, the costs of undergraduate instruction is typically higher in engineering departments when compared with those in social science departments. Such findings in determining the costs of instruction have important policy implications regarding tuition, subsidy, and other forms of appropriation. This is especially true in cases where an institution might have cost-related tuition policies and average cost funding directives (see James, 1978; Hoenack and Weiler, 1975; Berg and Hoenack, 1987).

Clearly, the results from a single-output or instructional-cost study that ignores research costs is probably biased, if not misleading, in the case of the multiproduct nature of higher education. Moreover, one of the most important features of American research universities as multiproduct firms is their difference from many other multiproduct industrial organizations because they also employ their graduate students (i.e., outputs) as inputs to produce other outputs (i.e., research and undergraduate instruction). Although many cost advantages may come from fixed costs and the joint utilization of resources, the utilization of outputs as inputs for teaching and research may provide additional cost advantages for some departments in their production of both instruction and research. This can be called the "*dual role of graduate education*" because of the utilization of graduate students as an input, substituting for faculty, and as an output as graduate students. As a consequence, the costs of teaching by level of instruction may *not* necessarily increase as the level of output increases, as commonly found in most single-output or instructional cost studies. In contrast, for example, the costs of graduate level instruction may be lower than undergraduate instruction in departments in which a large number of graduate students are used as teaching assistants. Similarly, if we were able to measure precisely the output of research and its costs and the contribution of graduate students, we might also find overestimation of the costs of graduate education.

To illustrate this possible bias in the estimation of costs due to the dual roles of graduate education, consider the following hypothetical cases from the two academic fields of engineering and social sciences. Each department produces four outputs as undergraduate students (y_1), master students (y_2), doctoral students (y_3), and research output (y_4), with joint utilization of three inputs such as faculty (x_1), administrative and support staff (x_2), and equipment and services (x_3), while holding the quality of outputs and prices of inputs constant. The question becomes, what are the likely costs of each output in the case of such joint production of these four outputs? The answer depends in part on the joint utilization of the inputs.

First, consider the production of engineering departments. In this case, if engineering departments employ only three identified inputs, x_1, x_2, and x_3, and do not use any other output (i.e., graduate students) in their production of teaching and research, the costs of each output will be dependent upon the level and the composition of the outputs, and any prospective economies of scale and scope arise from the joint utilization of shared inputs independent of graduate student use in teaching. Therefore, the cost structures of such departments may indicate significant differentiation in the costs of outputs by level and across the engineering departments. For example, graduate students may be more expensive to educate than undergraduates because of smaller class sizes at the graduate level, or engineering departments may have higher marginal costs for their outputs (compared with the social sciences) because of smaller class sizes and higher utilization of equipment and services. Alternatively, we could assume that the engineering departments start to increase the number of their doctoral students and use doctoral students as research assistants for the production of research output, as such departments often do. If we are able to measure research output, we probably will have an increase in research without substantial increases in other inputs or costs. Thus, the natural question becomes, what might be the change in the marginal costs of doctoral level students? It is possible that they could decline!

Consider as a second case the social science departments. In this case the question is essentially the same. What happens to the costs of outputs if such departments utilize doctoral students as teaching assistants, as they often do? Would we still have higher marginal costs for doctoral education? Could there be material differences in terms of the marginal costs of outputs across departments when they are compared according to their utilization of doctoral students? The answers are not clear. De Groot et al. (1991) raised this issue but did not examine it when they found a statistically significant interaction term between undergraduate and doctoral education, suggesting cost complementarity between these two outputs. However, the question of what would be the marginal costs of doctoral level instruction compared with master level instruction or undergraduate education remains to be answered. One likely explanation is that increasing the number of doctoral students and subsequently their employment as teaching and research assistants may, in fact, reduce departmental costs, suggesting lower marginal costs for doctoral students compared with the costs of master or even undergraduate students. On the other hand, an increase in master level students who are not utilized as input in the production of teaching and research, might have a greater negative effect on costs than doctoral level production. Obviously, this line of reasoning about the costs of higher education is intuitively contradictory but applicable when we consider higher education as a multiproduct firm. It deserves much more attention since cost-related funding policies and cost-related tuition policies may provide significant economic benefits for improving internal efficiencies in higher education.

Sources of Multiproduct Economies in Higher Education

A review of the sources of multiproduct economies in the higher education industry will be helpful in understanding the nature and the extent of economies of scale and scope in the higher education industry, and for better understanding the spiraling price of attending a college or university since the early 1970s.

Economies of scale in higher education. With respect to the utilization of inputs and scale economies, departments and institutions are typically characterized by large fixed costs. Expenses for minimum levels of libraries, administration, and academic staffing are necessary for both institutional and departmental production and for maintenance of quality within departmental outputs. The expenses for these minimum levels of inputs may be relatively fixed after a certain level of output; any increase in costs will be dependent upon the output level and composition. This description is based on the assumption that the quality of outputs will not change as the scale increases. If the rate of increase in total costs is less than the rate of growth of the outputs, it is said that there exist ray-economies of scale, suggesting that a college or university will enjoy some degree of internal efficiencies due to an increase in their output levels. This scale economy will largely come about from the presence of their fixed costs.

It should be emphasized that the cost savings due to the presence of scale economies only appear if the quality aspect of the output remains the same. For example, institutions may adapt to variations in the demand for higher education over a relatively short period of time in which the size of their inputs (e.g., faculty, and the like) remains constant. Although increased enrollment may suggest cost-efficiency with respect to a decline in the average cost of teaching, it may also result in a decline in the quality of departmental production with respect to both teaching and research output. As Hoenack and his colleagues (1986) have argued, whether such a decline takes place "depends on the ways that a higher teaching work load fits in with a faculty member's other activities" (p. 336). Obviously, forgone research productivity will incur for amounts of time and personnel effort devoted to instruction. For instance, "the instruction of more undergraduate students may reduce the research outputs of faculty, but research output may be enhanced by additional high quality graduate students working as research assistants. These economic costs of extra students can differ substantially from cost measures obtained by multiplying the number of additional enrollment by the costs per student obtained via accounting formulas" (Hoenack et al., 1986, p. 336).

Economies of scope in higher education. Although there could be economies associated with the scale of operations, there may also be economies associated with the composition of outputs which measure whether there are cost advantages associated with the simultaneous production of many products (Wang, 1981). The diversity of products within a single firm, known as scope, may raise internal efficiency by providing cost advantages in a situation in which a single firm produces a given level of output for each product level while spending less in total than a combination of specialized separate firms. Scope economies may arise when there exist some inputs, networking, and intangible assets which are shared in the production of two or more outputs (Bailey and Friedlaender, 1982). The presence of shared inputs results in multiproduct economies. The sharable inputs which were once employed for the production of one output also would be available (either wholly or in part) to aid in the production of the other outputs (Panzar and Willig, 1979).

In the case of production within higher education institutions, a research university can be viewed as a typical multiproduct firm. Two major types of scope economies can result from the joint production of outputs:

1. Scope economies can arise from the joint production of teaching and research and from the joint production of undergraduate and graduate instruction within a university or single academic unit (i.e., college, school or department).

2. Scope economies can also result from the joint production of a number of subjects and programs between two or more programs (Lewis and Dundar, 1995).

In the first case, in the production of research and graduate education at most universities there is typically joint production and interactive use of graduate students. All public research universities produce three major products, namely teaching, research, and public service through the sharing and joint utilization of their inputs. There is typically shared uses of faculty (via their time on both research and teaching), equipment, library, plant facilities, and other educational inputs. Scope economies arise when individual members of the academic staff diversify their activities rather than specialize in a single output. Economies of scope exist in most research universities because of the direct interaction between research and teaching, the non-linear character of most inputs (e.g., equipment), diminishing returns to specialization (e.g., to the faculty), and because of market imperfections and transaction costs (involving, for example, graduate assistants) (James, 1978, p. 162).

It is often argued that one advantage of American higher education compared with the European higher education model is the presence of cost advantages in the U.S. due to their joint production of teaching and research output. Consequently, any study analyzing the costs of American universities needs to examine their degrees of economies of scope through measurement of the effects of joint production. These forms of scope economies have become the focus of several recent studies in the U.S. (Cohn et al., 1989; de Groot et al., 1991, Nelson and Heverth, 1992; Dundar and Lewis, 1995). They all empirically confirmed the existence of economies of scope in the joint production of undergraduate teaching, graduate studies, and research. Nevertheless, there are some limitations to these findings if we do not control for the quality of outputs. Although the results of several studies indicate that undergraduate and doctoral instruction can be produced more cheaply when combined than when conducted separately, ignoring the quality dimension of instruction will result in biased estimates for economies of both scale and scope. It is commonly agreed, for example, that employment of teaching assistants might influence the quality of undergraduate instruction. Moreover, any answer to the question about whether "the cost to the institution of educating a Ph.D. who has served as a teaching assistant is considerably greater than educating one who has not" is still largely unknown (James, 1978, p. 411).

In the second case, which has not received the attention of any study in the United States, scope economies can arise when universities produce a number of programs and subjects (such as the arts, sciences, social sciences, engineering, and health sciences) jointly rather than separately (Lewis and Dundar, 1995). This type of economies of scope has been the focus of studies for Australian universities (Lloyd et al., 1993) and for U.K. universities (Johnes, 1994). "The source of economies of scope for this case type would be largely depended upon jointly used inputs such as central administration and support services, libraries and laboratories. Additionally, cross-college teaching production could be an important source of such economies because fewer courses would be provided by other colleges within a university instead of employing full-time teaching staff within each college" (Lewis and Dundar, 1995, p.139).

Complementarity of faculty time on academic outputs. The most important input for the joint production of teaching and research outputs is faculty time. Because research and instructional activities of the faculty are not inherently tied together in fixed proportions, faculty time can be considered as a variable input to a variety of academic outputs. As Becker (1979) has argued, faculty must produce teaching, research, and other professional activities through the allocation of their time. The exact mix of faculty time on one activity varies among institutions and departments. The amount of time devoted to one activity affects the production of the other output. However, the direction of the effect is not always clear. Assume, for example, that there will be an increase in teaching loads at the undergraduate level within a given department. The likely result may be a reduction of the faculty's time on research, resulting in an economic cost for the departmental production of research output. The impact can be seen as a shift in product mix resulting in a higher undergraduate teaching/research ratio. The results also may be a lower quantity of research and an increase in the quality of undergraduate instructions. Simply ignoring research output and the quality of other outputs will overstate undergraduate instructional costs and understate the social rate of return resulting from undergraduate education (James, 1978).

Hoenack and his colleagues (1986) have argued that instructional activities can also increase a faculty member's research productivity. They asserted that the benefits of teaching a graduate course depend in part on the individual's personal enjoyment of teaching, which is often greater the closer one's subject matter is to the faculty member's current research interest and activity. They noted that it can also be productive to talk about one's research with interested and intelligent students. The gain from teaching such a course can thus vary with the quality of the enrolled students. Becker (1979) has similarly argued that time spent in discipline-based teaching, such as graduate teaching, may increase the quantity and the quality of the faculty's research. The participation of graduate students in the faculty's research activity is clearly complementary to the production of research. While this complementarity in the production of research might be more defined in the field of engineering or the biological sciences, it is not so clear in the social sciences and humanities since such research usually requires less participation of graduate students in its production.

The joint supply of graduate education and undergraduate instruction is often said to provide complementarity since graduate students can also serve as teaching assistants. Employment of graduate students as an input in the production of undergraduate teaching is often practiced by research universities as an efficiency measure. This hypothesis has been confirmed by recent studies (e.g., de Groot et al., 1991; Dundar and Lewis, 1995) in their analysis of cost structures of American research universities. They found that producing undergraduate and doctoral students together reduces the overall costs of teaching in a given department. However, when the quality of undergraduate instruction is considered as a separate output, then the employment of graduate students as teaching assistants might possibly reduce the quality of undergraduate education and thus suggest that the cost efficiency due to joint production may not be as great as it is often assumed.

Countervailing influences on economies of scope. Countervailing influences on economies of scope in higher education can take place when public and institutional policies prescribe or stimulate the development of independent research institutions outside of departmental or institutional agencies. When graduate teaching takes place independent of opportunities for students to participate in sponsored research activities, such independence precludes both the joint sharing of such costs as well as opportunities for students to gain the skills and experience necessary to conduct such research after their program completions.

Using government-sponsored independent research agencies is especially appealing to countries undergoing economic development. Unfortunately, such sponsorship effectively increases the costs of graduate training and at the same time reduces the effectiveness of future faculty. Often these events take place at the same time that the country is attempting to expand its own higher education institutions with expectations about the increased research capacity of these institutions. The joint production of both graduate education and research has important effects on both costs and outcomes.

Additional countervailing influences on economies of scope arise within the institutions themselves. For example, institutions may elect not to use graduate students, especially doctoral students, in undergraduate instruction as has happened in several countries (Lewis and Dundar, 1995). Such restrictive activities can arise when institutional policies and practices are based on the assumption that graduate students do not have sufficient knowledge or expertise to deliver instruction to undergraduates. These practices, in turn, preclude the joint production of graduate with undergraduate instruction and any prospects for economies of scope. They also prevent any opportunities for graduate student instructional training as well.

Finally, countervailing influences on economies of scope arise when different departmental or collegiate faculties do not join together in the offering of common courses. Such cross-department and cross-college teaching production is often precluded because the respective faculty perceive a loss of student control or instructional quality taking place. Often, this lack of interdepartmental curricular planning takes place simply because of institutional inertia or historical tradition. Limiting strategic and curricular planning only to self-contained instructional units is not only dysfunctional for prospective economies of scope and contributes to enhanced costs, but it also limits the breadth and experiences of students.

THEORETICAL FRAMEWORK FOR COST STUDIES IN HIGHER EDUCATION

The conceptual framework for cost functions comes from past studies in institutional microeconomics. The theory of cost concepts in the case of multiproduct firms and organizations has been well developed during the past two decades, with applications to a large number of industries including higher education. This subsection provides a brief review of the econometric theory of the costs and measurements of economies of scale and scope with a particular focus on higher education.

Cost Functions

The cost function is considered to be a classical concept in economic theory for studying the economic behavior of a firm. Typically, the cost function is defined as a relationship between costs and outputs, in which total costs are a function of a set of outputs that give the least cost of producing a level of output (y) when factor prices are given (p). A typical cost function can be defined as

$$(1) \qquad C(y) = (y,p)$$

where $C(y)$ represents the total costs of producing a vector of output y, and p is a vector of the prices of inputs. Since the prices of the factors (e.g., mainly wages in the case of higher education) that the firm employs will affect the total costs, the prices of factors are also entered into the model. Since costs are viewed as being dependent on the levels and prices of inputs of the production process, this function is often described as

(2) $C = (\mathbf{x}, \mathbf{p})$

where C is the total cost of producing a given level of output y, $\mathbf{x}$ $(x_1,\dots,x_n)$ is a vector of input quantities, and $\mathbf{p}$ is a vector of the prices of factors, $x_1,\dots,x_n$ respectively (Varian, 1990). For a profit- or efficiency-maximizing organization of any sort, the goal is to minimize the cost of producing a given output or maximize the output derived from a given level of cost. If inputs are substitutable in production, a cost for a given level of output can be minimized after examining different combinations of x's. On the other hand, since the inputs, x_1, will be dependent upon the output vector, y, the cost function can also be described as a function of y, x_1, and their prices, $\mathbf{p}$

(3) $C = f(\mathbf{x}, \mathbf{y}, \mathbf{p})$.

An analysis of the structures of costs by equation (2) is appropriate only if there is a single output. Thus, as the work of Baumol et al. (1982) and a number of other empirical studies since the early 1980s have demonstrated, this conventional measure of a single-product cost function and the concept of scale economies based upon these functions do not accurately describe the cost structures of multiproduct firms and will produce misleading conclusions. In the case of multiproduct production, this concept does not provide much insight regarding scale economies. In the case of multiple outputs, the generalized model of the costs becomes

(4) $C = (\mathbf{y}, \mathbf{p}\}$

where C represents the total costs, y is a vector of outputs, and $\mathbf{p}$ is a vector of the prices of inputs.

Describing total cost. In examining institutional costs in higher education, the dependent variable for the total cost model includes all the costs for the (departmental or organizational) production of teaching and research. In this regard, many studies have followed procedures used in other similar studies through the use of institutional expenditures as the costs of higher education. Costs to students are excluded since our focus is on departmental and institutional cost comparisons. The typical costs of the departments include faculty and support salaries, computer and equipment expenditures, and unrestricted research funding. The costs of central administration, library, and the other maintenance and operations are excluded when examining only departmental profiles. Restricted research funding for organized and sponsored research are also often excluded. For example, total departmental costs could be described as the costs of all inputs employed for the production of y in a given academic year in the ith department, and could be noted as

(6) $C = \sum_i C_i, \ i = 1, \dots, 5$

where C_i is the total cost of employing the ith input. The cost of departmental inputs could be specified as

C_1 = annual total faculty wages and fringe benefits in the ith department.
C_2 = annual salaries and fringe benefits of support staff in the ith department.
C_3 = annual expenditure for services and supplies in the ith department.
C_4 = annual expenditure for equipment in the ith department.
C_5 = annual expenditure for computers in the ith department.

Identifying outputs. All of the multiproduct cost studies in higher education have concentrated only on the teaching and research outputs of higher education institutions. Although the importance of other outputs relating to public service and outreach have been generally recognized, the studies could find no reliable measure for this output dimension. Student-credit hours at three teaching levels (i.e., undergraduate, master, and doctoral) are recommended and should be used as proxies for teaching output for each academic year. With respect to research output, the most reliable proxy has been the number of articles produced by each department in an academic year. It is generally assumed that the research output produced is largely a result of departmental and internally funded activities, rather than organized and externally funded research production. Thus, the four outputs for cost functions could be noted as follows:

y_1 = annual undergraduate student-credit hours in the ith department.
y_2 = annual master student credit-hours in the ith department.
y_3 = annual doctoral student credit-hours in the ith department.
y_4 = the number of publications in the ith department.

The utilization of student credit hours as proxies for the teaching outputs of each department has a noteworthy implication from the point of view of departments. As noted above, in most studies the number of students or graduates has been used as a proxy for educational outputs. Because these latter data on head counts are specific to individuals who register in a particular department and do not measure the departmental resources spent for the cross-departmental production of teaching, the cost estimates for the departmental production of teaching output are likely to be distorted. Therefore, student-credit hours produced by each department are a more accurate proxy for teaching.

Addressing the quality of outputs. It is assumed that there exist differences in the quality of outputs produced by departments. A quality variable about graduate programs in the U.S. can be obtained from the National Research Council's studies on research-doctorate programs (Goldberger et al., 1995) and used in order to control for the quality effect on departmental costs. The judgments of peers in every field on the effectiveness of the program in educating research scholars/scientists could be used as a proxy for the quality of graduate education in the ith department.

It is often observed that public research universities may have differentiation in their quality of undergraduate and graduate products. For example, public research universities may have an open-access policy at the undergraduate level, while competing to obtain the best and most able students into their graduate programs. This paradox has resulted in more variation in the quality of products at public higher education institutions than at private research universities.

The selectivity of institutions at the undergraduate level can be tested through the use of a proxy measure for the quality of the undergraduate teaching product. One could obtain undergraduate selectivity indexes of institutions, for example, from Barron's Profiles of Colleges and Universities (1986). Nevertheless, if the sample of institutions selected for the study is relatively homogeneous then it is likely that these undergraduate quality indexes may not discriminate well across the institutions.

Economies of Scale

The conventional concept of economies of scale indicates the reduction in the average cost of a product or a product-set as the level of output expands in the long run. Economies of scale are said to exist if total cost increases proportionately less than output. Findings of economies of scale are represented in several ways in the literature. The most common have been noted by Brinkman and Leslie (1987) as "the shape of the average and marginal cost curves, the difference between average and marginal costs, the sign and magnitude of correlation or regression coefficients, and unit costs in relation to size intervals" (p. 5).

The most conventional way to estimate for economies of scale is to examine the relationship of average costs to marginal costs (see Figure 1, 148). As noted above, assuming that the prices of inputs (p) do not vary significantly, a total cost function is defined as $c = C(Y)$, where Y is a number representing aggregate output, and C is the total cost for producing that amount of output. From this function, average cost [AC] and marginal cost [MC] are defined as $C(Y)/Y$. and ($\partial C / \partial y$) respectively. Since AC will decrease as long as MC is less than AC, scale economies are measured as $S = AC / MC$, which also gives the elasticity of cost with respect to output. When scale elasticity becomes $s \geq 1$ or $s \leq 1$ economies or diseconomies of scale, respectively, are said to exist (Bailey and Friedlaender, 1982).

In the case of a multiproduct setting, Baumol and his colleagues (1982) make a distinction between two different types of economies of scale. First, *ray-economies of scale* indicates the reduction in average costs relative to marginal costs when a composition of output is assumed to remain fixed while its size is allowed to vary. This concept is analogous to economies of scale in single-product firms, and measures overall economies of scale. Ray economies of scale are generated by the existence of fixed costs (α_0); however, as outputs expand, diseconomies of scale become evident at some point (Mayo, 1984). The ray average cost of producing the output vector is defined to be $C(\mathbf{y}) / \sum_{j=1}^{n} y_j$. The ray represents composite output and the behavior of ray average costs is like the case of the single output. Ray economies of scale are defined over the entire output set, N = {1,...,n), at **y**, and are noted by

$$(7) \qquad S_N = \frac{C(y)}{\sum_{i=1}^{n} y_i C_i(y)}$$

where $C_i(y) = \partial C(\mathbf{y}) / \partial y_i$ and represents the marginal cost of producing the ith output. In other words, in the case of multiproduct production, the marginal cost of output is given by

$$(8) \qquad MC_i = \partial C(y)/\partial y_i = \alpha_i + \sum_j a_{ij}(y_j - \bar{y}_j) \quad .$$

While each α_i indicates the marginal costs of output type i (evaluated at the sample output mean), α_{ij} indicates changes in the marginal cost with respect to output type i. Since in a multiproduct cost function α_{ij} coefficients can be either positive or negative, negative estimates for marginal costs are also possible (Friedlaender, Winston, and Wang, 1983).

Ray economies (diseconomies) of scale are said to exist if S_N is greater (less) than unity. S_N is interpreted as the elasticity of the outputs of the relevant composite outputs with respect to the cost needed to produce them (Baumol et al., 1988, pp. 50-51). Increasing the level of production for each output from the mean level would result in an increase in cost-efficiency. From the estimated coefficients of a multiproduct cost function, the degrees of economies of scale at a given point of production can be computed.

Second, *product-specific economies of scale* for output i, (S_i) indicates the reduction in average costs relative to marginal costs for each of the outputs. The existence of product-specific economies of scale is said to exist when one element of a vector of output is changed and the composition of the other outputs remain fixed. An elasticity of economies of scale can measure how costs change as the output and composition of commodities changes. This second dimension of economies of scale is referred to as product-specific economies of scale. Ray economies of scale assume that output is expanded proportionally along a ray emanating from the origin. However, the magnitude of a multiproduct firm's operations may change through variation in the output of one product, holding the quantities of other products constant. Therefore the product-specific expansion in a product set becomes an important feature of multiproduct cost concepts. The incremental cost of a multiproduct firm for producing an additional output i is noted by

$$(9) \qquad IC(y_i) = C(y_N) - C(y_{N-i})$$

where $IC(y_i)$ denotes the total cost of producing all of the multiproduct firm's outputs, excluding the ith one. From this concept we compute the average incremental cost [*AIC*] due to additional production of the ith output as follows:

$$(10) \qquad AIC(y_i) = [C(y_N) - C(y_{N-1})] / y_i = IC(y_i) / y_i.$$

Returns to scale that are specific to a particular output can be derived from the above specification as

$$(11) \qquad S_i(y) = AIC(y_i) / C_i(y) = AIC_i / MC_i$$

where S_i is the elasticity of the product-specific economies (diseconomies) of scale, AIC_i is the average incremental cost for the product i, and MC_i is the marginal cost for the product i. If $S_i \geq 1$ or $S_i \leq 1$, economies or diseconomies of scale are said to exist for the product i. Increasing the level of production for each output with the presence of economies of scale would result in cost advantages. In the production of teaching and research output, if there exist some product-specific fixed costs, then we would expect that product specific economies of scale would exist. The existence of such economies for product i suggest that an increase in the level of output i would result in cost efficiency.

Economies of Scope

The presence or absence of complementarity between outputs in production becomes a crucial matter in the case of multiproduction. This concept is quite new, appearing first in the papers of Baumol (1977), and Panzar and Willig (1975, 1979), and has been introduced as a complement to the older concept of "economies of scale". Economies of scope measures "the cost advantages to firms of producing a large number of diversified products as against specializing in the production of a single output" (Bailey and Friedlaender, 1982, p. 1025). Two types of scope economies are distinguished as either global or product-specific scope economies.

Global-economies of scope (S_G) simply measure whether the cost of producing two or more products jointly will be less than the cost of producing them separately. If $S_G \geq 0$, global economies of scope are said to exist and the cost of producing a bundle of outputs jointly is less than the cost of producing them separately. Complementarities in the production of the university's multiple outputs while using a set of shared inputs result in scope economies. Weak global economies (diseconomies) of scope are present when

(12) $C(y) \leq (\geq) C(y_{N-t}) + C(y_t)$

where $C(y_t)$ is the cost of producing the product set t, and $C(y_{N-t})$ is the cost of producing all products but those in the product set t. The degree of economies of scope is given for a product set t by

(13) $SC_G = [C(y_t) + C(y_{n-t}) - C(y)] / C(y)$

where SC_G denotes the degree of global economies of scope. If $SC_G \geq 0$ then cost advantages accrue for producing the output bundles jointly.

Global economies of scope in higher education production suggest that a single institution (or a department) can produce a given bundle of outputs less costly than specialized teaching or research institutions, each producing smaller output levels with the same proportions. In the four-product case of our illustration, global economies of scope exist with respect to the product sets of y_1, y_2, y_3, and y_4 (i.e., undergraduate, master level, doctorate level, and research, respectively) if

(14) $C(y_1, y_2, y_3, y_4) \leq C(y_1,0,0,0) + C(0,y_2,0,0) + C(0,0,y_3,0) + C(0,0,0,y_4)$

The degree of global-economies of scope S_G, can be noted as

(15) $S_G = \dfrac{y_1,0,0,0) + C(0,y_2,0,0) + C(0,0,y_3,0) + C(0,0,0,y_4) - C(y_1,y_2,y_3,.}{C(y_1,y_2,y_3,y_4)}$

If SG is equal to or less than 0, then there will be cost advantages in producing the output set jointly rather than separately.

There also may be some cost advantages due to production of each output jointly with the other outputs.

Product-specific economies of scope (SC_i) measure whether it would cost less to produce output type i separately and the remaining types in combination than to produce all product types together (Wang Chiang and Friedlaender, 1985, p. 253). If $SC_i \geq 0$, associated with output type i, then the production of i with the combination of the other products will be more efficient. If this is the case, then the joint production of one of the outputs (say undergraduate instruction) with the others is an efficient way to produce, rather than to produce the output independently. Thus, the degree of product-specific economies of scope (SC_i) measures the proportional increase or decrease in costs from producing all of the outputs except the ith product. Product-specific economies of scope can be noted as

(16) $SC_i = [C(y_i) + C(y_{n-i}) - C(y)] / C(y)$

where $C(y_{n-i})$ represents the total costs of producing all the outputs jointly except the ith one. Product-specific economies of scope are said to exist if $SC_i \geq 0$, indicating cost advantages for producing the ith output jointly with the other products. Thus, there will be cost advantages to producing outputs simultaneously, resulting largely from the existence of common fixed costs.

In the case of a department conducting both instruction and research production, how can we specify the existence of product specific economies of scope? Since a typical department in a research university produces various levels of outputs and appears to have product-specific economies of scale associated with these outputs in all disciplines, it is important to ask whether economies of scope are associated with the production of each type of output. Suppose, for example, that some departments were to specialize and only produce research and others were to produce only a combination of all teaching outputs, could we expect there would be cost savings from such a specialization? The answer to such a question could be found if we examine the cost effect of the existence of separate research centers or institutes within research universities. If such research units within universities were allowed to exist with separate inputs to produce only research outputs while academic departments were focused on the teaching outputs, the question of efficiency from such a specialization could be answered. The question can also be addressed by estimating the product-specific scope economies associated with the production of research output. In the case of four outputs, product-specific economies of scope associated with y_1 exists, for example, if

(17) $C(y_1,y_2,y_3,y_4) \leq C(y_1,0,0,0) + C(0,y_2,y_3,y_4)$

and the degree of product-specific scope economies is written as

$$(18) SC_i = \frac{'(y_1,0,0,0) + C(0,y_2,y_3,y_4) - C(y_1,y_2,y_3,y_4)}{C(y_1,y_2,y_3,y_4)}$$

where SC_i represents the scope economies for y_1. Cost advantages accrue to the department producing y_1 jointly with another product if $SC_i \geq 0$.

Cost Complementarities

With respect to the joint supply of the outputs, cost function interaction terms can also provide some important insights about the existence of cost complementarities in the joint production of the outputs. For a twice continuously differentiable cost function, weak cost complementarities between two products i and j are said to be present at y' if

(19) $\partial^2 C(y') / \partial y_i \partial y_j \leq 0, \quad i \neq j.$

As an example, we report in Table 2 the results from a recent Dundar and Lewis (1995) study to illustrate the signs of the cost complementarities between four outputs for each of three fields. While the positive signs imply discomplementarities, the negative signs imply possible cost complementarities. Comparisons of cost complementarities in the production of the four outputs within the three disciplines examined in this particular study provide observations regarding the possible existence of joint supply effects in the production of multiple outputs.

Table 2. Cost Complementarities between Departmental Outputs

Fields	y_1y_2	y_1y_3	y_1y_4	y_2y_3	y_2y_4	y_3y_4
Social Sciences	-	-	-	+	+	+
Physical Sciences	+	+	+	-	+	-
Engineering	-	+	-	-	+	-

Note: The sign of the cost-complementarity between output y_i and output y_j is indicated by the sign of $C_{ij} = \partial^2 C(y) / \partial y_i \partial y_j$. For a four-output model we have (y_1, y_2, y_3, y_4) = (Undergraduate, Master, Doctorate, Research), respectively.

A particularly important question is whether the utilization of doctoral students in the joint production of outputs results in any efficiencies. For example, it is commonly known that departments in the social sciences utilize more graduate students to teach at the undergraduate level, while departments in physical sciences and engineering may utilize graduate students more as research assistants. Do these academic departments achieve cost savings due to such joint production of outputs?

Although such a theory has long been argued, there is little empirical support regarding cost complementarities of such utilization of graduate students in the various disciplines. A recent study by de Groot et al. (1991) argued that such cost complementarity existed between graduate education and undergraduate education. However, little is known about whether such a joint supply effect actually exists for each discipline. This question can be answered by examining interaction terms of the cost functions for each discipline. Such results should illustrate the degree to which various forms of cost complementarities might exist between outputs for each discipline.

Utilization of doctoral students as teaching assistants is a widespread phenomenon in research universities, in particularly social science departments, and this is, indeed, cost effective. In Table 2, the negative sign of y_1, y_3 illustrates that there *does* exists a joint supply effect for producing undergraduate and doctoral students in the social sciences. Producing these two outputs jointly provides cost savings for departments in the social sciences. These findings are consistent with findings from previous studies at the institutional level (Cohn et al., 1989; de Groot et al., 1991). De Groot et al. (1991) explained that such cost savings were obtained by employing graduate students as teaching assistants at a relatively low price. However, Dundar and Lewis (1995) in their departmental study did not find such a cost complementarity between undergraduate teaching and doctoral teaching (i.e., y_1, y_3) in the physical sciences and engineering, suggesting that these departments do not use graduate students as much as social science departments in the production of their undergraduate teaching.

Regarding the general assumption that graduate education is complementary to research, as reported by the interaction term (i.e., y_3, y_4) for doctoral studies and research in Table 2, the findings indicate that such complementarity does not exist with respect to costs between the two outputs in social science departments. This sign is both positive and statistically significant. On the other hand, such complementarity was found in the physical sciences and engineering. These findings are important because it is often assumed that the marginal cost of producing one product decreases when the quantity of the other product is increased. The reason for this assumption is that faculty can use graduate students as research assistants. As noted above, Hoenack et al. (1986) also make the argument that higher quality students may enhance the research productivity of the faculty due to students participating in faculty research activities (p. 345). Cohn et al. (1989) and de Groot et al. (1991) reported similar findings at the institutional level for the cost complementarity between production of research and graduate instruction, but they did not differentiate by fields. The findings by Dundar and Lewis (1995) indicate that such cost complementarity is field specific and not true across all fields.

In social science departments faculty apparently prefer to produce research more by themselves, and utilize fewer graduate students in the production of research output. The engineering or physical science departments, on the other hand, require closer collaboration between faculty and graduate students in their research production. Production of doctoral students and research output jointly in these two disciplines results in cost advantages.

In summary, our review of the theoretical foundations of the production and costs of higher education suggests that the failure of most past studies to analyze the costs structures of higher education by adjusting for their multiproduct nature has apparently resulted in biased, if not misleading, conclusions regarding costs and economies of scale and scope. Even those studies that examined only instructional costs and found that costs differ by level and across departments (without also adjusting for their multiproduct nature) should be interpreted with caution. We can only conclude that, despite formidable data problems, examining the cost structures of higher education while using micro level data and new multiproduct cost concepts will provide better estimates for such costs.

Issues and Limitations of Cost Analysis in Higher Education

In spite of the increasing number of empirical studies estimating cost functions in higher education, a number of methodological shortcomings still exist in the field.

Unclear definitions of costs. In many cases, the definition of cost is not clear. There exist many kinds of costs and costs can be estimated in many ways (Brinkman and Leslie, 1986; Halstead, 1991). For example, Adams, Hankins, and Schroeder (1978) provide a list of different definitions of the costs of higher education. Costs can be calculated as input or output, historical or projected, direct or indirect, total, average, or marginal, fixed or variable and so on. Because cost function studies deal with the estimation of relationships between costs and outputs, the most frequently used direct costs are those that are immediately related to a cost objective or full costs, and are the sum of direct and indirect costs. These costs are generally derived from institutional expenditures records (Brinkman and Allen, 1986). As such, some costs such as forgone earnings are always excluded because they are usually beyond the scope of these type of studies.

Black-box production functions. The production function of higher education is still largely a "black-box." It is not explicitly known which inputs and what kind of technical requirements are necessary for producing optimum outputs in order to derive a mathematically sound cost function (Brinkman and Leslie, 1986; Gilmore, 1990; Hopkins, 1990). In light of the difficulties in dealing with costs, a common approach has been to use statistically best fitting techniques in order to find an appropriate functional form (Cohn and Geske, 1990; Brinkman, 1990). Therefore, the definition and choice of cost function plays a critical role in providing more reliable information with respect to the cost structure of higher education institutions.

This notion of ill-defined production functions in higher education has been noted by several writers on the topic (Dolan, Jung, and Schmidt, 1993; Cohn and Geske, 1990). Conflict can arise because it is unclear what functional form should be used in order to estimate the best generalized cost function. As noted by Cohn and Geske (1990), the correct theoretical functional form of costs in higher education cannot be determined since relatively little is known about the shape of most institutional production functions. As such, a number of studies estimating the cost functions of higher education institutions have used either very different forms of cost functions from previous studies or have estimated a number of cost function forms in order to derive the best curve-fitting form from available data.

Outcomes are not clearly defined. The outputs and outcomes of education are typically not clearly defined and measured. The four most commonly expected outputs of higher education institutions are undergraduates, graduate education, research (such as producing new knowledge or applying existing or produced knowledge) and public services. However, there are no clear-cut measures to indicate the quality and quantity of these outputs. Despite the fact that value-added measures for teaching and research outputs (such as the added knowledge and skills of students and the effects of research in extending knowledge and enhancing technology) are most desired, it is very difficult, if not impossible, to obtain direct measures characterizing the outputs of higher education institutions. Accordingly, almost all studies have employed either only approximate or proxy variables for teaching and research outputs. Because this makes it very problematic to find a direct relationship between costs and outputs and to test it empirically, the models in these types of studies are often considered as "surrogate functions" (Sengupta, 1975). The lack of certain data regarding the quality of outputs, non-budgeted research output, and non-budgeted public service output further precludes the use of qualitative measures for higher education institutions (Smith, 1978).

Higher education does not minimize costs. A fourth problem area is related to the fact that most higher education institutions as non-profit organizations may *not* work to minimize their costs. This results from the fact that not only the quantity of outputs, but also their qualities are desirable outputs (James, 1978; James and Rose-Ackerman, 1986; Bowen, 1981). It is often argued that, rather than minimizing their costs, higher education institutions spend all their available revenue for the sake of increasing quality and prestige (Bowen, 1981; Galvin, 1981). Colleges and universities have limited incentives to reduce costs in quest of profit since profit is not their goal. They are not forced by competitors to reduce their costs in order to survive. This behavior is partly a result of funding by government and philanthropy and partly because they are protected from competition by geographic location and by diversification of services. It is also because institutions know little about the relationship between their expenditures and their educational outcomes, and it is also a belief that increased expenditures will automatically produce commensurably greater outcomes with higher quality (Bowen, 1981, p.15).

In order to control costs, numerous funding methods have been implemented. Some states have tried to regulate educational activities and expenditures in great detail. Line-item appropriations and detailed supervision by the state is a result of such interest in controlling costs. However, as many have later realized, excessively detailed financial control brings about a false efficiency and threatens institutional autonomy in academic decisions. For the small sum saved due to such budgeting, the much greater efficiency resulting from local initiative and common sense is constrained and discouraged.

Bowen (1981) defined this economic behavior of higher education institutions as a "revenue theory of costs," at least in the short run. Although Brinkman (1990) has argued that this explanation for the cost behavior of higher education institutions has some validity, it is probably an overstatement without substantial empirical evidence. Verry (1987) has observed that "the assumption that education institutions act as cost minimizers is not absurd; after all the teachers and administrators in such institutions do have certain objectives and are constrained by limited resources, so that departures from cost minimization imply that whatever objectives are being pursued will not be attained to the full extent possible" (p. 408). Therefore, most observers would agree that higher education institutions neither minimize nor maximize their costs, and "the true relationship between costs and outputs in higher education institutions must await improved models of the behavior of nonprofit organizations" (Verry, 1987, p. 408). Our lack of understanding about cost minimization requires one to be very careful in arriving at definitive conclusions, and in interpreting results as being approximate rather than actual representations of cost minimization principles.

Selection of unit of analysis can be problematic. The selection of the unit of analysis can be a serious limitation. While the relationship between costs and outputs in higher education can be examined from a broader perspective (i.e., college or university) or from a narrower perspective (i.e., department or faculty work groups), the department as the unit of production seems to be most appropriate because it is the basic decision making unit in research universities. Departments are the locus of inputs and outputs affiliation and the accounting unit for most academic expenditures in a university. Thus, a cost function for the production of teaching and research for a department or departments in a field (e.g., social science, engineering, and the like) in a number of universities (i.e., cross-sectional analysis) or a department in a university for a period of time (i.e., time-series analysis) should be estimated. Using this methodology, as Verry (1987) has noted, central costs can be allocated to individual departments.

Although both Cohn et al. (1989) and de Groot et al. (1991) used institutions as the unit of analysis for their cost functions, previous studies have found that such cost functions vary significantly across disciplines in relation to outputs. Tierney (1980), Nelson and Heverth (1992), and Lewis and Dundar (1995) all justified their positions when they employed departments as their unit of analyses by noting that departments are the fundamental producing units of colleges and universities. For example, decisions regarding curriculum, academic standards, and the recruitment and promotion of faculty are generally made at the departmental level. In addition, departments are relatively autonomous despite an increase in their interdependencies in a time of decreasing organizational slack. The most important problem seems to be that different production functions between academic disciplines is likely to generate problems in analyzing cost functions across departments. For example, the results may be misleading if a single cost function is estimated for both a chemistry and an English department, because they have quite dissimilar production processes. Departments, as the fundamental organizational units of colleges and universities, are relatively autonomous, make decisions on the curriculum, determine academic degree standards, and recruit and promote faculty. Even if a multiproduct cost analysis at the institutional level provides important insights about existing economies of scale and scope between institutions, it has little to offer policy makers at the institutional level because of the differing production processes of each department.

Differences in the quality of outputs are problematic. Differences in the quality of outputs can result in biased estimates of the costs of higher education. However, the quality of educational experience or research outputs cannot be easily measured.The quality of an educational environment for students that requires teachers, facilities, equipment, programs, services and the mixture of these educational resources clearly affects the quality of its teaching output (Gilmore, 1990). Nerlove (1972) emphasized the importance of measuring quality differences in outputs across institutions or disciplines to obtain reliable results in a multiple-product production function. Even the recent multiple-product cost function studies by Cohn et al. (1989), de Groot et al. (1991), Nelson and Heverth (1992), and Lewis and Dundar (1995) have been criticized for their lack of attention to quality concerns. Quality of teaching is of particular concern.

Over two decades ago, Nerlove (1972) asked, "Can…quality differences be quantified…among different types of institutions?" (p. 215). Then, the answer was no. Two decades later, Massy (1990) still remarked that there were no data representing a useful measure of quality differences in teaching between programs and institutions (p. 18). How, then, can cost functions be generalized to include them?

Although infrequently used, there are several ways for measuring the quality of teaching. First, the opinion of the faculty about other institutions may be a partial proxy for the quality of teaching at various levels. Such studies called "reputational-quality" measures have been used since the work of Cartter (1966) on the assessment of graduate education. Jones, Lindzey, and Coggeshall (1982) provided a comprehensive reputational rating of graduate education in a select number of programs among research universities. Recently, Goldberger et al. (1995) have also provided a similar reputational survey of doctoral programs. The major weakness of these studies for the purpose of providing data with respect to teaching is their focus only on the quality of graduate education. It can be argued that the quality of graduate education does not necessarily reflect the quality of undergraduate education since the inputs used for both products may often vary considerably. We still lack a comprehensive reputational study on the quality of undergraduate education in research universities.

A recent study by Gilmore (1990) is an advancement for finding a measure for the quality of undergraduate education, and it seems to be helpful for measuring the impact of the quality of undergraduate education on costs. Gilmore developed an "educational progress" variable, which is a composite of freshman GPA, sophomore retention, and graduation rates, to specify institutional characteristics and the structural elements that can explain institutional impact and performance on student outcomes.

Public service is often ignored. Public service is often seen as one of the three main functions and outputs of higher education institutions, and 10-20 percent of the total budget is often spent on it. Even so, none of the studies reviewed has ever employed a measure or even an estimate for public service output. Public service is an especially important segment of public research universities. Although, the importance of the public service function of research universities is often acknowledged (e.g., de Groot et al., 1991), all existing cost function studies in higher education excluded public service because there was no apparent way to measure its output. It should be kept in mind that failure to account for differences in public service across departments and institutions undoubtedly leads to biased estimates of costs.

Other limitations and problematic issues. Beyond the limitations mentioned above in the application of the cost concepts to higher education, a number of additional problematic issues emerge pertinent to the data and estimation of almost all of the models in each of the studies reviewed. For example, Dundar and Lewis (1995) noted two likely sampling errors. First, in their American sample they drew their data disproportionally from research-oriented universities. Although this may be seen as a problem of selection bias, it is also one of the strengths of the study because such a detailed examination of more homogeneous institutions in terms of their production technology (or quality) may provide important insights about the cost structures of these types of institutions. Second, their sample included only the 18 research institutions that were members of AAUDE. Exclusion of other member universities which did not report the necessary data for the 1985-1986 academic year and other nonmember research oriented institutions may also contribute to a sampling bias. Caution should also be given to interpreting their results, since no attempt was made to control for and analyze the costs of inputs shared by all the department fields in their study (e.g., central administration, libraries, buildings, central computer centers, and the like).

Although it is readily acknowledged that there are still a number of unresolved theoretical and data problems in defining the measurement of the outputs and efficient cost structures of higher education institutions, we also side with other researchers who have suggested that any enhanced understanding of the economic behavior of higher education institutions will necessarily be advanced in small steps (Verry, 1987; Dolan et al., 1993). Fortunately, recent estimates of production functions as well as cost functions now receive relatively more attention with increasingly available data in terms of outputs and inputs (Massy, 1990). Baumol et al. (1982) discussed three promising multiproduct cost functions: the translog function, the quadratic cost function, and the constant elasticity of substitution multiproduct cost function. The quadratic cost function was employed by Cohn et al. (1989), Dundar and Lewis (1995), and Lewis and Dundar (1995), the translog cost function was employed by de Groot et al. (1991) and Nelson and Heverth (1992), and Johnes (1997) used a constant elasticity of substitution type of cost function.

The models employed in almost all higher education cost studies do not control for any prospective differences in factor prices. It has been argued that the absence of any uniform and exogenously provided set of prices for the inputs and outputs of higher education makes it difficult to capture cost differences due to the price effect of the inputs and outputs (Hopkins, 1990). On the other hand, the main ingredients for departmental production in research universities are the faculty and administrative staff. Since the national labor market for faculty and administrators at the top public research universities is very competitive, wages are highly correlated with average (research) productivity. Therefore, price measures are almost always omitted in higher education cost functions wherein it is assumed that wages corrected by productivity differences are essentially constant across institutions. The prices of other purchased goods and services are almost never included due to their alleged small share of nonlabor costs as a part of variable costs.

REVIEW OF THE EVIDENCE ON COST EFFECTS

Although the literature on cost analysis in higher education goes back as far as a study by Stevens and Elliot (1925), and a number of studies have accumulated over the past two decades with the appearance of statistically estimated cost functions, there has been relatively little quantitative analysis of the nature of higher education cost functions associated with multiple production. Some empirical findings from previous cost studies in higher education have been provided by Allen and Brinkman (1983), Brinkman and Leslie (1987), Brinkman (1990), Hoenack (1990), Cohn and Geske (1990), and Olson (1996); but these findings need to be updated especially in light of the more recent multiproduct studies.

In general, cost functions can be seen to provide information in many ways regarding the costs of higher education to improve internal efficiency and to plan the growth of higher education. Nonetheless, most previous studies have concentrated almost exclusively on two important roles of cost functions: To estimate the presence and the extent of economies (or diseconomies) of scale and to determine the marginal costs of teaching—e.g., the number of students or the number of student credit hours (Allen and Brinkman, 1983; Nelson and Heverth, 1992). The focus of recent cost-function studies utilizing multiproduct cost concepts also have been on unit and marginal costs, but in addition they have attempted to address prospective concerns about economies of scale and analysis of expected economies resulting from the joint production of several outputs wherein they could assess for economies of scope. Accordingly, our review of findings is based on the employment of cost functions to study the existence and magnitude of (a) marginal costs, (b) economies of scale, and (c) economies of scope in higher education.

Marginal Costs in Higher Education

There has been a particular interest in estimating the unit and marginal cost of outputs in higher education for financing higher education since in many states a large amount of unrestricted revenue in higher education is tied to students (either through state appropriation or tuition and fees). As noted by Allen and Brinkman (1983), the marginal cost of an additional output (i.e., per student or student credit hour) has been the most widely used type of cost analysis in higher education.

Cost functions typically are used to estimate both marginal and average costs that are critical in determining the costs of instruction by level of instruction and across departments, colleges and institutions. Additionally, estimating marginal costs (*MC*) and average costs (*AC*) can provide information about the existence and extent of economies of scale in a production unit. If a ratio of *AC/MC* is greater than one, there is an indication of prospective economies of scale, suggesting that an increase in the amount of output would be cost-efficient. Similarly, if a ratio of *AC/MC* is less than one, then there are prospective diseconomies of scale, suggesting a decrease in the amount of output for achieving cost-savings. As a result, most cost function studies in higher education have attempted to estimate both the average and marginal costs of teaching.

Most previous studies have indicated that unit costs of instruction differ by (a) level of instruction and (b) across academic fields (Allen and Brinkman, 1983; Berg and Hoenack, 1987). As noted by Nelson and Heverth (1992) and summarized in their findings of earlier cost studies, graduate students may be more expensive to educate than undergraduates, and upper level undergraduates may be more expensive than lower level undergraduates, despite the existence of a large variation in the magnitude of many cost estimates. Higher costs of graduate education are attributed largely to the fact that graduate programs have smaller class sizes and require the use of more expensive inputs.

With respect to variations of costs between the fields, the departments which involve laboratory classes have higher costs than departments that do not. Moreover, most studies have concluded that there is a difference between the marginal costs of arts and social sciences at both undergraduate and graduate levels and those of engineering and physical sciences. Brovender (1974), for example, estimated the determination of marginal costs of teaching by using linear cost functions at a large public research university. Two linear models were estimated, one for aggregated total credits for lower-level, upper level undergraduate and graduate credits, and a second model for desegregated graduate and undergraduate enrollments. The unit of analysis was academic programs and was defined as a "final degree conferred on the student upon graduation, conceptually many departments participate in each program" (Brovender, 1974, p. 657). Two important conclusions were derived from his estimation of cost functions for the humanities, natural sciences, and social sciences. First, marginal program costs per credit hour were substantially lower than those of most programs' average costs. Second, humanities had the lowest cost, social sciences were the most expensive, and the natural sciences were intermediate (Brovender, 1974, p. 663). Brinkman (1990) has speculated that the unusually high costs in the social science departments probably resulted from the fact that enrollments in the social sciences were very high at that time in history and it was likely that such departments had little unused capacity.

One of the more noteworthy studies includes an estimate by Tierney (1980) of departmental costs through the use of quadratic cost functions. His analysis is one of the few studies that employed longitudinal data for estimating cost functions. Seven academic departments at 31 selected private liberal arts colleges were examined. He argued that colleges and universities have a limited ability to alter inputs and the technological conditions of the production process. Therefore, a long-run cost function ought to include a reasonable period of time so that all departmental inputs can be varied. On the basis of this assumption, he pointed out that a long-run cost function may be longer than one year but it is considerably shorter than the life span of tenured faculty. In an empirical implementation of his non-linear regression model, longitudinal data for a four year period, 1972-1973 through 1975-76, were examined. The only variable Tierney employed as a measure of output was total full-time equivalent students as a combination of undergraduate and graduate students in each department. One of the significant features of the study was the inclusion of a measure of departmental quality in order to control for cost differences that were unrelated to output differences among the departments. The results of Tierney's study indicated that all departmental marginal costs were less than average costs, which also indicated that there existed prospective economies of scale. Estimated departmental marginal and average costs varied significantly across the departments.

Verry and Davies (1976), by using a number of different cost functions, also found that there exist wide differences between departmental marginal costs in the production of British universities. For six departments they found marginal costs for undergraduate education varying from £120 in mathematics to £450 in engineering. Corresponding graduate education marginal costs were estimated to be very high, especially in the science programs, differing from £470 in arts to £1,550 in physical sciences.

Marginal cost estimates of multiproduct cost studies. De Groot et al. (1991) calculated the marginal cost of each of several outputs for an average research university in the U.S. as $2,400 for a FTE undergraduate student, $10,000 for a FTE graduate student, $4,100 per student for all students, and $96,000 per research publication. These estimates for teaching outputs (i.e., undergraduate and graduate students) came as no surprise, since the empirical results of the earlier studies showed that producing a FTE graduate student typically costs more than a FTE undergraduate student. This study also confirmed the earlier studies with respect to the ratio of the costs of graduate education to undergraduate education. The ratio of costs for graduate students to undergraduate students was about four to one. That is much higher than the usual ratio of graduate to undergraduate tuition. Thus, they argued that graduate education is cross-subsidized by undergraduate education because the average revenue per student in their sample was $3,700. However, they presented no information with respect to the marginal cost of upper-and lower-level undergraduates.

One of the most interesting and important results from the de Groot et al. study was their estimation of the cost of research output. The costs of research output in American research universities was found to be surprisingly high compared with undergraduate and graduate education because the marginal costs of research output (per publication) were placed at 31.2 and 7.5 times that of undergraduate and graduate students. They offered two explanations for this high marginal cost of research output. First, there was a large potential cost savings from expansion of research for an average university, suggesting inefficiency within most research universities. For instance, they reported that the marginal costs per publication for the typical top private university were about $70,000. Second, traditional cost estimates do not recognize the possibility that the production of research output could be cross-subsidized from non-research revenues. Consequently, it is difficult to verify the conclusions of this study concerning the costs of research output because we still lack other comparative studies measuring the costs of research. Nevertheless, the results of this study have illustrated for the first time the importance of research output in determining costs in higher education. As James (1978) noted, failure to account for differences in research output may result in specification bias, overestimation of the costs of teaching, and misleads estimates of scale and scope economies.

More recently, Nelson and Heverth (1992) also analyzed the marginal costs of teaching by levels (i.e., lower-, upper- and graduate-level instruction). They estimated a multiproduct translog cost function employing data from a single university and adopted departments as their unit of analysis. Following Verry and Davies (1976), they also accounted for differences in research activity across departments by a measure for research input (i.e., the percent of faculty time devoted to research). Although such a methodology controlling for research activity does not permit estimating the marginal cost for research, they justified their position by avoiding the problems associated with the existence and measurement of research output. They also found that marginal costs rise with the level of instruction. The marginal costs of graduate students were between 4.3 and 8.9 times that of undergraduates (Nelson and Heverth, 1992, p. 481). They reported that these estimates were slightly higher than the range of 2.4 to 7.6 estimated by Verry and Layard (1975) for British universities, and materially exceeded those estimated earlier by Bowen (1981) and the Carnegie Commission (1972). They also estimated the marginal costs of outputs with respect to type of instruction within departments. They reported, as expected, that laboratory classes were generally more expensive than lecture classes and confirmed earlier findings by Brovender (1974), Verry and Layard (1975) and Verry and Davies (1976) who also presented significantly higher costs for science and engineering courses.

In conclusion, both single and multiple output cost function studies have provided important information concerning estimates on marginal costs. First, there are significant cost differences between the levels of instruction (e.g., graduate education being more expensive than undergraduate education and lower level undergraduate education is generally more expensive than upper level undergraduate education). And second, there are indeed substantial cost differences between fields.

Economies of Scale in Higher Education

Early cost function studies paid considerable attention to the effects of enrollment size on average costs per student (Allen and Brinkman, 1983; Nelson and Heverth, 1992). A meta-analysis of economies of scale studies by Brinkman and Leslie (1986) provided a summary of such cost studies over a sixty-year period. Their evidence indicates that, in general, potential and substantial economies of scale actually exist in all types of higher educational institutions. These summary findings were later confirmed by others (e.g., Cohn et al., 1989; Cohn and Geske, 1990).

One of the first studies on economies of scale in the higher education industry was done by Maynard (1971) who employed data from 123 American four-year colleges in thirteen states in 1967-68. Economies of scale were examined through the use of a parabolic long-run cost function. The most important finding of the study was its estimation that optimal economies of scale could be realized when an average four-year undergraduate institution had about 5,363 FTE students. On the shape of the long-run cost function, a substantial disagreement with a number of other studies exists since a decline in long-run average costs typically will be seen as the scale of production increases from zero and then it appears to remain steady over some longer range. What the optical scale of plant might be within this longer range is the point at issue. Despite the fact that Maynard focused on four-year colleges and a separate long-run cost function for universities was not estimated, a conclusion, nevertheless, was drawn based on the assumption that universities typically have more academic programs at more instructional levels than four-year colleges. Maynard expected that a typical university would have decreasing unit costs over a wider range of size owing to a larger threshold of faculty, and optimal economies of scale could be realized between 9,000 and 10,000 FTE students (Maynard, 1971). Because many public research universities exceeded these points they were consequently recognized as operating within highly inefficient ranges of scale. These early estimates of economies of scale for universities that were estimated by Maynard are possibly of doubtful validity since no empirical study was conducted at the time and most subsequent multiproduct cost studies of universities have estimated much higher levels of enrollment for optimal scales of plant.

On analyzing departmental cost functions, Smith (1978) employed a non-linear, weighted regression model. He included the squares and cubic terms for four teaching outputs in order to estimate instructional cost functions at Michigan's public colleges and universities to explore for economies and diseconomies of scale, and to examine the question of interaction among four student levels. Efficient economies of scale were found for each discipline at the undergraduate level, but his graduate programs indicated a mixture of economies and diseconomies of scale.

An early comprehensive study of the costs of higher education institutions was made for six types of departments in British universities by Verry and Davies (1976). By applying multiple regression analysis, they estimated for economies of scale and the marginal costs of undergraduate education, graduate education and research output. Their study shed considerable light on the structure of departmental costs. Recognizing the fact that universities not only produce teaching output but also research output, an attempt to control for research output was made by using proxy variables of self-reported allocations of time by faculty and their number of publications.

Among the most original features of this study was their recognition of the fact that the quality of output often changes with the size of the institution. One of the major limitations of most earlier studies was that the quality aspects of products were often ignored because they assumed that outputs were relatively homogeneous. What happens to institutions, for example, if they become larger and larger? Evidence from economies of scale studies over the past sixty years indicates that, generally, unit costs for two-year and four-year institutions decline with an increase in the number of students, and after a certain size, become relatively constant. However, the next legitimate question is: What is the relationship between costs, size, and quality? Fluctuation in the quality of output with size, for example, in undergraduate teaching may have two different consequences. For example, if a change in size affects and reduces the quality of instructional programs, costs in terms of the effectiveness of learning will be incurred by students. In fact, Bowen (1981) early on observed this issue as a source of diseconomies of scale in higher education. Nonetheless, as noted by Brinkman and Leslie (1986), few other cost studies have addressed this issue. Maynard (1971) acknowledged the same problem by noting that both quantity and quality of measurable unit output ought to be taken into account in any cost study. He noted that the measurement of output at a higher education institution "must go beyond measure of numbers of students and consider the nature of the learning experience made available to the students" (p. 50). However, the perplexing problem with the definition of what higher education institutions produce, and thus the lack of reliable data on both quantity and quality of outputs, makes it difficult to make a direct application of microeconomics theory to the estimation of costs in higher education.

Despite problems with the measure of the quality of teaching, several authors have attempted to control the quality of teaching to estimate cost functions by using completion rates, tests and measurement of learning outcomes, and crude measures of value added based on labor market effects. The attempt of Verry and Davies (1976) was an important advance for the application of theory to analyze the affect of size on quality of output. Their results for departments in the arts and engineering fields and in the biological sciences, somewhat surprisingly, provided evidence that the size associated with optimal economies of scale would be underestimated unless the quality dimensions of undergraduate teaching output were included.

Verry and Davies (1976) found that British colleges and universities exhibit modest economies of scale with often statistically insignificant results when they regressed enrollments only on expenditures. Interestingly, economies of scale did not increase when they entered the research activity of faculty. Verry and Davies suggest that the cause of this unexpected pattern is that, contrary to what is often supposed, the ratio of research to teaching falls, rather than rises, as departments get larger. On the other hand, Hoenack (1990) has argued that "the weak findings of economies of scale could also result from the estimated equations reflecting demands for and supplies of departmental instructional services, rather than the opportunity costs directly facing faculty" (p. 137). Hoenack, noticing the distinction between economies of scale for faculty and administration as a result of the difference between the opportunity cost of instruction faced by faculty and administration, suggests that "although faculty may have substantial economies of scale in the opportunity costs of instruction directly facing them, these economies may not be revealed by regressing departmental budgets, which instead reflect the opportunity costs of instruction faced by administrators, against enrollments" (p. 137).

While preliminary and tentative, Verry and Davies (1976) concluded that the extent of scale economies depends on the size of fixed costs. One of the most important findings of their study was that omitting any measure of research output from their cost functions did not necessarily cause an underestimation of economies of scale because larger departments concentrated on more research relative to teaching than smaller departments. Their empirical findings indicated that the incidence of fixed costs, and therefore economies of scale, were reduced by the inclusion of research.

There are two major shortcomings in Verry and Davies' widely acclaimed research on cost functions in higher education. As a typical cost function study in higher education, they dealt with overall economies of scale rather than with both the overall and particular products; their results often were limited to explanation of the effect of the overall institutional size on unit costs. This is partially a result of their lack of theoretical tools for examining the joint, multiple outputs of education. They also failed to address adequately the issue of scope economies.

So far we have reviewed only the most important earlier studies that lacked analyses of the multiproduct nature of higher education institutions. However, the focus of more recent studies has been on utilization of recently developed multiproduct cost concepts. Following is a brief review of these most recent studies.

Estimates of multiproduct cost function studies. Multiproduct cost studies in higher education, the first by Cohn et al. (1989) and then by de Groot et al. (1991), Nelson and Heverth (1992), Lloyd et al. (1993), and most recently by Dundar and Lewis (1995), Lewis and Dundar (1995), and Johnes (1996, 1997), are seen as important advances since they each separately estimated the two types of multiproduct economies—i.e., ray economies and product-specific economies. A few also examined for economies of scope. Nevertheless, substantial differences between these studies with respect to their levels of analysis, sample populations, data structures, and econometric techniques continue to be obstacles in our having clear confirming results regarding the presence of economies of scale in higher education.

Cohn and his colleagues (1989) were the first to conduct a multiproduct study on the costs of higher education by estimating flexible-fixed cost quadratic functions for 1,195 public and 692 private institutions of higher education in the United States, essentially covering most four-year undergraduate institutions. They estimated two separate cost functions for public and private institutions on the basis of the assumption that public and private institutions have different cost structures as a result of differing missions and employing different production technologies. Their particular interest was to eliminate any systematic differences in teaching quality between these two systems in the absence of any reliable measure of teaching quality (p. 285). Full-time equivalent undergraduate enrollments and full-time equivalent graduate enrollments were used as proxy measures of teaching outputs, and research grants and contracts were used as a proxy measure of research output.

The second attempt to analyze higher education utilizing multiproduct-product cost concepts was made by de Groot and his colleagues (1991). There are several major differences between the two studies with respect to their methodology and data. First, de Groot et al. (1991) analyzed cost functions of a subsample of 147 doctorate-granting universities with a major emphasis on research. By selection of only research universities as their subsample, their results were intended to provide substantial insights regarding the cost structure of research universities with similar production functions. In the case of the study by Cohn et al., their institutional sample was much larger and comprised almost all four-year institutions in the United States. This larger more heterogeneous sample may have created problems with the results of their study since different institutions within their public or private subsamples undoubtedly had different missions and production functions. The study by de Groot and his colleagues, on the other hand, was intended to provide more specific conclusions of multiproduct cost functions only for research universities.

Beyond sample differences, other differences in measurement and method also existed. For example, de Groot et al. employed number of publications as a proxy measure of research output instead of research grants and contracts as in the study of Cohn and his colleagues. One of the most striking differences between the two studies was the inclusion of a program quality measure for graduate programs in the study by de Groot et al., whereas Cohn et al. did not attempt to control for the quality of undergraduate instruction. Although Cohn et al. were aware of the problem, they did not include any such variable based on their argument that there was no reliable measure of teaching quality. To control for quality differences between public and private institutions, Cohn et al. estimated two different cost functions. De Groot et al., on the other hand, attempted to study the impact of graduate program quality by introducing peer ratings of program quality. Another major difference in the study by de Groot et al. was the inclusion of a dummy variable for the presence of a medical school to control for the impact of "expensive" medical education on the cost structure of research universities. This further assumed that different production functions of medical schools may result in a biased estimation of cost functions. Unfortunately, Cohn et al. made no attempt to control for such variables. Finally, the intensity of state regulation of personnel and administrative practices on the production efficiency in public higher education was investigated by de Groot et al. wherein they utilized an explicit measure of the degree of state regulation.

In spite of these differences in the use of samples, methodology and data between these two multiproduct cost function studies in higher education, their results shed important light on the presence of scale economies in higher education. While Cohn et al. (1989) reported that ray economies of scale are probably fully exhausted in the public sector at their current output means, de Groot et al. (1991) found ray economies up to about 50,000 FTE students and 17,000 FTE students in public institutions and private institutions, respectively. De Groot et al. offered two possible explanations for their study differences. First, even though Cohn and his colleagues estimated separate public and private samples, they used a very small number of research universities in their samples and their data were probably submerged within the very large number of small institutions with little or no graduate instruction or research. This might have resulted in misleading conclusions for their estimated high output levels. Second, the research grants and contracts used by Cohn et al. as a proxy measure of research output appear to perform poorly and probably lead to overestimations in instructional costs. Although Cohn et al. found evidence that the cost structures of private and public institutions were different and they reported prospective economies of scale separately for both private and public sectors, de Groot et al. reported that there were no differences in their sub-sample of research universities regarding type of control and thus no attempt was made to provide separate estimates for the public and private sectors. While Cohn et al. reported the existence of ray economies of scale at the sample output mean for the private sector, they estimated that ray economies of scale for the public sector were probably exhausted at their current output mean.

Product-specific economies of scale were also reported in both studies. De Groot et al. (1991) found evidence for product specific economies of scale for the average institution in the production of both teaching and research output. The found that an average institution with large undergraduate enrollments, graduate enrollments and a fairly large research output would be the least costly research university. They also reported that product-specific economies of scales for research and graduate enrollment were almost fully exhausted for institutions with large numbers of undergraduate and graduate students. Interestingly, they found product-specific economies of scale for undergraduate institutions with only a small number of undergraduates and graduates and a large volume of publications. Although scale economies could be obtained from expanding undergraduate enrollments alone, de Groot et al. noted that a possible decline in the quality of undergraduate instruction makes this expansion possibly problematic. Comparing these results with those of Cohn et al. reveals that there were substantial differences in their estimates for product-specific economies of scale. Cohn et al. found no evidence for the existence of prospective product-specific economies of scale for increasing undergraduate enrollments in public institutions. Their only cost savings could be obtained by expanding graduate enrollments and research output. Moreover, product-specific economies of scale did not appear to exist in the private sector. One of the most striking findings of the study by de Groot and his colleagues was that no significant efficiency gains were made in the production process because of state regulations of personnel and administrative practices, such as a ceiling on the number of faculty positions, returning year-end surpluses, prescribing salary schedules, regulating investment decisions, and the like.

In their final conclusions, Cohn and his colleagues estimated that the most efficient institution would have about thirty thousand FTE students and research grants and contracts amounting to roughly $80 to $100 million in 1982 dollars. De Groot and his colleagues, on the other hand, estimated an optimal institution as having an output vector of over 42,000 undergraduate enrollments, graduate enrollments of almost 12,000, and 2,158 publications. The University of Minnesota, having respective output vectors of 36,372, 12,325, and 2,373 was said to operate very close to their optimal scale conditions (de Groot et al., 1989, p. 17).

Recently, Nelson and Heverth (1992) employed data from a single university to analyze departmental costs and the effect of class size on marginal costs and economies of scale and scope. Their findings are obviously limited in generalizability with respect to the presence of economies of scale and scope in higher education. Nonetheless, the study is important because of its analysis of departments in the costs of higher education institutions and the role of class size on the existence of economies of scale and scope in single universities utilizing multiproduct cost concepts. Nelson and Heverth only reported information regarding ray (or overall) economies of scale. Estimates indicated the existence of scale economies with and without average class size in both lecture and laboratory classes. However, the extent of the scale economies varied according to the average class size and type of department (i.e., lecture or laboratory oriented). As expected, both large classes and extensive use of lectures contributed to prospective economies of scale. They concluded that failure to account for average class size in estimating cost functions appears to bias upward the estimates of overall economies of scale. They also reported little effect of research intensity on the estimates of economies of scale, confirming the earlier findings of Verry and Layard (1975) and Verry and Davies (1976).

In 1993, Lloyd and his colleagues reported on their multiple output cost study with 1988 data across 69 institutions within the system of higher education in Australia. They included five fields or disciplines and examined three levels of instruction across various clusters of these institutions. There primary intent was to estimate for expected economies of scale and scope that might result from representative amalgamations (i.e., institutional mergers) across the system. They found that in all cases there would be resulting cost savings. In their sample clusters, they found such cost savings to vary from 4.5 percent to over 17 percent. They similarly decomposed the cost savings into those due to economies of scale and those due to economies of scope. They found with only two exceptions that all of their estimates for economies of scale were both significant and material.

More recently, Dundar and Lewis (1995) analyzed the departmental cost structures of American public research universities. Their study estimated quadratic multiproduct cost functions and examined the degree of economies of scale and scope for the social sciences, physical sciences, and engineering fields using cross-sectional data from 18 public research universities. Estimates were made for determining the most efficient level and product-mix for different departments. The study considered universities as multiproduct firms producing three teaching outputs (full-time equivalent undergraduate, master, and doctoral student credit hours) and research output (measured by number of publications). In contrast with earlier higher education cost function studies which examined only institutional level data, this study focused on academic departments as the unit of analysis.

The estimated cost functions of the study provided insight into the nature of multiproduct economies in higher education. From a methodological point of view, the results of the study indicated that it is appropriate to analyze the structures of costs in higher education using multiproduct quadratic cost functions. With respect to the costs of outputs, both marginal and average incremental costs for each of four outputs were estimated. Previous studies found that the cost of instruction increases by level (e.g., graduate education costs more than undergraduate, doctoral education costs more than master level education). In contrast, the estimates of this study do not lend support to some findings of the previous studies. It was found, for example, that graduate education does not necessarily cost more than undergraduate instruction across all departments. Findings of the study suggested that the costs of doctoral level education were lowest in both the social and physical sciences, while they were the highest in engineering. Findings from the study also showed significant economies associated with both the scale and joint production of teaching and research. Similar results were also found by Lewis and Dundar (1995) in a subsequent departmental multiproduct cost study of all 38 universities in Turkey. These departmental findings imply that some higher education institutions indeed can reap greater efficiencies by an expansion of their departmental outputs and by producing teaching and research outputs jointly.

Most recently, two related comprehensive studies were undertaken by Johnes (1996; 1997) within the United Kingdom. In the first study Johnes (1996) estimated a quadratic multiproduct cost function for all universities in the U.K. while employing 1989-90 data sets. He included three outputs (i.e., undergraduate students, graduate students, and research grants) for the two broadly defined fields of 'arts' and 'sciences.' His estimated results largely confirmed work from previous studies wherein he found that there did indeed exist economies of both scale and scope within the system. However, he found product-specific economies of scale present for only two (graduate education and research in the sciences) of his six outputs.

In his most recent study, Johnes (1997) extended his earlier work to include former polytechnics in the U.K. and employed more recent data from the 1994-95 academic year. In this latest more comprehensive study he modified his model and used a constant elasticity of substitution [CES] cost function instead of the more common quadratic function. His estimated results again confirmed the existence of both economies of scale and scope in the U.K. Although he reported that it appeared that the number of institutions in the U.K. system was at about the right number, there appeared to be too many universities involved in research if cost-effectiveness was a major consideration in the system.

In conclusion, both the earlier single-output and the more recent multiproduct cost function studies reveal that prospective economies of scale do exist at both institutional and departmental levels for an average size institution or department. Although there were some modest field related differences in the evidence, the most recent studies utilizing multiproduct cost concepts appear to strengthen our understandings about economies of scale, particularly product-specific economies of scale. Nevertheless, the single most pervasive limitation of all these studies is their inability to control adequately for the quality of undergraduate instruction as size increases.

Economies of Scope in Higher Education

Although there could be economies associated with the scale of operations, there also may be economies associated with the composition of outputs, which measures whether there are cost advantages associated with the simultaneous production of many products. It is often argued that one advantage of American higher education compared with most other countries is the presence of cost advantages due to the joint production of teaching and research. This can be empirically tested by examining for prospective global and product specific economies of scope in the production of teaching and research.

A number of early studies recognized the fact that higher education institutions produce multiple outputs and therefore economies of scope from the joint production of multiple output may exist. For example, Nerlove (1972) intuitively argued that it is more efficient to produce undergraduate teaching and research within the same institution and by the same faculty than in entirely separate ones because the various activities for teaching and research are mutually supportive and fewer scarce resources are needed to produce the total product together rather than apart.

From a comparative perspective it has been argued that American higher education, which has relatively more emphasis on jointness in production than European higher education, may have the most efficient production. In this sense, Balderston (1990) observed that "combining a wide range of academic programs and linking the conduct of large-scale research with graduate education, American universities differ from institutions in Europe and the Soviet Union, where a great deal of research is done in separate institutes and academies while instruction of students is the dominant function of universities" (p. 33). This multiplicity of functions in American universities is clearly seen as a strength by many. In spite of such a belief, empirical findings and reports relative to scope economies are still relatively limited.

In the absence of using more sophisticated econometric techniques to measure economies of scope, interaction terms were first used in linear regression production models to examine possible joint effects. Positive and statistically significant coefficients for the interaction terms are said to indicate the absence of economies of scope. For instance, Verry and Davies (1976) estimated interaction terms among outputs of higher education institutions to test for the joint supply effects for producing undergraduate, graduate and research outputs jointly. By adding interaction terms to a simple linear cost function they concluded that the results were inconclusive as to whether producing undergraduate and graduate education, and graduate education and research activity together would indicate economies of joint production. Their estimated interaction coefficients were not statistically significant nor did they have the expected minus sign, which would have suggested that a joint supply of the two outputs would cost less. De Groot et al. (1991) interpreted these findings as resulting from the fact that graduate students are not employed as teaching or research assistants at relatively low prices in most British Universities. Nevertheless, Verry and Davies (1976) did estimate production functions in which they found that interdependence in production significantly affected the joint production of graduate education and research.

Only a few recent studies have examined whether economies of scope exist in producing multiproduct-outputs in higher education (Cohn et al., 1989; de Groot et al., 1991; Nelson and Heverth, 1992; Lloyd et al., 1993; Dundar and Lewis, 1995; Lewis and Dundar, 1995). These six recent multiproduct studies are an important advance in our understanding of the cost structure of higher education since they are the first studies to truly estimate economies of scope in higher education beyond just using interaction terms.

De Groot and his colleagues (1991) in their classic study of American universities were one of the first to report on economies of scope resulting from the joint production of undergraduate teaching, graduate instruction and research outputs. They found evidence for economies of scope between undergraduate and graduate instruction. Comparing their results with the findings of Verry and Davies (1976), they argued that the research universities in the United States obtain cost savings largely from employing graduate students as teaching assistants. However, they found no evidence from interaction terms or for scope economies between graduate training and research output even though it was assumed that there would be such cost savings due to the utilization of graduate students as research assistants.

Interestingly, Cohn and his colleagues (1989) found positive and statistically significant interaction terms between undergraduate instruction and research and between graduate training and research, indicating the absence of economies of scope for these respective outputs. However, their subsequent analysis of economies of scope with their multiproduct cost function indicated that economies of scope did, in fact, exist for both public and private institutions at almost all output levels. These findings are important because they indicate clear complementarity between teaching and research outputs. Nelson and Heverth (1992) found more mixed results regarding economies of scope at departmental levels. Controlling for class size, their results indicated diseconomies of scope for both lecture and laboratory classes between the three teaching outputs, but the results were not statistically significant.

As noted in the previous section, Lloyd and his colleagues (1993) in Australia also carefully examined the likely outcomes for cost savings from economies of scope as a result of prospective institutional mergers. They concluded that there would be such results but that they would be much smaller than those resulting from scale economies. For example, with mergers involving a large or extra large university (with another university or college) diseconomies of scope almost always occurred. The only case where economies of scope were almost as important as economies of scale was in the amalgamation of a teachers college with a technical college. Economies of scope from merging small colleges with more diverse institutions were negligible.

Both departmental studies by Dundar and Lewis (1995) in the United States and by Lewis and Dundar (1995) in Turkey tend to confirm these results. Their findings indicated that for all faculties in the fields of social sciences, engineering and health sciences, there appear to be material opportunities for economies of joint production from combining the production of teaching and research. In short, they found that in all three fields the costs of producing undergraduates, masters, doctorates and research simultaneously are smaller than the costs of producing them separately within normal ranges of production. The statistical evidence pertaining to the existence of economies of scope arising from the joint production of teaching and research appears to be confirmatory.

POLICY IMPLICATIONS AND FUTURE RESEARCH NEEDS

There has been much public debate about increasing costs, declining productivity, and the quality of higher education (Buckles, 1978; Bowen, 1981; Getz and Siegfried, 1991). Indeed, due to rising costs, the costs of higher education have been the center of much criticism. Accountability and efficiency have become the center of many reform attempts. To a certain extent, such criticism of higher education because of its spiraling costs has some validity. However, what is missing in much of the ongoing debate and in many studies that have examined the costs of higher education is attention to the multiproduct nature of higher education institutions. Although this chapter did not attempt to analyze the causes of changes in costs, it does provide major findings with respect to the cost behavior of institutions. The costs of higher education can be explained best through the utilization of multiproduct cost concepts. Such cost models that estimate total costs as a function of the major outputs of higher education provide more reliable and accurate measures regarding costs. Exclusion of research output, for example, has frequently resulted in an overestimation of the costs of teaching outputs.

Massy and Wilger (1992) have recently argued that the change in the output mix of higher education organizations has significantly affected their increasing costs. They argue that "many colleges and universities, particularly research institutions, have lost sight of their essential mission—the teaching of undergraduate students—as faculty members spend more time away from the classroom engaged in research and other professional activities" (p. 367) and this behavior has contributed to increasing costs. James (1978) likewise has presented evidence that faculty are spending more time on research. She reports, for example, that in 1953-54 faculty spent on average 12 percent of their time on research while in 1975-76 this figure was about 29 percent (p. 164). She found evidence of a resource shift away from undergraduate teaching toward graduate instruction and research. Specifically, in 1953-54, the research/teaching effort allocation was 2:1 but by the late 1960s it had risen to 6:1 (p. 165). Obviously, some part of faculty research time may be paid for out of externally funded projects and therefore should not be considered as institutional and departmental research production. However, as James (1978) observed, this kind of effect is probably small because only 7 percent of all university faculty positions were located in organized research settings and most of these were concentrated in a few institutes and fields.

Increasing time devoted to research activities in higher education is considered one of the most important reasons for increased costs in higher education over the last two decades. Massy and Wilger (1992) articulated this concept in their explanation of the causes of cost increases in higher education and coined the term "output creep" to explain the cost escalation. "By output creep we mean the slow change in product-mix observed at many colleges and universities….No longer do faculty members devote the majority of their time to teaching and related activities such as academic advising and mentoring. Rather, the primary focus of faculty effort increasingly is research, scholarship, and other professional activity" (p. 367). They also noted that this phenomenon occurs most dramatically at elite research universities.

Implications for Policy

Cost studies can play a critical role in allocating resources across and within higher educational institutions. Past cost studies, particularly multiproduct studies, have indeed indicated the existence of differences in the costs of higher education by types of outputs and disciplinary fields, by levels of instruction, and by internal resource management. Scale, scope of the output and number of institutions can all be addressed through appropriate uses of multiproduct cost studies (Johnes, 1997).

Findings from the studies reviewed in this chapter permit us to examine empirically the arguments about "output creep." In this chapter the importance of research output in determining departmental cost structures was examined across several fields. Our findings indicate, for example, that research output in engineering departments had the highest marginal costs, while it was the lowest in the social sciences. Although these results are tentative, they suggest that there are important differences among the costs of research output across different fields. Our summary findings also indicate that the estimated marginal costs of research are much lower than many previous estimates. These differences can be attributed largely to the unit of measurement. While several multi-product cost analyses focused on departmental cost functions, most previous studies focused on the institutional level.

With respect to the costs of various types of instructional outputs, the departmental cost functions revealed that undergraduate instruction had the lowest costs among all levels of instruction. Although most previous cost studies have suggested that the cost of graduate education was consistently more than undergraduate education, the findings from two of the departmental level studies provide some preliminary evidence that the assumption that the costs of graduate education are higher than the costs of undergraduate education does not hold for every field or department. Although it was found that there were cost differences by level of instruction and across departments, these findings do not suggest advanced education is inherently more expensive than undergraduate education in each discipline or department. Findings of lower marginal costs for doctoral level output in the social sciences at the sample output mean, as found, for example, in the Dundar and Lewis (1995) study, is important because, as often assumed, educating doctoral students at the margin does not cost more than educating other level students in all fields. This can be partly explained by the theory of duality in the production of graduate education.

These findings have particularly important policy implications for research universities. As commonly assumed, it might not be the case that the cost of instruction increases by level of instruction across every field. The low costs of doctoral level education compared with master level education in the social and physical sciences supports the notion that is often argued that doctoral students are not only output but also input for teaching at other levels and research.

Empirical results that suggest that the production of research in most departments in research universities accounts for a large amount of total departmental costs need to be interpreted with caution. Since only cross-sectional data were used in all of the studies, it is premature to suggest that increasing costs in higher education are largely due to a shift in the output mix from teaching to research activities. What is important from such a finding is that focusing on instructional costs in research universities without examining the output mix misses the point of the price effect of the research output on educational costs. Much of the debate has focused on spiraling costs within higher education institutions, while limited attention has been given to the production of research and other activities at departmental levels.

Concerns about improving efficiency should also be raised as an important issue in the policy debate. In this respect, examining scale economies and scope economies sheds important light on efforts for increasing the internal efficiency of higher education institutions. In the studies of this chapter we found for the United States that ray economies of scale and global economies of scope exist up to 200 percent respectively of their sample mean outputs, suggesting that a simultaneous growth in all outputs might be economically efficient. Product-specific economies of scale were found to exist for all outputs except doctoral instruction. There might also be cost advantages resulting from increasing the size of departmental production for undergraduate and master teaching outputs and for expanding research beyond the point where ray economies of scope are exhausted. Although it is recognized that there is currently a reform movement in which it has been argued that there should be greater restrictions for access to undergraduate programs in research universities in order to increase the quality of undergraduate education, the findings in this chapter clearly suggest that there are, nevertheless, cost efficiencies in raising undergraduate teaching output; assuming, of course, that the quality of such output can at least be maintained.

With respect to economies of scope, our findings support the commonly understood notion about the efficiency likely resulting from the joint production of higher education teaching and research. The existence of global economies of scope suggests that cost savings will likely result in most institutions from jointly producing both undergraduate and graduate education and from jointly producing graduate instruction and research rather than specializing in producing only one or a sub-set of the outputs. The existence of global scope economies up to 300 or even 600 percent of the sample output means in the physical sciences, engineering and social sciences, respectively, in research universities clearly suggests that the costs of producing these outputs jointly are less than producing them separately.

Our findings indicate that more attention should be paid to the concept of economies of scope since it may be at least as important as the scale effect in designing more efficient departmental production. Flourishing specialized research centers and research institutes within or outside of institutions of higher education will result in less efficiency in the production of the same outputs.

If graduate students are also considered to be an input into research production, as is often assumed, one should expect the existence of economies of scope between these two outputs. Empirical evidence does suggest, however, that in some fields this complementarity may not exist, as was found in one study for the social sciences. However, cost complementarities were found between doctoral level teaching production and research output production in both the physical sciences and engineering, suggesting that in the hard sciences doctoral students are used more as research inputs while in the social sciences they probably are used more in teaching.

It should be emphasized that estimating cost functions in higher education has been quite limited due to a number of data and methodological problems. Our reporting of studies in this chapter is a natural extension of other cost reviews that have appeared in recent years. As in most all studies in higher education, the number and measurement of outputs are often limited by the data. Thus, the results in this chapter should be suggestive rather than definitive in nature.

Specific Policy Recommendations

Estimating multiproduct cost functions in higher education and utilizing their results to analyze the existence of multiproduct scale and scope economies can provide important tools for policy analysts in higher education. Our ultimate concern in this chapter was to examine whether economies of scale and scope existed in higher education and, if they did exist, to what extent. The results presented in this chapter have a number of important and practical implications for policy makers. First, our literature review indicates the existence of both economies of scale and scope for most fields of scholarship in American, United Kingdom, Australian, and Turkish higher education. Many institutions will enjoy cost advantages with the expansion of their outputs due to the presence of ray-economies of scale. While all departments operating at an output range smaller than their sample output mean will enjoy cost savings due to an increase in outputs, ray-economies of scale do exhaust at some point. Obviously, any attempt to expand levels of production to increase cost savings in higher education through scale economies needs to be carefully examined and attention needs to be given to quality.

Second, the empirical evidence found in this review indicates that there are cost advantages associated with the joint production of teaching and research. These economies of scope arise from the joint utilization of faculty, administrators, support staff, and equipment and services for the production of both teaching and research outputs. However, global economies of scope are also exhausted at some point at larger levels of output production.

Third, it also has been estimated in both institutional and departmental studies that average incremental and marginal costs for research outputs are at their highest in a multiple output cost function model. These findings suggest that excluding research from any cost study will result in underestimating or overestimating the costs of other outputs. Studies focusing on the instructional costs of higher education need to be especially careful in any policy designed for financing tuition policies. One implication of the findings with respect to cost-related tuition policy is that disciplines have very different cost structures within research universities, with relatively high variations in their average and marginal costs. For example, undergraduate education generally has the lowest average and marginal costs in the social sciences, while the physical sciences have the highest average costs. With respect to research output, while the social sciences have the lowest average incremental and marginal costs, engineering has the highest average costs, and the physical sciences typically have the highest marginal costs. The existence of high cost variation across departments also supports policies for having cost-related tuition policies.

Implications for Future Research Needs

The literature on cost functions in higher education over the past two decades has provided substantial insight regarding scale economies and the costs of instruction. However, there is only limited evidence on the related questions of product-specific economies of scale and economies of scope. Such evidence is needed before arriving at more definitive policy conclusions. These results did not arise because of any lack of interest by economists or policy analysts, but rather because of a lack of appropriate methodology to analyze multiproduct output firms until only very recently. Although most of the earlier studies, (e.g., Sengupta, 1975; Southwick, 1969; Verry and Davies, 1976; Verry and Layard, 1975; Bear, 1974; Brinkman, 1981; James, 1978) considered higher education institutions, particularly universities, as multiproduct firms, only seven recent studies have analyzed the cost functions of higher education in the United States, the United Kingdom, Australia and Turkey by employing recently developed multiproduct cost functions techniques.

The lack of studies employing these new techniques puts several obstacles in front of our understanding the cost structures of higher education institutions. Despite the ample evidence regarding scale economies, a particular limitation of most early studies was that they were limited to single-output cost functions. In the case of the multiproduct nature of higher education the results of most single or aggregated output cost function studies should be read with caution. Despite the substantial body of literature on economies of scale in higher education over the past sixty years and the recognition of the multiproduct-product nature of higher education (e.g., Brinkman, 1981; Verry and Davies, 1976, Tierney, 1980), almost all of the earlier studies fell short of a rigorous analysis of both scale and scope economies. Although many of the early studies attempted to estimate ray economies of scale, product-specific scale economies have been estimated only in a few recent studies, and estimates on economies of scope have been limited to only five of these recent multiproduct studies.

Interest in the costs of higher education through the utilization of multiproduct cost functions has materially increased during the past few years. The seven recent multiproduct studies focused on both institutional (Cohn et al., 1989; Lloyd et al., 1993; and de Groot et al., 1991) and departmental or field based (Nelson and Heverth, 1992; Dundar and Lewis, 1995; Lewis and Dundar, 1995; Johnes, 1996 and 1997) levels and they have given us understandings about both undergraduate four-year colleges and research universities across both public and private domains in several countries. As Brinkman (1990) and others have recommended, our understanding of the cost behavior of higher education institutions depends upon more such empirical cost function studies. Nevertheless, as can be seen from the literature review of this study, we are still at the very early stages of our understanding costs of higher education with respect to the existence and nature of both their economies of scale and scope. We need to have a larger number of studies examining costs of higher education utilizing data from differing samples, time periods, and countries. Moreover, since statistical fitting is an accepted form of most cost function studies, additional types of multiproduct cost functions of the sort identified in this chapter need to be examined.

The availability of detailed cost and research output data from the 1980s was a major advantage and permitted all of the multiproduct studies to estimate cross-sectional cost functions for higher education and to examine for the most recent existence of economies of scale and scope. It is encouraging to note that new, detailed data bases soon will be available with respect to costs, enrollments, and research output at departmental levels in American research universities. Beyond the recurring cost and enrollment data of the Association of American University Data Exchange, a new survey study of the National Research Council examining the quality and research outputs of research universities is shortly forthcoming and will provide extensive new data sets for further research of this type. Most importantly, future studies will need to give more careful attention to the issue of appropriately measuring the quality effects that might result from changing the size of enrollments.

Most multiproduct cost studies have examined only the cost structures of American higher education institutions with respect to economies of scale and scope. It is imperative that we have more comparative studies, especially in developing countries, before arriving at firm conclusions concerning economies of scale and scope in the production of higher education institutions around the world. A most important question is whether the cost savings arising from the American model of higher education that produces teaching and research jointly might also be accruing in other like settings around the world. Our findings from the U.K., Australia and Turkey indicate that this is likely, but we clearly need more evidence on this and other related questions. Since Verry and Davies (1976) and Verry and Layard (1975) in their early studies in England did not find such economies from their examination of joint production, it would be very instructive and provide highly useful policy information to have other studies examining multiproduct cost functions utilizing data from other countries where research is often done in separate enterprises outside of the university as in Eastern and Western Europe today.

The literature is now limited to studies examining only American higher education, with only a few studies coming from British and Australian universities and one from Turkey. The expansion of higher education throughout the world over the last three decades is one of the most important developments of the twentieth century. The existence and the extent of economies of scale and scope are virtually unknown in most other developed and developing countries despite the fact that higher education is one of their largest industries. This does not mean that there are no comparative cost studies in higher education outside the United States and England. For example, several World Bank studies have examined the cost structures of higher education in developing countries (Psacharopoulos, 1980; Bellew and DeStefano, 1991; Tan and Mingat, 1992). However, as in the case of earlier studies in American higher education, they have all only examined homogeneous output and thus have limited findings. Little is known, for example, about the impact of research on the costs of higher education in most other developing and developed countries around the world. Studies utilizing cost and output data of several countries would be extremely helpful for our understanding of comparative costs of higher education and empirically estimating the true costs of higher education products.

REFERENCES

Adams, C. R., Hankins, R. L., and Schroeder, R. G. (1978). The literature of cost and cost analysis in higher education. In C. R. Adams, R. L. Hankins and R. G. Schroeder (eds.), in *A Study of Cost Analysis in Higher Education: Volume I*. Washington, DC: American Council on Education.

Allen, R., and Brinkman, P. (1983). *Marginal Costing Techniques for Higher Education*. Boulder, Colorado: National Center for Higher Education Management Systems, Inc.

Bailey, E. E., and Friedlaender, A. F. (1982). Market structure and multiproduct Industries. *Journal of Economic Literature,* 20, 1024-1048.

Bailey, E. E. (1988). Foreword. In W. J. Baumol, Panzar, J. C.,and Willig, R. D. (eds.), *Contestable Markets and the Theory of Industry Structure* (Revised Edition). New York: Harcourt Brace Jovanovich, Inc.

Balderston, F. E. (1990). Organization, funding, incentives, and initiatives for university research: a university management perspective. In S. A. Hoenack and E. L. Collins (eds.), *The Economics of American Universities*. Albany, NY: State University of New York Press.

Barrons Educational Service (1986). *1985 Barron's Profiles of Colleges and Universities*. New York: Barron's Educational Service Inc.

Baumol, W. J. (1977). On the proper cost tests for natural monopoly in a multiproduct industry. *American Economic Review* 67: 809-822.

Baumol, W. J., Panzar, J. C., and Willig, R. D. (1982). *Contestable Markets and the Theory of Industry Structure*. New York: Harcourt Brace Jovanovich, Inc.

Baumol, W. J., Panzar, J. C., and Willig, R. D. (1988). *Contestable Markets and the Theory of Industry Structure* (Revised Edition). New York: Harcourt Brace Jovanovich, Inc.

Bear, D. V. T. (1974). The university as a multi-product firm. In K. G. Lumsden (ed.), *Efficiency in Universities: the La Paz Papers*. New York: Elsevier Scientific Publishing Company.

Becker, W. E. (1979). Perspectives from economics: the economic consequences of changing faculty reward structures. In D. R. Lewis and W. E. Becker (eds.), *Academic Reward Structures in Higher Education*. Boston: Ballinger Publishing.

Bellew, R., and DeStefano, J. (1991). *Costs and Finance of Higher Education in Pakistan*. The World Bank Population and Human Resources Department Working Papers No. WPS 704. Washington, DC: The World Bank.

Berg, D. J., and S. A. Hoenack (1987). The concept of cost-related tuition and its implementation at the University of Minnesota. *Journal of Higher Education* 58: 276-305.

Bottomley, A. (1972). *Costs and Potential Economies: Studies in Institutional Management in Higher Education*. Paris: Organization for Economic Co-Operation and Development.

Bowen, H. R. (1980). *The Costs of Higher Education*. San Francisco: Jossey-Bass Publishers,

Brinkman, P. (1981). Factors affecting instructional costs at major research universities. *Journal of Higher Education* 52: 265-79.

Brinkman, P.,and Allen, R. (1986). Concepts of cost and cost analysis for higher education. *AIR Professional File,* 23(Spring).

Brinkman, P. (1990). Higher education cost functions. In S. A. Hoenack and E. L. Collins (eds.), *The Economics of American Universities*. Albany, NY: State University of New York Press.

Brinkman, P., and Leslie, L. L. (1986). Economies of scale in higher education: sixty years of research. *Review of Higher Education*, 10(1).

Broomall, L. W., Mahan, B. T., McLaughlin, G. W., and Patton, S. S. (1978). *Economies of Scale in Higher Education*. Blacksburg, VA: Virginia Polytechnic Institute and State University, Office of Institutional Research. ERIC Document Reproduction Service NO. ED 162604.

Brovender, S. (1974). On the economics of a university: toward the determination of marginal cost of teaching services. *Journal of Political Economy* 82(May/June): 657-664.

Buckles, S. (1978). Identification of causes of increasing costs in higher education. *Southern Economics Journal* 45: 258.65.

Butter, I. H. (1967). *Economics of Graduate Education: An Exploratory Study*. Ann Arbor: The University of Michigan Department of Economics.

Carlson, D. E. (1972). *The Production and Cost Behavior of Higher Education Institutions*. Ford Foundation Program for Research in University Administration. Berkeley: University of California.

Carnegie Commission on Higher Education. (1972). *The More Effective Use of Resources*. New York: McGraw-Hill.

Cartter, A. M. (1966). *An Assessment of Quality in Graduate Education*. Washington, DC: American Council on Education.

Clotfelter, C. T., Ehrenberg, R. G., Getz, M. and Siegfried, J. J. (1991). *Economic Challenges in Higher Education*. Chicago: The University of Chicago Press.

Cohn, E., and Geske, T. (1990). *The Economics of Education* (3rd Ed.). New York: Pergamon Press.

Cohn, E., Rhine, S. L., and Santos, M. C. (1989). Institutions of higher education as multi-product firms: economies of scale and scope. *The Review of Economics and Statistics* 71: 284-90.

De Groot, H., McMahon, W. W., and Volkwein, J. F. (1989). *The Cost Structure of American Research Universities*. Discussion Paper Series, 8915/P. Rotterdam: Institute of Economic Research, Erasmus University.

De Groot, H., McMahon, W. W., and Volkwein, J. F. (1991). The cost structures of American research universities. *The Review of Economics and Statistics* 73: 424-431.

Dolan, R. C.,. Jung, C. R., and Schmidt, R. (1993). *Modeling the Production of Higher Education*. Manuscript submitted for publication.

Dundar, H. and Lewis, D. R. (1995). Departmental productivity in American universities: Economies of scale and scope, *Economics of Education Review 14*: 119-144.

Friedlaender, A. F., Winston, C., and Wang, K. (1983). Costs, technology, and productivity in the U.S. automobile industry. *The Bell Journal of Economics* 14.

Galvin, D. A. (1980). *The Economics of University Behavior.* New York: Academic Press.

Getz, M. and Siegfried, J.J. (1991). Cost and Productivity in American colleges and universities. In C. T. Clotfelter, R. G. Ehrenberg, M. Getz, and J. J. Siegfried (eds.), *Economic Challenges in Higher Education.* Chicago: The University of Chicago Press.

Gilmore, J. L. (1990). *Price and Quality in Higher Education.* Washington, DC: U.S. Department of Education.

Goldberger, M. L., Maker, B.A., and Flattaki, P.T. (1995). *Research-Doctorate Programs in the United States: Continuity and Change.* Washington, DC: National Academy Press.

Graham, P. A., Lyman, R.W., and Trow, M. (1995). Accountability of colleges and universities: an essay. *The Accountability Study.* New York: The Trustees of Columbia University in the City of New York.

Gumport, P.J. and Pusser, B. (1995). A case of bureaucratic accretion: Context and consequences. *The Journal of Higher Education* 66:493-520.

Halstead, K. (1991). *Higher Education Revenues and Expenditures: A Study of Institutional Costs.* Washington, DC: Research Associates of Washington.

Hoenack, S. A. (1990). An economist's perspective on costs within higher education institutions. In S. A. Hoenack and E. L. Collins (eds.), *The Economics of American Universities.* Albany, NY: State University of New York Press.

Hoenack, S. A., and Weiler, W. C. (1975). Cost-related tuition policies and university enrollments. *The Journal of Human Resources* 10: 332-360.

Hoenack, S. A., Weiler, W. C., Goodman, R.D., and Pierro, D. J. (1986). Marginal costs of instruction. *Research in Higher Education* 24: 335-417.

Hopkins, D. (1990). The higher education production function: theoretical foundations and empirical findings. In S. A. Hoenack and E. L. Collins (eds.), *The Economics of American Universities.* Albany, NY: State University of New York Press.

Hopkins, D., and Massy, W. F. (1981). *Planning Models for Colleges and Universities.* Palo Alto, CA: Stanford University Press.

James, E. (1978). Product mix and cost disaggregation: a reinterpretation of the economics of higher education. *Journal of Human Resources* 13: 157-86.

James, E., and Rose-Ackerman, S. (1986). *The Nonprofit Enterprise in Market Economics.* New York: Harwood Academic Publishers.

Johnes, G. (1988). Research performance indicators in the university sector, *Higher Education Quarterly,* 54-71.

Johnes, G. (1996). Multi-product cost functions and the funding of tuition in U.K. universities, *Applied Economic Letters,* 3: 557-561.

Johnes, G. (1997). Cost and industrial structure in contemporary British higher education, *The Economic Journal,* 107: 727-737.

Jones, L. V., Lindzey, G., and Coggeshall, P. E. (eds). (1982). *An Assessment of Research-Doctorate Programs in the United States.* Washington, DC: National Academy Press.

Leslie, L.L. and Rhoades, G. (1995). Rising administrative costs: Seeking explanations. *The Journal of Higher Education* 66: 187-212.

Lewis, D.R. and Dundar, H. (1995). Economies of scale and scope in Turkish universities, *Education Economics 3*: 133-157.

Lloyd, P. J., Morgan, M. H., and Williams, R. A. (1993). Amalgamations of universities: Are there economies of scale and Scope? *Applied Economics* 25: 1081-1092.

Massy, W. F. (1990). A paradigm for research on higher education. In J. C. Smart (ed.), *Higher Education Handbook of Theory and Research,* Volume 6. New York: Agathon Press.

Massy, W. F. (1991). Improving productivity in higher education: Administration and support costs. *Capital Ideas* 6.

Massy, W. F., and Wilger, A.K. (1992). Productivity in postsecondary education: a new approach. *Educational Evaluation and Policy Analysis* 14: 361-376.

Maynard, J. (1971). *Some Microeconomics of Higher Education: Economies of Scale.* Lincoln, Nebraska:

University of Nebraska Press.

Mayo, J. W. (1984). Multiproduct monopoly, regulation, and firm costs. *Southern Economic Journal* 51(July): 208-218.

McLaughlin, G. W., Montgomery, J. R., Smith, A. W., and Broomall, L. W. (1980). Size and efficiency. *Research in Higher Education* 12: 53-66.

McPherson, M.S., and Winston, G. C. (1993). The economics of cost, price, and quality in U.S. higher education. In M. S. McPherson, M. O. Schapiro, and G.C. Winston (eds.). *Paying the Piper: Productivity, Incentives, and Financing in U.S. Higher Education.* Ann Arbor: The University of Michigan Press.

Nelson, R., and Heverth, K. T. (1992). Effect of class size on economics of scale and marginal costs in higher education. *Applied Economics* 24: 473-482.

Nerlove, M. (1972). On tuition and the costs of higher education: prolegomena to a conceptual framework. In T. W. Schultz, (ed.), *Investment In Education: The Equity-Efficiency Quandary.* Chicago: University of Chicago Press.

Olson, J. E. (1997). The cost-effectiveness of American higher education: The United States can afford its colleges and universities. In J. Smart (ed.), *Higher Education: Handbook of Theory and Research*, Volume 12. New York: Agathon Press.

Panzar, J. C., and Willig, R. D. (1975). *Economies of Scale and Economies of Scope in Multi-output Production.* Bell Laboratories Economic Discussion Paper No.33.

Panzar, J.C., and Willig, R. D. (1979). *Economies of Scope, Product-specific Economies of Scale and the Multiproduct Competitive Firm.* Bell Laboratories Economic Discussion Paper No. 152.

Panzar, J. C., and Willig, R. D. (1981). Economies of scope. *American Economic Review* 71: 268-272.

Psacharopoulos, G. (1980). *Higher Education in Developing Countries: A Cost-benefit Analysis.* Discussion Paper No. 440. Washington, DC: World Bank.

Schapiro, M. O. (1993). The concept of productivity as applied to U.S. Higher Education. In M. S. McPherson, M. O. Schapiro, and G.C. Winston (eds.). *Paying the Piper: Productivity, Incentives, and Financing in U.S. Higher Education.* Ann Arbor: The University of Michigan Press.

Sengupta, Jati K. (1975). Cost and production functions in the university education system: an econometric analysis. In H. Correa (ed.), *Analytical Models in Educational Planning and Administration.* New York: David McKay Company, Inc.

Shoesmith, G. L. (1988). Economies of scale and scope in petroleum refining. *Applied Economics* 20: 1643-1652.

Smith, N. S. (1978). *An Economic Analysis of the Costs of Instruction in the Michigan System of Higher Education.* Unpublished doctoral dissertation, Michigan State University.

Southwick, L. Jr. (1969). Cost trends in land grant colleges and universities. *Applied Economics* 1: 167-182.

St. John, E. P., *Prices, Productivity and Investment: Assessing Financial Strategies in Higher Education.* An ASHE-ERIC Higher Education Study, no. 3. Washington, DC: George Washington University.

Stevens, E. B., and Elliot, E. C. (1925). *Unit Costs of Higher Education.* New York: Macmillan.

Tan, J.-P., and Mingat, A. (1992). *Education in Asia: A Comparative Study of Cost and Financing.* World Bank Regional and Sectoral Studies. Washington, DC: The World Bank.

Tierney, M. (1980). An estimate of departmental cost functions. *Higher Education* 9: 453-468.

Tsang, M. C. (1989). Cost analysis for educational policymaking: A review of cost studies in education in developing countries. *Review of Educational Research* 58: 181-230.

Varian, H. R. (1990). *Microeconomic Analysis* (third edition). New York: W. W. Norton and Company.

Verry, D. W., and Layard, P. R. G. (1975). Costs functions for teaching and research. *The Economic Journal* 85: 55-74.

Verry, D. W., and Davies, B. (1976). *University Costs and Outputs.* Amsterdam, The Netherlands: Elsevier.

Verry, D. W. (1987). Educational cost functions. In G. Psacharopoulos (ed.), *Economics of Education: Research and Studies.* New York: Pergamon Press.

Wang Chiang, J. S., and Friedlaender, A. F. (1985). Truck technology and efficient market structure. *The Review of Economics and Statistics* 67: 250-258.

Wang, J. C. (1981). *Economies of Scale and Scope in Multiproduct Industries: A Case Study of the Regulated U.S. Trucking Industry.* Unpublished Doctoral Dissertation. Cambridge, MA: Massachusetts Institute of Technology.

Witmer, D. R. (1972). Cost studies in higher education. *Review of Educational Research* 47: 99-127.

Epilogue

Over the course of the past two to three years since this chapter was first published, several of the cost and productivity foci in our chapter have continued to be pursued. At least four major concerns and areas of research are noteworthy: A continuing concern with uncovering those cost factors that may have contributed to extraordinary price rises to students; the re-emergence of demands for performance indicators for assessing accountability and enhancing efficiency in resource use; a renewed focus upon cost accounting and the budgetary process; and the continued examination of institutional productivity and costs so as to uncover better understandings about economies of scale and scope.

Perceived rising costs. First, and most important, issues surrounding the increasing rise of college costs in the United States have continued across the land with many parts of the media (e.g., *Newsweek, Time, U.S.A. Today*, the *Wall Street Journal*, and *U.S. News and World Report*, along with several regional papers) posting headline stories about the "price tags" of both elite private schools and public universities (Paulsen, Chapter 6). Congress even established a National Commission on the Cost of Higher Education and its final report came out in 1998. Its most important findings indicated that students and their families are paying a larger share of the rising cost of higher education, while state support of public institutions has been decreasing (Toutkoushian, Chapter 1). As noted by Flowers (1998) in *Academe*, the professional journal of AAUP, the commission paid close attention to its task of identifying "cost drivers." Though it found no obvious or outrageous factors, it did note that part-time students have been increasing and such students require more services with student service costs (in real terms) increasing over 35 percent during the past 15 years, administrative expenditures per student increased during the 1980s but leveled off during the 1990s, and complex state and federal regulations on such matters as health, safety, and reporting requirements have imposed increasing financial burdens at almost every institution. Along with several other recommendations, two points relevant to our discussion were noted: (1) more research was needed to uncover better those factors that have been contributing most directly to rising costs; and (2) both funding authorities and accrediting agencies needed to look more carefully at "outcomes" rather than just "resources" as they make judgments about quality and educational productivity. This latter recommendation has, in turn, led to renewed attention being given to the use of performance indicators in higher education.

Using performance indicators. The whole notion and use of performance indicators in higher education clearly has taken on greater importance (Lasher and Greene, Chapter 14). Despite doubts raised in many academic quarters, the pressures for productivity reform, cost containment and change coming from governments and other critics of higher education have been considerable. This has been especially critical in the United Kingdom (UK) where they have placed a great deal of their reform efforts in higher education on the development and use of outcome indicators. The use of performance indicators for both accreditation and resource allocation (or reallocation) have acquired a much "higher profile" in the UK and in several other Northern European (Cave, et al., 1997) and Commonwealth countries (Davis, 1996) during the 1990s. Performance budgeting has also taken on increased importance in many of the reform agendas of developing countries where there are currently movements away from negotiated budgets (Johnstone, 1998).

In the United States a similar push for using performance indicators has also re-arisen within the 1990s. Just before 1989, there was only one state (i.e., Tennessee) in the U.S. that had tied its allocation of state resources to institutional performance. Today, more than ten states have some form of performance funding programs in place and several others are considering adopting such policies. The driving forces have been to focus on enhancing quality and rewarding institutions that demonstrate accountability and improvement in achieving statewide goals and priorities (Burke and Serban, 1997). Variations on using performance indicators within institutions in the US are also evident in the recent emergence of "incentive-based resource allocation" systems within some of the leading public universities (e.g., Michigan, Minnesota, Indiana, and UCLA).

The key pressures behind the international introduction of performance indicators have been largely focused on demands for greater accountability, strengthening institutional management, and developing greater efficiencies in the delivery of both instructional and research activities. A useful summary of both the prospective benefits and problems resulting from performance indicators along with some evidence relative to their use as measures of productivity and efficiency, especially within the UK, the Netherlands, and Scandanavia, can be gotten from Cave et al. (1998). A similar summary of performance indicators as tools for state higher education policy in approximately one-third of the United States is also given in Ruppert (1994), wherein detailed case studies are reviewed. In Tennessee, for example, with over two decades of experience with performance indicators (and the linkage of outcomes with budgeted allocations from the state) these developments there have been the focus of international attention. Unfortunately, surprisingly little attention in the use of performance indicators has been directed to the examination of equality of educational opportunity for historically disadvantaged students.

Cost accounting and continuing studies on expenditures. Since the early 1970s, cost accounting and searches for the main determinants of costs have been core issues across most of higher education. Several recent articles have continued our pursuit of more accurate approximations of both educational cost and production functions (Pritchett and Filmer, 1999; Robst, 1997; King, 1997; Toutkoushian, 1998; Losco and Fife, 1997). Much of this work in the 1990s has attempted to address several of the cost issues raised by Hoenack and Collins (1990), especially with respect to the likely differential effects on costs of alternative combinations of resources in instruction and research.

Extensive concerns have been raised over the past decade about the comparative efficiency of higher education institutions in the United Kingdom. The governmental initiatives of the last 15 years within this sector have given major emphasis to issues of accountability, productivity and cost control. Several recent studies in the UK have arisen in order to gain further insights into the operations of its universities relative to these issues (e.g., Athanassopoulos and Shale, 1997; Glass, McKillip and Hyndman, 1995; Groot and Maasen van den Brink, 1997; Johnes, 1992, 1995). One of their most important findings was that the high output efficiency of benchmarked institutions did not, in general, equate with low unit (i.e., per FTE student) costs.

Equally important has been the recent publication by Hans Jenny (1996), *Cost Accounting in Higher Education*. This manual supplements and expands James Hyatt's earlier (1983) publication on cost accounting published by the National Association of Colleges and University Business Officers (NACUBO). Prior to 1983, NACUBO and others had recognized the need for developing consistent cost information and costing techniques that could be applied throughout higher education in the US. Of special interest is the joint work on costing performed by NACUBO and the National Center for Higher Education Management Systems in 1977 (NACUBO and NCHEMS, 1977).

Cost accounting and continuing explorations on economies of scale and scope. Finally, additional work has continued on attempting to better understand and explain to what extent prospective economies of scale and scope exist within higher education. Cormack (1995), for example, has extended the earlier work of Nelson and Hevert (1992) and Lloyd, Morgan, and Williams (1993) in further examining the likely scale and scope effects of class size in the context of its labor input, course characteristics and administrative decisions. Prospective economies of scale in the context of quality factors were further examined through the use of ordinary least-square regression techniques with four groups of 195 Carnegie type research and doctoral granting universities in the United States by Koshal and Koshal (1995). They found that the size of minimum efficient scale ranged from 11,758 for group IV Carnegie type institutions to 30,957 for group I institutions. The results of their study also imply that the quality of education is an important variable in the explanation of the variation in average total cost.

The efficiency effects resulting from economies of scale and scope were further confirmed by four additional studies by Hashimoto and Cohn (1997), Koshal and Koshal (1999), Abbott (1996), and Heaton and Throsby (1997). Hashimoto and Cohn employed a flexible fixed-cost quadratic function to estimate multiple-output cost functions for 94 private universities in Japan. Koshal and Koshal used a similar method to estimate multiple-output cost functions for 158 private and 171 public comprehensive (as compared with research and Ph.D. granting) universities in the United States. Abbott examined the likely cost effects of institutional mergers in Australia, while Heaton and Throsby found strong evidence in Australia that suggested that the size of a university was a major determinant of average and marginal costs and that there were indeed optimal sizes for such institutions. Although some minor differences and variations with exceptions were found when comparing these four results with our previous reviewed studies, all four of these studies found that there were indeed varying degrees of economies of scale and scope in Japanese, American, and Australian higher education.

References

Abbott, M. (1996). Amalgamations and the changing costs of Victorian Colleges of Advanced Education during the 1970s and 1980s. *Higher Education Research and Development* 15(2), 133-144.

Athanassopoulos, A. and Shale, E. (1997). Assessing the comparative efficiency of higher education institutions in the UK by means of data envelopment analysis. *Education Economics* 5(2), 117-134.

Burke, J. and Serban, A. (1997). *Performance Funding of Public Higher Education: Results Should Count.* New York: Public Higher Education Program, Rockefeller Institute.

Cave, M., Hanney, S., Henkel, M. and Kogan, M. (1997). *The Use Of Performance Indicators in Higher Education* (3rd edition). London: Jessica Kingsley Publishers.

Cormack, P. (1995). A comment on some recent estimates of economies of scale in higher education. *Applied Economic Letters* 2: 227-230.

Davis, D. (1996). *The Real World of Performance Indicators: A Review of Their Use in Selected Commonwealth Countries.* London: Commonwealth Higher Education Management Service.

Flower, R. (1998). Quantifying cost and quality: The national commission on the cost of higher education. *Academe* July-August, 37-41.

Getz, M., Siegfried, J.J., and Zhang, H. (1991). Estimating economies of scale in higher education *Economics Letters* 37: 203-208.

Glass, J., McKillip, D., and Hyndman, N. (1995). Efficiency in the provision of univesity teaching and research: An empirical analysis of UK universities *Journal of Applied Econometrics* 10: 61-72.

Hashimoto, K. and Cohn, E. (1997). Economies of scale and scope in Japanese private universities. *Education Economics* 5(2): 107-115.

Heaton, C. and Throsby, D. (1997). *Cost functions for Australian universities: A survey of results with implications for policy* (Discussion Paper No. 360). Canberra, Australia: Centre for Economic Policy Research, Australian National University.

Hoenack, S. and Collins, eds (1990). *The Economics of American Universities: Management, Operations, and Fiscal Environment.* Albany, NY: State University of New York Press.

Hyatt, J. (1983). *A Cost Accounting Handbook for Colleges and Universities.* Washington, DC: NACUBO.

Jenny, H. (1996). *Cost Accounting in Higher Education.* Washington, DC: National Association of College and University Business Officers.

Johnes, G. (1992). Performance indicators in higher education: A survey of recent work. *Oxford Review of Economic Policy* 8: 19-34.

Johnes, G. (1995). Scale and teaching efficiency in the production of economic research. *Applied Economics Letters* 2: 7-11.

Johnstone, D. B. (1998). *The Financing and Management of Higher Education: A Status Report on Worldwide Reforms.* Washington, DC: The World Bank.

King, W. (1997). Input and output substitution in higher education. *Economics Letters* 57: 107-111.

Koshal, R. K. and Koshal, M. (1995). Quality and economies of scale in higher education. *Applied Economics* 27: 773-778.

Koshal, R. K., and Koshal, M. (1999). Economies of scale and scope in higher education: A case of comprehensive universities. *Economics of Education Review* 18: 269-277.

Losco, J. and Fife, B. L. (1997). *Exploring the Costs of Higher Education: Priorities and Policies* (ED 418 663). Washington, DC: Educational Resources Information Center (ERIC).

NACUBO and NCHEMS (1977). *Procedures for Determining Historical Full Costs.* Washington, DC: NACUBO.

National Commission on the Cost of Higher Education (1998). *Straight Talk About College Costs and Prices.* New York: Oryx Press.

Pritchett, L., and Filmer, D. (1999). What education production functions really show: A positive theory of education expenditures. *Economics of Education Review* 18: 223-239.

Robst, J. (1997). *Cost Efficiency in Public Higher Education* (ED 422 758). Washington, DC: Educational Resources Information Center (ERIC).

Ruppert, S. (ed) (1994). *Charting Higher Education Accountability: A Sourcebook on State-level Performance Indicators.* Denver: Education Commission on the States.

Toutkoushian, R. (1998). *The Value of Cost Functions for Policymaking and Institutional Research* (ED 422 813). Washington, DC: Educational Resources Information Center (ERIC).

Chapter 6

ECONOMIC PERSPECTIVES ON RISING COLLEGE TUITION:
A Theoretical and Empirical Exploration[1]

Michael B. Paulsen

Each year since 1980, tuition charged by both private and public four-year colleges and universities has increased at a rate faster than that of the consumer price index (College Board, 1997; Lewis, 1989). In response, administrators, researchers, students, parents, politicians, and others have expressed persistent concern in their search for answers to questions about the causes of rising tuition (National Commission on the Costs of Higher Education, 1998). Empirical studies of the causes of rapid tuition growth have emphasized both institutional factors, such as increasing instructional or administrative expenditures, and environmental factors, such as job market opportunities for college graduates and federal student aid; and a variety of economic theories has served as the basis for seeking understanding of these phenomena, such as human capital theory, labor market theory, price theory, and theories of production and costs (Coopers & Lybrand, 1997; Koshal, Koshal, Boyd, and Levine, 1994; McMahon, 1974; McPherson and Schapiro, 1991, 1993; National Association of Independent Colleges and Universities, 1997; Paulsen, 1991; Rusk and Leslie, 1978; To and Olson, 1996). Theoretical and empirical inquiries have assumed a variety of perspectives and have provided opportunities for better understanding of the problem (Frances, 1990; Halstead, 1989; Hauptman, 1990; Lee, 1988). However, such analyses remain relatively separate, segregated, and disconnected in both the

---

[1]I would like to thank Jim Hearn, Professor and Chair of the Department of Educational Administration and Policy at the University of Minnesota, Walter Lane, Associate Professor of Economics at the University of New Orleans, Jim Paulsen, Chief Investment Officer and Economist at Norwest in Minneapolis, and Sarah Turner, Assistant Professor in the Department of Leadership, Foundations, and Policy at the University of Virginia for their careful readings of and helpful comments on earlier versions of this chapter. This chapter was originally published in Volume XV of *Higher Education: Handbook of Theory and Research,* © 2000 by Agathon Press. It has been updated with an Epilogue written especially for this volume.

perspectives they have taken and in the products, outcomes, or results they have generated. What is needed is a conceptual framework that can be productively used to integrate and elucidate the different perspectives taken—and the conclusions that have been drawn—in the various theoretical and empirical analyses reported in the existing literature.

Therefore, this chapter is not a conventional literature review. Instead, it has two distinct but mutually reinforcing, purposes: (1) to develop and present an economic model of the pricing behavior of a college or university selling educational services in a marketplace context; and (2) to apply the model as a heuristic device and conceptual framework within which the impacts of possible causes of rising tuition can be meaningfully explored and examined, and the findings of a somewhat fragmented set of related empirical studies can be meaningfully integrated. The exploration presented in this chapter is based on selected theoretical and empirical perspectives that I believe to be representative of the themes that characterize a vast existing literature on the causes of college tuition. Like many higher education researchers, I advocate the use of concepts, theories, and models from the appropriate underlying disciplines to serve as frameworks or heuristic devices in reviews of the research literature in higher education. Theory and research inform one another, and it is interesting that higher education researchers have drawn much more from the concepts and theories of disciplines such as psychology, sociology, and political science, while drawing much less from a wide range of potentially useful theories in the discipline of economics, one of the prominent policy sciences. I believe the higher education literature in the area of finance can be enriched by bringing economic concepts and theories into the mainstream in more explicit and elaborate forms. This would give higher education scholars a greater range of foundations and perspectives from which to do theoretical and empirical work that would expand our understanding of higher education finance and associated policies.

The price theory that constitutes a substantial portion of microeconomic theory would appear to be an appropriate choice as a useful conceptual framework for these purposes (Halstead, 1991). This approach is consistent with the view of Rothschild and White (1993) that the competitive market context provides a reasonable, important, and useful framework for the analysis of college and university behavior and understanding current issues such as costs and allocation in higher education. However, the choice of the type of market structure that best characterizes or approximates the features of the marketplace in higher education is somewhat more problematic. Some important contributions to the literature on the economics of higher education have been accomplished within a framework that assumes the presence of a perfectly competitive marketplace for higher education (Hopkins and Massy, 1981; James, 1978, 1990; Rothschild and White, 1995). The assumptions underlying this model have helped simplify the analysis of organizational behavior in many markets, including higher education, and it has become conceptually and empirically clearer that the higher education marketplace has become a more competitive environment (Hoxby, 1997) in which even public institutions are being shaped by trends toward—and the search for balance in—the process of privatization (Massy, 1996; Zemsky, Wegner, and Iannozzi, 1997).

No one economic model of the marketplace appears to offer an ideal framework for exploring college and university behavior. And unfortunately, the assumptions of the perfectively competitive market in some ways fall short of providing a close approximation of the features that characterize higher education (Leslie and Johnson, 1993). However, in his recent study of institutional costs in higher education, Halstead (1991) recommended and used a theory of imperfect competition called "monopolistic competition" as a model of the marketplace. Similarly, Garvin (1980), in his study of university behavior, also recommended monopolistic competition as a model whose underlying assumptions provide a more realistic approximation for some of the key characteristics of higher education. The monopolistically competitive market structure more closely matches the characteristics of the higher education marketplace than does the perfectly competitive model that is typically used, and also provides a more complex and flexible model—one that is more consistent with the economic realities of higher education and therefore, more fitting for the analysis of higher education using an economic analogy.

Although the models of both perfect and monopolistic competition assume a market with many sellers and buyers, perfect competition assumes that sellers' products are homogeneous—that is, they are undifferentiated, perfect substitutes for one another. For example, one farmer's corn is perceived to be pretty much the same as any other farmer's corn. On the other hand, monopolistic competition assumes that sellers' products are differentiated in the eyes of buyers and are close, but not perfect, substitutes for one another; for example, consumers often prefer one type of breakfast cereal over others (Binger and Hoffman, 1988; Henderson and Quandt, 1980; Waud, 1992). The assumption of product differentiation is far more characteristic of higher education than the assumption of product homogeneity. Potential students and their families perceive the product (educational package) offered by an individual college or university to possess characteristics that help make it appear unique and distinguishable compared with those offered by other institutions.

Furthermore, due to product homogeneity, the perfectly competitive seller faces a perfectly elastic demand curve. This means the seller is a price-taker and cannot influence the price charged for its product. That is, the seller must take or accept a single overall market price as given, and although it could sell all it desired at that price, it could sell none of its product at a higher price. In other words, if the seller raised its price above the overall market price, it would be abandoned by all of its customers, who could buy what they perceived to be the "identical" product elsewhere at a lower price. So, an individual seller that faces a perfectly elastic demand would find that customers would be infinitely or completely responsive to any increase in product price.

However, due to product differentiation, the monopolistically competitive seller faces a downward-sloping demand curve. In this case, customers perceive each individual seller's product to possess unique or distinguishing characteristics. As a result, each individual seller can charge or "set" a unique price for sale of its relatively unique product. In other words, when a monopolistically competitive seller raises its price, only those customers who were already on the borderline regarding their preferences for that seller's product over another's are very likely to switch brands. Because most of its customers prefer its relatively unique product over others, the monopolistically competitive seller possesses some degree of monopoly power in the marketplace. In higher education, colleges and universities typically face downward-sloping enrollment demand curves, and possess and exercise some degree of control over the setting of the price of their product (tuition). Private colleges and universities as well as public institutions or systems of public institutions are often more like the price-setters of monopolistic competition than the price-takers of perfect competition.[2]

Finally, product differentiation also leads to some non-price competition on the part of the seller, often taking the form of advertising, marketing, program development and related expenses intended to positively influence the position and slope of the seller's demand curve. On the other hand, the homogeneous product marketed in perfect competition provides no incentive or reason for institutions to engage in non-price competition. Once again, higher education is often characterized by not only product differentiation, but colleges and universities also regularly engage in non-price competition through ongoing, established programs for advertising, marketing, fund raising, recruitment, retention, and program development and expansion.

An important conceptual feature of market entry in monopolistic competition is especially relevant to, and descriptive of, the higher education marketplace: market entry can occur either through the formation or start-up of new organizations or through what Rothschild and White (1993) call "product extensions—new programs or schools begun by existing universities" (p. 32). In either case, the assumption that entry or exit in the market serves to sustain a more or less continuous process of

---

[2]Both logic and evidence suggest that some colleges and universities—in certain sectors and geographic settings—may be operating in a marketplace that is somewhat "closer" to a perfectly competitive market structure. For example, it is possible that for colleges in the same urban setting, some potential students and their families may view the bachelor's degree programs in business as fairly close substitutes. This possibility raises several interesting issues and questions. First, to the extent that some students view several colleges' business programs as very close substitutes, the colleges may face a demand curve that is somewhat more elastic. In other words, if one member of such a group raises its tuition, a substantial number of students may decide to enroll at a competing college. Second, the behavior of colleges in such sectors would still represent what the theory of monopolistic competition is intended to address; that is, it describes the market behavior of organizations in industries where sellers are characterized by "some amount" of product differentiation with respect to their competitors and therefore, face downward-sloping demand curve. However, even if colleges in some sectors and locations may be characterized by a "smaller degree" of product differentiation, it is difficult to imagine instances in which a college would lose all—or even nearly all—of its students if the institution raised its tuition above that of its nearby competitors. Rather, such institutions would be appropriately viewed as characterized by monopolistic competition and would face downward-sloping demand curves, but their demand curves would be more elastic than those faced by sets of colleges in markets characterized by greater college-to-college product differentiation, as perceived by potential students. An astute reviewer of an earlier version of this chapter offered the insight that rates of increase in tuition might be related to the market structure in which a college operates or alternatively, to the elasticity of the demand curve faced by colleges in that market. This is an empirical question, of course, and poses an interesting challenge for future research in the economics of higher education.

adjustment that moves monopolistically competitive sellers toward a natural equilibrium in which the average seller experiences little or no savings or budget surplus, provides a reasonable approximation that is suitable for use in the analysis of college and university behavior.[3,4]

The next (second) section of this chapter, "Revenues and Costs: A Monopolistically Competitive Model," develops and presents, in some detail, the assumptions, definitions, concepts, specifications, and relationships that, in combination, constitute an economic model of the ways in which revenue and cost structures of institutions help explain the pricing behavior of colleges and universities operating in a monopolistically competitive market setting. The third section of the chapter, "Revenues, Costs and Tuition: The Role of Institutional Subsidies in the Model," examines and illustrates those features of the economic model that highlight the important roles that institutional subsidies from public (e.g., state appropriations) and private (e.g., private giving) sources play in making it possible for public and private colleges and universities to supply or provide enrollment places at sticker-price tuition charges that are far below the actual per-student cost of a year's worth of college education. The fourth section of the chapter, "Revenues, Costs and Tuition: A Diagrammatic Exploration," is the largest; its primary purpose is to review the higher education literature on the possible causes of rising tuition, with special emphasis on the period from 1980 to the present. An important secondary purpose of this section is to employ the economic model as a conceptual framework and heuristic device for integrating, examining, and interpreting the results of empirical studies and related data about the causes of rising college tuition. More particularly, the economic model is used to explore and examine the possible ways in which supply-side or cost-and-subsidy-based factors and demand-side or revenue-based factors may have acted both independently and interdependently to promote increases in tuition. Depending on background and interests, some readers may elect to focus their attention on this section and the final section, both of which may be read without the need for careful study of the development of the economic model in previous sections. The fifth and final section of the chapter presents the results of the analyses conducted in the chapter to explore the possible causes of the rapid inflation of college tuition since 1980. In this section I present a set of tentative conclusions, based on the combined

---

[3]It might seem, in the case of higher education, that even when existing colleges experience surpluses or savings (profits) in the short run, that there would be substantial barriers to the opening of new colleges or the closing of existing colleges; however, based on data from the U.S. Department of Education, Rothschild and White (1993) report that between 1975 and 1990, 58 new public four-year and 72 new public two-year colleges were established, as were 203 new private four-year and 198 new private two-year colleges. And between 1970 and 1990, 34 public institutions and 242 private institutions closed their doors. For details about this data, see Rothschild and White (1993, pp. 30, 32-33).

[4]It is beyond the scope of this chapter to thoroughly investigate the acclaim or the criticism that surrounded the theory of monopolistic competition when first introduced (Chamberlin, 1965). However, many of the early questions raised about the possible shortcomings or inadequacy of Chamberlin's assumptions, analytical and mathematical rigor (e.g., see Blaug, 1985), have been rigorously and usefully addressed—and in some cases convincingly resolved—as a product of the resurgence of theoretical interest and research on monopolistic competition since the late 1970s (e.g., Hart, 1979, 1985a, 1985b; Perloff and Salop, 1985; Wolinsky, 1986).

results of the theoretical and empirical analyses conducted in the chapter, and express them in the form of propositions, or more precisely, testable hypotheses about the causes of recent tuition growth, each rated according to the probable strength of its impact. The final section also articulates additional suggestions for future theoretical and empirical research in this important area.

REVENUES AND COSTS: A MONOPOLISTICALLY COMPETITIVE MODEL

In this model I assume, following Migue and Belanger (1974), Niskanen (1975, 1991), Blais and Dion (1991) and others, that nonprofit organizations such as colleges and universities seek to maximize the administration's discretionary budget. The administration's discretionary budget (DB) represents the institution's budgetary surplus or saving. It is defined as the difference between the total revenues and the total costs of producing the institution's educational services. However, total revenue consists of tuition revenue from market sources—what Hansmann (1986) calls "commercial" income—and non-tuition revenue from nonmarket sources, including government appropriations, private gifts, and endowment income, an expanded version of what Hansmann (1986) calls "donative" income. This distinction between revenue sources is an important one because colleges and universities face more than just a market demand for their services in which revenue comes from commercial sources or sales alone, as in the case of the typical for-profit organization. Instead, a substantial portion of college and university revenues comes from public donative resources—that is, government appropriations—and private donative resources including gifts, grants and endowment income, where the latter are actively pursued—and with considerable success—by both private and public institutions through fundraising expenditures and efforts directed toward increasing donations from a variety of private sources.[5]

The assumption that colleges and universities seek to maximize their administrations' discretionary budgets or savings is also consistent with the perspective and criteria used to assess the economic performance of several highly selective and financially healthy colleges with large endowments between 1988 and 1993 (Weber and Winston, 1994).

> The 'bottom line' in an evaluation of a year's economic performance in global accounts is a college's *saving*. Saving is simply total income less total current spending, it is what is left over for future use from a year's resources....A college whose year's real saving is exactly zero has had an OK year—is in a 'financial equilibrium' in that it's saving enough that it can go on like that forever. A college that had positive real saving has had a good year....If it's saving less, it will fall behind in wealth and in what it can do for its students (pp. 2-4).

---

[5]Of course, public institutions also actively pursue state appropriations through lobbying efforts. However, expenditures for lobbying are very difficult—perhaps impossible—to measure and difficult to model in a meaningful way. Furthermore, the share of revenue for public institutions from state appropriations is steadily shrinking while the share of their revenue coming from private donative sources is rapidly rising in an era of rapidly increasing privatization of public institutions (Breneman and Finney, 1997). Therefore, the pursuit of voluntary gifts through fund-raising expenditures and activities is viewed as the more important and relevant "strategic" element in the financial futures of both private and public institutions, and the mathematical model is specified accordingly.

Non-profit organizations such as colleges and universities commonly experience budgetary surpluses or savings and are certainly permitted to experience a surplus of revenues over costs, but of course, they are not legally permitted to distribute such surpluses or savings to any owners such as the stockholders, proprietors or partners that own for-profit organizations (McPherson, Schapiro and Winston, 1996). This is what Hansmann (1986) calls the "nondistribution constraint". However, while colleges and universities must use all revenues to finance current or future production of educational services, budget surpluses or savings increase an institution's opportunities to add to their endowment so that the income or payout from it may be used to finance other educational services in the future (Breneman, 1994), or to cross-subsidize the production of educational services in one area by internal re-allocations of surplus revenues from a more profitable area in the current period (James, 1990).[6]

The various institutional goals that have been proposed as arguments in a university's utility function—such as prestige, student quality, faculty quality, or enrollment (see for example, Garvin, 1980; James, 1978, 1990)—are captured in the institutions' pursuit of a discretionary budget that offers the administration the flexibility to pursue such important and valued goals beyond the mere provision of educational services. For example, colleges can use their discretionary budgets to supplement their current spending on marketing, advertising and other activities in order to increase the uniqueness of their educational package—that is, to differentiate their product from that of other colleges—in the eyes of potential students and their families (Kotler and Fox, 1985; Paulsen, 1990a). When they are successful, this will increase students' demand for their product (an outward or rightward shift in the demand curve) and reduce the elasticity of that demand (increase the steepness of the demand curve). As a result, students would demand a larger number of places at the college for a given tuition, permitting the college to be more selective in their admissions, thereby enhancing student quality, diversity and institutional prestige; and for a given level of enrollment, students would be willing to pay a higher tuition than before. In combination, these outcomes of discretionary spending would generate more tuition revenues due to the perception that the college offers a more distinctive package of educational services than it did previously.

Colleges and universities in both the private and public sectors can also use their discretionary budget to support increases in current fund-raising activities, in their pursuit of additional revenue from private donative sources (Dunn, 1986; Duronio and

---

[6]Although it may in some ways appear that public universities are not allowed to experience budgetary surpluses or positive discretionary budgets, this is not accurate. Administrators, faculty and students in most public colleges and universities have witnessed the excitement that surrounds a mid-year or spring announcement that there is a bit of a surplus that the institution has no trouble finding ways to spend—essentially increasing their costs to match their revenues—that will help the institution pursue its important goals before the end of the fiscal year. Such behavior is quite consistent with Bowen's (1980) revenue theory of costs. Of course, many have also experienced the heartbreak of budget shortfalls—which can happen just as surpluses can—at which time institutions seek ways to cut costs before the fiscal year ends. As donative resources from private giving become a larger percentage of the budget of public institutions over the next 5-10 years, it seems likely that even some of the peculiarities that still distinguish between how public and private institutions conceptualize and use their savings will diminish.

Loessin, 1990; Grunig, 1995; Leslie and Ramey, 1988; Paton, 1986). The more successful a college has been in enhancing the distinctiveness of its educational product, the more effective its fund-raising activities will be. In combination, both additional marketing expenditures and fund-raising expenditures can be viewed as investments that institutions typically make in their "search" for more revenue to cover, or even exceed, their current costs. In summary, the discretionary budget can be used to supplement institutional expenditures in the pursuit of university goals in the current period, or it can supplement an institutions' endowment, the income from which can be used to supplement such spending in future periods.

The Mathematical Model

The model used to explore ways in which the relationships between the demand configuration and costs faced by a college impact the level of tuition or sticker price is presented formally below. Equation 1 below is the maximand for the discretionary budget of a representative college or university.

Eq. 1[7] $DB = P(Q,M(Q))Q - C(Q) - mQ - fQ - aQ + d^P fQ + d^G Q + rE$

where

DB = the administration's discretionary budget, equal to the difference between revenues from commercial sources and the costs of providing its educational product, adjusted for subsidies from donative resources.

P = sticker price or tuition

Q = undergraduate enrollment

PQ = gross revenue from commercial sources, that is, due to sales of enrollment spaces at sticker prices to undergraduate students

C = costs of providing the college's desired educational product, undergraduate education, equal to educational and general expenditures (E&G), adjusted for—that is, after subtracting out—expenditures expressly dedicated to funded research, public service, or restricted externally funded scholarships (such as federal Pell grants, in which cases the institution has no discretion in their use). The largest components of adjusted E&G expenditures include the costs of instruction, institutional and academic support—which, in combination, account for most of an institution's admin-

---

[7]Note that the explicit functional form of M(Q) is M(Q) = mQ, where "m" equals marketing expenditures per student; therefore, M is proportional to, and a linear function of, undergraduate enrollment (Q) and is expressed in its explicit functional form in the last or total-cost portion of the objective function, as a vertical adjustment to C(Q) in the maximand, when m>0. However, in the first or total-revenue part of the maximand, the notation M(Q) is employed. These equivalent, but alternative notations are used to increase the clarity of exposition, which can be more readily seen by inspection of the first-order conditions below. Briefly, the use of M(Q) in the expression for total revenue yields, among other things in the first-order conditions, the term P_M, which represents the change in sticker price students are willing to pay—for a given enrollment level—due to a unit increase in marketing expenditures per student, and is correspondingly assumed to be greater than zero. The use of mQ in the expression for total costs yields, in the first-order conditions, marketing expenditures per student, m, which is one of a set of parameters that represent the vertical magnitudes of equal shifts in marginal and average costs curves.

istrative costs—plant operations, and students services (Getz and Siegfried, 1991).

m = marketing expenditures per undergraduate student, one of the components of E&G expenditures, usually distributed across the subcategories of E&G expenditures, but noted separately here because of its strategic importance in the revenues and costs, and enrollment and pricing decisions of colleges and universities.

mQ = total marketing expenditures

f = fund-raising expenditures per undergraduate student, one of the components of E&G expenditures, usually included in the subcategory of institutional support but noted separately here because of its strategic importance in the revenues and costs, and enrollment and pricing decisions of colleges and universities.

fQ = total fund-raising expenditures

a = amount of institutional aid per-student, one of the components of E&G expenditures, usually referred to as the subcategory of unrestricted scholarships, but noted separately here because of its strategic importance in the revenues and costs, and enrollment and pricing decisions of colleges and universities.

aQ = total expenditures for institutional aid

d^P = donative resources from private donations per dollar of fund-raising expenditures

d^PfQ = total donative resources from private donations

d^G = donative resources in the form of government appropriations per student.

d^GQ = total donative resources from government appropriations

E = current market value of endowment

r = rate of payout on—or rate of spending from—endowment

rE = total donative resources from endowment income

In this model, an institution is assumed to engage in marketing expenditures (m) in an effort to differentiate or distinguish its educational product from those of other colleges. This accomplishment will cause the position and slope of its demand curve to increase—that is, an outward shift and a steepening of the demand curve would occur—resulting in greater revenue from commercial sources (tuition revenue). The purpose of such an undertaking is to increase revenues from commercial sources by more than the increase in marketing expenditures.[8]

Similarly, an institution is assumed to engage in fund-raising expenditures (f) in an effort to increase the level of donative resources available from private giving, to assist the institution in pursuing its goals. As noted above, f equals the dollars spent on fund raising per student. This amount essentially indicates the "intensity" of fund-raising efforts. As stated above, d^P equals donative resources from private giving per dollar of fund-raising expenditures. Therefore, d^P reflects the "receptivity" of the community to fund-raising efforts, and indicates the "effectiveness" of fund-raising activities and expenses. It is also possible to view d^P as the "return" on a dollar of fund-raising expenditures per student, so that d^P must be greater than 1 for fund-raising expenditures to be profitable or yield a positive return per dollar.[9] Private donative resources take the form of private gifts, grants and endowment income, acquired in either a past or the current period through fund-raising efforts. These private donative resources are non-tuition revenues that are viewed as cost-reducers or subsidies to cover institutional costs in the present model.

Finally, d^G, defined above as donative resources in the form of government appropriations per student, can be viewed as an indicator of a state's commitment to the financial support of higher education. Government or public donative resources are another non-tuition source of revenue, and are also viewed as cost-reducers or subsidies to cover institutional costs in the present model.

There are two possible ways to view institutional aid in a model of revenues and costs for a college or university (Bowen and Breneman, 1993; Getz and Siegfried, 1991). One approach is to view such aid as an expenditure or cost of production and the other is to view it as a reduction in revenue. The difference between the two approaches is related to differences in the semantics and viewpoints of accounting and economics. Viewing institutional aid as an expenditure is consistent with standard accounting practices in institutions of higher education (Breneman, 1994; Getz and Siegfried, 1991), in which case colleges report "gross" tuition revenue—inclusive of revenue "paid" by students from the institutional aid they "receive" in the form of scholarships—on the revenue side of the ledger, and include institutional aid as an expenditure on the cost side of the ledger. In this approach, institutional aid is essentially viewed from an accounting perspective as an equal amount added to both revenues and costs. Gross tuition revenue is defined as sticker price times total enrollment, while institutional aid is defined as expenditures from the institution's unrestricted funds on scholarships to selected students that help them pay a portion of the sticker price.

When institutional aid is viewed as a reduction in revenue, the relationships between revenues and costs would be essentially unchanged because the amount of such institutional aid would simply be excluded from both the revenue and cost sides of the ledger. This approach is inconsistent with standard accounting practices of col-

---

[8]The way in which marketing expenditures (m) can lead to either an upward and outward shift and/or a steepening in the slope of the institution's demand curve can be illustrated by specifying the following linear demand curve for the institution: $P = a + a'm - bQ - b'mQ$, where $(a + a'm)$ is the vertical intercept of the demand curve and $(-b - b'm)$ is the slope of the demand curve. When $m = 0$ (no marketing expenses), then the demand curve becomes the simpler linear form before any shifts or changes in slope: $P = a - bQ$ However, when there are marketing expenditures ($m > 0$), then the resultant changes in the demand curve—an upward and outward shift and/or a steepening in slope—will depend on whether a' and b' are greater than or equal to zero. If $b'=0$ and $a'>0$ then the demand curve will become $P = a + a'm - bQ$, and the intercept increases vertically by the amount a'm, resulting in an upward and outward shift in demand. If $a'=0$ and $b'>0$ then the demand curve will become $P = a - bQ - b'mQ$, and the slope of the demand curve steepens by the amount b'm. This is a clockwise rotation in demand and would result in less elasticity of demand; that is, the percentage change in enrollment per 1% change in sticker price would decrease and students attracted to the relative uniqueness of this institution's educational product would become less price-responsive. Finally, if $a'>0$ and $b'>0$ then the full linear specification is relevant: $P = a + a'm - bQ - b'mQ$, and the demand curve shifts upward by amount a'm and steepens in slope by amount b'm. In other words, for a unit increase in marketing expenditures per student (m) the intercept of the demand curve shifts up by a' and the slope steepens by -b'Q. In combination, these effects would enhance the institution's opportunity to increase revenue from commercial sources—tuition revenue. It should also be noted that upward and outward shifts in demand create greater opportunities for institutions to be more selective in their admissions decisions, for a given enrollment level, which in turn, could increase the quality and diversity of students at the institution. A greater quality and diversity in the student body can serve to further enrich the educational experiences of admitted students.

leges and universities, but is economically meaningful. Institutional aid is more likely to be viewed as a reduction in revenue when additional students are charged lower prices than the sticker price in order to increase enrollment toward an institution's target level (Bowen and Breneman, 1993). This is possible when an institution knows so much about a student's financial status that it can identify the maximum price each student would be willing and able to pay and still attend their college. Economists describe colleges or universities who engage in this practice as perfect price-discriminating sellers who are exercising some degree of monopoly power in the marketplace (Bowen and Breneman, 1993; Breneman, 1994).

Colleges and universities use institutional aid for two different purposes (Bowen and Breneman, 1993). One purpose is to attract selected students because of the quality and diversity they bring to the student body. In these instances, institutional aid may be more appropriately viewed as an expenditure in the form of an investment in quality on the part of the institution—that is, as an economic cost of producing the educational product. The other purpose is to attract students who cannot afford the sticker price in hopes of expanding enrollment closer toward a desired target level. In this case, institutional aid may be more appropriately viewed as a reduction in revenue—that is, some students are offered enrollment places at lower prices than others merely because they would not otherwise attend. Such lower prices are commonly referred to as tuition discounts. As Bowen and Breneman (1993) explain, the great majority of colleges use institutional aid for both purposes.

> of course, many colleges and universities occupy intermediate positions along what is a continuum....[A] liberal arts college may not be able to fill all its places without some use of student aid as a price discount, but it may spend considerably more on student aid than it would need to spend if it were concerned only with meeting an enrollment target. Many colleges invest some of their limited institutional resources in student aid to achieve a stronger and more diverse student body than they could attract otherwise....In mixed cases of this kind, student aid functions partly as price discount and partly as an educational investment" (p. 305).

Because both purposes and viewpoints about institutional aid are important, both will be used in this chapter to examine the behavior of colleges and universities in a monopolistically competitive marketplace. In most instances, whether institutional aid is viewed as a cost or as a reduction in revenue, the model will make similar predictions about the direction of change in tuition due to demand-induced changes in the revenue structure or cost-induced changes in the cost structure of an institution. Therefore, I have used the criteria of simplicity and clarity of exposition to decide which approach will be taken first and most often in this chapter to explore the relationships between changes in revenue and cost structures and the direction of change in tuition. Viewing institutional aid as an expenditure or cost provides a much simpler

---

[9]Inspection of the first-order conditions (FOC) below indicates that $(-f + d^P f) = (d^P - 1)f$, where $(d^P - 1)$ is essentially the "net return" on a dollar of fund-raising expenditures per student. And d^P is the reciprocal of a measure of fund-raising effectiveness that is commonly used in the literature, "costs per dollar raised" (Grunig, 1995).

and clearer framework for exploring the ways in which changes in revenues and costs affect tuition. Viewing institutional aid as a reduction in revenue requires the use of a far more complex and complicated variation of the basic model to illustrate the behavior of the perfect price-discriminating monopolistically competitive institution (Binger and Hoffman, 1988; Breneman, 1994; Henderson and Quandt, 1980; Salvatore, 1986).

For these reasons, the model will view institutional aid as an expenditure or cost for most of the forthcoming analyses, However, because of the additional understanding of tuition-discounting and enrollment-expanding behavior that can occur by viewing such aid as a reduction in revenue, a special section of the chapter will be devoted to one possible variation of the model in the examination of the behavior of a perfect-price-discriminating monopolistically competitive institution.

Equation 1 views expenditures for institutional aid as part of the adjusted E&G expenses that constitute the overall costs of producing an institution's educational product in this model. In this way, the model assumes that the discretionary-budget-maximizing—or target level of—enrollment is comprised of (a) some students who are willing and able to pay the full sticker price without institutional aid and (b) other students who are willing and able to pay the full sticker price only with the help of the institutional aid they receive. This approach explicitly includes the amount of institutional aid as part of the total educational costs of production *and* as part of "gross" tuition revenue. The effect of this approach—which is consistent with the accounting practices of colleges and universities—is to simplify the model in ways that make it much more effective for its intended purpose: to serve as a heuristic device and conceptual framework for integrating a wide range of theory and research relevant to our understanding of the causes of rising tuition. This approach also makes it possible to focus analysis on increases in the sticker price of college, which is important because it has been the rate of increase in the sticker price that has been the source of society's deepest concern.[10] As shown in Equation 1, institutional aid is addressed separately and explicitly in the model, with the symbol "a" representing institutional aid per student and "aQ" measuring total expenditures on institutional aid, because in our era of rising tuition, this has become the fastest-growing category of educational costs (Getz and Siegfried, 1991) and an important strategic element in budgeting and enrollment management (Hossler, Bean and associates, 1990; Hubbell, 1992).

---

[10]An optimizing, perfect-price-discriminating seller would engage in price discrimination across the entire range of the demand curve from the highest possible sticker price to the marginal price—that is, the lowest price charged in the tuition-discounting process, where MC = D. (Binger and Hoffman, 1988; Henderson and Quandt, 1980). However, such a model would tend to shift the focus of the analysis away from the determination of the sticker price to the determination of the marginal price. And the added complexity of such an approach would tend to work against the purpose of the model used in this chapter: to serve as a simple, clear heuristic device and conceptual framework for integrating a wide range of research relevant to our understanding of the causes of rising sticker-price tuition. The development of such a model would be an important contribution, but its purpose would be to enhance our understanding of the internal financial behavior of colleges and universities. See the section on Conclusions and Implications for Future Research, and the accompanying footnotes, for suggestions about the nature and value of such a model in future research.

The first-order conditions necessary for the college to maximize its administration's discretionary budget appear in Equation 2 below.[11]

Eq. 2 $DB_Q = P + P_Q Q + P_M M_Q Q - C_Q - m - f - a + d^P f + d^G = 0$

where

$[P + P_Q Q + P_M M_Q Q]$ = marginal revenue (MR) from commercial sources; $[-1(C_Q + m + f + a - d^P f - d^G)]$ = marginal cost (MC = C_Q) plus a series of vertical shift parameters representing the magnitudes of the identical vertical shifts in marginal cost (MC) and average cost (AC), due to changes in specified per-unit costs or subsidies (m + f + a - $d^P f - d^G$); and rE does not appear in the first order conditions (DB_Q) because it is income in the current period—specified as the rate of payout on endowment (r) times the market value of endowment (E)—and although it serves as another source of donative resources or revenue, it is viewed, and specified, as a lump-sum institutional subsidy or cost-reducer so that when it changes, only the AC curve and not the MC curve would shift in the model.

The following first-order conditions formally express some important assumptions of the model: $P_Q < 0$, $P_M > 0$, $M_Q > 0$, $C_Q > 0$. First, $P_Q < 0$ means that sticker price (tuition) and enrollment are inversely related; that is, for a given demand, enrollment (Q) can be increased only by decreasing price, ceteris paribus. Of course, it also represents a critical characteristic of a monopolistically competitive seller: that each institution possesses some degree of monopoly power, due to its relatively unique product that is differentiated from others in the eyes of students and their families, and the downward-sloping demand curve it faces ($P_Q < 0$) is evidence of this. $P_M > 0$

---

[11]The second-order conditions (SOC) can also be derived, and they reveal some other interesting features of the specified model.

$DB_{QQ} = [(P_Q + P_M M_Q) + (P_Q + P_{QQ} Q + P_{QM} M_Q Q) + (P_M M_Q + P_{MQ} M_Q Q + P_{MM} M_Q^2 Q + P_M M_{QQ} Q)] - [(C_{QQ})] < 0$

or, collecting and rearranging terms, yields the expression

$DB_{QQ} = [2 P_Q + 2 P_M M_Q + P_{QQ} Q + P_{QM} M_Q Q + P_{MQ} M_Q Q + P_{MM} M_Q^2 Q + P_M M_{QQ} Q] - [C_{QQ}] < 0$

where

$P_{QQ} = 0$, $P_{QM} < 0$, $P_{MQ} < 0$, $P_{MM} = 0$, $M_{QQ} = 0$, $C_{QQ} > 0$

Most of the second-order conditions have quite interesting interpretations which shed additional light on the behavior of colleges as displayed in their revenue and cost structure and clarify assumptions of this model's specification. P_{QQ} indicates the effect that increased enrollment (Q) would have on the slope of the demand function. Because the functional form of demand is assumed to be linear, the slope would be constant; therefore, $P_{QQ} = 0$ and the third term in the SOC drops out to zero. P_{QM} indicates the effect that an increase in marketing expenditures would have on the slope of the demand function. The derivative of the slope of the linear demand function specified in footnote number 7 with respect to m is negative. The negative effect ($P_{QM} < 0$) would be expected because increases in marketing expenditures would tend to increase the uniqueness of a college's product compared to that of other colleges, which in turn, would increase the slope (decrease the elasticity) or steepness of the demand curve (P_Q), which requires that the slope become more negative. The negative effect of increased Q on the first-order positive effect ($P_M > 0$) of marketing expenditures on the prices students will pay at various enrollment levels (($P_{MQ} < 0$) is also understandable in terms of the steepening of the demand curve (reduction in elasticity and slope becoming more negative) as Q rises along the linear demand. P_{MM} indicates the effect of increased marketing expenditures on the positive change in price due to increased marketing. Because the demand curve expresses a linear relationship between price and m and Q, its slope would be constant and the second derivative of the linear relationship between marketing price and marketing expenditures would be zero; therefore, $P_{MM} = 0$. Because M(Q) = mQ, indicating a proportional linear relationship with a constant slope, $M_{QQ} = 0$. Finally, C_{QQ} is positive ($C_{QQ} > 0$), indicating a marginal cost curve whose slope continues to increase with enrollment (Q), and is consistent with the U-shaped marginal and average cost curves which appear in the geometric exposition of the model.

means that sticker price and marketing expenditures are directly related; that is, marketing expenditures shift the demand curve up and to the right and reduce the elasticity of demand (increase its steepness or slope) due to the increased distinctiveness of the college's product in the eyes of potential students. $M_Q > 0$ indicates that marketing expenditures and enrollment are directly related; that is, higher enrollment levels are associated with larger volumes of marketing expenditures. $C_Q > 0$ states that costs of production are directly related to the level of enrollment (standard marginal costs are positive); that is, total costs increase with enrollment.

Two of the most distinctive features of this monopolistically competitive model of college and university behavior are expressed in two assumptions based on the first-order conditions shown in Equation 2 above: $P_M > 0$ and $(-f + d^P f) = (d^P - 1)f$, where $(d^P - 1)$ represents the net return from fund-raising expenditures per student (f), and such expenditures are worthwhile assuming that $d^P > 1$. These behavioral assumptions declare, respectively, that (1) institutions pursue increases in their revenue from commercial sources (tuition revenue) through marketing and related expenditures that enhance the configuration (position and elasticity or slope) of student demand for their educational services; and (2) institutions pursue increases in their revenue from donative sources in the form of private giving (non-tuition revenue)—specified here as institutional subsidies from donative sources that reduce their costs of providing a given level of educational services $(d^P fQ)$—through fund-raising expenditures (f) that enhance such private contributions. Of course, institutional revenues from non-tuition sources include private donations per-unit $(d^P f)$, endowment income (rE) and government per-unit appropriations (d^G); however, in the present model, both private and public colleges and universities are assumed to actively pursue private donations through fund-raising expenditures (fQ), while government appropriations—especially important for public institutions—are assumed to be determined by, and change due to, legislative decision-making in state capitols. Nevertheless, both private donations $(d^P fQ)$ and government appropriations $(d^G Q)$—along with endowment income (rE)—are viewed as important major sources of non-tuition revenue for colleges and universities in the model specified above.

As indicated by the positive signs in front of $d^P fQ$, $d^G Q$, and rE in the maximand, Equation 1, both private and governmental sources of donative resources are assumed to have an additive effect on the second-half or cost-related portion of the maximand.[12] In other words, in the present model, private and governmental donative resources are viewed as cost-reducers or institutional subsidies that cover a substantial portion of total institutional costs of providing educational services to undergraduate students. This focuses the model on one of the most distinctive characteristics of the revenue and cost structures of the monopolistically competitive colleges and universities that populate the higher education marketplace (Winston, 1998).

---

[12]Equation 1 defines the discretionary budget for a representative college or university. However, the parameters for some components of the equation, such as the subsidies per student of $d^P f$ and d^G, could have different values for public and private institutions. Nevertheless, the structure of the equation would be the same for both public and private institutions.

REVENUES, COSTS AND TUITION: THE ROLE OF INSTITUTIONAL SUBSIDIES IN THE MODEL

One of the most remarkable and distinctive features of the higher education marketplace is that institutions typically charge sticker prices (tuition) that are far below the costs of educating an undergraduate student. "This sustainable separation of cost and price...is surely a defining economic characteristic of higher education, both public and private (Winston, 1996, p. 5). This is possible due to large subsidies made available to institutions of higher education in the form of donative resources (non-tuition revenues) provided by private and government sources, symbolized by $d^P f Q$, rE, and $d^G Q$ in the model presented in the previous section. In his research, Winston (1998) refers to the difference between educational costs per student, excluding institutional aid, and sticker price as the "general subsidy" that is made available to all students once sticker price is determined. According to recently assembled 1995 data for 2,739 institutions (almost evenly divided between public and private institutions), this general subsidy accounted for 50.5% of educational costs per student, while the sticker price accounted for the other 49.5% of per-student educational costs (Winston, 1998).[13]

Of course, the actual net price that some students pay is less than the sticker price due to the institutional aid that is, in fact, awarded according to student financial need, merit, or other individual characteristics (Hubbell, 1992). As explained above, the model used here views such individualized, institutional aid as a component of educational costs. In this model, such aid can be offered to selected students—when desired by the institution—when donative resources in the current period are at least sufficient to cover those portions of educational costs that correspond to the general subsidy made available to all students according to where the sticker price is set. The remaining educational costs would then be covered by commercial or tuition revenues (McPherson, Schapiro and Winston, 1996).

The primary purpose of the model initially specified in the previous section, and illustrated and applied diagrammatically below, is to explore the various ways an institution's revenue and cost structures—where costs can include expenditures for institutional aid—interact in their impact on the direction of change in an institution's sticker price. The logical and diagrammatic framework for this analysis is presented below.

At a given point in time, each institution faces a particular demand configuration or "commercial" revenue structure, represented by its average and marginal revenue curves, that indicates the number of undergraduate students who meet admissions standards and would be willing and able to pay various sticker prices. However,

---

[13]Of course these percentages represent averages across all types of institutions. In fact, the percentages of educational costs per student that are accounted for by the general subsidy and the sticker price differ between public and private institutions. Just as one would expect, due in large part to the role of state government appropriations, the general subsidy as a percent of educational costs per student at public institutions is considerably higher than at private institutions. Accordingly, the percent of educational costs per student at private institutions accounted for by the sticker price is considerably higher at private institutions (Winston, 1998).

because educational costs per student are so high relative to the prices most students are willing and able to pay, the great majority of institutions—all but a few highly selective institutions who consistently face great excess demand for enrollment places—realize that the number of qualified students who would be willing to pay a sticker price high enough to cover the full costs of their education would constitute an enrollment that would be well below that which would be appropriate for their scale of operation. Donative resources are made available to institutions of higher education for the purpose of encouraging them to make higher education of good quality accessible to larger numbers of qualified students than would be possible if commercial revenue (tuition income) were the only source of revenue with which institutions could attempt to cover their educational costs of production.

The presence and magnitude of donative resources provided for higher education—like for other forms of investment in human capital such as health—are often attributed to the existence of positive "externalities" in the provision of higher education (Breneman and Nelson, 1981; Thurow, 1970). External benefits, those that will accrue to society in general, such as those resulting from a more educated citizenry or a general increase in workforce productivity (Bowen, 1977; Paulsen, 1996a, 1996b), are typically not considered by individual student consumers of higher education. Instead, an individual student consumer considers only the benefits of college that would accrue to her—that is, are internalized, captured or appropriated by the student—when comparing benefits with costs in the college investment decision-making process (Paulsen, 1998). In the presence of positive externalities, individual students who view their investment decisions in this way will consistently underinvest in higher education, unless subsidies are given to colleges and universities as donative resources that cover or reduce their educational costs so they can offer enrollment spaces to more students at a lower sticker price. Donative resources from private and public sources are given to colleges and universities in the form of subsidies that institutions can use to cover or pay for a substantial portion of their educational costs. This typically has the effect of reducing their educational costs so that the remainder can be covered by commercial revenues, that is, through the collection of tuition income from their students, the capacity for which is expressed in their revenue structure (demand and marginal revenue curves). An institution's cost structure will shift downward in the model represented diagrammatically below. For per-unit subsidies, such as $d^P f$ (private giving) and d^G (government appropriations), marginal cost (MC) and average cost (AC) will shift down by identical amounts. For lump-sum subsidies, such as rE (endowment income), only average cost will shift downward and the vertical amount of the shift will vary with enrollment because as enrollment rises, a fixed sum of endowment income must be distributed over the instructional costs of educating more students, yielding a progressively smaller per-student amount of endowment income.

A re-examination of Equation 1 will indicate the sizes of the vertical downward shift in the cost structure that will occur under various conditions. Re-writing Equation 1 in a somewhat simplified functional form (Eq. 1a) facilitates the logical identification of the magnitudes of the vertical shifts.

Eq. 1a $DB = PQ - cQ - mQ - fQ - aQ + d^P fQ + d^G Q + rE$

Re-writing Eq. 1a in per-unit or per-student form yields

Eq. 1b $db = P - c - m - f - a + d^P f + d^G + rE/Q$

where db = DB/Q or discretionary budget (saving) per student.

Collecting and grouping terms and re-writing Eq. 1b, so that the right-hand side shows a sequence of average commercial revenue (ACR) minus average cost (AC) plus average donative subsidy (ADS), yields

Eq. 1c $db = [P] - [c + m + f + a] + [d^P f + d^G + rE/Q]$

A more efficient statement of what appears in each pair of brackets on the right-hand side yields

Eq. 1d $db = ACR - AC + ADS$

If saving or discretionary budget equals zero (db=0), then

Eq. 1e $AC = ACR + ADS$

or

Eq. 1e' $AC - ADS = ACR$

Eq. 1e states that AC is exactly covered by the combination of ACR and ADS when db=0 (saving is zero)—the break-even scenario; or alternatively expressed, Eq. 1e' states that when ADS is used to reduce or cover AC, the amount of AC remaining will be exactly covered by ACR. However, if saving is positive (db > 0), the situation is a bit more complicated, but also probably a bit more common and realistic as well. In its simplest form, if there is positive saving (db > 0), then

Eq. 1f $db = ACR + ADS - AC$

or

Eq. 1f' $AC + db = ACR + ADS$

where Eq. 1f and 1f' state that the size of the discretionary budget (db) is equal to the excess of ACR and ADS over AC. Alternatively expressed, this would yield:

Eq. 1g $[(AC - ADS) + db] = ACR$

This restatement suggests an interesting interpretation, and one that is especially consistent with the format of the model used here. When donative subsidies (ADS) are substantial enough to cover or reduce average costs (AC) so that they are now below the sticker price (ACR or P), the commercial revenues alone (ACR) would be sufficient to cover the remaining average costs and still leave a surplus, saving or a positive discretionary budget for the administration. The administration, in turn, can elect to add the db to wealth (endowment) to increase the availability of donative resources in future periods or can increase spending on valued institutional goals by spending the db in the current period and break even.

The last possibility is that of a shortage, shortfall, or negative discretionary budget

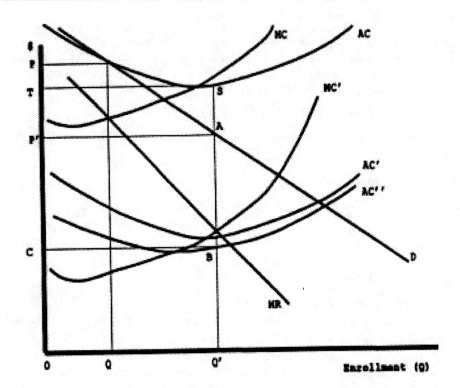

Figure 1. Effect of Donative Subsidies on Cost, Tuition, and Enrollment

so that Eq. 1g becomes

  Eq. 1g' $[(AC - ADS) - db] = ACR$

This means that donative subsidies are not enough to cover or reduce average costs (AC) so that they are at least below the sticker price (ACR or P); therefore, the commercial revenues alone (ACR) would not be sufficient to cover the remaining average costs, and the result would be a shortage or a negative discretionary budget for the administration. The administration, in turn, can elect to cover the shortfall by drawing on its wealth (endowment) from previous periods, decrease spending on valued institutional goals in the current period, or carry more debt, where each of these options ultimately leads to a break even scenario for the current period.

  The ways in which institutional subsidies from donative sources affect the institution's cost structure can be readily illustrated in a diagrammatic framework. Figure 1 compares two cost structures, one without, and another with, institutional subsidies from donative sources, and illustrates how costs interact with an institution's demand configuration—that is, its demand (average revenue) and marginal revenue curves—to indicate the direction of change in an institution's tuition (sticker price).[14] Based on the demand curve (D), the marginal revenue (MR) curve indicates the amount that each additional student enrolled would add to revenues from commercial sources or tuition income. The cost structure represented by MC and AC is very high across varying levels of enrollment (Q) because they have not yet been reduced by donative subsidies. MC and AC constitute the cost structure for an institution that receives no donative subsidies from either public or private sources. Given D and MR, the incremental revenue (MR) exceeds the incremental cost or marginal cost (MC) up to an enrollment level of only Q. In order to maximize its discretionary budget or surplus, the institution portrayed in the figure would not enroll students beyond Q, given its current revenue and cost structure. They would enroll Q students and the demand curve indicates that those students are willing and able to pay tuition P to attend. In this instance, for Q students, the revenue per student (P) is the same as the cost per student (AC) so the institution, technically speaking, could actually open its doors and break even (TR = TC). However, this is a very small enrollment, and for this institution—and the great majority of others—this would fall far short of the level of enrollment that would be consistent with its scale of operation. In the absence of donative resources to provide a general subsidy to all students and/or tuition discounting in the form of financial aid for selected students, probably only a small number of wealthy students (Q) could afford the very high sticker price (P).

But now is when donative subsidies enter the picture. The lower cost structure of MC' and AC' represent MC and AC after they have been shifted vertically downward by the per-unit amounts of donative resources available to subsidize, cover and reduce the institution's educational costs of production. Per-unit donative subsidies shift both marginal and average cost downward by identical vertical amounts. However, the final average cost curve, after all donative subsidies have been applied to reduce cost, is AC". The vertical difference between AC' and AC" is greater at lower levels of enrollment and gets smaller as enrollment expands. The reason for this is that the difference is due to the presence of the lump-sum donative subsidy that comes from the total amount of endowment income available in the current period to help subsidize or reduce costs. A fixed total amount of endowment income (rE) for the current period, when expressed in terms of reductions in per-unit or average costs rE/Q, decreases as enrollment expands. That explains the smaller difference between the two AC curves at higher levels of enrollment. This effect is evident in Figure 1 merely because it shows the effect of reducing cost curves by the full amount of donative subsidies

---

[14]Most textbooks on microeconomics present clear and thorough explanations of the rationales for the relative positions and shapes of the MC and AC curves, how and why the cost curves are inversely and, in the case of marginal and average variable cost curves, symmetrically related to the marginal and average product curves; and the relative positions and slopes of the demand and marginal revenue curves. However, interested readers who are relatively new to microeconomic theory, but very familiar with higher education settings, may wish to consult Halstead's (1991) monograph on his study of institutional costs, in which he explains and illustrates these economic concepts using concrete examples that are specific to college and university settings. More detailed and comprehensive presentations are available in good textbooks on microeconomics, such as Waud (1992) at the introductory level, Salvatore (1986) at the intermediate level, Binger and Hoffman (1988) for a combination of mathematical and diagrammatic exposition, or Henderson and Quandt (1980) for a purely mathematical exposition.

when all three types considered in the model are introduced for the first time. In subsequent diagrammatic analyses, when changes in costs are due to changes in per-unit costs or subsidies, the MC and AC curves will shift by identical vertical amounts at every level of Q.[15]

Given the new and much lower cost structure of MC' and AC", the institution would now find that additional students add more incremental revenue (MR) than incremental cost (MC) up to a much greater level of Q' enrollment spaces, for which the institution would charge a much lower price, P', which is the market-clearing price (that is, there is no excess demand at that price) and what the demand curve indicates students are willing and able to pay. Figure 1 illustrates how and why the substantial donative subsidies provided to colleges and universities by private and public sources lead to reduced tuition and greater access in higher education, relationships that have been clearly demonstrated in empirical work on the tuition-effects of state appropriations (Wittstruck and Bragg, 1988) and gift and endowment income (National Association of Independent Colleges and Universities, 1997). It is a portrayal of the impact of donative subsidies on the level of investment in higher education: an increase in access at a lower price to ensure the continued production of the external benefits that are desired by society (Leslie and Brinkman, 1988; Paulsen, 1998).

Figure 1 also illustrates the importance of the insights produced by the excellent work completed through the Williams College Project on the Economics of Higher Education (WPEHE). For example, WPEHE economists have advanced our understanding of the key elements of the finance of higher education. In particular, they have argued that the conventional business firm analogy urges us to think in terms of Price = Costs + Profits, while higher education is best understood in terms of Price + Subsidy = Cost (Winston, Carbone, and Lewis, 1998). The WPEHE model views institutional aid as a reduction in revenue rather than as an element of the cost of educational production; therefore, their "price" is sticker price less institutional aid and their cost is full cost less institutional aid. Alternatively, as discussed previously, the model used in this analysis views institutional aid as a cost; therefore it would be added to costs and to price to yield full cost and sticker price in the equation, without altering the fundamental logic of the relationships involved. However, in the case of years in which an institution experiences budget surpluses, the latter expression would be written as Price + Subsidy = Cost + Saving. Figure 1 illustrates the second relationship, but expresses it in a slightly rearranged format: Cost − Subsidy + Saving = Price. This means that if donative subsidies cover or reduce costs sufficiently, then the remaining costs plus some amount of saving would be covered by sticker price, with all measures expressed on a per-student basis. Winston (1997a) summarizes the basic

---

[15]In the model used here, one of the rare times that a non-parallel shift in AC would occur would be if an institution decides to increase either the payout rate on its endowment or reduce the principal value of the endowment in order to increase available donative subsidies for use in a particular academic year. This could and has happened, for example, in the case of an academic year in which the institution experiences a budget shortfall, that is a negative discretionary budget, one that must be covered either by incurring additional debt or making additional donative resources available by reducing the institution's wealth in the form of endowment.

elements of the relationships among price, cost, and subsidy that are represented in a more detailed format in Figure 1.

> The most fundamental anomaly in the economics of higher education is the fact that virtu-
> ally all US colleges and universities sell their primary product—education—at a price that is
> far less than the average cost of its production. The subsidy that that gives to nearly every
> college student in the country is neither temporary nor small nor granted only by govern-
> ment institutions: student subsidies are a permanent feature of the economics of higher edu-
> cation; they represent a large part of total costs; and they are only slightly smaller in private
> than in public institutions (p. 2).

REVENUES, COSTS AND TUITION: A DIAGRAMMATIC EXPLORATION

This section explores the interaction between revenue and cost structures and their implications for increases in tuition under a variety of conditions. In this section, the probable impacts of changes in revenue or cost structures on tuition are examined using comparative statics. In other words, typical queries would include: (1) "For a given demand and revenue configuration, what would be the probable impact on tuition of changes in per-student costs or subsidies?"; (2) "For a given cost structure, what would be the probable impact on tuition of changes in the demand and revenue structure?" This is a simplification used for purposes of clarity in exposition. In the real world, there are, of course, simultaneous changes in a wide variety of factors that would tend to shift costs, subsidies, and revenues upward and downward, with various and possibly contra-dictory effects on tuition. As a result, in a more dynamic analysis, explanation and pre-dictions about the direction of change in tuition would necessarily be ambiguous and speculative. The best that economic analysis can do is provide insight into the effects of a change in either the cost or revenue structure on the direction of change in tuition, *ceteris paribus*. However, such analyses yield important and useful insights, with implica-tions and guidelines for policy formation.

First, various sources of change in the per-unit costs or per-unit subsidies in higher education—such as rising costs of instruction and faculty, administration and student services, institutional support, academic support, institutional aid, program-matic changes, in combination with stable productivity or production technology; or decreases in the real value of state appropriations—are examined in terms of their implications for increases in tuition. The second section addresses the ways in which various sources of change in the demand configuration (revenue structure)—such as the job market for college graduates, increases in the numbers of potential college-bound students, the incomes of students and their families, the prices of related educational products, federal and state aid to students—are related to rising tuition. Then the third section addresses the importance of non-price competition—such as marketing expenditures which impact both cost and revenue structures—and ways they may have contributed to rising tuition. This section also examines the way in which the model predicts that in the long run, if the typical college is experi-encing annual saving or a positive discretionary budget, existing colleges will expand or extend their products or new colleges will be formed that will attract some student demand away from those colleges with saving.   The result of these factors, in combination, would be a natural tendency of the monopolistically competitive marketplace to reduce or eliminate saving or positive discretionary budgets for the typical college.

The fourth section explores the implications of institutional investments in fund raising, their impact on the availability of donative subsidies, and the resultant opportunities for cost reduction and quality enhancement. Next, the fifth section explores the implications for revenues and costs of the use of a more complex variation of the monopolistically competitive model in which institutions are viewed as perfect price discriminators.

Increases in tuition at both public and private four-year institutions have exceeded the rate of inflation in every year from 1980 to the present (The College Board, 1997; Lewis, 1989). Therefore, in most cases, the exploration of possible causes of tuition increases will focus on trends that began in the 1980s and have continued into the 1990s, albeit with somewhat less intensity in some instances. Most of the analyses in forthcoming sections will be presented in a sequence of several steps: (1) based on the literature on college tuition, a general hypothesis about a factor or a set of factors that appears to have lead to increases in tuition will be introduced and explained; (2) the monopolistically competitive model of the college or university will be used as a heuristic device or analytic framework for integrating and exploring the ways in which the revenue and cost structures of a typical institution would have interacted to promote increases in tuition; and (3) when possible, each general hypothesis about the causes of increasing tuition and the way in which the interaction of the revenue and cost structures can help explain such increases, will be compared with available empirical work related to the hypothesis.[16] The coverage of the vast literature on college costs and tuition in the succeeding sections is intended to be even and representative, but certainly not comprehensive, in its approach.

The Cost Structure and Increases in Tuition

An exploration of the impact on tuition of changes in per-student costs or subsidies is well summarized in the notion that when tuition goes up, "it *might* be because costs went up, but it might also be because *subsidies went down*" (Winston, Carbone, and Lewis, 1998, p. 7).

---

[16]Empirical studies that provide insight into the possible effects of either cost-side and/or demand-side factors on increases in college tuition have been conducted using national, state, institutional, and student-level data. Furthermore, these studies have been conducted using time-series data, cross-section data, or pooled time-series and cross-section data. To be sure, the primary focus of this chapter is on the changes in tuition that are likely to be made by an individual college or university, due to changes in its cost and revenue structures. However, I take the view that our understanding of the nature and direction of relationships between tuition and a cost-based or demand-based factor, can be enhanced from the results of research conducted from a variety of perspectives, using a variety of methods and types of data. Therefore, as an example, I cite empirical work indicating a significant, positive relationship between consumers' income, their demand for higher education, and the level of college tuition—whether based on national, state, institutional or student-level data—as relevant to our understanding of what is likely to lead an individual institution to increase its tuition. Clearly, however, for findings based on a variety of methods and types of data, it is the nature and direction of such relationships, and not their magnitudes, that have the capacity to enhance our understanding of the causes of rising tuition in the context of this chapter.

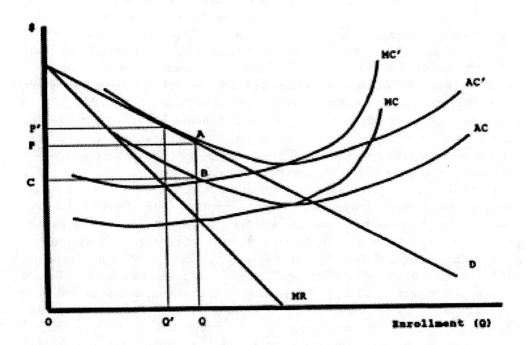

Figure 2. Effect of Changes in Per-Unit Subsidies on Tuition and Enrollment

Decreasing Shares of Subsidies from Donative Sources: The Case of State Appropriations
One of the most compelling arguments regarding causes of increases in tuition is based on
the decreasing share of state appropriations—$d^{G}Q$ in the present model—in current fund
revenues at public institutions (Frances, 1990; Hauptman, 1990; Mumper, 1996; National
Commission of the Costs of Higher Education, 1998). Beginning in the 1980s, and continuing—even intensifying—in the 1990s, state legislatures have had to contend with budget
shortfalls and cutbacks in—and expanding, competing claims on—state budgets due to the
politics of federal budget-balancing and the accompanying devolution of federal programs,
transferring responsibility for them to state and local governments (Zemsky and Wegner,
1997). Between 1980 and 1994, the share of state appropriations in total current fund revenues at public institutions fell from 44% to 33.3%, while tuition's share of revenues
increased from only 12.9% to 18.4% (Digest of Education Statistics, 1996, Table 322). In
other words, between 1980 and 1994, the primary source of donative subsidies for public
institutions—as a percent of current fund revenues—fell by 24.3%; while the share of revenues from tuition rose by 42.6%. Figure 2 indicates the effects that such changes in state
appropriations per student have on the cost structure, the interaction of cost and revenue
structures, and the ultimate impact of this interaction on tuition in the monopolistically competitive college or university.

In Figure 2, AC and MC represent the cost structure of the public institution before the
reductions in the proportion of current fund revenues from institutional donative subsidies took

place. Under such circumstances, the institution portrayed in Figure 2 would find that additional students would add more to revenue than to costs up to the point where MR = MC. Therefore, in seeking to maximize its discretionary budget (savings or surplus), the institution would enroll 0Q students and charge a sticker price of 0P. Some students, of course, would pay a net price less than 0P, due to the institutional aid awards to some students, which are included in the initial cost structure (MC and AC). The institution's educational cost per student, given 0Q students, would be the amount BQ, as measured off the relevant AC curve, or equivalently, amount 0C, measured on the vertical axis. In this short-run equilibrium, the institution would experience a positive discretionary budget or saving of amount AB = PC per student. This occurs primarily because donative resources, mostly from state appropriations per student, subsidize or reduce costs by enough to permit commercial revenues to exceed that necessary to cover the remaining costs, thereby making a surplus possible.

However, Figure 2 portrays the reduction in the proportion of revenues from state appropriations per student as equal to the vertical amount AB = PC. This is the amount by which both average and marginal cost curves would shift up to yield the new cost structure of MC' and AC'. The new cost structure is higher, of course, because the proportion of donative subsidies from state appropriations per student is less than before and fewer such subsidies means that a smaller portion of educational costs per student (AB = PC) would be covered by donative resources. Under this new set of circumstances, the institution would find that additional students would add more to revenue only up to 0Q' students, where MC = MR, and they would charge the sticker price that the unchanged revenue structure indicates students are willing and able to pay.[17] The new sticker price would be 0P', clearly higher than before the reduction in state appropriation subsidies per student. Once again, some students may pay a net price that is less than the sticker price due to expenditures on institutional aid that are included in the new, higher cost curves.

The institution would no longer experience a positive discretionary budget or saving, because commercial revenue per student (0P') is now just enough to cover the remaining educational costs per student, but not enough to leave a budget surplus for the institution. In other words, the smaller proportion of donative resources has raised the remaining, unsubsidized, uncovered, educational costs to a level that can be just exactly covered by commercial revenue (gross tuition income). The net effect of the change in appropriations per student would be to raise sticker price, *ceteris paribus*.[18] While this is the clear result of the comparative statics analysis, it should be emphasized, that in highly complex, dynamic analyses of this phenomenon, the cost and revenue structures would be shifting upward and downward for a variety of reasons, so that the net effect of changes in per-unit subsidies could well get lost in an inter-temporal shuffle of a multitude of opposing and contradictory cause-effect relationships. It is because of this possibility that exploring the effect on tuition of one cost-related or revenue-related factor at a time—that is, using the *ceteris paribus* assumption—can be a useful source of understanding the causes of rising tuition.

---

[17]In this model, an increase in the cost structure, in this and subsequent examples, appears to reduce enrollment, when all else remains unchanged. In fact, such enrollment declines were not common among institutions of higher education, because all else did not remain unchanged. As illustrated in later sections of this chapter, there were a variety of demand-side changes that would have served to offset the enrollment-reducing tendency of the cost increases illustrated here.

The conclusion that when smaller shares of current fund revenue are derived from state appropriations, tuition can be expected to increase, is consistent with—and supported by—empirical work that has examined this relationship (Gumport and Pusser, 1995; McMahon, 1974; Paulsen, 1991; Rusk and Leslie, 1978; Wittstruck and Bragg, 1988). This result is also quite consistent with the tuition-setting practices of public institutions, a process in which students, administrations, governing boards, legislatures and other powerful groups interact (Fenske, Besnette, and Jordan, in press).

Tuition-Setting Practices at Public Institutions

First of all, the traditional practice of tuition-setting at public institutions has viewed tuition as the "residual calculation from the difference between operating budget [cost] requirements and state appropriations (Van Alstyne, 1977, p. 66). In other words, "when state or local government revenues are restricted, states will seek increased revenues from other sources, including tuition and fees for higher education" (Viehland et al., 1982, p. 333). Based on their case study of the University of California (UC), Gumport and Pusser (1995) reported that when faced with a substantial decline in state funding beginning in the late 1980s, one of the first responses of the UC was to "raise student fees, which were increased over 120% between 1989/90 and 1993/94" (p. 507).

These are largely cost-based approaches to tuition setting—that is, when the costs of providing a college education rise faster than offsetting non-tuition revenues, tuition at public institutions is increased in response to rising costs of production. A recent SHEEO survey and analysis has indicated that some "linkage to the cost of providing higher education or to the instructional expenditures per student" is the most common, but not universal approach used (Lenth, 1993, p. 12). Other cost or expenditure-based approaches that are common include setting tuition in various relationships to state appropriations per student, that tend to result in inverse relationships between appropriations and tuition; and setting tuition in relation to changes in the higher education price index (a measure of the costs of the resources that an institution must acquire to provide its educational services).

Interestingly, some of the other common approaches focus on linking tuition to demand-side factors, such as the growth in personal income in the state, or the consumer price index; in each case, paying particular attention to the demand side and the ability to pay of students and their families (Lenth, 1993). And in most states, tuition at public institutions is related to tuition charged by a carefully identified set of peer institutions. In other words, tuition is set to be comparable with charges at competing institutions, another demand-side factor. Lenth (1993) interprets the results of his survey to mean that most states use a combination of these methods for setting tuition at their public institutions. Finally, one of the most interesting

---

[18]In Figure 2, the position of the cost structure before and after the change in the share of revenues from state appropriations is intended only to illustrate that a decreasing share of appropriations raises an institution's cost structure, which in turn, puts upward pressure on tuition. The presence of substantial donative subsidies from appropriations, by itself, does not necessarily lead to a surplus, and a decrease in the share of revenues from appropriations does not necessarily eliminate an existing surplus. However, for most institutions operating in a monopolistically competitive marketplace, a surplus is only a short-run phenomenon. The long-run adjustment process is illustrated in some detail in a subsequent section of this chapter, "The Long Run Adjustment and Zero Saving." See that section for an illustration and explanation of the natural tendency for monopolistically competitive institutions to experience zero saving, on average, in the long run.

developments in price-setting strategies at public institutions has been the move—either by design or default—toward a much more market-based approach, often referred to as the high-tuition/high-aid approach (Griswold and Marine, 1996; Hearn and Anderson, 1989, 1995; Hearn, Griswold, and Marine, 1996; Hossler et al., 1997; Mumper, 1998; Mumper and Anderson, 1993). These findings, in combination, are especially important for the analyses in this chapter, because they indicate that there is a reasonable amount of consistency between the underlying demand- and cost-based assumptions about tuition setting in the model used here and the actual cost- and demand-based practices of contemporary public institutions.

Increases in Per-Student Costs of Education
So far, the analysis has only explored the effects on tuition of reductions in donative subsidies in the form of per-student state appropriations; therefore, the next task is to explore the possible effects on tuition due to increases in the educational costs of production. The great majority of educational costs are represented by $C(Q)$ in the mathematical presentation of the model, with several smaller components expressed with separate symbols—aQ for expenditures for institutional aid, mQ for marketing expenditures, and fQ for fund-raising expenditures—because of their particular significance for institutional strategies regarding such expenditures. Increases in the per-student costs of providing a quality education have been consistently emphasized as a source of increases in tuition (Clotfelter, 1996; Frances, 1990; Halstead, 1989; Hauptman, 1990; Hansen, 1988; Mumper, 1996; St. John, 1994). Of course, educational costs are comprised of many separable components of expenditure, and whether or not per-student costs of education increase is also dependent on fundamental measures of educational productivity, such as student-faculty ratios, class sizes and teaching loads.

Getz and Siegfried (1991) have made the most detailed and thorough study of the, growth in the various categories of educational and general expenditures during the 1980s. The fastest growing categories of educational expenditures were in the areas of institutional aid, administration, and student services, where expenditures in each area grew at rates well in excess of the rate of inflation in the general price level. Although instructional expenditures were not among the fastest-growing categories, instructional expenditures did increase rapidly—and a good deal faster than the rate of inflation—and more importantly, they continue to account for the largest share (40-50%) of overall educational expenditures. Although the patterns of increasing costs were similar, expenditures per student increased at a much faster rate at private than at public institutions.

Increases in Instructional Costs per Student
Increases in instructional expenditures—the largest component of $C(Q)$ in the model—are especially important in understanding the high rates of increase in overall educational spending because they account for what is by far the largest component of such spending (Getz and Siegfried, 1991; Mumper, 1996). Faculty compensation, in turn, constitutes the largest component of instructional expenditures and has a weighting as high as 75% in the Higher Education Price Index (Halstead, 1991). After faculty had experienced a substantial loss of purchasing power due to salary increases well below the high rates of inflation in the 1970s, institutions made efforts to restore some of that lost purchasing power with salary increases that exceeded inflation rates in the 1980s (Frances, 1990; Hauptman, 1990; Hal-

stead, 1989). At the same time that salaries were rising, so were the costs of fringe benefits for faculty (Mumper, 1996). The results of a set of case studies of highly selective private institutions indicated that due to intense competition for highly qualified, often more senior faculty, rates of increase in faculty salaries may have been intensified even more for some institutions (Clotfelter, 1996). Increases in faculty compensation have continued to exceed the rate of inflation in the 1990s, but by a smaller amount than they had in the 1980s (National Commission on the Cost of Higher Education, 1998).

Increases in faculty compensation are important because of their prominent role in instructional costs, as well as because such increases can have an exaggerated or disproportionate effect on expenditures because of what Baumol and Blackman (1995) refer to as the "cost disease."[19] The cost-disease construct is used to explain the existence of a relatively high degree of rigidity in some of the technological requirements that tend to constrain or inhibit growth in productivity in higher education, medical care, the performing arts, and other personal-service industries that are characterized by labor-intensive processes of production.[20] For example, colleges and universities often view the student-faculty ratio and the number of students per class as aspects of educational quality, such that if the student-faculty ratio or average class size were increased, the quality of students' educational experiences would be diminished. Therefore, increases in faculty compensation, with no change in the number of students being educated, would raise per-student educational costs, but would probably be perceived by institutions as maintenance of important features of the quality of education they offer. As a result, institutions tend to resist increases in student-faculty ratios and class sizes, even though they would tend to reduce educational costs per student.[21]

The inverse relationship between student-faculty ratios and instructional costs has been consistently observed in the results of empirical work on the estimation of higher education cost functions; and has been observed for a wide range of institutional types, from large universities to small liberal arts colleges (Brinkman, 1981; Paulsen, 1989). Getz and Siegfried (1991) found that institutional types with the largest student-faculty ratios—such as comprehensive, doctoral, and two-year colleges—also have the lowest costs per student; and those with the lowest ratios—such as liberal arts colleges and, to a lesser extent, research universities—have the highest costs per student. Comparisons between public and private institutions are also revealing. Between 1978 and 1988, on average, student-faculty ratios increased at public institutions and decreased at private

---

[19]Instructional expenditures can also be increased because of the effects of the "growth force," a construct originally articulated by Bowen (1980) and more recently expanded and applied in explaining the increases in educational costs by Massy (1996) and others. While it would not be inappropriate to discuss the effects of the growth force on costs at this point, I have elected to discuss its impact on educational costs within the context of increases in administrative costs in the next section of the chapter.

[20]The interested reader may wish to consult St. John (1994), who presents some creative insights regarding the meaning of instructional and institutional productivity and improvements in productivity. For example, see his distinctions between marginal, meaningful, and deceptive gains in productivity on pages 82-83.

[21]Nevertheless, the advances and experiments with technology in the service of teaching and learning have already begun to challenge our longstanding assumptions about the nature of the technology of instruction and students' capacities to learn in non-traditional environments, through non-traditional media. In time, it would seem that the cost disease may not have as comprehensive an influence as it seems to have now and has had in the past (Baumol and Blackman, 1995; Chickering and Ehrmann, 1996; Van Dusen, 1997).

institutions, notably at private liberal arts colleges, faculty salaries increased faster at private than at public institutions; and as expected, overall educational and general expenditures increased faster at private than at public institutions (Getz and Siegfried, 1991).

Between 1988 and 1994, data from the National Center for Education Statistics (NCES) on instructional expenditures per student indicate that they have continued to grow at a pace that exceeds the rate of inflation, but less so than previously, for private and public universities and for liberal arts colleges; while increases in instructional spending have stayed more in line with increases in the general price level at public four-year and two-year institutions (U.S. Department of Education, 1996, Tables 338-342). Concerns about the continuing growth in instructional expenditures has lead states and institutions to conduct faculty workload studies to assess how faculty spend their time, especially relevant to teaching productivity (Layzell, 1996; Meyer, 1998; Wergin, 1994) and recent research, based on the National Survey of Postsecondary Faculty (NSOPF), has helped scholars, administrators, and policy makers to achieve a better understanding of the nature and amount of faculty work (Fairweather, 1996).

The National Commission on the Cost of Higher Education (1998) has reported some interesting results based on a comparison of the 1988 and 1993 NSOPF surveys, illustrating not only how faculty spend their time, but also indicators of possible increases in the teaching-related component of faculty productivity and accompanying impacts on the related instructional costs. Between 1987 and 1992, the number of hours that faculty spent in contact with students, measured as the number of hours spent in the classroom per week times the number of students in those classes, increased from 300 to 337; the average number of hours spent in the classroom per week increased from 9.8 to 11 hours (National Commission on the Cost of Higher Education, 1998); and the proportions of faculty who were part-time, untenured, not on tenure track, or were of low rank, all increased. In combination, these changes also resulted in a small increase in average class size over the period, rising from 30 in 1987 to 30.6 in 1992 (U.S. Department of Education, 1997). Research suggests that increases in instructional productivity, such as an increase in class sizes in higher education may help explain why instructional costs—and perhaps tuition as well—are not increasing as fast in the 1990s as they were in the 1980s (Koshal, Koshal, Boyd and Levine, 1994).

On the other hand, just as Getz and Siegfried (1991) observed that student-faculty ratios at liberal arts colleges decreased between 1978 and 1988, Clotfelter (1996), in his in-depth case studies of several highly selective private universities (Harvard, Chicago, and Duke) and one highly selective private liberal arts college (Carleton), observed that those institutions experienced a reduction in faculty teaching loads, apparently without commensurate increases in class sizes, during the period of analysis from 1977 and 1992. Perhaps these are the institutions that set the standard for quality that other institutions often do their best to emulate. The major difference might be that these highly selective institutions are representatives of that small proportion of institutions that are wealthy enough to consistently cover the highest of expenditures to maintain that quality or at least, the public's perception of quality.

However, instructional costs continue to increase at rates exceeding the rate of inflation, especially at the large doctoral and research universities, as well as some liberal arts colleges. The phenomenon known as the "academic ratchet" (Massy and Wilger, 1992; Massy, 1996) may be responsible for this trend, especially because it is believed to be far more prevalent at the large research universities and liberal arts colleges than at other institutional types. Massy (1996) explains the meaning of this construct—which has also received recent empirical support (Massy and Zemsky, 1994)—as a plausible basis for increased instructional costs.

> The *ratchet*...describes the steady, irreversible shift of faculty allegiance away from the goals of a given institution, toward those of an academic specialty. In pursuit of prestige, some faculty have developed an independent, entrepreneurial spirit leading to increased emphasis on research and publication and on teaching their own specialty instead of general introduction courses, often at the expense of coherence in an academic curriculum. The increasing outputs or primary gainers from the ratchet are research, publications, professional services (consulting), and curriculum specialization. Diminishing outputs or the primary losers include teaching quality, advising, mentoring, tutoring, and curriculum structure....The influence is felt throughout the research and doctoral-granting sector...[and] has progressed to the point that even a few liberal arts institutions have begun referring to themselves as research colleges (p. 81).

Increases in Administrative Costs per Student

One of the fastest growing components of educational and general expenditures—and one that has been talked and written about at great length—is administrative costs, measured primarily as the "institutional support" category of educational and general expenditures (Mumper, 1996). Administrative costs—explicitly defined as a portion of $C(Q)$ in the model—have been such a source of concern and an important feature of the enterprise that proposals for re-conceptualizing the meaning and measurement of such costs are appearing in the literature (Rhoades, 1998). Between 1978 and 1988, this category of expenditures was second only to institutional aid in its rate of increase, growing at a rate much higher than the rate of inflation (Getz and Siegfried, 1991). Between 1988 and 1994, NCES data on administrative expenditures indicate that they have continued to grow, slowing a little, so that they have increased only somewhat faster than the rate of inflation at public and private universities and four-year colleges, and have been close to right on pace with the inflation rate at public two-year colleges (U.S. Department of Education, 1996, Tables 338-342).[22]

A recent study of budget documents for a twenty-five year period at the University of California revealed that administrative positions grew two-and-one-half times as much as instructional positions, accompanied by commensurate differences in the rates of growth in expenditures for administration and instruction (Gumport and Pusser, 1995). An interesting set of theories and propositions—only some of which have been empirically tested and supported—have appeared in the literature to explain why administrative costs have risen so much in American higher education. Some of the most prominent themes in the various explanations of the escalation of administrative costs include growth in the overall enterprise of higher education, administrative responses or adaptations to technological, regulatory, and economic changes in a complex environment, the increasing use of more participatory management styles in changing governance structures, changing roles of and tasks performed by faculty and administrators, and adaptations to budget constraints, including the allocation of additional resources to administrative units—such as the development or fund-raising office[23]—who are able to sustain or increase donative resources from public or private sources (Gumport and Pusser, 1995; Leslie and Rhoades, 1995; Massy, 1996; Massy and Wilger, 1992).

For example, one theory is referred to as the "growth force"—essentially a reconceptualization of Bowen's (1980) revenue theory of costs—which addresses the mediating forces that yield constant increases in administration expenditures in response to—and in step with—growth of the enterprise.

> Many a university president has pointed out that the opportunities for education and research—and, indeed, knowledge itself—grow without limit. They say that, because their universe is expanding, universities and colleges must grow continually in order to maintain their excellence and their place in the academic pecking order....A continuous stream of new academic programs is required for an institution to maintain its vitality: each decade brings new scientific discoveries and literatures, with little diminution of the old (Massy, 1996, p. 54).

And the theory of the "administrative lattice" proposes that administrative costs expand because faculty turn their attention away from undergraduates and toward their research, leaving administrative staff to perform tasks—such as advising undergraduates—that have been forsaken by faculty; contemporary forms of participative management require more administrative staff; and administrations are self-perpetuating, creating additional work and a demand for additional administrative staff to perform these additional tasks (Massy and Wilger, 1992).

Increases in Student-Services and Related Costs

Spending on student services—shown as a portion of C(Q) in the model—grew at a pace well in excess of the rate of inflation, and, with the exceptions of institutional aid and administration expenditures, grew faster than any of the other categories of educational

---

[22]The analysis of trends between 1988 and 1994 is based on the NCES measure of the "administration" component of educational and general (E&G) expenditures. While Getz and Siegfried (1991) use only the institutional support category of expenditures to measure growth in administrative expenses, NCES provides a more comprehensive measure of the administration component of E&G expenditures. The NCES measure includes the categories of institutional support *and* academic support (less library expenses), which is the measure used successfully by Stanley and Adams (1994) in their study of administration costs at research universities. The main reason this measure of administration expenses is more comprehensive is because it includes the substantial component of academic support that is due to academic administration, which includes expenditures related to the activities performed by academic deans in the central administrative offices of each college of a university. Getz and Siegfried (1991) report on a study of 12 private research universities in which 43% of expenditures on academic support were for administration, 40% for libraries, 10% for computing, and 7% for all other such expenditures. Because the NCES measure of administration used here excludes libraries, administration represents the great majority of academic support expenses. It should also be noted that academic support grew at a slower rate than institutional support from 1988 to 1994 (U.S. Department of Education, 1996, Table 334); therefore, the more comprehensive NCES measure may understate the growth in administrative expenses as measured by institutional support alone. This poses no problem, however, because the growth in the NCES measure of administration expenditures still exceeds even the rate of inflation for the great majority of institutions.

[23]Fund-raising has long been a practice of considerable importance and expense at private institutions and is rapidly becoming very important for public institutions as well. Therefore, this component of costs [C(Q)] has its own separate term in the mathematical model [fQ] and will be addressed more fully in a later section of the chapter.

expenditures in the 1980s (Getz and Siegfried, 1991). Expenditures for student services grew more at private than at public institutions (Mumper, 1996) and grew especially fast at private, four-year colleges (Getz and Siegfried, 1991). Between 1988 and 1994, NCES data regarding spending on student services indicate that they continued to grow at rates in excess of the inflation rate, but somewhat more slowly than the rates at which they grew in the 1980s; and the growth in spending at private institutions continued to exceed that at public institutions (U.S. Department of Education, 1996, Tables 338-342).

A broad view of student services would include all "activities whose primary purpose is to contribute to students' emotional and physical well-being and to their intellectual, cultural, and social development outside the context of the formal instructional program" (Getz and Siegfried, 1991, p. 293). This would include expenditures for admissions, recruitment, and retention, administration of financial aid, services of the office of the registration, career guidance, counseling and student health centers, learning-resource or learning-skills centers, freshmen orientation programs, disabled student services, tutoring and mentoring programs, computer labs with technical support, child care centers, international student offices, ESL programs, housing and residence life, food services, athletics, and support for various student organizations and activities (Komives, Woodard and associates, 1996). When it comes to educational and general expenditures, some of these aspects of student services—such as housing, food services, and athletics—would be viewed as auxiliary enterprises and included in an expenditure category separate from student services expenditures (Getz and Siegfried, 1991). It is also easy to see that much of what is formally classified as student services expenditure is essentially administrative in nature—that is, most of the student affairs functions require additional administrative positions and expenses (Whitt, 1997).

Much of the expansion in the budget for student services in the 1980s—a trend which has continued, but at a slower rate in the 1990s—has been attributed to changes in the demographics of the student body, which is comprised of much larger proportions of older and part-time students (Hauptman, 1990). In addition to increased enrollment of part-time students and students of non-traditional age, the decline in the expected number of potential traditional-age students has been offset by increased participation rates of students of traditional age (Halstead, 1989), including increased participation rates of students from minority groups, and from students representing all income and ability categories (U.S. Department of Education, 1997, Tables A9 and A10, pp. 64, 66). Colleges and universities have responded to this growing participation of diverse groups of students by adding new forms of student services, such as child care services, and expanding existing services, such as remedial programs in math or language skills (Halstead, 1989; Hauptman, 1990; Mumper, 1996).

Some of the increases in student services expenditures are closely related to the heightened non-price competition among colleges and universities that coincided with the "student-as-consumer" movement that seems to have substantially changed the higher education marketplace for the foreseeable future (Riesman, 1980). The increases in expenditures associated with non-price competition include those related to the intensification of admissions, recruitment, and retention efforts (Hossler, Bean and associates, 1990) and those related to enhancing the distinctiveness and/or quality of the educational product of an institution in the eyes of its potential students, such as the large investments that many private colleges and universities—and a growing number of public institutions—have made in the area of access to the latest in computer technology for their students (Clotfelter, 1996; National Association of Independent Colleges and Universities, 1997). Because of both the magnitude and strategic importance of these "marketing" costs, they are given their own separate mathematical component of the educational cost function (mQ) and will be addressed more fully in a subsequent section of this chapter.

In Figure 3, AC and MC represent the cost structure of the institution before the increases in the per-student expenditures on instruction, administration, and student services—all represented as portions of C(Q) in the model—took place. Under such circumstances, the institution portrayed in Figure 3 would find that additional students would add more to revenue than to costs up to the point where MR = MC. Therefore, in seeking to maximize its discretionary budget (savings or surplus), the institution would enroll 0Q students and charge a sticker price of 0P. Some students, of course, would pay a net price less than 0P, due to the institutional aid awards to some students, which are included in the initial cost structure (MC and AC). The institution's educational cost per student, given 0Q students, would be the amount BQ, as measured off the relevant AC curve, or equivalently, amount 0C, measured on the vertical axis. In this short-run equilibrium, the institution would experience a positive discretionary budget or saving of amount AB = PC per student. This occurs

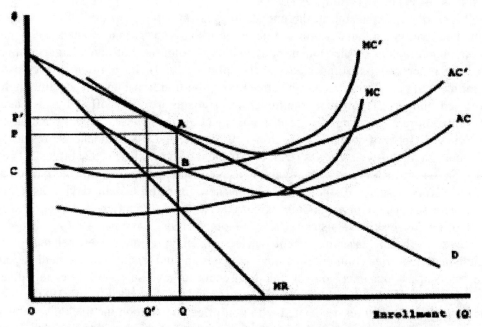

Figure 3. Effect of Changes in Per-Unit Costs on Tuition and Enrollment

because donative resources—primarily from state appropriations for public institutions and gifts and endowment income for private institutions—subsidize or reduce costs by enough to permit commercial revenues to exceed that necessary to cover the remaining costs.

However, Figure 3 portrays the increases in per-student educational costs as equal to the vertical amount AB = PC. This is the amount by which both average and marginal cost curves would shift up to yield the new, higher cost structure of MC' and AC'. Due to the increases in educational costs, the institution would find that additional students would add more to revenue only up to 0Q' students, where MC = MR, and they would charge the sticker price that the unchanged revenue structure indicates students are willing and able to pay. The new sticker price would be 0P', clearly higher than before the increase in per-student costs. Once again, some students may pay a net price that is less than the sticker price due to expenditures on institutional aid that are included in the new, higher cost curves.

The institution would no longer experience a positive discretionary budget or saving, because given no concomitant increase in donative subsidies, commercial revenue per student (0P') is now just enough to cover the higher educational costs per student, and not enough to leave a budget surplus for the institution. In other words, the increase in the costs of instruction, administration, and student services has raised the remaining, unsubsidized, uncovered, educational costs to a level that can be just exactly covered by commercial revenue (gross tuition income). The net effect of the change in educational costs [C(Q)] per student would be to raise sticker price, *ceteris paribus*.

Once again, while this is the clear result of the comparative statics analysis, it should be emphasized, that in highly complex, dynamic analyses of this phenomenon, the cost and revenue structures would be shifting upward and downward for a variety of reasons, so that the net effect of changes in per-unit costs (or subsidies) could easily get lost in an inter-temporal shuffle of a multitude of opposing and contradictory cause-effect relationships. It is because of this possibility that exploring the effect on tuition of one cost-related or revenue-related factor at a time—that is, using the *ceteris paribus* assumption—can be a useful source of understanding the causes of rising tuition.

The conclusion that when components of the educational and general expenditures—that is, the costs of instruction, administration, and/or student services—increase, tuition can be expected to increase, is quite consistent with—and supported by—empirical work that has examined this relationship (Koshal, Koshal, Boyd, and Levine, 1994; McMahon, 1974; National Association of Independent Colleges and Universities, 1997; Paulsen, 1991; To and Olson, 1996). Furthermore, in a study of doctorate-granting institutions, Koshal, Koshal, Boyd and Levine (1994) found that average class size—one of the measures of instructional productivity discussed above—was significantly and inversely related to tuition.

Increases in Expenditures on Institutional Aid Per Student
The fastest growing category of E&G expenditures or educational costs per student, during the 1980s, for all public and private institutions combined, was institutional aid (Getz and Siegfried, 1991), and that fact extends to the most highly selective private colleges and uni-

versities as well (Clotfelter, 1996).[24] Getz and Siegfried (1991) measured institutional aid using the sub-category of E&G expenditures called scholarships and fellowships from unrestricted funds and "these are funds that are allocated to scholarships at the discretion of the institution" (p. 295). Other researchers have measured institutional aid in terms of scholarships from unrestricted plus restricted funds, minus federal Pell and SEOG grants (Basch, 1997; Breneman, 1994; McPherson and Schapiro, 1993).[25] Regardless of which measure is used, institutional aid per student grew far in excess of the general rate of inflation during the 1980s. For example, during the nine-year period from 1979 through 1988, figures from Getz and Siegfried's analysis show a constant-dollar increase in per-student institutional aid of about 97% for public and private institutions combined. During the ten-year period from 1979 to 1989, figures from McPherson and Schapiro's (1993) analysis show a constant-dollar increase in per-student institutional aid—from unrestricted and restricted funds, less Pell and SEOG grants—of about 66% for public universities and 71.8% for private universities. For the six-year period from 1988 through 1994, NCES data show a constant-dollar increase in per-student institutional aid from unrestricted funds of about 60% at private institutions and 64% at public institutions (U.S. Department of Education, 1996, Tables 24, 25 B8, 318).

These rates of increase in institutional aid exceed the constant-dollar increases in tuition during comparable time periods (College Board, 1997; Lewis, 1989). This has heightened the importance of the analyses of scholars who have consistently argued that increases in institutional aid contribute to higher levels of tuition (Frances, 1990; Mumper, 1996; Pearson and Baldi, 1998; Reynolds, 1998), and economists have offered counsel regarding how administrators should view their use of institutional aid to make it an appropriate and effective element of their institutions' financial strategies (Breneman, 1994; Hubbell, 1992). Mumper (1996) presents the basic elements of the argument that increases in institutional aid contribute to increases in tuition in the following way:

> As colleges increase the amount of internal financial aid they award, they must find revenues to cover these new expenditures. The ironic consequence has been that institutional efforts to provide grants to disadvantaged students have driven up college costs and, in turn, driven up tuitions (p. 35).

To and Olson (1996), in their recent study of the determinants of tuition at private liberal arts colleges, articulated these practices in terms of an analogy that has become a popular way to describe the relationship between sticker price and institutional aid: "institutions often overcharge regular students to get additional money to provide institutional aid to target students whom they particularly want to attract, the Robin Hood Effect" (p. 18). Winston, in his colorful essay, "Robin Hood in the Forests of Academe," (1993) provides an insightful analysis of

---

[24]See the earlier subsection of this chapter on "the mathematical model" for a detailed explanation of why expenditures on institutional aid are viewed as additions to educational costs rather than reductions in revenue in this model. Also, as previously noted, the alternative view will be examined in a later section of the chapter that applies a variation of the model that views perfect price discrimination as a characteristic or feature of the behavior of monopolistically competitive colleges and universities.

[25]The only substantial difference between this and the former approach is that institutional grants from restricted funds have experienced somewhat smaller growth than institutional grants from unrestricted funds (U.S. Department of Education, 1996, Table 334).

both the strengths and shortcomings of using the "Robin Hood Effect" as an analogy; nevertheless, it has by now assumed a firm place in the professional jargon, and for better or worse, it does convey some aspects of the essential processes involved in tuition discounting.

A number of scholars have attempted to estimate the effect of increases in institutional aid on tuition (Frances, 1990; Hauptman, 1990; National Association of Independent Colleges and Universities, 1997). For example, the National Association of Independent Colleges and Universities (NAICU) (1997) employed data on year-to year changes in institutionally provided aid as a percentage of year-to-year growth in tuition and fees to reach the following conclusion and estimate:

> The increase in institutionally provided aid is the fastest growing determinant of tuition and fees at Independent colleges and universities. By itself, the expansion of student aid from independent higher education's own resources currently represents one-third of the growth in tuition (p. 13).

The NAICU estimate is representative of—and reasonably similar to—those obtained by others (Frances, 1990; Hauptman, 1990); however, such methods seem limited and problematic in the face of a very challenging and complex task.

A much more appropriate and effective way of estimating the effect of increases in institutional aid on tuition has been illustrated—or at least approximated—by recent efforts to estimate the parameters of appropriate equation systems (Coopers & Lybrand, 1997; McPherson and Schapiro, 1991, 1993; To and Olson, 1996). Ideally, there should be specified demand and specified cost or supply functions, distinct sets for private and public institutions, and the use of appropriate simultaneous equations estimation procedures. Then, the effect of institutional aid, or growth in institutional aid, and a set of other independent variables—for both theoretical purposes and for the purposes of control and complete specification—on tuition or tuition growth could be more meaningfully estimated. McPherson and Schapiro (1991, 1993) acknowledge that the interplay of the variables in appropriate equation systems would include variables that are endogenous in one equation as explanatory variables in another, and use an appropriate method of two-stage least squares estimation. Coopers & Lybrand (1997) fashion their method after that of McPherson and Schapiro, To and Olson (1996) employ equations to estimate both institutional aid and the effect of growth in aid and other factors on tuition growth; however, they use OLS rather than 2SLS for estimation—and the NAICU study (1997) uses a single multiple regression, but examines the effect of both demand- and supply-side variables on tuition.[26]

Each of these empirical studies has found that institutional aid has a positive and statistically significant effect on tuition (Coopers & Lybrand, 1997; McPherson and Schapiro, 1991, 1993; To and Olson, 1996). The findings of these studies are quite consistent with what the monopolistically competitive model of the college or university would predict regarding the effect of institutional aid on tuition. This analysis can be readily incorporated into the relationships portrayed in Figure 3, by viewing the vertical, upward shifts in the marginal and average cost curves—from MC and AC to MC' and AC'—as due to some combination of increases in the per-unit costs of institutional aid—symbolized by "a" in the model—and increases in the other educational costs—such as those for instruction, administration and student service, and symbolized by C(Q) in the model—that were examined in the previous three subsections of this chapter. The increase in institutional aid would be expected to affect tuition in much the same way as changes in the other components of per-unit costs, resulting in an increase in the sticker price from 0P to 0P' in Figure 3.

Demand, the Revenue Structure, and Increases in Tuition

The factors that influence student demand for enrollment places have been studied more extensively than the cost or supply-side of the marketplace for higher education. Such studies typically provide estimates of the effect of a variety of factors on the demand for enrollment places, while holding the level of tuition constant. Research has shown that for a given level of tuition, the most prominent determinants of increases in enrollment demand include (a) improvements in the labor market opportunities for college graduates relative to those of high school graduates, the latter being viewed as the opportunity cost of attending college; (b) increases in the number of potential college-bound students; (c) increases in the income of students and their families; (d) increases in the presence of, and tuition charged by, substitute institutions; and (e) increases in federal and state financial aid to students (Clotfelter, 1991; W. Becker, 1990; Paulsen, 1990a; Weiler, 1984).

The findings of a recent study of the determinants of tuition at 76 liberal arts colleges in the 1989-90 academic year (To and Olson, 1996) are useful as a framework for interpreting the results of other studies and analyses in this section. Although To and Olson found that cost-related factors were significant as determinants of the level of tuition among their sample institutions, the variable that had the largest positive and direct impact on tuition was "excess demand," measured as "the ratio of the number of applicants (demand for college admissions) to the number of enrollments (available enrollment slots)" (pp. 11-12). Because excess demand was consistently related to higher levels of tuition in their study, one useful way to view the various factors that are discussed in this section as determinants of increases in student demand is to think of them in terms of generating excess demand, which in turn, leads to upward adjustments in tuition, as indicated by the results of the To and Olson study.

---

[26]McPherson and Schapiro (1991, 1993) employ a wide set of supply-side variables as explanatory variables in their three-equation system, and although they estimate a model in which the growth in instructional expenditures is an endogenous variable, neither instructional expenditures nor any other related measure of institutional costs such as faculty salaries is used as an explanatory variables in their estimated equations. Also, their model does not adequately consider the demand side of the determination of tuition, but of course, that is not their intention. They make it clear that they are examining supply-side behavior. As far as one can tell from their report, Coopers & Lybrand (1997) take a similar approach, although they do not appear to have included a control variable comparable to McPherson and Schapiro's change in state income per capita. To and Olson (1996) do not use 2SLS squares, which would seem to be the more appropriate estimation procedure for their study; however, their approach is clearly based on the specification of both demand- and supply-side influences on tuition growth. Their use of a measure of excess demand as a proxy for a range of possible demand-side variables, in combination with a measure of E&G expenditures, as a broad proxy for cost-related variables, and their explicit inclusion of growth in institutional aid, constitutes an interesting, and apparently effective, if parsimonious, specification. The NAICU (1997) study estimates the parameters of a single multiple regression equation, includes a comprehensive set of supply-side measures, including measures of educational costs, but considers only one demand-side measure based on income levels of applicants. These studies have made important contributions to the literature on the causes of tuition, but also pose a variety of challenges for other researchers to address in future studies.

Labor Market Opportunities for College Graduates Relative to High School Graduates
Human capital theory contends that students' decisions to purchase, or invest in, units of a college education depends on their valuation of the benefit-cost ratio of such an investment, relative to alternative uses of their resources (G. Becker, 1993; Mincer, 1993). Research has consistently demonstrated that, holding tuition constant, job market opportunities for college graduates relative to such opportunities for high school graduates are directly related to students' enrollment decisions (Clotfelter, 1991; Hoenack and Weiler, 1979; Krakower and Zammuto, 1987; Paulsen and Pogue, 1988; Quigley and Rubinfeld, 1993; Tannen, 1978) and to the levels of tuition in both the public and private sectors of higher education (Paulsen, 1991).

A number of economists have argued that one of the leading causes of the increase in enrollment demand in the 1980s was the substantial increases in the economic payoff for a college education (Clotfelter, 1991, 1996; Kane, 1995; McPherson and Schapiro, 1998). After the earnings differential between college and high school graduates deteriorated in the 1970s (Freeman, 1975), reaching a low point at which the earnings of college graduates exceeded those of high school graduates by only 38%, it soared to a 58% differential by 1989 (Murphy and Welch, 1992a); with similar patterns of improvement in differentials observed for whites and blacks and men and women (W. Becker, 1992; Murphy and Welch, 1992b). Using Current Population Survey (CPS) data on median annual earnings of college graduates aged 25-34, the earnings differentials for the 1970s, 1980s, and 1990s can be examined separately for men and women. In 1978, the college-high school earnings differential was 18% for men and 55% for women; in 1988, it was 42% for men and 81% for women; and in 1995, it was 52% for men and 91% for women (U.S. Department of Education, 1997, p. 120). As the data shows, the earnings differential for college graduates has continued to increase in the 1990s, albeit at a somewhat slower rate.

The Number of Potential College-Bound Students
The forecasts of substantial decreases in the population of 18-year-olds in the population after 1979, and of concomitant decreases in enrollment in higher education concerned more than a few administrators and faculty (Cartter, 1976; Dresch, 1975; Freeman, 1976). However, enrollments increased throughout the 1980s, due in large part to increases in the population of potential students of non-traditional age, increases in the participation rates of students of traditional age, and increases in the enrollment of part-time students (Clotfelter, 1991).

Overall, FTE enrollment in institutions of higher education increased by 13.4% between 1978 and 1988 and by 9.3% between 1988 and 1994, distributed between corresponding increases in the public sector of 13 and 9.7% and increases in the private sector of 14.4 and 8.3% (U.S. Department of Education, 1996, Table 196). In addition to the increases in enrollment among students of non-traditional age and in part-time enrollment, the participation rates of students of traditional age increased substantially among white, black and Hispanic students and across all income and ability levels during similar time periods (U.S. Department of Education, 1997, pp. 64, 66).

These increases constitute substantial and sustained increases in the demand for enrollment places in higher education throughout the 1980s and into the 1990s; and the growth is distributed fairly evenly between the public and private sectors. In hindsight, these increases are consistent with—but also give a new and fuller meaning to—the statistically significant role played by the population of potential students of traditional age in explaining the enrollment demand of students—holding tuition constant—in previous empirical work in this area (Campbell and Siegel, 1967; Hoenack and Weiler, 1979; Paulsen and Pogue, 1988; Quigley and Rubinfeld, 1993; Tannen, 1978).

The Income of Students and Families

A college education, as a product or service, is income-elastic (Clotfelter, 1991); that is, studies of enrollment demand have consistently observed that, while holding tuition constant, there is a positive effect on enrollment due to the income level of potential students (Campbell and Siegel, 1967; Clotfelter, 1991; Corazzini, Dugan, and Grabowski, 1972; Handa and Skolnick, 1975; Hopkins, 1974; Mattila, 1982; McMahon, 1974). Furthermore, in a four-equation, demand-and-supply, private-and-public-sector model of tuition determination, income of families was found to be significantly and positively related to tuition in both the private and public sectors (Paulsen, 1991). However, examining the effect of income on demand and increases in tuition in the 1980s and 1990s is a fairly complicated issue.

Median family income, measured in constant dollars and viewed across all income levels combined, rose very little during the 1980s and the early 1990s (College Board, 1997; Lewis, 1989). However, families in the highest or fifth income quintile experienced substantial increases in their real (inflation-adjusted) incomes, families in the second-highest or fourth income quintile experienced modest increases in their real incomes, families in the lower, third and second, quintiles experienced income that increased at about the rate of inflation, and those in the lowest quintile experienced a decrease in their real income (Mumper, 1996, p. 54).

Based on his in-depth case studies of highly selective, elite private colleges and universities, Clotfelter (1996) attributes the "surge in demand" for education at the elite colleges, at least in part, to "the rapidly advancing affluence of the affluent" (p. 256). Clotfelter elaborates on this income-induced increase in demand, with the help of CPS data, as follows:

> The most prominent bellwether of this improvement was a robust increase in incomes at the top of the income distribution. During the 15-year period covered in the present study, between 1977 and 1992, the mean income of families in the top quintile of the income distribution increased at an annual rate of 1.1%, after inflation. By comparison, the incomes of the remaining four-fifths of families barely grew, increasing at only 0.2% per year" (p. 59).

Perhaps undergirded by the early formation of cultural capital and habitus (Bourdieu, 1977), research has consistently demonstrated that when controlling for a variety of background and ascribed characteristics, even within high and exceptionally high ability groupings, students from higher-income families are more likely to attend the most elite institutions of higher education and have become increasingly concentrated in such schools (Cook and Frank, 1993; Hearn, 1984, 1988, 1990, 1991; Kingston and Lewis, 1990). In combination, these factors make the changes, between 1980 and 1994, in the proportional representations of students from different income groups in the enrollments at different types of institutions especially revealing.

McPherson and Schapiro's (1998) analysis of data from the American Freshman Survey illustrate these changes. Between 1980 and 1994, the following shifts in "relative" enrollment demand at different types of institutions were evident: (1) middle- and upper-income students shifted away from two-year colleges toward four-year colleges and universities, while students in the lowest-income groups became more concentrated among the enrollments at two-year institutions, and the net effect was to produce a relative decrease in demand at both public and private two-year colleges in general; (2) the decrease in the relative demand at two-year colleges resulted in increases in the relative demand at public and private, four-year colleges and universities; (3) upper-income and the richest-income groups shifted away from private four-year colleges and toward private and public universities; and (4) all three middle-income groups increased their relative demand for education at private four-year colleges. McPherson and Schapiro (1998) contend that point (4) "undoubtedly accounts for the intense financial pressure that private four-year colleges have appeared to be under over the past decade, as no-need students have become increasingly rare" (p. 46).

It is important to remember, however, that in "absolute" numbers, public two-year and four-year institutions and public four-year institutions all experienced substantial increases in their enrollments from 1980 to 1994, and only private two-year colleges experienced more or less stable enrollments during the period (U.S. Department of Education, 1996, Table 196). Furthermore, as noted above, research has consistently shown that when tuition is controlled for, increases in student income are associated with increases in enrollment demand.

The Tuition Charged by Substitute Institutions

Another one of the typical determinants of the demand for enrollment at a particular institution is the tuition charged—and the enrollment at—a competing or substitute institution or group of institutions (W. Becker, 1990; Weiler, 1984). Research has consistently demonstrated that, for a given tuition at a particular college or group of such colleges, an increase in tuition charges at a substitute institution or group of such institutions will lead to an increase in demand for enrollment places at the particular college or group in question (Heller, 1996; Kane, 1995; McPherson, 1978).

For example, McPherson (1978) examined the effect of changes in tuition at public colleges on enrollment at private colleges, observing a direct or positive relationship; while both Kane (1995) and Heller (1996) observed that when tuition at a state's public two-year colleges is increased, the demand for enrollment places at its public four-year colleges increases. This may explain why peer group inter-institutional comparisons are a prominent feature of tuition-setting practices at both public (Lenth, 1993) and private institutions (Mulugetta, Saleh, and Mulugetta, 1997; Warner,

1984).[27] While an individual institution might like to be on the receiving end of the increases in demand due to increases in the prices charged by its closest competitors, it would certainly not want to risk over-pricing its competitors, only to see student demand to attend their college decrease.

The importance of the pricing strategies used by peer institutions can also be detected in the behavior of Ivy League institutions and MIT since the formal charges of price fixing were made against these institutions by the Justice Department—that is, since those institutions signed the consent decree to cease their longstanding tradition of sharing information about sticker prices and institutional aid awards planned for each year. In particular, Mulugetta, Saleh, and Mulugetta (1997) found that among the Ivy League institutions and other highly selective institutions in their sample—the 31 highly selective private institutions of the COFHE (Consortium on Financing Higher Education), which includes the Ivy institutions and MIT — "recycling tuition to finance institutional grants has become more institution-specific during the period after the consent decree, reflecting institutional characteristics and strategies....evidence that the institutions have become more strategic and less collective in their financial aid practices" (p. 61). Of course, previous research on the relationship between the pricing strategies of fairly close competitors and demand for attendance at one's own college would lead us to suspect that these kinds of uncoordinated pricing- and aid-setting strategies were just what the Ivy League institutions had long sought to avoid.[28]

The positive or direct relationship between tuition charges at a competing institution or set of institutions—such as private colleges—on the "demand" for enrollment places at another college or set of colleges—such as public institutions, has also been observed in research that has sought to explain the demand- and supply-

---

[27]In their recent examination of the tuition- and aid-setting practices of public and private institutions for the National Commission on the Cost of Higher Education, Hauptman and Krop (1998) summarized what their experiences have taught them about the setting of tuition at such institutions as follows: "The thrust of our argument in this paper is that college officials set their tuitions each year and then gauge whether students and their families are willing and able to pay the higher prices. In those instances where demand slackens, colleges then either reduce the rate of increase in tuition and other charges in the next year or become even more aggressive with their student aid strategies" (p. 78). Although sensitivity to costs factors would appear to be implicit in their view of the initial round of tuition-setting practices, Hauptman and Krop (1998) make clear the explicit attention that college officials would pay to the demand-side factors in terms of the adjustments they would make in response to such factors as they reveal themselves more clearly over time.

[28]Of course, at the time, the Justice Department was actually investigating several small groups of very similar institutions in terms of product, price, and location. These included the Ivy institutions, the group of 12 Midwestern colleges known as the Great Lakes Colleges Association, a group of eight mostly Southern women's colleges, and at least one other small group of universities charging very high tuitions (see Rothschild and White, 1993, and the references cited by them for more information). It should also be noted that when such small groups of institutions can so clearly identify each other as very close competitors that they cannot resist the temptation to collaborate on pricing decisions and/or market share decisions, the appropriate market structure to describe the behavior of such groups would probably move toward some form of oligopolistic model (see for example, Kuenne, 1992; Tirole, 1988). Clearly, additional research is needed in this area, and the subject is not addressed in more detail here.

side determinants of tuition in the two sectors (Paulsen, 1991; Rusk and Leslie, 1978). Between 1980 and the mid-1990s, tuitions have increased substantially at all types of institutions; therefore, these constant interactions could have been somewhat mutually reinforcing in their net effect, promoting more or less ongoing, incremental increases in demand for enrollment places at various types of colleges and universities.

Financial Aid to Students from Government Programs

By far the largest portion of non-institutional aid that is given to students to help finance their postsecondary educational investments comes from the federal programs for grants, loans and work-study (Clotfelter, 1991).[29] Economists typically conceptualize federally funded financial aid to students as an example of a subsidy that goes directly to the consumer in a market, and is therefore, customarily viewed as an important determinant of demand for the educational product (W. Becker, 1990; Clotfelter, 1991; Weiler, 1984). Technically, a subsidy to students as consumers would shift the demand curve upward, by a vertical amount equal to the per-unit subsidy or subsidy per student. This shift would be logically the same as a downward shift in consumer demand due to the government charging consumers a per-unit tax on consumption, in which case the demand curve would shift down by the vertical amount of the per-unit tax (Binger and Hoffman; Henderson and Quandt, 1980; Musgrave and Musgrave, 1984; Salvatore, 1986). Based on the usual—though unrealistic—assumption that students have perfect access to, and complete understanding of, information on the availability of government sources of financial aid, the demand curve should shift vertically upward by the amount of the per-student subsidy value of the increase in aid. This would equal the average value of Federal grants, such as Pell grants, and the subsidy portion of a government-subsidized loan[30]—estimates of the latter having ranged from about 30 to 50% (Clotfelter, 1991; Coopers & Lybrand, 1997).

Although reviews of the literature have revealed ample evidence that, for a given level of tuition, increases in financial aid tend to increase enrollment demand, especially among low-income students (Leslie and Brinkman, 1988; Paulsen, 1990a), and furthermore, that student demand for enrollment places is more likely to increase in response to increases in grants than in loans (Heller,

---

[29]The states have also made a variety of attempts to support the attendance of their students at postsecondary institutions, often through the use of grant programs. State grant programs, have, in most cases, been somewhat more successful than the large federal grant programs in keeping up with increases in tuition growth; although this means not falling as far short of such growth as have the federal programs. Although states' efforts to support students' enrollment is not addressed fully in this chapter, the interested reader should see the excellent summaries of such efforts by Mumper (1996, 1998) and Mumper and Anderson (1993).

[30]Of course, government loans actually do little to reduce the price a student pays for higher education. Rather its two primary effects are to postpone the payment of the price of education and to increase the overall price by the total amount of the interest the student must pay on the loan. Nevertheless, among different types of loans, the Perkins and Stafford-Subsidized programs make it possible to purchase units of college education at less than would be possible through Stafford-Unsubsidized loans.

1997)[31]; exploring the relationship between federally funded financial aid and tuition levels is more complex. Since the beginning of the heightened federal budget-consciousness that characterized the early 1980s, scholars and policy-makers have debated the merits of what has come to be called the "Bennett Hypothesis (Bennett, 1987)." The hypothesis has been expressed in many ways, but the essence of it is based on the contention that colleges and universities—especially in the private sector—have raised their tuitions at a fast pace, in large part, because this has enabled them to capture increased federal aid in the form of enhanced tuition revenue (Hauptman, 1990; Hauptman and Krop, 1998; McPherson and Schapiro, 1991, 1993, 1998; Pearson and Baldi, 1998).

The basic elements of the argument revolve around the possible tuition-sensitivity of federal aid, and the importance of making appropriate distinctions between the tuition-sensitivity of aid in the forms of grants versus loans. Based on federal program requirements, as well as their empirical and theoretical research on this issue, McPherson and Schapiro (1998) explain these factors as follows:

> And the fact that federal aid dollars are keyed to student financial need—which rises with tuition—makes it appear that colleges should be able to capture more federal aid by raising prices. However,...in the main federal grant program, the Pell program, the amount of aid awarded to a student is a function of the student's need, up to a limit imposed by the student's family's income. Thus the largest grant any student can receive for 1997-98, no matter how needy, is $2,700, and maximum grant size declines with family income. At current Pell funding levels, these income-graded award maxima are a very severe constraint, with the result that virtually no students in private higher education and relatively few in pubic higher education have their full need met by Pell....The most plausible place to look for an impact of tuition increases on available federal funds is in the federal loan programs....At present, more students are below the loan maximum in the public sector than in the private sector, and it is therefore more likely that federal aid increases would drive tuition higher in public rather than in private institutions" (pp. 82-83).

The reasoning in this argument receives some support from the limited amount of empirical work that has been completed to investigate the nature and magnitude of the effect of federal aid on tuition. McPherson and Schapiro (1991, 1993) analyzed the relationship between changes in federal grant aid to students and tuition increases at institutions between 1978 and 1986. They found that changes in federal grants were not related to tuition increases at private institutions, but were positively related to tuition increases at public institutions. The Coopers & Lybrand (1997) study was a follow-up to the empirical work of McPherson and Schapiro with the notable changes including data covering the period from 1989 to 1995 and separate data for both federal grants and federal loans. They found no significant relationship among these variables for public institutions, but did find that increases in federal loans were positively associated with increases in tuition at private institutions. Furthermore, both the McPherson and Schapiro and the Coopers & Lybrand studies found that federal grants were positively related

---

[31]The major shift from grants to loans in federal programs since 1980 constitutes one of the most dramatic shifts in financial policy related to higher education in the U.S. Although beyond the scope of this chapter, the patterns of change in federal aid programs have been insightfully and thoroughly analyzed in two previous chapters in this series (Hearn, 1993; St. John and Elliott, 1994).

to increases in institutional aid at private institutions, and in separate models, found that increases in institutional aid were positively related to increases in tuition at private institutions. These findings, in combination, suggest the presence of both direct and indirect effects of increases in federal aid on increases in tuition.

However, additional findings introduce some possible limitations and/or contradictions. For example, in the Coopers & Lybrand (1997) study, they also found that federal grants had a negative direct effect on tuition at private institutions. In some respects this tends to contradict their own finding about the positive effects of federal loans on tuition, but is supported by findings from the NAICU (1997) study, indicating a negative relationship between federal grants to students and tuition. Furthermore, it appears that each of these studies has significant shortcomings in its specifications and/or estimating procedures. The McPherson and Schapiro (1991) and Coopers & Lybrand (1997) studies both estimate separate sets of equations to estimate the effects of federal aid on tuition and on institutional aid, but neither has any measure of institutional costs, which would be an important variable, not only for purposes of control, but would also be of considerable theoretical interest in modeling the causes of tuition growth. And while the NAICU (1997) study does include a strong measure of educational costs, it does not report any evidence of having estimated separate equations to examine the effects of federal aid on institutional aid as well as on tuition. Standard microeconomic theories would predict increases in demand and upward pressure on tuition due to a government subsidy given to student consumers, and there is clearly empirical work to support those predictions. Nevertheless, there are apparently other supply-side factors and behaviors that need to be more fully addressed in future research, before such predictions can be made with confidence.

Figure 4 portrays the revenue and cost structure of an institution before and after it experiences an increase in its demand and corresponding marginal revenue curves due to improvements in the labor market opportunities for college graduates relative to those of high school graduates, increases in the number of potential college-bound students, increases in the income of students and their families, increases in the presence of, and tuition charged by, substitute institutions, and increases in federal financial aid to students. Before the changes, the revenue structure of the college portrayed in Figure 4 is represented by demand and marginal revenue curves D and MR, and AC and MC represent the cost structure of the institution. Under such circumstances, the institution portrayed in Figure 4 would find that additional students would add more to revenue than to costs up to the point where MR = MC. Therefore, in seeking to maximize its discretionary budget (savings or surplus, if possible), the institution would enroll 0Q students and would find that students would be willing and able to pay a sticker price of 0P. Some students, of course, would pay a net price less than 0P, due to the institutional aid awards to some students, which are included in the cost structure (MC and AC). The institution's revenue per student, given 0Q students, would be the amount 0P—measured on the vertical axis—which is exactly the same as educational cost per student. Therefore, the institution would not experience a positive discretionary budget or saving, because donative subsidies cover only enough of

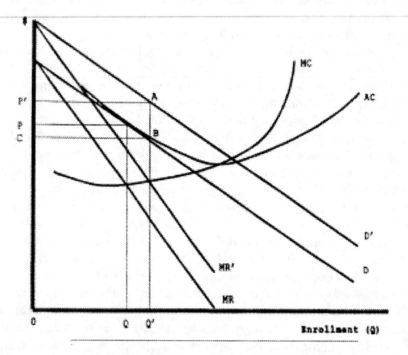

Figure 4. Effect of Changes in Demand and Marginal Revenue on Tuition and Enrollment

the educational costs per student so that commercial revenue per student (0P) is just
enough to cover the remaining costs, and not enough to leave a budget surplus for the
institution. The increase in demand and revenue is illustrated by the new, higher revenue structure of D' and MR'. Given the new revenue structure, the institution would
enroll 0Q' students and would find that students would be willing and able to pay a
sticker price of 0P'. In this new short-run equilibrium, the institution would experience a positive discretionary budget or saving of amount AB = P'C per student.

The new sticker price would be 0P', clearly higher than before the increase in the
demand and marginal revenue for the educational services of the institution portrayed
in Figure 4. Once again, some students may pay a net price that is less than the sticker
price due to expenditures on institutional aid that are included in the new, higher cost
curves. The net effect of the increase in demand—and corresponding marginal revenue— would be to raise sticker price, *ceteris paribus*.[32]

The conclusion that increases in student demand, due to increases in the relative job

[32]Once again, while this is the clear result of the comparative statics analysis, it should be emphasized,
that in highly complex, dynamic analyses of this phenomenon, the cost and revenue structures would be
shifting upward and downward for a variety of reasons, so that the net effect of changes in per-unit costs (or
subsidies) could easily get lost in an inter-temporal shuffle of a multitude of opposing and contradictory
cause-effect relationships. It is because of this possibility that exploring the effect on tuition of one cost-
related or revenue-related factor at a time—that is, using the *ceteris paribus* assumption—can be a useful
source of understanding the causes of rising tuition.

market opportunities for college graduates, numbers of potential college-bound students, incomes of students and their families, tuition charged by competing institutions, and federal financial aid to students, lead to tuition increases, is quite consistent with—and supported by—empirical work that has examined these relationships (McMahon, 1974; McPherson and Schapiro, 1991, 1993; National Association of Independent Colleges and Universities, 1997; Paulsen, 1991; Rusk and Leslie, 1978; To and Olson, 1996).

Expensive Non-price Competition: Trading Marketing Costs for Revenues

By the end of the 1970s, American colleges and universities had many concerns, but two of the most prominent were the dramatic decline in the job market opportunities of college graduates and the forthcoming decrease in the pool of potential students of traditional college-going age (Cartter, 1976; Dresch, 1975; Freeman, 1976). Many institutions reacted to these developments by engaging in a variety of expensive forms of non-price competition for the shrinking pool of students. Each college or university needed to find ways to enhance potential students' awareness of opportunities to attend their college, and good reasons to view their institution as unique or distinctive in ways that would attract them not only to college, but to their specific college out of so many.

More colleges and universities began to view students as consumers or as potential customers who sought information to aid them in their decision-making and who expected to have their needs met by the college of their choice (Riesman, 1980). The use of terms such as "strategic marketing" (Kotler and Fox, 1985) and "enrollment management" (Hossler, 1984; Paulsen, 1990a) became part of the new market-oriented jargon of higher education. Many colleges invested more money and effort in the recruitment and retention of students of traditional age and students from non-traditional age groups (Frances, 1990; Hauptman, 1990). The changing demographics of the student body also lead to greater spending for corresponding changes in services to meet the changing needs of students, such as child-care centers, remedial, learning skills, tutoring and counseling programs (Halstead, 1989; Mumper, 1996). Colleges added new programs, most of them more vocational or career-oriented than in the past (Rehnke, 1987; Roemer, 1982; Stadtman, 1980), and many of these new programs—for example, in business, computer science, or engineering—were more expensive than the standard liberal arts and sciences curriculum (Frances, 1990; Hauptman, 1990). Although the new career-oriented programs were expensive, research has indicated that when conditions in the job market for colleges graduates deteriorated, institutions that placed more emphasis on career-oriented programs not only maintained, but actually increased their enrollment levels at a substantial rate (Paulsen, 1990b). Furthermore, the dramatic redistribution of student enrollment and degrees conferred away from traditional arts and sciences and toward career-oriented fields is well-known throughout higher education (Frances, 1990, p. 18).

Of course, we now know that colleges and universities were not only able to maintain, but were able to increase the demand for their educational products, by trading increases in expenditures for increases in revenues. The economic theory of monopolistic competition is designed to illustrate the effects of simultaneous increases in costs and demand on tuition and enrollment decisions. In his analysis of the causes of rising tuition for the National Center for Postsecondary Governance and Finance, Hansen (1988) explains this important and realistic connection between the economic theory of monopolistic competition and some prominent features of the behavior of colleges and universities in the marketplace.

> If institutions can sufficiently differentiate their product, they gain some flexibility as monopolistic competitors in setting their prices; this occurs because of the emergence of strong preferences on the part of consumers for 'name brands.' Hence, as colleges and universities have tried to differentiate themselves, they may have gained some ability to raise prices without worrying about enrollment losses" (p. 7).

The model used in this chapter can be readily applied to illustrate this behavior and its effects on costs, demand and tuition. When a college or university increases its expenditures for recruitment, retention, and program development with the intention to further differentiate its educational product or package from that of other colleges in the eyes of potential students and their families, this model uses the separate component of educational costs called marketing expenditures (mQ), expressed on a per-student basis by the symbol "m". As noted in an earlier section on "the mathematical model," "m" refers to marketing expenditures per undergraduate student, one of the components of E&G expenditures, usually distributed across the appropriate subcategories of E&G expenditures, but noted separately here because of its strategic importance in the revenues and costs, and enrollment and pricing decisions of colleges and universities.

Figure 5 portrays a college or university that is typical of those who were among the first to increase their per-student marketing expenditures (m) in an effective tradeoff of marketing

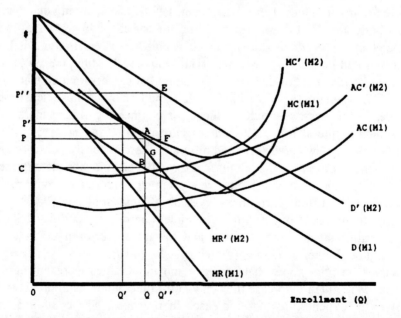

Figure 5. Expensive Non-Price Competition: Trading Marketing Costs for Revenues

costs for commercial revenues from matriculating students. Before the college's investment in "marketing" for product differentiation purposes, its revenue structure is represented by demand curve D, corresponding to only a nominal level of M1 dollars of per-student marketing expenditures, and marginal revenue MR. Its cost structure is represented by AC, also corresponding to only a nominal level of M1 dollars of per-student marketing expenditures, and MC. Under such circumstances, additional students would add more to revenue than to costs up to 0Q students, where MR = MC, and the college would charge the sticker price that the initial demand curve D indicates 0Q students are willing to pay, 0P = QA. Revenue per student would be 0P = QA and cost per students would be 0C = QB, and the college would experience savings or a positive discretionary budget of PC = AB.

Next, the college increases its marketing expenditures on some combination of recruitment, retention, and program development designed to increase the differentiation of the college's product relative to that of other colleges. The new cost structure is represented by AC', corresponding to a "strategic," and higher level of M2 dollars of per-student marketing expenditures, and MC', corresponding to the same strategic level of marketing expenditures, M2. Now, MR = MC' at 0Q' students, who would be willing to pay a sticker price charged by the college of 0P'. Both revenue per student and cost per student equal 0P' and no savings or positive discretionary budget would be experienced; however, the increase in per-student costs, by themselves would tend to increase the sticker price from 0P to 0P', consistent with the higher cost structure due to the strategic level of marketing expenditures.

Of course, it only makes sense for a college to increase its marketing expenditures from M1 to M2 if they expect that it will result in an increase in their demand by either an equal or greater amount—that is, if an equal or greater vertical shift in the demand would be the expected outcome. For this college, as for many others constituting the first several waves of institutional investments in strategic marketing expenses, it is reasonable to assume that such an increase in demand would be very likely to occur. For the college portrayed in Figure 5, the increase in the revenue structure—that results from the increase in "m" and is due to greater perceived distinctiveness of this college's product relative to that of others—is represented by demand curve D', corresponding to the new strategic and higher level of M2 dollars of per-student marketing expenditures, and the associated marginal revenue curve MR'. Under these circumstances, students would add more to revenue than to costs up to an enrollment level of 0Q", and the college would charge the sticker price that the new demand curve indicates students are willing and able to pay, 0P" = Q"E. As usual, the cost curves contain some expenditures for institutional aid offered to selected students who would not otherwise be able to pay the full sticker price. The revenue per student would now equal 0P" = Q"E and the cost per student would equal Q"F = 0P; which leaves saving or positive discretionary budget per student of FE = PP".

Finally, one of the most important results illustrated in Figure 5 is the fact that the college portrayed was successful in shifting its demand curve by more than its cost curves. In terms of vertical shifts, the demand curve increased by the amount GE, while the cost curves shifted by the amount BA, where BA is clearly much less than GE. For the college portrayed in Figure 5, their risk paid off—that is, their increase in expenditures per student (BA) was more than offset by the resultant increase in revenue per student (GE), and the college even ended up with net saving in the process. As can be readily seen in Figure 5, both the increase in marketing costs, reflected in the upward shift in the cost structure (AC and MC), as well as the increase in demand, reflected by the increase in the revenue structure (D and MR), had the effect of contributing to rising tuition. The combination of increase in tuition due to both higher educational costs and increased demand creates substantial upward pressure on tuition. Indeed, non-price competition is capable of being quite "expensive" for the students who elect to attend a college such as this one.[33]

The Long Run Adjustment and Zero Saving

However, there is another very important chapter in this story of colleges and universities operating in a monopolistically competitive marketplace, and it is illustrated in Figure 6 below. Figure 6 presents the probable "future" of the college portrayed in Figure 5 after some time—probably several years—has passed. The same college in Figure 6 is portrayed as having a cost structure represented by AC and MC and faces a revenue structure represented by demand D and marginal revenue MR. Enrollment will be based on the number of students that add more to revenue than to costs, indicating that 0Q students would be enrolled (where MR = MC), and the college would charge tuition 0P = QA, which the demand curve indicates students are willing to pay. The difference between revenue per student (0P = QA) and costs per student (0C = QB) is CP = BA, which indicates that the college is experiencing a positive discretionary budget or saving. The important part of this chapter in the story of our representative college is that after a few years, many other colleges, seeing the success of the peer institutions as a result of their strategic marketing (increased expenditures for recruitment, retention and program development), make similar investments. Under such circumstances, a given pool of enrollment is redistributed among those colleges in the first wave of such strategic marketing and those who have now matched their efforts. In other words, for each college that was among the first to add new programs in business, computer science, or engineering, there are now others who have matched their advances and have also learned how to better market their product to differentiate it in a favorable fashion in the eyes of potential students. The impact on the college portrayed in Figure 6 can be seen in the reduction in its demand curve that would result from intense non-price competi-

---

[33] In fact, for colleges whose experience is portrayed in Figure 5, there is even one more very likely development that would contribute even more to increases in tuition. When a college is successful in differentiating its product from others in the eyes of students as consumers, the demand curve often does more than just shift upward, as shown in Figure 5. It also rotates clockwise as it shifts upward and outward. The clockwise shift is due to a steepening of its slope which accompanies an increase in the distinctiveness of the college's product in the eyes of the student. Because the students place a high value on attending this particular college—due to their perceptions of its unique characteristics—they will not only be willing to pay a higher sticker price than others, but would also be less sensitive to increases in the price compared to others as well. The result would be that the new demand would be in a position something like what is illustrated in Figure 5, but as it shifts up and outward it will also become steeper so that students would be willing and able to pay a price even higher than 0P" = Q"E, consistent with how much steeper the demand curve becomes at enrollment Q". This is a realistic appraisal of the more probable final outcome of the analysis; however, it is not shown on Figure 5, because the figure is already quite cluttered when illustrating only eight revenue and cost functions, without adding even more.

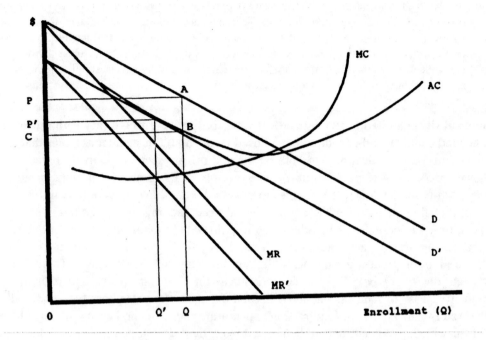

Figure 6. The Long-Run Adjustment and Zero Saving

tion from other peer institutions. The college's new revenue structure is represented by demand D' and marginal revenue MR'. Now, MR' = MC when 0Q' students are enrolled, and those students are only willing to pay the sticker price of 0P'. The result for this and other such colleges is that, in the long run, the typical college or university in monopolistic competition will tend to experience zero savings or no positive discretionary budget (Binger and Hoffman, 1988; Halstead, 1991; Henderson and Quandt, 1980; Salvatore, 1986).

Once again, this analysis is based on comparative statics. In a fuller, dynamic analysis, both the cost and revenue structure of the college portrayed in Figure 6—which illustrates the experiences of the vast majority of America's public and private institutions—would be rising consistently over time; however, in the case of this representative college, the cost structure would be rising somewhat faster than the revenue structure (demand curve), resulting in the long-run adjustment process and the outcome of zero saving for the typical college in the short run. Although the great majority of American colleges and universities would tend toward zero saving or surplus, that is, no positive discretionary budget, in the long run; some relatively small number of institutions that are very wealthy, highly selective, with high levels of donative subsidies from private sources in the form of endowment and gifts, may experience a positive discretionary budget on a more consistent basis. In other words, colleges and universities do not compete on a level playing field, and a very few elite institutions are largely sheltered from market forces (Winston, 1997b).

So the higher education market, already separated along *regional* lines—and sometimes *ideological* lines among denominational schools—is also highly hierarchical, differentiated by *donative wealth* into vaguely delineated and over-lapping bands that have little competitive interaction. At the top are schools characterized by large subsidies, excess demand, and student selectivity; at the bottom are schools characterized by excess supply; in the middle are the schools facing quality/quantity tradeoffs and the unpleasant choices of enrollment management (p. 36).

Fund Raising and Donative Subsidies: Cost Reduction and Quality Enhancement

The mathematical and economic model used throughout this chapter assumes that institutions of higher education—in both public and private sectors—actively pursue additional donative resources from private giving. This gives institutions a greater opportunity to use donative resources to cover additional expenses in pursuit of valued institutional goals in either the current period or, by adding to the institution's endowment, in future periods. The model uses the symbol "f" to indicate per-student expenditures on fund-raising activities. The symbol d^P equals the amount of donative resources acquired from private giving per dollar of fund-raising expenditures. Therefore, d^P reflects the "receptivity" of the community to fund-raising efforts, and indicates the "effectiveness" of fund-raising activities and expenses. It is also possible to view d^P as the "return" on a dollar of fund-raising expenditures per student, because d^P must be > 1 for fund-raising expenditures to be profitable or yield a positive return per dollar. Total expenditures for fund raising are indicated by the expression $d^P fQ$.

The mathematical model used here assumes the pursuit of donative resources to be of strategic importance for both public and private institutions. Although many individuals would tend to associate fund raising primarily with private colleges and universities, the acquisition of donative resources from private sources has grown tremendously in both public and private sectors. After adjustment for inflation, the amount of voluntary support for higher education experienced a "real" increase of 86%, between 1980 and 1995 (U.S. Department of Commerce, 1997, Table 294; U.S. Department of Education, 1996, Table 37). This was distributed between a 54% increase in giving for the private sector and a 164% increase for institutions in the public sector.

A substantial literature exists on the determinants of the giving behavior of donors in higher education (Dunn, 1986; Duronio and Loessin, 1990; Harris, 1990; Jacobson, 1990; Leslie and Ramey, 1988; Okunade and Beri, 1997; Taylor and Martin, 1995; Willemain et al., 1994). Of special interest here, however, is research on the return on institutional investments in fund raising; that is, estimates of how much is raised in gifts per dollar of fund-raising expenditures. A recent survey of seventy public and private universities revealed that, on average, total giving was about $8.00 per dollar of fund-raising expenditures—an estimate of "d^P" in the model used here—indicating a substantial rate of return per dollar invested in pursuing increases in donative resources from private sources (Grunig, 1995). However, the total amount of gift revenue raised per dollar of fund-raising expenditures is directly related to measures of an institution's size (e.g., FTE enrollment or total E&G expenditures) and the size of its existing endowment. These differences are evident in Paton's (1986) review of research on giving per dollar of fund-raising expenditures—"d^P" in the model used here. For highly selective liberal arts colleges, apparently those with large endowments, total giving is about $14.00 per dollar spent on fund raising and for private universities, the return is about $12.50 per dollar spent. But at private four-year colleges of moderate selectivity, total giving is approximately $5.55 per dollar of fund-raising spending and for public universities the figure is $5.00 per dollar of fund-raising costs (p. 31).

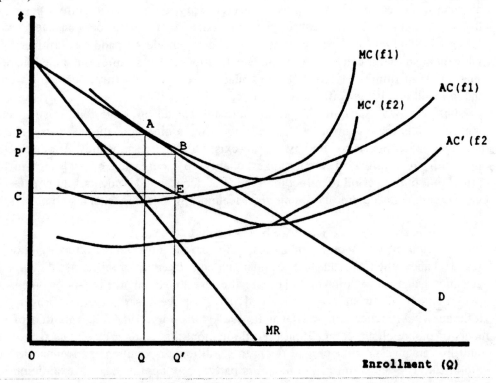

Figure 7. Fund Raising and Donative Subsidies: Cost Reduction and Quality Enhancement

Figure 7 illustrates the effects of fund-raising expenditures and increases in donative resources on the cost structure of a typical college or university. The initial cost structure for the college portrayed in Figure 7—before any increase in fund-raising expenditures per student—is represented by AC and MC, corresponding to the initial lower level of per-student fund-raising expenditures f1, and the demand configuration is represented by demand curve D and marginal revenue MR. Initially, the college would find that students add more to revenue than to costs up to enrollment of 0Q students and those students would be willing to pay the institution's sticker price from the demand curve, 0P = QA. Revenue per student, 0P = QA is the same as cost per student; therefore no saving or positive discretionary budget occurs—the college breaks even.

However, if an increase in fund-raising expenditures per student (f) yields a return of d^P that is greater than zero, then the increase in "f" will be more than offset by the amount of giving per dollar spent (d^P), and the cost structure will shift downward by an amount equal to the excess of giving per student over fund-raising expenditures per student. This is shown by the new lower cost structure, represented by AC' and MC', which correspond to the higher level of fund-raising expenditures f2.

Under these circumstances, students would add more to revenue than to costs up to enrollment level 0Q' and these students are willing to pay the college's sticker price of 0P' = Q'B. Revenue per student is 0P' = Q'B and cost per student equals 0C = Q'E, leaving a surplus or positive saving of CP' = EB per student. The college or university can elect to either spend its surplus or discretionary budget in the current period to advance the university toward its valued goals—this would be consistent with Bowen's (1980) revenue theory of costs—or they can elect to add the surplus to its endowment so that it can be used to pursue additional expenditures on valued institutional goals in future periods. All else equal, increases in donative subsidies would tend to result in a lower tuition, as illustrated in Figure 7.

There are two especially important outcomes of an effective fund-raising campaign. One is the reduction in an institution's remaining educational costs—that is those that haven't been covered by the pre-existing donative subsidies. Another is the opportunity to improve an institution's "quality" by increasing expenditures in the current or a future period to attract more talented faculty and students, add new facilities, increase the accessibility of computer technology on campus, and so on.

A Variation of the Model: Perfect Price Discrimination

Unlike organizations in other industries, colleges and universities typically know a great deal about the financial status of their students. Because of this unusual degree of such knowledge, some colleges and universities are able to engage in—or engage in an approximation of—what economists call perfect price discrimination (Binger and Hoffman, 1988; Henderson and Quandt, 1980; Salvatore, 1986). A variation of the model of monopolistic competition used throughout this chapter can be used to illustrate this practice and its effects on tuition, tuition discounting, and expansion of enrollment. This variation of the model is particularly appropriate for examining the behavior of a college or university that has low or moderate selectivity, does not experience excess demand, and can only meet its enrollment target for its scale of operation by offering tuition discounts to attract students through price discrimination, who will still add more to revenue than to costs. This variation of the model is presented here because its additional complexity helps to better illustrate some of the enrollment-expanding, tuition-discounting behavior of relatively unselective institutions. However, this variation was not used previously in this chapter, because its added complexity would have complicated the exposition, but added relatively little to the model's predictions about the direction of changes in tuition due to changes in the demand-side and cost-side factors examined.

Figure 8 represents a typical monopolistically competitive college or university, but with one important difference: institutional aid is no longer viewed as an educational cost and is no longer a component of the cost structure, represented by AC and MC. Instead, institutional aid is viewed as a reduction in potential revenues per student (Bowen and Breneman, 1993). In this example, I do not assume that the institu-

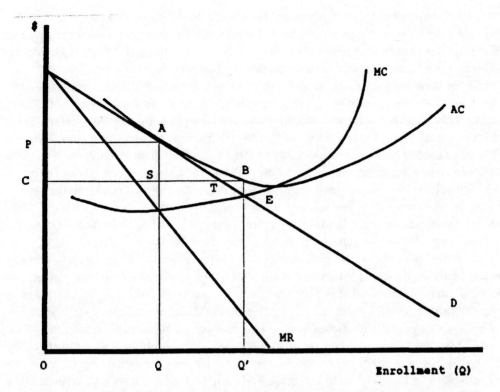

Figure 8. Effect of Perfect Price Discrimination on Revenue, Cost, Tuition, and Enrollment

tion price discriminates across the entire range of the demand curve, which is how economic theory would model the optimizing behavior of a perfect price discriminating seller.[34] Instead, I use the simplifying assumption that the institution engages in a two-phase process. First, the institution identifies its enrollment and sticker price for full-pay students; and then, the institution price discriminates, beyond that point to increase its enrollment. With these assumptions, the model illustrates the institution's behavior the way it has in previous analyses in this chapter, especially for the first phase, introducing the new view of the institution's behavior only in the second phase.

In phase one, the college portrayed in Figure 8 would find that students would add

---

[34]Microeconomic theory views the perfect-price-discriminating seller as an optimizer who engages in price discrimination across the entire relevant range of the demand curve. This range would run from the highest possible sticker price where demand intersects the vertical axis to the "marginal price," that is the lower price charged to the last consumer (or student) who adds more to revenue than to costs (Binger and Hoffman, 1988; Henderson and Quandt, 1980). Such a model would provide added insight into the relationships between revenues and costs. It would also enable the analyst to examine the effects of cost-side and demand-side changes on the highest possible sticker price, the marginal price (the lowest price, charged to the student who receives the largest tuition discount), and the range of prices charged to other students—including the median tuition charged—between the highest and the lowest tuition charged. Changes in revenue and cost structures would yield predictions about the direction of change in tuition due to demand-side or cost-side changes that would, in most instances, be similar to those predicted using the model in this chapter; however, the perfect-price-discriminating model would yield additional insights about the nature and meaning of tuition-discounting for enrollment expansion.

more to revenue than to costs up to an enrollment of 0Q students (where MR=MC), and that number of students would be willing to pay the institution's sticker price of 0P = QA. Revenue per student and cost per student are both equal to 0P = QA and the college experiences zero saving or discretionary budget.

Given their existing revenue and cost structures and their current scale of operation, some institutions may have a preference for a higher enrollment goal of 0Q' students. This can be achieved through the capacity to engage in perfect price discrimination. This capacity assumes that the institution can identify the highest possible price each student is willing to pay to attend. As they identify students who meet their admissions requirements but are only willing and able to attend at a lower price, they can selectively offer price or tuition discounts—that is, prices below the sticker price—to students they wish to have attend their institution. As long as each additional student adds at least as much (or more) to revenue as she or he does to cost, the college can maintain or even improve upon its current break-even status.

In phase two, the institution engages in price discrimination, which literally means charging different prices to different students. Under these circumstances, the demand curve indicates that 0Q students are willing to pay the full sticker price to attend, but the demand curve also indicates that additional students would attend at various prices below the sticker price. The essence of price discrimination is that after 0Q students choose to enroll, an additional student would be willing to enroll by paying a price somewhat below the full sticker price, but the remaining 0Q students are still willing to pay the sticker price and will still attend without discounts like those necessary to attract additional students. As a result, the addition to revenue as each additional student enrolls beyond 0Q, is equal to the maximum price that the demand curve indicates each student is willing to pay. In effect the demand curve—which indicates the maximum price each student is willing to pay—becomes the marginal revenue curve for enrollment beyond 0Q. Students are offered tuition discounts of the appropriate amounts as indicated at various points along the demand curve between points A and E. Students now add more to revenue than to costs up to the point where MC = D, which is at point E. Enrollment of 0Q' is now the enrollment that will make it possible for the institution to maximize its discretionary budget or saving. The full sticker price is paid by only 0Q students and the additional QQ' students enrolled will pay various prices somewhere between the maximum of 0P = QA and the minimum of Q'E.

A comparison of total revenues and costs before and after the additional students are enrolled illustrates the advantage of price discrimination for the institution portrayed in the figure. Total revenue was initially equal to the area PAQ0, the same as total cost. After the additional enrollment, total revenue is equal to the area PAEQ'0 and total cost is equal to the area CBQ'0. At enrollment of 0Q', total revenue and total costs actually "share" the area CSTEQ'0. However, total revenue also includes the area PATSC, while total costs also includes the area TBE; and PATSC > TBE so that the institution is now experiencing saving over which it has discretion in its use. Of course, the relative shapes and positions of an institution's revenue and cost structure will determine just how much additional enrollment would be possible for the college to attract through tuition discounts before reaching the enroll-ment level at which additional students add more to costs than to revenues. Furthermore, with appropriate adjustments in the relative shapes and positions of the revenue and cost structure, Figure 8 could also illustrate the achievement of an enrollment goal of 0Q' students with institutional aid per student included in the cost curves, as in all other analyses in this chapter (Figures 1-7), and the institution could be shown to experience a saving or positive discretionary budget.

CONCLUSIONS AND IMPLICATIONS FOR FUTURE RESEARCH

This chapter has combined analyses based on the economic theory of monopolistic competition with related empirical work in the higher education literature to explore the possible causes of the rapid inflation of college tuition since 1980. The model of monopolistic competition has been employed as a heuristic device and conceptual framework within which to integrate many of the separate and disconnected analyses of the causes of tuition growth in the higher education literature. The effects of a vari-ety of demand-side and cost-side factors on tuition have been examined. The results of the analysis of the causes of tuition growth based on economic theory have been found to be consistent with, and supported by, the findings of empirical work in higher education for a number of probable causes of tuition growth.

Tentative Conclusions About the Causes of Rising Tuition

Some tentative conclusions based on the combined results of the theoretical and empirical exploration conducted in this chapter can be expressed in the form of propositions about the causes of recent tuition growth. Because of the relatively small number of comprehen-sive empirical studies of the causes of tuition growth that have been conducted to date, I view each of these propositions as "testable hypotheses," each of which constitutes a call for future research. The most probable causes of tuition inflation based on *cost-side fac-tors* include the following, each of which is rated in terms of the probable degree of its impact (strong, moderate, or weak), based on available theory and research:

- decreases in the share of institutional revenues from state government appropria-tions (strong).
- increases in the constant-dollar value of instructional expenditures per-student (moderate).
- minimal or no growth in conventional measures of instructional productivity, such as the student-faculty ratio (moderate).
- increases in the constant-dollar value of administrative expenditures per-student (strong).
- increases in the constant-dollar value of student-services expenditures per-student (strong).
- increases in the constant-dollar value of per-student expenditures on institutional aid (moderate to strong).

The most probable causes of tuition inflation based on *demand-side factors* include the following, each of which is rated in terms of the probable degree of its impact (strong, moderate, or weak), based on available theory and research:

- increases in the job-market opportunities for college graduates relative to high school graduates (strong).
- increases in the numbers of potential college-bound students, especially due to increases in the participation rates of students of traditional age, across different levels of income, levels of ability, and racial/ethnic groups; and increases in the numbers of students of non-traditional age and students attending part-time (moderate).
- increases in the constant-dollar income of students and their families in the top income quintile, and to a lesser extent, in the next-to-the-top income quintile (moderate).
- increases in the tuition among all members of groups of institutions that view themselves as good substitutes for one another, which initiates and sustains a mutually reinforcing pattern of tuition inflation (moderate).
- increases in the constant-dollar value of federal grants and loans to students (weak).

A probable cause of tuition inflation due to a combination of demand-side and cost-side factors was the increase in marketing expenditures (e.g., recruitment, retention, and program development) that financed a substantial amount of nonprice competition designed to increase both the cost structure and the demand configuration for a specific college, and thereby increase the distinctiveness of an individual college's product in the eyes of potential students. This effect was most likely stronger in the 1980s than in the 1990s.

Future Directions in the Economic Modeling of College and University Pricing Behavior

Most colleges and universities, as non-profit organizations, just like most for-profit business organizations, do not necessarily set their enrollment and tuition in accordance with careful estimates of their revenue and cost functions, even though research reviewed in this chapter indicates that tuition increases are consistently related to changes in such demand- and cost-side factors. Therefore, the economic model developed and used in this chapter should be viewed with due circumspection and emphasis on its primary role in serving as a heuristic device and conceptual framework for integrating a wide range of theory and research relevant to our understanding of rising tuition. The consistency between the model's predicted increases in tuition and the findings of empirical work on such relationships lends credibility to both the economic model presented in this chapter as well as to the tentative conclusions about the causes of rising tuition presented above. However, although the model presented in this chapter appears to have been useful and effective as a conceptual framework within which to integrate, examine, and interpret the findings of existing research on the causes of rising tuition, I believe that the model represents, at best, only a first approximation of college and university pricing behavior and the ways in which environmental and institutional factors operate through changes in revenue and cost structures to drive up tuition.[35] In addition to its use as a conceptual framework for organizing the review of literature, I have also presented the economic model in this chapter as a first step and possible foundation to encourage other higher education scholars to develop and test better, more complex and comprehensive economic models of the financial behavior of colleges and universities, in the form of contributions to the mainstream of higher education literature.

For example, with the help of more in-depth case studies of tuition-setting behavior, I believe that one of the next steps for research in this area should emphasize the development of a more comprehensive and more realistic model of college and university pricing behavior. One especially important undertaking would be the development and refinement of a model of the perfect, price-discriminating monopolistically competitive college or university. While the specification of the cost structure for such a model may be similar to that used here, the specification of the demand or revenue configuration has the potential to reveal additional insights into the nature of tuition-discounting and enrollment-expanding aspects of college and university financial decision-making behavior. Models that view institutions as price-discriminating along the entire demand curve would raise interesting questions and provide added insights about factors that influence the marginal price charged to the student receiving the largest tuition discount, the range of intermediate prices, including the median tuition charged, and the maximum possible sticker price. Such a model would focus future analysis and research on issues of net price, which is gradually assuming more importance relative to sticker price. Although many of the general conclusions from a full, price-discriminating model about how changes in demand- and cost-side factors affect tuition would probably be similar to those produced with the simplified model used in this chapter, a new comprehensive model, like that suggested above, would view the role of institutional aid as more central to our understanding of institutional pricing behavior. Also, such a model would view institutional aid as a reduction in revenue, rather than as an expenditure—the latter serving adequately as a meaningful, but simplified, and workable approach to serve the purposes of this chapter. Viewing institutional aid as a reduction in revenue may be more economically meaningful and yield added insights in our pursuit of a deeper understanding of the internal methods of tuition-setting, tuition-discounting, and enrollment-expanding behaviors that are

---

[35]For example, the model presented in this chapter does not explicitly specify any detailed and technical features of the production process. That is, the production function is only indirectly and implicitly specified in the model. One of the most recent, and especially insightful, specifications of the relationships between the production process and pricing behavior at colleges universities is that presented by Rothschild and White (1995). Using the simplifying assumptions of a perfectly competitive marketplace, they specify a production process that views students of different types as inputs into the production process, to be combined with a set of features of a college's instructional technology, in the production of a college's primary output, human capital. In such cases of a customer-as-input technology, the student as customer would pay a net price that reflects the relationship between the value of the student's characteristics as an input into the production process and the value of the human capital that is the output of the college's production process. Although Rothschild and White (1995) admit that currently, "there are few resemblances between universities' pricing behaviors and the predictions of our model," the increasingly widespread practice of pursuing quality and diversity among students through price discrimination at all types of postsecondary institutions makes it seem increasingly likely that such relationships between production and pricing may become more "descriptive" of actual practices in the near future.

growing in prominence at most postsecondary institutions.

Yet another variation on the price-discriminating model is to view a college as facing a perfectly elastic demand curve at its sticker price for full-paying students and a downward-sloping demand curve for the range of enrollment that represents partial-paying students. This kinked-demand-curve model would raise other interesting questions and may yield additional insights into the financial behavior of colleges and universities. Moreover, as suggested in a previous section, modeling the behavior of small groups of institutions who are intensely aware of each other as close substitutes for their students, so that in the absence of collusion, the actions of one member of the group would result in strong related reactions from others, calls for adapting models of oligopoly and oligopolistic competition. Good examples of such groups would be the Ivy League institutions and perhaps the COFHE group as well.

Finally, the possible relevance of the perfectly competitive model for understanding college and university pricing behavior should not be overlooked or dismissed. As noted in a previous section, students attending some sets of institutions—for example, a set of similar colleges and universities offering similar programs at similar prices in the same geographic, especially urban, area—may perceive relatively little product differentiation among the colleges in this set. In such cases, it may well be that if any one of these colleges were to substantially increase its tuition above the local average—overall market price—for the set of similar colleges, the result may be a substantial reduction in enrollment at the college that raised its price, and a redistribution of enrollments among other members of the group. Such colleges would still be characterized by monopolistic competition and would still face downward-sloping demand curves, but those demand curves, while not perfectly elastic, may be highly elastic. This means that the pricing behavior of colleges in some markets may actually be closely approximated by the model of perfect competition.

Future Research on the Causes of Rising College Tuition

Cures come from understanding causes. Tuition inflation and reduced affordability pose substantial threats to the equity of access and choice in American higher education (Heller, 1997; McPherson and Schapiro, 1998; Mumper, 1996; Paulsen, 1998). Obviously, rapid rates of increase in the tuition that students and their families are charged for college education, and the concomitant and relentless increases in the costs faced by the institutions that provide such education, are problematic matters of major importance in the formulation and evaluation of public policy at the national, state, and institutional levels. This chapter has used an economic model of the pricing behavior of colleges and universities, based on an adaptation and application of the microeconomic theory of monopolistic competition to the context of the higher education marketplace, as a framework within which to address and examine a wide range of both the relevant theoretical and empirical research that has been reported in the higher education literature. Nevertheless, there is so much more to be done. For proper testing of the tentative conclusions or propositions about the causes of rising tuition presented above, as well as for the development of solid empirical bases to better inform the process of policy development, there is a great need for more comprehensive empirical studies of the determinants of tuition.

Based on close examinations of previous empirical work on the causes of rising tuition, I would make the following recommendations for consideration by those who wish to pursue additional research in this area. First, we need more studies that explicitly specify constant-dollar tuition or changes in tuition as their primary dependent or outcome variable. Second, studies should fully specify separate structural equations representing the demand-side or revenue-related variables and the supply-side or cost-related variables. Third, the effects on tuition of demand-side and cost-related variables should be estimated for both the private and public sectors. Fourth, in research on the determinants of tuition, it is methodologically important to formally acknowledge the nonrecursive and interdependent nature of the relationships between some demand and cost-side variables and some private- and public-sector measures of certain variables, by using some form of simultaneous equations or similarly appropriate estimation techniques. Fifth, studies based on aggregated national or state data are important, just as are studies that rely on institutional data—each level of data offers different perspectives on the complex of relationships involved. Sixth, both time-series and cross-sectional data can be useful in such studies, and indeed, pooled time-series and cross-section databases may provide a particularly rich opportunity for more comprehensive examinations of the causes of rising tuition in particular or the determinants of tuition in general.

In an effort to deepen our understanding of the causes of rising tuition, this chapter has combined analyses based on a wide range of economic concepts, theories, and perspectives with the methodologies and findings of research reported in the higher education literature. As a result, a dozen tentative conclusions about the causes of rising tuition were presented in this concluding section in the form of testable hypotheses. The remainder of this section has presented a variety of specific suggestions for future advancements in the economic modeling of college and university pricing behavior, as well as a set of concrete recommendations to assist researchers in the planning of empirical studies to test the tentative conclusions of this review with more comprehensive research designs than those used in the previous studies that constitute the existing state of research in this field. Ideally, through advances in theory development as well as the implementation of more comprehensive research designs, the emergence of a critical mass of new theoretical and empirical work will empower higher education scholars and policy-makers with both the understanding and the resolve to reverse the trends of tuition inflation and reduced affordability and their destructive effects on the equity of access, choice, persistence, and attainment in higher education in the not-too-distant future.

References

Basch, D. L. (1997). Private colleges' pricing experience in the early 1990s: The impact of rapidly increasing college-funded grants. *Research in Higher Education* 38 (3): 271-296.

Baumol, W. J., and Blackman, S. A. B. (1995). How to think about rising college costs. *Planning for Higher Education* 23: 1-7.

Becker, G. S. (1993). *Human Capital*. Third edition. Chicago: University of Chicago Press.

Becker, W. E. (1990). The demand for higher education. In S. A. Hoenack and E. L. Collins (eds.), *The Eco-*

nomics of American Universities. (pp. 155-188). Albany, NY: State University of New York Press.

Becker, W. E. (1992). Why go to college? The value of an investment in higher education. In W. E. Becker and D. R. Lewis (eds.), *The Economics of American Higher Education.* (pp. 91-120). Boston: Kluwer Academic Publishers.

Bennett, W. (1987). Our greedy colleges. *New York Times,* February 18, p. A31.

Binger, B. R., and Hoffman, E. (1988). *Microeconomics with Calculus.* Glenview, IL: Scott, Foresman, and Co.

Blais, A., and Dion, S. (Eds.) (1991). *The Budget-maximizing Bureaucrat: Appraisals and Evidence.* Pittsburgh: University of Pittsburgh Press.

Blaug, M. (1985). *Economic Theory in Retrospect,* Fourth Edition. Cambridge: Cambridge University Press.

Bourdieu, P. (1977). Cultural reproduction and social reproduction. In J. Karabel and A. H. Halsey (eds.), *Power and Ideology in Education.* (pp. 487-551). New York: Oxford University Press.

Bowen, H. R. (1977). *Investment in Learning: the Individual and Social Value of American Higher Education.* San Francisco: Jossey-Bass.

Bowen, H. R. (1980). *The Costs of Higher Education.* San Francisco: Jossey-Bass.

Bowen, W. G., and Breneman, D. W. (1993). Student aid: Price discount or educational investment? In D. Breneman, L. L. Leslie, and R. E. Anderson (eds.) (1993). *Finance in Higher Education.* (pp. 303-307). ASHE Reader Series. Needham Heights, MA: Ginn Press.

Breneman, D. W. (1994). *Liberal Arts Colleges: Thriving, Surviving, or Endangered?* Washington, DC: The Brookings Institution.

Breneman, D. W., and Finney, J. E. (1997). The changing landscape: Higher education finance in the 1990s. In P. M. Callan and J. E. Finney (eds.), *Public and Private Financing of Higher Education: Shaping Public Policy for the Future* (pp. 30-59). Phoenix, AZ: The American Council on Education and The Oryx Press.

Breneman, D. W., and Nelson, S. C. (1981). *Financing Community Colleges: An Economic Perspective.* Washington, D.C.: The Brookings Institution.

Brinkman, P. T. (1981). Factors affecting instructional costs at major research universities. *Journal of Higher Education* 52: 265-279.

Campbell, R., and Siegel, B. N. (1967). The demand for higher education in the United States, 1919-1964. *American Economic Review* 57: 482-484.

Cartter, A. M. (1976). *Ph.D.'s and the Academic Labor Market.* New York: McGraw-Hill.

Chamberlin, E. H. (1965). *The Theory of Monopolistic Competition: A Re-orientation of the Theory of Value.* Cambridge, MA: Harvard University Press.

Chickering, A. W., and Ehrmann, S. (1996). Implementing the seven principles: technology as lever. *AAHE Bulletin.* 49 (2): 3-6.

The College Board. (1997). *Trends in Student Aid: 1987 to 1997.* New York: College Entrance Examination Board.

Clotfelter, C. T. (1991). Demand for undergraduate education. In C. T. Clotfelter, R. G. Ehrenberg, M. Getz, and J. J. Siegfried (eds.), *Economic Challenges in Higher Education.* (Part I, pp. 19-139). Chicago: The University of Chicago Press.

Clotfelter, C. T. (1996). *Buying the Best: Cost Escalation in Elite Higher Education.* Princeton, NJ: Princeton University Press.

Cook, P. J., and Frank, R. H. (1993). The growing concentration of top students at elite schools. In C. T. Clotfelter and M. Rothschild (eds.), *Studies of Supply and Demand in Higher Education* (pp. 121-140). Chicago: The University of Chicago Press.

Coopers & Lybrand (1997). *The Impact of Federal Student Assistance on College Tuition Levels.* Washington, DC: Coopers & Lybrand, L. L. P.

Corazzini, A. J., Dugan, D. J., and Grabowski, H. G. (1972). Determinants and distributional aspects of enrollment in U.S. higher education. *Journal of Human Resources* 11 (1): 39-59.

Dresch, S. P. (1975). Demography, technology, and higher education: Toward a formal model of educational adaptation. *Journal of Political Economy* 83 (3): 535-569.

Dunn, J. A. (ed.) (1986). *Enhancing the Management of Fund Raising.* New Directions for Institutional Research No. 51. San Francisco: Jossey-Bass.

Duronio, M. A., and Loessin, B. A. (1990). Fund-raising outcomes and institutional characteristics in ten types of higher education institutions. *The Review of Higher Education* 13 (4): 539-556.

Fairweather, J. S. (1996). *Faculty Work and Public Trust: Restoring the Value of Teaching and Public Service in American Academic Life*. Boston: Allyn and Bacon.

Fenske, R. H., Besnette, F. H., and Jordan, S. M. (in press). The process of setting tuition in public university systems: A case study of interaction between governing board and campus management. In A. Hoffman (ed.), *Managing Colleges and Universities: Issues for Leadership*. Maryville, MO: Prescott.

Frances, C. (1990). *What Factors Affect College Tuition? A Guide to the Facts and Issues*. Washington, DC: American Association of State Colleges and Universities.

Freeman, R. B. (1975). Overinvestment in college training? *Journal of Human Resources* 10 (3): 287-311.

Freeman, R. B. (1976). *The Overeducated American*. New York: Academic Press.

Garvin, D. A. (1980). *The Economics of University Behavior*. New York: Academic Press.

Getz, M., and Siegfried, J. J. (1991). Costs and productivity in American colleges and universities. In C. T. Clotfelter, R. G. Ehrenberg, M. Getz, and J. J. Siegfried (eds.), *Economic Challenges in Higher Education*. (Part III, pp. 259-392). Chicago: The University of Chicago Press.

Griswold, C. P., and Marine, G. M. (1996). Political influences on state policy: Higher-tuition, higher-aid, and the real world. *The Review of Higher Education* 19 (4): 361-389.

Grunig, S. D. (1995). The impact of development office structure on fund-raising efficiency for research and doctoral institutions. *Journal of Higher Education* 66 (6): 686-699.

Gumport, P. J., and Pusser, B. (1995). A case of bureaucratic accretion: Context and consequences. *Journal of Higher Education* 66 (5): 493-520.

Halstead, D. K. (1989). *Higher Education Tuition*. Washington, DC: Research Associates of Washington.

Halstead, D. K. (1991). *Higher Education Revenues and Expenditures: A Study of Institutional Costs*. Washington, DC: Research Associates of Washington.

Handa, M. L., and Skolnick, M. L. (1975). Unemployment, expected returns, and the demand for university education in Ontario: Some empirical results. *Higher Education* 4: 27-43.

Hansen, W. L. (1988). The high and rising costs of college: Is there a problem? In J. B. Lee (ed.), *College Costs and Tuition: What Are the Issues?* (pp. xiii-17). Washington, DC: National Center for Postsecondary Governance and Finance.

Hansmann, H. (1986). The role of nonprofit enterprise. In S. Rose-Ackerman (ed.), *The Economics of Nonprofit Institutions* (pp. 57-84). New York: Oxford University Press.

Harris, J. T. (1990). Private support for public, doctorate-granting universities: Building a theoretical base. *The Review of Higher Education* 13 (4): 519-538.

Hart, O. D. (1979). Monopolist competition in a large economy with differentiated commodities. *Review of Economic Studies* 142: 1-30.

Hart, O. D. (1985a). Monopolistic competition in the spirit of Chamberlin: A general model. *Review of Economic Studies* 52: 529-546.

Hart, O. D. (1985b). Monopolistic competition in the spirit of Chamberlin: Special results. *The Economic Journal* 95: 889-908.

Hauptman, A. M. (1990). *The College Tuition Spiral*. Washington, DC: The American Council on Education.

Hauptman, A. M., and Krop, C. (1998). Federal student aid and the growth in college costs and tuitions: Examining the relationship. In National Commission on the Cost of Higher Education. *Straight Talk About College Costs and Prices*. (pp. 70-83). Phoenix, AZ: The Oryx Press and the American Council on Education.

Hearn, J. C. (1984). The relative roles of academic, ascribed, and socioeconomic characteristics in college destinations. *Sociology of Education* 57: 22-30.

Hearn, J. C. (1988). Attendance at higher-cost colleges: ascribed, socioeconomic, and academic influences on student enrollment patterns. *Economics of Education Review* 7(1): 65-76.

Hearn, J. C. (1990). Pathways to attendance at the elite colleges. In P. W. Kingston, and L. S. Lewis (eds.), *The High-status Track: Studies of Elite Schools and Stratification* (pp. 121-145). Albany: State University of New York Press.

Hearn, J. C. (1991). Academic and nonacademic influences on the college destinations of 1980 high school graduates. *Sociology of Education* 64: 158-171.

Hearn, J. C. (1993). The paradox of growth in federal aid for college students, 1965-1990. In J. C. Smart (ed.), *Higher Education: Handbook of Theory and Research*, Volume IX. (pp. 94-153).

Hearn, J. C., and Anderson, M. S. (1989). Integrating postsecondary education financing models: The Minnesota model. In R. H. Fenske (ed.), *Studying the Impact of Student Aid on Institutions*. (pp. 55-73). New Directions for Institutional Research No. 62. San Francisco: Jossey-Bass.

Hearn, J. C., and Anderson, M. S. (1995). The Minnesota financing experiment. In E.P. St. John (ed.), *Rethinking Tuition and Student Aid Strategies*. (pp. 5-25). New Directions for Higher Education, No. 89. San Francisco: Jossey-Bass.

Hearn, J. C., Griswold, C. P., and Marine, G. M. (1996). Region, resources, and reason: A contextual analysis of state tuition and student aid policies. *Research in Higher Education* 37 (3): 241-278.

Heller, D. E. (1996). *Rising Public Tuition Prices and Enrollment in Community Colleges and Four-year Institutions*. Paper presented at the annual meeting of the Association for the Study of Higher Education, Memphis, TN.

Heller, D. E. (1997). Student price response in higher education: An update to Leslie and Brinkman. *Journal of Higher Education* 68 (6): 624-659.

Henderson, J. M., and Quandt, R. E. (1980). *Microeconomic Theory: A Mathematical Approach*. New York: McGraw-Hill.

Hoenack, S. A., and Weiler, W. C. (1979). The demand for higher education and institutional enrollment forecasting. *Economic Inquiry* 17: 89-113.

Hopkins, D. S. P., and Massy, W. F. (1981). *Planning Models for Colleges and Universities*. Stanford: Stanford University Press.

Hopkins, T. D. (1974). Higher education enrollment demand. *Economic Inquiry* 12 (1): 53-65.

Hossler, D. (1984). *Enrollment Management: An Integrated Approach*. New York: College Entrance Examination Board.

Hossler, D., Bean, J. P., and Associates. (1990). *The Strategic Management of College Enrollments*. San Francisco: Jossey-Bass.

Hossler, D., Lund, J. P., Ramin, J., Westfall, S., and Irish, S. (1997). State funding for higher education: the Sisyphean task. *Journal of Higher Education* 68 (2): 160-190.

Hoxby, C. M. (1997). *How the Changing Market Structure of U.S. Higher Education Explains College Tuition*. NBER Working Paper Series No. 6323. Cambridge, MA: National Bureau of Economic Research.

Hubbell, L. L. (1992). *Tuition Discounting: the Impact of Institutionally Funded Financial Aid*. Washington, DC: National Association of College and University Business Officers.

Jacobson, H. K. (1990). Research on institutional advancement: A review of progress and a guide to the literature. *The Review of Higher Education* 13 (4): 433-488.

James, E. (1990). Decision processes and priorities in higher education. In S. A. Hoenack and E. L. Collins (eds.), *The Economics of American Universities*. (pp. 77-106). Albany, NY: State University of New York Press.

James, E. (1978). Product mix and cost disaggregation: A reinterpretation of the economics of higher education. *Journal of Human Resources* 13: 157-186.

Kane, T. J. (1995). *Rising Public College Tuition and College Entry: How Well Do Public Subsidies Promote Access to College?* Cambridge, MA: National Bureau of Economic Research Working Paper Series No. 5164.

Kingston, P. W., and Lewis, L. S. (1990). Undergraduates at elite institutions: The best, the brightest, and the richest. In P. W. Kingston, and L. S. Lewis (eds.), *The High-status Track: Studies of Elite Schools and Stratification* (pp. 105-120). Albany: State University of New York Press.

Komives, S. R., Woodard, D. B., and Associates. (1996). *Student Services: A Handbook for the Profession*, Third Edition. San Francisco: Jossey-Bass.

Koshal, R. K., Koshal, M., Boyd, R., and Levine, J. (1994). Tuition at Ph.D.-granting institutions: A supply and demand model. *Education Economics* 2 (1): 29-44.

Kotler, P., and Fox, K. F. A. (1985). *Strategic Marketing for Educational Institutions*. Englewood Cliffs, NJ: Prentice-Hall.

Krakower, J. Y., and Zammuto, R. F. (1987). Enrollment projections: the case against generalizations. *The Review of Higher Education* 10 (4): 333-356.

Kuenne, R. G. (1992). *The Economics of Oligopolistic Competition: Price and Nonprice Rivalry*. Cambridge, MA: Blackwell Publishers.

Layzell, D. T. (1996). Faculty workload and productivity: Recurrent issues with new imperatives. *The*

Review of Higher Education 19 (3): 267-281.

Lee, J. B. (1988). (ed.), *College Costs and Tuition: What Are the Issues?*. Washington, DC: National Center for Postsecondary Governance and Finance.

Lehr, D. K., and Newton, J. M. (1978). Time series and cross-sectional investigation of the demand for higher education. *Economic Inquiry* 16: 411-422.

Lenth, C. S. (1993). *The Tuition Dilemma: State Policies and Practices in Pricing Public Higher Education.* Denver, CO: State Higher Education Executive Officers.

Leslie, L. L., and Brinkman, P. T. (1988). *The Economic Value of Higher Education.* New York: Macmillan.

Leslie, L. L., and Johnson, G. P. (1993). The market model and higher education. In D. Breneman, L. L. Leslie, and R. E. Anderson (eds.), *Finance in Higher Education.* (pp. 69-83). ASHE Reader Series. Needham Heights, MA: Ginn Press.

Leslie, L. L., and Ramey, G. (1988). Donor behavior and voluntary support for higher education institutions. *Journal of Higher Education* 59 (2): 115-132.

Leslie, L. L., and Rhoades, G. (1995). Rising administrative costs: Seeking explanations. *Journal of Higher Education* 66 (2): 187-212.

Lewis, G. L. (1989). Trends in student aid: 1963-64 to 1988-89. *Research in Higher Education* 30 (6): 547-561.

Massy, W. F. (1996). Productivity issues in higher education. In W. F. Massy (ed.), *Resource Allocation in Higher Education.* (pp. 49-86). Ann Arbor: University of Michigan Press.

Massy, W. F., and Wilger, A. K. (1992). Productivity in postsecondary education: A new approach. *Educational Evaluation and Policy Analysis* 14 (4): 361-376.

Massy, W. F., and Zemsky, R. (1994). Faculty discretionary time: Departments and the 'Academic Ratchet.' *Journal of Higher Education* 65 (1): 1-22.

Mattila, J. P. (1982). Determinants of male school enrollments: A time series analysis. *Review of Economics and Statistics* 64: 242-251.

McMahon, W. W. (1974). *Investment in Higher Education.* Urbana: University of Illinois Press.

McMahon, W. W., and Wagner, A. P. (1982). The monetary returns to education as partial social efficiency criteria. In W. W. McMahon and T. G. Geske (eds.), *Financing Education: Overcoming Inefficiency and Inequity.* Urbana, IL: University of Illinois Press.

McPherson, M. S. (1978). The demand for higher education. In D. W. Breneman and C. E. Finn (eds.), *Public Policy and Private Higher Education.* (pp. 143-196). Washington, DC: The Brookings Institution.

McPherson, M. S., and Schapiro, M. O. (1991). *Keeping College Affordable: Government and Educational Opportunity.* Washington, DC: The Brookings Institution.

McPherson, M. S., and Schapiro, M. O. (1998). *The Student Aid Game.* Princeton, NJ: Princeton University Press.

McPherson, M. S., Schapiro, M. O., and Winston, G. C. (1993). *Paying the Piper: Productivity, Incentives, and Financing in U.S. Higher Education.* Ann Arbor: University of Michigan Press.

McPherson, M. S., Schapiro, M. O., and Winston, G. C. (1996). The economic analogy. Williams Project on the Economics of Higher Education Discussion Paper No. 37. Williamstown, MA: Williams College.

Meyer, K. A. (1998). *Faculty Workload Studies: Perspectives, Needs, and Future Directions.* ASHE-ERIC Higher Education Report Volume 26, No. 1. Washington, DC: The George Washington University, Graduate School of Education and Human Development.

Migue, J-L., and Belanger, G. (1974). Toward a general theory of managerial discretion. *Public Choice* 17: 27-47.

Mincer, J. (1993). *Studies in Human Capital.* Brookfield, VT: Edward Elgar Publishing.

Mulugetta, Y., Saleh, D. A., and Mulugetta, A. (1997). Student aid issues at private institutions. In R. Voorhees (ed.), *Researching Student Aid.* New Directions for Institutional Research No.95 (pp. 43-64). San Francisco: Jossey-Bass.

Mumper, M. (1996). *Removing College Price Barriers.* Albany, NY: State University of New York Press.

Mumper, M. (1998). State efforts to keep public colleges affordable in the face of fiscal stress. In J. C. Smart (ed.), *Higher Education: Handbook of Theory and Research*, Volume XIII (pp. 148-180). New York: Agathon Press.

Mumper, M., and Anderson, J. (1993). Maintaining public college affordability in the 1980s: How did the states do? *Journal of Education Finance* 19: 183-199.

Murphy, K. M., and Welch, F. (1992a). The structure of wages. *Quarterly Journal of Economics* 107 (1):

285-326.

Murphy, K. M., and Welch, F. (1992b). Wages of college graduates. In W. E. Becker and D. R. Lewis (eds.). *The Economics of American Higher Education.* (pp. 121-140). Boston: Kluwer Academic Publishers.

Musgrave, R. A., and Musgrave, P. B. (1984). *Public Finance in Theory and Practice*, Fourth Edition. New York: McGraw-Hill.

National Association of Independent Colleges and Universities (1997). *Ten Facts About Tuition At Independent Colleges and Universities.* Washington, DC: NAICU

National Commission on the Cost of Higher Education. (1998). *Straight Talk About College Costs and Prices.* Phoenix, AZ: The Oryx Press and the American Council on Education.

Niskanen, W. A. (1971). *Bureaucracy and Representative Government.* Chicago: Aldine Atherton.

Niskanen, W. A. (1975). Bureaucrats and politicians. *Journal of Law and Economics* 18 (3): 617-643.

Niskanen, W. A. (1991). In Blais, A., and Dion, S. (eds.), *The Budget-maximizing Bureaucrat: Appraisals and Evidence* (pp. 13-31). Pittsburgh: University of Pittsburgh Press.

Okunade, A. A., and Berl, R. L. (1997). Determinants of charitable giving of business school alumni. *Research in Higher Education* 38 (2): 201- 214.

Paton, G. J. (1986). Microeconomic perspectives applied to development planning and management. in Dunn, J. A. (ed.), *Enhancing the Management of Fund Raising.* New Directions for Institutional Research No. 51 (pp. 17-38). San Francisco: Jossey-Bass.

Paulsen, M. B. (1989). Estimating instructional cost functions at small independent colleges. *Journal of Education Finance* 15(1): 53-66.

Paulsen, M. B. (1990a). *College Choice: Understanding Student Enrollment Behavior.* ASHE-ERIC Higher Education Report No. 6. Washington, DC: The George Washington University, School of Education and Human Development.

Paulsen, M. B. (1990b). Enrollment management with academic portfolio strategies: Preparing for environment-induced changes in student preferences. *Journal of Marketing for Higher Education* 3 (1): 107-119.

Paulsen, M. B. (1991). College tuition: Demand and supply determinants from 1960 to 1986. *The Review of Higher Education* 14 (3): 339-358.

Paulsen, M. B. (1996a). Higher education and productivity: An afterword. *Thought and Action: NEA Higher Education Journal* 12 (2): 135-139.

Paulsen, M. B. (1996b). Higher education and state workforce productivity. *Thought and Action: NEA Higher Education Journal* 12 (1): 55-77.

Paulsen, M. B. (1998). Recent research on the economics of attending college. *Research in Higher Education* 39 (4): 471-489.

Paulsen, M. B., and Pogue, T. F. (1988). Higher education enrollment: the interaction of labor market conditions, curriculum, and selectivity. *Economics of Education Review* 7 (3): 275-290.

Pearson, R. J., and Baldi, S. (1998). Student aid and tuition: Toward a causal analysis. In National Commission on the Cost of Higher Education. *Straight Talk About College Costs and Prices.* (pp. 93-101). Phoenix, AZ: The Oryx Press and the American Council on Education.

Perloff, J. M., and Salop, S. C. (1985). Equilibrium with product differentiation. *Review of Economic Studies* 52:107-120.

Quigley, J. M., and Rubinfeld, D. L. (1993). Public choices in public higher education. In C. T. Clotfelter and M. Rothschild (eds.), *Studies of Supply and Demand in Higher Education* (pp. 243-278). Chicago: The University of Chicago Press.

Rehnke, M. A. F. (ed.) (1987). *Creating Career Programs in A Liberal Arts Context.* New Directions for Higher Education No. 57. San Francisco: Jossey-Bass.

Reynolds, A. (1998). The real cost of higher education, who should pay it and how? In National Commission on the Cost of Higher Education. *Straight Talk About College Costs and Prices.* (pp. 103-116). Phoenix, AZ: The Oryx Press and the American Council on Education.

Rhoades, G. (1998).Reviewing and rethinking administrative costs. In J. C. Smart (ed.), *Higher Education: Handbook of Theory and Research*, Volume XIII (pp. 111-147). New York: Agathon Press.

Riesman, D. (1980). *On Higher Education: the Academic Enterprise in An Era of Rising Student Consumerism.* San Francisco: Jossey-Bass.

Roemer, R. E. (1981). Vocationalism in higher education: Explanations from social theory. *The Review of Higher Education* 4 (2): 23-46.

Roherty, B. M. (1997). The price of passive resistance in financing higher education. In P. M. Callan and J.

E. Finney (eds.). *Public and Private Financing of Higher Education: Shaping Public Policy for the Future* (pp. 3-29). Phoenix, AZ: American Council on Education & the Oryx Press.

Rothschild, M., and White, L. J. (1993). The university in the marketplace. In C. T. Clotfelter and M. Rothschild (eds.), *Studies of Supply and Demand in Higher Education* (pp. 11-37). Chicago: The University of Chicago Press.

Rothschild, M., and White, L. J. (1995). The analytics of the pricing of higher education and other services in which the customers are inputs. *Journal of Political Economy* 103 (3): 573-586.

Rusk, J. J., and Leslie, L. L. (1978). The setting of tuition in public higher education. *Journal of Higher Education* 49 (6): 531-547.

Salvatore, D. (1986). *Microeconomics: Theory and applications*. New York: Macmillan Publishing.

St. John, E. P. (1994). *Prices, Productivity, and Investment: Assessing Financial Strategies in Higher Education*. ASHE-ERIC higher Education Report No. 3. Washington, D.C.: The George Washington University, School of Education and Human Development.

St. John, E. P., and Elliott, R. J. (1994). Reframing policy research: A critical examination of research on federal student aid programs. In J. S. Smart (ed.), *Higher Education: Handbook of Theory and Research*, Volume 10. (pp. 126-180). New York: Agathon Press.

Stadtman, V. A. (1980). *Academic Adaptions*. San Francisco: Jossey-Bass.

Stanley, E. C., and Adams, J. W. (1994). Analyzing administrative costs and structures. *Research in Higher Education* 35 (1): 125-140.

Strickland, D., Bonomo, V., McLaughlin, F., Montgomery, J., and Mahan, B. (1984). Effects of social and economic factors on four-year higher education enrollments in Virginia. *Research in Higher Education*. 20 (1): 35-53.

Tannen, M. B. (1978). The investment motive for attending college. *Industrial and Labor Relations Review* 31 (4): 489-497.

Taylor, A. L., and Martin, J. C. (1995). Characteristics of alumni donors and nondonors at a research I, public university. *Research in Higher Education* 36 (3): 283-302.

Thurow, L. C. (1970). *Investment in Human Capital*. Belmont, CA: Wadsworth Publishing.

Tirole, J. (1988). *The Theory of Industrial Organization*. Cambridge, MA: The MIT Press.

To, D-L., and Olson, J. E. (1996). *Why College Tuition Increased: A Supply-demand Model*. Paper presented at the annual meeting of the American Education Finance Association, Salt Lake City.

U.S. Bureau of the Census. (1997). *Statistical Abstract of the United States: 1997*. Washington, DC: U.S. Government Printing Office.

U.S. Department of Education, National Center for Education Statistics. (1997). *The Condition of Education 1997*. Washington, DC: U.S. Government Printing Office.

U.S. Department of Education, National Center for Education Statistics. (1996). *The Digest of Education Statistics 1996*. Washington, DC: U.S. Government Printing Office.

Van Alstyne, C. (1977). Rationales for setting tuition levels at public institutions. *Educational Record* 58: 66-82.

Van Dusen, G. (1997). *The Virtual Campus: Technology and Reform in Higher Education*. ASHE-ERIC Higher Education Report Volume 25, No. 5. Washington, DC: The George Washington University, Graduate School of Education and Human Development.

Viehland, D., Norman, W., Kaufman, S., and Krauth, B. M. (1982). Indexing tuition to cost of education: the impact on students and institutions. *Research in Higher Education* 17 (4): 333-343.

Warner, T. (1984). Priorities, planning, and prices. In L. H. Litten (ed.), *Issues in Pricing Undergraduate Education*. New Directions for Institutional Research No. 42 (pp. 35-45). San Francisco: Jossey-Bass.

Waud, R. N. (1992). *Microeconomics*, Fifth Edition. New York: HarperCollins.

Weber, V., and Winston, G. (1994). *The Economic Performance of Williams, Amherst, Swarthmore, and Wellesley 1988-9 to 1992-3: A Global Comparison*. Williams Project on the Economics of Higher Education Discussion Paper No. 28. Williamstown, MA: Williams College.

Weiler, W. C. (1984). Using enrollment demand models in institutional pricing decisions. In L. L. Litten (ed.). *Issues in Pricing Undergraduate Education*. (pp. 19-34). New Directions for Institutional Research, No. 42. San Francisco: Jossey-Bass.

Wergin, J. F. (ed.) (1994). *Analyzing Faculty Workload*. New Directions for Institutional Research No. 83. San Francisco: Jossey-Bass.

Whitt, E. (ed.) (1997). *College Student Affairs Administration*. ASHE Reader Series. Needham Heights,

MA: Simon and Schuster Custom Publishing.

Willemain, T. R., Goyal, A., Van Deven, M., and Thukral, I. S. (1994). Alumni giving: the influences of reunion, class, and year. *Research in Higher Education* 35 (5): 609-629.

Winston, G. C. (1993). Robin Hood in the forests of academe. In McPherson, M. S., Schapiro, M. O., and Winston, G. C. *Paying the Piper: Productivity, Incentives, and Financing in U.S. Higher Education* (pp. 229-231). Ann Arbor: University of Michigan Press.

Winston, G. C. (1996). *The Economic Structure of Higher Education: Subsidies, Customer-inputs, and Hierarchy.* Williams Project on the Economics of Higher Education Discussion Paper No. 40. Williamstown, MA: Williams College.

Winston, G. C. (1997a). *College Costs: Subsidies, Intuition, and Policy.* Williams Project on the Economics of Higher Education Discussion Paper No. 45. Williamstown, MA: Williams College.

Winston, G. C. (1997b). Why can't a college be more like a firm? *Change* 29 (5): 33-38.

Winston, G. C. (1998). College costs: Subsidies, intuition, and policy. In National Commission on the Cost of Higher Education. *Straight Talk About College Costs and Prices.* (pp. 117-127). Phoenix, AZ: The Oryx Press and the American Council on Education.

Winston, G. C., Carbone, J. C., and Lewis, E. G. (1998). *What's Been Happening to Higher Education? Facts, Trends, and Data 1986-87 to 1994-95.* Williams Project on the Economics of Higher Education Discussion Paper No. 47. Williamstown, MA: Williams College.

Wittstruck, J. R., and Bragg, S. M. (1988). *Focus on Price: Trends in Public Higher Education.* Denver, CO: State Higher Education Executive Officers Association.

Wolinsky, A. (1986). True monopolistic competition as a result of imperfect information. *The Quarterly Journal of Economics* 89 (4): 493-511.

Zemsky, R., Wegner, G. R., and Iannozzi, M. (1997). A perspective on privatization. In P. M. Callan and J. E. Finney (eds.), *Public and Private Financing of Higher Education: Shaping Public Policy for the Future.* (pp. 74-77). Phoenix, AZ: Oryx Press/American Council on Education.

Epilogue

Over the course of the past two or three years since this chapter was first written and then published, tuition at four-year public and private institutions has continued to increase at annual rates in excess of the rate of inflation (College Board, 2000). More specifically, between 1997-98 and 1998-99, tuition at public four-year institutions (in current dollars) increased by 4.4 percent (from $3,111 to $3,247), between 1998-99 and 1999-00, tuition at public four-year institutions increased by 3.4 percent ($3,247 to $3,356), and between 1999-00 and 2000-01, tuition at such institutions increased by 4.6 percent ($3,356 to $3,510). At private four-year institutions, the corresponding increases were 7.6, 4.6, and 6.2 percent (College Board, 2000, Table 5, p. 7).

Earlier in this chapter, I identified a number of "tentative conclusions" about the effects of selected cost-side and demand-side factors on the growth in college tuition since 1980. At the time of my original analysis, the data available on most of these factors did not extend beyond the early-to-mid 1990s. Now, the available data on most of these factors extend through either the middle or late 1990s. Because annual tuition growth has continued at rates in excess of inflation through the year 2000-01, it might be informative to see whether the patterns of growth—based on more recent data through the late 1990s or even 2000—for some of the factors identified as potentially "causal" are consistent with continued rapid tuition growth. This brief essay will examine recent developments regarding five of these factors, including two of the cost-side factors, state appropriations and institutional aid, and three of the demand-side factors, job-market opportunities, income of students and their families, and numbers of potential college-bound students of traditional age. These particular factors were chosen both because very recent data are available on them—either through the late 1990s or 2000—*and* because there have been noteworthy changes in the patterns of the data in the second half of the 1990s that permit modest, but meaningful, assessments of their consistency with the continued high rates of tuition growth throughout the 1990s. Therefore, the following sections will consider the latest developments in each of these five factors.

However, first it is important to point out a change in the patterns of tuition growth between the first half and the second half of the 1990s. From 1990 to 1995, tuition at public four-year institutions increased by 37 percent in constant (adjusted for inflation) dollars; however, from 1995 to 2000, tuition at such institutions increased by only 9.9 percent. Although still well in excess of inflation, there is, nonetheless, a noteworthy reduction in the annual rate of growth between the first and the second half of the 1990s. Both the reduction in the rate of growth in tuition, as well as the sustained rate of tuition growth in excess of inflation, after 1995, need to be explained. The pattern of growth among private four-year institutions is more balanced across the two periods, increasing by 14.7 percent between 1990 and 1995 and by 17.6 percent from 1995 to 2000; however, there is still an increase in the annual growth in tuition in the second half of the 1990s that needs to be explained (College Board, 2000).

State Government Appropriations

State appropriations to public institutions in the 1990s have been predictably related to the fortunes of the business cycle. In the early 1990s, many states were struggling with recessions in their economies. But during the second half of the decade, most state economies flourished with the economic expansion experienced nationwide. This generated budget surpluses, lower unemployment rates, higher household incomes, and therefore, greater tax revenues. Some of the increase in tax revenues resulted in substantial constant-dollar increases in state appropriations to public institutions between 1994-95 and 1999-00 (AASCU, 1999; Hines, 2000; McKeown-Moak, 2000). More specifically, between fiscal year 1990 and fiscal year 1995, state appropriations (in constant dollars) decreased by 7.7 percent. However, between fiscal year 1995 and fiscal year 2000, appropriations increased by 17.7 percent (Hines, 2000). These data—which represent a substantial increase in the rate of growth in state appropriations between the first and second halves of the 1990s—would be consistent with the substantial reduction in the rate of growth in tuition in the second half of the 1990s and supportive of the earlier conclusion of this chapter—also supported by the findings of previous research (e.g., Paulsen, 1991; Rusk and Leslie, 1978)—that growth in state appropriations, a cost-side factor, is inversely related to tuition growth.

Institutional Aid: Tuition Discounting

Another tentative conclusion I reached about a cost-side factor was that increases in institutional aid or tuition discounting contribute to increases in tuition, a hypothesis that has been supported by previous research (e.g., Coopers and Lybrand, 1997;

McPherson and Schapiro, 1991; To and Olson, 1996). In his recent book, *Tuition Rising*, Ehrenberg (2000) describes the intensification of this very pattern at Cornell.

> [Between] the academic years 1987-88 and 1997-98...grant dollars going to Cornell undergraduate students from Cornell's own funds—endowment income, annual giving, or tuition dollars--rose from $20.5 million to $56.2 million, an increase of almost 174 percent. As a result, the share of financial aid grant dollars that came from the university's own funds rose from .618 to .760. Increasingly, financial aid grants were the responsibility of the university and increasingly its financial aid dollars came from its own tuition revenues. Hence the need for more funds to provide grant aid to students was partially responsible for tuition's continuing to rise at rates greater than the rate of inflation during the period" (pp. 80-81).

Indeed, there is a good deal more evidence of the continued growth of institutional grants and expansion of tuition discounting practices during the 1990s, based on a recent NACUBO survey of 275 private colleges and universities (NACUBO, 1999). On average, the percentage of gross tuition revenue used for institutional grants (the tuition discount rate) increased from 27.7 percent in 1990 to 37.3 percent in 1999 (Lapovsky and Hubbell, 2000). In their study of the tuition-discounting practices of the 223 institutions that responded to the NACUBO surveys in 1993 and 1998, Breneman, Doti, and Lapovsky (chapter 12) report that while the sample colleges increased their tuition by 27.9 percent, they increased their total institutional grants (tuition discounts) by 56.4 percent—nearly twice the rate of increase in tuition. These data are certainly consistent with the increase in tuition at private colleges and universities of 14.7 percent between 1990 and 1995 and by an even greater 17.6 percent from 1995 to 2000.

Job Market Opportunities for College Graduates Relative to High School Graduates

A number of economists have asserted that the attractive earnings differentials between college and high school graduates in the 1980s and early 1990s were an important determinant of the increase in enrollment demand, which, as economic theory would suggest, would tend to promote upward pressure on the price of education—tuition (Kane, 1999; McPherson and Schapiro, 1998; Paulsen, 1998). When earnings differentials began to climb upward after the recession in the college job market of the early 1970s (Freeman, 1976), the college-high school earnings differential reached 19 percent for men and 52 percent for women by 1980. By 1985, the premium for men reached 50 percent and for women, 69 percent. The premium for men remained relatively stable at 48 percent in 1990, while the premium for women soared to 92 percent. Then, the premium for women remained stable at 91 percent in 1995, but the premium for men increased to 55 percent by 1995. Between 1995 and 1998, the latest year for which data is available, the premium for men increased only slightly to 56 percent, while the premium for women increased to 100 percent (U.S. Department of Education, 2000b, Table 23-3, p. 144).[36] In each of the periods examined here, the college-high school earnings differential

---

[36]The earnings differential is measured here as the ratio of median annual earnings of all wage and salary workers ages 25-34 whose highest education level was a bachelor's degree or higher compared with those with a high school diploma or GED (see U.S. Department of Education, 2000, Table 23-2, p. 144).

increased while tuition in the public and private sectors was increasing at rates in excess of inflation. Sometimes the increase in the premium applied to both men and women; other times the increase in the earnings premium was experienced by either men or women, but not both. Even though the premium for men remained relatively stable from 1995 to 1998, the premium for women increased by another 9.9 percent. This latest data, for the second half of the 1990s, shows that increases in earnings premiums are continuing in a way that would be quite consistent with the concomitant growth of tuition. Therefore, the earlier conclusion of this chapter that rising earnings premiums could be one of the demand-side factors contributing to rising college tuition receives modest support from an examination of these latest developments.

The Income of Students and Their Families

Studies of enrollment demand have consistently demonstrated that student demand for a college education is income-elastic (Clotfelter, 1996; Paulsen, 1991). An earlier conclusion of this chapter was that the tuition growth in the 1980s and early 1990s might be attributable, in part, to the substantial inflation-adjusted increases in income among families in the top income quintile, supported by a smaller, but not inconsequential increase among those in the second-highest quintile. During the 15-year period from 1980 to 1995, these increases were 36 and 14 percent, respectively. Between 1980 and 1995, families in the bottom three quintiles experienced very little, if any, constant-dollar increases in their incomes; these were 8.1, 4.3, and –1.5 percent, respectively (College Board, 2000, Table 8, p. 15). However, during the five-year period from 1995 to 2000, due to the persistent strength of the U.S. economy, families in all five quintiles experienced increases in their incomes of 18, 13.3, 12.8, 11, and 7.9 percent, respectively. Given the income-elasticity of enrollment demand, this pattern of income increases (after inflation) across all income quintiles would be consistent with the continued tuition growth, in excess of inflation, between 1995 and 2000.

The Number of College-Bound Students of Traditional Age

Economists and other researchers have often observed the population of potential students to be a significant determinant of enrollment demand (Hoenack and Weiler, 1979; Paulsen and Pogue, 1988; Quigley and Rubinfeld, 1993). The most recent year for which FTE enrollment data are available is 1997 (U.S. Department of Education, 1999, Table 203, p. 228). For the two ten-year periods, 1977-87 and 1987-97, FTE enrollment grew by 8.5 and 13 percent at public institutions and 13.5 and 15.4 percent at private institutions. Hidden in the middle of the second ten-year period are the low points of growth; between 1990 and 1995, FTE enrollment increased only 2.6 percent at public and 6.5 percent at private institutions. If other factors had remained constant, economic theory would have predicted a reduction in upward pressure on tuition. Nevertheless, that short period of relatively slow growth in enrollment does not appear to have slowed tuition growth, which continued at double-digit rates, even after adjustment for inflation, in both public and private sectors. However, there are some forthcoming changes in demographics that are expected to increase enrollment demand, and theoretically, upward pressure on tuition.

According to the U.S. Department of Education's (2000a) *Projections of Educa-*

tion Statistics to 2010, the 18-24-year-old population passed its lowest point in the mid-1990s and the number of 35-44-year-olds is expected to reach its peak in 2000. While the growth of enrollment in the 1980s and 1990s was fueled primarily by the substantial growth in the number of students of non-traditional age, it is the number of students of traditional college-going age (18-24 years old) that is expected to increase by 18 percent or more, between 1998 and 2010. Also, between 1998 and 2010, the population of 25-29 year olds is forecast to increase by 7 percent, the 30-34-year-old population is forecast to decrease by 6 percent, and the 35-44-year-old population is expected to increase by 1 percent from 1998 to 2000 and then it is forecast to decrease by 12 percent by 2010 (U.S. Department of Education, 2000a, Table B4).

Comparing two 12-year periods, enrollment grew by about 17 percent between 1985 and 1997, and is now expected to grow by about 20 percent between 1998 and 2010 (U.S. Department of Education, 2000a, Tables 10, 13A, 13B). If these projections prove to be accurate, the next ten years would be characterized by an increase in enrollment demand, more-or-less balanced between public and private sectors, as a result of which, all else equal, economic theory would predict an upward pressure on tuition.

Conclusion

This epilogue has served as an opportunity to reflect on some of the conclusions drawn earlier in this chapter about the probable causes of tuition inflation since 1980. These included state appropriations and institutional aid, two of the cost-side factors, and job-market opportunities, income of students and their families, and numbers of potential college-bound students of traditional age, three of the demand-side factors. Noteworthy changes in the patterns of more recent data about each of these five factors for the second half of the 1990s made it possible to conduct modest, but meaningful, assessments of the consistency of these patterns with the continued high rates of tuition growth throughout the 1990s.

In general, recent developments regarding state appropriations, institutional aid, job-market opportunities, and income of students and their families, were quite consistent with the continuing growth in inflation throughout the 1990s, and provided modest support for the earlier conclusions drawn about their probable role as causes of rising tuition. The examination of actual and projected numbers of students of traditional age, from 1985-97 and 1998-2010, raised the prospect of an increase in enrollment demand, and potential upward pressure on tuition, over the next decade.

References

American Association of State Colleges and Universities. (1999). *State Fiscal Conditions.* Washington, DC: AASCU.

Clotfelter, C.T. (1996). *Buying The Best: Cost Escalation In Elite Higher Education.* Princeton, NJ: Princeton University Press.

College Board. (2000). *Trends in College Pricing 2000.* New York, NY: The College Board.

Coopers & Lybrand (1997). *The Impact Of Federal Student Assistance On College Tuition Levels.* Washington, DC: Coopers & Lybrand, L. L. P.

Ehrenberg, R.G. (2000). *Tuition Rising: Why College Costs So Much.* Cambridge, MA: Harvard University Press.

Freeman, R.B. (1976). *The Overeducated American*. New York: Academic Press.

Hines, E. (2000). *Grapevine*. Bloomington, IL: Illinois State University.

Hoenack, S.A., and Weiler, W.C. (1979). The demand for higher education and institutional enrollment forecasting. *Economic Inquiry* 17: 89-113.

Kane, T.J. (1999). *The Price of Admission: Rethinking How Americans Pay for College*. Washington, DC: Brookings.

Lapovsky, L., and Hubbell, L.L. (2000). Positioning for competition. *Business Officer*, March.

McKeown-Moak, M.P. (2000). *Financing Higher Education in the New Century: The Second Annual Report from the States*. Denver, CO: SHEEO.

McPherson, M.S., and Schapiro, M.O. (1991). *Keeping College Affordable: Government And Educational Opportunity*. Washington, DC: The Brookings Institution.

McPherson, M.S., and Schapiro, M.O. (1998). *The Student Aid Game*. Princeton, NJ: Princeton University Press.

National Association of College and University Officers. (1999). *1999 NACUBO Tuition Discounting Survey*. Washington, DC: NACUBO.

Paulsen, M.B. (1991). College tuition: Demand and supply determinants from 1960 to 1986. *The Review of Higher Education* 14 (3): 339-358.

Paulsen, M.B. (1998). Recent research on the economics of attending college. *Research in Higher Education* 39 (4): 471-489.

Paulsen, M.B., and Pogue, T.F. (1988). Higher education enrollment: The interaction of labor market conditions, curriculum, and selectivity. *Economics of Education Review* 7 (3): 275-290.

Quigley, J.M., and Rubinfeld, D.L. (1993). Public choices in public higher education. In C. T. Clotfelter and M. Rothschild (eds.), *Studies Of Supply And Demand In Higher Education* (pp. 243-278). Chicago: The University of Chicago Press.

Rusk, J.J., and Leslie, L.L. (1978). The setting of tuition in public higher education. *Journal of Higher Education* 49 (6): 531-547.

To, D-L., and Olson, J.E. (1996). *Why College Tuition Increased: A Supply-Demand Model*. Paper presented at the annual meeting of the American Education Finance Association, Salt Lake City.

U.S. Department of Education, National Center for Education Statistics. (2000a). *Projections of Education Statistics to 2010*. Washington, DC: U.S. Government Printing Office.

U.S. Department of Education, National Center for Education Statistics. (2000b). *The Condition of Education 2000*. Washington, DC: U.S. Government Printing Office.

U.S. Department of Education, National Center for Education Statistics. (1999). *The Digest of Education Statistics 1999*. Washington, DC: U.S. Government Printing Office.

Part III

Federal and State Policies and the Finance of Higher Education

Chapter 7

THE PARADOX OF GROWTH IN FEDERAL AID FOR COLLEGE STUDENTS, 1965-1990[1]

James C. Hearn

One group of federal programs for education has experienced well over two decades of extraordinary growth despite the significant changes taking place in the nation's political climate since the 1960s. In 1963-64 the federal government awarded a little over $100 million in aid dedicated to needy college students.[2] In the following year, Congress passed the Higher Education Act of 1965, a central element in the Democratic leadership's domestic-policy agenda.[3] Fueled by broadening interpretations of the Act and its Amendments, federal awards of generally available student aid grew to approximately $19 billion by 1989-90, a figure 24 percent greater than that of 1980-81, at the start of the Reagan years, and 40 times greater than that of 1963-64, in constant-dollar terms.[4] By any standard, overall growth in these programs has been remarkable.

---

[1]This chapter was originally published in Volume IX of *Higher Education: Handbook of Theory and Research,* © 1993 by Agathon Press. It has been updated with an Epilogue written especially for this volume.

[2]See Gillespie and Carlson (1983).

[3] See Brubacher and Rudy (1976), Gladieux and Wolanin (1976), Leslie (1977), Brademas (1987), and Fenske (1983) for details of the development of the Act. For key participants' personal reflections on the history of the Act from its beginnings, see Fields (1985a,b).

[4]See College Board (1990). The analysis for this chapter focuses upon the federal government's "generally available" student-aid programs, which should be distinguished from other student-aid programs specially targeted for specific populations. For ease of reading, the phrase "generally available" is not used everywhere it applies in the text. Unless otherwise noted, however, the text refers solely to this kind of aid. The federal generally available aid programs, as of 1989-90, were Stafford Loans (formerly Guaranteed Student Loans [GSL]), Pell Grants, Supplementary Educational Opportunity Grants [SEOG], State Student Incentive Grants [SSIG], College Work Study [CWS], Perkins Loans, Income Contingent Loans, Supplemental Loans for Students [SLS], and Parent Loans for Undergraduate Students [PLUS]. Among the specially targeted programs, which are not considered in this analysis, are Veterans' aid programs, military aid programs, Social Security aid programs (which had been fully phased out by 1985-86), and certain other small grant and loan programs for those in special populations or targeted occupational groups. In 1989-90 the total outlays for the federal government's specially targeted programs were approximately one-fourteenth of those for its generally available aid programs (College Board, 1990).

But equally remarkable is the absence of many of the ideal—or, in some respects, even the usual—philosophical, managerial, political, fiscal, and demographic bases for such growth. Numerous theorists, including Rodgers and Bullock (1972, 1976), Weatherly and Lipsky (1977), Johnston et al. (1978), Cerych (1979), and McDonnell and Elmore (1987) have suggested that policy success and growth require certain desirable conditions, including coherence in policy goals, programmatic clarity, and a rich information-base to support management decisions. Such characteristics are advanced not solely as ideals but as feasible achievements for governmental efforts: California's 1972 Coastal Initiative, the development of the British Open University, and the emergence of the aggressive U.S. space program in the 1960s are presented as primary examples. When failures are presented in this literature, the absence of rationally valued conditions is often inferred to have been a primary cause of the policy failure.[5]

The analysis presented here addresses the historical roots of the paradox of significant growth in the federal aid programs in concert with an ongoing absence of many of the contextual characteristics assumed, under rationalist models of policy development, to be prerequisites for such growth. The chapter seeks to illuminate the ways in which well-intentioned and capable policy advocates and administrators, backed by continuing pro-student-aid sentiment among the American public and most of their representatives, have succeeded in securing substantial funding growth for the student-aid programs but have not succeeded in substantially improving the programs themselves. After consideration of the historical emergence of the paradox, the chapter proceeds to an evaluation of five explanatory frameworks that may aid understanding of this paradox. The essay concludes with consideration of possible policy implications and discussion of recent developments in federal student-aid.

THE PARADOX OF FEDERAL STUDENT-AID POLICY

Analysts of the federal government's programs of financial aid for college students confront a system that defies the ideals of logical policy development and implementation, as described in the classic texts (e.g., Sabatier and Mazmanian, 1979). Lacking to a significant degree are *philosophical coherence, well-considered patterns of policy development, programmatic clarity and distinctiveness, access to managerially needed information, a strong and supportive interest-group coalition, a beneficent resource environment,* and a *robust client base.* These points are elaborated in turn below.

In place of *philosophical coherence,* federal support for student aid is motivated by a multiplicity of somewhat unconnected goals. Legislation has been passed under a variety of logics, most visibly including advancing equality of opportunity for the socioeconomically disadvantaged, but also including protecting the financial position of the middle class, rewarding worthy institutions, rewarding worthy students, fostering national economic development, protecting private institutions, and developing human

---

[5]Hall (1982) examines "great planning disasters" in public policy, with particular attention to the Anglo-French Concorde, the Sydney Opera House, and London's failed plans for a third airport. Advocating a rationalist perspective while accepting the inevitabilities of incrementalism, Hall outlines some ways to avoid planning disasters. He emphasizes the aggressive pursuit of reliable advance information on the likely behavioral and political outcomes of policies.

capital (Gladieux, 1983; Smith and Jenkins, 1983; Leslie and Brinkman, 1988). Typical of many national efforts in education, the federal aid programs have often been designed and modified in response to a variety of non-educational concerns (Schuster, 1982). As William Van Dusen (1978, p. 5) has noted,

> The development of publicly-funded student aid in the United States is an example of the type of compromise common in our pluralistic, democratic society. Often competing and occasionally conflicting public and private goals have been modified and amalgamated into a series of student aid programs which fulfill, or attempt to fulfill, a variety of purposes.

In that light, it is unsurprising that there are few signs of improvement in policy coherence. Indeed, two developments point in opposite directions. The Higher Education Act's original programmatic focus on lower-income and lower-middle income students has become increasingly blurred to include increased numbers of the middle and even upper-middle classes (see McPherson and Schapiro, 1991). In addition, despite the increasing federal fiscal commitment to student aid, there has been a breakdown in consensus regarding the basic federal role in student aid. Since the 1970s, the federal government has retreated somewhat from the role of dominant, agenda-setting partner in the aid enterprise, asking states to take up more of the burden of financing student aid (College Board, 1990). Many states have done so (see, for an example, Hearn and Anderson, 1989). Yet the philosophical debate still rages. In particular, Congress has acted to resist executive-branch hostility to the centrality and growth of federal student aid (Keppel, 1987).

Beyond questions of mission, there has also been an absence of *well-considered patterns of policy development* in the delivery of federal student aid. Instead of a rationalized pattern of development in operational goals and program specifics, the federal financial aid system is by unanimous definition jerry-built (Fenske et al., 1983; Fitzgerald, 1991). There is no reason to dispute the contemporary validity of an observation made well over a decade ago by Van Dusen (1978, p. 5): "Rube Goldberg might have been the architect for the current configuration of student aid programs." Despite concerted efforts during each of the periodic reauthorizations of the Higher Education Act since 1965, there has been no systematic "housecleaning" to reduce the policy and program contradictions, inefficiencies, and illogics accumulated in the years since the Great Society era. Longtime financial-aid analyst Bruce Johnstone, now Chancellor of the State University of New York, noted recently that the Title IV student-aid programs seem mired in a "political and administrative gridlock" that dooms to failure any efforts to make fundamental improvements in the programs.[6]

Instead of fundamental change, it is change in the operational details that has characterized the federal aid programs' history. The pace of such changes has often been characterized as dizzying. Program regulations, including eligibility criteria and reporting requirements, have been modified almost yearly since inception. A recurring complaint of financial-aid officers on campuses, state policy officials, and policy analysts at

---

[6] The quote is from a conversation reported in Johnstone, Evans, and Jerue (1990, p. 29). It should be noted that Johnstone adds that the seeming disarray of the programs should not distract from their clear successes in improving students' access to higher education.

state and national levels is that the development and delivery of basic program services are unduly complicated and burdened by the absence of a federal commitment to some measure of stability (Fenske et al., 1983; Advisory Committee on Student Financial Assistance, 1990). A typical problem of the past few years has been controversial, last-minute changes in eligibility criteria for federal aid, imposed from the U.S. Department of Education. Many campus aid officers say that they are "being buried under growing mounds of paperwork that the government has required in recent years" ("Student Aid Administrators Seek Relief," 1990, p. A21).[7] Recently, even the Department of Education itself has admitted publicly that its aid programs suffer from poor management (DeLoughry, 1991b). The increased role of the Congress in forming program regulations over the past few years has, by all accounts, not lessened the problem (Fitzgerald, 1991; Flint, 1991). The consistency necessary for organizational and political effectiveness in campus and state-government settings has been missing.

Programmatic clarity and distinctiveness have also been lacking in federal student-aid programs. Instead of an array of clearly discrete programmatic efforts addressing in distinctive fashion a set of overarching policy objectives, constituents for the programs (including students, families, financial-aid officers, and state policy officials) confront an array of overlapping efforts with rather vaguely differentiated objectives (Fenske et al., 1983; Smith and Jenkins, 1983; Doyle and Hartle, 1985). For example, several student-loan programs currently are funded under the Act, and even members of the student-aid community would be hard pressed to distinguish among these individual loan programs' goals (Gladieux, 1983). The complexity of the system exacts a particularly large price on those students and families encountering it for the first time in efforts to expand their own educational opportunities. A bewildering array of forms, procedures, and regulations confront the unwary, and may actually serve to hinder the purpose of aiding those disadvantaged students with undeveloped educational talents. Clinging to the margins of the educational system, such students may become discouraged by the complexities of it all (Carnegie Council, 1979, Evangelauf, 1988; Collison, 1988; Post, 1990).

Despite intensified accountability pressures in governments generally, and in the federal government in particular, *access to managerially needed information* has been deficient. There has been an ongoing absence of desirable information on student clients, as well as an ongoing absence of credible indicators of efficiency and effectiveness. Instead of a working decision-support system providing targeted information at the student level for policymakers and administrators of the programs, the programs have been run without unduplicated counts, year-to-year matches, and many of the other management-information prerequisites of welfare-type programs (Palmer, 1986;

---

[7]An article in the *Chronicle of Higher Education* ("17 Changes in 4 Years...," 1990) recounts the seemingly typical tale of the aid director of Johns Hopkins University. She noted that a new rule on Stafford Loan delivery was the latest of 17 changes in the past four years in the Stafford Student Loan Program alone. That count did not include changes in the Pell Grant, SEOG, and CWS programs, which she and her staff members also administered. The aid director estimated that she spent four nights a week reading proposed regulations, financial-aid newsletters, and other publications to prepare herself for forthcoming changes from the Department of Education. She concluded, "We want so badly to do what we're supposed to do, but sometimes it's hard to tell what that is." (ibid., p. A24)

Stampen, 1987). Recent federal efforts are beginning to address these problems (DeLoughry, 1991b), but much room for improvement remains. In addition, in the absence of defensible indicators of efficiency and effectiveness in pursuing such goals as equality of opportunity in student access, choice, and persistence in higher education, analysts are reduced to making no more than informed guesses as to the success of the massive federal investment in student aid (McPherson, 1988a,b; Stampen, 1984). Thomas Wolanin, staff director of the House Subcommittee on Postsecondary Education, commented in 1986 that "We think [student aid] makes a difference, but most of what we know is anecdotal... Students come to testify and tell us it's made a difference, but there isn't much research to confirm that...[The absence of data] has really hindered our efforts at making policy, but we have to go ahead doing it. We can't sit around here twiddling our thumbs" (Palmer, 1986, p. 17). In a similar vein, Arthur Hauptman, a consultant and author on higher education student-aid issues, suggests that "We spend billions and billions of dollars on aid, but we don't know how effective it is" (Evangelauf, 1988, p. A37). More recently, the need for greatly improved data for guiding policy decisions has been stressed by the Department of Education's own advisory committee (Advisory Committee on Student Financial Assistance, 1990).

Many classic texts in political science (e.g., Dahl, 1961; Lowi, 1969) suggest that a *strong and supportive interest-group coalition* is central to the growth of fiscal support for programs. Instead, the federal aid programs enjoyed relative harmony among various interest groups for only a brief period in the 1970s. In the earliest years of the programs, controversies over aid to students versus aid to institutions reigned (Hansen, 1977). More recently, there has been a clear breakdown of the relative consensus of the 1970s. Divisions between public and private institutions, vocational and traditional institutions, and other entities have emerged within the coalition of interest groups supporting growth in the programs (Finn, 1990; Mumper and Vander Ark, 1991).

No one would argue that the period of the 1970s, 1980s, and early 1990s has been one of a *beneficent resource environment* for social and educational programs. Instead of the relatively unconstrained resources usually seen as necessary for substantial program growth, the recent period has been one of increasing fiscal constraint at the federal level. Most directly relevant is the pattern of federal spending on elementary, secondary, and vocational education. Such spending has become severely restricted in keeping with federal expenditures for most social programs. But spending for postsecondary education resisted the trend, growing both in absolute and relative terms. Between 1972 and 1980 federal spending on postsecondary student aid grew from 19 percent of total federal education outlays to 34 percent (Hartle and Stedman, 1986). In the 1980s this relative growth continued (U.S. Department of Education, 1990). That the programs have grown so heartily in a strained fiscal context adds to the paradox.

A *robust client base* is usually viewed as essential for growing fiscal support. Certainly, the number of students in postsecondary education has not decreased in recent years, contrary to earlier forecasts. Yet, by any definition, there has been a greatly slowed expansion of the overall client base for the student-aid programs. The number of 18-year-olds began to shrink yearly in the 1980s, and the number of people in the 18-40 year-old age range (which comprises the vast majority of those in postsecondary education) has begun to grow at a greatly decreased rate in recent years as well (U.S. Bureau of the Census, 1980-90). Thus, the increasing number of students receiving aid represents not so much an increase in the target population as an increase in the proportion of those in the target population taking advantage of the programs. The programs have thus not fueled their fiscal growth on "automatic" benefits from an immutable demographic destiny. Such would have been the case in the 1960s, but comparable demographic advantages for the programs were lacking in the past 15 years.

In rational theories of decision making and budgeting, the absence of so many of the usually assumed preconditions for increasing fiscal support is highly problematic (see the review by Wildavsky, 1984). To be sure, the contradictions of parallel growth and disorder fit within the literatures of disjointed incrementalism and organized anarchy, as they relate to government bureaus (Lindblom, 1980; Pressman and Wildavsky, 1984; Cohen, March, and Olsen 1979). Nevertheless, the emergence of this pattern within the seemingly straightforward policy context of need-based student aid, as opposed to the more open-ended decision contexts of a National Institute of Education (Sproull, Weiner, and Wolf, 1978) or a research university (Cohen and March, 1986), poses an especially interesting puzzle for historical, political analysis.

THE ANALYTIC APPROACH OF THIS ESSAY

Although a quarter of a century would normally seem an adequate period for policy maturation, federal student-aid policy is characterized by most observers as being well short of maturity. Because the continuing fiscal growth of the programs in this context is striking, the history of the aid programs in their first 25 years is traced in some detail here. The analysis is based on a review of historical documents and recollections (e.g., Cohen, 1977), public debate (e.g., "The Great Society...", 1985), descriptive data (e.g., Gillespie and Carlson, 1983), political analyses (e.g., Gladieux and Wolanin, 1976; Hansen, 1977), and policy-evaluation efforts (e.g., Leslie, 1977; Haveman, 1977; Murray, 1984; McPherson, 1988a,b).

The selected quantitative data presented here are for years chosen on two criteria. First, the year had to immediately precede, correspond to, or illustrate significant political developments. Second, the year had to be one for which solid information was available. Those criteria led to the presentation here of data for the fiscal years 1963-64, 1972-73, 1975-76, 1977-78, 1980-81, 1983-84, and 1989-90. More extensive quantitative data on the topic may be found in reports by Gillespie and Carlson (1983), the U.S. Department of Education (1988, 1990), and the College Board (1990).

As an attempt at integrative "political history", the chapter seeks to build from available historical and political sources a profile of persistent themes and emerging developments in federal student-aid policy. No new data are presented here, and the chapter provides neither a detailed historical account of the year-to-year evolution of the federal aid programs since 1965 nor a fully developed political analysis of federal-level conflicts, compromises, and policies during the time period covered. Instead, the chapter places existing sources into a new framework. Its overarching goal is expanding our understanding of the paradox of the programs' political history: ongoing growth in the face of seemingly contrary conditions. Historical and political evidence is considered, analyzed, and interpreted only as it helps address that paradox.

In investigating the genesis and perpetuation of the focal paradox, the review pursues two specific objectives. First, it seeks signs of distinctive historical phases in the programs' target populations, policy objectives, Congressional support, interest-group status, and other characteristics. Second, the review investigates how these changing circumstances relate to the glaring contradictions to rational policymaking models in the federal student-aid arena. The chapter is, thus, based more in an exploratory perspective than a theory-testing perspective. Nevertheless, the chapter concludes with some tentative consideration of five alternative explanations for the paradox, based on the evidence at hand. Ideally, the analysis will contribute to new ways of understanding national educational policy in the quarter century stretching from the optimistic, expansionist mid-1960s into the more constrained years of the Reagan and Bush presidencies.

THE POLITICAL HISTORY OF THE 1965 HIGHER EDUCATION ACT AND ITS AMENDMENTS

The years 1964 and 1965 brought the seeds of extraordinary change to federal policy in education. In those years, the 89th U.S. Congress undertook a wide-ranging initiative in education, passing more than two-dozen acts aimed directly at American schools and colleges. Each of those acts was philosophically and politically connected to the Democrats' "War on Poverty" and "Great Society" efforts, as well as to the Civil Rights Act of 1964. In fact, President Lyndon Johnson and the Democratic leadership in the House and Senate saw educational change as the most powerful, as well as the politically most acceptable, mechanism for achieving their ambitious goals. The President repeatedly stressed that, in his view, "The answer for all our national problems, the answer for all the problems of the world, comes down, when you really analyze it, to one single word - education" (cited in Gladieux and Wolanin, 1976, p. 17).

Like other levels of education, higher education was to benefit appreciably from this linkage of educational improvement to emerging national priorities. In both its form and its scope, the U.S. Higher Education Act of 1965 was not out of character for the 89th Congress. The Act encompassed two approaches to federal support for higher education: aid to states and institutions for construction of academic facilities and for support of a variety of academic activities, and aid to needy students (Aaron, 1978; Gladieux and Wolanin, 1976; Leslie, 1977; Fenske, 1983).[8] The focus of the present chapter is

---

[8] Support for federal action in higher education in 1965 was widespread, but debate over appropriate means to agreed-upon ends was spirited. Naturally, the Act finally resulting represented a compromise of sorts. In this context, ongoing political rivalries were certainly not forgotten. An indication of the conflicts lying just beneath the surface at the birth of the Higher Education Act is provided by the following anecdote (related by Frederic Jacobs in a symposium at the annual meeting of the Association for the Study of Higher Education in St. Louis, November 1988). Upon learning from U.S. Office of Education official Frank Keppel that Robert Kennedy was planning to propose the following day a program of special federal aid to colleges for blacks, President Johnson suddenly decided to travel to the National Education Association convention in Atlantic City that very afternoon to announce his own program for the same purpose. Thus was conceived Title III of the Higher Education Act. Johnson commented to Keppel before his hurried departure for New Jersey, "I want to take that piece of candy out of Bobby Kennedy's mouth and chew on it myself."

solely on the second of these approaches. For college student-aid, the passage of the Higher Education Act in 1965 was a landmark event destined to make earlier need-based student-aid award levels seem trivial by comparison.[9]

The transition in the federal government's funding of generally available student aid from a minor, tightly focused loan effort in the 1960s to a mammoth fiscal commitment in the 1990s merits politically focused historical examination. Prior to undertaking that analysis, however, it is useful to consider in broad outline the first 25 years of this federal effort. Prior to the passage of the Act, need-based, generally available federal student aid came entirely in the form of National Defense Student Loans [NDSLs]. Spending on the NDSL program totaled $114 million in 1963-64. Under the following year's U.S. Higher Education Act, both the NDSL program and a variety of new student-aid programs were to be encompassed under the Act's Title IV. Title IV established the College Work Study [CWS] Program, the Guaranteed Student Loan [GSL] Program, and the Educational Opportunity Grants Program. The latter two programs were later renamed the Stafford Loan Program and the Supplemental Educational Opportunity Grants [SEOG] Program, respectively. Each of these Title IV student-aid programs was, in essence, delivered or initiated via campus offices, so even the student-focused aspects of the Act were embedded within institutional arrangements. Later, this institutional focus was muted and other, more portable forms of aid were emphasized. Of particular significance in this transition to portability are the developments of 1972, when Congress established the Basic Educational Opportunity Grants [BEOG] Program, which was later renamed the Pell Grants Program. A student's award eligibility level under this program is calculated independently of the actual institutions under consideration. Then, once the student chooses an institution, his or her eligibility index and data on the costs of the institution chosen are combined formulaically to produce the final amount of the grant.

Spurred particularly by growth in the Pell and Stafford Programs, total federal outlays for aid grew steadily and significantly in the 1970s, then grew more moderately in the 1980s. Table 1 presents, in constant-dollar terms, a quantitative history of funding for all of the federal government's generally available student-aid programs. As may be noted from the table, these programs were over 32 times larger in 1980-81 than in 1963.9 Most of the total outlays went into Pell Grants and Stafford (Guaranteed Student Loan) awards. The programs' growth slowed in the mid-1980s but surged again in the latter years of the decade. In constant-dollar terms, outlays in 1989-90 were about 24 percent larger than in 1980-81, and about 40 times larger than in 1963-64. By the late 1980s approximately one-third of all U.S. undergraduates received some form of federal

[9]The total is for the federal government's expenditures for generally available aid for college attendance by needy students. All of this money was in the form of National Defense Student Loans [NDSLs]. The total is equivalent to $456 million in 1989 dollars. National Defense Student Loans later were renamed National Direct Student Loans, and then renamed again as Perkins Loans. This program's two name changes are merely the most dramatic of a long series of name changes for the federal government's generally available aid programs (an interesting political phenomenon in itself). Basic Educational Opportunity Grants [BEOG] were renamed as Pell Grants in the early 1980s. Most recently, in 1988, Guaranteed Student Loans were renamed as Stafford Loans. Stafford, Pell, and Perkins, each a member of the U.S. Senate, contributed notable support and leadership for federal student-aid legislation in the era of the Higher Education Act.

Table 1. Total awards for generally available federal student aid, selected years 1963-1990 (in millions of 1989 constant dollars)

	1963-64	1972-73	1975-76	1977-78	1980-81	1983-84	1989-90 (est.)
Pell Grants (formerly BEOG)	-	-	2092	3145	3418	3401	4370
Supplementary Educational Opportunity Grants (SEOG)	-	503	449	482	527	440	432
State Student Incentive Grants (SSIG)	-	-	44	118	104	73	70
College Work Study (CWS)	-	769	659	929	945	833	762
Perkins Loans (formerly NDSL)	456	1152	1028	1218	993	831	824
Income-Contingent Loan	-	-	-	-	-	-	5
Stafford Loans [formerly GSL]	-	3393	2831	3441	8878	8843	9431
Supplemental Loans for Students (SLS)	-	-	-	-	0	180	795
Parent Loans for Undergraduate Students [PLUS]	-	-	-	-	3	204	783
Total Generally Available Aid	456	5817	7103	9334	14868	14805	18473

Note: The data of Table 1 are adapted from Gillespie and Carlson (1983) and College Board (1990).

financial aid (U.S. Department of Education, 1988). This coverage of the population far exceeded that envisaged by the Act's initiators in 1965.

Figures 1, 2, and 3 supplement Table 1 with further details.[10] Figure 1 graphically portrays trends in the proportional distribution of federal student-aid funding. The percentage of all such funding going to grants peaked in 1977-78 at 40 percent, then quickly retreated to about 25 percent in the later years of the Carter presidency. It has remained at roughly that level ever since. Conversely, proportional funding for all of the loan programs together has followed a U-shaped pattern, bottoming out at about 50 percent in the mid- and later-1970s. Interestingly, proportional college work-study funding has shrunk gradually but consistently from rather humble beginnings, owing perhaps to the work-study program's lower profile and "stepchild" position in relation to the more visible grant and loan programs associated with the Higher Education Act (Gladieux, 1983; Doyle and Hartle, 1985). Relating Table 1 and Figure 1, we can conclude

---

[10]The data of Figures 1, 2, and 3, like those of Table 1, are adapted from Gillespie and Carlson (1983) and the College Board (1990).

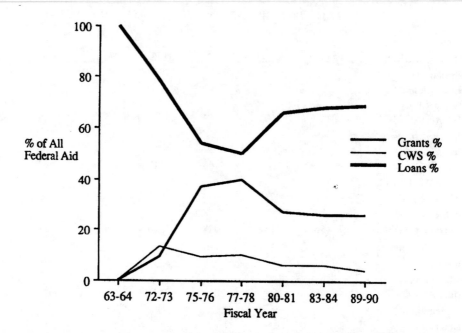

FIGURE 1. Percentage breakdown of federal student awards, selected fiscal years 1963–1990.

Note: Federal grants programs included here are the Pell, SEOG, and SSIG programs. Federal loan programs included here are the Stafford [formerly GSL], Perkins, Income-Contingent, SLS, and PLUS programs.

that federal student-aid policy made a transition from the relatively modest NDSL program of the early 1960s, to a substantially larger effort with a mixed grant and loan focus in the 1970s, then to an even larger effort with a renewed emphasis on loans in the years since.

The explosive growth of the federal grant and loan programs has been concentrated in the two largest federal aid programs, the Pell Grant and Stafford Loan programs. The precise nature of this growth is explored in Figures 2 and 3, which highlight data on the number of recipients and average award size.[11] Significantly, the data suggest that increases in numbers of students served, rather than increases in award size, have driven the striking growth since the mid-1970s in total outlays for these two critical programs. Indeed, award sizes shrank between 1977-78 and 1989-90 in both programs, in terms of constant (1989) dollars. For example, the average size of Pell Grants decreased from $1,687 to $1,366 during the period while the number of students served by the program was rising from 1.9 million to 3.2 million (see Figure 2). Similarly, the average size of Stafford awards decreased in those years

---

[11]Outlays for Stafford Loans and Pell Grants together in 1989-90 composed 75 percent of the total outlay that year for generally available aid (College Board, 1990). Outlays for Supplementary Educational Opportunity Grants [SEOG], State Student Incentive Grants [SSIG], College Work Study [CWS], Perkins Loans, Income Contingent Loans, Supplemental Loans for Students [SLS], and Parent Loans for Undergraduate Students [PLUS] loans contributed the remaining 25 percent of generally available aid (ibid.).

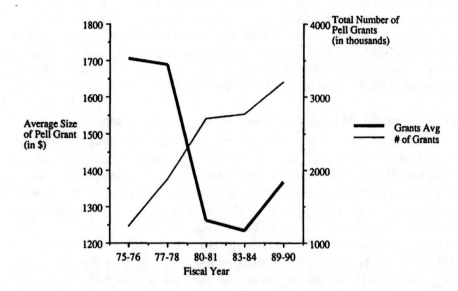

FIGURE 2. Average Pell Grant awards and total number of Pell Grants, selected fiscal years 1975-1990.

Note: This table has two vertical axes. The average size of Pell Grants is portrayed on the left axis, with the yearly data represented by a broad line. The number of Pell Grants is portrayed on the right axis, with the yearly data represented by a narrow line. Award figures are in constant 1989 dollars.

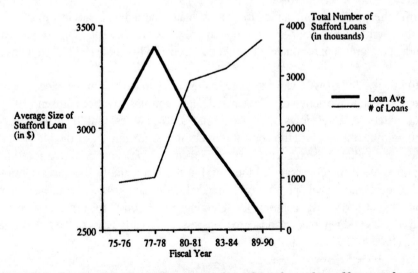

FIGURE 3. Average Stafford Loans awards and total number of loans, selected fiscal years 1975-1990.

Note: This table has two vertical axes. The average size of Stafford Loans is portrayed on the left axis, with the yearly data represented by a broad line. The number of Stafford Loans is portrayed on the right axis, with the yearly data represented by a narrow line. Loan figures are in constant 1989 dollars.

from $3,392 to $2,552, but the number of Stafford recipients rose threefold, from a little over one million in 1977-78 to approximately 3.7 million in 1989-90 (see Figure 3). The increase in the number of students served by these two programs seems to be related more to increasing college costs and to the increasing number of financially independent (and, therefore, usually more needy) college students rather than to any major expansion of the programs into widened eligibility for students from the higher-income ranges. Indeed, financial eligibility requirements for the programs generally tightened in real terms over period.

Phases in the Political Evolution of the Act and Its Amendments

The history above presents relatively straightforward data regarding the fiscal, programmatic, and population-coverage characteristics of activities under Title IV of the Act. Of greater potential interest are the substantive patterns underlying these data. As policy objectives, target populations, Congressional support, interest-group status, and other factors have shifted, at least four identifiable phases have occurred in the political history of the aid programs under the Act. Table 2 presents an overview of these phases.

The first phase was initiated with the passage of the Act in 1965. Funds in this initial *"policy emergence"* phase were focused mainly on lower-income and lower-middle income students and delivered mainly via campus officials. This initial phase is notable for introducing two new kinds of federal aid: need-based grants (the Educational Opportunity Grants) and federal work-study aid. Loan programs were, nevertheless, the dominant vehicles for the new aid efforts: the already existing NDSL program was expanded, and the GSL program was initiated. In light of later developments, it is worth noting that the latter program was designed to provide some limited federal help for the more needy among the middle class by easing the cash-flow problems associated with college attendance, and that the program was to do so via a relatively unsubsidized approach (Gladieux, 1986). Clearly, in setting up the GSL program, the government aimed to be a facilitator more than a provider of funds. Through the combination of grant, work-study, and loan programs, federal spending for generally available student aid grew approximately tenfold between 1963-64 and 1972-73, in constant-dollar terms.

Intriguingly, this growth was due more to the policy initiatives of the executive branch and the Congress than to the activities of organized interest groups.[12] Janet Hansen (1977), on the basis of extensive interviews with participants, concludes that the Congress and the Johnson administration were the central players in the formation of the aid programs.

She argues that the executive branch played a significant formative role in the years leading up to the 1964-65 passage of the Act, but the Act actually was passed "only when a rationale (equal educational opportunity) coincided with a congressional consensus that the federal government had a responsibility for fostering opportunity" (p. vi). The executive branch then played a diminishing role, secondary to Congress, in the early years of the federal grant-in-aid programs (1964 to 1972).

---

[12]It would be erroneous, however, to assume that unorganized, unexpressed interests have had no effects on federal student-aid policy, either in the 1960s or afterwards. As Gary Rhoades noted in response to an earlier draft of this chapter (personal communication, November 2, 1991), one cannot ignore aggregates of interest that possess significant political potential but are as yet unmobilized. Rhoades suggests that unmobilized interests favoring improved educational equity and opportunity were instrumental in the expansion of the community colleges in the 1960s.

Table 2. Aspects and phases of federal student-aid policy under the U.S. Higher Education Act, 1965-1990

POLICY ASPECT	POLICY PHASE			
	Phase I: 1965 to 1972-73 *Policy emergence*	*Phase II: 1972-73 to 1977-78* *Policy refinement and expansion*	*Phase III: 1977-78 to 1980-81* *Destabilization of policy agenda*	*Phase IV: 1980-81 to 1989-90* *Policy drift*
Policy Objective(s)	access objective	access, choice, and persistence objectives	continuing focus on access, choice, and persistence objectives	de-emphasis of choice and persistence objectives
Target Population	targeted on needy students, most (but not all) from lower-income ranges	targeted on needy students, from lower and middle-income ranges	expansion under MISAA of "need" to include more middle-income and upper-income students, then retreat	retreat from MISAA, narrowing of definition of "need" to exclude many middle-income and upper-income students
Primary Program Vehicle(s)	loans	mix of grants and loans	return to loans	loans
Delivery System	campus-oriented delivery system	increased student-orientation in delivery system	continuing student-orientation in delivery system	continuing student-orientation
Congressional Status	seeds of consensus on student aid in Congress	growth of consensus on student aid in Congress	some breakdown of consensus on student aid in Congress, with tax-credit advocates emerging	continuing threats to consensus on student aid in Congress
Interest-Group Status	clash of institutional-aid and direct-student-aid advocates	growth of the "student-aid coalition" after defeat of the institutional-aid advocates	some breakdown of the "student-aid coalition," as public and private institutions, and others, note diverging interests	increased pressures on the "aid coalition", breakdown of consensus
Federal/State/Institution Relationships	federal government becomes the new partner of states and institutions in the aid enterprise	federal government becomes the dominant partner in the aid enterprise	federal government continues as the dominant partner in the aid enterprise	federal government retreats as the dominant partner in the aid enterprise, state role increases
Spending Growth (Constant $)	App. tenfold over eight years	60% over five years	59% over three years	24% over nine years

In contrast to Congress and the executive branch, interest groups were apparently not especially influential in the emergence and early development of the student-aid programs under the Higher Education Act (Moynihan, 1975b; Hansen, 1977).[13] To the extent the longstanding, general-purpose interest groups (such as the American Council on Education) had positions on student-aid issues, those positions tended toward support and development of institutions. Student aid was a concern for them mainly as it happened to benefit institutional agendas. During this first phase in the political history of the programs, higher-education interest groups other than the ACE were splintered, not yet fully formed, or poorly positioned. As a result, Hansen (1977, p. vi) observes, interest groups were "almost completely ineffectual" in those years: largely disorganized and unsure of their positions and their role, they simply reinforced the disagreements within Congress. The weakness of the higher-education interest groups became more pronounced over the federal aid programs' early years and culminated in an especially painful debate over the 1972 amendments to the Act.

That debate in 1972 culminated with what are, arguably, the most dramatic amendments and additions in the history of the Act's Title IV. Accordingly, that year can be viewed as marking the beginning of a new, second phase in the political history of the aid programs. The phase is notable for its *policy refinement and expansion.* As the debates of 1972 approached, there was general agreement over establishing a new, expanded program of aid for college attendance, but conflict had emerged among institutions, policy analysts, interest groups, and politicians over the question of delivering the aid directly to students versus using institutions to deliver the aid (Gladieux and Wolanin, 1976; Brademas, 1987). After forceful and telling deliberations on the issues by respected and experienced policy analysts like Alice Rivlin, some consensus was reached over the directions of expansion in the aid programs: toward more direct channels of aid to students, toward greater emphasis on facilitating student choice and persistence, toward an expanded pool of eligible applicants for aid, and toward a distinct, *foundational* role for the federal government in the enterprise of building aid packages for the needy student. The advocates of a continued emphasis on institution-focused aid, including prominent Congresswoman Edith Green of Oregon, suffered a major, and to this date lasting, defeat.[14]

Viewing this debate in retrospect, Gladieux and Wolanin (1976) suggest that two critical "charter" provisions for federal student aid were laid down in the amendments of 1972: (1) equal opportunity underlies all federal higher-education activities, and (2) student needs come before institutional needs. Noting the broadening of the definition of eligible institutions and students with the 1972 amendments, Schuster (1982) suggests a third, central implication of the amendments: they brought the transformation of "higher education" into "postsecondary education"

---

[13] At the level of individuals seeking access to postsecondary education, Karen (1991) argues, student-aid issues have never received as much organized interest-group attention as more general issues of access. In particular, interest groups representing women and minorities have played a role since the 1960s in building popular and political support for expanding access into the system of higher education. That mobilization has had its most significant influence on the legal climate surrounding admissions and the funding of some institutional sectors. In contrast, Karen argues, lower-SES students have not mobilized in equivalent strength and, therefore, not affected the specific directions of federal student-aid policy.

[14] Apparently stunned and discouraged by her defeat at the hands of a bipartisan Congressional group led by Brademas, Quie, Perkins, and Reid, Mrs. Green relinquished her chairmanship of the House's Higher Education Subcommittee in 1973 and retired the following year (Gladieux and Wolanin, 1976).

as an area of federal policy, expanding the pool of policy beneficiaries to students and institutions not previously included in federal largesse.

The most important programmatic development of 1972 was the establishment by Congress of the BEOG Program, a program with many of the characteristics of a voucher or an entitlement, in that grants were to be "portable" from institution to institution. In this sense, the BEOG Program was the first student-based, as opposed to institution-based, program funded under the Act. Its general impetus was to disengage federal student-aid efforts under the Act from their heavy reliance on institution-based delivery. Students' BEOG eligibility levels, based on family finances, and their parallel right to an aid award for a certain percentage of their college costs, "went with them" regardless of the institution they chose to attend. The making of informed choices by students among competing institutions was, therefore, favored. The assumption was that such an approach would make institutions more sensitive to market forces favoring efficiency and quality.

Philosophically, therefore, the Basic Grants program was a very significant development. The new program was equally significant fiscally. Daniel Patrick Moynihan, then a White House aid for domestic legislation, was struck by the fact that the new Basic Grants program was extraordinarily generous but largely invisible to the general public:

> The FY 1974 budget requests $959,000,000 for [BEOGs]. One billion dollars for a program of great equalizing intent and probable result. In the whole of the War on Poverty nothing came near this by way of direct income redistribution. Yet I should imagine that six months after its enactment, at most a handful of Americans knew the program even existed, much less its dimension. (Moynihan, 1975a, p. 313)

Part of the reason for this ignorance no doubt lies in the absence of concerted interest-group focus and success at the time. Hansen argues that for higher-education interest groups, the debate of the early 1970s was a "debacle" (1977, p. 242) of disunity and frustrated hopes. In a similar vein but a more partisan spirit, a campus-based observer of the time suggested that:

> The Higher Education Amendments of 1972, passed with bipartisan support and White House approval, will profoundly affect the character and quality of education beyond high school for a long, long time. The failure of the Washington-based spokesmen for higher education to contribute significantly to the shaping of those amendments verges on the scandalous. (Honey, 1972, p. 1243)

Thus, although the political-science literature often suggests that mobilized interest-group strength is a central factor in policy emergence and development (e.g., Dahl, 1961; Lowi, 1969), examination of the student-aid arena in the early 1970s casts doubt on this proposition. In this respect, the aid programs seem similar to other federal policy initiatives in education in the 1960s. As Peterson and Rabe (1983) note in their study of federal-level education politics after 1960, "Most [federal education] programs can best be attributed to a distinct set of political circumstances that enabled the legislative and executive branches to take new policy steps" (p. 709). Apparently, the relatively minor role of interest groups in federal higher-education policy in the 1970s is not uncharacteristic of the era.

After the dramatic, watershed debate and ultimate resolution in 1972, the expression of interest-group differences became even more muted. In fact, elements of unprecedented consensus began to emerge. The aid community witnessed the growth of what came to be termed the "student-aid coalition" or the "student-aid partnership." This group, which became broadly united behind the outlines of the Act's revisions of 1972 (Fenske, 1983), consisted of postsecondary institutions and their associations (mainly headquartered in Washington), state-government officials involved in state-level aid policy, federal officials in the U.S. Department of Health, Education, and Welfare [HEW], and organizations connected with the processing of aid applications (such as the American College Testing Program and the College Board's College Scholarship Service). In the mid-1970s this initially loose confederation of actors from a variety of settings began not only to voice similar views on the proper nature and delivery of student aid but also to lobby occasionally for those views at the state and federal levels. The needs for extensive lobbying by these groups, as well as the threats to their consensus, were slight, however, because few true policy controversies emerged in the years 1972-78. Instead, the coalition took on more of the form of a partnership working together toward technical (operational and bureaucratic) improvements in the programs (Fenske, 1983). It was, thus, a time of relative harmony and stability for the Title IV programs. Real federal aid outlays grew 60 percent over the five years of the second phase, 1972-73 to 1977-78. In this supportive climate, those changes that *were* made were mainly incremental and in keeping with a consensually supported focus on equal opportunity (Hansen, 1977).

In summary, the second phase in the political history of the aid programs began with the change and expansion of the programs' charge under the amendments of 1972 and progressed through a five-year period of greatly increased funding. In this period, there was little active executive-branch stake or effort in educational policy formation. As a consequence, most of the funding growth in this period came at Congressional initiative (Orfield, 1975) and was not aimed at substantially changed policy targets. The period was notable for the refinement and expansion of policy, not for dramatic conflict.

Nevertheless, the years of the Higher Education Act's second phase were years of increasing demographic, economic, and political tension in higher education (Hansen and Stampen, 1987), and the second phase ended in serious controversy. That controversy arose in part out of the emerging concern of Congress, apparently reflecting constituent pressures, over the perceived financial plight of middle-class parents of college-bound students (Hartle and Stedman, 1986; Brademas, 1987). As Murray (1984) and others note, broad-based opposition to many federal entitlement and quasi-entitlement programs began to appear in earnest in these years, so the Congressional controversy was by no means limited to the aid programs.[15] Unlike other domestic programs, however, the pressures in the aid arena were for more aid for more people rather than for abandonment or major retrenchments of the programs. Heated debate arose in Congress over the expansion of traditional aid programs versus the introduction of tuition tax-credits for college attendance. Both approaches would aid previously unaided populations, but the tax-credit approach would do so outside of the established need-based aid programs and mechanisms: regardless of income, students and their families would be able to claim a tax-credit for college expenses on their income-tax returns. Intriguingly, the usual political alli-

---

[15]Economics, or at least the economic perceptions of the general public, may have been a factor in the federal government's movement away from a focus on equality for the lower-income population. A central proposition of the formal theory of welfare program support posited by Wilensky (1975, p. 57) is as follows: "The greater the visible tax burden of the middle mass relative to the upper middle mass and the rich, the greater the resistance to health and welfare spending that appears to favor the poor."

ances within the aid partnership were split on the question. For example, Senator Kennedy of Massachusetts, a long-time ally of direct student-aid, favored the tax-credit approach.

In the end, the proponents of the general approach of the Higher Education Act were able to defeat the tuition tax-credit movement. Congress passed the Middle Income Student Assistance Act [MISAA] as the Higher Education Amendments of 1978. MISAA represented a compromise between the traditionalist coalition favoring need-based aid and a variety of other advocates favoring tuition tax-credits and alternative, non-need based approaches to the perceived crisis (Brademas, 1987). Like the rival tax-credit approach, MISAA greatly expanded aid for the middle- and upper-income groups, but it did so under the framework of the existing federal aid programs. Specifically, MISAA loosened the definition of need to include more middle-income families in the Basic Grants (Pell) program and removed the income ceiling on eligibility for GSLs, thereby making any student facing college expenses as needy enough, by definition, to warrant some federal support.

The passage of MISAA initiated the third phase in the political history of the federal aid programs. The expanded clientele for the programs brought on by MISAA, along with the rapid escalation in interest rates in the period, pushed total grant and loan award funding to unprecedented new highs in the three years of the third phase. Between 1977-78 to 1980-81, constant-dollar federal aid outlays grew a stunning *59* percent. Actual disbursements for the GSL program in the period regularly exceeded budgeted appropriations by large margins, as the middle (and upper) classes became increasingly attracted to what was then an easily accessible, non-need-based, quasi-entitlement. Nevertheless, program growth in this phase was less directed and laden with far greater controversy than the growth characterizing the immediately preceding phase. The era is best summarized as a period of *destabilization of the policy agenda*. To understand why that phrase appropriately characterizes this phase, it is necessary to consider the nature of the MISAA as political action. In a sense, MISAA was a political defeat only for the proponents of tax credits. As noted above, MISAA did not represent a fundamental change in the Higher Education Act's programmatic array or delivery mechanisms: students rather than institutions were still the delivery target of choice, the budget rather than the tax system was utilized, and the federal role as the dominant partner in the nation's increasingly organized aid enterprise was further reinforced. Why, then, might one consider MISAA one of the more significant shifts in a policy history notable mainly for refinements at the margins?

Underneath its surface appearance of incremental change, MISAA represented a striking defeat for the aid coalition and its value consensus favoring lower-income targeted, need-based, grants-oriented aid. In the late 1970s, federal aid policy's "era of good feeling" clearly came to an end. The new phase initiated by MISAA brought several developments contributing to policy destabilization. First, the clientele of the programs was substantially expanded. The stated goals of the MISAA legislation were to promote educational choice and persistence, as well as access, for both lower and middle-income students. As it turned out, upper-income students and families also benefitted substantially from the MISAA legislation. In this sense, MISAA was a clear departure from the aid coalition's need-based dogma in that it instituted a substantially more liberal definition of "need" for the federal aid programs.

It is important to remember that attention had indeed been paid to the middle-class in both the 1965 and 1972 debates on federal student aid, and therefore was not a new phenomenon.[16] Nevertheless, the middle-class had never before 1978 occupied so central a place in aid debates in Washington. Congress' expansion of GSL eligibility to the middle and upper classes was especially out of keeping with program history. Most participants and analysts attribute that move to the combination of middle-class pressure for relief from college costs and intense lobbying efforts by banking-industry officials, who would receive substantial returns from their federal administrative allowances on an expanded pool of eligible GSL borrowers (e.g., see McPherson, 1989). Stampen (1987, p. 10) suggests that resistance to government regulation was also a factor:

> Senator Jacob Javits of New York argued, to a room charged with certainty about the excess of government regulation, that the ceiling on Guaranteed Student Loans should be eliminated so that middle- and upper-income students could become eligible. He reasoned that it was costing the government more to enforce the regulations excluding them than to remove the ceiling. The government's fiscal note, which turned out to be wildly inaccurate, estimated a cost of $9 million. Senator Javits concluded by saying he was not worried that a Rockefeller or two might receive a loan because they would repay many times through higher taxes after graduation.

However they might have come to be, MISAA's magnanimous terms represented a real change in policy from earlier years in the federal aid programs.

The increased attention in MISAA to the needs of the middle-class may have indirectly had some effects on college attendance. By the late 1970s, lower-income and lower-middle-income populations had made significant gains in their enrollment rates, relative to other groups (McPherson and Schapiro, 1991). The retreat under MISAA from aid support of solely their attendance (and not the attendance of others) may have come as a political reaction to a perception of threat by those in other parts of the population. If so, the pattern would seem to fit a central proposition of the formal theory of welfare-program support posited by Wilensky (1975, pp. 54-55): "The greater the educational opportunity (measured by enrollment rates or fraction of the children of lower strata who go on to higher education), the more chance that the middle-mass parents of college students

---

[16]Janet Hansen (personal communication, February 14, 1992) stresses that the aims of MISAA were not at all without precedent. She notes that, even at their birth, the Title IV programs were not exclusively lower-income oriented, and that, in fact, the potential for extending the programs to the middle-class has always been a source of their appeal:

> Certainly the War on Poverty provided the environmental context in which it first became politically feasible to enact federal student aid. But it's also true that the Senate had passed a tuition tax credit in 1964 or 1965. (To my mind) wiser heads realized that student aid was a better model. The debate over tuition tax credits in 1978 was not so much a new debate over aid to the middle class but a continuation of a debate that had existed since the programs' inception....Similarly, in 1972 Senator Pell argued explicitly that the new BEOGs should be available to middle-income as well as to low-income student because you needed political support from the middle class for the program to thrive. If you look at the actual legislation, you'll see that it called for maximum grants in the early years of $11,400, an amount that would have made a goodly number of low-middle class and probably middle-class kids eligible. In fact, because funding levels were not large, the early grant maxima were far below that, so the aid was more targeted on the lower-income students than Congress explicitly agreed to when it authorized the program. I don't think Congress ever directly saw student aid as just for the poor.... This failure to explicitly identify the target group is another of those ambiguities that I believe allowed many different people to support the program, perhaps because they could each think that it was addressing their own particular concerns.

as well as a large number of the highly educated will resist the push from below for equality." Whatever the reason, the gains of the lower-income and lower-middle-income population in college attendance, relative to other groups, began to shrink soon after the "counter-revolution" of the late 1970s (Mortenson, 1990). Whether this enrollment reversal was caused by a parallel lessening of funds for student aid for the very most needy (a "zero-sum" hypothesis), by needy prospective students having a perception of growing federal inattention or abandonment (an attitudinal hypothesis), or by some other factor is impossible to discern. The rigorous policy analysis necessary to discover causation has not yet been done, and may well be impossible. Still, the pattern is provocative, and worthy of further discussion and investigation.

A second factor associated with policy destabilization in the third phase was the shift to loans in the overall balance of program allocations under Title IV, after several years of expanded emphasis on grants. MISAA marked the beginning of the dramatic return in federal student-aid policy to an emphasis on loans over grants (see Table 1 and Figure 1). As noted earlier, this shift was due in large part to the removal of the family-income ceiling on GSL eligibility in the context of dramatically rising interest rates. This action created new and substantial incentives to families to participate in the program: fixed-rate seven-percent loans were extraordinarily attractive, and too tempting to resist. Relatedly, in the same period as the MISAA enactment, the government removed the cap on the special financial allowance for banks and others participating in the GSL program, and implemented a more liberal, variable special allowance instead. This provided financial institutions with an inflation-proof, government-guaranteed investment. Because they had suddenly become a far more attractive investment instrument, GSLs were soon heavily marketed by the financial institutions, thus further fueling the loan explosion and, indirectly, the dominance of loans over grants in federal aid efforts.[17]

A third destabilizing factor in this phase was the breakdown of consensus among the aid partnership. The tuition tax-credit controversy revealed the seeds of the conflict among the aid partnership, and whatever consensus remained after the passage of MISAA further broke down in the latter years of the third phase. Controversies arose over questions of program efficiency (e.g., the control of fraud, abuse, and waste) and program fairness, with special attention to the apparent misuse of the GSL program by some upper-income families.[18] The interests of public and private institutions, of higher-cost and lower-cost institutions, and of selective and open-admissions institutions were increasingly perceived as divergent (Finn, 1980; Schuster, 1982; Gladieux, 1983; Mumper and Vander Ark, 1991). In addition, student lobbies and such professional groups as the National Association of Student Financial Aid Administrators became more independent, more active, and more influential with Congress.

Policy destabilization in the third phase was also brought on by a fourth factor, a growing awareness among those in the aid community that there were still unresolved philosophical issues underlying the programs since the reforms of 1972 and 1978 (Hartle and Stedman, 1986). Speaking for a group of aid authorities from a variety of sectors, Van Dusen commented in 1978 (p. 6) that, "The current system still contains fundamental conflicts of purpose. The Congressional debates of tax credits versus 'middle-income assistance' programs—with their contradic-

---

[17]I am indebted to Janet Hansen (personal communication, February 14, 1992) and, indirectly, to Arthur Hauptman for this insight.

[18]There was concern that some wealthy parents were using the program, with its low, deferred interest rate and absence of any limitations on eligibility, as an attractive source of new capital for investments or consumption.

tory philosophies, strategies and goals—demonstrate the programmatic conflicts which can occur in the absence of a unified public policy and approach to the financing of students."

A fifth and final contributor to policy destabilization in these years was financial. Growing fiscal pressures narrowed the range of feasible options and reduced the feasible levels of outlays for federal student-aid. Congress and the Carter administration would no longer tolerate rapidly expanding budgets for the programs in a time of increasing inflation, high interest rates, and a troubling budget deficit. Control of costs became a primary concern. Not surprisingly, it was in this period that direct federal oversight of student-aid award processes began to increase at a notable rate. One indicator of that growth was changes in the printed length of the U.S. Office of Education's official student-aid regulations: that length grew from fewer than 20 pages in the early 1970s to 238 pages in 1980 (Flint, 1991).

The emerging context of conflict and fiscal concern led naturally to the rescinding of the major reforms of MISAA and the end of the third phase in the programs' political history. The timing of the retreat from the MISAA initiative and the growth of Congressional and administration concern over issues of program efficiency and effectiveness should be noted. The emergence of those changes began not as a controversial assault on federal largesse under the banner of the "Reagan revolution" but, rather, in the later years of the Carter administration. By the time Ronald Reagan entered office in early 1981, much of the expansive potential of MISAA had been dismantled or was under reconsideration by Congress, and questions of programmatic direction and control were high on policymakers' education agenda (Gladieux, 1983; Hartle and Stedman, 1986).

It would be wrong, therefore, to assume that a mere liberal/conservative, or Democrat/ Republican, standoff fueled the paradoxes of federal student aid's recent political history. Stampen and Reeves (1986) conducted an extensive analysis of political decisions in the 96th and 97th Congresses (1979-81 and 1981-83), a period that crosses from the Carter years into the early years of the Reagan administration. The authors found profound consistency in the coalitions favoring and opposing various student-aid initiatives over that period. They conclude that Congressional attitudes to aid exhibited rather stable, across-party patterns of accord and division over the period, despite the absence of comparable stability in presidential politics during the period. Specifically, Congressional supporters of preserving and expanding student aid always included liberal Democrats but often included the more conservative Democrats (the "Boll Weevils") and the more domestically progressive Republicans (the "Gypsy Moths").

The fourth phase in the life of the Higher Education Act, from 1980-81 to 1989-90, may be termed a period *of policy drift.* Although the overall size of the federal aid commitment increased, growth was appreciably slower than in earlier times. Real federal outlays increased only 24 percent in the nine years of this phase. Congress responded to continuing complaints about the wastefulness of the aid programs (e.g., U.S. Office of Management and Budget, 1985; Bennett, 1985) by acting to control such problems when feasible. Congress also regularly debated the excesses of the loan programs, especially GSL/Stafford (Gladieux, 1986). Only minimal concrete policy action was taken during the period, however. Mumper and Vander Ark (1991, p. 62) note that "the process of reauthorizing the Higher Education Act in 1985 began with the consideration of proposals for a comprehensive overhaul of what was then the GSL program. But it ended in frustration, stalemate, and only minor adjustments in the programmatic status quo." Similarly, efforts of Congress to undertake some trimming of the aid agenda, stressing a return to need and access as central concerns, and eliminating some aid for some middle-income students, met with resistance among various sectors of the higher-education community in the 1980s—higher-cost institutions, for example, claimed clear harm from the loss of funding for needy students' attendance at such schools (Finn, 1990). On the basis of such concerns, the aid agenda remained largely unchanged from earlier years.[19]

All told, therefore, the major story of the fourth phase was not one of dramatic overall growth or shrinkage in the programs, as had been the case in earlier phases. Neither was the story one of consistent, consciously grafted policy reform. Instead, the major story would seem to be the remarkable stability of the programs in the face of dramatic changes in the overall climate for educational and social spending. The most striking aspects of the stability of the period were the continuing dominance of loans over grants in the composition of federal aid and the failure of Congress to undertake concerted and serious reform of the loan programs. The dominance of loans over grants, begun in the Carter years, continued at consistent levels throughout the 1980s, as highlighted in Figure 1. The complaints about the loan programs also continued, largely without redress. Mumper and Vander Ark (1991) argue that political power most clearly accounts for this pattern of loan-program stability in the midst of a turbulent policy context. They suggest that Pell Grants suffered, relative to loan programs, because they appealed mainly to the poorest students and the politically weakest colleges and because middle-income students, banks, and expensive private colleges composed significant interest groups with well-paid, talented lobbyists. Janet Hansen (personal communication, February 14, 1992) downplays the role of political interest groups and the middle class in loan-programs' strength in the 1980s, however. Instead, she stresses Congress' efforts to control the overall federal budget deficit, culminating in the Gramm-Rudman Act and its descendants:

> Keeping a lid on Pell costs while letting GSL rise didn't just happen because it was politically easier. Given that GSL is an entitlement, it was almost impossible to cut its costs without making structural changes in the program. Pell grants, on the other hand, depend on appropriations and could not easily be left out of across-the-board efforts to cut appropriated programs or limit their growth. Such cuts and limits weren't necessary directed at any particular program but rather got caught up in larger debates.

The drift of the fourth phase was brought on in part, therefore, by the emerging dominance of the federal budget deficit as an issue. Because deficits are broad rather than narrow concerns, higher-education interest groups were not central players in deficit-oriented debates. There was no absence of political conflict over student aid in the period, however. The central foci of that conflict were not the details of aid programs themselves, but the proper funding levels of those programs relative to other social and educational programs. What is more, the central parties to the conflict were not so much opposing members of Congress as distinct branches of government. In short, the fourth phase in the political history of the aid programs was marked by an ongoing, almost ritualized battle of wills between the Reagan administration and Congress. Democratic Congressman William Ford of Michigan related the outlines of that battle in 1985 at the twentieth anniversary celebration of the signing of the Higher Education Act (Fields, 1985b, p. 13):

---

[19]Further dissensus emerged in the 1980s over a proposal by Senators Nunn and McCurdy that those receiving federal aid be required to perform national service. Resistance from what remained of the aid coalition (see Pell, 1989) led to tabling of the proposal.

The competition for federal dollars is fiercer than ever before in my experience and probably going to get worse. In addition, we have a President in the White House who does not share the bipartisan commitment of his most recent seven predecessors going back to President Truman (including four Democrats and three Republicans) that the federal government has a responsibility to open the doors of educational opportunity not only for the sake of the individuals who will benefit but also as President Johnson said, "for the nation's sake."...President [Reagan] says "Look at all the money we've spent on education and there still are problems. I say, "My God, where would we be if we hadn't spent it?"

The conflict Ford recounts continued over the remaining years of the Reagan presidency, until the final year of that administration. Then, special political circumstances apparently softened the administration stance toward federal student aid.

Figure 4 highlights this striking tale of administration/Congress conflict, focusing upon Pell Grants and GSL (Stafford) Loans. Until 1988-89 the administration would regularly submit budgets calling for major cuts in aid, and these requests would be regularly rejected by a Congress intent on preserving levels at roughly the *status quo*. For example, in 1986 the Senate rejected, by margins consistently near to two-to-one, a variety of Reagan proposals to cut aid and end certain Title IV programs like State Student Incentive Grants [SSIGs] (see "Senate bars Reagan plan...",1986).[20] Keppel (1987) has noted that one result of such standoffs between the executive and legislative branches was, ironically, to bring the majority and minority parties of Congress into closer collaboration in opposition to the administration. In this way, the federal role in student aid was largely preserved, despite a more general federal movement toward "devolution" of educational activities from the federal to the state and local levels (Whitt et al., 1986). Although the relative proportion of total student aid paid by states and institutions increased in the 1980s after a long downward trend, the overall size of that shift was not nearly so dramatic as one might have expected on the basis of administration rhetoric. In the end, the opposing forces reached something of a balance, or an impasse.

The Core of the Paradox—The Third and Fourth Phases

The phase-by-phase history above suggests that the natural development of the federal student-aid programs was, in a sense, short-circuited in the late 1970s. The third and fourth phases, in the late Carter years and into the Reagan-Bush era, would normally have been years of policy maturation and institutionalization, but the analysis here suggests that program maturation was instead stifled. Politically, there was a breakdown of the previous consensus among administrations, Congress, and interest groups. Philosophically, the original focus of the programs on lower-income and lower-middle income students became blurred as a political response to perceptions of middle-class revolt in the late 1970s. Structurally, the federal government retreated from the role of dominant, agenda-setting partner in the aid enterprise in the 1980s. Managerially, information on programmatic effectiveness and efficiency, although demanded by some, proved elusive. Economically, the programs' maturation was hindered

---

[20]Saunders (1991) notes that the chairman of the Senate Subcommittee on Education, Senator Robert Stafford, began the hearings on the reauthorization of the Act in 1986 with the stated aim of maintaining the *status quo* in the face of the Reagan administration's attacks on student aid.

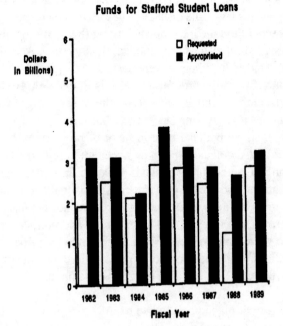

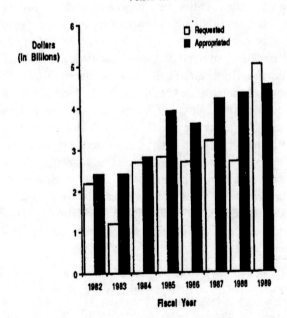

FIGURE 4. Administration/Congress conflict over student aid in the Reagan era: Administration requests and Congressional appropriations.

Note: The figure is adapted with permission from the *Chronicle of Higher Education* (November 9, 1988, page A23). The dollar figures are not inflation-adjusted. Prior to the 1988-89 fiscal year, the Stafford Loan Program was known as the Guaranteed Student Loan Program (GSL).

by budgetary constraint.[21] Of course, the political, philosophical, structural, managerial, and economic problems facing the programs in the late 1970s and 1980s were linked. The roots of each of these problems lay in the distinctive history of the programs. In the 1960s, federal student aid for the poor (and the most needy among the lower middle-class) represented to Congress a previously radical idea whose time had finally come. According to Hansen (1977) and others who have studied the issue or were personally involved (e.g., Keppel, 1987), there was not a sizable interest-group commitment to this innovation. In the following years, a core constituency developed, and in the 1970s this constituency was successively joined by other interest groups also favoring student aid, but for a variety of other purposes. The results were two-fold. First, the political base in favor of program expansion was strengthened and secured, and the added dollars came in unprecedented volume. Second, however, the seeds of disorder, conflict, and doubt were laid. As constraints on the federal budget multiplied and competing political agendas emerged, the consensus that had fueled student aid's rise began to break down in all but the vaguest outline. Aid remained popular with the general public and continued to grow. Nevertheless, the bureaucratic and political infrastructure, which would ideally become more knowledgeable and more powerful in periods of policy maturation a decade or so after initial emergence of a policy direction, never coalesced sufficiently to serve as a spur for effective, ongoing program development. A kind of drift of indecision set in.

Given the weight placed on the use of information in traditional rational models, it is especially important to consider the fate of policy-evaluation studies in the third and fourth phases. Significantly, such studies were cancelled, underfunded, or diverted to other purposes in this period.[22] The many difficulties inherent in analyzing the impacts of social programs (Levin, 1977; Weisbrod, 1977; Wirt, 1980; Murray, 1984; Hearn and Wilford, 1985; McPherson, 1988a; Weiss, 1991) may be partly to blame for the problem of inadequate evaluation efforts in student aid. Budgetary challenges are clearly also involved. David Longanecker, former director of education policy analysis for the Congressional Budget Office and now Executive Director of the Colorado Commission on Higher Education, suggests (Palmer, 1986, p. 17) that "Ever since the mid-1970s, evaluation of the programs has been left to atrophy. The Carter administration ran out of money, and one of the first things that always gets cut when budgets are tight is program evaluation. That's probably the last thing that should be cut. You have to know what's working and what's not."[23] Beyond the undeniable methodological and budgetary constraints, it is also clear that ideological reservations played a role in limiting evaluation research in the 1980s. Reginald Wilson, a senior scholar at the American Council on Education, suggested in 1988 that "During the Reagan-Bennett years, higher edu-

---

[21]Allan W. Ostar, who was involved in 1965 and in recent years in the politics of the Act, suggested that "The issues then were political, philosophical, and even constitutional. The issues today are more budget-driven" ("With warmth and nostalgia...", 1990, p. A26).

[22]In the late 1970s a multimillion-dollar series of studies, labeled the "SISFAP" studies, was begun (see Fenske et al., 1983; Hearn and Wilford, 1985). The results of these studies were inconclusive, like much of the work in this area. Also inconclusive were the results of the more recent National Commission on Student Financial Assistance (Brademas, 1987), which began as a comprehensive look at the programs' effectiveness before the most recent reauthorization but ended with a series of reports which were skillfully done but provided little that was not already known by analysts in the research area.

cation [has been] under siege. We haven't had the time to find out if what we've protected is worth protecting" (Evangelauf, 1988, p. A37).

The ideological developments that limited policy-evaluation efforts in the 1980s were also reflected in changes in the overarching goals of the federal aid programs, according to some observers. Hansen and Stampen (1987) suggest that the aid programs' maturation was affected importantly by a national shift away from an equity emphasis and toward a "quality" emphasis. Hansen and Stampen, noting the many reports and commissions in the early 1980s on restoring excellence to higher education, characterize those years as a period in which the quality emphasis became ascendant. Because the aid programs of the Higher Education Act of 1965 and its 1972 amendments were designed in an era emphasizing access, their fundamental goals and organizational roots were naturally destabilized by what was arguably a wholesale return to the quality emphasis of the 1950s.

In a similar analysis, James Guthrie (1985) also discerns a federal turn away from a concern with equality in the 1980s, but Guthrie sees the resulting national education-policy focus as more one of efficiency than of quality *per se:*

> In the quarter of a century between 1955 and 1980, American education policy was dominated heavily by a concern for expanding equality.... The 1980 election of Ronald Reagan symbolized a turning point in American educational policy. His campaign opponent, President Jimmy Carter, attracted the electoral support of conventional advocates of expanded educational equality.... At least for a time, concern for equality was to be eclipsed by efficiency. (Guthrie, 1985, pp. 328-9)

Guthrie attributes this shift, at least in part, to economic difficulties faced by governments and weighing heavily upon middle-class taxpayers.

Such analyses provide useful insight into the changing sociopolitical context during the third and fourth phases of the federal aid programs. Nevertheless, none attempts to address how the need-based federal aid programs were able to *grow* in such a context, i.e., in the face of an increasingly hostile executive branch and other threatening social and economic developments. Therein lies the paradox of interest in this essay. One hypothesis might be that the programs simply became something entirely different in this period and, thus, were able to survive under a different set of rules. The late Francis Keppel, who was intimately involved in legislation on the Higher Education Act over virtually the entire 25-year period covered by this chapter, rejected this interpretation, however. Keppel concluded in 1987 (p. 51) that the Act then was still a recognizable extension of its origins: "Title IV of the 1986 Act...was a continuation of its 1965 predecessor; it was expanded to include the middle class, it relied far more heavily upon loans, it was far more expensive, and more federally driven—but it was a continuation nevertheless." Keppel made this judgment in 1986 because he believed three philosophical pillars for federal student aid were still quite strong: (1) the responsibility of parents to

---

[23]To the extent evaluation *was* conducted, it seems more often to have been directed to quality control than to improving effectiveness. Greg Jackson, who has done extensive evaluation of Title III of the Higher Education Act, has noted that there is an endemic conflict in federal agencies, including those focusing on higher education, between an "auditing evaluation" orientation and an "impact evaluation" orientation (comment at a symposium at the annual meeting of the Association for the Study of Higher Education, St. Louis, November 1988). In the last 15 years, the auditing-evaluation orientation clearly began to prevail in federal student-aid efforts. Such analyses fall well short of the more ambitious standards of impact evaluation.

contribute to offsprings' college expenses; (2) the orientation to need-based aid, rather than aid based on merit; and (3) the expectation that student earnings from summer employment, term-time employment, and career earnings (the last via loan repayments) contribute to college expenses. Keppel's conclusion is reasonable and suggests that the origins of the focal paradox of this chapter lie deeper than a simple matter of radical displacement of the government's original aid policy. That is, change has occurred, but not change so fundamental as to support an argument that the puzzling patterns emerging in the Act's third and fourth phases are simply the inevitable manifestations of newly introduced policies, or the artifactual manifestations of different policies playing under different rules. Instead, what took place in the programs' stated overarching directions between 1978 and 1990 was a logical extension of what had come before in the 1960s and the earlier years of the 1970s.

Yet what took place in the programs' actual development was not what either previous history or the rationalist policy literature would lead us to expect. Analyses written in the mid- and later 1970s tend to portray the history and performance of Title IV aid programs with positive, upbeat themes of progress, growth, and control (e.g., Fife, 1975; Leslie, 1977). It is in subsequent years that the paradox has fully emerged. It is thus the third and fourth phases of the political history of the programs that represent the core of the paradox. Twenty-five years of growth in real spending for a set of federal programs suggest that there must have been a consistent underlying context of highly favorable philosophical, political, structural, managerial, and economic conditions for those programs. Why the progressive breakdown of such conditions seems largely irrelevant to the federal aid programs' fiscal fortunes is a question well worth further consideration.

FIVE POTENTIAL EXPLANATIONS OF THE PARADOX OF FEDERAL STUDENT AID

The paradox of funding growth for a set of programs in concert with an absence of many of the usually assumed prerequisites for such growth is striking. Although a variety of perspectives may have potential for explaining the paradox, five seem especially promising. First, entrenched governmental bureaucracies, supported by the institutionalization over time of certain policies associated with those bureaucracies, maintained enough structural and procedural weight to deflect and defuse reform. Second, relevant interest groups were sufficiently united in their *general* support of federal student-aid efforts to thwart efforts at budgetary cuts but were so divided over other, more specific issues that serious reform efforts failed. Third, Congress in the 1980s, facing other matters of overriding national significance, but still zealously opposed to efforts by powerful administrations to cut student-aid programs, settled for maintenance of the status quo in federal student aid. Fourth, the simple popularity of student aid with the middle class may have made both reform and retrenchment politically difficult and unlikely. Fifth, reform and cutback efforts may have failed because of the nonlinear, "organized-anarchy" qualities of federal policy-making in education. Each of these five explanations will be explored in turn.

Entrenched Government Bureaucracy

The first potential explanation for the paradox is that *entrenched governmental bureaucracies, supported by the institutionalization over time of certain policies associated with those bureaucracies, maintained enough structural and procedural weight to deflect and defuse reform.*

Here, the hypothesis is that such deflecting and defusing occurred not through overt political channels but, rather, through the tenacity and persistence of the formal organizations associated with the delivery of a policy or program to the public. The focus of this explanation for the paradox is, therefore, not on political factors but rather on the institutionalization of certain policy frameworks within sizable public organizations.

John Brandl, in a presidential address to the Association for Public Policy Analysis and Management (1988), has pursued this line of reasoning on a generic level, arguing that our standard analytic lenses too often prove incapable of helping us understand how seemingly unsuccessful efforts continue to receive funding and support. Brandl suggests that recent years have exposed the deficiencies of traditional linear models for understanding the development, funding, and delivery of government programs. Focusing on governmental bureaucracy, in particular, as a hindrance to fundamental policy change along rational lines, Brandl argues that rational policy development tools, like the economist's "production function" metaphor, were invented for goal-directed, efficient enterprises, which government bureaus clearly are not. Such highly rationalized approaches rely upon assumption-laden and necessarily abstract calculations of public and private costs and benefits. When used in a governmental context, he argues, they will tend to present only part of the full picture of programs' overall context, costs, effects, and prospects. Such approaches will tend to overlook forces within the bureaucracy, such as self-interest and the appeal of routinization, that complicate and ultimately defeat a purist's focus on policy rationality. To the idealist who asks how it is that clearcut policy failure can lead to budgetary success, Brandl counsels a redefinition of policy failure. Adopting Brandl's perspective, one can argue that the federal student-aid programs' growth despite deviation from the rational ideal is less paradoxical than we first supposed. Viewed from the perspective of fuller knowledge of governmental bureaus, the paradox may disappear.[24]

Weiss (1991) pursues a similar line of argument, arguing that policy development and funding can achieve a level of organizational institutionalization that compromises analyses driven purely by efficiency-driven concerns. Program administrators, she suggests, may develop agendas only partly intersecting with the need for evaluation. Weiss argues (1991, p. 215) that administrators are not "irrational," but instead "have a different model of rationality in mind," one focused on organizational survival, program funding, staff development and loyalty, and so forth. Evaluation, and particularly evaluation that might lead to negative outcomes, is not especially welcome under this form of rationality:

> Evaluators tend to assume that accomplishing the objectives for which the program was established is the overriding imperative. But for program managers, the priority is usually to keep the agency going....The view that some managers hold about their programs is *"nil nisi bonum,"* speak nothing but good; it is a phrase usually reserved for the dead. (1991, p. 215)

Padgett (1981) agrees with Brandl and Weiss that bureaucratic factors can cripple rationalized policy development but adds broader ecological constraints as well. In a theoretically grounded analysis of federal policy in the Department of Housing and Urban Development [HUD], he suggests that analysis of federal budgeting and programming must attend to at

---

[24]Of course, Brandl is not arguing that the rational metaphors are flawed as ideals but rather that they provide flawed descriptions of the ways real government bureaus work.

least three hierarchical levels within the federal bureaucracy: (1) the *macroeconomic* determination of federal spending at the presidential level, which is particularly sensitive to defense and overall domestic spending targets; (2) the *distributional* determination of relative spending priorities at the level of the Office of Management and Budget and upper echelons of the cabinet departments, which is particularly sensitive to political and tactical issues, as well as to substantive debate; and (3) the *administrative* determination of "proper" allocations to meet individual program needs, which is particularly sensitive to technical, legal, administrative, and efficiency issues. Bureaucratic conflict exists within each level, Padgett argues, and also across the levels, as conflicts over targets and priorities are played out.[25] Padgett adds, however, that more than simple bureaucratic conflict is present: each of the three levels of organization is embedded in a distinctive cultural context of "ecological control." The premises of that controlling context "reflect, in highly compressed form, the historical residues of past political struggles—program controllability, whose roots lie in the legal structure; organizational priorities, whose roots lie in institutional roles and constituency relations; and presidential fiscal targets, whose roots lie in macroeconomic and defense issues" (1981, pp. 122-23). In Padgett's view, these pressures on program development and funding act to make programmatic outcomes different from those one might expect from purely "rational" organizational or policy models.

Although Padgett's empirical analysis was based on HUD funding in the Vietnam War years, the hypotheses may well hold in an analysis of student-aid funding in the same period and beyond. One facet of the agan administration's efforts against the federal role in education was an attempt to shrink and eventually close the Department of Education from the inside via strategic placement of conservative operatives within the bureaucracy. There is evidence that this plan ultimately failed because of the greater numbers, longer experience, and superior organizational skills of civil service personnel in the Department (Clark and Astuto, 1988). Clearly, as the programs begun under the Higher Education Act have been extended from the 1960s through to the 1990s, they have acquired organizational resonance, and unique organizational moorings, within the federal government. The programs begun under the Higher Education Act are the product not only of a variety of historical, political, economic, and social forces, but also of distinctive organizational forces in the federal bureaucracy. That they may fail under one, limited, highly contextualized definition of success does not preclude their having offsetting, and ultimately determinative, support within the other contexts in which they operate. The momentum of aid-program growth continued through periods in which executive-branch support faltered, evaluation research was underfunded and inconclusive, and a single, coherent, widely shared philosophical rationale was lost. That growth must reflect distinctively nurturing organizational and ecological conditions, perhaps even a nascent institutionalization.[26]

---

[25]Wildavsky (1984) also addresses these conflicts and tensions

[26]Institutionalization is meant here in the sociological sense, that of a process in which some activity, value, attitude, or form becomes taken-for-granted, deeply imbedded, and resistant to change. The process may take place in societies, but the focus here is on organizations. Certain innovations within organizations may become institutionalized features that command a high degree of acceptance and loyalty from those within and without the organization and that seem to be protected from narrow, rationalized analysis (Perrow, 1986). The student-aid programs may have become institutionalized features of the Department of Education, and within the federal government in general.

Kagan (1991) pursues a related line of analysis but focuses on the legal aspects of government organization and action. He proposes that governmental decision-making in the U.S. is shaped powerfully by the likelihood of legal action during and subsequent to policy initiation and change. Kagan begins his analysis with the suggestion that governmental decision-making varies along two dimensions, hierarchical versus party influenced, and formal versus informal. He terms the resulting four possible decision styles alternative "modes of policy making and dispute resolution." Hierarchical/informal relies on expert or political judgment, hierarchical/formal relies on bureaucratic rationality, party-influenced/informal relies on negotiation and mediation, and party influenced/formal relies on adversarial legalism. Internationally, there is variation in which style is dominant, Kagan suggests, with the U.S. most clearly in the party-influenced/formal mode: "Compared to other economically advanced democracies, the United States is uniquely prone to adversarial, legalistic modes of policy formulation and implementation, shaped by the prospect of judicial review" (p. 369). Obviously, there are high costs to this tendency, including the frequent violation of expert-driven, bureaucratically rational norms. Specifically, "[T]he American policymaking system encompasses, on average: more complex legal rules; more formal, adversarial procedures for resolving political and scientific disputes; slower, more costly forms of legal contestation; stronger, more punitive legal sanctions; more frequent judicial review of and intervention into administrative decisions; and more political controversy about (and more frequent change of) legal rules and institutions" (p. 372). Kagan notes that the federal efforts aimed at ensuring equal educational opportunity compose a primary example of this administrative style in government. For those in the federal government focusing on postsecondary student aid, in particular, the slow, defensive, legally circumspect style of policy development may have been at first necessary, then familiar, and now, ultimately, institutionalized. Fundamental change under these circumstances could involve prohibitive organizational, professional, and personal risks.

The argument that organizational factors hinder the develop of coherent federal policy in student aid is a variation of a familiar line of criticism of federal education policy. On the basis of a review of the literature, Peterson and Rabe (1988) argue that there are two general lines of criticism of federal policy in elementary and secondary education: the *implementation* line and the *capture* line. Both lines focus on organizational factors as hindrances to success. The implementation line suggests that federal programs impose burdensome regulations, guidelines, and requirements on their "producer groups" (e.g., schools). These constraints preclude the development of coherent, sustainable, defensible programs. Confusion, conflict, and occasional failure are the results. The Brandl and Padgett approaches, although not always overtly critical in tone, contain elements of the implementation line, focusing on the federal government as a source of seeming irrationality. In contrast, the "capture" theme in the education-policy literature sees federal authorities not as overcontrolling but as weak and passive relative to other bureaucracies and groups. Specifically, it suggests that other organizations (especially producer groups, as opposed to beneficiary groups) capture federal policy after it is initiated and shape its ongoing implementation and reform. In concluding their review, Peterson and Rabe suggest that both the implementation and capture lines are overdrawn and conclude that, at least in elementary-secondary education, cooperative, adaptive, consensual, mutually accommodating behaviors are the emerging norm at the federal level, with all parties searching for "a reasonably safe path between the Scylla of organized interests and the Charybdis of excessive proceduralism" (p. 470).

The path from Peterson and Rabe's review of recent K-12 policy to better understanding of federal postsecondary policy is not straightforward, but is revealing. Regarding the potential power of the "capture line," there certainly is a significant non-federal organizational infrastructure underlying and surrounding the federal student-aid programs. That infrastructure is at the national, state, and local levels, and contains both public and private elements. Along the latter lines, the Student Loan Marketing Association ("Sallie Mae"), the College Scholarship Service, and the American College Testing Program are examples of large enterprises intimately tied to federal efforts in student aid. As substantial organizations with innumerable standard operating procedures and notable structural differentiation, they face high "transaction costs" in making changes. In the terms of organizational theory (see, for example, Pfeffer, 1981), their level of resource dependency on the federal government's aid policies is extreme. In the private sector, the resistance of these organizations to change often takes the form of interest-group activity. Stability in interorganizational relations, not fundamental change, tends to be in their interest. Regarding the potential power of Peterson and Rabe's "implementation line," there is no denying the impressive organizational skills, longevity, and culture within the federal education agency.

Nevertheless, there are some problems with purely organizational interpretations of the aid paradox. As noted earlier, although there are certainly a variety of organizationally complex interest groups surrounding federal student-aid policy, few analysts have adopted a pure "capture" line in assessing those groups' influence on policy development. The evidence for their having substantial power is not strong. Similarly, the extent to which the federal aid bureaucracy has been buffeted over the years by political appointments and constraints on personnel budgets makes the assignment of ultimately *determinative* power to them, in keeping with the strict "implementation" line, questionable.

Patterns of Unity and Disunity Among Interest Groups

A second potential explanation for the paradox of the aid programs between 1965 and 1990, and particularly for the programs' third and fourth historical phases, is that *relevant interest groups were sufficiently united in their general support of federal student-aid efforts to thwart efforts at budgetary cuts but were so divided over other, more specific issues that serious reform efforts failed.* This explanation focuses not on the creative, pro-active capabilities of higher-education interest groups (which, as we have already noted, have been weak through much of the programs' history) but on the restraining capabilities of those groups. From the perspective of this explanation, those restraining capabilities emerged from both the groups' unanimous opposition to sweeping budget cuts and from their divisions among themselves over the nature of appropriate program reform. Opposition to the budget cuts proposed by the Reagan administration was virtually unanimous among postsecondary interest groups. At the same time, as noted earlier, striking interest-group divisions developed in the third and fourth phases of the history of the Act. For example, public institutions disagreed with private institutions over proper levels of funding for attendance at the latter schools, and proprietary institutions disagreed with traditional institutions over the validity of policies for non-degree-granting programs. In the 1980s it began to appear that at least one significant sector would arise to oppose *any* reform proposal generated. One can argue that this situation, of interest-group consensus on general issues and dissensus on specific ones, produced a kind of stalemate in which neither serious reforms nor significant cutbacks were possible.

In their analysis of the absence of reform in the Stafford Loan program in the 1980s, Mumper and Vander Ark (1991, p. 74) argue that such reform was hampered by the absence of a well-developed policy reform alternative and by the increased number of Congressional and executive-branch participants compared to earlier years. They go on to argue, however, that the primary reason for the lack of reform was political: the divergence of interests among established, as well as newly professionalized and newly mobilized interest groups. Mumper and Vander Ark suggest that the consensus necessary to maintain the original intent and focus of the Stafford program withered in the face of entry into the arena by new interest groups such as the National Student Lobby, the National Association of Independent Colleges and Universities, and in the face of splintering of the membership organizations of the American Council on Education away from that association's formerly inclusive umbrella. As a result, reform was deterred by a lack of consensus. In this context, the Stafford program simply grew, without systematic reform and without substantial grounding in the original purposes of the program.

Writing critically on general federal aid policy in the 1980s, Mortenson (1990) follows a similar path, concluding that the lines of agreement among interest groups were thin indeed and that reform efforts suffered in this context:

> The enterprise of "financial aid" consists of many players, each with distinct programs and goals that only overlap at providing financial resources to students to enroll in higher education. The distinct interests of the different parties must be clearly identified before one can hope to understand how the whole system "works." A fundamental axiom of political budgetary analysis is: listen not to what politicians announce to be the goals of a program but look instead at who benefits from the program. While all in the financial aid enterprise profess service to students, in fact little else binds us to that common theme. In fact,…politicians seek votes for re-election, lenders seek profits from making loans, colleges seek enrollments that maximize revenues and/or academic reputation, guarantors seek jobs, budget makers seek ways to stretch dollars, and students seek ways to finance college educations. Only in the last item do we find a common ground for our commitment to financial aid for students. (Mortenson, 1990, p. 58)

Along the same lines, Gladieux (1986, p. 4) observed in the mid-1980s that "Vested interests have naturally emerged, creating a kind of gridlock that I think we all at one time or another find frustrating because it seems to block constructive change and adjustment that may be needed. Any significant change creates winners and losers….The status quo seems to be the path of least resistance." The analysis by Gladieux is convincing. Of course, conflicts among interest groups do not necessarily ensure gridlock. After all, one or more groups may be sufficiently strong to overwhelm the opposition of an assortment of opponents. Still, the absence of clearly dominant interest groups probably helped to preclude significant action in the third and fourth phases.

The truth regarding interests groups in this period is, therefore, complex. Interest groups in the 1980s may have had only circumscribed influence in federal *policy-making* in education but may have exerted more notable influence through keeping reform proposals off the agenda, or helping defeat them once they reached the agenda. Such an interpretation would seem to contradict the viewpoint discussed and largely accepted earlier: that interest-group's influence on federal student-aid policy has been limited (Hansen, 1977; Moynihan, 1975b). In reality, it is best considered a revision in keeping with the notion that those studying policy should pay as much attention to the generation or encouragement of *nondecisions* as to the making of decisions (Bachrach and Baratz, 1962). There is evidence from the the general political-science literature that, once a potential reform is on the agenda for consideration, interest groups may be more effective at retarding innovation than at promoting it (Lowi, 1969). In the 1980s a "contested stalemate" of this kind seems to have been the defining characteristic of the politics of federal student aid.

The Vagaries of Congressional Attention Patterns

A third potential explanation for the paradox of federal student-aid policy also focuses on the politics of the 1980s: *Congress in the 1980s, facing other matters of overriding national significance, but still zealously opposed to efforts by powerful administrations to cut federal student-aid programs, settled for maintenance of the status quo in those programs (i.e., continuing, albeit slowed, funding growth without significant structural change).* This interpretation argues, as does the interpretation above, that politics are central to resolving the paradox. Unlike the second interpretation, however, this one focuses more squarely on Congress, and more broadly on the nature of legislators' attention to aid in the larger context of other pressing national concerns. To oppose the Reagan administration, the majority and minority parties of Congress came into closer collaboration on aid issues in the 1980s, but Congress seemed not to have the time or energy to deal with more fundamental issues in aid policy. Keppel's description of the reauthorization of 1985-86 is illustrative:

> Congress did not deal with the "imbalance" between grant and loan funds…[or] the growing concern over the rising costs of higher education. The budget problems of the institutions and the federal government were of course affected by forces beyond the reach of the congressional committees: the economic machinations of OPEC, institutional appetites for bigger and better facilities, the widespread public concern over eroding academic quality.…The higher education community was sufficiently troubled with its own affairs to make united recommendations on such difficult issues as costs and quality almost impossible. Finally, looming over the whole scene was the huge and growing federal budget deficit, reflected in the administration-supported Gramm-Rudman legislation. Unlike 1965, a year in which the deficit was not an issue, 1985 seemed scarcely the best time to chart the unknown. (Keppel, 1987, p. 66)

This explanation is in essence one of a "domain defense" approach by Congress in the face of assaults from the Reagan administration and others who saw cuts in educational and social programs as essential for solving the nation's problems. Miles and Cameron (1982) suggest such an approach was adopted by successful tobacco companies after external threats to their survival. One aspect of the domain-defense approach pursued by the Congress involves its attitude toward evaluation of the aid programs. Ironically, steady Congressional roots may help to explain both the absence of systematic evaluation of the programs and the failure to employ what evaluation evidence did exist. Congressional support of the aid agenda has been strong throughout the history of the aid programs, regardless of changes in administration, and regardless of ebbs and flows in the level of interest-group consensus. One might surmise that the combination of a hostile administration and interest-group conflict in the 1980s might have spurred pressures for systematic policy evaluation, analysis, and assessment, yet these years of turmoil in federal policy directions in education led to little public attention to evaluation efforts. Indeed, in some instances, a variety of often conflicting interest groups united with Congress to dilute and deflect efforts by the Reagan administration and its contractors to evaluate the programs in traditional cost-effectiveness terms, on the grounds that such educational programs have payoffs not measurable, and perhaps systematically underestimated, by such approaches (Doyle and Hartle, 1985; McPherson, 1988a,b).[27]

In effect, the Reagan administration's radical proposals may have created a higher-level agreement among the 1980s' otherwise factionalized interest groups and Congress. That macro-level, pro-student-aid consensus—backed by the extensive and substantial policy infrastructure of aid officers, institutions, students, processors of financial-aid applications, state governments, and politicians of many persuasions—may have deferred efforts at targeted, information-based policy improvement in order to win larger, more immediate battles. However visible the interest groups may have been in the media, they seem not to have created major pressures for rigorous policy-analysis efforts. In turn, the Congressional leadership, faced with the challenges of ritualized yearly battles over Reagan-era cut proposals, was not wont to invest heavily in evaluations that might bring analytic support to opposing forces operating on largely ideological rather than empirical foundations. With the largely non-ideological conflict among student-aid interest groups subsumed by the broader, ideological conflicts over general aid policy fomented by the Reagan administration, the paradox of growth and disorder continued unabated.[28]

The stiff resistance of Congress to cutbacks was facilitated by the diverted political attention and ineptitude of the Reagan administration in its student-aid efforts. Former U.S. Education Secretary Terrell Bell (1988), as well as Clark and Astuto (1988), have suggested that the Reagan administration's lack of success in educational reform was in good part due to an imbalance between the rhetoric, presence, and commitment of conservative operatives and the power and skill they wielded in shaping educational policy outcomes. On the one hand, President Reagan, Martin Anderson, Edwin Meese, and David Stockman all made significant public commitments to diminishing the federal role in education and succeeded in putting in place a committed group of conservative partisans in the Department of Education bureaucracy. On the other hand, as Clark and Astuto (1988, p. 51) note:

> [T]he danger they posed to the federal government's role in education was lessened by their insignificant numbers in contrast to the numbers in civil service and by their naivete in attempting to carry out their mission. They were too radical to gain and sustain power. Those who had the power to threaten the existence of a federal role in the field (e.g., Anderson, Stockman, and Meese) had too little interest in the battle. Throughout the struggle over…eliminating basic programs

---

[27]In a more general analysis, Weiss (1991) suggests that high-level policymakers such as cabinet secretaries or legislators may favor and initiate evaluation under a number of agendas (for example, the public's right to know, or increasing efficiency), but other concerns may conflict with their actual *uses* for evaluation (for example, getting re-elected, maintaining the cooperation of the target group, negotiating a compromise among competing factions, gaining prestige and repute among members of their professional guilds, gaining legislative support, paying off political debts, satisfying constituents, and so forth). In federal student-aid policy, Congressional zeal for evaluation apparently has operated under limits of this kind.

[28]For intriguing discussions of the limited role of interest groups in recent federal education policy, see Peterson and Rabe (1983) and Rabe and Peterson (1988).

in education…, Congress was the balance wheel. Congressional leaders, it seems, were…[not] willing to modify the federal role in…radical terms.

With the administration's philosophy and overall agenda for education abundantly and publicly clear, but its attention and skills largely focused elsewhere, student-aid programs continued to persist and even grow, absent any substantial executive-branch support.

Thus, the Congress continued to dominate aid policy-making through the 1980s. Its efforts did just enough to stem the tide of the critics of the programs while not bowing to pressures to create pure, politically defining, win/lose situations for either the advocates or critics of the programs. The aid programs occupied only as much Congressional attention as was necessary to their continuation in roughly unchanged form. Writing in 1977 (p. 241), Janet Hansen noted that "[T]he politics of federal scholarships…don't seem likely to change dramatically. Incremental in movement, dominated by the equal opportunity rationale, engineered by Congress, only marginally affected by interest groups: these traits probably describe the process in the future as they have in the past…." Subsequent experience has in no way invalidated Hansen's prescient observation.

The Popularity of Student Aid

A fourth potential explanation for the paradox of concern in this chapter is that *the simple popularity of student aid with the middle class may have made both reform and retrenchment politically difficult and unlikely.* A rational model of policy action would suggest that available resources, supportive information, and demonstrable need would drive program development. That is, a program would not grow without the existence of budgetary slack, credible evidence of its effectiveness, and ongoing demand by the target population. Absent one or more of those foundations, reform and retrenchment would be expected.[29] Of course, that expectation was not met in the case of student aid. Both budgetary freedom and supportive evaluation evidence were slight. Demand, however, continued. Indeed, demand from the original target group was augmented by increasing attention to the programs from the middle class. The political popularity of education, and especially federal aid for college students, may have contributed to its persistence in the face of tight budgets and inadequate evaluation evidence. The aid programs may have been spared the axe by their attractiveness to newly served groups. In placing heavy weight on finances and information and attending little to raw politics, the rational model may slight the significance of mass public opinion.

The point has been made before. Among the more notable critics of assumptions that programs will be rationally responsive to information and that ineffective programs will be terminated and effective ones preserved are Carol Weiss (1973, 1981, 1987) and Joseph Wholey (1983).[30] They argue that, for one thing, federal social programs rarely are allowed to die: even in tight budgetary environments, although some programs may be cut, few programs are eliminated (Wholey, 1983). For another, the process of evolution is largely independent of effectiveness. Weiss reviewed the histories of federal social and educational programs over

---

[29]Shadish, Cook, and Leviton (1991) suggest that the work of Michael Scriven and Donald Campbell, in particular, fits within this general rational model.

[30]In similar, albeit more general, analyses, Lindblom (1980), Wildavsky (1979), and Ellwood (1991) have each noted that attractively rationalized decision-making processes can lead to poor political outcomes, and vice versa.

a number of years. She consistently found that "evaluative data seemed to have little effect on either budgetary allocations or the selection of programs for expansion or reduction" (1987, p. 42). Why might findings of "no-effect" not lead to program termination, or at least reform and retrenchment? The answer, Weiss suggests, lies in the political context. Even "devastating evidence of program failure has left some policies and programs unscathed, and positive evidence has not shielded others from dissolution. Clearly, other factors weigh heavily in the politics of the decision process. ... A considerable amount of ineffectiveness may be tolerated if a program fits well with prevailing values, if it satisfies voters, or if it pays off political debts" (1973, p. 40).

Such definitely seems to have been the case with the federal aid programs. A convincing argument may be made that it was neither new evidence of programmatic effectiveness nor the sudden emergence of ingenuous largesse on the part of politicians that encouraged growth in the aid programs but, rather, increasing popular demand. The sources of the demand for the aid programs expanded over time and increased the programs' political support. Consider the decline through the 1980s in the nation's number of high-school graduates aged 18 to 24. Left solely to utilization by traditionally aged college attenders enrolling in college at traditional rates, the programs would probably have actually shrunk in size over the late 1970s and the 1980s. That the programs, in fact, grew over that period shows that the programs have not fueled their growth on "automatic" benefits from an immutable demographic destiny, as noted earlier. Instead, the programs benefited from a rise in enrollment rates among the traditionally aged population for college attendance and among older cohorts as well. Of course, the quasi-entitlement nature of the programs meant that outlays would roughly parallel the growth in enrollment, and potentially even exceed that growth as increasing proportions of students enrolled as "independents" without parental support. More subtly, though, the programs attracted additional political support as their rates of client utilization expanded and as their domain of influence expanded into older groups. Many families came, for the first time, to have a college attender or college graduate in their midst. Thus, although a dilution of target-group focus might seem to make the programs more vulnerable, it actually may have made their base of support wider. The population of college students and the general population of citizens (and voters) came into substantial overlap.

In this fashion, by attending to a change in the political winds, advocates of federal-aid programs helped ensure their continuing success in budgetary deliberations. A liberal-poor coalition garnered votes for politicians in the 1960s and helped provide the initial spark for the programs. But, as Gladieux (1986) has suggested, public attention and discourse soon ceased to focus on the problems of the poor. The anti-poverty origins of the initial student-aid legislation largely faded into history, and eligibility for federal aid stretched up the economic scale. That stretching, Gladieux argues, helped popularize the programs and broadened their political base, preserving them from dire cuts, but also diluted attention to politically progressive agendas. By the late 1970s and into the 1980s, politicians' election and reelection success began to hinge more closely upon their paying attention to groups other than the poor.

Clark Kerr, widely respected higher-education leader and scholar, notes somewhat ruefully this development of the late 1970s and beyond:

I was surprised at how quickly and how greedily middle- and higher-income families insisted on sharing, at the higher educational level, the federal largesse for student aid, particularly in the Higher Education Amendments of 1978. This reduced the funds potentially available for support for students from lower-income families. Middle-class hedonism and middle-class political power triumphed. The "American dream" was interpreted less as equality of opportunity and more as "me too" than I had expected it would. (Kerr, 1991, p. 374)

Obviously, politicians in those years needed to avoid becoming victims of a nascent middle-class revolt fueled by fears of unemployment and by a sense of unfairness in entitlement and welfare programs (Wirt, 1980). Probably of equal significance, however, was politicians' need to be in tune with a dramatic upward trend in public opinions about higher-education attendance. Increasingly in the 1970s and 1980s, the nation's lower and middle classes began to view obtaining a college education as the critical pathway to individual development, opportunity, and prosperity (Elam, 1983; Yankelovich, 1987). Now, as we enter the final years of the century, the general public's faith in higher education attendance as a pathway to learning and opportunity seems largely unabated. Yankelovich (1987), for example, suggests that a growing majority of the public believes obtaining a college education is "very important," and Gallup (1985) reports that the percentage of adults believing that such education is "very" or "fairly" important rose to over 90 percent in the 1980s. According to the latter source, the percentage believing college education was "not too important" shrunk to only seven percent. That public faith seems to be valid: econometric evidence suggests that the returns to higher education attendance are good and getting better (Leslie and Brinkman, 1988).[31]

Those most in a position to know do not deny the power of mass politics in the aid programs' continuing strength. Mark Heffron, director of student-aid programs for the American College Testing Program (personal communication, March 25, 1991), says the reason for the program's growth in the face of adversity is the growing popularity of education with the general public, not solely the poor. Policy analyst Arthur Hauptman has argued that, if the aid programs are to continue, providing federal aid for the middle-class is essential; lawmakers in the 1990s, he suggests, cannot ignore the "political clout of the middle class" (Hauptman, 1991, p. B2). In a similar vein, Thomas Wolanin, staff director of the House Subcommittee on Postsecondary Education, has stressed that lawmakers are generally elected on the strength of middle-class votes and are inclined to support programs that serve that constituency. Simply put, Wolanin notes, "If you make the programs purely poverty programs, there won't be any programs" (Blumenstyk, September 11, 1991, p. A30). One can argue that Wolanin's point applies not only to the programs' political future, but also to their financially robust past as well, throughout the political challenges of the late 1970s and 1980s.

The Anarchic Qualities of Federal Policy Making

A fifth potential explanation for the paradox at the heart of this chapter is that *the failure of reform and cutback efforts may be traced to the nonlinear, "anarchic" qualities of federal policy making in education.* This explanation shares with the preceding explanation a focus on the dominance of politics over mechanical rationality. In both explanations, reform and cutback

---

[31]There are, of course, some doubts associated with the public's general faith in the merits of higher education (see the review by Alfred and Weissman, 1987).

pressures have not been matched to the politics of the time. The organized-anarchy explanation diverges from the preceding "public-popularity" explanation in its focus on organizational structure and process rather than popular roots for interpreting the paradox. Here, the idea is that the political system is insensitive to contrary evidence regarding a policy because of the nonlinear way the legislative/bureaucratic apparatuses go about getting their business done. Simply put, "selection" mechanisms for putting items on the public (political) agenda often allow good ideas to go unrewarded and weak programs to go unpunished.

As in the preceding example, a contrast with rational theory is instructive. Sabatier and Mazmanian (1979) are often cited as proponents of a linear view of policy implementation. Among the necessary ingredients for successful implementation, they propose, are a foundation of sound theory, unambiguous policy directives, leadership exhibited through managerial and political skill, support by all relevant constituencies, and continuing priority of the policy. As noted earlier, several of those ingredients have been missing to a significant degree in federal-aid policy. Rationally, one would expect such seeming failures in policy implementation to be "punished," that is, to lead to policy decline. But why, then, has that punishment not come? Why is it so hard to dismiss the argument that the Higher Education Act's first 25 years compose a history of unpunished failure in policy implementation?

Some analysts suggest that failure in federal policy implementation occurs far more often than traditionally assumed. Ideal-type rationality, they argue, is largely absent in policy implementation in the real world. For decades, scholars have noted the U.S. political systems' toleration of incrementalist decision-making, a clear violation of rational models (see, of course, Lindblom, 1980). Certainly, the aid system has been fertile ground for incrementalism. The politics in this arena are notable for the regular emergence and partial implementation of certain prescriptions: a dose of free-market privatizing here; a dose of bureaucratic/legalistic control there; a dose of error, fraud, and abuse control here; a dose of incentive management for institutional financial control here; a dose of Gramm-Rudman here; a dose of the "paperless office" there; and so on. Lost in all of these year-to-year changes are some fundamental philosophical directions that are effectively being pursued by default, in the absence of much conscious thought. Yet incrementalism falls short in describing those shifts that *have* occurred in the system, such as the rapid expansion of the programs' clientele in the 1970s to include larger numbers of the middle class.

A more radical deviation from rational models may be necessary. Several analyses have suggested that policy implementation is, in fact, *regularly,* not irregularly, unpredictable, uncertain, and chaotic. For example, Geller and Johnston (undated) note that implementation is indeed sometimes affected by the purposive actions of leaders and others, but not always and not always in directions predicted. Apropos of that, they cite the wisdom of the comic-strip character Moon Mullins (p. 8): "what you want is results, what you get is consequences." From the perspective of such analyses, there is no necessary connection between the behavioral effectiveness of a policy and its political fortunes. This point has been developed most fully in the work of John Kingdon (1984).

The Kingdon model is derived from Cohen and March's theory of organizational choice (1986). The model suggests that traditional rational or even incrementalist notions are inadequate to explain the realities of federal policy development as it typically takes place. Instead, Kingdon posits that a version of Cohen and March's organizational anarchy is present in governmental policy making. Most relevant for the present analysis are Kingdon's suggestions that comprehensive, rational policy-making is impractical, for the most part, and that incrementalism describes parts of the process but does not describe more sudden, discontinuous changes in policy agendas. Such shifts, he argues, occur often enough in federal policy to merit greater attention than they have been given in the past. In Kingdon's model, policy shifts occur when the three "process streams" flowing through the system—the streams of problems, policy proposals, and politics—are coupled. These streams are largely independent of each other, each developing according to its own dynamics and rules. When the streams do join on occasion, however, significant policy changes grow out of that connection.

At the heart of Kingdon's conception is the notion of a political selection system that, in Darwinesque fashion, determines which policy alternatives merit serious legislative attention. Problems, policies, and politics are mixed over time in unpredictable ways into "garbage cans" of policy considerations. The resulting outcomes are not necessarily connected to rationalist expectations. Regarding the policies stream, Kingdon says:

> The generation of policy proposals...resembles a process of biological natural selection. Many ideas are possible in principle, and float around in a "policy primeval soup" in which specialists try out their ideas in a variety of ways—bill introductions, speeches, testimony, papers, and conversation. In that consideration, proposals are floated, come into contact with one another, are revised and combined with one another, and floated again. But the proposals that survive to the status of serious consideration meet several criteria, including their technical feasibility, their fit with dominant values and the current national mood, their budgetary workability, and the political support or opposition they might experience. Thus the selection system narrows the set of conceivable proposals and selects from that large set a short list of proposals that is actually available for serious consideration. (p. 21)

Regarding the politics stream, Kingdon notes that it is

> composed of such factors as swings of national mood, administration or legislative turnover, and interest group pressure campaigns. Potential agenda items that are congruent with the current national mood, that enjoy interest group support or lack organized opposition, and that fit the orientations of the prevailing legislative coalitions or current administration are more likely to rise to agenda prominence than items that do not meet such conditions. (p. 21)

In Kingdon's view, items come up for action only if all three streams are coupled together in a package: problems, policies, and politics. Alternatives are generated in the policy stream, but action takes place only when there are openings in the political stream. Policy windows open and close quickly, so if action is delayed, it may never take place. In Kingdon's model, events do not proceed in stages or phases. Instead, independent streams with lives of their own become coupled when a window opens. Rationalists would expect agendas to be set first, then alternatives generated. Kingdon's view is that, in contrast, alternatives tend to be advocated fruitlessly for months or years. They become active agenda items only when a short-run opportunity, a policy window, emerges.

Returning now to the paradox of federal student aid, we can apply Kingdon's perspective to the rationalist reform proposals at the heart of the paradox of this chapter. Those reforms that *have* occurred have been in directions not generally expected from rational models. For example, the MISAA reforms of the late 1970s did not fit especially well with the policy foundations of the Higher Education Act of 1965, yet succeeded in passage through Congress. On the other hand, the efforts of a variety of reformers to simplify the programs, improve their management, and return their focus to the most needy have almost universally failed, regardless of whether the reform advocates came from the bureaucracy, the professional associations, or the interest groups, and regardless of the advocates' location on the left-right political spectrum. Using Kingdon's model, one might argue that the politics of these rationalist reform proposals have never become closely coupled to the politics of the Congressional agenda, which was focused most squarely on resistance to retrenchment and maintenance of support for existing recipient classes. What reform did occur was in response to pressures from legislators for expanded program coverage rather than in response to concerns regarding needs for greater accountability, better management information, and so forth.

In Kingdon's terms, therefore, the pattern was not atypical: a highly visible cluster of legislative and administration actors controlled the federal *agenda*. A more hidden cluster, including specialists in the bureaucracy and in professional communities, continually generated *alternatives* from which authoritative choices could be made, but none of these putatively rationalist reforms ever achieved status as a true agenda item. Policy proposals may have been rather well coupled to the problems of the programs, but they remained largely uncoupled from the ongoing politics of the programs.

Evaluating the Five Explanations

It would be simplistic to attempt here to choose one and only one explanation. Our knowledge base of the evidence is still incomplete, and there are aspects of truth in each of the five perspectives. They vary in their intended explanatory scope, with the entrenched-bureaucracy perhaps the narrowest and the organized anarchy perhaps the broadest. There is also overlap in the models. For example, there is attention to politics in each of the models, but especially in the last four: the interest-group model, the Congressional model, the public-popularity model, and the organized-anarchy model. In addition, several of the models feature aspects of the pioneering organizational theories of Simon, March, Cohen, and Allison (e.g., the focus on standard operating procedures in the entrenched-bureaucracy model, the focus on bounded rationality in the entrenched-bureaucracy model and the organized-anarchy model, the focus on limits on attention in the Congressional model and, of course, the focus on independent streams of decision making in the organized-anarchy model).[32]

Forced to choose one of the models, one would necessarily have to choose a perspective encompassing *both* the internal and external politics of the situation, as well as the institutional context out of which policies are implemented. Because the politics of Congress are undeniably paramount in the specific nature of aid legislation, the Congressional-attention model certainly cannot be dismissed. Longtime aid analyst Janet Hansen (personal communication, August 25, 1989) notes that the federal debate on student aid has been always a matter of indirection and lack of focus and suggests that a policy process dominated by Congressional rather than executive or interest-group politics may almost inevitably result in a policy arena with the paradoxical characteristics described here in the aid arena. The Congressional-attention model also has the advantage of particularity to the distinctive political context of the

---

[32]See March and Simon (1958), Allison (1971), Cohen, March, and Olsen (1979), and Cohen and March (1986).

1980s. Although inattentive to internal politics and to institutional factors, the public-pop-ularity model is strengthened by its parsimony and by its consideration of the unique place of education in the nation's core values, a factor largely unconsidered by the other perspectives. In contrast, the entrenched-bureaucracy and interest-group models largely ignore grassroots public support, focusing instead on institutionalized constraints on linear policy development and implementation. These two models add significantly to our understanding of organiza-tional and contextual factors behind the paradox. Of all the models, the organized-anarchy model, as the most inclusive, most closely fits the criterion of broad scope. Its view of the para-dox as the predictable outcome of a game involving multiple legislative, bureaucratic, and interest-centered agents is persuasive in its sweep, and resonates especially well with gen-eral perceptions of the contested aid arena of the 1980s. Therefore, although it would be a dif-ficult choice, the organized-anarchy model seems the most sensible discrete explanation. Nevertheless, one cannot dismiss the distinctive contributions of the other four models to our understanding of the processes at work in the federal aid programs' survival and growth. The analogy of different explanations to different "lenses" for viewing some phenomenon is without doubt overused in the social sciences but seems unavoidably appropriate. Each lens pro-vides some new insight on the subject at hand, and none alone is sufficient. The development of a single, more comprehensive theoretical model for understanding the paradox necessarily must await another analysis and, most likely, another analyst as well.

IMPLICATIONS

What implications flow from this analysis? Assuming that the diagnosis is essentially correct, we might simply suggest that movement toward resolving the paradox in the direction of ratio-nal public policy making is the only acceptable alternative. Hence, immediate efforts to incor-porate all of the more *controllable* aspects of the traditionally valued features of public policy would be imperative. That is, although it is impossible for policymakers to improve directly the client base, the political context, or the resource environment, it would be possible and advis-able to move the programs toward greater philosophical coherence, more linear policy devel-opment, greater programmatic clarity and distinctiveness, and expanded access to managerially needed information. This response is in many ways attractive, but it is in good part flawed: advocates' efforts along these lines have not been successful in this arena before, and such efforts may not be sufficiently sensitive to the realities of current federal policy-making. The linear, putatively "rational" model may be as problematic as we have portrayed the federal aid system itself to be. Anyone assuming such a model is both achievable and optimal may be seri-ously out of touch with what can and cannot be accomplished in Washington, and exactly how effective policy is achieved there. We are left with two workable alternatives. First, we might accept the reality of the problems but respond to the critique solely with a spirited defense of the programs' success as public policy. Second, we might accept the reality of the problems, accept the arguable success of the programs, *and* advance a vision of improvement in the arena.

Let us turn to the first response. Nothing in the present analysis is meant to preclude the very real possibility that there are substantial positive benefits from the federal effort in student aid, or even the possibility that those benefits are being achieved at socially acceptable costs.[33] Unquestionably, the programs *are* succeeding on some levels: for some people, some of the time, the programs are clearly essential for meeting legitimate educational goals, and for many they are virtually so (Leslie and Brinkman, 1988). Viewing the student-aid programs solely as clear-cut examples of failed policy implementation sells them far short. Veteran aid-policy observer Bruce Johnstone suggests,

> What we must keep in our minds is that the programs, for all of their inadequate dollars and patchwork appearance, *do* work. The system might look a little funny, at least to the first-time observer. But it is *not,* I submit, fundamentally broken. Let us fix it up. But let us not begin with the assumption that anything short of radical restructuring will represent a failure, (from an interview reprinted in Johnstone, Evans, and Jerue, 1990, p. 33, italics in original)

Johnstone's point, and the similar argument by Keppel (1987), are in keeping with a growing literature challenging the pessimistic accounts of the effectiveness of "Great Society" social and educational policy. Several analysts have suggested that it has become far too easy in recent years to accept the notion that such policies have failed: the conventional wisdom notwithstanding, such conclusions are based on inadequate0 understanding of the complex evidence on program effects, misinterpretation of the original expectations of policymakers, and reliance on an excessively short time perspective (e.g., see Haveman, 1977; Aaron, 1978). Peterson and Rabe (1988, p. 484) note that:

> [Much of the recent criticism of federal policy [is] overdrawn. The spate of criticisms of federal programs was spawned by an era that had both the highest expectations and the most severe cynicism about U.S. institutions. To be sure, such reactions were invited by the lofty claims of Great Society enthusiasts who wrote extraordinarily far-reaching objectives into the laws they passed. That no serious government official ever expected these objectives to be more than decently approached was, however, underappreciated by those analysts who found a great disjunction between what Washington promised and what Peoria experienced.

Advice that we be cautious in scientific and historical analyses of federal programs, proud of their accomplishments, and zealous in our defense of their continuation, is certainly proper and welcome. Is the muting of any criticism of the programs also proper and welcome, however? Some partisans of the federal student-aid programs undoubtedly would answer yes, fearing that any criticism of the programs within the political context of the 1980s and 1990s will serve mainly to weaken Congressional support for the programs, and that curtailing that support could disadvantage innumerable deserving students. This argument for avoiding any direct, visible criticisms of the federal student-aid programs is more subtle than one might first surmise. Federal aid to higher education has always been rather indirect, granted more in the service of other goals than as part of any truly comprehensive higher-education policy (Moynihan, 1975b; Schuster, 1982). David Reisman has suggested to Daniel Patrick Moynihan (cited in Moynihan, 1975b, p. 130) that higher education actually benefits from the indirectness and invisibility of the federal government's aid to it, noting that higher education's vulnerability to assault is so great that the more "obscurity and obscurantism in the forms in which aid is channeled to higher education," the more secure that aid will be. Scrutiny of higher education is not always in its best interest, this view implies. From this perspective, we seem best advised to continue in largely uncritical reaffirmations of the programs, thereby avoiding the possibility that we might inadvertently provide the tools for their ultimate demise.

---

[33]Indeed, I believe that systematic evaluation evidence, once collected, will tend to support the defense of the programs as social policy.

An alternative response to this chapter's critique seems more comprehensive, more reasonable, and more constructive, however. The alternative response begins in agreement with the first response: there is much to be praised and preserved in the current efforts. The response diverges in its movement toward prescription. Rather than accept the paradox and settle for tinkering at the margins with admitted programmatic flaws, this response conceives of movement toward a more reflective policy-making, policy-delivery, policy-evaluation style.

At the heart of the response is the notion of not simply ignoring the paradox or adjusting grudgingly to it but, rather, embracing it and working productively within its constraints. The response seeks to blend somehow the appeal of the traditional rational focus on information, deliberation, and calculation, on the one hand, with the necessity and undeniable value of politicized and market-driven decision-making in democratic society, on the other. The genesis of this idea lies in the work of Lindblom (1977) and Wildavsky (1979) in the years after the discovery of "incrementalism" in public policy and planning. In separately conceived, but similarly focused essays in the late 1970s, these well-respected theorists suggested that there are two general ways in which public policy proceeds: one the more rational style of planning and analysis, the other the more rough and tumble style of politics and the marketplace. Wildavsky terms these, respectively, the "intellectual cognition" and "social interaction styles." The intellectual-cognition style proceeds as though society functioned with a single mind, was comprehensive in its concerns, systematically acted to avoid error, chose what was correct, and executed its decisions via orders. In contrast, the social-interaction style proceeds as though largely ungoverned political and economic interplay among people and organizations is the societal norm, without community concern over collective consequences, without substantial forethought, and with achieving agreement (rather than correctness or probity) as the criterion for successful decision-making. Neither decision style is ideal, Wildavsky argues, and each has it place. In the real world of day-to-day political struggle, Wildavsky asserts, cognition should serve to restrain, but not replace, social interaction. Social interaction is often imperfect as a problem-solving approach, but it is also usually essential.

Placed in the context of federal student aid, Wildavsky's idea of dual modes may help inform our understanding of the paradox. It seems reasonable to argue that the paradox stems from an excessive domination of the social-interaction mode over the cognition mode. In the rationalist terms of Sabatier and Mazmanian (1979, 1983), implementation problems certainly exist in federal student aid. Those problems may, nonetheless, be more a matter *of imbalance in the two decision-making modes* than a matter of fatal implementation failure—a case of political and market forces overpowering the intellectual mode. What may be necessary is not so much a full-scale retreat from these largely unexamined, inadequately managed, and heavily politicized federal programs as a re-emphasis on the necessity of cool-headed analysis to support them.

In keeping with that view, Browne and Wildavsky (1984a and 1984b) suggest that policy implementation is best conceived not as a well-planned, linear journey, from a clear policy to a predictable institutionalization in national life but, rather, as an ongoing process of learning and adaptation. Because there are complex interactions between policies and their implementation, successful implementation includes both forward and backward "mapping," that is, prospective and retrospective assessments of obstacles to policy success.[34] Prospective mapping allows one to design policies in advance in ways that minimize the risks of failure; retrospective mapping allows one to cope once failures have begun to occur. Here, failures are part of an ongoing exploratory process which forsakes the traditional "unquestioning, uninquiring, myopic stance" of the organization that solely seeks to impose its own predetermined techniques on eternally intractable social problems (Browne and Wildavsky, 1984b, p. 255). Browne and Wildavsky's ideal is a process of mutual learning and adaptation wherein policy means, and even policy goals, are continually revised in light of policy experience. In Browne and Wildavsky's vision, ongoing evaluation that is inclusive of both forward and backward mapping is critical for the organization:

> Evaluation that is insensitive to the problems of transforming policy makers' ideas into implementers' actions is obtuse; it leaves the best bits...unexamined. Evaluators who hold implementers accountable for each increment of this transformation and nothing else are, in essence, only accountants. Without denying the importance of evaluation studies, there should also be an appreciation of evaluation as continuous learning. Locating all evaluation along a continuum, accountability will approach one extreme while learning-oriented evaluation, searching for experience, falls toward the other....Accountability seeks to preserve existing relationships by holding the actors at the bottom responsible to the expectations at the top. Learning evaluation strives to unearth faulty assumptions, reshape misshapen policy designs and continuously redefine goals in light of new information derived during implementation, (ibid.)

In reconceptualizing implementation as "an exploratory rather than an unquestioning, instrumental, or even subservient type of behavior," Browne and Wildavsky (1984b) suggest that those who hold the federal programs to a traditional accountability standard are, in essence, asking less of them, not more.[35] To be poorly accountable is less harmful, and less dangerous, than to be poorly evaluated.

From this perspective, the seeming paradox in the federal student-aid programs may be due to the adoption of an overly limited vision of policy success and policy development. Policy partisans and foes alike may legitimately be saddened by the existence of the problems highlighted in this chapter. But to focus upon the most manipulable of those problems (i.e., philosophical coherence, policy development, programmatic clarity and distinctiveness, and access to managerially needed information) merely as matters of specific managerial failings is to miss the point. The need to be addressed is more a matter of improving governance than of improving management. The maw of politics and markets is not to be eliminated or avoided, only confronted more directly. Good decisions need not, and do not, flow only from purely rationalist contexts and premises, and good politics need not, and do not, flow only from good politicians. Wildavsky (1979) introduced and championed the concept of the "self-evaluating" public organization. In doing so, he did not mean to imply that it was reasonable to assume that public bureaucracies and legislatures could somehow be moved to place evaluation analysis at the heart of their affairs, as the sole guide to their actions. Rather, he meant to suggest that knowledge could and should play a greater role in those affairs, as a counterbalance to the ongoing play of politics and markets. In federal student aid, successfully addressing the paradox may be more a matter of correcting an imbalance by emphasizing

---

[34]The mapping notion employed by Browne and Wildavsky is the creation of Richard F. Elmore (1982).

[35]Also see Browne and Wildavsky, 1984a. In a similar vein, Liggett (1990), in an essay also questioning the traditional valuing of foresight and stability in policy development, suggests that the tendency for a given social policy to "wander off" and generate new meanings at various stages in its history is generally condemned by both practitioners and analysts but should, in fact, be praised as both adaptive and useful.

self-critical knowledge development than a matter of abandoning an essentially defensible policy direction.

In concluding this essay, and especially in considering its broader implications, it seems important that I re-emphasize a point stressed by Lindblom, Weiss, Wildavsky, and innumerable other policy theorists: there is nothing new about discovering contradictions, complexity, disorder, and indirection in government policy. The intentions of the present analysis are not to disabuse anyone of wide-eyed notions of the dominance of rationality in policy design and delivery. In this arena, few naifs remain. What *is* needed, however, is more comprehensive understanding of the emergence of such patterns and of the imperviousness of some policies to their persistence. Historically and politically directed analysis can help to provide that understanding.

That having been said, it seems reasonable to suggest that the approach taken in this inquiry may well be applied to other policy-related paradoxes in higher education. In particular, the five hypothesized explanatory lenses may well be extended or modified to address perplexing questions in such other arenas as university planning (e.g., why do certain academic programs persist despite unfavorable external reviews, small enrollments, and noncentral missions?), research funding (e.g., why do universities, foundations, and the federal government sometimes provide a continuing stream of scarce resources to research efforts seemingly having only marginal payoffs?), and the coordinating efforts of states and accrediting agencies (e.g., why do some small, underenrolled institutions continue to be certified and allowed to stay open?). The influences of politics, bureaucratic infrastructures, and anarchic decision contexts may play no small role in the persistence of such seeming paradoxes. It is neither difficult nor especially comforting to draw these parallels between these higher-education paradoxes and the aforementioned paradoxes in federal educational policy efforts, but doing so may be profoundly useful.

Returning to the present analysis, it appears that *25* years may have been far too long a time to hold fast to consistent policy goals and delivery approaches in a broadly defined, value-laden, bureaucratically complex, politically sensitive domain like postsecondary educational policy at the federal level. At a critical time in their development, federal student-aid policies were set adrift from some of their original moorings. That they survived this transition, endured the absence of many hypothetically necessary policy features, and persisted in their fiscal support makes for a remarkable story worth ongoing scholarly attention.

EPILOGUE[36]

Although the history recounted in this chapter ended in 1990, developments since that time merit attention. As the reauthorization of 1992 approached, there was ample promise of rationally oriented reform on the horizon, emanating from both political parties (see Saunders, 1991; DeLoughry, 1990, 1991a, b, c, and d; "Washington Update," February 6, 1991; "Middle-class maneuvers...," 1991). Congressional debates concerning the federal student-aid programs were focusing on some of the core issues behind the paradox introduced in this chapter. The Bush administration was suggesting shifting some aid resources from middle-income

---

[36]This Epilogue was written for the original 1993 version of this chapter. The new Epilogue, written especially for this volume, begins on page 316.

families to lower-income families. Administration officials were also seeking to improve program development, management, and delivery by taking "tougher" attitudes, focusing on program cost-effectiveness, and more closely involving the Office of Management and Budget [0MB] in deliberations concerning student aid. While Republican legislators generally lined up with the administration on such reforms, those in the majority party did not. Democratic leaders on student-aid issues were suggesting that Congress consider making freshmen ineligible for loans but eligible for larger Pell Grants, making Pell Grants an entitlement for all students who needed them, phasing out the Perkins Loan program (formerly the NDSL program) to simplify the programs and create savings for SEOGs, making all postsecondary students (regardless of family income) eligible for federally guaranteed loans, and paying for any additional spending by instituting a new "millionaire's tax." In late 1991 and early 1992, leaders of both parties were also seriously considering a proposal to make a financially significant distinction in federal student-aid policy between the offerings, certification, and students of purely vocational institutions (e.g., proprietary schools) and the offerings, certification, and students of more traditional higher-education institutions.[37]

Of course, rationalizing reform has always been in the air when the legislative calendar calls for reauthorizing the Higher Education Act. As the actual reauthorization legislation of 1992 took final shape, each of the above proposals died aborning (DeLoughry, 1992b). The one bold proposal that did not die outright, a call for eliminating private financial institutions' participation in the loan programs by making loans directly through colleges, won approval only in a significantly watered-down "demonstration" format. The final result of the reauthorization of 1992 was, therefore, essentially reform at the margin of existing program and policy features.[38] In response to the disappointments of 1992, aid analyst Art Hauptman noted that "It just seems that this process is in microcosm what's wrong with the American government (DeLoughry, 1992a, p. A34). At the time of this writing (mid-1992), the prospects for significant change in the federal student-aid programs seem quite limited. Widely lamented problems in aid policy have been left unaddressed, and no federal leaders are proposing substantial movement toward a greater knowledge-building orientation in the aid programs. Most likely, the paradox will persist.

Acknowledgments

Janet Hansen, formerly of the Washington office of the College Board and now of the National Research Council, read two earlier versions of this chapter and made innumerable valuable suggestions, especially focusing on the history of student financial aid as a concern of federal policy. Mark Heffron of the American College Testing Program, Robert Fenske of Arizona

---

[37]Aid-policy expert Janet Hansen (personal communication, November 2, 1991) has suggested that major policy change in the federal student-aid arena tends to take place largely *outside* of Congressional reauthorization hearings nowadays, unlike 20 years ago. There currently seems to be no major reform activity in the non-Congressional arena, however.

[38]Saunders (1992) is more sanguine about the results of the 1992 reauthorization, but even he expresses disappointment about the "gridlock" frustrating further reform. Koltai (1992) also blends disappointment and hope. Blaming the failures of the 1992 reauthorization effort both on the lack of a federal "blueprint" on aid policy and on the strength of anti-reform lobbying, he expresses optimism regarding for the work of the recently formed National Commission on Responsibilities for Financing Postsecondary Education

State University, and Thomas Flint of Robert Morris College also provided useful first-hand perspectives on that history. Melissa Anderson, John Bryson, David Karen, Tim Mazzoni, Gary Rhoades, John Smart, and Robert Stout each helped with conceptual criticisms and suggestions at various stages of the work. Sharon Wilford provided excellent research assistance on the direct predecessor of this chapter—a 1985 consulting project undertaken for the Twentieth Anniversary Observance of the Signing of the U.S. Higher Education Act. Finally, Sammy Parker provided fine editorial assistance. The author gratefully acknowledges the contributions of each, while holding none responsible for the final product.

References

Aaron, H. J. (1978). *Politics and the Professors: The Great Society in Perspective.* Washington, DC: Brookings Institution.

Advisory Committee on Student Financial Assistance. (1990, July) *Ensuring Access: Challenges in Student Aid in the 1990s.* Washington, DC: Author.

Alfred, R. L., and Weissman, J. (1987). *Higher Education and the Public Trust: Improving Stature in Colleges and Universities.* (ASHE-ERIC Higher Education Report No. 6.) Washington, DC: Association for the Study of Higher Education.

Allison, G. T. (1971). *Essence of Decision.* Boston: Little-Brown.

Bachrach, P., and Baratz, M. S. (1962). Two faces of power. *American Political Science Review* 86: 947-952.

Bell, T. H. (1988). *The Thirteenth Man: A Reagan Cabinet Memoir.* New York: Free Press.

Bennett, W. J. (1985, April 15). Letter to the Honorable George Bush, President of the Senate.

Blumenstyk, G. (1991, September 11). States urged to redirect spending on public colleges from tuition subsidies to support for needy students. *Chronicle of Higher Education* XXXVIII(3): A29-30.

Brademas, J. (1987). *The Politics of Education: Conflict and Consensus on Capitol Hill.* Norman: University of Oklahoma Press.

Brandl, J. E. (1988). On politics and policy analysis as the design and assessment of institutions. *Journal of Policy Analysis and Management* 7(3): 419-424.

Browne, A., and Wildavsky, A. (1984a). Implementation as mutual adaptation. In J. Pressman and A. Wildavsky, *Implementation* (3rd ed.). Berkeley: University of California Press.

Browne, A., and Wildavsky, A. (1984b). Implementation as exploration. In J. Pressman and A. Wildavsky. *Implementation* (3rd ed.). Berkeley: University of California Press.

Brubacher, J. S., and Rudy, W. (1976). *Higher Education in Transition* (3rd ed.). New York: Harper and Row.

Carnegie Council on Policy Studies in Higher Education. (1979). *Next Steps for the 1980s in Student Financial Aid.* Berkeley: Author.

Cerych, L. (1979). Higher education reform: The process of implementation. *Education Policy Bulletin* 7: 5-21.

Clark, D. L., and Astuto, T. A. (1988, September/October). The accidental secretary: Education policy and the Reagan years (review of *The Thirteenth Man*, by T. Bell). *Change* 5(20): 50-52.

Cohen, W. J. (1977). Discussion of Henry Levin's paper, "A decade of policy developments in improving education and training for low-income populations." In R. H. Haveman (ed.), *A Decade of Federal Antipoverty Programs: Achievements, Failures, and Lessons.* New York: Academic Press.

Cohen, M. D., and March, J. G. (1986). *Leadership and Ambiguity: The American College President* (2nd ed.). Cambridge, MA: Harvard Business School Press.

Cohen, M. D., March, J. G., and Olsen, J. P. (1979). People, problems, solutions and the ambiguity of relevance. In J. G. March and J. P. Olsen (eds.), *Ambiguity and Choice in Organizations.* Bergen, Norway: Universitetsforlaget.

College Board, The. (1990). *Trends in Student Aid: 1980 to 1990.* Washington, DC: The College Board.

Collison, M. (1988, July 6). Complex application form discourages many students from applying for federal financial aid, officials say. *Chronicle of Higher Education* XXXIV(43): Al, A30.

Dahl, R. A. (1961). *Who Governs?* New Haven: Yale. Dearman, N. B., and Plisko, V. W. (1979, April). Comparisons of public perceptions of education with the current status of education. Paper presented at the annual meeting of the American Educational Research Association, San Francisco.

DeLoughry, T. J. (1990, October 3). Administration eyes linking student aid to academic record. *Chronicle of Higher Education* XXXVII(5): Al, A28.

DeLoughry, T. J. (1991a, March 20). Budget office makes crucial decisions on education policy. *Chronicle of*

Higher Education XXXVII(27): A23, A26, A27.

DeLoughry, T. J. (1991b, April 17). U.S. seeks overhaul of its student aid management; Poor supervision has added to abuses, report says. *Chronicle of Higher Education* XXXVII(31): A20, A26.

DeLoughry, T. J. (1991c, November 13). A tough-talking former businessman rankles colleges with his effort to clean up U.S. student-aid programs. *Chronicle of Higher Education* XXXVIII(12): A31, A34.

DeLoughry, T. J. (1991d, December 18). Congress preparing "Get tough" rules on aid to students. *Chronicle of Higher Education* XXXVIII(17): A1, A28-29. DeLoughry, T. J. (1992a, April 22). College officials say politics and budgetary constraints have doomed Reauthorization bill's promise of reform. *Chronicle of Higher Education* XXXVIII(33): A29, A34-35.

DeLoughry, T. J. (1992b, July 8). President and Congress agree on bill to reauthorize Higher Education Act. *Chronicle of Higher Education* XXXVIII(44): A15, A25.

Doyle, D. P., and Hartle, T. (1985, July/August). Facing the fiscal chopping block: It's time to rethink student aid. *Change* 17(4): 8-10, 54-56.

Elam, S. M. (1983). The Gallup Education Surveys: Impressions of a poll watcher. *Phi Delta Kappan* (September): 26-47.

Elmore, R. F. (1982). Backward mapping: Implementation research and policy decisions. In W. Williams et al. (eds.), *Studying Implementation: Methodological and Administrative Issues.* Chatham, NJ: Chatham House.

Ellwood, J. W. (1991). Symposium comment: On the new politics of public policy. *Journal of Policy Analysis and Management* 10(3): 426-433.

Evangelauf, J. (1988, November 9). Revamping of financial aid called vital for low-income and minority students. *Chronicle of Higher Education* XXXV(11): A1, A37.

Fenske, R. H. (1983). Student aid past and present. In R. H. Fenske, R. P. Huff, and Associates, *Handbook of Student Financial Aid.* San Francisco: Jossey-Bass.

Fenske, R. H., Huff, R. P., and Associates. (1983). *Handbook of Student Financial Aid.* San Francisco: Jossey-Bass.

Fields, C. M. (1985a, November 13). 20th birthday of Higher Education Act celebrated in Texas. *Chronicle of Higher Education* XXXI(11): 20.

Fields, C. M. (1985b, November 20). Texas celebration is tinged with fear Johnson's legacy may be dissipated. *Chronicle of Higher Education* XXXI(12): 1, 12-14.

Fife, J. D. (1975). *Applying the Goals of Student Financial Aid.* (AAHE/ERIC Higher Education Research Report No. 10.) Washington, DC: American Association for Higher Education.

Finn, C. E. (1980, September). The future of education's liberal consensus, *Change* 12(6): 25-30.

Finn, C. E. (1990, March/April). Two decades inside the Beltway. *Change* 22(2): 58-63.

Fitzgerald, B. K. (1991, Summer). Simplification of need analysis and aid delivery: Imperatives and opportunities. In Jamie P. Merisotis (ed.) *New Directions for Higher Education: The Changing Dimensions of Student Aid,* No. 74: 43-63. San Francisco: Jossey-Bass.

Flint, T. A. (1991). Historical notes on regulation in the federal student assistance programs. *Journal of Student Financial Aid* 21 (1): 33-47.

Gallup Organization, The. (1985). *Public Opinion Survey: Attitudes Toward Higher Education.* Princeton, NJ: Author.

Geller, H. A., and Johnston, A. P. (undated). Exploring the limits of policy science. Unpublished monograph, University of Vermont, Burlington, VT.

Gillespie, D. A., and Carlson, N. (1983). *Trends in Student Aid: 1963 to 1983.* Washington, DC: The College Entrance Examination Board.

Gladieux, L. E. (1983, Winter). The future of student financial aid. *The College Board Review* 126: 2-12.

Gladieux, L. E. (1986, May). Student aid and educational opportunity: Past commitments, future uncertainties. Paper presented to the New Jersey Board of Higher Education Conference on Student Financial Assistance, Jamesburg, New Jersey.

Gladieux, L. E., and Wolanin, T. R. (1976). *Congress and the Colleges: The National Politics of Higher Education.* Lexington, MA: Lexington (Heath).

The Great Society: An exchange. (1985, April 8) *New Republic.* 21-23.

Guthrie, J. W. (1985). The educational policy consequences of economic instability: The emerging political economy of American education. *Educational Evaluation and Policy Analysis* 7(4): 319-332.

Hall, P. (1982). *Great Planning Disasters.* Berkeley: University of California Press.

Hansen, J. S. (1977). The politics of federal scholarships: A case study of the development of general grant assistance for undergraduates. Unpublished doctoral dissertation, The Woodrow Wilson School, Princeton University.

Hansen, W. L., and Stampen, J. O. (1987). Economics and financing of higher education: The tension between quality and equity. In P. G. Altbach and R. O. Berdahl (eds.), *Higher Education in American Society* (revised ed). New York: Prometheus.

Hartle, T. W., and Stedman, J. B. (1986). Federal programs: A view of the Higher Education Act. In M. P. McKeown and K. Alexander (eds.), *Values in Conflict: Funding Priorities for Higher Education.* Cambridge, MA: Ballinger.

Hauptman, A. M. (1991, March 20). Financial incentives, not regulation, are needed to reform the student-aid process. *Chronicle of Higher Education* XXXVII(25): B2-B3.

Haveman, R. H. (ed.). (1977). *A Decade of Federal Antipoverty Programs: Achievements, Failures, and Lessons.* New York: Academic Press.

Hearn, J. C., and Wilford, S. (1985, November). *A Commitment to Opportunity: The Impacts of Federal Student Aid Programs.* Invited report prepared for the Twentieth Anniversary Observance of the Signing of the U.S. Higher Education Act of 1965, San Marcos, Texas, November, 1985. Report submitted under a consulting contract with the Texas Guaranteed Student Loan Corporation.

Hearn, J. C., and Anderson, M. S. (1989). Integrating postsecondary education financing policies: The Minnesota model. In R. H. Fenske, (ed.), *New Directions in Institutional Research: Studying the Impact of Student Aid on Institutions,* No. 62: 55-73. San Francisco: Jossey-Bass.

Honey, J. C. (1972, December 22). The election, politics, and higher education. *Science* 178(4067): 1243.

Johnston, R. A., Schwartz, S. I., and Klinkner, T. (1978). Successful plan implementation: The growth phasing program of Sacramento County. *AIP Journal* 44:412-423.

Johnstone, D. B., Evans, S. V., and Jerue, R. T. (1990, Summer). Reauthorization: What's important, what's not. *Educational Record* 71(3): 29-33.

Kagan, R. A. (1991). Adversarial legalism and American government. *Journal of Policy Analysis and Management* 10(3): 369-406.

Karen, D. (1991, February). The politics of class, race, and gender: Access to higher education in the United States, 1960-1986. *American Journal of Education* 99(2): 208-237.

Keppel, F. (1987). The Higher Education Acts contrasted, 1965-1986: Has federal policy come of age? *Harvard Educational Review* 57(1): 49-67.

Kerr, C. (1991). *The Great Transformation in Higher Education: 1960-1980.* Albany, NY: SUNY Press.

Kingdon, J. W. (1984). *Agendas, Alternatives and Public Policies.* Boston: Little Brown.

Koltai, L (1992, May 20). Letter to the Editor. *Chronicle of Higher Education* XXX-VIII(37): B5.

Leslie, L. L. (1977). *Higher Education Opportunity: A Decade of Progress.* (ERIC/ AAHE Higher Education Research Report No. 3.) Washington, DC: American Association for Higher Education.

Leslie, L. L., and Brinkman, P. (1988). *The Economic Value of Higher Education.* New York: Macmillan.

Levin, H. (1977). A decade of policy developments in improving education and training for low-income populations. In R. H. Haveman (ed.),/4 *Decade of Federal Antipoverty Programs: Achievements, Failures, and Lessons.* New York: Academic Press.

Liggett, H. (1990). The verbal usury model: A post-structuralist approach to policy analysis. In J. N. Stanfield II and P. Takich (eds.), *Research in Social Policy,* Volume 2. Greenwich, CT: JAI Press.

Lindblom, C. E. (1977). *Politics and Markets: The World's Political and Economic Systems.* New York: Basic Books.

Lindblom, C. E. (1980). *The Policy-Making Process* (2nd ed.). Englewood Cliffs, NJ: Prentice-Hall.

Lowi, T. J. (1969). *The End of Liberalism.* New York: Norton.

March, J. G., and Simon, H. A. (1958). *Organizations.* New York: Wiley.

McDonnell, L. M., and Elmore, R. F. (1987). Getting the job done: Alternative policy instruments. *Educational Evaluation and Policy Analysis* 9(2): 133-152.

McPherson, M. S. (1988a). On assessing the impact of federal student aid. *Economics of Education Review* 7(1): 77-84.

McPherson, M. S. (1988b). *How Can We Tell If Federal Student Aid Is Working?* Washington, DC: The College Entrance Examination Board.

McPherson, M. S. (1989). Appearance and reality in the Guaranteed Student Loan Program. In L.E. Gladieux (ed.), *Radical Reform or Incremental Change?: Student Loan Policy Alternatives for the Federal Government.* Washington, DC: The College Entrance Examination Board.

McPherson, M. S., and M. O. Schapiro (1991). *Keeping College Affordable: Government and Educational Opportunity.* Washington, DC: Brookings.

Middle-class maneuvers: How the Democrats are playing for new voters. (1991, August 12). *Newsweek:* 27.

Miles, R. H., and Cameron, K. S. (1982). *Coffin Nails and Corporate Strategies.* Englewood Cliffs, NJ: Prentice-Hall.

Mortenson, T. G. (1990). *The Reallocation of Financial Aid from Poor to Middle Income and Affluent Students - 1978 to 1990.* Iowa City, IA: American College Testing Program.

Moynihan, D. P. (1975a). *Coping: On the Practice of Government.* New York: Random House, Vintage Books.

Moynihan, D. P. (1975b, Winter). The politics of higher education. *Daedalus* 104: 128-147.

Mumper, M. and Vander Ark, P. (1991). Evaluating the Stafford Student Loan Program: Current problems and prospects for reform. *Journal of Higher Education* 62(1): 62-78.

Murray, C. (1984). *Losing Ground: American Social Policy, 1950-1980.* New York: Basic.

Orfield, G. (1975). *Congressional Power: Congress and Social Change.* New York: Harcourt, Brace Jovanovich.

Padgett, J. F. (1981). Hierarchy and ecological control in federal budgetary decision making. *American Journal of Sociology* 87(1): 75-129.

Palmer, S. E. (1986, January 22). How many students got aid from U.S.? Nobody knows, and that's worrisome. *Chronicle of Higher Education* XXXI(19): 13, 17.

Pell, C. (1989). A two-tiered system is unfair. *The College Board News* (Summer): 5-6.

Perrow, C. (1986). *Complex Organizations: A Critical Essay* (3rd ed.). New York: Random House.

Peterson, P. E., and Rabe, B. G. (1988). The evolution of a new cooperative federalism. In N. J. Boyan (ed.), *Handbook of Research on Educational Administration.* New York: Longman.

Peterson, P. E., and Rabe, B. G. (1983). The role of interest groups in the formation of educational policy: Past practice and future trends. *Teacher's College Record* 84(3): 708-729.

Pfeffer, J. (1981). *Power in Organizations.* Boston: Pitman. Post, D. (1990). College-going decisions by Chicanos: The politics of misinformation. *Educational Evaluation and Policy Analysis* 12(2): 174-187.

Post, D. (1990). College-going decisions by Chicanos: The politics of misinformation. *Educational Evaluation and Policy Analysis* (12)2: 174-187.

Pressman, J., and Wildavsky, A. (1984). *Implementation* (3rd ed.). Berkeley: University of California.

Rabe, B. G., and Peterson, P. E. (1988). The evolution of a new cooperative federalism. In N. J. Boyan (ed.), *The Handbook of Research on Educational Administration.* New York: Longman.

The Reagan Years: How much the President requested for 5 education and research programs, and how much Congress appropriated. (1988, November 9). *Chronicle of Higher Education* XXXV(ll): A23.

Rodgers, H. R., and Bullock, C. S. (1972). *Law and Social Change.* New York: McGraw-Hill.

Rodgers, H. R., and Bullock, C. S. (1976). *Coercion to Compliance.* Lexington, MA: Heath.

Sabatier, P., and Mazmanian, D. (1979). The conditions of successful implementation: A guide to accomplishing policy objectives. *Policy Studies Review Annual* 4: 181-203.

Sabatier, P., and Mazmanian, D. (1983). Policy implementation. In S.S. Nagel (ed.), *Encyclopedia of Policy Studies.* New York: Marcel Dekker.

Saunders, C. B. (1991, April 3). The broadest changes in student aid in 25 years could be part of education amendments of 1992. *Chronicle of Higher Education* XXX-VII(29): B1-B2.

Saunders, C. B. (1992, June 3). Letter to the Editor. *Chronicle of Higher Education* XXXVIII(39): B4.

Schuster, J. H. (1982). Out of the frying pan: The politics of education in a new era. *Phi Delta Kappan* (May): 583-591.

Senate bars Reagan plan to curb aid; Votes $11.2 billion extra for education. (1986, April l 30). *Chronicle of Higher Education* XXXII(9): 11, 13.

17 Changes in 4 years: Johns Hopkins grapples with new loan rules. (1990, December 5). *Chronicle of Higher Education* XXXVII(14): A24.

Shadish, W. R. Jr., Cook, T. D., and Leviton, L. C. (eds.). (1991). *Foundations of Program Evaluation: Theories of Practice.* Newbury Park, CA: Sage.

Smith, M. S., and Jenkins, J. W. (1983). Higher education legislation. In H. E. Mitzel (ed.), *The Encyclopedia of Educational Research* (5th ed.). New York: Free Press (Macmillan).

Sproull, L. S., Weiner, S. S., and Wolf, D. (1978). *Organizing an Anarchy: Belief, Bureaucracy, and Politics in the National Institute of Education.* Chicago: University of Chicago.

Stampen, J. O. (1984). Evaluating student aid in a political advocacy system: In search of a better way. *Journal of Student Financial Aid* 14(3): 3-18.

Stampen, J. O. (1987). Historical perspective on federal and state financial aid. In California Postsecondary Education Commission, *Conversations about Financial Aid.* Sacramento, CA: California Postsecondary Education Commission.

Stampen, J. O., and Reeves, R. W. (1986). Coalitions in the Senates of the 96th and 97th Congresses. *Congress and the Presidency* 13(2): 188-208.

Student aid administrators seek relief from rules designed to cut defaults. (1990, December 5). *Chronicle of Higher Education* XXXVII(14): A21, A24.

U.S. Bureau of the Census. (1980 through 1990). *Current Population Reports.* Washington, DC: U.S. Government Printing Office.

U.S. Department of Education. (1988). *Undergraduate Financing of Postsecondary Education.* Washington, DC: U.S. Government Printing Office.

U.S. Department of Education. (1990). *Digest of Education Statistics.* Washington, DC: U.S. Government Printing Office.

U.S. Office of Management and Budget. (1985). *Background on Major Spending Reforms and Reductions in the FY 1986 Budget.* Washington, DC: U.S. Government Printing Office.

Van Dusen, W. D. (1978). *The Coming Crisis in Student Aid.* Queenstown, MD: Aspen Institute for Humanistic Studies.

Washington Update. (1991, February 6). *Chronicle of Higher Education* XXXVII(21): A24

Weatherly, R., and Lipsky, M. (1977). Street-level bureaucrats and institutional innovation: Implementing special-education reform. *Harvard Education Review* 47: 171-197.

Weisbrod, B. (1977). Discussion of Henry Levin's paper, "A decade of policy developments in improving education and training for low-income populations." In R. H. Haveman (ed.),/4 *Decade of Federal Antipoverty-Programs: Achievements, Failures, and Lessons.* New York: Academic Press.

Weiss, C. H. (1973). Where politics and evaluation research meet. *Evaluation* 1: 37-45.

Weiss, C. H. (1981). Measuring the use of evaluation. In J. A. Ciarlo (ed.), *Utilizing Evaluation: Concepts and Measurement Techniques.* Beverly Hills, CA: Sage.

Weiss, C. H. (1987). Evaluating social programs: What have we learned? *Society* 25(1): 40-45.

Weiss, C. H. (1991). Evaluation research in the political context: Sixteen years and four administrations later. In M. W. McLaughlin and D. C. Phillips (eds.), *Evaluation and Education: At Quarter Century,* Part II. Chicago: The National Society for the Study of Education.

Whitt, E. J., Clark, D. L., and Astuto, T. A. (1986, December). An analysis of public support for the educational policy preferences of the Reagan administration. Published as Occasional Paper No. 3 by the Policy Studies Center of the University Council for Educational Administration, University of Virginia, Charlottesville.

Wholey, J. S. (1983). *Evaluation and Effective Public Management.* Boston: Little-Brown.

Wildavsky, A. (1979). *Speaking Truth to Power: The Art and Craft of Policy Analysis.* Boston: Little, Brown, and Company.

Wildavsky, A. (1984). *The Politics of the Budgetary Process.* Fourth edition. Boston: Little, Brown, and Company.

Wilensky, H. L. (1975). *The Welfare State and Equality: Structural and Ideological Roots of Public Expenditures.* Berkeley: University of California Press.

Wirt, F. (1980). Neoconservatism and national school policy. *Educational Evaluation and Policy Analysis* 2(6): 5-18.

With warmth and nostalgia, Lyndon Johnson's admirers recall his campaign for the Higher Education Act of 1965. (1990, April 11). *Chronicle of Higher Education* XXXVI (30): A23, A26.

Yankelovich, D. (1987). Bridging the gap. *CASE Currents* 13(9): 25-27.

Epilogue[39]

The "Paradox" examined in this chapter emerged in an unusual, and perhaps instructive, way. In the late 1980s, a talented University of Minnesota doctoral student with strong interest in postsecondary educational opportunity issues was gracefully navigating her way through her oral preliminary examination. Her answers to faculty questions were well-considered and largely unassailable. As a member of her examining committee, I was straining to come up with a question that would enliven our time together. As she answered yet another of our questions skillfully, I jotted down what would become the

---

[39]The author appreciates the helpful comments of Ed St. John on an earlier version of this Epilogue

core question of this chapter's essay: why did federal student-aid programs exhibit such remarkable growth in the face of a welter of problematic characteristics? When I asked this question, the student did at least pause a bit, and our ensuing discussion was a bit more lively than before. None of us felt we had reached closure, however, and afterwards, a fellow committee member from the university's public-policy program suggested that I write something about this topic. Playfully if not assuredly, I took up that suggestion. The eventual product was the "Paradox" essay.

Reflecting on all this nearly a decade after this chapter was first published, I must conclude that the paradox still looms, and still invites our engagement and investigation. Of course, much has changed since the late 1980s. At the federal level, loans and tax benefits have increasingly replaced grants as vehicles for promoting college opportunity, aid efforts have shifted somewhat away from a need-based orientation, and direct lending to students has ascended as a delivery approach (Baum, Chapter 2). At the institutional level, tuitions have continued to rise in both the public and private sectors (Paulsen, Chapter 6; Toutkoushian, Chapter 1) and colleges and universities have increasingly utilized tuition discounting and more sophisticated aid packaging as tools in student recruitment (Breneman, Doti and Lapovsky, Chapter 12). Students themselves have become more financially and academically discerning in their institutional choices. And, of course, governments at all levels have increasingly asked tough questions of the institutions and systems benefiting from their largesse.[40]

Yet, how much has changed in the various specific components of the paradox? Simply stated, the paradox noted in the original essay was that, as of the early 1990s, federal student aid was continuing to grow despite the fact that federal policies in that arena lacked *philosophical coherence, well-considered patterns of policy development, programmatic clarity and distinctiveness, access to managerially needed information, a strong and supportive interest-group coalition, a beneficent resource environment,* and a *robust client base.* To update the "Paradox" essay, let's revisit the question of growth, then address the status of the previously lacking elements one by one.

Is Growth Continuing? The latest year of federal aid funding covered in the original essay was 1989-90. The latest year for which at least preliminary data are available now is 1998-99 (see College Board, 1999b). Over those years, total generally available federal aid grew 129 percent, from \$19.0 billion to \$43.6 billion. In constant-dollar terms, this translates into 77 percent growth over the period. The Pell Grant program grew only 17 percent in constant-dollar terms and federal work-study funding grew even less. Clearly, the bulk of real growth has come in the federal loan programs. Most notable sources of growth were the loans provided through the new direct student loan program (from nothing in 1989-90 to just over \$11 billion in volume in 1998-99) and the new unsubsidized guaranteed loans provided through traditional channels (from nothing in 1989-90 to over \$8.4 billion in 1998-99). Thus, albeit in concentrated areas, real growth has indeed continued in federal aid programs over the years since the original essay.[41]

Has Philosophical Coherence Been Achieved? Bruce Johnstone (1999, p. 3) has argued recently that "the fabric of the American 'system' of financial assistance and

---

[40]See McPherson and Schapiro (1998), College Board (1999 a and b), Spencer (1999), and Winston (1999).

tuition policy seems to be unraveling." That may be overstating the case, but certainly not by much. Continuing debates over grants versus loans as vehicles of educational opportunity, direct versus traditional forms of loan provision, the use of tax breaks as aid mechanisms, the place of merit in aid efforts, and other philosophical issues indicate that the answer to the question of philosophical coherence must be in the negative.[42]

Have Well-Considered Patterns of Policy Development Emerged? Policy development has been energetic and often innovative in the past decade. We have seen the emergence of the federal direct lending programs, growth in unsubsidized loans as a policy approach, improvements in the technology of aid applications and delivery, and enhanced controls over default rates and award errors. Regardless, however, integrated policy development has been as hard to achieve as ever.

Have Programmatic Clarity and Distinctiveness Been Developed? The ongoing difficulty of describing loan programs simply illustrates the ambiguities of the federal aid portfolio. In 1989-90, the federal government supported five loan efforts: Perkins loans, Income Contingent loans, Subsidized Stafford loans, SLS loans, and PLUS loans. In 1998-99, the government supported eight loan efforts: Perkins loans, subsidized Stafford loans under the Ford Direct Loans program, unsubsidized Stafford loans under the Ford Direct Loans program, PLUS loans under the Ford Direct Loans program, subsidized Stafford loans under the Family Education Loans program, unsubsidized Stafford loans under the Family Education Loans program, SLS loans under the Family Education Loans program, and PLUS loans under the Family Education Loans program. While distinctions within this variegated portfolio become arguably clear upon inspection, the array is unquestionably daunting to students and families. Disputes over which programs merit the most substantial investment at the federal level continue to fuel ambiguities.[43]

Has Access to Managerially Needed Information Been Provided? There has been clear improvement in the management information systems and research data supporting the student-aid programs. Transactional information (e.g., counts and averages for awards made through different channels) is superior to that provided in the past. What is more, useful information is accumulating on the effects of student aid on students (e.g., see St. John's influential 1994 work on the impacts of different aid packaging approaches on needy students). We know more about aid effects than we did a decade ago.

It seems warranted here to clarify my view of the evidence on effects. In the original "Paradox" essay, I did not in any way mean to imply that substantial positive aid effects

---

[41]One might argue that the growth has even been understated by the above analysis, particularly if the next few years are considered. Recent estimates place the value of the tax breaks for college expenses provided under the Taxpayer Relief Act of 1997 at $12-15 billion a year (College Board, 1999b). These lost federal revenues are not student aid in the usual sense, however, and are also difficult to calculate. For those reasons, these funds are not considered in this analysis.

[42]Indeed, as Spencer (1999, p. 116) has perceptively argued, we in higher education may be in a new era in which even "the federal commitment to 'access' for low-income students can no longer be taken for granted."

[43]Policy developments in federally supported student loans, at least up to the mid-1990s, are covered in more depth in Hearn (1998).

don't exist, or that doing away with the federal programs would be a good idea. My view on this issue remains the same. In fact, I have always been committed to the necessity, on equity grounds, of substantial federal investment in student aid. The point also holds now on pragmatic grounds: I believe students, institutions, and others are increasingly dependent on these programs. We could not slash or remove them without dire implications. My point in the original chapter, and my point now, is simply that I wish we knew more. Given the multibillion-dollar investment, we are research-shy. We invest without having enough evidence on how we might best fashion the investment.

Regrettably, we also invest without sufficiently *using* extant evidence on how we might best fashion the investment. This problem, one of policymakers' attitudes toward using research, may precede their attitudes toward commissioning research, and raises broader issues. Work by Wildavsky (1979) and others provocatively addresses this continuing, and very fundamental, question.

In summary, the database and technological improvements of the past decade, and the expanded research literature base, have not fully addressed the aid arena's daunting information challenges. Indeed, new developments like direct loans and aid delivered through tax breaks have posed distinctive and difficult new analytic challenges. This aspect of the paradox remains.

Has a Strong and Supportive Interest-Group Coalition Emerged? Policy decisions regarding federal student-aid continue to be marked by interest-group infighting. Notably, the debate over perhaps the single watershed policy innovation of the decade, direct student lending, was marked by bitter disputes among lobbyists over the proper role of private-sector firms in aid delivery (Cook, 1998; Parsons, 1997). This issue-driven discord is supplemented by institutional discord over policies that differentially affect the various institutional sectors. Thus, no cohesive interest-group perspective has emerged in the politics of federal student aid. Indeed, in light of the divisiveness of the past few years, the notion of a national student-aid "consensus" or "coalition," an idea widely accepted in the 1970s and actually formalized at that time, now seems quaint and hard to imagine.

Has a Beneficent Resource Environment Developed? The improvement in the U.S. economy since the late 1980s and early 1990s is perhaps the major national news story of the succeeding decade. Personal incomes and wealth grew annually and government coffers benefited in concert. These favorable trends continue at the time of the present writing. Yet federal spending on social and educational programs has been less robust than might be expected from the magnitude of the economic growth. Overall spending on such programs has grown at only modest rates, in the face of pressures to reduce federal debt and provide tax breaks. Thus, while one might argue that the aid programs have benefited from a greatly improved resource environment, it would be hard to portray recent Congresses and the Clinton administration as especially munificent toward social and educational programs in general. Indeed, partisan battles over such funding have generally ended in compromises toward rather static levels of investment. The growth in student-aid investments over the period, however modest, is thus notable.

Has a Robust Client Base Appeared? On this question, the answer may be in the affirmative. Past years' declines in the size of the nation's 18-24 year-old population are reversing as baby boomers' children age. This demographic development has brought increased numbers of high-school graduates considering postsecondary enrollment, and increased attention to aid policies among families nationwide. At the same time, adult interest in attending continues to be strong. Among both adults and traditional-age students, growing proportions believe that having a postsecondary degree is necessary (Spencer, 1999). These developments, in parallel with the increasing costs of attendance (College Board, 1999a), have propelled increasing rates of aid utilization over the past decade in all segments of the population.

CONCLUSION

It would be folly not to conclude that the elements of the original paradox remain largely in place. In some ways, the paradox has grown even more striking. Yet polls reveal the U.S. public is remarkably united in its belief that college expenses for needy students should be met in part by government-supplied student aid (Spencer, 1999). Many families and students have real need for federal student aid. The ongoing divisions and disorder in aid policy reflect not a lack of support for meeting that need but rather ongoing dissension over how best to meet the need and manage it. Clearly, the combination of policymakers' sensitivity to the public's strong support for student aid and a robust tax base provided by a booming economy have been sufficient to buffer aid policy from crippling paralysis over specific policy characteristics. Thus, if straining for a bit of intellectual excitement in a too-quiet doctoral exam, I would have little hesitation in posing the same question as before. It is still fascinating to contemplate the "just do it" mentality that drives our multi-billion dollar investment in federal student aid.

References

College Board, The. (1999a). *Trends in College Pricing*. Washington, DC: The College Board.

College Board, The. (1999b). *Trends in Student Aid*. Washington, DC: The College Board.

Cook, C. E. (1998). *Lobbying of Higher Education: How Colleges and Universities Influence Federal Policy*. Nashville: Vanderbilt University Press.

Hearn, J. C. (1998). The growing loan orientation in federal financial-aid policy: A historical perspective. In R. Fossey and M. Bateman (eds.), *Condemning Students to Debt: College Loans and Public Policy*. New York: Teachers College Press.

Johnstone, D. B. (1999). Introduction. In J. King (ed.), *Financing a College Education: How It Works, How It's Changing*. Phoenix, AZ: American Council on Education and Oryx Press.

Kane, T. J. (1999). *The Price of Admission: Rethinking How Americans Pay for College*. Washington, DC: Brookings Institution.

McPherson, M. S. and Schapiro, M. O. (1998). *The Student Aid Game: Meeting Need and Rewarding Talent in American Higher Education*. Princeton: Princeton University Press.

Parsons, M. D. (1997). *Power and Politics: Federal Higher Education Policy Making in the 1990's*. Albany, NY: SUNY Press.

Spencer, A. C. (1999). The new politics of higher education. In J. King (Ed.), *Financing a College Education: How It Works, How It's Changing*. Phoenix, AZ: American Council on Education and Oryx Press.

St. John, E. P. (1994). Assessing tuition and student aid strategies: Using price response measures to simulate pricing alternatives. *Research in Higher Education, 35*(3), 301-335.

Winston, G. C. (1999). College costs: Who pays and why it matters so. In J. King (ed.), *Financing a College Education: How It Works, How It's Changing*. Phoenix, AZ: American Council on Education and Oryx Press.

Wildavsky, A. (1979). *Speaking Truth to Power: The Art and Craft of Policy Analysis*. Boston: Little, Brown, and Company.

Chapter 8

STATE EFFORTS TO KEEP PUBLIC COLLEGES AFFORDABLE IN THE FACE OF FISCAL STRESS[1]

Michael Mumper

After more than a decade of relative stability, the price of public colleges and universities began to rise rapidly in the early 1980s. While these price increases slowed somewhat in the last half of the 1980s, rapid tuition inflation returned in the 1990s. Today, public higher education in most states is more expensive than it has ever been. As college prices rise, so too does public concern over them. Few issues now concern American families as much as the spiraling price of college (Gallup, 1991). This combination of rising prices and public concern over them has, in turn, generated substantial pressure on policy makers to take action to address the problem.

Most of the public debate over declining college affordability has focused on the astronomical costs of the most expensive private colleges. Certainly, few American families can afford the full $30,000 per year now charged at many of these institutions without depleting their retirement savings, remortgaging their homes, or going far into debt. However, much less attention has been directed at the growing problem of public college affordability. In 1980, states like California, New York, North Carolina, and Texas provided public higher education to state residents for virtually no charge. Even the public colleges in high tuition states like Pennsylvania, Ohio, and New Hampshire were bargains by today's standards. But after nearly two decades of tuition inflation, prices have risen to the point that average public college tuition in several states is more than $6,500 a year. When living expenses and books are included, the price tag for four years at a public university can easily exceed $40,000 per student.

Beginning in 1965, with the enactment of the Higher Education Act, the federal and state governments joined in an implicit partnership to make higher education affordable to all

---

[1] I would like to acknowledge the support of the Ohio University Research Committee in completing the research for this chapter. The project was also aided substantially by the careful and conscientious research assistance of Lisa Eiserman. This chapter was originally published in Volume XIII of *Higher Education: Handbook of Theory and Research,* © 1998 by Agathon Press. It has been updated with an Epilogue written especially for this volume.

Americans. The states would keep tuition at public colleges low and the federal government would provide a means-tested system of grants and loans to insure that all students could meet those costs. In recent years, however, that partnership has come unraveled. Faced with public pressure to reduce taxes and balance the budget, national policy makers have frozen the size of the grant programs and forced more and more students to rely on loans to finance their higher education (Gladieux and Hauptman, 1995). As the federal government has backed away from its traditional responsibility for insuring college access for the lower income and disadvantaged, that role has been largely given over to the states and to families. Today, it is clear that if the nation's public colleges are to remain affordable to all Americans—even the lowest income families—it will be the result of actions taken by state level policy makers.

The states, however, have followed quite different paths in their efforts to insure equal college opportunity. This chapter will examine how state governments have addressed this complex problem in the 1990s[2]. Specifically, it will consider:

- 1) Why have public college prices increased so rapidly? And what accounts for the variation among states both in tuition levels and in the levels of tuition inflation?
- 2) How have states responded to these pressures? What actions have they taken to try to insure that their public colleges will be affordable to lower income and disadvantaged students?
- 3) Which state actions have proven the most effective? As states struggle to do more with fewer resources, which approaches seem to provide the greatest hope for improving college affordability?

The Public College Affordability Problem[3]

While public college prices have increased everywhere in the past decade, those increases have varied tremendously across the states and across time. Table One shows the average tuition at four-year public colleges for selected years between 1984-85 and 1994-95. It shows that all but five states have experienced tuition inflation of greater than 100 percent during the decade. The states with the fastest rates of increase (California, Texas, Massachusetts, and Connecticut) were all hit hard by the recession of the early 1990s and were among the last to recover. Moreover, because California and Texas had maintained such low tuition at the beginning of the period, their price increases of 557 and 318 percent, respectively, still did not move them to among the most expensive states. Indeed, in spite of this dramatic price increase, Texas remains among the states with the least expensive public colleges.

At the other end of the spectrum, Nevada, Idaho, and Georgia were the states with the lowest rates of tuition inflation. In the case of Georgia and Nevada, this is the result of both a healthier than average state economy and a growing population base.

---

[2]The focus of this chapter will be limited to the affordability of undergraduate education at public institutions. The issues of access and affordability to graduate professional and private institutions of higher education are certainly important. But they are substantially different than those discussed here.

[3]Data in this section are drawn from the *Digest of Education Statistics 1995* (Washington, DC: Government Printing Office).

Table One illustrates that in spite of some high profile news accounts of a leveling off of tuition inflation, the price of public colleges increased more rapidly in the last half of the decade than it had in the first. New York, Michigan, Maine, and Minnesota, in particular, were able to maintain their low levels of tuition inflation between 1985 and 1990. But each experienced dramatically greater growth in the following years. New York, in particular, was able to maintain tuition increases at its four-year colleges to less than 10 percent in the last half of the 1980s (Mumper, 1993). But prices there more than doubled between 1990 and 1995.

TABLE 1. Four-year Public College Tuition

State	1984-1985	1989-1990	1994-1995	5 yr. percent change	10 yr. percent change
California	411	1,123	2,703	173	558
Texas	384	959	1,608	150	319
Massachusetts	1,130	2,052	4,131	82	266
Connecticut	1,044	2,017	3,746	93	259
Wyoming	567	1,003	1,908	77	237
Washington	849	1,710	2,686	101	216
New Jersey	1,225	2,511	3,773	105	208
North Carolina	494	1,015	1,503	106	204
Illinois	1,060	2,370	3,197	124	202
Oregon	1,024	1,738	3,063	70	199
Missouri	944	1,532	2,787	62	195
Maryland	1,175	2,120	3,318	80	182
Rhode Island	1,322	2,281	3,718	73	181
Virginia	1,345	2,532	3,769	88	180
Arizona	680	1,362	1,894	100	179
South Carolina	1,085	2,162	3,021	99	178
Michigan	1,368	1,484	3,729	9	173
Delaware	1,405	2,768	3,817	97	172
Louisiana	816	1,768	2,214	117	171
Mississippi	903	1,858	2,448	106	171
Alaska	768	1,280	2,045	67	166
Oklahoma	631	1,309	1,675	107	166
New Mexico	717	1,326	1,836	85	156
Montana	833	1,535	2,110	84	153
Hawaii	596	1,293	1,508	117	153
Pennsylvania	1,870	3,210	4,512	72	141
Vermont	2,427	3,641	5,752	50	137
Florida	759	na	1,786	na	135
Kentucky	879	1,316	2,056	50	134
Tennessee	812	1,406	1,897	73	134
Arkansas	837	1,376	1,955	64	134
Maine	1,425	1,980	3,319	39	133
Alabama	911	1,522	2,106	67	131

TABLE 1. Four-year Public College Tuition (Continued)

State	1984-1985	1989-1990	1994-1995	5 yr. percent change	10 yr. percent change
Iowa	1,082	1,823	2,462	69	128
Wisconsin	1,087	1,861	2,470	71	127
North Dakota	992	1,604	2,245	62	126
West Virginia	886	1,591	1,963	80	122
New Hampshire	1,814	2,196	4,003	21	121
New York	1,355	1,460	2,957	8	118
Ohio	1,577	2,432	3,405	54	116
Kansas	954	1,467	2,019	54	112
DC	496	664	1,046	34	111
Indiana	1,371	1,975	2,864	44	109
South Dakota	1,243	1,718	2,557	38	106
Colorado	1,162	1,830	2,377	57	105
Utah	974	1,429	1,960	47	101
Minnesota	1,500	2,063	2,919	38	95
Nebraska	1,059	1,519	2,058	43	94
Georgia	1,084	1,631	1,965	51	81
Idaho	889	1,119	1,583	25	78
Nevada	915	1,100	1,601	20	75
U.S. Total	971	1,781	2,689	84	177

Source: U.S. Department of Education (1995)

Table Two shows average tuition at two-year public colleges by state between 1990 and 1995. The pattern here is the same. Every state has experienced tuition increases in the last five years, although the rate of inflation in this sector remained substantially lower than it was among four year colleges. Again, those states with the highest rates of tuition inflation were either those, like California, Maine, and Massachusetts, which were hit especially hard by the recession and/or states like North Carolina and California where 1990 tuition levels were far below those charged in other states.

While, in general, the trends in four-year and two-year college tuition inflation are moving in the same direction, there are a few notable exceptions. Both Illinois and South Carolina have held tuition increases at their two-year colleges substantially below those experienced at four-year colleges. By holding down tuition inflation at two-year colleges, these states can insure that lower income families have access to more affordable public higher education and still allow their research universities to generate the revenues which result from higher tuition. A similar approach has been used in California which has always kept tuition at two-year colleges very low. This represents an implicit strategy to maintain college affordability by encouraging students to attend institutions which provide an education at the lowest price.

A great deal can be learned from examining trends in aggregate tuition rates in the states. But these figures may also mask important differences in public college affordabil-

TABLE 2. Two-year Public College Tuition

State	1989-1990	1994-1995	5 yr. percent change
California	112	365	226
North Carolina	288	582	102
Maine	1,134	2,137	88
Massachusetts	1,332	2,441	83
Oregon	753	1,324	76
Virginia	813	1,384	70
Alabama	662	1,123	70
Rhode Island	1,004	1,686	68
Connecticut	915	1,520	66
Washington	802	1,314	64
West Virginia	803	1,312	63
Colorado	792	1,279	62
Nevada	522	842	61
Maryland	1,172	1,848	58
Kentucky	693	1,080	56
New Jersey	1,130	1,755	55
Florida	729	1,112	53
New York	1,412	2,152	52
Montana	877	1,329	52
Texas	455	680	50
Missouri	815	1,203	48
Kansas	711	1,044	47
Wyoming	613	893	46
New Hampshire	1,608	2,316	44
Delaware	882	1,266	44
Wisconsin	1,160	1,649	42
Arizona	519	734	41
Iowa	1,225	1,699	39
Arkansas	644	888	38
Mississippi	680	935	38
Oklahoma	840	1,153	37
Illinois	871	1,194	37
Michigan	1,047	1,432	37
New Mexico	496	678	37
Vermont	2,120	2,877	36
Indiana	1,374	1,854	35
Ohio	1,636	2,164	32
North Dakota	1,286	1,689	31
South Carolina	807	1,048	30
Minnesota	1,499	1,928	29
Idaho	779	990	27

TABLE 2. Two-year Public College Tuition (Continued)

State	1989-1990	1994-1995	5 yr. percent change
Pennsylvania	1,419	1,751	23
Louisiana	837	1,027	23
Hawaii	410	500	22
Tennessee	803	975	21
Nebraska	919	1,097	19
Georgia	852	1,015	19
Utah	1,136	1,340	18
Alaska	na	1,320	na
South Dakota	na	3,430	na
U.S. Total	758	1,194	58
California	112	365	226
North Carolina	288	582	102

Source: U.S. Department of Education (1995)

ity. Tuition at public colleges within a state may vary widely among institutions. This may even occur within a single sector. As such, the average tuition may not accurately represent the amount most students must pay. Some students will pay more than the average. Others will pay much less.

Perhaps more important, low tuition is not the same as affordability. By providing need-based financial aid, states can substantially reduce the real price of college for lower income students. If the rising tuition in a state is paid only by more wealthy students, those increases may have little or no impact on the college prices paid by the most disadvantaged. Complicating matters further, institutions themselves offer financial aid that may also mitigate the impact of tuition increases. As such, rising tuition cannot be equated with declining affordability in a state. And even stable tuition is no guarantee that public college access for lower income students is not declining.

The States and Public Higher Education

The fact that public college tuition has increased rapidly in recent years is undeniable. The causes of these increases, however, remain the subject of much dispute. Some see rising prices as the product of insufficient support from the federal and state governments (Hauptman, 1990, p. 59-64). Some see them as driven by wasteful and unnecessary expenditures by campus leaders (Sowell, 1992). Some see them as the product of bloated bureaucracies and red tape (Bergmann, 1991). Still others see rising college prices as a direct result of the rising costs of purchasing and maintaining new technology, providing health care for employees, and covering the costs of complying with federal regulations (Francis, 1990). As these costs of offering a quality education rise, institutions raise their prices in order to balance their budgets.

Putting aside these disagreements over causes, there are three things that all sides agree have played a role in causing public college prices to rise. First, due to the fiscal pressures they have experienced in the past few years, states have been unable to significantly increase their appropriations to higher education. Steven Gold (1995), one of the most careful observers of state spending patterns, found that in the early 1990s "higher education took a worse beating than any other spending category" (p. 25) in state budgets. In several states, the level of support has actually declined. In Virginia, for example, state support for higher education fell by $500 million or 27 percent between 1990 and 1995 (Hsu, 1995). Second, public colleges have increased their spending on such things as student services, computing facilities, and faculty and administrative compensation. Finally, as more students are going to college, and more of them begin with academic deficiencies, colleges are spending more time and money providing remedial courses to prepare students to do introductory college work. This combination has forced college leaders to provide more students with a wider array of services, to pay higher prices to provide those services, and to do so with stable or reduced levels of state support. The result has been tuition inflation.

But there is something more than just these forces at work. There is also evidence of changing state priorities. Several states seem to have decided to shift the responsibility of paying for higher education from taxpayers to students and their families. Sandra Ruppert puts it this way:

> To some extent, high tuition values reflect the state's position that the individual is the primary beneficiary of his or her education and so students and their families should bear more of the cost. Conversely, high state appropriations suggest a state's position that higher education provides social and economic benefits for states and localities so government should bear more of the cost (Ruppert, 1996, p. 35).

State Government's and Public College Prices

When viewed in aggregate, state spending on higher education dwarfs the combined efforts of federal and local governments. States provide most of these dollars directly to public colleges and universities as instructional subsidies. Colleges, in turn, use these subsidies to keep their tuition considerably below the full cost of providing a higher education. Another large portion of those state funds is allocated for need-based grants which are awarded directly to lower family income students. These grants are given with the express purpose of providing students with the resources necessary to attend the college of their choice. As such, the level of state support is a central factor in the affordability of public higher education in a state.

While state governments are major players in the financing of public higher education, the relationship between state governments and public colleges is complex and multifaceted. While states provide more than half of the revenues currently used to operate public institutions of higher education, these colleges retain substantial autonomy in their administrative and financial operations. In most states, it is the colleges themselves, acting through boards of trustees, who determine the tuition they will charge.[4]

In only a few states, like New York, Texas, and Washington, does the legislature actually set the tuition level charged at public colleges. But even in these states, it is usually set

---

[4]For a discussion of the different approaches, see Lenth, 1993.

in careful consultation with the state's board and college presidents (Lenth, 1993).

There is a clear relationship between levels of state support and the tuition charges at a state's public colleges. Public colleges receive their funding from a combination of state support, tuition, private contributions, and sales and services. When state support declines, colleges plug the revenue gap by increasing tuition charges. That is exactly what has happened since 1990. As Thomas Mortenson (1994) describes it:

> As states' governors and legislators have chosen to shift state appropriations away from higher education into more "important" budget priorities like corrections and Medicaid, public institutions have raised tuition charges to students to offset the loss of state appropriations (p. 7).

A 1996 study by the National Education Association (NEA), which reports the findings of a survey of the chairs of education committees in state legislatures, makes a similar point. It found that a part of the reason higher education has been a low budgetary priority is that the burden of these cuts can be easily shifted. Many legislators are aware that a share of the cuts to the higher education appropriation can be shifted to others primarily in the form of tuition and fee increases. Indeed, a strong majority of committee chairs (68 percent) agreed that a significant factor on determining how much money the legislature will appropriate for higher education is the ability of colleges and universities to raise their own money through tuition, research grants, and gifts (Ruppert, 1996, p. 9).

While the link between state appropriations and tuition at public colleges is a real one, it is far from lockstep. The determination of the tuition level charged each year at public colleges is the product of countervailing pressures. Long traditions of institutional autonomy from direct government control mandate that campuses retain at least some control over expenditure and pricing decisions. But growing public pressures for accountability in the use of public funds demand that state governments act to control or limit price increases (Berdahl and McConnell, 1994). Whether or not those public pressures are translated into explicit governmental action, campus decision makers are certainly aware that rapidly rising tuition makes them the target of increased scrutiny by governors and state legislatures (Lenth, 1993, p. 7-15). As such, public colleges must establish their own price levels within the context of limited state appropriations and the need to be responsive to broad public and political pressures.

The Fiscal Condition of the States

The 1990s have been a difficult time for state governments. Gold (1995) recently termed the period "the fiscal crisis of the states." The most important cause of the fiscal problems faced by the states was the recession of the early part of the decade. This created a squeeze in which state tax revenues were declining as the demand for many public services was increasing. Although the national recession ended in early 1991, many states experienced its effects for a much longer time. A few appear to have not yet recovered.

While important, the recession was not the only cause of the fiscal problems faced by the states in the 1990s. The explosive growth of Medicaid and the increased impact of federal mandates required all states to spend more in these areas without generating any additional revenue to cover those costs (Miller, 1993). Many states experienced significant increases in public school enrollment or faced court orders to reduce disparities in spending among school districts (Zumeta and Looney, 1993, p. 8-9). Similarly, mandatory sentencing requirements and tougher practices in the criminal justice system forced states to greatly increase their spending on corrections and prison construction (Gold, 1995, p. 27).

The ability of a state to support its public colleges is a function of both the state's capacity to raise revenue and the willingness of the legislature to appropriate funds. Edward Hines (1996) describes it this way:

> The amount of revenue available depends on the capacity of the tax system and the overall health and level of activity in the economic system. State appropriations take place in a system characterized by tradeoffs and choices. At a time when states' finances are under strain by increasing demands on state services, the willingness of lawmakers to appropriate to one area may mean lawmakers will be unable to support another area of need (p. 6).

In combination, these factors have forced states to reallocate the shares within their annual budgets. As shown in Table Three, since 1990 there were increases in all of the major state expenditure categories except higher education. This is no accident. State policy makers were trapped between pressures to increase spending on K-12 education, prisons, medical care, and welfare on the one hand and pressures to hold down taxes and legal requirements to balance their state budgets on the other. Given these cross-pressures, many policy makers felt as though higher education was the only place they could reduce spending without producing a short-term disaster (Ruppert, 1996, p. 9). As such, even when not accounting for inflation, state spending on higher education experienced an annual decline of 0.6 percent per year between 1990 and 1995.

TABLE 3. Mean Annual Change in Major Expenditure Categories from State General Funds: 1990-1995

Major State Expenditures	Mean Annual Change
Medicaid	10.0%
Prisons	8.5%
K-12 Education	3.7%
AFDC	1.6%
Higher Education	-0.6%

Source: Mortenson, 1994.

These trends seem likely to remain evident at least through the end of the century. Even in those states which are experiencing rapid economic growth, the need for additional spending on health care, prisons, and elementary and secondary education will continue to attract the bulk of the new resources. In those states where the economy is weak, higher education is likely to experience disproportionate reductions (McGuinness, 1994, p. 159).

The Specter of Enrollment Increases

Complicating matters further, many states are facing the forecast of an increasing demand for higher education in the next decade. These states, many of which are already operating their systems at or near full capacity, must find ways to accommodate these new students without the funds necessary to open new campuses or dramatically expand the physical capacities of their existing campuses (Ruppert, 1996, p. 27-28).

This new student demand is coming from two places. First, the number of nontraditional students returning to school has been growing for more than two decades. This group now significantly outnumbers the traditional 18-21 year old now enrolled in American higher education. The vast majority of these nontraditional students are enrolled in public colleges and universities. During the last decade, public colleges were able to absorb this new demand because the number of high school graduates was declining. Thus, even as the participation rates of high school graduates was growing, their absolute number in colleges was increasing more slowly.

But over the next decade, the number of high school graduates in many states will increase rapidly. As shown in Table Four, ten states will have an increase in the number of graduates of more than 30 percent. If these new graduates plan to attend college at the same rates as current graduates (and forecasts are that they will), and the number of nontraditional students continues to grow (and forecasts are that they will), the challenge will be enormous. How will states continue to provide affordable higher education to all their residents in the face of rising costs, scarce resources, and rapidly expanding demand? In many states the answer will be higher tuition at the public colleges.

TABLE 4. Projected Changes in the Number of High School Graduates Between 1995-1996 and 2005-2006

Nevada	71%
Florida	51%
Arizona	46%
California	43%
New Hampshire	36%
Alaska	33%
Colorado	33%
Delaware	32%
Washington	32%
Maryland	30%

Source: Ruppert (1996). Appendix C: State Date Table, pp. 57-58.

The Policy Responses of the States

States have not been passive in the face of the growing strain on public college affordability. Voters, taxpayers, parents, and students all demand that states take action to keep public colleges affordable. As a result, policy makers in most states have been forced to respond, in one way or another, to those pressures. Their responses, however, have varied widely. Few states have developed a comprehensive strategy or policy to control college prices (Hearn, Griswold, and Marine, 1996). Most states have undertaken piecemeal, ad-hoc, incremental changes on several fronts simultaneously. In some states the response came directly from the state legislature or the governor's office. In others, it came from the Board of Regents or the state's higher education coordinating board. In others, it came as informal pressure on campus leaders from state policy makers to induce them to change their behavior or policies.

In general, the state responses can be divided into four categories. States have sought to (1) alter the expenditure patterns of public colleges, (2) increase the revenues available to public college leaders to offset their rising costs, (3) redesign the delivery of higher education in order to make it more efficient and thus reduce its cost, and/or (4) increase the resources available to students and their families to pay for those costs. The next section of this chapter looks more closely at these responses. It is important to remember, however, that these are not mutually exclusive categories. States can choose to respond in a variety of ways at once. Many states have done a little of each. Other states have concentrated their efforts in one or two of them.

RESPONSE #1: Controlling Institutional Expenditures

As state policy makers struggle to address more and often more serious problems with a limited pot of funds, they often begin by attempting to insure that existing funds are spent in the most productive way. This pressure to do more with less has caused legislatures and governors to demand increased accountability from their public colleges. In most cases, states want to insure that colleges are spending their state funds, and also the funds they generate from tuition, in ways that they feel are serving the state's interests (Mathesian, 1995).

These efforts have renewed old tensions between states and campuses over institutional autonomy. To some, they may have fundamentally altered the relationship between capital and campus. William Shkirti, Vice President for Finance at Ohio State University, puts it this way: "the assumption used to be that higher education was a good investment...now we're being asked to prove that we're not inefficient" (Mathesian, 1995, p. 21).

Mandated Price Controls

The ways public college prices are set vary widely from state to state. But in almost every state, the legislature and the governor can, if they choose, exert a powerful influence on the process. Indeed, legislatures in almost every state have the power to freeze tuition increases either directly by statute or indirectly through appropriations negotiations. By taking actions to limit the tuition charged by public colleges, states are indirectly limiting the revenue available to those colleges to provide educational programs and services. Indeed, by limiting tuition increases, states are implicitly ordering campus leaders to change their spending priorities.

Legislative action to limit public college price increases is especially easy in states where public college tuition is actually set by the state legislature. By keeping tuition very low, many state legislators feel that they maintain the widest possible access to their public colleges. But low tuition generates little revenue to cover educational costs and state legislatures often provide colleges with little additional revenue to cover their rising costs. As a consequence, public college leaders in these states have complained bitterly that they are being squeezed in such a way that they have little choice but to compromise program quality.

In Texas the low tuition policy is more complex than it might appear. To insure that colleges have adequate revenues, and also maintain their policy of very low tuition, the state legislature and public colleges have reached an uneasy compromise. Colleges have been allowed to establish a number of student fees and charges which cover the cost of a specific activity or service. These fees are then used to supplement the campus budget and serve to replace the funds which are not appropriated by the state. For many, perhaps most, Texas students, these fees are now larger each term than their total tuition bill (Texas House Research Organization, 1995).

In states where tuition is set by a state board or by individual campuses, the process of state control is slightly more difficult. In Virginia and Ohio, for example, the legislature has established annual tuition caps for all public institutions. These caps, which were set at the level of consumer inflation in Virginia and slightly higher in Ohio, establish the maximum percentage of tuition increase that the state will accept each year. In both states frustrated legislators saw tuition caps as a way to show campus leaders they were serious about controlling costs. In the view of many legislators, this was the only way to force unresponsive campuses to limit their wasteful spending and set reasonable priorities. When coupled with reductions in state appropriations, legislators felt that such caps were the only way to insure that necessary belt-tightening took place on campus and the budget cuts were not simply passed on to students in the form of higher tuition.

Few people see state mandated tuition freezes as a long term solution to the college affordability problem. They are simply a way for state policy makers to force campus leaders into adjusting their spending priorities. Often such actions are the first step in a renegotiation of the relationship between campus and state leaders. Ohio State Representative Robert Hagen puts it this way, "those in the ivory tower have to come down, get a little muddied and explain the whole process of what it is they do" (Mathesian, 1995, p. 22).

Performance Funding

A more positive way for states to alter the spending patterns of public colleges is performance funding. This approach ties state funding levels to measures of institutional performance. In theory, high performing institutions will be rewarded with funding increases while low performing institutions will be punished with funding reductions (Nedwek, 1996).

During the 1980s, a few states developed "incentive funding" programs that added dollars to the base budgets of institutions that implemented an approved plan that fit state priorities. Tennessee was the first state to adopt such a program, followed by Florida, New Jersey, and Ohio (Zumeta, 1995, p. 83). These incentive plans link increased funding with improving undergraduate teaching, increasing classroom use of technology and improved job training at community and technical colleges among others. In Colorado, the legislature passed an incentive funding plan which rewards colleges and universities that improve in five statewide priority areas: productivity, growth in enrollment, expanded job training, strengthened ties to public schools, and increased financial aid (Colorado Commission on Higher Education, 1994).

In 1993, the Texas legislature was poised to enact a performance-based budgeting system to distribute 5 percent of the state's higher education funds. But when the plan was revised to increase the share to 10 percent, the consensus behind it evaporated. It died in committee and has never been revived (Mathesian, 1995, p. 24).

In South Carolina the legislature has taken a much more comprehensive approach to performance funding. The state's higher education commission developed a set of performance indicators for each state college. By 1999, the plan would base all of the funds it gives to each public college on how well they perform according to those indicators (Schmidt, 1996).

- These efforts to improve the accountability of public higher education through performance funding are not directly related to the problem of rising tuition. They do, however, illustrate significant state efforts to alter the funding priorities of public colleges. In general, performance funding seeks to reward institutions that focus on undergraduate education, effective teaching, and job preparation (Zumeta, 1995). In doing so, states are implicitly discouraging more spending on research, public service, and graduate education.

The survey of education committee chairs conducted by the NEA shows substantial support for performance measures in funding higher education. Nearly half of the respondents think that their legislatures are likely in the next few years to "link funding to campus efforts to increase enrollment, graduation rates, or other measures of student or institutional performance" (Ruppert, 1996, p. 37).

Improved Efficiency and Productivity

Another way for states to alter the expenditure patterns of campus leaders is to mandate improved efficiency and productivity. While the goals of these mandates are similar to performance funding, they are much more intrusive. Rather than simply measuring performance on predetermined criteria, governors and legislators can simply require that colleges change their spending priorities. These state efforts can range from mandated increases in faculty workloads to adjustments in the types and availability of courses offered. In some states, legislatures have overhauled campus purchasing procedures and/or mandated reductions in specific spending categories. In other states, these efforts were more broadly designed to bring campus spending in line with available revenues and reduce the need for tuition increases.

Virginia has been among the most aggressive states in their efforts to improve efficiency and productivity. In 1994, the Governor appointed a Commission on Government Reform to search for ways to improve efficiency across the entire state government. This Commission ominously called itself the Blue Ribbon Strike Force. As part of their work, and with the support of the General Assembly, the Commission required all public colleges and universities in Virginia to submit extensive restructuring plans:

to effect long term changes in the deployment of faculty, to insure the effectiveness of academic offerings, to minimize administrative and instructional costs, to prepare for the demands of enrollment increases, and to address funding priorities as approved by the General Assembly (Virginia Council on Higher Education, 1994, p. 1).

These plans were to follow strict criteria developed by the state's Council on Higher Education.

As part of this process, each public institution was required to conduct a comprehensive review with an eye toward reducing programs, eliminating expenses, and saving money. While the language of the plan stresses quality enhancement, participants in the process viewed the focus of the plan as on improving efficiency and reducing the size and scope of the higher education system (Lively, 1995). The entire process was met with stiff opposition from college and business leaders in the state (Hsu, 1995).

One institution where this process had a significant impact was James Madison University. After conducting the state mandated review, the University's president recommended the elimination of the physics major. His reasoning was that as institutions more clearly define their missions, not every college needed to offer every program. Indeed, the purpose of the review had been to eliminate weak and unnecessary programs. While in the end, the physics major was restored, the battle illustrated the determination of the state to take dramatic action to reduce spending on higher education (Magner, 1995).

A similar study was conducted in Ohio between 1990 and 1993. Under orders from the state legislature, the Ohio Board of Regents examined ways to reduce costs and prepare for the future needs of Ohio students and taxpayers. The report focused on the need to reduce duplication of high cost programs, increase cooperation between sectors of the higher education system, and increase faculty productivity (Cage, 1995). Perhaps its most controversial recommendation was to require all public colleges to increase faculty teaching loads by 10 percent. However, measurement of what constituted teaching, and how the requirement would be enforced, was left to campus officials (Tucker and Voelker, 1995).

In Colorado, the Commission focused its attention on the need to accommodate projected enrollment increases. But unlike in Ohio, the Commission's proposals were designed around positive incentives rather than threats and mandates. Their recommendations included steps to encourage students to choose community college over research universities, and the elimination of subsidies for remedial courses and courses which were avocational rather than academic or vocational in nature (Colorado Commission on Higher Education, 1994).

These efforts by legislators and governors to alter the spending patterns of public colleges are symptoms of a broader tension. Campus and state leaders often have starkly different views of the appropriate priorities and practices. In particular, legislators began to question how faculty members spend their time. In 1993-94, 24 states conducted studies of faculty workload or productivity (Chronicle, 1994). As Daniel Layzell (1996) describes it:

> The logic in the minds of state legislators is clear: the more time faculty spend in the classroom, the more undergraduate students who can be accommodated at (lower cost), and the higher quality education received by those students (p. 164).

This concern over faculty teaching loads represents a fundamental tension between state lawmakers and campus leaders. The NEA survey of education committee chairs found that 86 percent felt strongly that college and university faculty should focus more on undergraduate education. The same survey found that 67 percent of legislators think that college faculty should teach more courses. Further, more than one in four education committee chairs think that their legislature will take action to mandate higher teaching loads in the next three to five years. As long as the gulf between the views of campus administrators and state leaders remains so wide, states are likely to continue to seek ways to alter campus spending patterns to more closely fit state priorities.

RESPONSE #2: Increasing Institutional Revenues

Rather than focusing on campus expenditures, some states have responded to increasing college prices by making adjustments in the revenue streams available to campus leaders. In its most straightforward manifestation, this means increasing the state appropriations to public colleges. By providing colleges with additional revenues, states can reduce the fiscal squeeze facing campus leaders and lessen the need for tuition increases. Such a response makes sense if the root cause of tuition inflation is that colleges have insufficient resources to provide a quality education at a stable price.

From a state's perspective, increasing institutional revenues is a very costly solution to the problem of tuition inflation. Even in states where policy makers see insufficient state support as the cause of rising college prices, limited state resources and shifting state priorities make increasing instructional subsidies unrealistic. There is simply not enough money to increase spending on higher education and still meet other state demands.

Generally, states build each year's budget by making incremental adjustments to last years budget. As such, the level of budgetary increase or reduction experienced by higher education often is a function of nothing more than how much money the state legislature has to allocate. Sandra Ruppert (1966) quotes one legislator who put the situation clearly "the most significant factor in whether we appropriate more money is if we have more money to appropriate" (p. 31). Complicating matters further, increasing state appropriations to higher education alone does not guarantee stable college prices. Unless state support increases more rapidly than campus spending, schools may still feel the need to raise tuition. Indeed, in recent years, public college expenditures have increased rapidly in some states even as public college prices were rising.

On the other hand, New Mexico has successfully expanded their public support of higher education. Beginning in the 1980s, state policy makers undertook a massive increase in state spending on higher education which continued into the early 1990s. This was made easier by the relative health of the state's economy. But rather than reduce taxes or expand other state services, policy makers increased appropriations to higher education by 81 percent between 1984-85 and 1994-95 (New Mexico Commission on Higher Education, 1994).

In most states, however, the prospects of colleges benefiting from additional state tax revenues is bleak. The NEA survey of education committee chairs found that less than 10 percent thought it likely that their state would increase taxes in the next 3 to 5 years (Ruppert, 1996, p. 35). A more likely source of new state revenue for public colleges are bond issues and the proceeds from state lotteries. Bond issues may be proposed to expand or renovate campus facilities. Several states already earmark lottery funds for education and several more are considering the option. One example is the HOPE program in s which uses lottery revenues to pay 100 percent of tuition and fees for all Georgia residents who attend an in-state college and who meet certain other eligibility requirements (Ruppert, 1996, p. 35).

In this difficult fiscal situation, often the best that higher education can hope for, is protect existing funding levels from cuts. In Louisiana, for example, the legislature debated creation of a "floor" for higher education funding. This action would have amended the state's constitution to guarantee that higher education could not receive less funding than it had in the previous year without a two-thirds vote of the legislature. While the measure was not adopted in Louisiana, such earmarking may be a way for state's to stabilize the dramatic shifts which often occur in higher education appropriations (Ruppert, 1996, p. 30).

Changing Pricing Practices

Faced with the realization that there is unlikely to be substantial new nontuition revenue available to them, public college leaders have sought to find ways to maximize their tuition revenues. One way to do this is to change the way they set prices without limiting the access available to lower income and disadvantaged residents. States have tried to do this in a number of ways. The most controversial is to abandon the long held commitment to low tuition.

Questioning the Value of Low Tuition

Historically, state governments and public colleges have shared a common interest in keeping public tuition charges low. States benefited from the economic and social development which accrued from increased participation in higher education, and states saw low tuition as the most direct way to increase the levels of participation in public higher education. Moreover, because colleges are attended disproportionately by higher income residents, a low tuition policy was an easy way to gain the political benefit of distributing public benefits to well-to-do residents.

Public colleges also saw low tuition as beneficial. Low tuition gave them an advantage in the competition with private schools for the best students, and also allowed them to attract large numbers of first generation college students who might otherwise not have attended college. The increase in college participation thought to result from low tuition was seen as fueling economic development and generating new revenues for state governments. More recently, however, as the budgets of both state governments and public colleges have been squeezed by rising costs and falling revenues, the interests of states and public colleges began to diverge. Their different views of how best to respond to this fiscal stress are the natural result of the different constituencies that each serve.

Governors and state legislators focus their attention on the big picture of state finance. They must generate sufficient revenue to provide the services demanded by state tax payers and still keep the state's operating budget in balance. But the dual pressures to expand public services and limit tax increases makes balancing state budgets a political mine field.

In order to reconcile these conflicting demands, state policy makers have few options. They can either raise taxes, cut state spending in other areas, increase the efficiency of service delivery, or develop alternative revenue sources. From the perspective of the governor's mansion and the statehouse, higher education looked like a good place to cut.

Public college leaders saw the slowing of state appropriations for higher education as the shortsighted and misguided efforts of state governments to shift the responsibility for funding higher education to students and their families. On campus, this raised concerns that a disastrous chain of events was being set in motion. Rising college costs would lead to lower college participation rates, which would lead to declining economic growth in the state, which would lead to reduced state revenues, which would require further cuts in all types of state services. In the end, students, colleges, and states, would all end up in worse economic condition.

Thus the relationship between states and public colleges in the 1990s is characterized by an unusually high degree of budgetary conflict. Both sides argue that the other does not understand the fundamental problem. But the differences of opinion are not simple misunderstandings. The college affordability problem, and the appropriate response to the problem, look quite different on the green at a public college than in the deliberations of a state appropriations committee (Mumper, 1996).

The High Tuition/High Aid Pricing Model

In order to generate additional revenue without limiting affordability, some states have abandoned their traditional commitment to low tuition and shifted to a high tuition/high aid pricing model. In doing so they shift their funding of higher education away from broad based state appropriations to institutions and towards need-based student aid. The changes forces public college prices to increase. But needy students will be able to pay those rising costs with the larger grants from the state they now receive. On the other hand, higher income students would find their college costs increasing as reduced state support to colleges led to higher tuition. This strategy, which has been followed in Vermont for many years, is now under consideration in several other states as a way of maintaining access for disadvantaged students while dramatically reducing the state's appropriation for higher education.

While the concept of high tuition/high aid funding has been around for more than three decades, it has emerged as a leading reform option in the 1990s. This rise to prominence was driven largely by the fiscal pressures facing state governments. As states searched for ways to reduce spending without producing negative social consequences, high tuition/high aid made sense. Supporters of this pricing strategy argue that low tuition policies are both inefficient and ineffective ways to fund higher education (Wallace 1992). State instructional subsidies allow public colleges to charge students the same low tuition regardless of their need. Students who can afford to pay the full cost of their education pay the same price as those who cannot. Further, low tuition policies insulate public higher education from the discipline of the marketplace (McPherson and Schapiro, 1991). Many students, especially low income students, have little choice but to attend a nearby public college. Thus public colleges do not face the competitive pressures which serve to increase performance and improve quality. They have a captive audience of lower income students who, even with federal financial aid, cannot afford to attend a private college or even another state institution.

Advocates of this approach see it as a way to simultaneously reduce government spending and increase educational quality. By reducing instructional subsidies state governments save money. By increasing student aid, lower income students experience no declines, or perhaps even increases, in college access (Fisher, 1990). And public colleges are forced to raise standards to compete with private colleges based on quality of education and not price.

While there has been a great deal written about the theoretical advantages of the high tuition/high aid model, it was not academic arguments which seem to be driving the shifting pricing strategies of the states. Instead, the change is almost always the product of fiscal stress. In discussing the decision to shift to a form of high tuition/high aid funding in Minnesota, Hearn and Anderson (1995, p. 18) quote a former state representative John Brandl, who observed that "when it came right down to it, we passed the legislation because we just didn't have any money". This view is echoed in the 1996 NEA survey of state education committee chairs found that "few legislators currently support shifting funds from institutional support to student financial aid programs, although many acknowledge that a high tuition/high aid strategy is being carefully examined" (Ruppert, 1996, p. 36).

Criticisms of High Tuition/High Aid Funding
Critics of the High Tuition/High Aid pricing strategy make several arguments against the plan. First, they say that as states allow their public college tuition to rise, lower income and disadvantaged students will conclude that higher education is beyond their financial reach. Well before they can fill out the forms to find out what financial aid they may receive, the "sticker shock" of higher tuition will drive them off of the college track. Others make a financial argument. Because there are more low and middle income students in public colleges, raising tuition for the upper income students will not generate sufficient revenues to cover the financial aid of the lower income students. Moreover, as public college prices rise closer to the level of private colleges, upper income students will be more likely to leave the public system. This will exacerbate the financial stress and force states to further raise tuition and/or reduce financial aid thus undermining the system (Lopez, 1993).

Another set of critics charge that high tuition/high aid pricing generates a political dynamic in state legislatures that will eventually lead to its reversal (Mingle, 1992). The political opposition to tuition increases is strong and broad based. As public college tuition rises, state's feel citizen pressure to moderate those increases. Political support for student aid is weak and narrowly based. Proposals to reduce state student aid meet with little opposition. When state's are under fiscal st

ress, and looking for ways to reduce spending, the logic of high tuition/high aid pricing asks them to take the heat for tuition increases without any political benefit. As a consequence, even when such plans are enacted, state support for them is likely to erode over time and under fiscal stress (Mumper, 1996). This seems to have been the fate of the approach in Vermont in recent years, where tuition increases have far out paced increases in student aid (Lenth, 1993, p. 36).

Linking Tuition Increases with Student Aid
One way to avoid this dynamic is to explicitly link tuition setting with financial aid. This is the approach taken in Minnesota where an effort was made to more systematically integrate the financing of postsecondary education. A key portion of this plan specified the relative shares of the costs of providing a higher education which would be borne by families and the federal and state government. Students were expected to pay 50 percent of the cost of attendance through income or loans. The remaining costs were to be covered by government assistance. After a student's Pell grant funds were counted, the state of Minnesota accepted the responsibility for any further costs (Hearn and Anderson, 1995).

Similarly, in Washington, the state legislature has taken actions to achieve proportionality between changes in tuition and student aid. In order to do so, they issued a guarantee that if tuition is raised, 24 percent of the increase must go to financial aid (Ruppert, 1996, p. 36-37). This was made easier since the Washington state legislature is responsible for setting tuition levels at the state's public colleges.

Many states have tried different ways to maintain the proportionality between tuition levels and student aid. In Illinois, New York, Rhode Island, and Virginia, the state student aid commissions explicitly attempt to compensate for tuition increases with additional funding for student aid. In Illinois, a rough 'rule of thumb' is employed in which 20 percent of all revenue generated by tuition increases go to student aid. Recently, however, the state has been unable maintain that rule in the face of rapid tuition inflation (Lenth, 1993, p. 24).

Another group of states, including Arizona, North Carolina and Texas, the coordinating or governing board define guidelines within which resources are to be allocated to student aid. But control over administration of the aid programs is decentralized to individual campuses. In Texas, for example, senior public institutions must set aside 15 percent of all tuition income for need based student. Community colleges must set aside 6 percent (Lenth, 1993, p. 25).

A recent study by Carolyn Griswold and Ginger Marine (1996) found that while such linkages do improve the power of the pricing strategy to improve equity within the state, the troubling political dynamic remains. They find that "When aid funding depends on state appropriations, it seems unavoidable that it will be cut during times of financial stress. Similarly, when tuition increases depend on the will of elected officials, such increases will be driven by fiscal considerations" (p.383). They conclude that any attempt to change to a high tuition high aid pricing policy will require extensive planning and coordination as well as strong political will.

Raising Non-Resident Tuition
Another way that public colleges can raise additional revenues is to increase the tuition

charged to nonresident students and use that money to subsidize resident students. Today almost every state charges nonresident students a tuition which approaches the full price of the education they receive (Lenth, 1993, p. 16). This is because state policy makers are generally unwilling to provide higher education, or any state service, to those who don't pay taxes in the state. But in both Vermont and Colorado, some public colleges have raised nonresident tuition rates to levels substantially higher than full-cost and use the additional revenue to subsidize in-state students.

Such an approach is unlikely to be successful in all states. Vermont and Colorado are popular destinations for prospective students from all corners of the nation. Public colleges which are located in less desirable places may find that raising tuition charges for nonresidents would reduce their enrollments. This would limit diversity on campus and potentially produce a reduction in campus revenues. Even in Vermont, the state Commission on Higher Education warned that "the rising tuition level charged to out-of-state students threatens the attractiveness of going to college in Vermont". They went on to recommend out-of-state tuition should be "sufficiently attuned to market conditions that a large number of students from outside Vermont are still attracted" (Vermont Higher Education Commission, 1989, p. 5).

RESPONSE #3: Redesigning Delivery Systems

States have also responded to pressures to control college prices by attempting to redesign their higher education system in ways that produce the same output at a lower price. These changes, ranging from comprehensive review of educational programs in order to reduce duplication and eliminate unnecessary offerings to the increased use of instructional technology, are intended to offer citizens the educational services they need at a lower cost to the state budget. While these efforts are quite popular with government leaders and voters, they are generally viewed with skepticism by more traditional higher education institutions (Blumenstyk, 1995).

Distance Learning and Virtual Universities

Perhaps the restructuring proposals that have received the most attention in recent years are those which focus on ways to use new technology to provide higher education to more and different students at a lower cost. These proposals range from two-way interactive television networks where traditional campus courses are brought to previously unserved areas by "virtual campuses" where entire programs are offered through the Internet.

Traditionally, distance learning initiatives have been aimed at nontraditional students and most of it offered through correspondence courses. Recently, however, technology has expanded the focus of distance learning to include more traditional students as well (Institute for Higher Education Policy, 1994, p. 7). To its supporters, these programs are seen as less expensive ways to offer educational services to more students or to handle the pressures of enrollment growth.

Improved technology has been largely responsible for this explosion of interest. The Institute for Higher Education Policy estimates that as recently as 1987, only ten states offered a distance learning program. By 1992, however, all 50 states were operating some type of program (1994, p. 1). The NEA survey of education committee chairs found a remarkable level of agreement on the hope that technology could be used to address a number of higher education problems, especially rising prices. All of the respondents endorsed the expanded use of technology for delivering higher education instruction and 95 percent believe that their legislature will continue to support such programs in the future (Ruppert, 1996, p. 35). James Mingle observes that: "Right now, technology seems to be the only thing states are willing to invest in" (Blumenstyk, 1994).

Perhaps the state which has developed the most elaborate system of distance education is Maine. The Education Network of Maine, a campus-less entity of the University of Maine, now employs an extensive microwave transmission system and a one way video network. The system is now available to over 100 locations and enrolls more than 7,500 students across the state (Blumenstyk, 1996).

West Virginia has also been active in pioneering distance learning. In 1988, West Virginia began a network to deliver one way video and interactive audio to test sites across the state. Today, courses are offered at up to fifty down link sites, including schools, libraries, and hospitals, across the state. The program has served more than 11,000 students and averages 2,100 annually (SHEEO, 1994).

But these programs are dwarfed in comparison to the ambitious plan now being developed by 11 western states. The governors of these states have agreed to explore the creation of a "virtual university" that would deliver courses through computer networks, television, and other technologies, and would award degrees of its own. Unlike traditional institutions that teach and offer credentials, the virtual university would simply award credentials using a set of measures that assess students' mastery of various subjects (Blumenstyk, 1995). In this way, it is similar to New York's Empire State College in offering competence based degrees.

Just how this new university will function is still unclear. But in these states where school-age populations are growing, and funding for new campuses is unlikely to be available, such alternative delivery systems have enormous appeal. Legislators and governing boards see higher education as too labor intensive and are looking to technology to improve productivity and reduce costs. Utah, which anticipates that the number of students attending its public colleges will double by 2010, is banking on such programs to accommodate that growth. Commissioner of Higher Education Cecilia Foxley admits that "you can't handle all of the growth through technology" but she goes on to make clear that Utah "is not planning to replicate nine existing campuses. We will keep building to a minimum" (Blumenstyk, 1994).

Still in spite of its promise, questions remain over whether technology based instruction really reduces costs and thus holds potential for reducing public college tuition. When compared to the expense of building campuses, virtual universities and distance learning plans certainly appear to be less expensive. But the start-up costs of such programs can be substantial. Maine has invested more than $15 million to set up its microwave transmission system. Fiber Network installation costs nearly $10,000 per mile and the setup of each classroom can run another $40,000 (Institute for

Higher Education Policy, 1994). Computer and Internet instruction are less expensive, but even here the costs are not insignificant. Moreover, the costs of student advising, electronically available library books, and royalties for copyrighted teaching materials will all increase substantially. As a result, these initiatives may serve to improve access to higher education, but it remains unclear whether they will lower costs as well.

Shifting to Lower Cost Providers

The cost of offering any educational course or program varies widely from institution to institution. If a state is able to shift enrollments from higher cost providers, like flagship research institutions, to lower cost four-year institutions or community colleges, they can reduce the cost of instruction to the student and to the state. In this way, state mandated enrollment caps have long been used to force students to attend less costly institutions. In an effort to shift enrollments to two-year and lower cost four-year colleges, California, Colorado, and Washington have had long standing enrollment caps. Oregon and North Dakota have recently followed suit (Zumeta, 1995, p. 88). While these limits may save money in the short term, they also raise substantial problems. Low income and disadvantaged students are likely to bear the brunt of the these limitations since remaining spaces are usually allocated by raising admission standards. While this would be troubling in any state, it is especially difficult in those states where the number of high school graduates is growing rapidly (Zumeta, 1995).

Differential tuition has also been used to shift enrollment to lower cost institutions. By widening the gap between the price of the flagship research university, where the per student cost of instruction is high, and community colleges, where costs are substantially lower, states can make it more attractive for students to choose the lower cost option. In this way market forces may work as well as state mandates. Sometimes this leads students to enroll in a community college rather than a research university. Other times it means that students will "double dip", taking classes at both institutions simultaneously. At the University of Nevada-Reno, for example, 30 percent of all undergraduates are enrolled concurrently at a community college. The same is true at Arizona State University. At Eastern Michigan University the percentage is about 20 (Gose, 1995).

For such plans to reduce the cost of higher education, however, students must be able to easily transfer those credits from one campus to another. If students are forced to take more courses, even if they are offered at a lower price, they may see their costs actually rise. Consequently, several states have also passed legislation to streamline the articulation and transfer process between two-year and four-year colleges. This is seen as a way of reducing net college prices by allowing more students to study at less expensive community colleges for two years and then transfer to a four year college with no loss of credit.

In Ohio, for example, all public four-year colleges are required to accept any "transfer module" which has been approved by the Board of Regents. In this way any student taking an approved module at a two-year college can be assured that it will transfer to any public four-year college in the state without the loss of credits (Ohio's Managing for the Future Taskforce, 1994).

Response #4: Increasing the Resources of Families and Students

Each of the responses discussed previously seeks to insure that state residents can afford higher education by holding down the prices charged by public colleges. But states have also responded to the affordability problem by developing mechanisms which help families to accumulate the resources necessary to pay those rising costs. Some states have done this by developing innovative mechanisms that allow families to more easily save the money they will need to pay for their children's higher education. By making it easier for families to save, states can shift the responsibility for paying for college from the taxpayers to families and still help those families to pay those higher costs.

State Prepayment and Savings Bond Programs

One way a state can increase the resources available to students and their families is to create state sponsored savings programs. These programs offer benefits to state residents who are willing to save for their children's education. By offering tax-free status to certain investments or a state match of funds placed in certain accounts, states can increase the pool of funds available to families.

These programs fall into two categories; college prepayment programs and college savings bond programs. Tuition prepayment programs allow people to purchase contracts that are guaranteed to cover a percentage of the future costs of attending college. Parents, relatives, and family friends can pay now for a future student's education. College savings bond programs use public relations campaigns and financial incentives to encourage families to save for college by investing in tax exempt government bonds. While neither type of program has much impact on college affordability in the short term, they are designed to change family savings patterns in the long term and make it possible for parents to re-assume a greater responsibility for the college costs of their children (Baum, 1990).

Both types of college savings programs have proliferated since the mid-1980s, at least in part, because they gave state policy makers politically and economically acceptable alternatives to more costly and controversial responses to increasing college prices (Mumper and Anderson, 1996). By creating college savings programs, policy makers could respond to public concerns that college was becoming unaffordable without having to appropriate new spending in the current year.

Michigan was the first state to enact such a program when it established the Michigan Education Trust (MET) in 1986. This program allowed parents and others to pay for the cost of tuition and fees at a state college years before a child reaches college age. The purchase was then guaranteed to cover those costs, no matter how high, when the child eventually enrolled. This program attracted a great deal of attention nationwide. Jeffrey Lehman (1993, p. 28) called the enactment of MET "the most widely publicized government action in the field of higher education finance during the 1980s". Soon programs like MET were under consideration everywhere. A recent survey by the General Accounting Office found that more than 40 states had considered enactment of some type of savings program and 30 of those had actually adopted some type of program. Of those, 12 have adopted a prepayment program and 7 of those have fully implemented that program (GAO, 1995).

The operation of a state prepayment program is a fairly complex matter[5]. The revenue from purchaser payments are pooled into one large fund and invested with the goal of achieving a rate of return that exceeds the inflation rate at participating institutions. Each semester that the beneficiary enrolls in a participating college, the program pays the school whatever it currently charges for tuition and fees and any other prepaid benefits. If the prepaid benefits are not used as intended, the funds are then refunded according to program stipulations.

In 1995, Massachusetts introduced a new type of prepayment plan. This program sells "tuition certificates" redeemable toward the cost of tuition and fees at any of the 67 public and private colleges in the state that agreed to participate in the program. The certificates are guaranteed by the state to hold their value until redeemed by the beneficiary. For example, if a $1,200 certificate is equal to 20 percent of tuition costs at a given college at the time of purchase, the certificate will cover that same percentage of costs when the beneficiary enrolls in that college in the future (Healy, 1995).

State prepayment programs have a number of limitations which have reduced their appeal to states in recent years. Most participants in these programs come from middle and upper income families. The GAO (1995) reported that:

> In Alabama, Florida, and Ohio, the majority of purchasers reported family incomes of over $50,000 in 1992, while the majority of state families with children had incomes under $30,000. In addition, Alabama state tax returns from 1992 and 1993 revealed that the median income among purchasers was about $61,200 while the Bureau of the Census data showed that the 1992 median family income for all families in the state was about $27,400 (p. 5).

Because of these participation patterns, the programs could subsidize their mostly well-off participants while doing little to help lower income families.

Another major concern over prepaid tuition programs is the degree of risk they pose for states. Critics worry that they could create an unfunded liability for the state if investment income is insufficient to cover the programs obligations (Lehman, 1995, p. 30-31). However, no state program has yet experienced such a shortfall and, if one did occur, it is unclear how the situation would be resolved. Because of these concerns, more states have chosen to establish a college savings bond program rather than a prepaid tuition program. Issuing college savings bonds are both less financially risky and easier to administer. About 20 states have sold college savings bonds, though relatively few have done so on a regular basis (GAO, 1995).

State college savings bond programs are quite straightforward. The state issues general obligation, zero-coupon bonds, and markets them to individuals wanting to saving for future educational costs. Because these bonds are state debt instruments, the interest earned is exempt from state and federal taxes. Although these bonds are marketed as college savings bonds, in practice they generally do not require the purchaser to spend the funds on higher education and the purchaser need not designate a beneficiary when the bond is purchased (Williams, 1993).

---

[5]Details of the development and operation of these programs are explained in Horvitz, 1993.

Finally, Kentucky has developed a college savings account program. People can save as much or as little as they like on behalf of a designated beneficiary, depending on their individual savings goals. Deposits may be as low as $25. The program guarantees a minimum 4-percent rate of return and the interest is exempt from state income taxes. When withdrawn, the funds can be spent at virtually any college in the country (GAO, 1995, p. 6).

Tuition Waivers and Exemptions

Many states offer some full or partial tuition waivers for certain types of students. This is quite different from need-based student aid in that the waivers are awarded based on some criteria other than financial need. Louisiana, North Dakota, Virginia, Wisconsin, and Wyoming among others, all provide tuition waivers to top high school students who attend their states public colleges. In Illinois, state statutes provide each member of the state legislature with two tuition waivers each year to be used at the discretion of the member at an Illinois public college or university (Lenth, 1993, p. 22-23). But it is Texas which offers the most extensive system of tuition waivers and exemptions. In 1993, nearly 23,000 students at Texas colleges and universities received tuition and fee exemptions totaling $9 million. These waivers go to war veterans and veterans who served at least 180 days during the cold war, children of disabled firefighters and peace officers, and the highest ranking graduate of each Texas high school (Texas House Research Organization, 1995).

These waivers and exemptions may serve an important social purpose by rewarding certain behaviors and life choices. But they do little to improve college affordability for those who are not part of the narrow group that is eligible for benefits. Indeed, by reducing the revenue flowing into public colleges, these waivers may actually cause some colleges to raise their tuition for other students in order to compensate for the lost revenue.

Evaluating the State Responses

There are a great many studies and reports which describe or analyze the efforts of particular states to keep their public colleges affordable. There are also many studies which examine the operation of a single reform strategy among a number of states. But there has been almost no systematic evaluation of the wide range of efforts which have occurred across the 50 states.

The only major study which attempts to explain the variations in public college affordability among all the states was conducted by Hearn, Griswold, and Marine (1996). Using 1990 data, they disaggregate the impact of several independent variables on public college tuition and student aid levels in the states. Their study makes several important findings. Region of the country is the variable which they identify as most closely associated with tuition and student aid in the states. States in the northeast and midwest have high tuition and high aid levels. States in the southwest and west have low levels of tuition and aid. Second, they find that economically developed states are more likely to have low-priced entry points into the postsecondary system. The higher the personal income in a state, the lower the tuition at two-year colleges. Finally, they found that states with planning agencies and strong coordinating boards were associated with higher tuition levels at four-year colleges (p. 267-269).

These findings point to important underlying factors that may drive changes in college affordability. The more fully the complex dynamics between tuition, student aid, state politics, and governance structure are understood, the easier it will be for policy makers to develop paths to productive policy change. But, at least in the short term, such findings provide limited guidance for policy makers. A state's region and its level of economic development are largely fixed. Even the governance structure of the state's colleges may be quite difficult to adjust.

There are still no studies which systematically examine the link between *specific policies* and college affordability across the states. In spite of the absence of such empirical analysis, however, it is clear that no policy, program or approach has fully addressed the problem. It persists, to one degree or another, in every state. This is not to say that the problem is unsolvable. Many of the responses discussed here have been in place for only a short time. Moreover, since the precise causes of the problem may vary considerably from state to state, it is perhaps unreasonable to expect to find a single solution that works everywhere. Still, with these limitations in mind, it is possible to draw some speculative regarding the effectiveness of these state efforts.

Paths to Improved Affordability

There are two sharply different paths that seem to have produced at least modest success in maintaining public college affordability. The first is for states to insure that their public colleges hold the line on tuition increases. A state can do this through generous support of its public colleges, or it can be done through threats and mandates to the colleges. This low tuition strategy, most evident in Texas, North Carolina, Idaho, Nevada, and Arizona, is generally a very costly approach. But it has had a long record of success in many states in the 1960s and 1970s. Low tuition reduces the need for states to provide financial aid to students or devise incentive programs to encourage families to save for college. This, in turn allows these states to direct all of their support for higher education to be directed to the single purpose of low tuition.

In addition to its possibilities, however, a low tuition strategy also involves substantial risks. If low tuition is achieved by starving a state's colleges of the funds necessary to maintain high quality programs or to attract the best faculty and students, it may prove a hollow victory. Policy makers must carefully answer the question "access to what?" when considering this approach. Similarly, if low tuition is achieved by limiting enrollments at some or all institutions, it may prove counter productive. Lower income and disadvantaged students may be denied access to a state's best colleges, not because they cannot afford it, but because all the slots are already filled.

Finally, even those states which have been able to maintain the lowest tuition at their public colleges have still experienced substantial price increases in the past few years. The average public college tuition in every state increased by more than 75 percent between 1985 and 1995. The average tuition doubled in all but five states. This is far greater than the increases in consumer inflation or family wages during the same time period. As prices begin to creep up, even the lowest price public colleges risk becoming unaffordable. This is because students do not only pay tuition when they go to school, they must also pay living expenses, buy books, and get back and forth to classes. Additionally, students must pay an opportunity cost to enroll in college. They must forgo earnings and job experience while they are in school. Unless there is student aid, family savings, or loans to offset these nontuition costs, even low tuition colleges may prove too costly and many potential students may simply decide not to enroll.

During the last two decades, state after state has abandoned this low tuition approach either because they could no longer afford its high cost, or because they had lost confidence in its effectiveness. California, New York, and Washington are recent examples. In its place, states have begun to employ a combination of steps that attack the problem from several sides at once. While the precise combination of steps varies from state to state, they usually include efforts to improve efficiency and productivity, to generate new revenues, and to protect the most vulnerable students from the impact of tuition increases. This incremental approach has also produced some success in maintaining public college affordability.

In most states, the first step in this approach has been to search for ways to offer the same or improved educational services at a lower price. This can be done through a redesigned delivery system, efficiency improvements, workload increases, and/or shifting students to lower-cost providers. It can also be done through performance funding. While these efforts alone are unlikely to solve the problem, over time they can reduce its magnitude. They can also help to restore the confidence of policy makers and the public that public college leaders can be trusted to spend their funds wisely.

The second step in this incremental strategy is to expect more affluent students to pay closer to the full price of their education. This will mean higher tuition for many students which will, in turn, generate new revenues for the state's public colleges. These new tuition revenues can then be used to fund need-based student aid programs or simply to replace those dollars which are no longer supplied by the state government.

The final step is then to insure that the most disadvantaged students are protected from the impact of rising prices. In most cases, this has been done by expanding the availability of need based financial aid. This can involve a full-scale shift to high tuition/high aid funding, or simply a more careful coordination between the levels of need-based aid and the rates of tuition increase. Regardless of how it is done, no effort to improve college access can be effective if it does not insure that the most disadvantaged students have access to the resources necessary to participate in the system. Some states have done this by tracking many such students into colleges with lower instructional costs. This can be done by a system of differential tuition where community colleges are priced much lower than research universities. It can also be done by a system of enrollment caps that close many of those students out of the most high cost institutions.

Like the low tuition strategy, this incremental approach also carries substantial risks. It is difficult for anyone to oppose improved efficiency and productivity. But what is an unnecessary or wasteful program to one person is often critically important to another. As such, the price of state efforts to improve efficiency may be discord and acrimony which can disrupt the smooth functioning of campuses and programs.

At the same time, rising tuition can undermine the political and public support for higher education funding. If more affluent families begin to abandon a state's public college in favor of private or out-of-state institutions, governors and legislators may lose interest in the need to maintain affordability. Similarly, during times of economic downturn, states may slash their financial aid programs because they are not protected by strong political interests. And too generous state savings programs may pull limited subsidy dollars away from programs which support all students to pay for benefits that go primarily to the richest families.

In the end, neither the low tuition nor the incremental approach represents a final solution. The myriad of social, political, and economic problems that have caused the fiscal problems now faced by state governments seem to be here to stay. As a consequence, no state is likely to have the resources necessary to turn the clock back to the era of no, or very low, tuition. As public colleges try to cover their increasing expenditure levels with more and more limited state dollars, they will be forced to raise tuition even further. Without sufficient funds to compensate for those increases with proportionate increases in need-based student aid, public college affordability will continue to decline. As long as these fundamental conditions remain in place, nothing appears likely to reverse the present trends. The best that states and institutions can hope to do is moderate the rate of declining affordability and to protect the most disadvantaged from its full effect.

References

Baum, S. (1990). The need for college savings. In J. Hansen (ed.) *College Savings Plans: Public Policy Choices.* New York: The College Board.

Berdahl, R., and McConnell, T.R. (1994). Autonomy and accountability: some fundamental issues. In P. Altbach, R. Berdahl, and P Gumport (eds.) *Higher Education in American Society* (3rd ed.). Amherst NY: Prometheus Books.

Bergmann, B. (1991). Bloated administration, bloated campuses. *Academe* 77 (November/December): 12.

Blumenstyk, G. (1994). Networks to the rescue? *Chronicle of Higher Education*, December 4, 1994. A21.

Blumenstyk, G. (1995). Campuses in cyberspace. *Chronicle of Higher Education*, December 15, 1995. A18.

Blumenstyk, G. (1996). Learning from afar. *Chronicle of Higher Education*, May 31, 1996. A15.

Cage. M. (1995). Regulating faculty workloads. *Chronicle of Higher Education*, January 20, 1995. A31.

Chronicle of Higher Education. (1994). Almanac issue. September 14, 1994.

Colorado Commission on Higher Education. (1994). *Access to Success: Accommodating Student Enrollment Demand For Colorado Higher Education.* Denver: Colorado Commission on Higher Education.

Fisher, F. (1990). State financing of higher education: a new look at an old problem. *Change* 22: 42-56.

Francis, C. (1990). *What Factors Affect College Tuition?* Washington, DC: American Association of State Colleges and Universities.

Gallup Organization. (1991). *Attitudes About American Colleges.* Washington, DC: Council for the Advancement and Support of Higher Education.

General Accounting Office. (1995). *College Savings: Information on State Tuition Prepayment Programs.* Washington, DC: General Accounting Office.

Gladieux, L. and A. Hauptman. (1995). *The College Aid Quandary.* Washington, DC: Brookings Institution.

Gose, B. (1995). Double dippers. *Chronicle of Higher Education*, August 4, 1995. A27.

Gold, S. (1995). *The Fiscal Crisis of the States.* Washington, DC: Georgetown University Press.

Griswold C., and Marine, G. (1996). Political influences on state policy: higher-tuition, higher-aid, and the real world. *Review of Higher Education* 19: 361-390.

Hauptman, A. (1990). *The College Tuition Spiral.* Washington, DC: The College Board and the American Council on Education.

Healy, P. (1995). Massachusetts Starts a Novel Program to Help Families Pay Tuition *Chronicle of Higher Education*. February 3, 1995. A 24.

Hearn, J., and Anderson, M. (1995). The Minnesota financing experiment. In E. St. John (ed.) *Rethinking Tuition and Student Aid Strategies*. San Francisco: Jossey Bass.

Hearn J., Griswold, C., and G. Marine, G. (1996). Region, resources, and reason: a contextual analysis of state tuition and student aid policies *Research in Higher Education* 37: 241-278.

Hines, E. (1996). *State Higher Education Appropriations 1995-96*. Denver: State Higher Education Executive Officers.

Horvitz, P. (1993). Prepaid tuition plans: an exercise in finance, psychology, and politics. In M. Olivas (ed.) *Prepaid College Tuition Plans: Promise and Problems*. New York: The College Board.

Hsu, S. (1995) Va. failing in funding, colleges say: business leaders warn of cuts' effect *Washington Post*. January 23, 1995. A1.

Institute for Higher Education Policy. (1994). Assessing distance learning from a public policy perspective. *Policy Steps* 3:7-9.

Layzell, D. (1996). Developments in state funding for higher education. In J. Smart (ed.) *Higher Education: Handbook of Theory and Research*, Vol. XI. New York: Agathon Press.

Lehman J. (1993). The distribution of benefits from prepaid tuition programs: new empirical evidence about the effects of program design on participant demographics. In M. Olivas (ed.) *Prepaid College Tuition Plans: Promise and Problems*. New York: The College Board.

Lenth, C. (1993). *The Tuition Dilemma—State Policies and Practices in Pricing Public Higher Education*. Denver: State Higher Education Executive Officers.

Lively K. (1995). Tough state budget line. *Chronicle of Higher Education*. January 20, 1995. A23.

Lopez, M. (1993), High tuition high aid won't work. *Chronicle of Higher Education*. April 7, 1993. B1.

Magner, D. (1995). Restructuring stirs outcry at James Madison. *Chronicle of Higher EducationI*. March 3, 1995. A15.

Massy, W., and R. Zemsky, R. (1990). *The Dynamics of Educational Productivity*. Denver: State Higher Education Executive Officers.

Mathesian, C. (1995). Higher ed.: the no longer sacred cow. *Governing*. March: 20-24.

McGuinness, A. (1994). The states and higher education. In P. Altbach, R. Berdahl, and P. Gumport (eds.) *Higher Education in American Society* (3rd ed.). Amherst NY: Prometheus Books.

McPherson, M., and Schapiro, M. (1991). *Keeping College Affordable*. Washington, DC: Brookings Institution.

Miller, V. (1993). State medicaid expansion in the early 1990s: program growth in a period of fiscal stress. In D. Rowland et. al. (eds.) *Medicaid Funding Crisis*. Washington, DC: American Association for the Advancement of Science.

Mingle, J. (1992). Low tuition, progressive taxation. *AGB Reports*. Washington, DC: Association of Governing Boards.

Mortenson, T. (1994). retrenchment in allocation of state resources to public higher education paused in FY 1995 *Postsecondary Education Opportunity*. November: 7.

Mumper, M. (1993). Maintaining public college affordability in the 1980s: how did the states do? *Journal of Education Finance*.19: 183-199.

Mumper, M. (1996). *Removing College Price Barriers*. Albany NY: State University of New York Press.

Mumper, M., and Anderson, J. (1996). Helping Families Save For College. In M. Mumper. *Removing College Price Barriers*. Albany NY: State University of New York Press. 175-190.

Nedwek, B. (1996). Public policy and public trust: the use and misuse of performance indicators in higher education. In J. Smart (ed.) *Higher Education: Handbook of Theory and Practice*, Vol. XI. New York: Agathon Press. 47-89.

New Mexico Commission on Higher Education. (1994). *The Condition of Higher Education in New Mexico*. Santa Fe, NM: New Mexico Commission on Higher Education.

Ohio Governor's Task Force. (1992). *Managing for the Future: Challenges and Opportunities for Higher Education in Ohio*. Columbus OH: Ohio Board of Regents.

Ruppert, S. (1996). *The Politics of Remedy: State Legislative Views on Higher Education*. Washington, DC: National Education Association

Schmidt, P. (1996). Earning appropriations *Chronicle of Higher Education*. May 24. A23.

SHEEO. (1994). *Access Through Distance Education: Collaborative Ventures in West Virginia*. Denver:

State Higher Education Executive Officers.

Sowell, T. (1992) The scandal of college tuition. *Commentary* 95:24.

Texas House Research Organization. (1995). *State Finance Report Number 74-2. Higher Education Tuition in Texas*. Austin, TX: Texas House of Representatives.

Tucker, J., and Voelker, J. (1995). Public higher education policy in Ohio. In C. Lieberman (ed.), *Government, Politics, and Public Policy in Ohio*. Akron, OH: Midwest Press.

U.S. Department of Education. (1995). *Digest of Education Statistics*. Washington, DC: U.S. Government Printing Office.

Vermont Higher Education Study Commission. (1989). *Recommendations and Findings*. Montpelier, VT: Vermont Higher Education Study Commission.

Virginia Council on Higher Education. (1994). *Restructuring Criteria*. Charlottesville: Virginia Council on Higher Education.

Virginia Governor's Commission on Government Reform. (1994). *Executive Committee Briefing*. Charlottesville: Governor's Commission on Government Reform.

Wallace, T. (1992). The inequities of low tuition. In *Tuition and Finance Issues for Public Institutions*. (AGB Occasional Paper #15), Washington, DC: Association of Governing Boards.

Williams, D. (1993). Taxation on prepaid tuition and other forms of college expense assistance. In M.A. Olivas (ed.) *Prepaid College Tuition Plans: Promise and Problems*. New York: The College Board. 55-77.

Zumeta, W. (1995). State policy and budget developments. *The 1995 NEA Almanac of Higher Education*. Washington, DC: National Education Association.

Zumeta W., and Looney, J. (1993). State Policy and budget developments in higher education. Working paper in public policy analysis and management. Graduate School of Public Affairs, University of Washington, Seattle WA

Epilogue

During the five years since I completed the original chapter, the American economy has experienced a period of unparalleled expansion. The resulting growth in revenue to state governments has significantly improved their fiscal situation. At the same time, welfare reform, declining crime rates, and low unemployment rates have reduced the demands on states for new expenditures. Today, the fiscal crisis of the states that characterized the early 1990s is only a distant memory. In many states, the difficult problem of avoiding a budget deficit has been replaced by the much less difficult problem of what to do with the budget surplus.

The improved economic situation of the states has produced a similarly positive change in the finances of public colleges and universities. The combination of fiscally healthy states, and the emphasis many state policy makers place on education, has brought state spending on colleges and universities to record levels. Appropriations to higher education have increased by almost six percent annually since 1997. A recent report by the National Center for Public Policy and Higher Education describes the present period as "as good as it gets in state funding for higher education" (2000, p. 7)

These improved levels of state support for higher education have translated into lower rates of tuition inflation at public colleges and universities. By the 1999-2000 academic year, price increases had slowed to about 3 percent a year. Such a rate seemed unimaginable as recently as five or six years ago. With wages in the nation growing again, the cost of attending a public college, as a percent of family income, has stabilized for the first time in nearly three decades.

But all this economic good news has not resulted in a period of tranquility in the relations between states and their public colleges. Public college leaders complain that state support has not grown fast enough to compensate for the budget pressures imposed by the states in the previous years. Today, state appropriations to higher education per $1,000 of personal income remain far below their 1990 level (Mortenson, 1999, p. 1). As a consequence, while tuition inflation has slowed, prices remain at levels that large segments of the public perceive to be too high. This has created ongoing public demands for new state initiatives to improve affordability and broaden access to colleges. In response to this pressure, states have continued and expanded many of the initiatives outlined in this chapter. But two recent developments deserve special attention: the growth in non-need resources available to students and the explosion of distance education programs. Both initiatives create the illusion of improved access and affordability. Unfortunately, their eventual impact may be quite different.

MORE AID TO THE LESS NEEDY

Even in times of budget surpluses, most states have continued to find it too expensive to return to an era of low tuition. A few states have experimented with tuition freezes or rollbacks. But most have continued to look for ways to provide residents with additional resources to pay these higher prices. Rather than expand the conventional aid programs, however, states have chosen to accelerate the flow of new resources to students and families. A recent report by the American Association of State Colleges and Universities characterizes these as a "new generation" of student aid programs (2000, p. 1). Such programs operate under broad eligibility requirements, often involving no needs-test. As such, they are designed to appeal primarily to middle income students. The most notable of these are merit scholarship programs and state sponsored savings programs.

The growth of merit scholarship programs can be traced to Georgia's HOPE (Helping Outstanding Pupils Educationally) scholarship program that began in 1993. This program earmarks state lottery funds to provide full tuition scholarships to all Georgia high school graduates who have a 3.0 grade point average. The scholarship covers full tuition at any public Georgia college or $3,000 per year to attend a private institution in Georgia. The scholarship continues as long as the student maintains a 3.0 GPA in college. Today, more than 150,000 Georgia students are receiving HOPE scholarships. At public colleges, like the University of Georgia and Georgia Tech, as well as leading private institutions like Spelman and Agnes Scott College, more than 95 percent of in-state students are receiving a HOPE scholarship.

In a very short time, HOPE has become an extremely popular program in Georgia. It appears to have the full support of both political parties, the Governor, and the legislature. HOPE's popularity has inspired similar innovations across the country, especially in the

South. More than a dozen states have either modeled the HOPE program or are actively considering such a plan. It is even credited with inspiring the HOPE Tax Credit enacted by Congress in 1998, although the final version of this program did not involve a merit scholarship provision.

Merit scholarship programs illustrate the costs and benefits of these new generation aid programs. Supporters see them as rewarding outstanding performance and encouraging students and high schools to set high academic standards. They also allow states to respond in a bold way to public demands for improved college affordability. But critics see them as inefficiently designed, unnecessarily expensive, and unlikely to improve college access for the disadvantaged. In particular, critics see the costs of these programs as diverting funds from lower income families toward middle and upper income families. Since lower income families are more likely to play state lotteries, they provide the bulk of the funds to run the program. This inherent inequity is made worse in Georgia because the value of any Pell grant received is subtracted from the HOPE scholarship. This has the effect of excluding low-income families from eligibility for the program. As a result, the rewards of HOPE go disproportionately to more wealthy families. Indeed, all such merit scholarships skew financial aid toward the non-needy because traditional merit measures are highly correlated with family income. As such, states are providing generous subsidies to upper and middle-income students who could easily afford higher education on their own. Thomas Mortenson (2000, p. 1) argues that programs like Georgia's HOPE Scholarship are serving to transfer income from poor families to middle-income and rich families, "just like plantation economics."

A similar explosion has taken place in state sponsored savings programs. During the mid-1990s, state interest in these programs seemed to have waned. But as the fiscal health of the states improved, the same dynamic that led to increased interest in merit scholarship programs has driven a renewed growth of these savings programs. Today, forty-four states and the District of Columbia have authority to operate and manage college savings programs. Currently, 19 states operate prepaid plans and 16 operate savings plans. Fourteen new savings plans and one additional prepaid plan are expected to begin operation within the next year. Every remaining state, except Georgia, has legislation pending or is actively studying the establishment of a college tuition plan. There are now nearly one million signed college tuition contracts. The estimated fair market value of these contracts is over $5 billion, and the numbers of participants and contracts have mushroomed in recent years.

These state savings plans have become so popular, in part, because they help middle-income families get a handle on rising college prices. This is good politics. But like merit scholarships, such programs offer little to those families who lack the resources to save for college. Some states have expressed an interest in increasing lower income participation in these programs. Michigan, for example, developed a monthly payment option in an effort to attract lower income participants. But the option did little to change the income distribution of purchasers. In spite of their good intentions, these new savings programs do little to help the most needy. Indeed, such state efforts will, at best, have a marginal impact because low-income families simply lack the disposable income necessary to take advantage of the opportunity such savings programs provide. College savings programs target their benefits to those families with discretionary income to set aside for higher education. Families with lower incomes, and already low marginal tax rates, find it difficult to save and thus receive little benefit from the programs.

A final important trend in state financing of higher education is the increased attention to distance education. The technological advances of the past decade are rapidly transforming the way that higher education is provided. The modest initiatives I described earlier in this chapter are now dwarfed by a tidal wave of distance learning programs. Today, nearly half of all institutions of higher education offer courses online. Students now can select from hundreds of degree options that do not require visiting a traditional campus. These programs hold great appeal to state policy-makers. They offer the prospect of significantly expanding access to public higher education. It makes it easier for full-time workers to return to school to upgrade their skills without quitting their jobs. Additionally, public college enrollments have increased steadily and the specter of an impending enrollment boom is on the minds of many state policy makers. Facing this need to increase the number of students that can be served, states view these new delivery systems as a way to accommodate more students without requiring large expenditures in new capital projects or expanding the number of full-time faculty and staff.

Yet, as with the new generation aid programs, these new generation delivery systems reinforce the troubling trend discussed earlier. Those in the best position to take advantage of the opportunities they provide are the best educated and have higher incomes. Conversely, lower-income students find the developments of these new delivery systems the least useful. A recent College Board (Gladieux and Swail 1999, p. 20) report concludes: "Not all students have equal access to computers and the Internet. In fact, there is evidence that students with the greatest need get the least access". The report goes on to note that "the most advantaged citizens – and schools – are most able to benefit from cutting-edge technologies. Advantage magnifies advantage" (Gladieux and Swail 1999, p. 20).

CONCLUSION

During the difficult fiscal times experienced by states in the 1980s and early 1990s, public colleges became less affordable. The impact of these trends hit lower income families especially hard. As the fiscal situation of the states improved, it might seem like the appropriate time to take action to reverse this trend. Unfortunately, the states did not choose to provide more help to the most needy. Instead, they bowed to political expediency and directed their new spending initiatives to middle and upper income families.

The result is a troubling dynamic for lower-income and disadvantaged students. During times of fiscal stress, states allow public college tuition to rise and allocate fewer dollars for need-based student aid. Affordability and access are reduced for everyone. During better times, however, states have not chosen to reverse these trends. Instead, they have targeted their new spending toward less needy residents. They have expanded the funds available for middle- and upper-income students through merit scholarships and savings programs and spent additional funds on new delivery systems. Affordability and access are improved for middle-income students, but the most needy are unable to take advantage of the opportunities created by these new state initiatives.

References

American Association of State Colleges and Universities. (2000). State Student Financial Aid: Tough Choices and Trade-Offs for a New Generation. *Perspectives* 2 (1).

Gladieux, L. and Swail, W.S. (1999). *The Virtual University and Educational Opportunity.* (Washington DC: The College Board).

Hovey, H. (1999). *State Spending for Higher Education in the Next Decade.* Washington DC: National Center for Public Policy and Higher Education.

Mortenson, Thomas. (December 1999). "State Tax Fund Appropriations for Higher Education, FY 2000" in *Postsecondary Education Opportunity.*

Mortenson, Thomas (2000). "Refocusing Student Financial Aid: From Grants to Loans, from Need to Merit, from Poor to Affluent". www.postsecondary.org.

Chapter 9

STATE POLICY AND
PRIVATE HIGHER EDUCATION:
Past, Present and Future

William Zumeta

INTRODUCTION

The title of this chapter implies that there are state policies which affect the private (independent, nonprofit) sector of higher education[1] and that these are worthy of attention. This may not be obvious to the casual observer who might well think that state higher education policies are concerned almost exclusively with public colleges and universities. Recent survey evidence indicates that a surprising number of state policymakers share such a public-only (or at least public-mostly) perspective (Zumeta, 1989; 1992; 1994; Education Commission of the States, 1990).

Nonetheless, as will be explained, many state policies do affect private higher education in important ways and this sector in turn can help to achieve public purposes. To the extent the independent sector is significant in American higher education, or in particular states, it is well that these policies and their impacts be examined. Also, many observers have been concerned for a number of years that the valuable resource represented by the private sector of American higher education has been imperiled by the combined forces of the long decline in the number of high-school graduates, rapid growth in the price of private higher education (especially relative to public alternatives), and the sluggish and erratic growth in federal student aid funding since the early 1980s.[2]

---

[1]The focus of this chapter is on private, *nonprofit*, or independent, colleges and universities, not (except peripherally) on private, for-profit and vocational postsecondary institutions. Hence, the terms *private* and *independent* higher education are used interchangeably. The chapter was originally published in Volume XII of *Higher Education: Handbook of Theory and Research,* © 1997 by Agathon Press. It has been updated with an Epilogue written especially for this volume.

[2] See Carnegie Council (1977), Education Commission of the States (1977; 1990), Breneman and Finn (1978), McPherson and Schapiro (1991), and Breneman (1994).

Further, the argument will be made in this chapter that the private sector's role in meeting emerging future demands on higher education—demands that will be increasingly difficult to meet in the accustomed ways—could be quite important, but only if state policies consciously facilitate this. It will also be argued, however, from both theoretical and empirical perspectives, that in many states there are powerful forces at play that tend to work against such explicit state recognition of the role and potential of private higher education.

Purposes and Approach of the Chapter

The purposes of this chapter are several. First, I will expand upon the above themes in order to explain why the topic of state policies affecting private higher education is important in an emerging era of increasing demands on higher education but also extreme pressures on its traditional sources of support. Then, I shall trace the development of public policies affecting private higher education historically and comparatively, emphasizing especially the period since about 1970. This review will cover the highlights of the pertinent literature and will attempt to assess in broad terms the consequences of policies, as well as of larger contextual conditions, on private higher education. The coverage includes federal as well as state policies, for in most periods in U.S. history, what the federal government was doing or not doing is critical to understanding the context for state higher education policy.

Next, I will offer a theoretical perspective seeking to comprehend and explain the variability in states' attention to the private higher education sector and, in particular, why many states tend to pay it little heed. I will argue that such a posture has had real consequences in the recent past and will, in general, not serve states well in the years to come, while other feasible postures should work better for many states. Finally, I will suggest key issues for further work in both theory development and empirical research and analysis in this field.

Why Private Higher Education and State Policies Affecting It Are Important

The private higher education sector in the United States is of historic and, it will be argued here, high current importance. The contributions of the private sector to broad public purposes date back to the colonial period (Rudolph, 1962; Veysey, 1965; Trow, 1993), and are well-known and widely envied around the world, where substantial private sectors are relatively rare (Clark, 1983; Geiger, 1986; Levy, 1986; Kerr, 1991). This admiration is in part due to the high quality of many of America's private institutions, which serves as a benchmark for their public counterparts. Ashby (1971), Clark (1983), and Kerr (1991), among others, have suggested that American private higher education has also provided important models of autonomous but socially responsible governance and behavior to public higher education both here and abroad. These are valuable public purposes served uniquely by independent higher education.

American private colleges and universities are a highly variegated lot, representing a wide variety of cultural, philosophical, and religious, as well as experimental academic, perspectives, and diverse and unusual combinations of subject area specialties. This provides a rich range of choices for students and potential sponsors and

supporters that the public sector, with its church-state and other political and bureaucratic limitations, could never match. This is a real virtue in a country as diverse as
the contemporary United States. Also, as nongovernmental, largely market-driven
entities, private institutions can often respond more quickly— and with more variety,
thus serving as a hedge against uncertainty— to new societal needs than can more
cumbersome, layered public systems. If some responses prove inappropriate, these
can also be more easily allowed to die out or pressured by the environment to adapt
than is usually the case in public systems (Thompson and Zumeta, 1981; Birnbaum,
1983).

Moreover, private colleges and universities also do more to serve the equity goals
of public policy than is widely appreciated. Nationally, these schools enroll nearly as
high a proportion of minority students as do public four-year institutions (National
Institute of Independent Colleges and Universities, 1992; Breneman 1994), and graduate a substantially higher percentage of those they enroll (Porter, 1989). Also,
according to studies in several states, the family income profile of private college students in the aggregate is very similar to that of students in the four-year public sector
and is substantially lower than that of the leading public research universities.[3]

Private higher education institutions are also broadly, if somewhat unevenly, distributed across the country. There are private, nonprofit colleges in the District of
Columbia and in 49 of the 50 states. In the fall of 1992, a total of more than 1,800
such institutions enrolled some 2.95 million undergraduate and graduate students
(Zumeta, 1994). Even limiting attention to four-year, Carnegie-classified, general-
purpose colleges and universities (thereby excluding hundreds of two-year, unclassi-
fied and specialized institutions[4]), the aggregate headcount enrollment in this narrowly defined private higher education sector is more than 2.4 million. Although their
market share has declined sharply since World War II, private colleges and universities still grant some 28 percent of all baccalaureate degrees, 36 percent of all Ph.D.s,
and 60 percent of all first-professional degrees, including a high percentage of teacher
education degrees (ECS, 1990).   Thus, the private sector is of real importance to
national goals in regard to skilled labor force development.

The proportion of statewide headcount enrollments (including two-year enrollments) in independent colleges and universities is small in some states but ranges to
above 50 percent in Massachusetts and to more than 80 percent in the District of
Columbia. In the fall of 1992, private sector enrollments were more than a third of the
statewide total in seven states (plus D.C.) and were 20 percent or more in 17 states
plus D.C.[5] The overall "market share" figure for the private higher education sector
in the nation was just over 20 percent in 1992, down from around 50 percent just after
World War II (McPherson and Schapiro, 1991, p. 22). If two-year institution enroll-

---

[3]In 1993, the estimated median family income of dependent students enrolled at independent colleges
and universities was about $46,000. Studies conducted in California, Florida, Minnesota, and Oregon gen-
erally show that, contrary to popular belief, the median family income of private-college students tends to
be similar to that of students enrolled in four-year public institutions, and below the median income of students attending "flagship" public research universities (National Institute of Independent Colleges and Universities, 1995).

[4]The "specialized" designation includes seminaries, free-standing law and medical schools, and the like.

ments are excluded, the nationwide private-sector share in 1992 jumps to 29 percent. It has been estimated that it would cost taxpayers an additional $12 billion annually (1990 dollars) to educate in the public sector all the students now attending private colleges and universities (ECS, 1990, p. 11). Most of this sum, of course, would be paid by state taxpayers.

Thus, there is ample reason for public policy to be concerned with the capacity and vitality of private higher education, given the key societal functions it performs uniquely (or particularly well) and the extent to which it eases burdens on the public fisc in many states. If the private sector continued to perform these functions in the absence of policy intervention or change, there would be no cause for concern. But, as will be argued below, there are reasons to think that important parts of the private sector will be unable to do so, indeed are already visibly slipping in their ability to serve key public purposes.

In light of the limited resources pragmatically available to governments today, the point about reducing burdens on the public fisc takes on added importance. Most importantly, although many state policymakers are not yet fully aware of it, a majority of states will soon face increases—some very substantial increases—in the demand for places in higher education simply by virtue of known demographic trends. In particular, the maturation to college age of the large "baby boom echo" cohort of children born in the 1970s and early 1980s and the effects of recent population growth patterns will be felt very strongly in many states by 2000 and in the years beyond. According to the latest state-by-state projections by the Western Interstate Commission on Higher Education (1993), the number of high-school graduates is projected to increase between 1994-95 and 2004-05 *by thirty percent or more* in ten states (including populous California and Florida), by 15 to 29 percent in 13 more, and by ten percent or more in yet another half-dozen states (Figure 1). These figures are a good rough, though probably conservative, indicator of pressures on enrollment capacity in higher education (hereafter termed simply "demand").[6]

Additional increases in demand for higher education may well be spurred by clear recent signs of strong labor market rewards for college graduates relative to their less-educated peers (Murphy and Welch, 1989), and by the growing interest of employers and employees in higher education as a means of increasing workers' human capital.[7]

---

[5]The state-level private market share figures reported here were developed by the author with the aid of Dr. Penelope Karovsky, University of Washington, and the National Institute of Independent Colleges and Universities, from the federal Integrated Postsecondary Education Data System (IPEDS) survey data. We have been careful to exclude the private proprietary and vocational schools included by the federal government in its reports from this data base.

[6]The figures are projected from trends in actual data on public and private high-school graduates through 1991-92 (WICHE, 1993). They are probably conservative as indicators of trends in higher education demand because they take no account of recent patterns of increased demand for higher education from older adults and employers seeking worker training, and of the effects of improvements in instructional technology and delivery systems on demand.

[7]There is evidence that the weak job market created by the recession reduced returns on investment for college graduates (Mishel and Bernstein, 1992), though economic returns remain high by historical standards. There is good reason to believe this is a short-term blip in a long-term upward trend in returns to investment in higher education (Marshall and Tucker, 1992).

In many cases high-cost professional school enrollment slots (e.g., in engineering and some health professions) will be in particular demand. Yet, in the face of this growing demand, many public higher education systems are at or near capacity to enroll students and would have to build additional buildings or whole campuses and hire additional faculty to expand enrollments significantly.[8] This is likely to be a very expensive proposition on a per-student basis at a time when public support for taxes and public spending is at a low ebb.

While some public sector expansion will no doubt be necessary in states with growing enrollment demand, many of these same states have private colleges and universities with apparent slack capacity after years of relatively stable or even declining enrollments. Six states[9] showed a decline over the 1980-92 period in undergraduate enrollments in private, four-year colleges and universities, and another seven experienced only modest aggregate increases (less than ten percent) over these twelve years, suggesting that some private institutions in these states may well have additional capacity.[10] Indeed if full-time-equivalent (FTE) enrollment counts are used instead of headcounts, the number of states showing declines in enrollment or only modest increases (<10%) over the 1980-92 period increases to 16.[11] Among these 16 states with sluggish recent enrollments in the private sector, four anticipate growth in high-school graduates over the next decade (1994-95 through 2004-05) in the twenty percent range or more, and four more expect growth in the 9-14 percent range.

Incremental costs to add students at private institutions with slack capacity should be relatively low, certainly lower than the per-student cost of building additional capacity in the public higher education sector.[12] Moreover, some private institutions wish to grow regardless of slack capacity considerations and it may well be in the tax-

---

[8]For example, California, Florida, Virginia, and Washington all face strong pressures to expand their already-full public higher education systems to accommodate large increases in the college-age population (Zumeta and Looney, 1994). Washington also seeks to increase its below average participation rate in upper-division and graduate education (Washington Higher Education Coordinating Board, 1992). Another large state, Pennsylvania, anticipates only modest increases in high-school graduates (14 percent between 1994-95 and 2004-05) but has made increasing participation in higher education a major priority and so is greatly concerned about capacity constraints in its public sector. These cases are only illustrative but they show that capacity constraints in the public sector are not a problem limited to small states or the "Sunbelt."

[9]For these purposes, the District of Columbia is considered a state.

[10]A recent survey by the author of state independent sector association executive officers provides further evidence of underutilized capacity in private higher education (Zumeta, 1994). Of 33 respondents (states) to a question about numbers of additional students that independent colleges and universities in the respondent's state could accept without a major additional investment in facilities and faculty, the median response represented a 10 percent increase over the sector's Fall 1990 enrollment (mean = +13%). When asked how many additional students private institutions *would be willing to accept assuming adequate quality students and government-funded student aid*, the median percentage increase relative to 1990 enrollment jumped to +14% and the mean to +21% (n=31).

[11]This difference, of course, reflects the trend toward greater proportions of part-time enrollments in private institutions (Zumeta, 1994). Significantly, in more than half the states (27), private-sector enrollments of *full-time* students either declined or grew by less than ten percent over the 1980-92 period.

[12]The comparative cost advantage of the private sector may disappear where public institutions also have slack capacity. Even so, funding arrangements for public institutions may not fully reflect this as they are often tied more closely to average than to marginal costs.

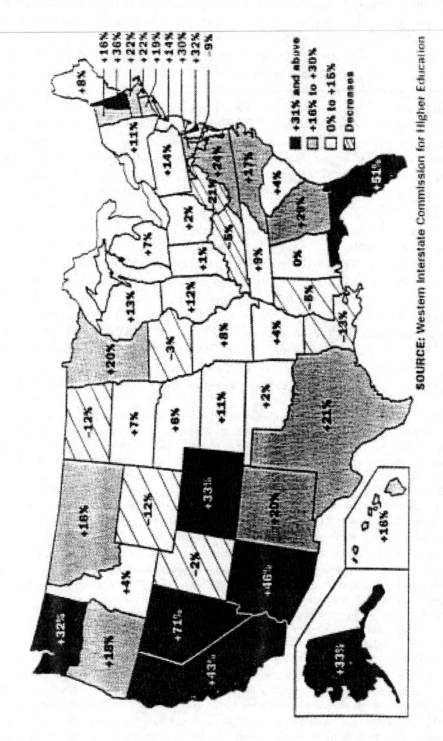

FIGURE 1. Projected Change in the Number of High-school Graduates, 1994–95 to 2004–05

Source: *The Chronicle of Higher Education Almanac Issue, Sept. 1, 1994*

payer's interest for them to do so where demand for higher education is strong, even if such growth requires some financial inducement from the state.[13] For present purposes, the primary point is that private higher education's capacity and vitality (that is, quality and capacity to grow) is, if anything, more squarely than ever a legitimate concern of policymakers.

Yet, even as its potential capacity is increasingly needed, private higher education faces threats to its ability to continue to serve public purposes well. These threats trace back, in their most serious form, to around 1980 when the number of high-school graduates began a decline that is just now coming to an end nationally (U.S. Department of Education, 1995); when there began a rapid increase in the private/public "tuition gap" (Clotfelter, 1991); and when the growth in federal student aid funds (particularly grants) slowed dramatically (College Board, 1994). These developments are in all likelihood a factor in the declines in private sector enrollments during the 1980-92 period in several states mentioned above, in the exodus of middle-income students from private institutions identified by Zumeta (1990) and McPherson and Schapiro (1991), and in the sharply increasing trend in private institutions' spending on student aid to attract students (National Institute of Independent Colleges and Universities, 1990; College Board, 1994; Breneman, 1994). These latter trends do suggest potential problems in the ability of the private higher education sector, or at least parts of it, to serve public purposes, problems which are sometimes exacerbated by public policy.[14]

It must be noted, however, that it is not at all clear that private higher education has fared terribly badly with the limited attention it has received from public policy during the recent period of very difficult contextual conditions. Nationwide, full-time-equivalent enrollments in private higher education grew by about eleven percent between 1980 and 1992, not far behind the growth rate over this period in public sector enrollments (Zumeta, 1994). As indicated earlier, there was some enrollment growth in the private sector in nearly nine-tenths of the states during this period and the coming years promise substantially more favorable underlying demographic trends in most states. In short, the evidence on private higher education's health and prospects is decidedly mixed.[15] The argument for enhanced public policy attention to the private sector thus hinges at least as much on the notion of states seizing an opportunity to meet their emerging needs cost-effectively as on any urgent need to rescue a valued sector of higher education that is in serious trouble.

It will be argued here that state policies toward private higher education have been, for most of U.S. history and with few exceptions, of a generally limited, largely

---

[13]This analysis assumes that the state does not have to pay as much per student-place for private sector capacity as it would pay for new public sector capacity. (It also assumes adequate quality in the private sector.) When the state payments approach a level equal to per-student subsidies (including capital costs) in the public sector, this would be a signal to cap these inducements.

[14]For example, state policies in the area of expansion and pricing of public higher education and in design and funding of student aid programs can have substantial impacts on private institutions. These and other specific policy issue areas are discussed in the analysis which follows.

[15]See also Breneman (1994) for a similar conclusion, following exhaustive analysis of financial trends for private liberal arts colleges.

"hands off" character. There are important variations—the major outlines of which will be sketched later—and there has been a clear tendency toward more state involvement in recent years. Still, by and large, most states until quite recently have left private higher education largely alone to both enjoy the benefits of limited state regulation and to weather the storms created by economic recessions and demographic changes. Part of the reason is that independent higher education is a form of private enterprise, which American political and economic philosophy favors leaving alone absent strong reasons to the contrary. And, of course, many in this sector have generally preferred a minimal relationship to government, at least as long as environmental conditions were mostly favorable.[16]

Thus, relatively few states have taken extensive advantage of the opportunities provided by these independent institutions to serve public purposes, beyond simply allowing them to educate as many students as they chose to in the competitive environment created by their coexistence next to heavily subsidized public institutions. The associated norms and habits are rather powerfully embedded in many states still. Hence, it will not be easy for states to behave differently even in circumstances which suggest that more active state partnerships with private institutions might well be cost-effective for higher education in the era now dawning of renewed demand growth but sharp constriction in traditional sources of financial support for the entire postsecondary enterprise. A key purpose of this chapter is to provide both comparative and historical background and a conceptual framework for understanding the state policies that affect private higher education, so as to make possible a broader view of both the possibilities and limitations for use of this sector as an instrument of public policy in this new era.

State Policies That Affect Private Higher Education

Before proceeding further, it seems appropriate to first describe the major types of state policies that touch private higher education to give the reader some concrete referents. This discussion will also seek to provide some practical insights into the varied arrangements by which states currently employ private colleges and universities to serve public purposes by bringing to bear some relevant, fairly recent survey data. Later in this chapter we will consider whether these policies can reasonably be thought of as part of a coherent *state policy posture* vis-a-vis private higher education and will consider some basic empirical evidence indicating that it makes sense to look for patterns of related policies in this field. Then, we will describe and seek to make sense of these state policy postures and their implications, both for policy science and for policy analysis.

A host of state policies affect private colleges and universities in some way. I will provide here a brief overview of these using some of the language of policy instruments familiar to students of public policy (see, for example, Dahl and Lindblom, 1953; Bardach, 1980; Hood, 1983; Elmore, 1987; Linder and Peters, 1989; Howlett,

---

[16]Private higher education's arms-length relationship to government in this country stems in part from the historical sensitivity of church-state relationships, which are often much closer in other countries. Everywhere that private higher education exists, religious motivations have played a part in the establishment of many of the private institutions (Geiger, 1986; Levy, 1986).

1991). This language is useful for thinking about whether and how policies in this area intentionally affect their targets or unintentionally impact private colleges and universities when these institutions are not their primary targets.

The empirical data referred to in this section come from three sources.[17] The major source is a pair of national surveys on state policies affecting private colleges and universities. These surveys of state higher education agency directors and statewide private college association heads were conducted by the author for the Education Commission of the States' Task Force on State Policy and Independent Higher Education in 1988.[18] The surveys covered all the major state policies affecting private colleges and universities except student aid funding levels and state policies influencing public institution tuition. These latter topics were well covered by the other two data sources referred to in this section—surveys by the National Association of State Scholarship and Grant Programs[19] and the State Higher Education Executive Officers (1988), respectively, to which I had access for the analyses summarized here.

The discussion below is organized by policy area.

Student Aid: According to those who represent them in state capitals (i.e., the state private sector association heads surveyed), the state policies most important to private colleges and universities as a group are, by a wide margin, those in the area of state student aid program design and funding. In response to federal funding incentives, virtually all states now have state student aid programs (i.e., state scholarships and the like) for which needy private college and university students are eligible (National Association of State Scholarship and Grant Programs, annual publication).[20] Many of these aid programs function as partial higher education vouchers from the state in that eligible students can carry them to either public or private institutions (including in some cases proprietary schools), and use them to offset tuition charges. But the level of state funding for the awards varies widely across the states, as do such key design features from the standpoint of the private sector as the extent of tuition sensitivity, the maximum award allowed, and the maximum family income level permitted for eligibility.

In addition, states may provide other student aid funds earmarked only for private or only for public college students. Six states provide "tuition equalization" aid grants to private college students regardless of their need status (NASSGP, 1994) on the theory that these students would receive non-need-based state subsidies in the form of below-cost tuition rates if they attended a public college or university. This approach clearly expands the pool of students for whom private institutions can compete and serves to target these state aid funds directly on them, but at the expense of the typical

---

[17]Note that these data are used illustratively here. The point of this section is to describe the nature of state policies that touch upon the private higher education sector.

[18]For a complete report on the data from these surveys, see Zumeta (1989).

[19]This survey of state student aid policy and funding by "NASSGP" is conducted annually, most recently for the 1993-94 academic year (NASSGP, 1994).

[20]In most cases these aid programs are restricted to undergraduates and about three-fourths of the award dollars are distributed on the basis of the recipient's financial need (NASSGP, 1994, p. 1).

policy goal of targeting aid funds to the needy. With this last consideration in mind, another twelve states make "tuition equalization" grants to private college students contingent on the student's need status.[21] In some states, student aid programs are large enough to, it would seem,[22] make a big difference in terms of the public/private competition for students. But Table 1, which summarizes state student aid funding per-student for the year 1993-94, shows that there is a great range in state funding levels for student aid.

TABLE 1. Estimated Grant Dollars to Undergraduates in 1993-94 per Full-Time Undergraduate Enrollment, by State

State	Undergraduate Grant Aid	State	Undergraduate Grant Aid
1. New York	$1,157	26. Oregon	$ 158
2. New Jersey	996	27. Missouri	153
3. Minnesota	783	28. Virginia	151
4. Illinois	727	29. Rhode Island	150
5. Pennsylvania	543	30. Arkansas	138
6. Vermont	504	31. Tennessee	129
7. Georgia	375	32. West Virginia	113
8. Ohio	356	33. Kansas	109
NATION	350	34. Louisiana	100
9. Iowa	340	35. North Dakota	82
10. Indiana	*338	36. Texas	66
11. Florida	332	37. Delaware	65
12. Washington	330	38. Alabama	63
13. Michigan	316	39. Nebraska	48
14. Connecticut	310	40. Alaska	46
15. Wisconsin	297	41. Dist. of Columbia	36
16. Maryland	286	42. Arizona	32
17. Colorado	269	43. South Dakota	29
18. California	268	44. Idaho	28
19. New Mexico	222	45. Hawaii	27
20. Massachusetts	215	46. New Hampshire	25
21. Kentucky	197	47. Nevada	18
22. North Carolina	190	48. Montana	16
23. Oklahoma	177	49. Wyoming	16
24. Maine	175	50. Mississippi	15
25. South Carolina	170	51. Utah	14

*Grant amounts for 1993-94 were not available. Calculation based on 1992-93 Grant Aid Dollars.
Sources of Data: Grant Aid dollars are from Column 1 and Column 3 in Table 1 of this report. Enrollment data are calculated from the U.S. Department of Education, National Center for Education Statistics, *Digest of Education Statistics, 1993,* Tables 188 and 192, pages 192 and 196. Enrollments for Fall 1992 were not available as this report went to press.
Source: National Association of State Scholarships and Grant Programs, 1994, p. 110

---

[21]This figure comes from an analysis developed by the author, with the assistance of John Fawcett-Long, from raw data in NASSGP (1994).

[22]This is a judgment, rather than an analytically based conclusion, for a recent survey by the author (Zumeta, 1995a) showed that few states have seriously studied such impacts of their student aid programs.

Direct State Payments to Independent Institutions: Nearly all the state student aid programs aid private colleges and universities *indirectly* by providing aid to their students or potential students, rather than providing funds directly to the private school. Such funding might logically be regarded as the purchase by the state of student enrollment slots at nonpublic institutions according to eligible students' choices of where to attend rather than as aid to these institutions, although it clearly has both effects and probably in most cases both purposes.

States can also contract *directly* with private colleges and universities to enroll students in particular fields, usually in practice high-cost graduate or professional fields, where the alternative is building additional public sector capacity. In addition, states may contract with private institutions for other services, such as research or technology development in particular fields, for enhancement of academic support programs for disadvantaged students, or for sharing the cost of building a capital facility. A small number of states provide fully discretionary and unabashedly direct aid without any contract involved to private institutions or a subset of them (such as medical or engineering schools which are part of private universities) explicitly in the name of preserving their educational capacity and other services to the state.

In total, according to the survey data, in 1988, 21 of the 50 states provided funds directly to private colleges and universities, whether by contract or other means.[23] Table 2 provides the results on the nature and distribution of these types of programs providing direct state support to private institutions, from the author's 1988 survey of state higher education agency heads. Note that only six states provided general institutional support to a broad range of private institutions. (A few others provided such support to a few schools.)

These data suggest both diversity in states' priorities and needs as these intersect with the capabilities of private colleges and universities, and also considerable variety in legal and fiscal arrangements for providing state support. Before this survey (since no similar survey had been done for many years[24]), it was widely thought that most state programs providing funds to private colleges and universities were contract-based with funding linked to numbers of students enrolled. Also, it was thought that most of these programs were specifically targeted at private colleges.

The survey revealed a considerably more complex picture. Only about half (27) of the 53 programs identified by the survey and with adequate data on funding arrangements for a judgment to be made were found to be *capitation-based* (i.e., funding linked to enrollments or degrees), and only eleven of these involved formal contracts. Another 16 instances of contract arrangements were identified, but in these cases the contracts were for something other than students or degrees, such as for a specific capital project or start-up support for a new program. Finally, ten programs provided support for a wide range of purposes without benefit of either a contract or any capitation formula. Many of these operated on something resembling a grant

---

[23]Excluded here are direct appropriations or contracts for student aid (to avoid double-counting of state student aid efforts affecting the private sector) and the occasional ad hoc project research grant, though substantial and ongoing research *programs* are included.

[24]The previous source was a series of annual surveys conducted by the Education Commission of the States (1971-1982).

TABLE 2.Types of Programs of Direct State Payments to Independent Institutions and Their Frequency

Type of Program	# of Such Programs	# of States w/Such Programs
General Institutional Support	6	6:IL, MD, MI, NJ, NY, PA
Support for Health Sciences & Health Professional Programs (Most common fields are medicine, dentistry and nursing)	22[a]	14:AL, FL, IL, MA, MI, NC, NH, NJ, NY, OH, PA, TN, TX, WI
Support for EducationalPrograms in Other Specific Fields (Most common fields are education and engineering)	12[b]	12:AL, FL, IL, MD, MO, NC, OH, PA, RI, SC, TN, VA[c]
Research/Technology Support	10	7:FL, GA, LA[d], NJ, NY, OH, TX
Program Support for Programs Serving Disadvantaged Students	6	6:AL, FL, MA, MI, NJ, NY
Support for Cooperative Ventures (Excludes technology ventures included above)	4	4:AL, IL, MA[e], RI[e]
Broad-purpose Capital Assistance	3	3:IL, MD, PA[d]
Support for Endowed Chairs Only	2	2: NJ, NY
Support for Instructional Quality Improvement Only	2	2: LA[c], SC[d]
Unclassifiable (Has supported very diverse activities)	1	1:NJ, (Dept. of Higher Education special-purpose grants)

Source: Zumeta, 1989.

[a]Includes cases where support for health fields is part of a larger program also supporting other fields.

[b]Includes cases of state appropriations to specialized institutions.

[c]First funding in 1988-89.

[d]Not funded in 1987-88.

[e]Higher education/K-12 cooperation.

basis: the state agency solicited proposals and funded the ones it found to best suit state needs, often with quite broad guidelines as to what types of projects might be eligible. A number of states had more than one program encompassing two or more of the above types of arrangements, suggesting again that states have a variety of instruments at their disposal in this policy arena to meet various objectives and state policymaker preferences as to approach.

Significantly and somewhat surprisingly, the survey also revealed that a substantial share of the state programs which provide funds directly to private colleges and universities were *not* limited to funding these institutions. In 29 of the 55 programs (53%) for which the relevant data were available from the survey, only private institutions were eligible for program funds. But in 21 cases (38%), covering 13 different states, the private schools shared eligibility for program funds with public institutions, and in five more cases (9%), covering three different states, for-profit institutions were eligible for state funding as well. The programs for which for-profit schools were eligible were all instances where the state essentially purchased enrollment slots in particular fields, but the programs including both private nonprofits and public institutions encompassed a number with other purposes. Even in the programs involving *only* private nonprofit institutions—most of which were programs in which the state purchased or subsidized enrollment slots, often in high-cost professional fields—the private schools are implicitly competing with public sector alternatives for use of these funds in that the state university system could be funded to open or expand a program in the field instead.

These data are at variance with the widely assumed view that programs providing state funds to private colleges are essentially "institutional aid." Rather, in many cases the private institutions appear to function more as alternative suppliers of services in a competitive marketplace, with decisions about whom to fund presumably made in substantial measure on the basis of judgments about comparative cost-effectiveness. The distinction is an important one for beginning to understand these state policies.

Other State Policies: States typically exempt colleges and universities, both private and public, from property, though such exemptions are increasingly under attack from financially hard-pressed local governments.[25] According to the survey data, they also occasionally provide exemptions from other taxes such as sales taxes, and they typically provide individuals and firms with deductions, or occasionally credits, against state tax liabilities for donations to higher education. Other policies are specifically designed to impact private higher education via creative use of policy instruments available to the state, such as making these institutions eligible for participation in state purchasing pools or eligible to take advantage of state tax-exempt bonding authority.

Also, states may provide by law or practice for private sector representation on the state higher education board itself, for participation in its formal planning activities for higher education, or for private sector participation in state review/approval of new academic programs or locations proposed by public institutions (and occasionally vice versa). There are often high stakes in these state planning and "program review" decisions for the long-term competitive position of private institutions. Yet, the survey evidence showed that many states do not include them very extensively or regularly in their planning and program review policy deliberations. Finally, states may include private colleges and universities more or less in their mandates and regulations governing higher education and in their data collection and analysis efforts. The survey evidence showed that, with the prominent exception of mandates in the area of teacher education, most states did not extensively regulate private higher education nor did they collect or distribute much information about it.[26]

State Policies Affecting Public Higher Education Tuition: Another area of state, or at least heavily state-influenced, policy decisions that is of great importance to private colleges and universities is decisions about tuition levels in public higher education.[27] Yet, a separate survey of state higher education agency heads showed that impacts on private

---

[25]See the discussion and sources cited in Zumeta (1995b, p. 83).

[26]A few states with substantial direct aid to private higher education did more regulation and monitoring of this sector. Also, most states subjected private colleges and universities to state regulation in nonacademic areas, such as labor relations, health and safety, environmental matters, and the like.

[27]Private sector representatives responding to the survey ranked this area second in importance to them behind only state student aid policies (Zumeta, 1989).

institutions received little or no consideration in these decisions in all but a very few states (State Higher Education Executive Officers, 1988). So, states seem to use the potent policy instrument of pricing of public higher education services in a way that virtually guarantees unintended consequences for the independent sector.

Thus, in sum, state higher education policymakers can be more or less conscious or strategic in their use of the various types of policy instruments at their disposal—some of which have much broader reach than the private higher education sector alone—heeding or not their impacts on private colleges and universities, as well as on the state's full range of needs and objectives in higher education. In general, policies whose primary targets are within higher education (e.g., student aid programs, tuition policies) can be more easily fine-tuned to take account of impacts on private higher education than can policies (e.g., many general tax and regulatory policies) made by noneducation agencies with multiple targets.

To come at this from another angle, in general, indirect instruments such as portable student aid grants, tax incentives, and information-based instruments[28] have important advantages, where they can get the primary job done, over mandates, regulations and even direct grants because they are less centrally directive and, critically in educational matters, less intrusive on institutional autonomy. They may also be expensive, so there will at times be hard tradeoffs to weigh among effectiveness, cost, and intrusiveness. The argument here is simply that the impacts on private institutions, which affect the ultimate achievement of reasonable state goals in higher education, seem often to get short shrift in the weighing of these tradeoffs. Policies affecting public institution tuition, student aid, program expansion, new initiatives (e.g., in economic development or new instructional technologies), information about higher education, and, sometimes, mandates and regulations tend to be made with the public higher education sector primarily in mind, with little regard to differential effects that may apply to the private sector. This is important background to keep in mind for the remainder of this chapter.

Structure of Remainder of the Chapter

The remainder of the chapter will proceed as follows. First, I will seek to place private higher education in the U.S. and its relations with government in some comparative perspective by taking a global, though not very fine-grained, view and looking a bit more closely at Japan—a nation of broad interest to the United States and one with an even larger private higher education sector. Next, I will review briefly the highlights of the early history of state-private-higher-education relations in the United States, beginning with the colonial period and continuing up to World War II. This discussion will illustrate the point that, after the *Dartmouth College* case in 1819 established strict limits on state claims on independent institutions, states generally paid little official attention to this sector of higher education, though it represented nearly 50 percent of all enrollments as late as 1950.

Then, the next section will review the postwar period, which saw drastic changes

---

[28]Included here, for example, would be information provided to student "consumers" so that they can better choose wisely among postsecondary education options.

in the scope of higher education in this country (Trow, 1974), with particular attention to the major role of government and public policy in these changes and to their impact on the relative place of the private sector. Because of its significance as the immediate backdrop for current dilemmas, the period since 1980 will receive most emphasis. In particular, in what shape do we now find independent higher education to face an increasingly demanding future, after a decade and a half of competing on uneven terms[29] for a shrinking pool of traditional college-age students? What role have state policies played during this recent period? We will see that it has generally been a limited one, though there is considerable variation from state to state.

The ensuing section will lay out the key dimensions of the future facing higher education in this country. In brief, federal resources will be sorely constrained and almost certainly largely limited to student aid and support for research and some research training. What student aid funding there is may well move even further in the direction of loans and away from grants. At the state level, on the basis of recent experience, governments seem likely to face both uneven potential revenue growth and, in many cases, inability to fully tap potential revenue due to legal or political limitations on taxing and spending (McIntire, 1995). Yet, states face continued powerful demands for spending on such items as replacement of aging physical infrastructure (e.g., roads and bridges), building and operating large amounts of new prison space, meeting the rapidly growing costs of health care for state employees and needy populations (especially through the Medicaid program), and meeting state commitments to fund much of the cost of elementary and secondary education, where demand is again growing rapidly (Zumeta and Fawcett-Long, 1996).

Thus, higher education's competition for state dollars is likely to be much keener than it has been in the past. Yet, as already indicated, in many states the demand for enrollment places in higher education is growing or soon will be (see Figure 1, p. 360). And, it can be cogently argued on grounds of both economic efficiency in the knowledge-based economy and equity for newly emerging groups in the population, that participation rates in higher education should be, if anything, targeted to increase. Certainly participation rates should not be allowed to fall, as the set of forces just described that are impinging on states' financial resources would seem to threaten. This section will conclude by observing that, where they are substantial, independent higher education sectors could have an important role to play here in expanding state capacity to meet demand for higher education, but only if state policies are conducive.

The last major section of the chapter will advance a conceptual framework for thinking about how in the contemporary context state policies interact with (i.e., affect and are affected by) the private higher education sector, and will reflect upon the possible determinants of the different *state policy postures* that are advanced within this framework. The purpose is to provide at least an initial basis for understanding states' policy configurations efficiently and also to provide a tool for assessing the prospects and possible means for changes to make fuller use of this sector. If the above scenario is at all accurate, states will need all the higher

---

[29]That is, as is documented more fully later, the gap between private and public tuition rates grew sharply and government-provided student aid funds did not keep up with tuition and demand growth.

education capacity they can muster to respond to the emerging forces at work. This section will also reference empirical evidence supporting the conceptual framework outlined and will suggest a program of research to more fully validate and refine it.

PRIVATE HIGHER EDUCATION IN THE UNITED STATES IN COMPARATIVE PERSPECTIVE

Research during the 1980s on higher education systems around much of the world found relatively few nations with substantial private collegiate sectors (Clark, 1983; Levy, 1985; 1986; Geiger, 1986). The significant cases are, in addition to the United States, Japan, the Philippines, and several countries in Latin America, notably Brazil (Geiger, 1986; Levy, 1986). The large Western European democracies and Canada sport a few of what Geiger (1986) calls "peripheral" private higher education sectors,[30] although several, including Great Britain and Canada, had more substantial private sectors in the past.

In the developed world outside the U.S. and Japan, most of twentieth century political history has reinforced historic state-centered tendencies in the development of major social institutions, and higher education has been no exception. Most nations have thought quite naturally in terms of national government action to expand educational opportunities and other social goods as their wealth has grown.[31] This fits with traditions emphasizing consistency with national goals and priorities, accountability of major social institutions, and equity across regions. In recent years, equity across other dimensions, in particular the socioeconomic class dimension, has become a more prominent concern in many nations and, in the main, equity goals are seen as more effectively pursued via national than via subnational (e.g., state) planning and policymaking. Also in recent years, many developing countries have tended to follow a similar path, seeing higher education as an engine of national development and a key part of national policies which at least claim to promote equity across regions, ethnic groups, and socioeconomic classes (Levy, 1986; Geiger, 1986).

Clark's (1983) sweeping analysis of higher education systems and their evolution suggests that such a pattern of development carries significant disadvantages, however. He points out that the presence of a substantial private higher education sector, which he defines as one enrolling at least 15 percent of the nation's college and university students, not only provides more diversity of choice for students and other clients of higher education, but also makes the national system more robust in several important ways. For one, it allows an alternate avenue for expansion of access in periods where this is too costly or politically complex for the public authorities to tackle. Such diversion of rapid growth to a private sector may even enhance public higher education's autonomy by reducing the intense scrutiny it

---

[30]Geiger (1986) classifies the private sectors in Belgium and the Netherlands, with their historical roots in the Roman Catholic Church, as cases of "parallel" public and private sectors (chapter 3). The United States and Japan he terms cases of "mass" private sectors (chapter 2).

[31]Postwar West Germany (now Germany) is a partial exception in that higher education is primarily a responsibility of the *lander* (states) rather than the federal government. Most significantly for purposes of this chapter, the institutions are all public.

would face under conditions of rapid growth and escalation of spending (Clark, 1983, pp. 161-171).[32]

In other cases, e.g., Japan, the Philippines, Brazil, the private sector has filled in gaps at particular quality tiers where public institutions were wanting (Clark, 1983; Geiger, 1986; Levy, 1986). More generally, the presence of a private sector adds to a system's capacity to innovate and otherwise respond to changing needs in society or the world of knowledge itself.[33] Finally, Clark notes that the presence of a substantial private sector tends to add to the competitive character of higher education systems in terms of the pursuit of academic prestige, which he notes, for all its faults, does serve to reward such values as scientific productivity[34] and high scholarly attainment by students (Clark, 1983, pp. 161-171).

The studies by Geiger (1986), of Japan and the Philippines, and Levy (1985; 1986) of Latin America, provide illustrations of the above point about the private sector's role in filling gaps, particularly gaps in enrollment capacity, left more or less deliberately by public authorities in the face of burgeoning social demand for access to higher education. Japan provides perhaps the readiest comparisons with the United States. According to Geiger's well-documented historical account,[35] the national government in Japan—particularly in response to the surge in demand for higher education after World War II—simply allowed the growing demand to be met by private institutions because of both lack of resources for massive public sector expansion and a concern for the maintenance of academic standards in the state institutions. Thus, by the 1970s, 78 percent of the nation's higher education enrollment was in the private sector.

Not surprisingly, by the late 1960s the trend in this direction had produced strong pressures to both improve standards in the private institutions and to bail them out of serious financial straits, which were leading to rapid escalation in tuition. The government addressed both these concerns simultaneously beginning in the early 1970s[36] with a program of formula-based grants to private colleges and universities designed to help and encourage them (via incentives built into the quite-detailed funding formulas) to spend more on the education of each student and on research and facilities,

[32]Elsewhere, Clark has argued that private higher education in the United States has enhanced public sector autonomy in a very fundamental way by providing the initial models for autonomous but public-spirited governance of institutions via independent boards of trustees composed of citizens of stature and influence (1987, pp. 5-6). Kerr (1991) makes a similar point. This governance model has had considerable influence beyond the United States.

[33]This is part of Clark's broader argument that systems with *decentralized authority*, e.g., in public-only systems where states or provinces rather than the national government make the critical decisions in higher education policy, are likely to be more innovative and flexible than systems with a central locus of decisionmaking (Clark, 1983, chapters four, five and six; see also Thompson and Zumeta, 1981).

[34]See also Ben-David and Zloczower (1962) on the point that decentralized and competitive national systems of higher education are likely to be more prone to scientific progress than highly centralized systems.

[35]See Geiger (1986, pp. 17-51).

[36]Prior to this, private institutions were subject to chartering and some other regulation by the national Ministry of Education but were eligible only for limited loans for capital purposes from public funds (Geiger, 1986, pp. 25-26). Few of these institutions had substantial sources of income other than student tuition and fees (which include substantial application and entrance testing fees).

and to limit enrollments to target ranges established by the national Ministry of Education (Geiger, 1986, pp. 46-47). According to Geiger, the law permitted the government to pay up to 50 percent of the operating expenses of private colleges and universities and in 1980 it actually provided enough to cover about 30 percent of these expenses (p. 47). Thus, the impact of the incentives built into the government's funding formulas could be expected to be quite substantial.

Indeed, Geiger believes that these incentives have had a profound effect on private higher education in Japan. They probably played a role in stabilizing enrollments after years of rapid, rather uncontrolled increases.[37] They also seem to have had the desired effect of improving academic quality—at least to the extent this can be equated with spending on faculty salaries and facilities per student.[38] But, Geiger argues, the incentives built into the funding formulas for private institutions rewarded them for increasing tuition revenue and thus led to sharp growth in tuition rates, not the slackening that government subsidies were expected to produce (p. 49).[39]

Predictably, the private institutions have become increasingly clients of the state and seek aggressively to make their influence felt in the deliberations of both the Ministry of Education and the Ministry of Finance. Finally, Geiger holds that, in spite of explicit efforts to the contrary and some minor successes, the net effect of the government's efforts to bring the private sector into the purview of its planning for higher education "...have powerfully induced greater institutional uniformity" (p. 49) in terms of the nature and aspirations of the institutions. Thus, in Japan public policy toward private higher education has been highly successful in terms of some of its immediate goals, but very likely at the expense of the dynamism and innovativeness of the sector, and certainly in terms of its "privateness." Geiger sees it as no longer a "mass" private sector in its historic free-form sense, but rather likely to grow only in a limited, controlled way as permitted by national policy (pp. 50-51). Thus, private higher education in Japan has become, in a real sense, an adjunct of the public sector and an important instrument of a carefully planned, if not foolproof, public policy regime in higher education. There may be lessons here for some states in the U.S.

GOVERNMENT RELATIONS WITH PRIVATE HIGHER EDUCATION IN THE UNITED STATES: EARLY HISTORY

The history of private higher education in the U.S. is quite different from that of most other nations which have sustained nonpublic colleges and universities in the past, or do

[37]Geiger notes, however, that the period of stability in private sector enrollments coincided with stability in the number of high-school graduates seeking admission (p. 48). Thus, the Ministry's efforts to cap enrollments may have had little independent effect.

[38]But, as Geiger notes, in Japan true changes in the quality of instruction in higher education are particularly hard to effect and to measure. This is so because the academic culture of classroom lecture with little student interaction or out-of-class contact is powerfully entrenched and because perceptions of quality (even by employers) are so closely equated with the test scores of students at entry (pp. 49-50).

[39]Geiger observes that this sharp growth in prices may well also have played a role in keeping enrollments from rising in the period after the government subsidies for private colleges and universities were introduced (p. 49).

so in the present. Rather than emerging to fill in gaps left by a dominant public university sector, in America private higher education in a very basic sense came first. This is true in that many of the early colonial colleges—Harvard, Yale, Princeton, Pennsylvania, Dartmouth—are now clearly private institutions, yet, in their early years were at least as much public as private. The early colleges were chartered by colonial, later state, legislatures, from which they received financial subsidies, and for a time had legislatively appointed members on their boards (Rudolph, 1962; Trow, 1993).

But, the early American colleges also possessed important elements of privateness. They were established by the initiative of private, often sectarian, groups separate from the state. As state-chartered corporate entities they had boards made up largely of private citizens which were granted considerable autonomous powers. And, they were not wholly financed by the state but drew their fiscal support from a variety of sources, including both private donations and student fees. These characteristics made them quite different from most European, and in particular English, colleges of the 17th, 18th, and early 19th centuries (Rothblatt and Trow, 1992). Also, the fact that the colonies and states which chartered the early colleges were different from one another led to the establishment of a pattern of differences in many aspects which seemed natural from the beginning in the American context, but which simply did not emerge in smaller countries with much longer common histories and the habit of thinking of higher education in national terms.

Trow (1993) and other authorities (e.g., Herbst, 1982) argue that the central ideas of the American Revolution and the westward expansion of a diverse population into remote areas together made for an environment most conducive to the emergence of a diverse range of higher educational institutions subject to little direction by the state, or by government in any form. Crucially, says Trow, "...the Revolution weakened all agencies of government by stressing the roots of the new nation in popular sovereignty, the subordination of the government to 'the people,' and the primacy of individual and group freedom and initiative" (1993, p. 51). Hence, neither the federal government nor even the states were much disposed to try to create key societal institutions "from the top down."[40] The diversity of the population (in terms of religion, national origin, geographic imperatives, and the like) and the relative sparseness of settlement combined with these ideas to make it inevitable that colleges would be created from the "bottom up" in this society and thus by diverse groups for a wide range of purposes and in diverse ways with limited governmental control. This is thus a rather unique historical backdrop for the emergence of forms of higher education in comparison to other, now-developed nations of the world. And its effects are still strongly felt in attitudes toward private higher education today in many states.

A watershed event in understanding the development of private higher education in the United States and its relationship to state government was the case

---

[40]An important illustration of this point is the failure of George Washington and his immediate successors in the presidency to generate much interest in chartering a national "University of the United States" (Trow, 1993, pp. 53-55). Such an institution would surely have exerted a powerful standardizing influence on models for higher education in the provinces as have institutions which play a similar role in other countries, such as Tokyo University, the University of the Philippines, or Oxford and Cambridge in England.

between Dartmouth College and the New Hampshire legislature (*Dartmouth vs. Woodward*) which came before the U.S. Supreme Court in 1819. The state had chartered the college for the benefit of the public, it argued, and now sought to alter the charter "...to improve the college as a place of learning by modernizing its administration, creating the framework for a university, and encouraging a freer, nonsectarian atmosphere...," while the college resisted this state intervention (Trow, 1993, pp. 55-56). In short, the legislature sought to make its creation more like what we would now call a public institution. Chief Justice John Marshall held for the Court, however, that the legislature must respect the sanctity of its original contract with the college (the charter) and could not change it unilaterally. In an important sense then the American *private* college was born here. Benefactors and trustees could now be sure that the fruits of their toil and treasure would not be taken over by the state, which surely did much to stimulate the subsequent proliferation of private colleges (Trow, 1993, p. 56), and sharp limits were placed on state control over this unique part of higher education.[41]

And great proliferation there was in the ranks of private colleges. In the colonial period, just nine colleges were created. Thirty-six more were added between 1789 and 1830, followed by another 136 before 1865 (Metzger, 1987, cited in Clark, 1987, p. 6), with most of these being what we would now call private institutions. Though many of these mostly small, struggling schools did not survive long, the urge to create institutions of higher education was very strong in America. By 1900 there were nearly 900 private colleges and universities spread out across the country (Clark, 1987, p. 7). At that point, relatively early in the development of the modern university, private higher education *was* much of American higher education, and it developed and thrived through the critical 19th century period with only a little help from government.

The next landmark in the history of American higher education was the Morrill Act of 1862. This Act provided for large-scale land grants to states for the purpose of establishing institutions of higher education.[42] The grants provided remarkable discretion to the states as to how they were to be used, specifying only that, in addition to the traditional, still largely classical, college curriculum of the time, the institutions provide instruction in "agriculture, mechanic arts, and military tactics" (Ross, 1942, cited in Trow, 1993, p. 57). This practical orientation was one of the innovations of American higher education.

Remarkably, the states were also left free to decide to whom the grant would be turned over for use. Thus, in some states private institutions were direct beneficiaries, e.g., Cornell in New York, M.I.T. in Massachusetts, Yale's Sheffield Scientific School in Connecticut. In Kentucky and Oregon private denominational colleges received the money from sale of much of the land grant. In California, an existing private liberal

---

[41]By so limiting state control over its creations, this decision probably also made the development of the different form we now call "public" colleges and universities inevitable (see Rudolph, 1962, chapter nine).

[42]It is worth noting that these were not the first federal land grants to the states for higher education. The Northwest Ordinance enacted under the Articles of Confederation provided for such land grants, but the Morrill Act grants were far more massive and broadly distributed (Trow, 1993, p. 57).

arts college was "merged" with the land-grant endowment to create the University of California (Trow, 1993, p. 57). In many states a new institution was founded, complete with not only a site but an endowment, and so also a new institutional form—the public state university—was solidified.[43] As suggested above, the creation of some form of public institution of higher education was probably made inevitable by the Supreme Court's ruling against the state legislature in the Dartmouth College case. A major part of the significance of the Morrill Act—and of particular importance for our purposes in this chapter—was that it once again confirmed that these institutions would be state- rather than federally owned and thus assured that the states would play a key role in higher education policy in this country. As Trow puts it, the federal government simply left the money "...on the stump and walked away..." (1993, pp. 57-58).[44]

In the interest of sticking to the highlights of most pertinence to a survey of public policy and private higher education in the United States, I will now pass over nearly a century of history and turn the reader's attention to the post-World War II period.

THE POSTWAR PERIOD

(1945 through the early 1970s)

The GI Bill and Growth of Public Higher Education

Although it gradually lost "market share" to public institutions as public universities grew, and especially as community colleges began to emerge and the old normal schools became teachers' colleges, private higher education thrived overall under the generally *laissez-faire* state regimes under which it lived during the years of the nation's rapid growth and development. It was not until the middle of the twentieth century that another major turning point was reached in public policy toward higher education that affected the private sector. This was the federal GI Bill[45] and the associated push by the states to greatly expand higher education opportunities for the legions of former soldiers who returned home needing something constructive to do in a peacetime economy.

The GI Bill itself was important not only in providing large scale federal support for higher education, but also for setting a key precedent by directing that support through students—in contrast to the approach taken by the national government in Japan somewhat later when that country faced a surge in demand for higher educa-

---

[43]State institutions of a continuing public character did not begin with the Morrill Act. A few trace their origins to the 18th century (Clark, 1987, p. 8), but it was the federal land-grants of the 19th century which led to the proliferation of this form across the country.

[44]By way of explanation, Trow (1993) points out that there was no federal education bureaucracy to oversee the use of the land grants and, at least as important, there was little agreement in Congress about what the new institutions should look like (p. 58). Thus, as with much else in American history, the key decisions simply were left to the states by a kind of institutionalized default.

[45]The "GI Bill" was known officially as the Servicemen's Readjustment Act of 1944.

tion—who carried the money to institutions of their choice, rather than supporting institutions directly. Trow points out that in 1944, as in 1862, the federal government opted to forgo an opportunity to manage and influence higher education more directly (1993, p. 59). Indeed, it once again exercised only the most limited oversight of the funds as one provision of the law stipulated, "no department, agency, or officer of the United States, in carrying out the provisions [of this Act] shall exercise any supervision or control, whatsoever, over any State, educational agency...or any educational or training institution" (Olson, 1974, 17-18, quoted in Trow, 1993, p. 59). Thus, students were allowed to take their GI Bill stipends to a wide range of institutions, including strictly vocational training schools and nonaccredited institutions, and there was some corruption and abuse of the funds (Trow, 1993, p. 59). But, Trow suggests, this tradeoff was a deliberate choice by the federal government to stay out of the details of the operations of higher education. The states did little more in the way of regulation.

The choice to provide GI Bill aid through students rather than institutions can also be seen as a boon to private higher education. It allowed the soldier-students to choose private institutions if they wished and provided many more of them than had ever had it in the past with the wherewithal to afford such a choice.[46] And it provided for this growth in demand without any significant strings attached, thus safeguarding the private sector's privateness. Yet, by initiating the first big surge in demand for higher education and helping to insure that the enterprise became too big and important for government to ignore for long, this first federal student aid program also marked the beginning of the end of the era of true independence from government for much of the private sector.[47]

State governments also reacted to the GI Bill-stimulated surge in demand for higher education with important steps of their own that were to have large, if mostly indirect, impacts on the private sector. After World War II, the pace at which states opened new community colleges, expanded the mission of public four-year institutions (largely the former teachers' colleges), opened new campuses, and expanded enrollments, including graduate enrollments, at their research universities leaped tremendously.[48] Thus, although private higher education enrollments grew at a healthy pace in numbers during the postwar period (1945-1970), the era witnessed a precipitous decline in this sector's "market share" of all higher education enrollments. This share fell from 49 percent in 1949 to 26 percent just twenty years later (U.S. Department of Education, 1989, shown in McPherson

---

[46] Of course, since the stipend was not pegged to tuition levels, public institutions with their state-subsidized tuition rates had a price advantage in competing for students funded under the GI Bill. It is not surprising that public institutions increased their share of the higher education market during this period.

[47] Some credit for this should also be assigned to a parallel federal postwar initiative — the development of the federally funded academic research complex. Here too the federal government chose to offer large-scale financing to private and public universities alike on a competitive basis. Given the relative stature of the country's great private universities at the time, this posture assured that they would continue to be key players in the growing research and graduate education enterprise. But it also eventually (one might say inevitably) led to much-increased governmental oversight of the institutions spending the taxpayers' money, private and public alike. (See Wolfle, 1972; Smith, 1990)

& Schapiro, 1991, p. 22).[49] These were momentous changes for they meant that higher education now involved far too many citizens and state dollars to escape government's notice any longer and that the responses of governments would, with the exception of a relatively small number of states with still-large private sector shares of the market, largely be shaped by the perceived needs, problems and demands of the public institutions.[50]

Significantly, by and large private higher education, decentralized as it was, passively accepted this development. Most colleges did not want to grow so dramatically as to maintain their market share—small size is part of the "charm" of many of these schools (Breneman, 1994). In any case, even though many new private colleges were founded during this period, it would have been almost impossible for the sector to maintain its overall share through it. The states were adding greatly to the size of the higher education market by opening hundreds of low-priced two-year institutions and building colleges in locations convenient to population centers, as well as by continuing the historic policy of subsidizing the prices of the four-year public schools. Thus, most private institutions were content for their own reasons to grow at a relatively modest pace and, inevitably, the private sector's overall share of the total fell steadily.

The expansion of both public and private higher education during this period was facilitated by reasonably prosperous economic growth with low inflation, and the fact that tuition rates grew only modestly in real terms. The fact that real incomes were rising steadily made it possible for a wider group in the population to consider higher education and to be willing to pay for it. Still, private-sector prices grew substantially faster than public during this period (Clotfelter, 1991, p. 70), and this probably contributed to the private sector's loss of market share.

The Beginnings of State Aid to Private Institutions and Their Students

This era, in particular the late 1950s and the 1960s, saw the beginnings of significant state student aid programs (Fenske and Boyd, 1981), which have since become a key part of state policy for the private higher education sector (Zumeta 1989; 1992). A

---

[48]Again, the contrast with other developed countries is notable. In Britain and Japan during this period, pressures for growth in the public higher education sector were held firmly in check by the national government for reasons of resource limitations and an effort to maintain high academic standards (Trow, 1993, pp. 58-59; Geiger, 1986, pp. 22-30). In the United States, while federal support was much more generous it was not continuous after the GI Bill expired. Here, competition among states to provide educational opportunities for citizens and for economic development played a key role. Growth in private colleges and universities in the United States was thus overshadowed by the dramatic burgeoning of the public sector, while in Japan the private sector was allowed to grow to alleviate pressure to expand the public segment. In Britain there was no private sector to turn to and participation in higher education remained very low relative to other advanced countries (Trow, 1993, pp. 58-59).

[49]As mentioned earlier, the private nonprofit sector's share of all enrollments in the Fall of 1992 was down to 20 percent. The government figures cited by McPherson and Schapiro include some private, for-profit institutions.

[50]It should be noted that this public sector dominance had always been the case in many of the Western states where private higher education had had little or no time to take root before the *Dartmouth College* decision and the Morrill Act land grants began to shift states' thinking in the direction of public sector provision.

few states, such as New York and Illinois, also initiated programs of direct support to private colleges and universities during this period.[51] Both these types of programs reflected a recognition by states—prodded to be sure by private higher education interests—that private higher education served a public purpose in educating students and that both the state and the students were well-served by having access to alternatives to the public system. The issue was, of course, sharpened by the competitive effects of proliferation of low-priced public alternatives to the private schools.

A notable example of recognition of the private higher education sector by a major state is to be found in the famed California Master Plan For Higher Education (Master Plan Survey Team, 1960). This landmark document is best known for its codification of the tripartite "division of labor" in the state's higher education system among the University of California, responsible for doctoral education and research, education in the "major" professions (law, medicine, etc.), and for educating at the undergraduate level the most academically qualified one-eighth of the state's high-school graduates; the California State Colleges (now Universities), responsible for undergraduates down to the top third of the high-school graduates, for education of teachers and for other "lesser" professions, and for some Master's-level programs; and the California Community Colleges, designed to be open-door institutions available to all adults in the state and providing a range of adult and vocational education programs, as well as an accessible route into baccalaureate-level academic education by means of articulated transfer programs (Smelser, 1993). Significantly, the Master Plan also embodied a commitment to very broad access (i.e., no tuition, many campuses spread across the state) and to world-class standards of quality (Pickens, 1995a).

Less widely heralded is that the Master Plan also established a prominent role for the independent sector in California's higher education system and made good on this commitment by establishing a state scholarship program (now called "Cal Grants") under which students could take their state grants to either public or private accredited institutions (Pickens, 1995a). In the early years these grants were clearly designed to facilitate attendance at private institutions. More than 90 percent of the awards in 1961 went to students selecting these schools. Also, the size of maximum grant awards was nearly equal to average tuition at independent colleges and universities as late as 1970 (Pickens, 1995a).[52] Thus, at the time of the Master Plan, the private sector in California was considered a significant piece of the state's capacity to meet the commitments embodied in the plan in the already-foreseeable impending period of rapid enrollment growth.

California was not alone in taking this view. As indicated above, during the 1950s, and especially in the latter years of the1960s, several other large states initi-

---

[51]However, in some cases (e.g., Alabama, Maryland), such direct state aid to private colleges actually goes back many years (Rudolph, 1962; Zumeta, 1989). Rudolph documents extensive state aid to private colleges in many states in the 19th century, and notes that in at least a few this continued into the early twentieth century (1962, pp. 177-200).

[52]The proportion of Cal Grant awards received by students attending private colleges and universities has fallen steadily over the years, to just over 30 percent in 1994-95. Similarly, the size of the largest grants available has fallen far behind tuition levels in the independent sector (Pickens, 1995a, pp. 10-11; 1995b, unpaginated).

ated substantial programs of aid to private colleges and/or their students. The major examples were states in the eastern half of the country (including the South and Midwest) who faced not only surging demand for higher education but also perceived threats to the viability or financial health of a venerable and well-connected part of the higher education enterprise in the private sector. Their responses included both state aid to students that could be used at private institutions and, in a small number of cases, new or expanded programs of direct state appropriations to private colleges and universities.[53]

The Higher Education Act of 1965 and Its 1972 Amendments

In 1965 the federal Higher Education Act was enacted. This was historically significant in that it represented, for the first time, a recognition by the federal government of a *permanent* national interest in higher education. The HEA provided for federal support of facilities construction, library development and personnel training, the strengthening of "developing institutions" (primarily, at least originally, the historically black institutions), teacher training, community service and continuing education programs, and financial assistance to students (Keppel, 1987).

Most significant of these provisions for our purposes here were the ones creating broadly based federal student aid programs (grants, loans and work-study under Title IV of the Higher Education Act) and funding them at a substantial level.[54] These were not the first federal student aid programs after the GI Bill, but they were the first to go beyond support of students in fairly narrow fields of specifically identified national need (as in the case of the National Defense Education Act of the 1950s), and were funded at a considerably higher level than the earlier, narrower programs which were limited to loans (Hearn, 1993, pp. 102-103). Reflecting its origins in the Johnson Administration Great Society period, the Act also set an important precedent in targeting federal aid on "needy" students who were thought to be not able to attend college without such aid (Keppel, 1987, pp. 56-57). Still, as is noted by Hearn (1993, p. 102), institutions decided which of their students were eligible and how much they received. Although the 1965 Act actually emphasized institutional aid more than student aid, this marked the high water mark for federal aid to higher education institutions in the United States. The broadly based student aid programs the Higher Education Act created paved the way for a sharp turn a few years later down the road which had been paved by the GI Bill's student-based approach.

The question of aid to students or aid to institutions was revisited with great intensity during the 1972 debate on major amendments to the Act.[55] There was broad support at this time for a sharp expansion of the federal commitment to higher education in response to then-strong societal commitments to expanding educational oppor-

---

[53]See Fenske and Boyd (1981), NASSGP (1994 and earlier annual survey reports), and Zumeta (1989) on the origins of state programs aiding private institutions of higher education.

[54]Still, the largest authorized spending for FY 1966 under the original Higher Education Act was for the construction of academic facilities for undergraduates. About 32 percent of the original $1.1 billion annual authorization under the Act was for student aid (Keppel, 1987, p. 58).

[55]For an account of this debate, see Gladieux and Wolanin (1976). See also Hansen (1977); Mumper (1991); Hearn (1993); Trow (1993, pp. 59-60).

tunities. One source of this support came from advocates of a big expansion of aid to needy students while another key group advocated direct federal aid to colleges and universities. In the latter camp were the national organizations representing the institutions and sectors of higher education as well as some influential members of Congress. But prominent on the side of those arguing for aid through students was the influential Carnegie Commission on Higher Education, led by former University of California President Clark Kerr (Trow, 1993, p. 60).

The Carnegie Commission and others made several telling arguments in favor of the aid-through-students approach. One was that aid to needy students—which was held to be an economic necessity as well as an equal opportunity policy—could be better and more efficiently targeted by federal control of the terms of the aid than if the money went through thousands of different institutions. Indeed, the original idea of the developers of the largest program created by the 1972 amendments, the Basic Educational Opportunity Grants (now Pell Grants) program, was to create a federal entitlement to aid for college for all financially needy students, with need to be established uniformly by a federal formula (Gladieux and Wolanin, 1976; Mumper, 1991, pp. 316-317; Hearn, 1993, pp. 109-110). In addition, less needy students were to have access to federally subsidized and guaranteed loans. Much of this program—with the important exception of the fully funded entitlement—was enacted.

Kerr, economist that he is, and others argued that aid to students rather than to institutions had the advantage of reinforcing market-like incentives for the colleges to respond to student preferences about courses of study and other matters, which they thought would better serve society in the long run than a system where institutional preferences, and inevitably inertia, were more influential. Of course, the GI Bill was cited as a precedent. Perhaps even more important, many on this side of the argument felt that federal aid directly to institutions was not in their own best interest (although the institutions wanted it) in the long run for it would inevitably lead to federal leverage over and interference in educational policymaking.[56] Finally, Trow points out that it was not lost on the advocates of aid-through-students that millions of aided students and their families would make a much broader and more effective constituency for continued federal support than would the higher education establishment alone (1993, p. 60).

In addition to whatever force these arguments may have had, chroniclers of the period observe that the institutional interests handled their legislative strategy and tactics quite poorly (Gladieux and Wolanin, 1976; Hansen, 1977; Finn, 1978; Mumper, 1991). The results then seem from this vantage point (with the benefit of hindsight) quite understandable—the major expansion in federal aid to higher education established in the 1972 Higher Education Act amendments routed the support overwhelmingly through students not institutions. Clearly, in the longer historical perspective traced here this seems quite understandable, even predictable, as well. In the United States the national government has paid relatively limited attention to higher education in comparison to the pattern in other countries. What it has paid is

---

[56]For example, there would have been more reason for the government to intervene to press institutions to reallocate resources among areas of study (i.e., manpower planning) were student choices less dominant in this process. Certainly, the national government would have been in a stronger position than it is now to try to influence substantive academic matters for political or bureaucratic reasons.

money for specific purposes—land grants to start institutions, support for research, aid to students to allow them to pursue higher education, and, more recently, substantial efforts to insure equity in employment practices. But, so far, all this has come with very little direction about what colleges and universities teach, how many of them there are, how much they charge, and so on. And, critically for our purposes, the federal government has welcomed private institutions into its programs[57] and has generally left oversight functions to the states.

One important elaboration on this last point is necessary in the context of the 1972 Higher Education Act amendments (Gladieux and Wolanin, 1976; McGuinness, 1975). This legislation influenced in two significant ways how states dealt with private institutions. First, it required that states strengthen and broaden their planning capacity for higher education as a condition for receipt of federal funds under the Act. In many cases states broadened the membership of their existing state higher education board or commission to qualify, but in some cases a separate planning body (or "1202 Commission" after the section number in the Act) was established with the requisite membership. These bodies were required to produce certain planning documents to satisfy Congress that new federal funds would be well-used.

The main significance for the present purpose is that the membership on the planning body now had to include representatives from both the private, nonprofit collegiate sector and the private postsecondary vocational training sector (often including for-profit institutions). These were new departures in many states—indeed, some had done little or no statewide planning for higher education before—and at least gave the private sector a place at this particular table. As we shall see, this did not necessarily insure that private institutions played a very meaningful role in all subsequent state higher education planning, but it did provide an officially sanctioned starting point.

Second, the 1972 HEA amendments provided modest federal funding for a new program of incentive grants to states, called the State Student Incentive Grant program or SSIG, to establish their own student aid programs (Gladieux and Wolanin, 1976; Hansen, 1979; Fenske and Boyd, 1981). Participating states were required to include students at private institutions in the program. This was a breakthrough for private higher education which had sought to get more states to establish student aid programs for which their students would be eligible. The federal incentive funding has led over the years to virtually all the states establishing such programs (Fenske and Boyd, 1981; Mumper, 1993), with many states providing much more than the required one-for-one match (NASSGP, 1994).[58]

---

[57]Notably, from the beginning of the BEOG program (now Pell Grants), the allocation formulas have been designed to insure that the aid funds could cover no more than a fixed percentage (first 50 percent, now 60 percent) of a student's cost of attendance (Mumper, 1993, p. 164). This restricts the amount of funds that might otherwise go to students choosing low-priced public institutions and insures that no student can get all costs covered by the grant.

[58]According to the most recent NASSGP publication (1994), the range across the states in terms of the share of their need-based grants that are provided by federal SSIG funds is from 50 percent (a one-to-one match) in two states, down to just one percent in New York. In addition, one state, Rhode Island, did not participate in the federal program. The figures are estimates for the 1993-94 academic year. States have not, however, always provided the matching funds themselves, but have at times required institutions to put up these funds, a particular problem for private schools.

Recent federal efforts to eliminate the SSIG program in the name of budget-cutting and the streamlining of federal student aid programs have cited the program's success in stimulating state student aid efforts as evidence that it is no longer needed.[59] Private higher education interests generally oppose such a step, fearing not only the loss of federal funds but also that some states will drop their need-based aid programs completely, or perhaps no longer assure the eligibility of students attending private colleges. It is widely agreed that the SSIG program has played a significant role in stimulating increased state support for student aid available to both private and public sector students (Hansen, 1979; Fenske and Boyd, 1981; Breneman, 1994). Together with the mandate to include the private sector in state higher education planning and the broader decision represented by the 1965 and 1972 actions on the Higher Education Act to minimize the federal government's direct involvement in higher education policymaking, we can look upon this period of federal action as important in shaping key dimensions of the states' role vis-a-vis private higher education in the succeeding years.

THE EARLY 1970S TO THE PRESENT

The 1960s, as well as the earlier postwar years to a lesser extent, were years of prosperity in American higher education. Enrollments grew dramatically, supported by expansive state appropriations to the public higher education sector. Strong federal support for research spilled over into support for facilities and graduate education (Smith, 1990). Private higher education was aided at the margins by the beginnings of federal and state student aid programs—and in the case of the private research universities very much by federal research support—but prospered primarily because there were plenty of students in the market in a period when the economy was providing enough for many of them to pay for a private education. Though, as in earlier periods, a number of private colleges failed during this period, many more were formed and thrived (Birnbaum, 1983; Zammuto, 1984).

The Seventies

But during a period of a few years on either side of 1970 many things changed. Enrollment growth rates slowed as the "baby boom" children began to graduate and as economic returns to college education took a nosedive (Freeman, 1976). Federal research funding also dropped off after a decade of rapid increases (Smith, 1990), thus making it harder to support graduate students who had provided a source of low-cost teachers of undergraduates. In addition, some graduate students were dissuaded by the first signs of the "Ph.D. glut" (Zumeta, 1982). The Vietnam War and then the first OPEC oil embargo in 1973 ended a long period of general economic prosperity with relatively low inflation and began an era during which real earnings have essentially stopped growing (Marshall and Tucker, 1992). This income stagnation, of course, makes it harder for students to pay for and donors to support higher education. Initially, during the 1970s, inflation and interest rates reached very high levels, leading to problems and dislocations throughout the economy, not least for higher education (Breneman, 1994).

---

[59]At this writing, it appears likely that the State Student Incentive Grant (SSIG) program will be eliminated when a budget for fiscal year 1996 is finally agreed upon by Congress and the President.

Private colleges and universities in particular faced worrisome fiscal circumstances as they contemplated huge, inflation-driven jumps in costs at a time when it was harder to recruit both students and private donations (Cheit, 1971; Carnegie Commission, 1973; Wynn, 1974). After several years of economic instability and after studying the projections of high-school graduates into the eighties and beyond, several groups of distinguished analysts offered a generally gloomy perspective on the future prospects for a healthy private sector (see Carnegie Council on Policy Studies in Higher Education, 1977; Education Commission of the States, 1977; Breneman and Finn, 1978; Behn, 1979). Basically, they feared a continuing rapid cost spiral with little prospect of offsetting growth in student revenues in light of the expected leveling and then decline in college-age students resulting from the "birth dearth" cohort of the 1960s reaching college-age. The uncertain economy seemed to offer little hope of a dramatic increase in private donations or help from the states, who would naturally be most concerned about taking care of "their own" public institutions in an "era of limits."

These analysts did, however, call for states to be attentive to the health of what they saw as a valuable resource in private higher education, and to help as much as they could. "Portable" student aid[60] and, significantly, higher and more predictable tuition rates in public higher education were generally the preferred routes for such help because of their more limited potential, as compared with direct institutional aid, for restricting the autonomy of *independent* institutions.[61]

In fact, while state student aid programs and expenditures grew substantially during the 1970s (McPherson and Schapiro, 1991, p. 29), they remained a modest part of the total student aid picture. Private institutions survived this decade as well as they did in large part because of the rapid growth in student aid from the federal government (Breneman, 1994, pp. 25-30; McPherson and Schapiro, 1991, pp. 25-43). McPherson and Schapiro, citing several sources, note that total federal student aid nearly doubled, after adjusting for inflation, during the 1970s (p. 26).[62] If only generally available aid is counted (thus excluding Social Security and Veterans' educational benefits), the real increase approached 200 percent over the decade, a rate of increase especially beneficial to private institutions with their unsubsidized (at least by the state) tuition rates.

Also during this period, unlike more recent times, federal grant aid grew about as fast as loan aid. An important factor in the rapid growth in federal student aid during this period was the liberalization of aid eligibility standards that culminated in the Middle Income Student Assistance Act (MISAA), enacted in 1978 (Mumper, 1991, pp. 319-320; McPherson and Schapiro, 1991, pp. 31-33; Hearn, 1993, pp. 111-116). MISAA was the product of an effort to head off a powerful movement toward tax

---

[60]"Portable" student aid in this context means that the recipient student may use the aid at either a public or an eligible private institution.

[61]On this point, in addition to the sources cited in the previous paragraph, see also Committee for Economic Development (1973) and National Commission on the Financing of Postsecondary Education (1973).

[62]See also Hearn (1993) for thorough documentation of the growth in federal student aid from 1965 through 1990.

credits for higher education tuition, the cost of which would have necessitated major changes in the federal student aid programs. To accomplish this, MISAA's framers raised the maximum family income permitted to qualify for a Pell Grant and, most importantly, removed the income ceiling entirely for federally guaranteed Stafford student loans, thus greatly expanding the federal aid available to middle-income students and families (Mumper, 1991, p. 320). Thus, the last half of the 1970s was a boon to a wide range of students seeking to attend college, including students interested in private institutions, compliments largely of federal largesse.

Meanwhile, in inflation-adjusted dollars, tuition rates grew modestly in the early 1970s, but then declined during the rapid inflationary period of the later years of the decade (McPherson and Schapiro, 1991, pp. 29-30). McPherson and Schapiro's analysis of the combined impact of the tuition and aid trends shows a decline in real net price (inflation-adjusted and net of aid) of higher education from the mid-1970s through 1979 for public institutions and through 1980 for independent schools (pp. 34-37). Thus, though the times were not without serious economic insecurities—caused by high interest and inflation rates and fears of energy shortages—conditions for higher education in retrospect look comparatively favorable. Also, private colleges and universities in particular were beginning to tap new student markets in earnest during the 1970s as they looked ahead to the period when demographic trends insured that there would be fewer potential students in the traditional age pool. Overall then, during the 1970s private higher education fared relatively well. According to the National Center for Education Statistics, enrollments in this sector climbed by nearly half a million (23%) between 1970 and 1980 (fall to fall), and its "market share" of enrollments in four-year institutions hardly changed (U.S. Department of Education, 1994, p. 177), after two decades of decline.[63]

The Eighties and Early Nineties

Through the early 1980s, federal student aid policies were quite generous and, if anything, especially so to students attending private colleges and universities. The half-cost limit provision remained in the Pell Grant program (until 1986 when the limit was increased to 60 percent of the costs of attendance), thus preventing students from attending public colleges at little or no out-of-pocket cost, and even students from affluent circumstances were able to obtain government-subsidized loans to attend high-tuition institutions during the MISAA years. But, the environment for the private institutions deteriorated rapidly with the recession of the early 1980s and the sharp changes in federal student aid policies brought about by the Reagan Administration. In addition, after 1980 the number of high-school graduates nationally began to decline, as had been forecast. Thus, although private higher education had staved off the worst of what analysts had predicted for it just a few years earlier, it looked as though this was merely a temporary postponement of the inevitable.

The Reagan Administration clamped down quickly and hard on what had become runaway growth in the guaranteed (Stafford) loan program (Mumper, 1991, p. 323). The

---

[63]Private higher education lost more than two percentage points in *overall* share of enrollments during this decade because of continued rapid growth in public two-year college enrollments.

Budget Reconciliation Bill of 1981[64] brought back limits on Stafford Loans related to income and educational costs. Also, the Pell Grant program was funded well below its estimated future costs, necessitating caps on the size of grants in subsequent years (*ibid.*). The other generally available student grant programs (Supplemental Educational Opportunity Grants, College Work-Study, and State Student Incentive Grants) were also cut back at this time and have never recovered the constant-dollar funding levels they enjoyed in the 1980s, much less their purchasing power relative to college costs (College Board, 1994). These cuts occurred just as funds available for student aid from Social Security and veterans' benefits were also declining sharply in magnitude. After a few years of absolute decline in the early 1980s, Pell Grant funding increased somewhat (even in constant-dollar terms) during the later eighties, but has fallen sharply again since 1992-93.[65] Thus, the nominal value of Pell Grants has increased only slightly over the years since 1980 (from $1,800 in 1979-80 to $2,300 in 1993-94), and the proportion of average college costs that the grant covers has declined steadily. For private universities, this proportion is down to ten percent (College Board, p. 3).

For private higher education in particular, the decline in the importance of federal grant programs has increasingly shifted their attention to the government's loan programs (Mumper, 1991), and with considerable success. Mumper points out that, throughout the 1970s, most federal aid was provided to students as grants (1991, p. 326). However, the loan proportion moved upward through most of the eighties, dropped back a bit for a few years when Pell Grant funding picked up, but has jumped sharply in the last couple of years.[66] Since the 1992 reauthorization of the Higher Education Act made substantially more loan funds available, especially to students with moderate rather than very low incomes, the College Board estimates that the dollar volume of federal direct and guaranteed loans has grown by a staggering 50 percent *after adjusting for inflation* between 1992-93 and 1994-95. This is in spite of the fact that a growing proportion of the loans (about one-third in 1994-95) are "unsubsidized" in that the federal government no longer absorbs interest costs for the years the borrower is enrolled (College Board, 1995, p. 3). Thus, although private higher education has aggressively sought access to federal loan funds for its students, student debt levels are now becoming a matter of increasing concern. (College Board, 1995, pp. 3-4; Education Resources Institute and Institute of Higher Education Policy, 1995, cited in Schoenberg, 1995).

A further problem facing the private colleges and universities in regard to federal stu-

---

[64]It should be noted that, because of "forward funding" of student aid programs, the cuts in support for these programs actually took effect in later academic years. Pell Grants and SSIG support, however, first decreased in current dollars in 1980-81 (College Board, 1994).

[65]According the College Board's latest figures, preliminary current-dollar figures for Pell aid awarded in 1994-95 are $5.65 billion, compared with $6.177 billion in 1992-93 (College Board, 1995). In constant-dollar terms, this is a two-year decline of 13 percent, and even this adjustment understates the true decrease in purchasing power relative to college costs. At this writing (late 1995), it seems all but certain in the current fiscal and political climate that the funding trend for this cornerstone program in the federal government's student aid effort will continue to be flat at best.

[66]The proportion of all student aid in 1994-95, including federal, state, and institutional sources, represented by loans is estimated at 56 percent with grants at 43 percent, compared with 49 percent for loans and 48 percent for grants ten years earlier (College Board, 1995).

dent aid in the 1980s was the large increase in the proportion of these federal funds going to students attending for-profit postsecondary schools, mostly vocational training schools. At a time when the total available student aid was lagging behind enrollment growth and college costs, the proportion of Pell Grants going to students attending proprietary schools jumped from about 10 percent in 1979-80 (up only slightly from 7 percent in 1973-74) to more than 26 percent in 1987-88.[67] The proportion of federal loans awarded to proprietary school students similarly skyrocketed (peaking at 35 percent of Stafford loans in fiscal 1987). These proportions have come down substantially in more recent years, largely as a result of the federal crackdown on schools with high numbers of loan-defaulting students. Nonetheless, proprietary-school students still receive a substantial share of the aid available (College Board, 1995), a development not foreseen by the framers of the federal student aid programs (Keppel, 1987; Mumper, 1991).

Many states made some effort to respond to the slowdown in federal student aid spending in the 1980s, but their efforts were largely cut short early in the decade by the national recession and consequent fiscal squeeze that beset most states. By and large, during the first half of the 1980s states imposed fiscal stringencies on all of higher education, including student aid programs. In many states, this worked a particular hardship on private colleges and universities, whose main (or only) source of state sustenance is these programs. Indeed, overall, student aid programs tended to be cut back more sharply than state appropriations to public colleges and universities, but this was followed by a stronger recovery in state support for them than of state support for public institutions during the generally prosperous years of the later eighties (Zumeta, 1993). Interestingly, during the state fiscal stringencies of the 1990s, states have generally increased the support of their student aid programs quite strongly (Mortenson, 1994a), though much of the increased support has gone to public higher education students to help offset the sharp tuition increases they have faced as state appropriations to their institutions have been cut (NAASGP, 1994; Hines and Pruyne, 1995).

Overall, the state share of all student aid has changed little over the years (6 percent of the total in 1993-94), although the states' share of grant aid has increased somewhat. In total, the states now provide more than $3 billion annually in grants to college students (NASSGP, 1994).[68] Given the likely prospect that the federal government, in its drive to balance its budget, will deemphasize student grants even more in the future, the role of the states in higher education affordability seems destined to become more crucial than ever. For private higher education then, the states' student aid programs are of particular importance in this environment in helping a wide range of students to seriously consider alternatives to low-priced public colleges and universities, should they so choose.

Student aid has taken on great importance in recent years, in large part because of the sharp run-up in tuition prices in both public and private higher education that began around 1980 (See Figures 2 and 3.) These graphs show tuition growth in each sector after adjustment for general price inflation, thus the consistency and overall

---

[67]Gillespie and Carlson (1983) and College Board (1989), cited in McPherson and Schapiro (1991), p. 28.

[68]More than 98 percent of this state aid goes to undergraduate students (NASSGP, 1994).

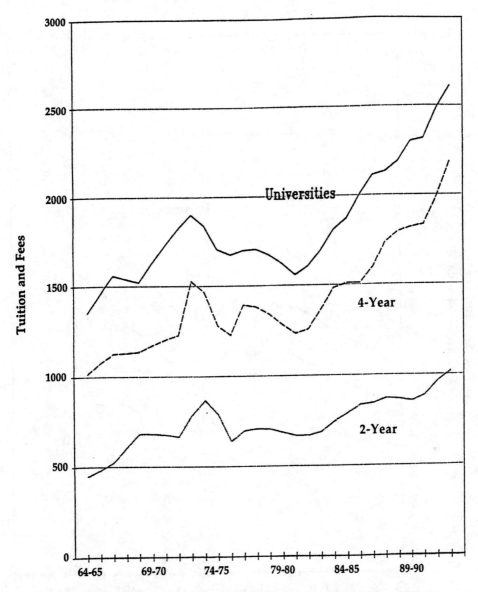

FIGURE 2. Tuition and Fees at Public Institutions, 1964-65 to 1993-93
Source: Mortenson, 1994b, p. 6.

magnitude of the increases are notable. The increases in the private sector are of particular interest here. Clotfelter (1991) compared tuition and other charges at private
and public institutions over nearly three decades and found a long-term growth trend
in the ratio of private-to-public tuition and fee levels. This ratio was 4.0 in 1959-60,
4.9 in 1974-75, and 5.9 in 1987-88 (p. 70). In relation to median family income, however, private tuition, room and board charges actually fell from 26.9 percent of
income in 1959-60 to 23.4 percent in 1979-80, but then jumped dramatically during
the 1980s to 32.3 percent in 1987-88. Average public institution charges as a percent-

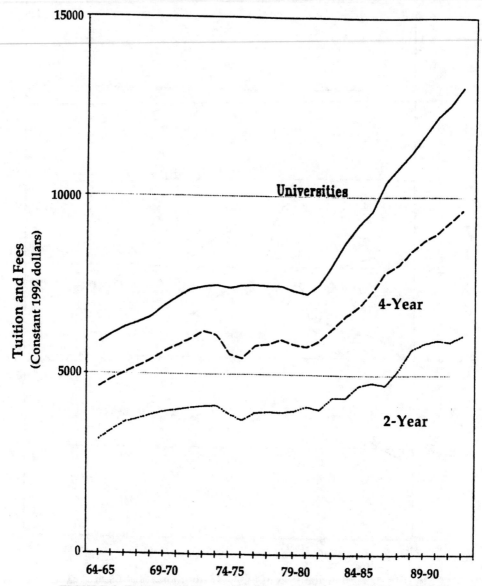

FIGURE 3. Tuition and Fees at Private Institutions, 1964-65 to 1992-93
Source: Mortenson, 1994b, p. 7.

age of family income also increased in the eighties, from 10.3 percent in 1979-80 to 12.3 percent in 1987-88, but remained well below the 14.6 percent level of 1959-60 (Clotfelter, 1991, p. 70).

In the private higher education sector, the rapid price increases of the early eighties were explained as being necessary to permit faculty and institutional maintenance expenditures to "catch up" after the period of dramatic inflation in the late 1970s (Breneman, 1994; St. John, 1994). Public higher education officials attributed large increases in these years to the need to generate revenue to offset recession-induced

slowdowns in their state appropriations (St. John, 1994, p. 2).

Nonetheless, year after year of relentless increases, well above the general rate of inflation and extending well beyond the end of the recession period, produced an unprecedented reaction from the federal government. Ronald Reagan's Secretary of Education, William Bennett, a former college professor, and his aides began to aggressively make the argument that colleges and universities were raising tuition and fees so regularly and sharply because they were full of waste and inefficiency and because this allowed them to take advantage of the government student aid available, since up to a point the formulas for distributing aid take tuition and fee levels into account in assessing a student's "need" (McPherson and Schapiro, 1991; Breneman, 1994; St. John, 1994).[69] These arguments certainly struck a populist nerve in some listeners and the point about institutions increasing prices to absorb increased government aid dollars has a superficial plausibility in microeconomic terms. However, the effective limits on income eligibility and grant (and loan) size built into the aid-dispensing formulas raise immediate doubts about the incentive effects on institutional pricing, since in many cases students and their families, not aid pools, would end up, at the margin, paying for the tuition increases.[70]

Private college interests in particular argued that the recent reductions in government aid simply meant that institutions would have to make up the difference for students, or reduce the number of needy students they enrolled.[71] They pointed to the sharp increases in aid from their own funds that they were providing.[72] They further noted that their main source of revenue for such increases in institutionally funded aid spending had to be tuition increases since this is their main source of flexible revenue. Thus, from the institutions' perspective, their large price increases were mainly attributable to reduced federal aid and their desire to continue to enroll diverse student bodies. They further argued that these steady price increases would indeed eventually affect their enrollments (or the income and ethnic composition of their student bodies), especially in an era when the size of the traditional age pool of college students was decreasing each year. One obvious problem is that, if institutions' aid budgets are mainly financed by tuition payments from relatively affluent students, at some point sharp price increases used mainly for redistribution among the student body seem sure to produce growing resistance from those paying the bills (Bowen and Breneman, 1993).

---

[69]For Secretary Bennett's sentiments unalloyed, see Bennett, 1986; 1987.

[70]For a careful analysis of the likely incentive effects built into the design of the aid programs, see McPherson and Schapiro (1991), pp. 67-69.

[71]With respect to moderate-income students, federally guaranteed loans were available during the 1980s, but the Reagan Administration imposed fairly stringent limits on who could get subsidized loans and how much they could borrow (Mumper, 1991). Thus, private institutions often had to supplement government aid funds heavily or "discount" their tuition prices selectively (whether or not these discounts were labelled officially as scholarships) to remain competitive for many moderate and middle-income students (Breneman, 1994, chapter three). For a helpful analysis of the debate between the Bennett position and that of private and other higher education interests, see St. John (1994, pp. 1-12).

[72]See in particular National Institute of Independent Colleges and Universities (1990); Breneman (1994, chapter three). Breneman, however, is critical of the standard way in which private institutions view and explain the issues at stake here.

Recent empirical research has made a contribution to sorting out the competing claims here. In order to increase understanding of the relationships between various forms of governmental support, including student aid, and key institutional behavior variables such as tuition pricing and discretionary spending on student aid, McPherson and Schapiro (1991) developed an econometric model incorporating the major financial variables for the fiscal years 1978-79 and 1985-86 to explore relationships among them for various types of colleges and universities (pp. 57-74). Contrary to suggestions by Secretary Bennett, these analysts find no empirical evidence for private four-year institutions of any relationship between federal student aid income and movements in tuition (pp. 70, 72).[73] They find a significant positive relationship between the rate of growth of federal student aid (as well as other income from government both state and federal)[74] and the growth rate of institutional spending on student aid, suggesting that "increased federal aid lowers the cost of admitting needy students sufficiently to allow private institutions to increase their own spending on aid in response..." (p. 72). This implies that the federal aid leverages an increased effect in the desired direction by motivating institutions to take advantage of it by doing more to attract more needy students. Plainly, there is no support here for the Bennett conjectures, though there is also no clear empirical evidence that reduced growth in federal financial support leads institutions to substitute their own funds for aid either.

On the other hand, the (mainly theoretical and conceptual) work of Massy (1990), Zemsky (1990), and Massy and Wilger (1992) also rings true to a considerable extent. These analysts, having observed academe's internal incentive structure and behavioral patterns over a long time and in many settings, point to several factors working to drive up costs over time.[75] To summarize briefly, these factors include the labor-intensive character of academic work given traditional definitions of quality based on close faculty-student contact and thus low student-faculty ratios;[76] lack of incentives for cost-saving innovations, in particular in faculty-reducing instructional technology;[77] professorial incentives toward research effort and output at the expense of teaching and advising responsibilities that have spread throughout most of academe and tend to increase costs per student; and incentives for bureaucratic entrepreneurs

---

[73]They do find a positive relationship between federal student aid received and *public* institution tuition pricing, however, probably because these institutions have prices low enough to be able to gain financially from increases in tuition-based aid eligibility of their students (pp. 70-73).

[74]These other relationships are significant because they suggest that private institutions use revenue from such sources as research grants and state appropriations and grants in part to replace some of their own funds spent on the supported activities, and that they move some of the freed-up discretionary funds into student aid (p. 73). According to the McPherson and Schapiro results, they also tend to raise tuition less than they would otherwise. Among public institutions, only the relationship between federal grant and contract funding and institutional student aid spending is statistically significant.

[75]See also Breneman (1994, pp. 32-33).

[76]See Bowen (1980) for a perceptive analysis of how these factors tend to drive up costs in higher education.

[77]Many faculty and institutional leaders are quite interested in investing in the latest educational technologies, but as an addition to the resources used in instruction to enhance quality, not as a way to teach more students per faculty member.

in academic administration to "build empires" that are costly as a route to advancement.[78] Another factor tending to increase costs on the administrative side is that institutions have had to respond in recent years to more and more mandates, regulation and information demands from federal and state governments.

These "inexorable" cost increases can be passed on to students, as long as they are willing and able to pay. In a macro sense, the availability of some $47 billion in aid annually (College Board, 1995)[79] no doubt does play a role in aggregate willingness to pay, as does the high private returns on investment available in the contemporary economy to those who complete higher education (Murphy and Welch, 1989; Marshall and Tucker, 1992; Breneman, 1994). Thus, there are few strong reasons to attack the powerful forces just described that tend to push costs and prices in higher education up steadily in real terms. (Attacks on these established ways of doing things would, of course, be met with fierce resistance from powerful and eloquent constituencies, so strong reasons are needed to produce impetus to act.)

For public institutions, there are signs that political forces, as well as improvements in the economy, are already bringing a halt to the most recent sharp jumps in tuition levels. (Zumeta and Fawcett-Long, 1996). But for the private sector this simply means that the "tuition gap" (best measured by the private/public price ratio used by Clotfelter, 1991) will likely resume its long-term growth pattern, and thus raises the question, How long will students and families be willing to pay staggering, and seemingly ever-growing, premiums for private higher education? Not surprisingly, the truly elite and most visible private colleges and universities, with plenty of surplus applicants of good quality from high-income families and large endowments, need not worry about this too much, though it does become increasingly expensive for them to maintain diverse student bodies.[80] Less-favored private schools with limited applicant pools and small endowments—the vast, if not very visible, majority of private institutions—have not been able to raise prices nearly as fast as their more-favored counterparts (Clotfelter, 1991), and so have had to be more resourceful in their survival strategies and do live more precariously. In short, many of them have not been averse to pushing aggressively for state assistance and, most importantly, have taken in many cases fairly dramatic steps on their own to revamp their programs and market them effectively to take advantage of whatever student markets they can find (Breneman, 1990; 1994; Zumeta, 1994).

While this resourcefulness in responding to the market is in many ways admirable—and quintessentially American—it is not without its price. With respect to the elite private institutions, there has been a substantial "middle-class melt" as students in this income group have faced steep price increases—even after aid is taken into account—that they have been unable or unwilling to pay (McPherson and Schapiro,

---

[78]Zemsky's (1990) terms for these last two phenomena are the "academic ratchet" and the "administrative lattice." The other points have been made for a long time by many others.

[79]This figure counts grant and loan aid from all sources, including federal, state, and institutional and private sources.

[80]McPherson and Schapiro (1994) have documented an apparent decline in proportions of private-college freshmen from high-income families in the last few years (1989-1993), however, suggesting that the point of serious price resistance on the part of such students may have been reached.

1991, pp. 78-89).[81] Significantly, though, the proportion of low-income students enrolling in these institutions has not decreased much, apparently because these students have continued to be prime targets for what grant aid is available from both governmental and institutional sources. Their proportions continue to be quite modest, however, as are the proportions of minority students in the elite schools (McPherson and Schapiro, 1991; Breneman, 1994). Thus, the place of the middle-income students in the top private schools has evidently been taken by even more students from affluent families who can afford to pay all or nearly all of their high prices (McPherson and Schapiro, 1991, pp. 78-89).[82] And these schools have maintained their liberal arts traditions and, by all accounts, continue to provide an extremely high quality of education to their favored clientele (Breneman, 1994). The elite private universities have also maintained their place in national rankings of quality in graduate education and research. There have been some signs of belt-tightening at some of these institutions (Chira, 1990; "Stanford to Lay Off...," 1990; Manger, 1991; De Palma, 1992; Celis, 1993), but few indications of major changes or that quality has been in any serious way affected.

As suggested above, more problematic (and elusive) are the effects of the difficulties of the recent era (i.e., since 1980) on the nonelite private colleges and universities.[83] Surprisingly, there is no evidence that the number of private institutions has declined as many expected it would. On the contrary, a careful comparison of numbers of private, nonprofit, degree-granting colleges and universities reporting enrollments in 1980 and 1992 shows a net increase of more than two hundred.[84] In terms of aggregate enrollments, the private nonprofit sector (including the elite institutions, whose enrollments have grown only a little), gained 13.4 percent in headcount enrollment over these twelve years (Zumeta, 1994).[85] But how have all these institutions survived and even grown in the face of fewer high-school graduates, a growing pri-

---

[81]McPherson and Schapiro point out (and emphasize further in their 1994 paper) that an important part of the "middle-class melt" phenomenon in private higher education simply results from the decline in the proportion of all students who are from families defined as middle-income (1991, p. 81).

[82]These authors point out that the same type of displacement has occurred in public universities (p. 88). Interestingly, their 1994 paper suggests some recovery in the proportions of private institution freshmen from lower- and middle-income backgrounds at the expense of upper-income students, but this analysis does not distinguish elite from other private institutions, as did the analysis published in 1991. Also, it shows a nearly two-percentage-point decline in the proportion of all freshmen enrolling in private institutions between 1989 and 1993 (1994, Tables 1 and 2).

[83]By this broad term, I mean private institutions lacking substantial endowments and comfortable numbers of "surplus" reasonably qualified applicants for admission.

[84]Calculated by the author with the assistance of Penelope Karovsky from an IPEDS-derived data base maintained at the University of Washington. This data base is the source of the enrollment figures for the private nonprofit sector cited in this section.

[85]These figures exclude Puerto Rico and U.S. territories. Over the same period, public college and university enrollments grew by 20 percent (calculated from NCES, 1994). If only four-year institutions are compared (since the fastest-growing segment in U.S. higher education is the large public community college sector, while private two-year colleges are a small part of the private sector), the two sectors' 1980-1992 growth figures are considerably closer: about 12 percent for the private, four-year institutions and 15 percent for the comparable public institutions.

vate/public tuition gap, and a less favorable federal student aid picture?

State student aid has probably helped a bit. After a period of very sluggish growth during the early and mid-1980s, these grant programs have increased quite strongly since the late 1980s (NASSGP, 1994; College Board, 1995). The total of state grant aid in constant dollars is now about twice the 1985-86 level (College Board, 1995).[86] Although public institutions' students have been claiming a gradually growing portion of this aid, especially in the last few years of sharp rises in public sector tuitions, the less-elite private schools, which enroll mainly students from their home state, are prime beneficiaries.[87]

Breneman (1990; 1994) points to the major process at work that accounts for the relative success of the private higher education sector.[88] A great many private institutions once called "liberal arts" colleges or universities have simply moved sharply away from this tradition in their programming in the direction of career-oriented fields. By Breneman's reckoning, by the mid-1980s only about two hundred colleges remained as liberal arts colleges, defined as baccalaureate-granting schools granting at least 40 percent of their degrees in liberal arts as opposed to professional fields. He documents large increases in the proportion of professional degrees awarded by baccalaureate institutions.[89]

Some analysis of recent enrollment trends in the broader private higher education sector is also pertinent. Table 3 (lower panel) shows that, while overall headcount enrollments in U.S. private colleges and universities grew by 13.4 percent over the years 1980-1992, full-time-equivalent (FTE) enrollments gained only 11.1 percent. This is because the strongest growth was in part-time rather than full-time students.[90] Part-time numbers in private colleges and universities grew by a robust 23.1 percent over the twelve years, while full-time students increased by less than half as much (9.6%). Another comparison is equally telling, and related to the first. The number of private-sector undergraduates grew by only 9.0 percent over these twelve years, while graduate and professional enrollments saw much stronger growth, at 28.0 percent. This is, it appears, because a large segment of the private sector has in recent years concentrated on enrolling professionally oriented students in postbaccalaureate programs, often part-time programs targeted at working students.[91]

This conclusion is consistent with Breneman's (1990; 1994) finding that many of the nonelite private colleges have moved away from the liberal arts tradition in terms of their

---

[86]These are preliminary figures for 1994-95.

[87]Most of the elite private schools have national student bodies, while most state student aid programs restrict eligibility to state-resident students. Thus, it is the locally oriented private schools that depend most on these programs to provide aid to their students.

[88]Breneman (1994) also attributes considerable importance to gains in endowment earnings and fundraising by private colleges, but these factors are of less import for the nonelite schools than for the best-known schools with large endowments.

[89]See Breneman (1994), pp. 138-142 for these trend analyses covering the Carnegie Foundation's Liberal Arts I and II categories of institutions.

[90]For purposes of computing full-time-equivalent enrollments, the National Center For Education Statistics (the source of the data used here) counts three part-time students as equal to one full-time student.

Table 3. Independent College and University Enrollments, 1980, 1985, 1990, &1992

	1980	1985	1990	1992	80-85	85-90	90-92	80-92	%80-85	%85-90	%90-92	%80-92
Headcount	2,593,130	2,669,553	2,852,194	2,953,558	76,423	182,641	101,364	360,428	2.9%	6.8%	3.6%	13.9%
Full-Time	1,867,646	1,882,889	1,990,062	2,060,400	15,243	107,173	70,338	192,754	0.8%	5.7%	3.5%	10.3%
Part-time	725,484	786,664	862,132	893,158	61,180	75,468	31,026	167,674	8.4%	9.6%	3.6%	23.1%
FTE	2,109,474	2,145,110	2,277,439	2,358,119	35,636	132,329	80,680	248,645	1.7%	6.2%	3.5%	11.8%
Undergraduate	1,983,693	2,015,084	2,130,764	2,174,438	31,391	115,680	43,674	190,745	1.6%	5.7%	2.0%	9.6%
Graduate+First Professional	605,235	648,883	721,430	779,120	43,648	72,547	57,690	173,885	7.2%	11.2%	8.0%	28.7%
Unclassified	4,202	5,586	0	0								
Independent College and University Enrollments, 1980, 1985, 1990, & 1992 (excluding Puerto Rico and Territories)												
	1980	1985	1990	1992	80-85	85-90	90-92	80-92	%80-85	%85-90	%90-92	%80-92
Headcount	2,522,428	2,576,223	2,763,747	2,859,498	53,795	187,524	95,751	337,070	2.1%	7.3%	3.5%	13.4%
Full-Time	1,813,656	1,808,355	1,922,393	1,987,220	-5,301	114,038	64,827	173,564	-0.3%	6.3%	3.4%	9.6%
Part-time	708,772	767,868	841,354	872,278	59,096	73,486	30,924	163,506	8.3%	9.6%	3.7%	23.1%
FTE	2,049,913	2,064,311	2,202,844	2,277,979	14,398	138,533	75,135	228,066	0.7%	6.7%	3.4%	11.1%
Undergraduate	1,915,959	1,917,595	2,049,104	2,088,126	11,636	121,509	39,022	172,167	0.6%	6.3%	1.9%	9.0%
Graduate+First Professional	602,485	643,206	714,643	771,372	40,721	71,437	56,729	168,887	6.8%	11.1%	7.9%	28.0%
Unclassified	3,984	5,422	0	0								
Source: Zumeta, 1994												

degree offerings. Table 4 provides some additional data that tend to confirm the point. This table shows the trends in private-sector enrollments by (1987) Carnegie classification of private institutions. The fastest-growing category (+30.6%) is the "Liberal Arts II," or less-selective "liberal arts" colleges, which Breneman argues are really small professional institutions (1994, pp. 11-15). Close behind is the "Comprehensive II" institutions category (+25.0%), which are also less-selective institutions dominated by vocationally and professionally oriented programs and students. Specialized private institutions,[92] largely professionally oriented, have also grown rapidly. "Comprehensive I" institutions, which also have substantial professionally oriented programs and students but are more selective than Comprehensive IIs, have also grown significantly (+10.5%). It appears that the strongest group of more traditional private institutions, the "Research I" universities, have also grown at a reasonable rate (+ 10.8%), but the other classifications in the more traditional mold have had sluggish enrollment growth or worse.[93]

These patterns suggest that, for institutions not at the top of the traditional quality hierarchy, the successful strategy in the eighties and early nineties has been to empha-

---

[91]Consistent with this is the finding from the author's (as yet unpublished) analyses of degree award data by field for various Carnegie classes of private institutions, that the fastest-growing fields in the fast-growing classes of institutions during the 1980s and early 1990s have been, by far, business and (since 1985 at least) education, with other professionally oriented fields (e.g., computer science, psychology) also among the leaders in growth rate, though of far less importance in quantitative terms.

[92]This is a composite category composed of a variety of Carnegie categories encompassing seminaries, schools of the arts, free-standing law schools, and various other types of specialized, largely professionally oriented institutions.

[93]Note that the least-demanding classification of doctorate-granting institutions, "Doctorate II" institutions, actually lost six percent of their 1980 enrollments by 1992, and the elite Liberal Arts I institutions gained only 0.5 percent. In the latter case, this enrollment stability appears to be largely by design (Breneman, 1994).

TABLE 4. Independent College and University Enrollments, Selected Years, 1980 through 1992, by 1987 Carnegie Classification of Institutions

HEADCOUNT	1980	1985	1990	1992	% 80-85	% 85-90	% 90-92	% 80-92
C1	608,360	634,765	665,950	672,388	4.3%	4.9%	1.0%	10.5%
C2	222,326	230,064	261,081	277,987	3.5%	13.5%	6.5%	25.0%
D1	188,343	184,104	196,742	200,216	-2.3%	6.9%	1.8%	6.3%
D2	183,385	178,927	172,326	172,266	-2.4%	-3.7%	0.0%	-6.1%
LA1	217,263	208,557	217,585	218,242	-4.0%	4.3%	0.3%	0.5%
LA2	330,088	332,622	402,831	430,961	0.8%	21.1%	7.0%	30.6%
R1	319,567	330,302	343,972	354,178	3.4%	4.1%	3.0%	10.8%
R2	88,524	87,945	90,756	90,427	-0.7%	3.2%	-0.4%	2.1%
Subtotal	**2,157,856**	**2,187,286**	**2,351,243**	**2,416,665**	**1.4%**	**7.5%**	**2.8%**	**12.0%**
2yr/Spec/Unc	364,572	388,937	412,504	442,833	6.7%	6.1%	7.4%	21.5%
Total	2,522,428	2,576,223	2,763,747	2,859,498	2.1%	7.3%	3.5%	13.4%
Source: Zumeta, 1994								

size professionally oriented programs accessible to part-time students. The fastest growth has been in such enrollments at the graduate level, but the underlying data (not shown here), as well as the import of Breneman's analysis, indicate that there have been substantial markets at the undergraduate level as well in many fields. It is also important to note, however, that the more traditional classes of private colleges and universities, with the exception of the small Doctorate II group of institutions, have at least held their own in enrollments during a very difficult era. This in itself is a significant accomplishment.

From a public policy perspective, the surprising resourcefulness and vitality of private higher education should be seen, in general, as a positive development. Stronger private-sector enrollments tend to be associated with higher overall participation in higher education and lower costs to state taxpayers (Zumeta, 1996). As suggested earlier, these relationships could be especially significant in the coming era of growing demands for higher education but limited tax revenues. On the other hand, Breneman rightly raises the question as to how small and inaccessible to broad groups of the population we wish to allow the "liberal arts core" of institutions in the country to become (1994, chapter one).[94] Perhaps policymakers should consider taking stronger steps to insure the survival and broader accessibility of more of the distinctively liberal arts institutions.

Secondly, the vigorous response to the demands of the student market by private institutions that live or die according to their attractiveness to students has potential for abuse, even when the institutions are not-for-profit. Governments, both state and federal, may need to consider creative ways to discharge their duty to the citizenry to insure reasonable quality and truth-in-advertising by these institutions without unduly circumscribing their freedoms as independent organizations and as institutions of higher learning. Certainly

---

[94]As Breneman and others have pointed out, virtually all liberal arts *colleges* (as distinct from universities with substantial liberal arts programs) are in the private sector. Thus, they are the only apparent source of their particular brand of undergraduate education available to students. These schools have long produced a disproportionate share of the nation's leaders and scholars (Breneman, 1994, ch.1).

this is a difficult balance to strike, but additional places in higher education are of little value if the programs are not sound and the students are not capable of profiting from them. The state role (or potential role) in this area is likely to grow in the foreseeable future as the federal government moves to devolve regulatory responsibilities to the states. States would do well to seek guidance from non-U.S., as well as home-grown, approaches in this delicate area (Geiger, 1986; Dill, 1995; van Vught, 1995).

WHAT THE FUTURE HOLDS FOR PRIVATE HIGHER EDUCATION

As we look ahead, it is important to think about the future of private higher education broadly, in the context of the challenges facing all of higher education. Indeed, as was suggested earlier, for more than a century it has made little sense in the United States to consider independent higher education separately from the public sector enterprise in this field. Now, as was argued in the early part of this chapter, the demand for higher education is growing for both economic (i.e., the needs of the modern economy) and social (i.e., demographic factors such as the "baby boom echo" and equity concerns) reasons. At the same time, the resources that have traditionally provided the bulk of support for higher education, state tax funds, are increasingly constrained by taxpayer resistance and pressures from other state functions with rapidly growing caseloads and a near-mandatory funding requirement: Medicaid, criminal justice and prisons, and elementary and secondary education. Impending devolution of responsibility for other human services from the federal government to the states adds to the competition for scarce state support.[95] In light of these trends, the prospects for higher education access and adequate funding per-student at the time the next recession hits the states may be grim indeed.

In many states private higher education can provide an important part of the answer to the dilemmas posed by this combination of forces and trends, but only if state policies are conducive. As I shall argue below, however, in a number of states the extant policy framework is not conducive to taking the independent sector seriously as a significant potential contributor to the achievement of state higher education policy goals. In the next section, I will present a conceptual framework for analyzing state policies that affect private higher education and the factors that influence them in an effort to begin to understand and account for the variation in how these institutions are treated in the policymaking process. I will also explain how this framework is helpful in thinking about policy outcomes, such as provision of cost-effective access to higher education in an era of growing demand, and will lay out a theory-building and research agenda related to it, as well as suggest its implications for policy analysis.

STATE POLICY POSTURES VIS-A-VIS PRIVATE HIGHER EDUCATION

Although state policies that affect private higher education are disparate, there are reasons to believe that within individual states such policies might be related to each other in a more or less coherent fashion. Rational policymakers seeking maximum

---

[95]For a more complete analysis of these developments, see Zumeta and Fawcett-Long (1996).

impact and minimum unintended consequences from the set of policies in place at any given time would be expected to try to select policies that meshed well with policies already in place or simultaneously enacted. Also, although the policies in place at any time have typically emerged during different periods, they arise from policymaking systems and cultures that are likely to be fairly stable over time in important respects (Gardner, Atwell, and Berdahl, 1985). Yet for all its apparent logic, policy coherence is hardly inevitable. Public policymaking processes do not always produce evidently rational results,[96] especially when a set of policies enacted over many years is viewed at a single point in time and in light of contemporary conditions. Moreover, since many state policies affect private higher education only secondarily in the course of pursuing other, more primary goals, the cumulative array of policies touching this sector could be virtually random.

Howlett (1991) describes a school of thought on the study of policy instruments (the "continuum" school), with its roots in such classics as Dahl and Lindblom (1953) and Kirschen et al (1964), which argues that conceptions of types of policy tools, and thus by extension policy regimes, such as those described in the next section are most useful in understanding instrument choice. The argument is that for most tasks a number of policy tools (e.g., instruments such as grants, mandates, or provision of information) are available, but that policymaker choices among them are driven more by the political, social, economic, and ideological variables at work than by rational assessment of which tool is right for which job. Such analysts as Linder and Peters (1989) in the contemporary "policy design" school, seek to blend the earlier ideas of scholars who emphasized a resource-based notion of policy instruments (i.e., distinguishing direct from indirect grants, information-based strategies from coercive regulations and the like) with those of the continuum school. Howlett concludes a discussion of these efforts by noting: "The basic assumption made by design theorists is that policy instruments are technically substitutable but context-ridden....For the design theorists, then, instrument choice is ultimately a political decision heavily influenced by the nature of beliefs, attitudes and perceptions held by political and bureaucratic decisionmakers" (1991, p. 8).

This line of argument suggests there is indeed some logic in searching for regularities among a state's policies in a particular field, such as those affecting private higher education. Surely, students of higher education are aware that some states pay more attention to their private higher education sector than do others. Elsewhere, I have provided empirical evidence that states' policies in such areas as the presence or absence of state programs providing direct funding to private colleges and universities (whether by contract or direct appropriation); the size of state student aid programs (per-enrolled-student); the level of public institution tuition (a key competitive parameter for private higher education subject to strong state influence); the extent of private-sector involvement in state higher education planning; consideration of impacts on private institutions (often covered under the heading of "program duplication") in state reviews of public sector programs and proposals; and the extent of state mandates, regulation, and data collection affecting private higher education are inter-

---

[96]See in particular Lindblom (1980) for a classic statement of the reasons behind this hoary truth.

correlated in predictable ways (Zumeta, 1992).[97] If they were not, there would be little point in searching for comprehensible state "policy postures."

Since there is reason to believe that state policies toward (or affecting) private higher education are not random, the next step is to theorize about how they might be linked and about what factors might determine particular patterns of policies. Conceptually, it seems convenient to begin this process by considering three distinct types of possible state policy orientations or *postures* toward private higher education, which I shall call the *laissez-faire*, *central-planning*, and *market-competitive* state policy postures.[98] Without some such framework concepts it is difficult to think systematically about the wide range of state policies that affect private higher education. Moreover, from a policy analytic standpoint, they facilitate thinking about options for intervening in a state's policy "system" in order to affect policy outcomes and about how to assess the feasibility of possible interventions. Thus, if it could be empirically validated, such a framework would have potentially valuable uses of both the positive and normative variety—i.e., it could help illuminate both policy science in this field and policy analysis.

The *Laissez-faire* Posture

A state taking the *laissez-faire* posture toward the private higher education sector is essentially choosing to leave this sector to its own devices, while the state pursues its policy ends in higher education strictly through public institutions. At the extreme, this would mean little or no state funds for student aid would be available to private college students; no tax incentives aiding private institutions would exist beyond those available to all nonprofits; little or no consideration would be given to independent campuses' concerns in establishing public college tuition and fee structures or their mission and program configurations; the state would provide no funds, either by direct appropriation

---

[97]For example, states with relatively high student aid spending levels are more likely to have programs providing direct state funding to private colleges and universities and to have relatively high tuition levels in public higher education. Each of these variables is also positively correlated with the extent of private-sector participation in state planning for higher education (Zumeta, 1992).

[98]For the roots of the latter two constructs, see Breneman (1981) and Spence and Weathersby (1981). In commenting upon a draft of this chapter, James Hearn points out that, if we conceptualize state policy frameworks in terms of a two-by-two matrix (as shown below), a fourth cell is manifest: *bureaucratic/regulatory planning,* which would fit a state that used direct state control mechanisms extensively, but did little in the way of providing incentives or seeking to integrate student aid, tuition, and other policies. I am indebted to Professor Hearn for this interesting suggestion, but will not try to pursue it in this chapter.

| | | USE OF DIRECT STATE CONTROL | |
		Low	High
USE OF DIRECT INCENTIVES	Low	Laissez-Faire	Bureaucratic/Regulatory Planning
	High	Market-Competitive	Comprehensive (Pro-Active) Central Planning

or by contract, to private institutions for any purpose beyond perhaps the occasional ad hoc research contract for a specific, limited purpose; the private sector would be excluded from a meaningful role in statewide higher education planning; the state would collect minimal information about independent institutions beyond that collected by the federal government; and the state's regulation of private higher education would be of the most limited conceivable scope, i.e., limited to licensing institutions to operate in the state and enforcing on them general state laws not specifically targeted at higher education.

In general, it seems likely that a state policy posture along these *laissez-faire* lines would be most plausible in states with a relatively small (in terms of enrollment share) and politically weak private higher education sector. Regional patterns should be prominent here because of historical factors (some suggested in the earlier discussion) leading to later and more limited development of private higher education west of the Mississippi (Trow, 1993). Other variables at work might include the wealth and general spending propensities of the state, since any proposed aid to private colleges or their students might look to a skeptical legislature much like any other new area of proposed state spending.[99] Also, a state's governance structure for higher education might play a role in that states where the state policy agency is also the governing board for the public institutions—an arrangement that obtains more or less in a number of states—might be expected to be little concerned with the private sector (i.e., behave as a *laissez-faire* state). On the other hand, other state governance arrangements, such as one of the coordinating board forms where the state agency has a meaningful policy and planning role for both sectors but no line management authority over the public institutions, should be more sensitive to the private sector's role and to potential impacts of policies on it.

What are the likely consequences of a state's pursuing laissez-faire policies vis-a-vis its private higher education sector? As suggested earlier, current competitive conditions facing private institutions, particularly those lacking large pools of surplus applicants and substantial endowments (i.e., the vast majority of private colleges), may imply some untoward consequences from the standpoint of the public interest, such as erosion of quality as funds are increasingly shifted from instruction and plant and equipment to student aid to compete for students; further increases in student debt burdens which may affect their career choices; likely further moves toward more narrow, vocationally oriented curricula; and, perhaps eventually, loss of capacity to enroll students (i.e., to provide access) and provide diversity to a state's institutional mix. If a particular state's private higher education sector is small and weak both academically and politically, the consequences may not be serious, practically speaking. In these circumstances, tragic though it may be for a few institutions and students, little quality enrollment capacity or meaningful diversity may be lost if some private institutions fail to survive the current competitive era without state help.

If, however, a state's independent sector does represent a substantial resource in terms of such publicly useful values as enrollment and research capacity, program

---

[99]In fact though, such spending might well offset state spending on public higher education and even lead to a net reduction in state spending on higher education (Zumeta, 1996).

quality, meaningful diversity and choice for students and other clients, and successful service to underserved areas and populations, then there is reason for public policy to be concerned about the implications of the laissez-faire posture. These implications should be of concern to policymakers, particularly in states that will soon need all the higher education capacity they can find (see Figure 1, p. 360).

The State *Central-Planning* Posture

At the opposite end of the conceptual continuum from the laissez-faire posture stands state *central-planning*. In this policy posture, instead of ignoring the private sector as in the laissez-faire regime, the state embraces this sector as an integral part of its higher education capacity. This model can only be fully developed in a state that practices strong central planning for its public higher education sector, which typically entails a well-developed "master plan" delineating institutional roles as well as extensive mandates, planning mechanisms, data collection, and use of funding leverage to enforce the grand scheme. In such a regime the private institutions are incorporated integrally in the extensive state planning and management of higher education that exists, get their share of attention when new state initiatives affecting higher education are planned, and receive a substantial share of the state's higher education dollars. Indeed the state's money presumably helps entice them into and cements them within this policy system. To better ensure adherence to its plans and designs, we would expect the central-planning-oriented state to channel some of its dollars directly to independent institutions, indeed perhaps to prefer direct funding of them at the margin to student aid and tax incentives as more effective levers to simultaneously aid and direct the private higher education sector to serve state purposes.

Central-planning also implies as a basic tenet efforts by the planners to limit apparent duplication in institutional missions and programs since this seems unnecessarily expensive.[100] Such efforts can be very significant to the private sector if taken seriously because they mean that duplication of private institution missions, programs, or geographic "turf" become legitimate considerations in state decisions about expansion in public higher education. This addresses one of the private sector's chief state policy concerns in the current competitive era, so this sector can be expected to actively support such vigilance by state authorities. Similarly, in the area of state policies affecting (or determining) public higher education tuition levels, the central-planning-oriented state would be expected to give attention to impacts on private institutions because it is dependent on them to play specific roles in the state's higher education "system." Thus, public tuition levels will tend to be biased upward, though this effect may be moderated by other factors, such as the relative political influence of the public and private sectors.

The price of solicitude from the state in program review matters, and of participation in its planning councils and funding largesse, seems likely to be increased state concern over time with private institutions' missions, program configurations, and performance with state funds.[101] Thus, the state practicing extensive central planning would be expected to collect increasing amounts of data from and about private insti-

---

[100]Whether or not this is always true is another question (Thompson and Zumeta, 1981).

tutions (as it would about its public institutions), and to oversee their financial operations and their efforts at new program initiatives more closely over time. It would also be likely to come to see these institutions as legitimately subject to more and more state regulation (e.g., with regard to student and institutional assessment, program review, perhaps tuition pricing), as well as to its fiscal largesse.

In short, "independent" institutions which choose to play in the state's game under a central-planning regime run the risk of becoming quasi-public. The negative side of this is that such quasi-public institutions, substantially dependent upon state dollars and subject to various formal and informal state controls, are likely to become less capable of sustaining the diversity of mission and approach, the flexibility and rapid market responsiveness, and the autonomy from a single central vision that is an important part of the reason public policy might seek to preserve an independent higher education sector.[102] Also, a centrally focused policy regime will tend to attract some of institutions' creative energies toward influencing the state authorities who control the resources and protections they seek, perhaps at the expense of direct attention to state service needs as reflected in student and market demands.

The state central-planning posture has some advantages as well. It permits the state considerable latitude to aid the independent higher education sector in a time when some (even many) private institutions may need help to continue serving public purposes well. Such aid need not be direct financial assistance from the state to private colleges and universities, though in some cases state help might take this form. Such direct state "institutional aid," more easily than student aid carried indirectly to institutions when students choose them, can be used to target state resources efficiently to particular purposes. Second, such a regime legitimizes use of private institutions to serve public purposes in situations where they may be more cost-effective tools for the particular task than public institutions (e.g., programs serving particular regions or high-cost specialty fields where the private sector already has capacity), or where the two sectors can work cooperatively. This could be increasingly important in an era of limited resources for higher education.

Third, the central-planning approach legitimizes extensive data-gathering on private institutions and their capabilities that should have many uses in managing an integrated state higher education system for optimal results. Fourth, it permits the state authorities to shield private institutions in various ways from subsidized public sector competition, if it is deemed to be in the public interest to do so. Finally, extending the state's regulatory net to include the private sector may have benefits to the extent these efforts succeed in enhancing educational quality, teacher preparedness, and the like, as they seek to do.

States tending in the direction of the central-planning model encompassing the private higher education sector are likely to have historical, cultural, and legal traditions that permit and encourage both strong central-planning and close state-private-sector relations.

---

[101]Geiger's (1986) accounts of the evolution of state-private-higher-education relations in Japan, Belgium, the Netherlands, and the Philippines over recent decades are instructive here.

[102]On these and related points, see Thompson and Zumeta (1981); Birnbaum (1983); Clark (1983); Ware (1989).

Also, the private sector has to be both willing to participate[103] and large enough to be worth taking into account. Empirically, one would tend to look for central-planning-oriented regimes with heavy independent sector involvement in policymaking among states with traditions of active state government and large, politically influential private higher education sectors. These considerations point toward the Northeast and upper Midwest states with large, long-established private sectors and traditions of governmental activism strongly influenced by affected interests. Other likely supportive factors are a coordinating board type of state governance structure, which tends to facilitate private sector involvement more than a statewide "board of regents" arrangement (Zumeta, 1992), and sufficient state wealth to make substantial student aid and programs channeling state funds directly to private colleges and universities seem affordable.

The *Market-Competitive* State Policy Posture

A third, distinctly different type of state policy posture is possible.[104] In the *market-competitive* regime, rather than letting the chips fall where they may as in the *laissez-faire* model, the state takes a more active posture toward private higher education and private/public relations. Although they avoid the detailed state direction characteristic of the *central-planning* approach just described, state authorities under the *market-competitive* regime nonetheless take a comprehensive view of the state's higher education resources, including its private institutions, but seek primarily to facilitate the workings of the marketplace and to promote evenhanded competition across sectors.

Under the pure market-competitive approach, state intervention would be limited to addressing the various market imperfections which characterize the higher education marketplace.[105] Thus state mandates and regulation would be quite limited. State interventions in this model would likely include tuition and student aid policies designed to more nearly equalize net prices (i.e., after student aid) between priva'' and public institutions;[106] encouragement, or at least no discouragement, of public/private competition not judged to denigrate quality or involve fraudulent claims; and efforts to disseminate widely and facilitate the use by students and their parents of comparative information about institutions' characteristics and performance.[107] This last point is in notable contrast to the central-planning regime where information pol-

---

[103]For example, nonsectarian and Roman Catholic institutions tend to be less standoffish with respect to state governments than are many Protestant institutions, especially conservative ones.

[104]Of course, so are many others. Empirical research and analysis should be helpful here (see Zumeta, 1996).

[105]These would include widely varying tuition subsidies not systematically related to policy objectives, the existence of near-monopolies in some markets, inadequate or no response to particular state needs by the higher education system, inadequate consumer information, and perhaps some quality control measures beyond information provision, if deemed necessary.

[106]We would expect the competitively oriented state to favor generous, but competitive or "portable" student aid grants tenable at both private and public institutions to *tuition equalization* grants available only to students attending private institutions. The latter, however, do serve to move state subsidies to private and public institution students in the direction of equality.

[107]See also Breneman (1981).

icy focuses on collecting data for managing the system from the center.

Where the state authorities saw a particular need not being adequately addressed by the public and private institutions (e.g., inadequate production of certain types of trained specialists, a need for new economic development initiatives), the true competitive regime would describe the type of program sought and offer it up for "bids" in a competition open to competent institutions from both sectors. Short of this, private institutions would at least routinely be offered the opportunity to compete to fill gaps not of interest to public colleges. Winning bidders would be granted time-limited, performance-based contracts, at least in theory subject to nonrenewal and rebidding, rather than essentially permanent institutional grant programs.[108] This would be the extent of direct state aid to private institutions in the true market-competitive regime, as the state would prefer aid mechanisms where the market selects who gets how much aid, such as tax incentives for donations to institutions of either sector and aid routed through students who can choose which college to attend.

Beyond the specific and carefully targeted interventions to "perfect" the market described above, the pure market-competitive state would, in sharp contrast to the central-planning regime, allow both public and private institutions (a) to plan and modify their own offerings within existing resources without close state regulatory oversight, and (b) to compete directly for students and the resources tied to them. An empirically plausible version of this model would almost certainly, however, entail some restrictions on the program configurations of public institutions (i.e., mission limitations and some state review of new program proposals), and some basic funding guarantees to public institutions independent of enrollments.[109]

One might summarize the differences between the state central-planning model and the market-competitive posture by observing that in the former the private institutions are treated by the state much like the public ones, while in the latter the public institutions face an environment deliberately designed to be somewhat like that now faced by the private schools. The basic point of the latter type of state policy regime is to focus institutions more on reacting to (or even anticipating) societal needs and demands by encouraging them to respond to market or quasi-market signals (i.e., enrollment-driven funding and performance contracting arrangements), and less on working state officials for favored treatment in centrally controlled decisions on missions, programs, and resource allocations.

This model has theoretical appeal but the full-blown market-competitive approach has a number of theoretical and practical difficulties. Two problems are paramount. First, the large costs involved in substantially reducing the effective price gap (tuition gap net of financial aid) between private and public institutions necessary to reduce the privates' sensitivity to direct public sector competition might well be seen as prohibitive in many states, though such expenditures could actually serve to offset in some measure public institutions' need for funds to serve more students

---

[108]For a fuller description, see Spence and Weathersby (1981). Several states have recently initiated on a limited basis performance contracting or incentive arrangements with their public institutions that resemble these ideas (Paulson, 1990; Jones and Ewell, 1993; Massy, 1994).

[109]Thus, this model falls short of complete privatization of the public higher education sector, a direction which has been talked about recently in a few states but seems unlikely to come about any time soon.

(Zumeta, 1996). Public higher education interests will surely argue that they have better uses for the state's limited funds than providing subsidies to more students to attend high-priced private schools. Second, the logic of encouraging in certain ways, rather than uniformly seeking to limit and constrain, intersector competition for students is difficult for many to understand, even in states with relatively strong pro-market attitudes in general. Competition can be noisy and unsettling and the other side of the competition coin is duplication of similar programs, which to many simply looks like waste.[110]

The market-competitive model's approach to information policy—emphasizing the dissemination of information in usable form to consumers to guide their choices rather than amassing it at the state level to inform centrally made decisions—is also unfamiliar to many and relatively untested, though there are recent signs of increased interest in it.[111] There are also legitimate doubts about the sustainability over the long run of a truly open and competitive bidding and rebidding process for performance-based contracts (Spence and Weathersby, 1981; Van Horn, 1991). Finally, one might well wonder what would happen under a market-competitive regime when competition threatened the demise of a public campus, or, for that matter, a politically well-connected private one. In short, the most important open questions about the viability of a market-competitively-oriented policy regime in higher education are likely to be ones of political economy rather than pure economics. Still, the nonintrusive nature of this approach makes it intriguing to those attracted to the market responsiveness, flexibility, and autonomy that characterize many institutions in the private higher education sector.

As with the other state policy posture models discussed here, one would expect historical and cultural factors to play an important role in determining which states might lean in the market-competitive direction with respect to policies toward private higher education. To the extent these factors are captured by regional differences, we might expect to see this posture come closest to fruition in the southern and western states where pro-market values are strong, especially in states where the private sector is large enough to attract policymaker attention but not so large as to successfully take a place in a cartel-like central-planning regime. The connection of the market-competitive orientation to state wealth is not entirely clear *a priori*, but one might expect it to be less attractive to the poorest states, where there will be resistance to large student aid programs benefiting the private sector, and to the wealthiest where concerns with cost-effectiveness in higher education may not be prominent, than to states in the middle-range on wealth measures. Finally, one would expect states with coordinating board governance arrangements to be more attracted to this rather hands-off, level-playing-field approach than would states with a board holding line authority over the public institutions.

---

[110]On the theory of desirable redundancy in public policy, however, see Landau (1969) and Bendor (1985). In higher education, moreover, programs with similar names may have different foci and serve different types of students, in part because providers seek to differentiate their products.

[111]Recent federal legislation, including the 1992 reauthorization of the Higher Education Act, has emphasized increased quantity and quality of consumer information to include data on student and institutional performance. States are likely to have a key role in enforcing this new policy thrust ("Focus on Accountability," 1994).

Utility of This Conceptual Framework

As was suggested at the beginning of this section, the type of conceptual framework advanced here seems to provide some useful leverage on the problem of understanding the disparate range of state policies (and nonpolicies) that significantly affect private higher education, while also providing a clear connection to state policies for all of higher education. Each of the ideal-type policy posture constructs proposed is designed to have internal consistency and overall coherence while also not being so far from reality as to seem hopelessly impractical. Therefore, they should be relatively understandable to policymakers. In each case, advantages and disadvantages seem fairly clear, as described above.

Normatively, if a state's policymakers prefer one or another of these ideal types (together with its likely consequences), the framework offered should give them a clearer idea of how to move in that direction, and how to think about modifications to the construct that may be pragmatically necessary. No doubt, the empirical reality of actual state policy configurations will prove considerably more complicated than the simple three-postures framework suggests. Many in-between configurations of policies are obviously plausible and even wholly different conceptualizations of policy coherence are possible, not to mention ad hoc, largely incoherent combinations of policies. The conceptualization sketched here simply represents one possible way of beginning the task of developing understanding of this policy landscape and of laying the groundwork for empirical analysis and testing.[112]

Once state policy postures have been successfully described and classified empirically, the next step would be to learn more about their origins, determinants, and dynamics over time, as well as their implications for policy outcomes of interest. Can *laissez-faire* regimes survive a long period of difficult environmental conditions for private higher education? If so, under what circumstances (e.g., given a small, weak private sector)? What are the consequences for system diversity (nationally as well as at the state level), participation rates in higher education, and costs to the taxpayer? Are *market-competitive* regimes cost-effective, as their proponents would claim? Do such policies undermine public support for public higher education or curtail participation in higher education overall? Is such a regime stable over time, or is it inevitably undermined by the efforts of the players to gain self-serving control over the rules of the game? Can the weaknesses of *market-competitive* and *central-planning* regimes be conquered by a hybrid approach? Is this what tends to occur to the purer models over time? What are the possible hybrid forms and under what circumstances does each tend to evolve? How will the emerging era of substantially increased demand affect the evolution of policy regimes? This is an agenda for a *policy science* of state higher education policy.

Additionally, this type of analysis, proceeding at once both conceptually and empirically, should help policymakers to think broadly but practically about how to achieve their long-range goals in higher education. In some states, deep-seated attitudes and realities related to historic market shares, constitutional provisions, and entrenched ways of doing things may limit the range of possibilities to those in the

---

[112]For a preliminary empirical analysis based upon this conceptual framework, see Zumeta (1996).

neighborhood of one of the above types of policy regimes. Together with precise analysis of the circumstances and needs of a particular state, the framework (especially after it has been validated or modified by empirical studies) should help to illuminate possibilities for modifications of the archetypical approaches that seem to make sense for a particular case. In general, the research program suggested here should eventually make the consequences of possible interventions more susceptible to broad-gauged but empirically grounded analysis, including consequences linked to longer-run political dynamics, as suggested in some of the questions raised in the previous paragraph. Thus, these models and the associated research agenda[113] can also make a contribution to policy *analysis* in higher education.

CONCLUSION

In this chapter, I have sought to survey the field of state policy and private (nonprofit) higher education. The chapter has provided both a fairly extensive historical and comparative perspective on the role of private higher education, and has indicated the reasons why public policy—in this country, state policy in particular—ought to pay some attention to this intriguing and socially valuable enterprise. I have also sought to make clear that, in current circumstances characterized by a growing private/public price gap not primarily of the private sector's making, by sluggish growth at best in the value of federal student aid, and, until very recently, by a steadily declining pool of traditional students, private higher education, though remarkably resourceful in its responses, has been considerably affected in its capacity to serve public purposes for higher education. In particular, the sector's capacity to serve students between the lowest- and highest-income groups has decreased, its focus on core liberal arts programming has declined dramatically, and, as many institutions have competed desperately for students via student aid offers (or tuition discounts) and vocationally oriented programs, it is at least arguable that quality has suffered.[114]

I have further asserted here that, as the demand for higher education rather suddenly turns sharply upward (at least in much of the country) while funds available to states for supporting the enterprise become ever more constricted, we will need all the quality higher education capacity we can get. Thus, more than ever, states need to pay attention to the health of their private colleges and universities, if for no other reason (though several others are offered) than simply to help them meet the coming surge in demand.

Finally, I have offered a preliminary conceptual framework to begin a research-based dialogue about how state policies affecting private higher education are and could be configured. I first suggest that *laissez-faire* state policies vis-a-vis private

---

[113]Or, perhaps, an alternative conceptualization that analysts find more compelling. The main point here is to argue for an effort to build and test broad conceptions of states' *approaches* to higher education policy.

[114]This is not to say that all private higher education should be focused on the liberal arts and that professionally oriented programs are necessarily of lower quality. Rather, I mean that the liberal arts core may be shrinking too fast and too much (Breneman, 1990; 1994), and that issues around the quality of the offerings of some of the rapidly growing institutions and programs merit more attention than they are receiving.

higher education are likely to have largely undesirable consequences.[115] I suggest that both the *market-competitive-* and *central-planning*-oriented state policy postures have attractions (as well as drawbacks of course), and may be rooted strongly enough in state political traditions and basic attitudes that new interventions may need to be conceived within these broad rubrics in many cases, at least in the near term.[116] I further suggest a research program, following at the same time and in a closely linked fashion both empirical and conceptual lines of development, designed to refine the ideal-type conceptions offered here of how states can approach policymaking affecting private higher education so that such constructs reflect empirical reality more closely and their dynamics over time can be studied and understood.

Such an effort should have payoff for both policy scientists and policymakers and analysts. If the future demands and pressures on higher education are anything like what appears at this juncture to be shaping up,[117] we shall need every bit of understanding we can muster to help make scarce dollars for higher education go as far as they can.

The author gratefully acknowledges support from the Lilly Endowment, Pew Charitable Trusts, Education Commission of the States, and National Institute of Independent Colleges and Universities for research relevant to this chapter. He also thanks John Fawcett-Long for research assistance and Handbook associate editor James Hearn for encouragement and helpful comments. The author bears sole responsibility for errors of fact or judgment.

References

Ashby, E. (1971). *Any Person, Any Study: An Essay on Higher Education in the United States*. First in a Series of Essays Sponsored by the Carnegie Commission on Higher Education. New York: McGraw-Hill.

Bardach, E. (1980). Implementation studies and the study of implements. Paper presented at the Annual Meeting of the American Political Science Association.

Behn, R. D. (1979). *The End of the Growth Era in Higher Education*. Statement presented to the Committee on Labor and Human Resources. United States Senate. Duke University, Institute of Policy Sciences and Public Affairs.

Ben-David, J., and Zloczower, A. (1962). Universities and academic systems in modern societies. *European Journal of Sociology* 3: 45-84.

Bendor, J. B. (1985). *Parallel Systems: Redundancy in Government*. Berkeley: University of California Press.

Bennett, W. J. (1986, November 26). Text of Secretary Bennett's speech on college costs and U.S. student aid. *The Chronicle of Higher Education*: 20.

Bennett, W. J. (1987, February 18). Our greedy colleges. *New York Times*: A31.

Birnbaum, R. (1983). *Maintaining Diversity in Higher Education*. San Francisco: Jossey-Bass.

Bowen, H. R. (1980). *The Costs of Higher Education*. San Francisco: Jossey-Bass.

Bowen, W., and Breneman, D. (1993, Winter). Student aid: price discount or educational investment?

---

[115]For empirical support, see Zumeta (1996).

[116]See Zumeta (1996) for empirical evidence about the relationships between these state postures — and of individual policies within them and of hybrid postures—and such variables of policy interest as state taxpayer spending per capita on higher education, overall adult participation rates, and spending per student in public institutions.

[117]For a fuller discussion of these pressures than could be presented here, see Zumeta and Fawcett-Long (1996).

Brookings Review: 95-97.

Breneman, D. W. (1990, Summer). Are we losing our liberal arts colleges? *The College Board Review*, 156: 16-21, 29.

Breneman, D. W. (1994). *Liberal Arts Colleges: Thriving, Surviving, or Endangered?* Washington, DC: The Brookings Institution.

Breneman, D. W. (1981). Strategies for the 1980s. In J.R. Mingle and Associates (eds.), *Challenges of Retrenchment: Strategies for Consolidating Programs, Cutting Costs, and Reallocating Resources*. San Francisco: Jossey-Bass.

Breneman, D. W., and Finn, C. E., Jr., (eds.), (1978). *Public Policy and Private Higher Education*. Washington, DC: The Brookings Institution.

Carnegie Commission on Higher Education. (1973). *Higher Education: Who Pays? Who Benefits? Who Should Pay?* New York: McGraw-Hill Book Company.

Carnegie Council on Policy Studies in Higher Education. (1977). *The States and Private Higher Education: Problems and Policies in a New Era*. San Francisco: Jossey-Bass.

Celis, W. (1993, October 14). Penn's fiscal plan would cut 3 departments. *New York Times*: A19.

Cheit, E. F. (1971). *The New Depression in Higher Education: A Study of Financial Conditions at 41 Colleges and Universities*. New York: McGraw-Hill Book Company.

Chira, S. (1990, July 9). Stanford takes plunge into budget smashing. *Seattle Post-Intelligencer:* A9.

Clark, B. R. (1983). *The Higher Education System: Academic Organization in Cross-National Perspective*. Berkeley: University of California Press.

Clark, B. R. (1987). *The Academic Life: Small Worlds, Different Worlds*. Princeton: The Carnegie Foundation for the Advancement of Teaching.

Clotfelter, C. T. (1991). Demand for undergraduate education. In Clotfelter, C. T., Ehrenberg, R., Getz, M., and Siegfried, J. (eds.), *Economic Challenges in Higher Education*. Chicago: The University of Chicago Press.

College Board, The. (1989). *Trends in Student Aid, 1980 to 1989*. New York: The College Board.

College Board, The. (1994). *Trends in Student Aid: 1984-1994*. New York: The College Board.

College Board, The. (1995, September 29). *1995-96 Increase in College Costs Averages Six Percent, Upward Trend in Student Borrowing Continues*. News from The College Board, New York, news release.

Committee for Economic Development. (1973). *The Management and Financing of Colleges*. New York: CED.

Dahl, R. A., and Lindblom, C. E. (1953). *Politics, Economics and Welfare: Planning and Politico-Economic Systems Resolved into Basic Social Processes*. New York: Harper.

De Palma, A. (1992, February 3). Hard times force many universities to rethink roles. *New York Times*.

Dill, D. D. (1995). Managerialism versus social capital: the regulation of academic quality in the United Kingdom. Paper presented at the American Association for Policy Analysis and Management, Annual Research Conference, Washington, DC, November 1995.

Education Commission of the States. *Higher Education in the States* series, annual surveys of state support of private higher education. Denver, CO: 1971 to 1982.

Education Commission of the States. (1977). *Final Report and Recommendations: Task Force on State Policy and Independent Higher Education*. Report No. 100. Denver, CO: The Commission.

Education Commission of the States. (1990). *The Preservation of Excellence in American Higher Education: The Essential Role of Private Colleges and Universities*. Report of the ECS Task Force on State Policy and Independent Higher Education. Denver, CO: The Commission.

Education Resources Institute, and Institute of Higher Education Policy. (1995). *College Debt and the American Family*. Boston: Author.

Elmore, R. (1987, Autumn). Instruments and Strategy in Public Policy. *Policy Studies Review* 7: 174-186.

Fenske, R. H., and Boyd, J. D. (1981). *State Need-Based College Scholarship and Grant Programs: A Study of Their Development, 1969-1980*. College Board Report No. 81-7. New York: College Entrance Examination Board.

Finn, C. E., Jr. (1978). *Scholars, Dollars and Bureaucrats*. Washington, DC: The Brookings Institution.

Focus on Accountability: State Accountability Efforts: The Emergence of Report Cards. (1994, March). *SHEEO/NCES Communication Network News* 13.

Freeman, R. B. (1976). *The Over-Educated American*. New York: Academic Press.

Gardner, J. W., Atwell, R. H., and Berdahl, R. O. (1985). *Cooperation and Conflict: The Public and Private Sectors in Higher Education*. AGB Special Report. Washington, DC: Association of Governing Boards of Colleges and Universities.

Geiger, R. L. (1986). *Private Sectors in Higher Education: Structure, Function, and Change in Eight Countries.* Ann Arbor: University of Michigan Press.

Gillespie, D. A., and Carlson, N. (1983). *Trends in Student Aid, 1963 to 1983.* New York: The College Board.

Gladieux, L. E., and Wolanin, T. R. (1976). *Congress and the Colleges: The National Politics of Higher Education.* Lexington, MA: Lexington Books.

Hansen, J. S. (1977). The politics of federal scholarships: A case study of the development of general grant assistance for undergraduates. Unpublished doctoral dissertation, The Woodrow Wilson School, Princeton University.

Hansen, J. S. (1979). *The State Student Incentive Grant Program: An Assessment of the Record and Options for the Future.* New York: College Entrance Examination Board.

Hearn, J. C. (1993). The paradox of growth in federal aid for college students, 1965-1990. In J. C. Smart (ed.), *Higher Education: Handbook of Theory and Research, Volume IX,* Bronx, NY: Agathon Press.

Herbst, J. (1982). *From Crisis to Crisis: American College Government, 1636-1819.* Cambridge, MA, and London, England: Harvard University Press.

Hines, E., and Pruyne, G., (1995). *State Higher Education Appropriations, 1994-95.* Denver: State Higher Education Executive Officers.

Hood, C. C. (1983). *The Tools of Government.* London: Macmillan.

Howlett, M. (1991, Spring). Policy instruments, policy styles and policy implementation: national approaches to theories of instrument choice. *Policy Studies Journal* 19: 1-21.

Jones, D., and Ewell, P. (1993) *The Effect of State Policy on Undergraduate Education.* Denver: Education Commission of the States, March 1993.

Keppel, F. (1987, February). The Higher Education Acts contrasted, 1965-1986: Has federal policy come of age? *Harvard Educational Review* 57: 49-67.

Kerr, C. (1991). *The Great Transformation in American Higher Education, 1960-1980.* Albany, NY: State University of New York Press.

Kirschen, E. S., et al. (1964). *Economic Policy In Our Time.* Amsterdam: North Holland.

Landau, M. (1969, July/August). Redundancy, rationality and the problem of duplication and overlap. *Public Administration Review* 29: 346-358.

Levy, D. C. (ed.), (1985). *Private Education: Studies in Choice and Public Policy.* New York: Oxford University Press.

Levy, D. C. (1986). *Higher Education and the State in Latin America: Private Challenges to Public Dominance.* Chicago: University of Chicago Press.

Lindblom, C. E. (1980). *The Policy-Making Process* (2nd ed.). Englewood Cliffs, NJ: Prentice-Hall.

Linder, S. H., and Peters, B. G. (1989, January-March). Instruments of government: perceptions and contexts. *Journal of Public Policy* 9: 35-38.

Manger, D. (1991, May 15). Smith College plans to cut 85 full-time positions. *The Chronicle of Higher Education*: A2.

Marshall, R., and Tucker, M. (1992). *Thinking For a Living: Education and the Wealth of Nations.* New York: Basic Books.

Massy, W. F. (1990, June). A New Look at the Academic Department. *Pew Policy Perspectives* 2.

Massy, W. F. (1994). Balancing values and market forces: perspectives on resource allocation. Paper presented at the Asia-Pacific Economic Community (APEC) Educational Forum, Chinese Taipei.

Massy, W. F., and Wilger, A. (1992, Winter). Productivity in postsecondary education: a new approach. *Educational Evaluation and Policy Analysis* 14: 361-376.

Master Plan Survey Team (1960). *Master Plan for Higher Education in California, 1960 to 1975.* Sacramento: California State Department of Education.

McGuinness, A. C., Jr. (1975). *The Changing Map of Postsecondary Education, State Postsecondary Education Commission (1202): Their Origin.* Report No. 66. Denver, CO: Education Commission of the States.

McIntire, J. L. (1995). *The Fiscal Policy Environment in Washington State: Trends, Restrictions, and Implications for Low-Income and Vulnerable Populations.* Seattle, WA: Fiscal Policy Center, Institute for Public Policy and Management, University of Washington.

McPherson, M. S., and Schapiro, M. O. (1991). *Keeping College Affordable: Government and Educational Opportunity.* Washington, DC: The Brookings Institution.

McPherson, M. S., and Schapiro, M. O. (1994). *College Choice and Family Income: Changes Over Time in the Higher Education Destinations of Students From Different Income Backgrounds.* Discussion Paper No. 29. Williams Project on the Economics of Higher Education. Williamstown, MA: Williams

College.

Metzger, W. P. (1987). The academic profession in the United States. In Clark, B. R. (ed.), *The Academic Profession: National, Disciplinary, and Institutional Settings* (Berkeley, Los Angeles, London: University of California Press.

Mishel, L., and Bernstein, J. (1992). *Declining Wages for High School and College Graduates*. Economic Policy Institute Briefing Paper. Washington, DC: Economic Policy Institute.

Mortenson, T. (1994a, September). FY1995 state appropriations for higher education: looking better, but that isn't saying much. *Postsecondary Education OPPORTUNITY* 27: 6-11.

Mortenson, T. (1994b, February). Institutional charges. Postsecondary education OPPORTUNITY 20: 10-14.

Mumper, M. (1991, Winter). The transformation of federal aid to college students: dynamics of growth and retrenchment. *Journal of Education Finance* 16: 315-331.

Mumper, M. (1993). The affordability of public higher education: 1970-1990. *The Review of Higher Education* 16: 157-180.

Murphy, K., and Welch, F. (1989, May). Wage premiums for college graduates. *Educational Researcher* 18: 17-26.

The Nation. (1994, September 1). *The Chronicle of Higher Education* XLI(1): 6.

National Association of State Scholarship and Grant Programs. *Annual Survey Report*. Harrisburg, PA: Pennsylvania Higher Education Assistance Agency for NASSGP, annual publication.

National Association of State Scholarship and Grant Programs. (1994). *NASSGP 25th Annual Survey Report, 1993-94 Academic Year*. Harrisburg: Pennsylvania Higher Education Assistance Agency for NAASGP.

National Commission on the Financing of Postsecondary Education. (1973). *Financing Postsecondary Education in the United States*. Washington, DC: National Commission on the Financing of Postsecondary Education.

National Institute of Independent Colleges and Universities. (1990). *A Commitment to Access*. Washington, DC: National Institute of Independent Colleges and Universities.

National Institute of Independent Colleges and Universities. (1992). *Independent Colleges and Universities: A National Profile*. Washington, DC: NIICU.

National Institute of Independent Colleges and Universities. (1995). *Independent Colleges and Universities: A National Profile*. Washington, DC: NIICU.

Olson, K. W. (1974). *The G.I. Bill, the Veterans, and the Colleges*. Lexington: University Press of Kentucky.

Paulson, C. (1990). *State Initiatives in Assessment and Outcome Measurement: Tools for Teaching and Learning*. ECS Working Paper. Denver, CO: Education Commission of the States.

Pickens, W. H. (1995a). Financing the plan: California's master plan for higher education, 1960 to 1994. Report prepared for the California Higher Education Policy Center, San Jose.

Pickens, W. H. (1995b). *Up-Date of Statistics for the Fiscal Data Base Maintained by the California Higher Education Policy Center: Following Adoption of the 1995/96 State Budget Act*. San Jose, CA: California Higher Education Policy Center.

Porter, O. F. (1989). *Undergraduate Completion and Persistence at Four-Year Colleges and Universities*. Washington, DC: National Institute of Independent Colleges and Universities.

Ross, E. D. (1942). *Democracy's College: The Land-Grant Movement in the Formative Stage*. Ames: Iowa State College Press.

Rothblatt, S., and Trow, M. (1992). Government policies and higher education: A comparison of Britain and the United States, 1630-1860. In C. Crouch and A. Heath (eds.), *Social Research and Social Reform: Essays in Honour of A. H. Halsey*. Oxford: Clarendon Press.

Rudolph, F. (1962). *The American College and University*. New York: Vintage Books.

St. John, E. P. (1994). *Prices, Productivity, and Investment: Assessing Financial Strategies in Higher Education*. ASHE-ERIC Higher Education Report No. 3. Washington, DC: The George Washington University, School of Education and Human Development.

Schoenberg, T. (1995, September 29). Student borrowing increases, following changes in federal policy. *The Chronicle of Higher Education* XLII(5): A56.

Smelser, N. J. (1993). California: a multisegment system. In A. Levine (ed.), *Higher Learning in America, 1980-2000*. Baltimore: Johns Hopkins University Press.

Smith, B. L. R. (1990). *American Science Policy Since World War II*. Washington, DC: The Brookings Institution.

Spence, D. S., and Weathersby. G. B. (1981). Changing patterns of state funding. In J. R. Mingle and Associates (eds.), *Challenges of Retrenchment: Strategies for Consolidating Programs, Cutting Costs, and Reallocating Resources*. San Francisco: Jossey-Bass.

Stanford to lay off 150 to 200 employees. (1990, April 25). *The Chronicle of Higher Education*: A2.

State Higher Education Executive Officers. (1988). Survey on Tuition Policy, Costs and Student Aid. Unpublished report. Denver, CO: SHEEO.

Thompson, F., and Zumeta, W. M. (1981, Winter). A regulatory model of governmental coordinating activities in the higher education sector. *Economics of Education Review* 1: 27-52.

Trow, M. (1974). Problems in the transition from elite to mass higher education. In *Policies for Higher Education*. General Report of the Conference on Future Structure of Post-Secondary Education. Paris: Organization for Economic Cooperation and Development.

Trow, M. (1993). Federalism in American higher education. In A. Levine (ed.), *Higher Learning in America, 1980-2000*. Baltimore: Johns Hopkins University Press.

U.S. Department of Education. (1989). *Digest of Education Statistics*. Washington, DC: U.S. Department of Education.

U.S. Department of Education. (1994). *Digest of Education Statistics*. Washington, DC: U.S. Department of Education.

U.S. Department of Education. (1995). *Projections of Education Statistics to 2005*. NCES 95-169. Washington, DC: National Center for Education Statistics.

Van Horn, C. E. (1991). The myths and realities of privatization. In W. T. Gormley, Jr. (ed.), *Privatization and Its Alternatives*. Madison, WI: University of Wisconsin Press.

van Vught, F. A. (1995). The Humboldtian university under pressure: New forms of quality review in Western European higher education. Paper presented at the American Association for Public Policy Analysis and Management, Annual Research Conference, Washington, DC, November 1995.

Veysey, L. R. (1965). *The Emergence of the American University*. Chicago: University of Chicago Press.

Ware, A. (1989). *Between Profit and State: Intermediate Organizations in Britain and the United States*. Princeton: Princeton University Press.

Washington Higher Education Coordinating Board. (1992). *A Commitment to Opportunity: 1992 Update of the Master Plan for Higher Education*. Olympia, WA: Author.

Western Interstate Commission for Higher Education, Teachers Insurance and Annuity Association, and The College Board. (1993). *High School Graduates: Projections by State, 1992-2009*. Boulder, CO: The Commission.

Wolfle, D. L. (1972). *The Home of Science: The Role of the University*. New York: McGraw-Hill.

Wynn, R. G. (1974). *At the Crossroads: A Report on the Financial Condition of the Forty-Eight Liberal Arts Colleges Previously Studied in the Golden Years, The Turning Point*. University of Michigan, Center for the Study of Higher Education.

Zammuto, R. F. (1984, March-April). Are the liberal arts an endangered species? *Journal of Higher Education* 55: 184-211.

Zemsky, R. (1990, July 13). The lattice and the ratchet: toward more efficient higher education systems. Presentation at the Annual Conference of the Education Commission of the States, Seattle, WA.

Zumeta, W. M. (1982). Doctoral programs and the labor market, or how should we respond to the "Ph.D. glut?" *Higher Education* 11: 321-343.

Zumeta, W. M. (1989). *State Policies and Independent Higher Education: A Technical Report*. Report to the Education Commission of the States, Task Force on State Policy and Independent Higher Education. Denver, CO: The Commission.

Zumeta, W. M. (1990, October 19). States and private colleges: new evidence and analysis from the policy arena. Paper presented at the annual Research Conference of the Association for Public Policy Analysis and Management, San Francisco.

Zumeta, W. M. (1992, July/August). State policies and private higher education: policies, correlates and linkages. *Journal of Higher Education* 63: 363-417.

Zumeta, W. M. (1993). Independent higher education and public policy: looking toward 2000. Final report to the Lilly Endowment. Seattle, WA: University of Washington, Institute For Public Policy and Management.

Zumeta, W. M. (1994). *Crisis Or Opportunity? Private Higher Education and Public Policy Looking Toward 2000 and Beyond*. Final Report to the Pew Charitable Trusts. Seattle, WA: University of Washington, Institute For Public Policy and Management.

Zumeta, W. M. (1995a, August 22). Review of Other States' Higher Education Structures and Public Funding for Private Higher Education. Report prepared for JBL Associates, Inc., for the Joint Legislative Budget Committee, State of Arizona.

Zumeta, W. M. (1995b). State policy and budget developments. In H. Wechsler (ed.), *The NEA 1995 Almanac of Higher Education.* Washington, DC: National Education Association.

Zumeta, W. M. (1996). Meeting the demand for higher education without breaking the bank: a framework for the design of state higher education policies for an era of increasing demand. *Journal of Higher Education,* forthcoming.

Zumeta, W. M., and Fawcett-Long, J. A. (in press). State policy and budget developments. In H. Wechsler (ed.), *The NEA 1996 Almanac of Higher Education.* Washington, DC: National Education Association.

Zumeta, W. M., and Looney, J. A. (1994). State policy and budget developments. In H. Wechsler (ed.), *The NEA 1994 Almanac of Higher Education.* Washington, DC: National Education Association.

Epilogue

In order to connect this brief essay to themes suggested in my earlier chapter, I focus here on how private colleges and universities could play a useful role in helping states respond to the emergent access/financing squeeze facing higher education policymakers in many states as the new century dawns, and on why seizing these opportunities has proven difficult. I would suggest at the outset, however, that there are other issues in the field of state policy and private higher education today that are well worth exploring. An obvious one is the implications for private higher education of the maturing of the Internet and World Wide Web and associated distance learning potentialities. How will states encourage and support public colleges and universities in this area and to what extent will they seek to monitor quality standards and competition among publics, private nonprofits, and for-profit providers? How can they hope to regulate such competition when providers can beam their programs from anywhere on the globe? Will states provide financial aid to distance learning students attending private nonprofit institutions in a way that allows them to compete with other providers in this market of rapidly growing importance, or will they simply permit *laissez-faire* competition for students? If so, what will be the implications for traditional private institutions, particularly smaller undergraduate colleges?

Another important issue in this field is the surprising growth of middle-class-friendly student aid policies including, at the state level, more "merit-based" aid programs, which seem to have grown in part at the expense of traditional need-based aid (National Association of State Student Grant and Aid Programs, 1999). How will this trend, if it continues, affect private colleges and particularly their commitment to broad access opportunities for a diverse range of students (Baum, Chapter 2; Breneman, Doti and Lapovsky, Chapter 12)? These are surely two of the most important issues that have emerged, or at least have appeared in sharper focus, in the four years or so since this chapter was first published. Space requires that I focus attention here on a single issue, however.

The Access/Financing Squeeze in Higher Education: Implications for States and Private Colleges

Higher education is now widely seen as more essential than ever in fueling states' economic growth (Mortenson, 1998) and, equally important, in meeting aspirations of lower-income and minority populations (which are the fastest-growing in many states) for opportunities to take full part in the economy and society. Meeting these aspirations is crucial for social equity policy goals and perhaps even for social stability. As had been forecast earlier, numbers of students seeking entry into higher education are growing rapidly in many states, especially the numbers of younger students, as children of the "baby boom echo" generation reach college age (Western Interstate Commission, 1998).[118] States' fiscal fortunes improved markedly in the late nineties and they have directed a modest portion of these increased resources into higher education (Zumeta, 1999a). Yet, there are good reasons to be concerned about the states' ability to stably finance higher education, much less to pay for a sharp ramp-up in capacity. This is because there is a fundamental structural imbalance in the way states provide for higher education as compared with their other major functions. In brief, elementary/secondary education, Medicaid, and criminal justice costs are largely driven by caseloads and federal and judicial mandates that make spending relatively uncontrollable. When school-age children, medical indigents, or sentenced criminals appear at the state's door adequate funds have to be budgeted to serve them. Until recently, this was also true of public welfare. Crucially, higher education has a different standing in state budgetary deliberations. There are few, if any, legal requirements that enrollment increases or student aid be funded at any particular level, or even funded at all.

Empirical evidence shows that this imbalance in budgetary standing does relatively little harm to higher education's fortunes in prosperous times. In the late nineties, for instance, state appropriations for higher education slightly outpaced gains in other areas of state general fund spending (Mortenson, 1999). Even so, the potential fiscal demands from health cost inflation and the aging of the Medicaid population and from tougher sentencing policies in the criminal justice system lurk on the near horizon. Problems emerge acutely, however, in times of economic stagnation or downturn. Then spending demands from Medicaid, the criminal justice system, and public assistance tend to rise sharply just as state revenues flatten out or fall. Policymakers casting about for areas of the budget to cut tend to look first at higher education because it is by far the largest discretionary item in the state budget. This is what happened in and for several years after the recessions of the early 1980s and early 1990s, and the cuts in appropriations to higher education were rather deep and painful. In response, tuition levels in public higher education escalated rapidly, which has helped to fuel the growth in criticism of higher education and calls for greater accountability (Zumeta, 1998). The next round of such recession-induced cuts in higher education is likely to be even more painful for several reasons: (1) public tax resistance and general skepticism about public spending is likely to lead to unusually strong pressures for major budget cutbacks in any economic downturn; (2) the response to increased needs for spending on public assistance is now *solely* the responsibility of the states; but (3) as already indicated higher education needs to invest in capacity for educating *more* students in the next few years not less if states are to prosper in the longer run.

---

[118]Projected increases in high school graduates between 1999-2000 and 2009-10 exceed 20% in such populous states as California, Florida, Georgia, New Jersey, and North Carolina, and range as high as 65% in Nevada.

How does all this relate to private higher education? States with large gains in numbers of students seeking entry and a desire to expand participation to meet economic and social policy goals will need all the higher education capacity they can find. Given the other demands on state budgets, few will be able to afford commensurate expansion in public higher education. The "solution" to this problem is likely to be multi-faceted, including some more public campus enrollment spaces; heavier use of existing space during summers, evenings, and weekends; more emphasis on distance learning delivery methods which *might* require less capital spending; increased emphasis on moving students through the educational system more efficiently; and, where the capacity and willingness exists or can be created, more use of the private higher education sector to serve the public purpose of providing expanded access opportunities. In states with a substantial private sector, perhaps particularly where this sector has had sluggish growth in the recent past so that schools are hungry for growth or where the sector is composed largely of high-growth-oriented categories of institutions (Zumeta, 1999b), there should be potential for it to assist in meeting the state's needs for increased enrollment capacity. Also, where private universities have capacity in high-cost professional fields such as the health professions and the state needs to expand enrollment capacity, it might want to consider encouraging private-sector alternatives to, say, building a new medical school. And, private colleges and universities have shown a good ability to reach out to, enroll, and graduate minority students, a concern for many of the states, such as California and Florida, with the highest projected enrollment demands.

To make any of these possibilities work, state authorities would need to work out mutually satisfactory arrangements with private colleges and universities to take on more students than they otherwise would. The tools available include enriched state student aid grants for students choosing private colleges; direct appropriations to or enrollment contracts with private institutions in return for commitments to enroll state-resident students; capital grants; and state master plans that reflect and enforce a policy of allocating by these means some of the anticipated enrollment growth to the private sector. All of these approaches have precedents in the array of state programs currently in place around the country. Moreover, survey data collected by the author just before the onset of the increased demand from the baby boom echo cohort but when it was well in sight, suggest that the majority of private schools would be ready to talk with state authorities about how the state might subsidize their ability to expand enrollment capacity (Zumeta, 1996).

Yet, the evidence of the last few years does not augur great optimism about the ability of states and private nonprofit institutions to negotiate such arrangements on a broad scale (Zumeta, 1999c). In some instances, many of a state's private institutions may be wary of closer involvement with the state partly on religious or ideological grounds but also partly on pragmatic grounds: if schools invest in physical and faculty capacity to meet a possibly temporary wave of student demand who will pay the ongoing costs when the state is no longer willing to? Equally important, state policymakers ask about the cost of enriching state student aid grants to attract more students to private colleges when many state-aided students who already attend these institutions will in fairness also have to be paid more. Direct appropriations and contracts can avoid this problem but are less familiar in most of the country and in some places are thought to run afoul of state constitutional strictures. Perhaps most fundamentally, survey evidence suggests that policymakers are simply not inclined to think much about measures for more proactively utilizing the private sector, and public institutions certainly do not encourage such thinking (Zumeta, 1999c).

One might point to the rapid growth in private, for-profit postsecondary enrollments and conclude that *laissez-faire* state policies will be adequate to meet the new demands. This may be true with respect to the groups of students seeking work-related courses and convenience to match their work schedules. But, unlike the recent past, much of the increased demand in the present decade will come from traditional-age students for whom campus-based education, both private and public, will still hold attraction and real educational benefit. Here, public policy has an obligation to respond to emerging needs and hard-pressed policymakers would do well to think creatively about ways to enlist the tried and true private nonprofit higher education sector in the effort.

References

Mortenson, T. (1998, June). Educational attainment in the states: status and importance to state economic welfare. *Postsecondary Education OPPORTUNITY* 72: 7-14.

Mortenson, T. (1999, September). A preliminary report: FY 2000 state appropriations for higher education. *Postsecondary Education OPPORTUNITY* 87: 11-13.

National Association of State Student Grant and Aid Programs. (1999, April). *29th Annual Survey Report: 1997-98 Academic Year.* Albany: New York State Higher Education Services Corporation for the association.

Western Interstate Commission on Higher Education and The College Board. (1998, February). *Knocking at the College Door: Projections of High School Graduates by State and Race/Ethnicity, 1996-2012.* Boulder, Colorado: author.

Zumeta, W. (1999a). Fiscal prospects for higher education: 1999. In H. Wechsler (Ed.). *The NEA 1999 Almanac of Higher Education.* Washington, D.C.: National Education Association.

Zumeta, W. (1999b, November 19). How did they do it? Private nonprofit higher education's enrollment response to adverse environmental conditions, 1980-1995. Paper presented at the annual conference of the Association for Study of Higher Education, San Antonio, Texas.

Zumeta, W. (1996). Meeting the demand for higher education without breaking the bank: a framework for the design of state higher education policies for an era of increasing demand. *Journal of Higher Education* 67(4): 367-425.

Zumeta, W. (1998). Public university accountability to the state in the late twentieth century: time for a rethinking? *Policy Studies Review* 15(4): 5-22.

Zumeta, W. (1999c). Utilizing private higher education for public purposes: policy design challenges facing efforts to help meet higher education access demands through the private sector. In S. Nagel (Ed.). *The Substance of Public Policy.* Commack, New York: Nova Science Publishers.

PART IV

Topics and Current Issues in the Finance of Higher Education

Chapter 10

THE ROLE OF FINANCES IN STUDENT CHOICE:
A Review of Theory and Research[1]

Edward P. St. John, Eric H. Asker,
and Shouping Hu

The role of finances in student choice processes has been the subject of debate over the past four decades. In the 1960s, when the *Higher Education Act* was first passed, there was a strong belief in the higher education research community that a goal of higher education was to promote individual development. In the 1960s, economists began the first wave of studies of the influence of public finance strategies on educational opportunity (e.g., Hansen and Weisbrod, 1969). In the early 1970s, the arguments of economists had a strong influence on the evolution of the federal role in student aid (Gladieux and Wolanin, 1976). However, the financial mechanisms through which prices and subsides were supposed to influence student choices were not yet well understood.

The idea that loans might expand educational opportunity was embedded in the theory of human capital (Becker, 1964; Paulsen, Chapter 3). Later a concept of student price response evolved in the 1970s, based largely on an adaptation of human capital theory (Paulsen, Chapter 4). Meta-analyses of student demand studies (both cross-sectional and longitudinal) were used to develop standardized price response coefficients (SPRCs), which provided an elasticity measure, a change in the probability of enrollment for every $100 change in net price (e.g., Jackson and Weathersby, 1975; Leslie and Brinkman, 1988; McPherson, 1978). SPRCs generally applied to grants and it was widely assumed that each incremental change in funding for need-based grants would result in an increase in enrollment as a result of price response in first-time enrollment and persistence. However, this metric did not predict the enrollment effects of aid very well and several analysts began to downplay the idea that the federal investment in aid had an impact (Hansen, 1983; Kane, 1995). By the early 1980s, few analysts still argued that financial aid played an important and direct role in college enrollment and persistence behavior. Consequently, the major

---

[1]We thank Michael B. Paulsen and James C. Hearn for their thoughtful comments on an earlier version of this chapter.

shift in federal policy from emphasizing grants to loans evolved without a widely accepted counter argument.

In the 1990s, new concepts of the differential effects of grants and loans have emerged. Policy analysts have traced the effects of declines in grant funding on decreasing opportunity at both the national (Mumper, 1996) and local (Orfield, 1992) levels. Economists have documented the effects of grants on educational opportunity for low-income students (McPherson and Schapiro, 1991, 1998). And higher education researchers have begun to test a theory of differential price effects (DesJardins, Ahlburg, and McCall, 1999; St. John, 1990a; St. John, Paulsen, and Starkey, 1996), an argument that students will respond to prices and subsidies based on their circumstances (Dresch, 1975; Paulsen and St. John, in press; St. John and Starkey, 1995). This new perspective illustrates that the role of finances is far more complex than originally assumed by economists. However, before it is possible to build a better understanding of the role of finances in college choice and persistence, it is necessary to develop a better theory of student choice processes.

This chapter suggests a theory of student choice that could better explain the role of finances. The concept of student choice used here is broader than the conception of college choice that is frequently used in higher education research (Hossler, Braxton and Coopersmith, 1989; Paulsen, 1990). First, we review evolving perspectives on student outcomes for higher education to situate this discussion of the student choice construct. Then we present the student-choice construct, as an alternative way of viewing the influence of policy decisions on student outcomes. Next, we review the new wave of research of the effects of finances using this reconstructed conceptual lens. Finally we conclude with reflections on the implications for policy formulation and research.

EVOLVING POLICY PERSPECTIVES ON STUDENT OUTCOMES

Theories of student outcomes also evolved during the past four decades. To build an understanding of the role of finances in student choice, it is appropriate to begin with a review of the theories of student outcomes that have been widely used in higher education research. Below we review the three perspectives on student choice research—developmental theories, change theories, and emerging choice theories—along with the ways these theories have complemented the policy goals that have been dominant in higher education policy.

Student Development and Equal Opportunity

Providing qualified students with the opportunity to develop personally, within the time-honored structure of the academy, provided an image of student outcomes that was compatible with the higher education policy discourse through the 1960s. Over time a set of developmental theories about college students evolved (e.g., Chickering, 1969, 1976; Perry, 1970) which provided the basis for working with college students that was consonant with the liberal arts tradition. These developmental theories were initially based on studies of students of traditional age and background. For example, Perry's theory of college student development was based on the study of college men at Harvard. These theories dealt with both the academic and student life experiences of students in college and they provided a basis for a discourse between faculty and the new professionals in student affairs.

As colleges expanded and became more diverse, attempts were made to adapt these base theories to include women, minority students, and adults. Research testing these theories assessed changes in students over time, using developmental schemes to interpret data. Initially the schemes were based on individual case studies, but a second wave of theories on ego development (Loevinger, 1976) and moral development (Kohlberg, 1981) used standardized instruments with measurable sequences of development. In spite of the fact that the movement toward mass higher education was predicated on the notion that higher education needed to respond to new demands from the labor market, the dominant notions of liberal education remained central to undergraduate education throughout most of the 20th century. Thus, the dominant beliefs of faculty about liberal education remained congruent with the developmental sequences embedded in the theories of college student development.

While these theories and related measurement instruments provided a way of focusing the discourse in the academic community on student development, they provided little opportunity to measure the ways academic practices influenced these outcomes. Further, these developmental outcomes did not link directly to the real educational choices confronting students. Rather, development was a goal that somehow happened in college, just as economic productivity—a goal of public investment in higher education—somehow happened as a result of public spending on this student-development process. These concepts were seldom criticized because they were so compatible with the beliefs of faculty about liberal education, as well as with the beliefs of the growing numbers of student affairs professionals who worked in support of student development. Both sets of beliefs fit very well with the progressive notions of education and the social and economic development goals that predominated in the public discourse about higher education throughout the late 1970s.

These beliefs have been fundamentally challenged since the late 1980s. On the one hand, new conservative academics began to raise questions about the loss of liberal arts traditions in the curriculum and experience of college (e.g., Bloom, 1987). They argued that there had been liberalizing influences that had changed the discourse in the academy. On the other hand, liberal critics pointed to the fact that many were marginalized or excluded from higher education because of the commonly held liberal arts traditions and notions of academic opportunities. These new perspectives provided a basis for exposing the limitations of the new conservative position and galvanized the new rightist academics in opposition to the broadening construction of inclusiveness and multiculturalism. Critical scholars then began to criticize core academic values as being unfair toward diverse populations (e.g., Hurtado and Carter, 1997; Tierney, 1992).

Change Theories and Accountability

Another notion of student outcomes gained broad acceptance in the 1980s, especially among state and federal policymakers. Change theories, which originated with the work of Alexander Astin (1975, 1993), focused on the explicit empirical links between college experiences and student outcomes. Theories of college choice (Jackson, 1978; Hossler, Braxton, and Coopersmith, 1989; Paulsen, 1990) and persistence (Bean, 1990; Tinto, 1987) emerged that provided well-specified ways of linking academic experience to student outcomes. Furthermore, national longitudinal databases were used to test models that linked student outcomes—access (Jackson, 1978; St. John, 1990a, 1991), choice of college (Jackson, 1978; Manski and Wise, 1983; Tierney, 1980), and persistence (St. John, 1990b; St. John, Andrieu, Oescher, and Starkey, 1994; Terkla, 1985)—to need-based aid programs. These newer theories provided a better empirical basis for evaluating the efficiency and effectiveness of the operations of student aid programs.

These models were also much tighter in the ways linkages between higher education experiences and student outcomes were conceptualized. Jackson's research on access and college choice (1978) represented an important conceptual and empirical breakthrough. Not only did he provide a new conceptualization of the choice process, but his research also provided a rationale for using student aid as an integral part of enrollment management. Pascarella and Terenzini's research on persistence (1979, 1980, 1991) provided that foundation for another breakthrough. They used structural equation models to test Tinto's persistence theory (1987). They also provided more systematic methods of linking college experiences to persistence. These new tighter models will provide a new foundation for researchers to explore; building better models became a preoccupation, a way of providing information that fueled a new academic discourse about the effects of college on students (Pascarella and Terenzini, 1991).

This new, more sophisticated way of thinking about the linkages between academic practices, public policy, and student outcomes was highly compatible with the new concerns about efficiency and accountability in higher education that emerged in the late 1970s and gained popularity among new conservative policy makers in the 1980s. The ideas that the outcomes of higher education could be routinely assessed (e.g., Astin, 1993) and that funding strategies could be developed to promote desired outcomes were advocated. While there are examples of state performance funding that have been viewed as successful, such as Tennessee's efforts to enhance learning outcomes (Banta, Rudolf, VanDyke, and Fischer, 1996), political coalitions in states have been difficult to hold together in part because of ambiguities about outcomes (Hossler, et al., 1997). The problems encountered with federal efforts to use default rates as a central outcome measure for the regulation of loan and other student aid programs illustrate the problem (St. John, 1994c). These initial efforts to use outcomes as a basis for public funding have been problematic for at least three reasons.

First, the conception of student outcomes embedded in the new market approach carried forward a perspective that did not adequately consider diverse groups. For example, the beliefs that institutions with high completion rates and high test scores should be rewarded biased the results of accountability schemes using these measures toward selective institutions with traditional clientele. It was only after higher education was extended to students with more diverse backgrounds in the 1970s that states began experimenting with student-outcome measures as a basis for funding. Further, the notion that funding should be based on persistence rates, an idea embedded in federal loan regulations, rewards schools that attract middle- and upper-income students who are more likely to afford the costs of attending. As loan defaults grew from excessive use of loans, limiting funding for schools with high default rates became a way of punishing schools that served students with the greatest need and who were in the highest risk situations. These new policy positions held an implicit class bias, based on progressive notions of success. Similar assumptions were embedded in the outcome measures commonly used in the research on which change theories were based.

Furthermore, the early research on college students focused nearly exclusively on students of traditional age and background (Pascarella and Terenzini, 1991). Not only were the original developmental theories based on studies of students of traditional age and background, but the dominant change theory (Astin, 1993) was also developed from studies of traditional students, as part of the Cooperative Institutional Research Program (CIRP). CIRP provides an annual survey of college freshmen in cooperating institutions and follow-up studies of four-or-so years later. These data sets have been widely used for studies of student outcomes and have been central to the construction of the major theories of student change.

Thus, while student-change theories were more compatible with the new market-oriented policies aimed at promoting accountability and improving efficiency, they were adapted to inform new public policy initiatives that actually rewarded traditional patterns. These policies actually discriminated against students who were more at risk either financially or academically, the population that most needed financial and academic support. This pattern is illustrated by the research finding that loan defaults are caused by factors related to student background: students at greater risk of dropping out or of not finding jobs were more likely to default (Flint, 1997; Wilms, Moore, and Bolus, 1987). Penalizing institutions for high default rates actually encouraged institutions to deny admission to students who were at more risk of dropping out. However, the issues raised by the new wave of conservative criticisms of higher education cannot be addressed by reconstructing the theories of student development and equal opportunity, as some have advocated (Kramer, 1993a, b; Mumper, 1996). Rather, a new model based on a fundamental rethinking of the underlying theory is needed.

Student-Choice Theory

Investigating how students actually make educational choices provides an alternative to the two competing perspectives on student outcomes. Student-choice theory is based on a critical review of sociological, economic, and educational (developmental and change) theories (Hossler, Schmit, and Vesper, 1999; Paulsen and St. John, 1997, in press; St. John and Hossler, 1998; St. John, Paulsen, and Starkey, 1996). The focus is on factors that influence students to make a sequence of choices that result in greater educational attainment. Rather than uncritically carrying forward progressive notions, these reviews examined outcomes from diverse ethnic and ideological perspectives in an attempt to identify factors that influence attainment. In other words, the idea that there could be diverse paths in the educational attainment process was integral to the formulation of the student-choice construct. The basic principles of the student choice construct are:

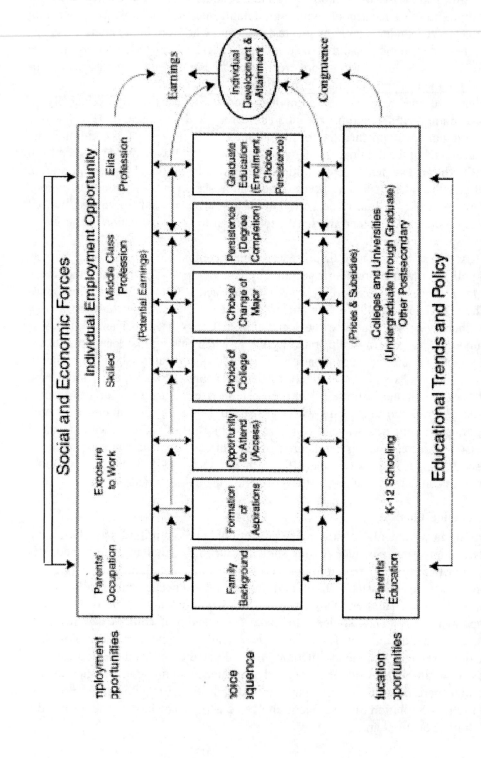

FIGURE 1. The Student Choice Construct: Linking Education and Employment Opportunities

- *There is a sequence of choices*: The formation of aspirations for college and career, the choice to attend college, the choice of college, the choice of major, the choice to persist, and choices about graduate education.
- *Students make choices in "situated" contexts*: The sequence of student choice can follow traditional or nontraditional patterns, but it results in gains in both attainment and employability whether traditional or nontraditional paths are followed. However, all of the educational choices students make are situated within their values and beliefs, and are constrained by financial means and enabled by financial incentives.
- *It is important to examine the effects of public policy, including finances, across student outcomes and in different contexts*: Policies aimed at promoting student choice and responsible use of resources can potentially optimize the returns on the public investment. The cumulative outcomes of choice processes include individual development and educational attainment, tax revenues and or the opportunity to reduce tax rates, and congruence (the consonance between individual development, education, and employment opportunity).

Given these principles, it is possible to envision how a theory of student choice can be used to reconstruct academic and financial policies in higher education. In a sense, the theory and practice of enrollment management (Hossler, 1984; Hossler, Bean, and Associates, 1990) has demonstrated how the theories and bodies of research in the areas of college choice and persistence could be used to build more integrated academic and student affairs policies. The student-choice construct provides a more integrated way of viewing the linkages between student outcomes and institutional, state, and federal policies related to academic and student affairs, as well as to resource management and the financing of postsecondary education. This alternative perspective merits further exploration, especially as it relates to the policy debates about accountability.

THE STUDENT CHOICE CONSTRUCT

The student choice construct (figure 1) provides a reconceptualization of the linkages between student-choice processes and the outcomes of higher education. This section provides an overview of the student-choice sequence; describes alternative patterns of student choices; and redefines the outcomes of student choice.

The Student-Choice Sequence

Postsecondary education opportunities unfold through life experiences, a process of developing aspirations and goals, pursuing those goals and aspirations through postsecondary educational choices, and making changes in these educational choices based on new experiences, successes, and failures. The sequence of postsecondary choices, which can be influenced by educators and policy makers concerned about improving educational attainment, include:

- *Formation of Postsecondary and Career Aspirations:* Aspirations can form in elementary school, or earlier, but usually take shape by middle school (Hossler, et al., 1999; Hossler and Stage, 1992). High school aspirations have long-term effects on educational attainment (St. John, 1991) and can be influenced by educational experiences, family and friends, and information provided by schools and education agencies (Paulsen, 1990). These aspirations are among the values and beliefs students use—tacitly and purposefully—to make educational choices.

- *Opportunity to Attend (Access):* The decision to attend is influenced by family background, aspirations, high school experiences, achievement, and affordability (Hossler, et al., 1999, Jackson, 1978, St. John and Noell, 1989). The opportunity to attend can be enhanced by: 1) developing accessible postsecondary systems, including community colleges and technical postsecondary programs (Voorhees, Chapter 13); 2) improving the quality of K-12 school systems; 3) disseminating information on postsecondary opportunities; and 4) promoting affordability through appropriate state and federal financing strategies (St. John, 1991).

- *Choice of College:* Frequently, college choice is characterized as a sequence of choices involving predisposition, search, and choice from among colleges to which a student is admitted (Hossler, et al., 1989; Hossler, et al., 1999). In addition to the factors that promote the predisposition to attend (similar to aspirations and opportunities as noted above), institutional marketing and student financial aid can influence the search and choice processes, the final stages of the college-choice sequence (Paulsen, 1990). Attending higher quality public colleges and private colleges improves student learning and earnings (Pascarella and Terenzini, 1991), which means there are both individual and social returns to the college-choice process.

- *Choice (and Change) of Major:* Student major choice is influenced by family background (including parents' occupations and aspirations for the child), student's aspirations and achievement, college experience, and college quality and characteristics, as well as labor market changes and expected earnings (Pascarella and Terenzini, 1991; St. John, 1994b; Smart, 1988). While there has been a tendency to view major choice as primarily an academic concern, the choice of major has historically been important in public policy because of the linkages between human resource planning and higher education finance.

- *Persistence:* Persistence in the college of choice, to the extent of aspirations and ability, represents completion of the undergraduate postsecondary attainment. Persistence is influenced by student and family background, student aspirations and commitments, academic and social integration processes in the college of choice, and affordability (Bean, 1990; Pascarella and Terenzini, 1991; St. John, Paulsen, and Starkey, 1996; Tinto, 1987).

- *Graduate Education Choices:* The choices about graduate education follow the same pattern of developing aspirations, having opportunity, making program/university choices, and persisting. Persistence in graduate education is influenced by student background, undergraduate experience, program and institutional characteristics, experiences in graduate school, expected earnings, and affordability (Andrieu and St. John, 1993; Pascarella and Terenzini, 1991). Choices about graduate study and professional development are situated in values and beliefs acquired over a student's lifetime (Kingston and Lewis, 1990).

Gains in all of these student-choice processes result in gains in student attainment.

Therefore, a focus on how policy decisions link to these choice processes provides a means of building workable linkages between postsecondary policy and student outcomes. These linkages have been used as a basis for assessing alternative desegregation strategies in higher education (St. John and Hossler 1998). They can also be used to construct a new way of viewing higher education finance and accountability (St. John, Kline, and Asker, 2001). Such policies can influence the opportunity to make informed educational choices and to attain personal college dreams.

The student-choice construct incorporates aspects of both the developmental and change perspectives. It represents a reconstruction of the developmental assumptions embedded in the original developmental theories. However, the sequence is more explicitly focused on interactions with the academic environment and employment, a perspective focusing more explicitly on policy concerns. The student-choice construct also uses a set of outcomes consistently examined by research conducted within the new tradition of change theory (Pascarella and Terenzini, 1991).

Alternative Patterns of Choice

For the student-choice construct to be useful in rethinking public policy in higher education, it must be applicable to students of nontraditional age and background as well as to traditional college students. Indeed, it is important to expand postsecondary opportunity beyond the one-third of the population that has attended consistently over the past three or four decades. Most of the research on the effects of college on students has focused on students of traditional age and background (Pascarella and Terenzini, 1991), and, therefore, the student-choice sequence is obviously applicable to these traditional students. However, the student-choice construct also provides insight into alternative patterns of enrollment.

First, we need to distinguish between traditional- and nontraditional-age students. For traditional students, that is, for the first round of educational choices, the student-choice sequence can be viewed as a lock-step process. Interestingly, in their recent longitudinal study, Hossler, Schmit, and Vesper (1999) found that there was equity in the development of aspirations, but that those with less-advantaged backgrounds were less likely to fulfill their postsecondary dreams, a finding that is consonant with recent studies of national longitudinal databases. However, the portion of older students attending college has been increasing over the past three decades, indicating that there are alternative ways through the sequence. That is, students who do not fulfill their postsecondary dreams when they first consider attending college or when they first enroll in college may find the opportunity later. Decisions to attend or reenter college may be delayed by life events (Hearn, 1992). Further, many adults change their aspirations and professional interests as they progress through the life cycle. Thus the number of citizens making postsecondary choices that lead to gains in attainment increases when we consider both traditional- and nontraditional-age students.

Second, most of the theory on student choice, especially that which pertains to college-choice processes, implicitly assumes geographic mobility. However, only a modest percentage of traditional-age students consider attending college away from home (Hossler et al., 1999) and most nontraditional-age students are locally situated. Thus, to expand opportunity to make educational choices, we need to consider the fact that many prospective college students are locally situated. Indeed, it is increasingly crucial that state policy planning for higher education recognize the need for *locally situated* high-demand programs; that is, programs for which there is local employment opportunity (St. John and Hossler, 1998). Yet, providing local access may not be sufficient if the programs offered are not the ones local citizens need. Clearly, the concept of congruence among career interests, education, and employment opportunity provides a way of linking these aspects of student choice to financial and academic policy.

Third, we need to consider ethnic differences in educational attainment as we develop new approaches to public policy in higher education. In particular, there is a need to promote opportunity for African-Americans, Latinos, and other groups that have been underrepresented in national systems of postsecondary education. Analyses of the impact of aid on affordability indicate great diversity in the ways students with different economic backgrounds view and respond to college costs (Heller, 1998; Kaltenbaugh, St. John and Starkey, 1999; Paulsen and St. John, in press; St. John, Paulsen, and Starkey, 1996). In addition, the student choice sequence can be used as a framework for promoting the choices made by students in ethnic populations that are historically underrepresented. Clearly there is a need for more research on how public policy decisions influence the integration process and attainment by minority populations (Allen, Epps, and Haniff, 1991; St. John and Hossler, 1998). Nevertheless, the student-choice construct provides a basis for promoting attainment by diverse populations.

The Outcomes of Student Choice

The student-choice construct (Figure 1) depicts the mechanisms through which citizens in American society, and other free societies, navigate their own paths through the educational system. There are four outcomes of the choice process that provide a basis for linking policy decisions about education to the social and economic goal of employability.

First, consistent with the early developmental theories, individual development is a primary outcome of higher education. The components of choice have links to individual development and self-actualization. While this developmental aspect of the student choice process may be hard to measure, there should be little doubt that the maturity of the individual plays a central role in life choices through adulthood.

Second, when students develop postsecondary aspirations and attain their college dreams, the result is gains in attainment. In the early 20th century, the postsecondary opportunities were distributed through three financial mechanisms: the direct payment of the costs of attending by families who could afford college: state subsidies to public institutions, which provided a means of lowering direct costs for families; and student aid, provided by institutions and some states, which expanded choices for some high-achieving, low-income students. In the second half of the 20th century, need-based student aid has been increasingly used to expand opportunity. However, due to the negative reaction of conservative policymakers to the growing public expenditures on higher education—a combination of taxpayers' support for institutions *and* students—in the last two decades of the twentieth century, there was a shift in the focus of need-based aid from grants to less-costly loans (Baum, Chapter 2). This shift in financial-aid policy, along with a detailed analysis of its implications for affordability (St. John, 1994c; in press), revealed that some of the gains in educational attainment that resulted from expanding student aid have now been eroded.

It is clearly evident that gains in postsecondary attainment result in gains in individual earnings (Leslie and Brinkman, 1988; Paulsen, Chapter 3; Pascarella and Terenzini, 1991). When we consider also that there are tax-revenue returns (social or public returns) from increased earnings, along with increased individual returns (Bluestone, 1993; St. John and Masten, 1990), the linkage between attainment and earnings provides an improved basis for rethinking public finance strategies. However, we also need a better way of linking student choices about field of study to postsecondary finance than that provided by social-attainment theory.

The notion that there is a linkage between tax revenues and investment in higher education provides another perspective on the new policy discourse as well. Given the importance of education to earnings—and taxes—why do so many taxpayers want to reduce tax rates rather than support higher education? To address this question we need to consider the congruence between higher education and employment.

The notion of congruence provides an alternative as a policy goal. Early social-attainment theory (Alexander and Eckland, 1974, 1977; Blau and Duncan, 1967) provided a biased view of status attainment that has limited utility in this construction of public finance strategy. The status-attainment perspective assigned a higher social value to the more elite professions, rather than valuing individuals attaining their own aspirations. Congruence between the individual's academic preparation, his/her employment opportunities, and aspirations and interests provided a more workable way of viewing the linkage between postsecondary education and employment. This new construct builds on the logic of Holland's vocational types (1980) and the related notion of congruence between major and employment (Smart, 1975, 1985, 1989). The inclusion of aspirations provides, in this construct, a way of linking the sequence of student choices to the academic programs in colleges and employment opportunities after college, without assuming one type of employment is inherently more valuable to society than another. This revised construct provides an improved basis for thinking about linkages between financial strategies, the professional academic work of faculty, and the choices individuals make in their efforts to develop personally and professionally. Congruence between education, employment opportunity, and individual interests represents a potentially important policy goal, one that merits further systematic exploration, as employability becomes a more central aim of educational and social policy.

UNDERSTANDING THE ROLE OF FINANCES

With the student choice construct as a lens and conceptual framework, it is possible to systematically review the recent research on the role of finances. There is a small but growing body of research that can inform our understanding of the role of finances across the choice sequence. In this section, we examine each component of the choice process with a focus on group differences in the choice process.

Family Background

Economic theory has held that there are differences in price response across income groups. Indeed, the emphasis on need-based financial aid within federal student aid programs reflects the general consensus that there are income differences in affordability. However, economic theory of student demand and sociological theory of attainment has tended to overlook ethnic and gender differences. Further, the focus on traditional age groups in research across these fields has further limited our understanding of choice process.

Research that examines the influence of prices for different income groups consistently finds that low-income students are more responsive to prices than middle- or upper-income students (McPherson and Schapiro, 1991; St. John, 1990a; St. John and Starkey, 1995). There is quite a bit of evidence that African-Americans are more sensitive to tuition charges even when the influence of family income is controlled for (Kaltenbaugh, et al., 1999). There is also difference in the ways students from different ethnic groups respond to loans, with loans having less direct influence on decisions by African- Americans (St. John and Noell, 1989). Therefore, there is growing evidence that it is important to consider group differences when the effects of finances on student choice are assessed.

Further, there is reason to consider locale as a factor. It has long been known that region of the country has an influence on postsecondary opportunity (Jackson, 1978). Urban higher education has historically been underdeveloped and with the increasing concentration of minorities and poverty in inner cities (Fossey, 1998; Jencks and Peterson, 1991) there is reason for more concentrated research on the ways the specific contexts where student reside may constrain opportunity.

Formation of Postsecondary Aspirations

Given the new emphasis on expanding the percentage of the population that attends college (Council for Aid to Education, 1997), there is reason to concentrate policy on increasing postsecondary aspirations. There is also a growing body of research that finds that aspirations can be influenced by information (Fenske, Geranios, Keller, and Moore, 1997; Hossler and Stage, 1992; Hossler, et al., 1999). There is also reason to consider group differences in the formation of postsecondary and career aspirations.

Research that considers group differences in formation of postsecondary aspirations has been limited. Prior research has documented that African-Americans have higher aspirations, controlling for their economic backgrounds, than do whites (St. John, 1991). However, there is also evidence that low-income students have more unfulfilled aspirations (Hearn, Chapter 7). Recent research indicates that financial aid—or perceptions of aid—influence aspirations more substantially for African-Americans than for Whites (Carter, 1999). Given the recent development of the federal Gaining Early Awareness and Readiness for Undergraduate Programs (GEAR UP), an HEA Title IV program that funds programs that provide outreach and information to aspiring students, it is now an opportune time to begin studying the impact of these programs. Do public interventions actually change aspirations, as some research suggests? With the expansion of these early intervention programs there should be new opportunities for research.

The formation of career aspiration may be an even more important issue. For decades social theory has argued that parents' careers influence the careers of their children (Blau and Duncan, 1964; Alexander and Eckland, 1974, 1977). This means that students from families and communities that have limited role models will have an embedded disadvantage. Norton Grubb's research (1996) indicates that some fields do not provide sufficient compensation to enable graduates to pay back their loans. However the process of forming career aspirations is problematic, especially given the difference in family contexts.

The Opportunity to Attend

There are several ways that public finance strategies influence the opportunity to attend. If there are not sufficient colleges then opportunity will be constrained. While America just passed through a period (the 1980s and the 1990s) during which there was an excessive capacity, at least according to historical projections (Carnegie Council on Policy Studies in Higher Education, 1980; Frankel and Gerald, 1980), there are still reasons why the opportunity to attend could have been constrained (Hearn, Chapter 11).

First, there is still reason to expect that in some locales and some states postsecondary opportunities may still be constrained by the lack of local institutions. For example, Indiana and Louisiana are among the states with low postsecondary attainment that have recently started community college systems under the theory that this will expand attainment. Further, there are many settings across the country where local postsecondary opportunities are limited.

Second, it is possible that the new high-tuition, high-loan environment could expand access for some students, including students whose aspirations and/or abilities might limit their ability to pay off loans. In fact, there is growing evidence that the opportunity to attend is related to the willingness to borrow and debt does not have a positive influence on persistence by all students (Kaltenbaugh et al., 1999). Furthermore, there is evidence that even in states with apparently adequate grants programs, students with low incomes are increasingly vulnerable and their opportunity to persist is limited by their reaction to debt (St. John, Hu, and Tuttle, in press).

Thus, there is reason to question whether the new federal efforts to expand access by providing better information about opportunities and finances will have their desired effect. If the access problem is a function of information but not affordability, then we could expect a substantial effect. If however, as the other evidence suggests, access is a function of information, preparation, and finances (St. John, 1991), then we could expect more limited effect from GEAR UP in states that have not made a sufficient investment in their grant programs.

College Choice

It has long been evident that finances have a direct effect on college choice. Historically, student price response was measured using a single indicator of price (tuition or net price), and it was widely believed that students responded to a single price (Jackson, 1978; Jackson and Weathersby, 1975; Leslie and Brinkman, 1988). More recent studies indicate that students actually respond differently to different types of prices (i.e., tuition and fees, room and board) and subsidies (e.g., grants, loans, and work) in their enrollment decisions (DesJardins et al., 1999; Paulsen and St. John, 1997, in press; St. John, 1991).

Further, it has been assumed that the receipt of an aid offer makes a difference in college choice, since Jackson (1978) concluded that the receipt of an offer rather than the amount of aid influenced college choice. This notion that the mere offer of aid could be used to induce more applicants and a greater yield of admitted applicants was integrated into the theory of enrollment (e.g., Hossler, 1984, 1987). For the past few decades, private colleges have strategically used aid to build their enrollments. Increasingly private colleges have leveraged their discretionary grant aid by targeting it on students who are more likely to be induced to enroll with aid subsidies (Breneman, Doti, and Lapovsky, Chapter 12). And, while this practice has been questioned because of its inherent inequities (McPherson and Schapiro, 1998), it is still widely used.

For the vast majority of students, choices are constrained before they ever apply to college or apply for student aid. Family background and educational experiences constrain the ranges of alternative most students consider (Paulsen, 1990). However, for most students the adequacy of aid offers is now an important issue, especially since the decline in federal grants. Indeed, it is increasingly apparent that, for some colleges, aid offers are not adequate to attract some accepted applicants with financial need (Somers and St. John, 1997). Thus, the strategies campuses use to supplement state and federal grant aid are also important because in many instances supplemental support is needed to provide access to many four-year colleges.

It has only more recently become evident that perceptions of finances have an influence on choice and subsequent persistence decisions. Indeed, many students consider financial factors as very important when they choose their college. Some researchers frame this as a continuous construct related to students' perceptions of their ability to pay (e.g., Cabrera, Nora, and Castañeda, 1992), while others consider the specific financial factors that influence choice. Research on the nexus between college choice and persistence reveals that:

- When the whole population of undergraduates was studied, there were distinct patterns of financial choice, with some students considering locale and earnings, others considering aid offers, and others regarding low tuition as very important (St. John, Paulsen, and Starkey, 1996).
- When undergraduate students enrolled in public and private colleges were separately examined, choosing a college because of high aid was more common among private college students, while low tuition, being close to home, and work opportunities were principal reasons for those choosing public colleges (Paulsen and St. John, 1997).
- When students were examined within income groups, a class-related pattern emerged. Poor students tended to choose their colleges so they would have low living costs and could work while attending. However, middle- and upper-income students tended to choose a college because high aid was important. And in general, financial factors were less important for upper-income than they were for lower-income students (Paulsen and St. John, in press).

These patterns of choice are important not only because they reflect the range of situated contexts in higher education, but also because these perceptions have a sustained influence on persistence (Paulsen and St. John, 1997, in press). Thus, the changed patterns of public finance and institutional strategy appear to have reshaped patterns of college choice. While there are limitations to the use of class-based concepts, we still need a better understanding of the role of social class in higher education finance.

Choice of Major

The idea that finances might influence major choice is rooted in both human capital and social attainment theories. Human capital theory argues that individuals consider prospective returns when they choose majors (Becker, 1964; Paulsen, Chapter 3), while social attainment theory links these considerations more directly to family background (Blau and Duncan, 1967). These theories provide a logical basis for considering the relationship between prices and subsidies and student choice of major field of study.

There is growing evidence that major choice is central to the role of loans. While research to date has not found a significant link between debt burden and major choice (St. John, 1994b), there is increasing evidence that debt interacts with major choice and loan repayment. Flint's finding (1997) regarding congruence between major and employment establishes this linkage. Indeed, it appears that students reevaluate the value of their education based on their employment experience after they have graduated.

Furthermore, there is evidence that the influence of majors on college persistence differs for different groups. For example, a recent study found that African-Americans with majors in engineering and computer science and health-related fields were more likely than their peers to persist, while Whites in undeclared majors were less likely to persist (St. John, Hu, Simmons, and Carter, forthcoming). Given that there are differences in the effects of student aid for these groups (Kaltenbaugh et al., 1999), there is reason to continue to explore the ways diverse groups are influenced by aid in their major choices.

Persistence

The changing public finance environment also has had an influence on persistence as well. A few decades ago, there were doubts about whether financial aid influenced persistence (Pascarella and Terenzini, 1991; Tinto, 1987). However, there is now a strong body of research confirming that finances influence persistence (Murdock, 1989; St. John, Cabrera, Nora, and Asker, in press). When attempting to untangle how aid affects persistence, it is important to consider both the direct and indirect effects.

First, there is growing evidence from students enrolled in the late 1980s and 1990s that student aid is generally not adequate unless federal grants are supplemented by grants from other sources. As a general pattern, it is evident that grant aid was inadequate by the late 1980s (St. John, in press). However, when the population was broken down by the type of institution attended, grants were adequate in private colleges but not in public four-year colleges (Paulsen and St. John, 1997; St. John, Oescher, and Andrieu, 1992), indicating that the private investment in grants had a sustained impact on persistence. More recently, state-level studies have found that state support of state grant programs has a substantial influence on keeping public colleges affordable (St. John, 1999; St. John, Hu, and Weber, in press). Thus, the different patterns of supplemental support for grant programs were not only having an influence on access, but also had a sustained pattern on persistence.

Second, there is also substantial evidence that the perceptions of finance influence persistence. In particular, Cabrera, Nora, and Castañeda (1992) have found that the ability to pay—a measure of the perceptions of college affordability—interacts with academic integration processes and has an indirect influence on persistence as a result. The nexus studies (Paulsen and St. John, 1997, in press; St. John, Paulsen, and Starkey, 1996) not only confirm that perceptions of affordability interrelate with academic experiences in college, but that they have a direct effect on persistence. Indeed, it is increasingly apparent that the opportunity to attain a college education is increasingly defined by social class, with poor and working class students facing constrained choices and reduced opportunity to persist due to financial constraints (Paulsen and St. John, in press).

Graduate Education

During the past decade, researchers have begun to examine the influence of finances on graduate school opportunity. Research to date does not provide consensus on the relationship between debt and the opportunity to attend graduate school. Some researchers point out that students with excessive educational indebtedness are less likely to go to graduate school (Weiler, 1994). However, others suggest that student educational debt has not reached the "excessive" level (Hansen and Rhodes, 1988) and has not limited student choice options to graduate school (Schapiro, O'Malley, and Litten, 1991). In higher education research, there is evidence that financial aid is not adequate to support continuous graduate enrollment (Andrieu and St. John, 1993). These linkages merit further investigation.

CONCLUSIONS

When the student choice construct is used as a lens for reviewing research on the effects of student aid and other financial factors, it is apparent that the role of finances is most appropriately examined in relation to the contexts in which students are situated. There are clearly differences across groups in the influence of tuition and student aid. Indeed, this review indicates that students make their educational choices in situated contexts. Not only does students' background influence the formation of their aspirations, but it also shapes the way they frame their educational options and make educational choices. More importantly, recent reviews leave little doubt that the new high-tuition, high-loan environment has different effects for different groups (St. John, in press). For middle-income families, the new environment has maintained the opportunity to make educational choices, while the choices for low-income families are more constrained, as is the opportunity to attain a college degree. These findings have implications both for research and public policy.

In the future, researchers should focus more on the choices made by diverse groups and the impact of finances on these choices. This represents a departure from an older pattern of research on the impact of finances, which focused on discovering universal estimates of the effects of tuition and aid (e.g., Leslie and Brinkman, 1988; Pascarella and Terenzini, 1991). It is time to move forward and consider the role of finances in valuing, promoting, and enhancing diversity and educational opportunities.

References

Alexander, K.L., and Eckland, B.K. (1974). Sex differences in the educational attainment process. *American Sociological Review* 59: 668-82.

Alexander, K.L., and Eckland, B. K. (1977). High school context and college selectivity: institutional constraints in educational stratification. *Social Forces* 56: 166-68.

Allen, W.R., Epps, E.G., and Haniff, N.Z. (eds.) (1991). *College in Black and White: African-American Students in Predominantly White and Historically Black Public Universities*. Albany: State University of New York Press.

Andrieu, S.C., and St. John, E.P. (1993). The influence of prices on graduate student persistence. *Research in Higher Education* 34: 399-418.

Astin, A.W. (1975). *Preventing Students From Dropping Out*. San Francisco: Jossey-Bass.

Astin, A.W. (1993). *Assessments for Excellence: The Philosophy of Assessment and Evaluation in Higher Education*. Phoenix, AZ: Oryx.

Banta, T.W., Rudolph, C.B., VanDyke, J., and Fisher, H.S. (1996). Performance funding comes of age in Tennessee. *Journal of Higher Education* 67: 23-45.

Bean, J.P. (1990). Why students leave: insights from research. In D. Hossler, J.P. Bean, and Associates (eds.), *The Strategic Management of Enrollment*. San Francisco: Jossey-Bass.

Becker, G.S. (1964). *Human Capital: A Theoretical and Empirical Analysis with Special Reference to Education*. New York: National Bureau of Economic Research.

Blau, P., and Duncan, O.D. (1967). *The American Occupational Structure*. New York: Wiley.

Bloom, A. (1987). *The Closing of the American Mind*. New York: Simon and Schuster.

Bluestone, B. (1993). *An Economic Impact Analysis*. Boston: University of Massachusetts.

Cabrera, A.F., Nora, A., and Castañeda, M.B. (1992). The role of finances in the persistence process: a structural model. *Research in Higher Education* 33: 571-593.

Carter, D.F. (1999). The impact of institutional choice and environments on African-American and White students' degree expectations. *Research in Higher Education* 40: 17-41.

Chickering, A.W. (1969). *Education and Identity*. San Francisco: Jossey-Bass.

Carnegie Council on Policy Studies in Higher Education. (1980). *Three Thousand Futures: The Next Twenty Years for Higher Education* (1st ed.). San Francisco: Jossey-Bass.

Chickering, A.W. (1976). Development as an outcome of education. In M. Keeton and Associates (eds.), *Experiential Learning: Rationale, Characteristics Assessments*. San Francisco: Jossey-Bass.

Council for Aid to Education (1997). *Breaking the Social Contract: The Fiscal Crisis in Higher Education*. Santa Monica, CA: RAND.

DesJardins, S.L., Ahlburg, D.A., and McCall, B.P. (1999). An event history model of student departure. *Economics of Education Review* 18: 375-390.

Dresch, S.P. (1975). A critique of the planning models for postsecondary education: current feasibility, potential relevance, and a prospectus for future research. *Journal of Higher Education* 46: 246-286.

Fenske, R.H., Geranios, C.A., Keller, J.E., and Moore, D.E. (1997). *Early Intervention Programs: Opening the Door to Higher Education*. ASHE/ERIC Higher Education Report, No. 6. Washington, DC: The George Washington University.

Flint, T. (1997). Predicting student loan defaults. *Journal of Higher Education* 68: 322-354.

Frankel, M.M., and Gerald, D.E. (1980). *Projections of Education Statistics to 1988-89*. Washington, DC: National Center for Education.

Fossey, R. (ed.) (1998). *Readings in Equal Education*. New York: AMS Press.

Gladieux, L.E., and Wolanin, T.R. (1976). *Congress and the Colleges: The National Politics of Higher Education*. Lexington, MA: Lexington Books.

Gose, B. (1997). A community college in Virginia attracts Ph.D.'s as students. *The Chronicle of Higher Education* July 11: A33-A34.

Grubb, W.N. (1996). *Working in the middle*. San Francisco: Jossey-Bass.

Hansen, W.L. (1983). Impact of student aid on access. In J. Froomkin (ed.), *The Crisis in Higher Education*. New York: Academy of Political Science.

Hansen, W.L., and Rhodes, M.S. (1988). Student debt crisis: are students incurring excessive debt? *Economics of Education Review* 7: 101-112.

Hansen, W.L., and Weisbrod, B.A. (1969). *Benefits, Costs, and Finance of Public Higher Education*. Chicago: Markham.

Hearn, J.C. (1992). Emerging variations in postsecondary attendance patterns: an investigation of part-time, delayed, and nondegree enrollment. *Research in Higher Education* 33: 657-87.

Heller, D. (1998, November). *A comparison of the tuition price and financial aid responsiveness of first-time enrollees and continuing college students*. Presented at the Association for the Study of Higher Education 23rd Annual Meeting, Miami, Florida.

Holland, A.S.B. (1980). *Complex function theory*. New York: Elsevier North Holland.

Hossler, D. (1984). *Enrollment Management: An Integrated Approach*. New York: College Entrance Examination Board.

Hossler, D. (1987). *Creating Effective Enrollment Management Systems*. New York: College Entrance Examination Board.

Hossler, D., Bean, J.P., and Associates. (1990). *The Strategic Management of College Enrollment*. San Francisco: Jossey-Bass.

Hossler, D., Braxton, J., and Coopersmith, G. (1989). Understanding student college choice. In J.C. Smart (ed.), *Higher education: Handbook of Theory and Research* 5: 231-288. New York: Agathon.

Hossler, D., Lund, J.P., Ramin, J., Westfall, S., and Irish, S. (1997). State funding for higher education: A Sisyphean task. *Journal of Higher Education* 68: 160-196.

Hossler, D., and Schmit, J. (1995). The Indiana postsecondary-encouragement experiment. In E.P. St. John (ed.), *Rethinking tuition and student aid strategies*, pp. 27-39. San Francisco: Jossey-Bass.

Hossler, D., Schmit, J., and Vesper, N. (1999). *Going to College: Social, Economic, and Educational Factors' Influence on Decisions Students Make*. Baltimore: Johns Hopkins University Press.

Hossler, D., and Stage, F.K. (1992). Family and high school experience factors influence on post-secondary plans of ninth grade students. *American Educational Research Journal* 29: 425-447.

Hurtado, S., and Carter, D. (1997). Effects of college transition and perceptions of the campus racial climate on Latino college students' sense of belonging. *Sociology of Education* 70: 324-45.

Jackson, G.A. (1978). Financial aid and student enrollment. *Journal of Higher Education* 49: 548-74.

Jackson, G.A., and Weathersby, G.B. (1975). Individual demand for higher education: a review and analysis of recent empirical studies. *Journal of Higher Education* 46: 623-52.

Jencks, C., and Peterson, P.E. (eds.). *The Urban Underclass*. Washington, DC: Brookings Institution.

Kaltenbaugh, L.S., St. John, E.P., and Starkey, J.B. (1999). What difference does tuition make? An analysis of ethnic differences in persistence. *Journal of Student Financial Aid* 29 (2): 21-31.

Kane, T.J. (1995). Rising public college tuition and college entry: How well do public subsidies promote access to college? Working paper series No. 5146. Cambridge, MA: National Bureau of Economic Research.

Kingston, P.W., and Lewis, L.S. (eds.) (1990). *The High Status Track: Studies of Elite Schools and Stratification*. SUNY Press.

Kohlberg, L. (1981). *The Philosophy of Moral Development: Moral Stages and the Idea of Justice*. San Francisco: Harper and Row.

Kramer, M. (1993a). Changing roles in higher education finance. In J.P. Merisotis (ed.), *Background Papers and Reports*. Washington, DC: National Commission on Responsibilities for Financing Postsecondary Education.

Kramer, M. (1993b). Toward a more stable allocation of financing roles. In J.P. Merisotis (ed.), *Financing Higher Education in the 21st Century*. Washington, DC: National Commission on Responsibilities for Financing Postsecondary Education.

Leslie, L.L., and Brinkman, P.T. (1988). *The Economic Value of Higher Education*. New York: Macmillan.

Loevinger, J. (1976). *Ego development: Conceptions and Theory*. San Francisco: Jossey-Bass.

Manski, E.F. and Wise, D.A. (1983). *College Choice in America*. Cambridge, MA: Harvard University Press.

McPherson, M.S. (1978). The demand for higher education. In D.W. Breneman and C.E. Finn, Jr. (eds.), *Public Policy and Private Higher Education*: 143-196. Washington, DC: The Brookings Institutions.

McPherson, M.S., and Schapiro, M.O. (1991). *Keeping Colleges Affordable*. Washington, DC: Brookings Institution.

McPherson, M.S., and Schapiro, M.O. (1998). *The Student Aid Game*. Princeton, NJ: Princeton University

Press.

Mumper, M. (1996). *Removing College Price Barriers: What Government Has Done and Why It Hasn't Worked.* Albany: State University of New York.

Murdock, T.A. (1989). Does financial aid really have an effect on student retention? *Journal of Student Financial Aid* 19(1): 4-16.

Orfield, G. (1992). Money, equity, and college access. *Harvard Educational Review* 62: 337-372.

Pascarella, E.T., and Terenzini, P.T. (1979). Interaction effects in Spardo's and Tinto's conceptual models of college drop-out. *Sociology of Education* 52: 197-210.

Pascarella E.T., and Terenzini, P.T. (1980). Predicting voluntary freshmen year persistence and withdrawal behavior in a residential university: a part analytic validation of Tinto's model. *Journal of Educational Psychology* 51: 60-71.

Pascarella, E.T., and Terenzini, P.T. (1991). *How college Affects Students.* San Francisco: Jossey-Bass.

Paulsen, M.B. (1990). *College choice: Understanding Student Enrollment Behavior.* ASHE-ERIC Higher Education Report No. 6. Washington, DC: The George Washington University, School of Education and Human Development.

Paulsen, M.B., and St. John, E.P. (1997). The financial nexus between college choice and persistence. In R.A. Vorhees (ed.), *Researching Student Aid: Creating an Action Agenda.* New Directions for Institutional Research, No. 95. San Francisco: Jossey-Bass.

Paulsen, M.B., and St. John, E.P. (in press). Social class and college costs: Examining the financial nexus between college choice and persistence. *Journal of Higher Education* 73.

Perry, W. (1970). *Forms of Intellectual and Ethical Development in the College Years.* New York: Holt, Rinehart and Winston.

St. John, E.P. (1990a). Price response in enrollment decisions: an analysis of the high school and beyond sophomore cohort. *Research in Higher Education* 31: 161-76.

St. John, E.P. (1990b). Price response in persistence decisions: an analysis of the high school and beyond senior cohort. *Research in Higher Education* 31: 387-403.

St. John, E.P. (1991). What really influences minority attendance? Sequential analyses of the high school and beyond sophomore cohort. *Research in Higher Education* 32: 141-58.

St. John, E.P. (1994a). Assessing tuition and student aid strategies: Using price-response measures to simulate pricing alternatives. *Research in Higher Education* 35: 301-34.

St. John, E.P. (1994b). The influence of debt on choice of major. *Journal of Student Financial Aid* 24(1): 5-12.

St. John, E.P. (1994c). *Prices, Productivity and Investment: Assessing Financial Strategies in Higher Education.* ASHE/ERIC Higher Education Report, No. 3. Washington, DC: The George Washington University.

St. John, E.P. (1999). Evaluating state grant programs: A case study of Washington's grant program. *Research in Higher Education* 35: 455-480.

St. John, E.P. (in press). The impact of aid packages on educational choices: High tuition/high loan and educational opportunity. *Journal of Student Financial Aid.*

St. John, E.P., Andrieu, S.C., Oescher, J., and Starkey, J. B. (1994). The influence of student aid on within-year persistence by traditional college-age students in four-year colleges. *Research in Higher Education* 35: 301-34.

St. John, E.P., Cabrera, A.F., Nora, A., and Asker, E.H. (in press). Economic influences on persistence. In J.M. Braxton (ed.), *Rethinking the Departure Puzzle: New Theory and Research.* Nashville, TN: Vanderbilt University Press.

St. John, E.P., and Hossler, D. (1998). Higher education desegregation in the post-Fordice legal environment: a critical-empirical perspective. In R. Fossey (ed.), *Readings in Equal Education.* New York: AMS Press.

St. John, E.P., Hu, S., Simmons, A., and Carter, D.F. (forthcoming). *What difference does a major make? The effects of college major field on persistence by African American and White students.* Policy Research Report, Bloomington, IN: Indiana Education Policy Center.

St. John, E.P., Hu, S., and Tuttle, T. (2000). Persistence in an urban public university: a case study of the effects of student aid. *Journal of Student Financial Aid.*

St. John, E.P., Hu, S., and Weber, J. (in press). State Policy and the Affordability of Public Higher Education: The Influence of State Grants on Persistence in Indiana. *Review of Higher Education.*

St. John, E.P., Kline, K., and Asker, E.H. (2001). The call for public accountability: rethinking the linkages to student outcome. In D. Heller (ed.), *The States and Public Higher Education Policy: Affordability,*

Access, and Accountability. Baltimore: The Johns Hopkins University Press.

St. John, E.P., and Masten, C.L. (1990). Return on the federal investment in student financial aid: an assessment of the high school class of 1972. *Journal of Student Financial Aid* 20(3): 4-23.

St. John, E.P., and Noell, J. (1989). The effects of student financial aid on access to higher education: an analysis of progress with special consideration of minority enrollment. *Research in Higher Education* 30: 563-81.

St. John, E.P., Oescher, J., and Andrieu, S.C. (1992). The influence of prices on within-year persistence by traditional college-age students in four year colleges. *Journal of Student Financial Aid 22*(1): 27-38.

St. John, E.P., Paulsen, M.B., and Starkey, J.B. (1996). The nexus between college choice and persistence. *Research in Higher Education* 37: 175-220.

St. John, E.P., and Starkey, J.B. (1995). An alternative to net price: assessing the influence of prices and subsidies on within-year persistence. *Journal of Higher Education* 66: 156-186.

Schapiro, M.O., O'Malley, M.P., and Litten, L.H. (1991). Progression to graduate school from the "elite" colleges and universities. *Economics of Education Review* 10: 227-244.

Slaughter, S., and Leslie, L.L. (1997). *Academic Capitalism: Politics, Policies, and the Entrepreneurial University.* Baltimore: Johns Hopkins University Press.

Smart, J.C. (1975). Environments as reinforcer systems in the study of job satisfaction. *Journal of Vocational Behavior 6:* 337-346.

Smart, J.C. (1985). Holland environments as reinforcement systems. *Research in Higher Education 23:* 279-292.

Smart, J.C. (1988). College influences on graduates' income levels. *Research in Higher Education* 29: 41-59.

Smart, J.C. (1989). Life history influences on Holland vocational type development. *Journal of Vocational Behavior* 34: 69-87.

Somers, P., and St. John, E.P. (1997). Interpreting price response in enrollment decisions: a comparative institutional study. *Journal of Student Financial Aid* 29(3): 15-36.

Terkla, D.G. (1985). Does financial aid enhance undergraduate persistence? *Journal of Student Financial Aid* 15(3): 11-18.

Tierney, M.L. (1980). The impact of student financial aid on student demand for public/private higher education. *Journal of Higher Education* 45: 89-125.

Tierney, W.G. (1992). An anthropological analysis of student participation in colleges. *Journal of Higher Education* 63: 603-618.

Tinto, V. (1987). *Leaving college: Rethinking Causes and Links of Student Attrition.* Chicago: University of Chicago Press.

Weiler, W. C. (1994). Expectations, undergraduate debt and the decision to attend graduate school: a simultaneous model of student choice. *Economics of Education Review* 13: 29-41.

Wilms, W.W., Moore, R.W., and Bolus, R.E. (1987). Whose fault is default? A study of the impact of student characteristics and institutional practices on guaranteed student loan default rates in California. *Educational Evaluation and Policy Analysis* 9: 41-54.

Chapter 11

ACCESS TO POSTSECONDARY EDUCATION:
Financing Equity in an Evolving Context[1]

James C. Hearn

Challenges to received wisdom, disruptive as they may be, can often serve larger purposes. We are approaching the twenty-year anniversary of a paper that shook the higher-education community's comfortable assumptions about the nation's efforts to use student financial aid to guarantee equitable opportunity for postsecondary education attendance. This chapter revisits, from a critical, contemporary perspective, the very fundamental questions raised by that paper. The intent is to draw us into a new consideration of the role of financing policy in ensuring postsecondary opportunity.

A preliminary word about scope is necessary. The chapter deals mainly with the influence of socioeconomic factors on entry into postsecondary education. The chapter uses a traditional, narrow definition of access: whether or not disadvantaged students enter postsecondary education.[2] Other chapters in this volume tackle the closely related questions of students' choices among various institutions and students' persistence to desired degrees or certificates (e.g., see St. John, Asker and Hu, Chapter 10). Similarly, although gender, race, and ethnicity intersect and interact with socioeconomic factors in influencing postsecondary attendance, this chapter focuses almost exclusively on students' socioeconomic backgrounds.[3] Finally, the chapter focuses only on undergraduate enrollment.

The chapter begins with a look at the controversy surrounding economist Lee Hansen's 1982 analysis of student financial aid and postsecondary access; then it presents

---

[1]The chapter benefited substantially from early critical readings by Mike Paulsen and Ed St. John. We may differ on some issues, but the dialogue with these two highly valued colleagues was enormously helpful.

[2]The chapter cannot deal with a prior question of great social importance: the high secondary-school drop-out rates of students from disadvantaged socioeconomic backgrounds. In noting rising postsecondary attendance among high-school graduates from lower-income backgrounds, for example, one should remember that this trend takes place in a pool reduced by disproportionately high drop-out rates in high school.

[3]Ed St. John, Erik Asker and Shouping Hu argue persuasively in Chapter 10 of this volume that the intersections of race/ethnicity and student financing of college are highly significant. I agree, and I regret that space is not available here for more intensive investigation of those connections.

a series of assertions regarding aid and access in contemporary U.S. postsecondary education. Next, the chapter reviews the many ways in which the current environment for postsecondary attendance differs from that in 1982. The chapter concludes with an examination of new questions and potential new solutions regarding equity in postsecondary opportunity.

A CONTROVERSIAL ANALYSIS

Virtually no one in higher education wanted to hear what Lee Hansen asserted in 1982: the federal government's massive investment in student financial aid was not working (Hansen, 1982).[4] More precisely, he argued that federal investment in need-based grants[5] was serving mainly as a "transfer payment," simply shifting funds between economic actors without having significant behavioral effects. In his view, tax-generated dollars being provided as grants to prospective postsecondary students were having little effect on their decision-making about whether to attend college:

> The evidence assembled here suggests that the expansion of federal financial aid programs and their targeting toward youth from lower income and lower status families did not alter to any appreciable degree the composition of…postsecondary education students or the college enrollment expectations of high school seniors over the 1970s (p. 50).

Hansen based his case on trends in the postsecondary expectations and participation rates of students in different socioeconomic groups, focusing on trends for the years after the explosion in federal student-aid funding that began with the passage of the U.S. Higher Education Act of 1965. Were the investment working, he argued, we would have seen by the early 1980s a dramatic narrowing of the gap in college expectations and attendance between students from disadvantaged backgrounds and other students. That not being the case, Hansen argued, the investment had been a failure on any grounds other than as a transfer payment. He ended his analysis with the suggestion that the nation had actually lost ground because of its investment in a need-based grants program:

> Aside from the lack of discernible impact, the program has entailed real costs. These include the administrative costs and the time costs (of students) associated with these programs. In addition, it can be argued that our focus on greater equality of opportunity in higher education has been costly because of the gap between our expectations and what has been accomplished. Thus, it appears that economic efficiency has been sacrificed in the pursuit of greater equity (p. 51).

Hansen's argument galvanized two camps: those favoring the federal government's efforts to achieve equality of educational opportunity via aid and those seeking to reduce federal spending on student aid. Among those pleased by the Hansen argument were the leaders of the then-new Reagan administration, who circulated Hansen's report approvingly. In a stinging series of rebuttals, Hansen was criticized convincingly on a variety of grounds, prominently including the limitations of his data sets in regard to

---

[4]The Hansen paper later appeared in a more widely disseminated and revised form: see Hansen (1983).

[5]Hansen focused on what were then Basic Educational Opportunity Grants but now are titled Pell Grants.

controls for confounding factors in college-going plans and decisions. Most in the higher-education community agreed with Breneman's conclusion (1982, pp. 12-13) that Hansen's data were "simply too deficient to allow strong causal connections to be made."

As it turned out, the Congress was largely resistant to the entreaties of the Reagan administration to cut grant funding, and the Pell program maintained slow but steady growth in most subsequent years (Baum, Chapter 2; Hearn, Chapter 7; College Board, 1999). Loans became a more dominant vehicle for federal investment, but the grants effort was by no means abandoned. Most higher-education leaders, analysts, and political figures realized evidence on the effectiveness of the federal grants effort in promoting enrollment equity was imperfect, but most were nonetheless unwilling to accept Hansen's null hypothesis (i.e., the hypothesis of no equity effects). Such a conclusion seemed both analytically premature and politically unacceptable.

Now, we find ourselves approaching the twentieth anniversary of the fervid debate over Hansen's thesis that our nation's massive grants investment was essentially for naught. Why revisit Hansen's argument? Two reasons emerge. First, as most observers already know, we still have not seen equalization in postsecondary enrollment rates across socioeconomic groups. As will be discussed below, lower-income students are appreciably less likely than others to attend college. Second, Hansen's argument still has a straightforward appeal for those in some philosophical camps. Notably, Hansen's suggestion in 1982 that we were then entering an era more attentive to efficiency and quality and less attentive to equality of opportunity proved prescient, and people who tend to view those as opposing rather than complementary policy directions may still resonate to the logic of his case. It therefore seems apropos to ask Hansen's core question again: does the nation's investment in need-based student financial aid make sense? Specifically, what do we know now that we did not know in 1982, and what is different now?

What Do We Know Now?

The years since 1982 have brought increasing evidence on the questions at the heart of Hansen's analysis. The field has benefited enormously from work by a very talented array of scholars and policy analysts (including Cliff Adelman, David Breneman, Larry Gladieux, Art Hauptman, Donald Heller, Thomas Kane, Mike McPherson, Mike Paulsen, Morton Schapiro, Ed St. John, Sarah Turner, and many others). We now have greatly improved our understanding of the two domains Hansen addressed: enrollment by lower-income students and the equity influences of need-based student aid. Those domains will be discussed in turn below.

Enrollment by Lower-Income Students

The evidence on enrollment by lower-income students may be summarized in the form of a series of assertions.

1. The gap between lower-income students and others in expectations for postsecondary attendance has become negligible. The existence of an income-based expectations gap was a major tenet of Hansen's argument that federal grants were having little or no effect. U.S. Department of Education data suggest support for this part of

Hansen's argument has been very seriously weakened.[6] In 1982, only 70 percent of high-school graduates from the lowest family income quartile stated an expectation to attend postsecondary education at some time, compared to 79 percent of middle-income graduates and 86 percent of upper-income graduates. In 1992, however, the comparable figures were 94, 97, and 99 percent. Expectations of postsecondary attendance were the norm across all income groups. Nothing suggests this trend has been reversed since 1992 (e.g., see Levine and Nidiffer, 1996; Kane, 1999). The expectations gap has effectively disappeared.

2. Lower-income students' participation rates in traditional postsecondary institutions have improved dramatically. In 1982, 42 percent of recent high-school graduates from the lowest-income quartile enrolled in a postsecondary institution directly after high-school graduation. In 1992, the figure was 53 percent.[7] In 1982, 49 percent of recent high-school graduates from the lowest-income quartile enrolled in a traditional postsecondary institution within two years of high-school graduation. In 1992, the figure was 64 percent. Since 1992, the trend appears to have continued. Census data are less targeted on the question at hand (postsecondary enrollment rates among recent high-school graduates), but do suggest that enrollment by lower-income people aged 18 to 24 continued to grow through the 1990s (Martinez and Day, 1999; *Postsecondary Education Opportunity,* July 2000). These gains are noteworthy and heartening.[8]

3. The enrollment gap between lower-income students and others, however, has grown. In 1982, while 42 percent of recent high-school graduates from the lowest income quartile were enrolling in a traditional postsecondary institution directly after high-school graduation, 68.5 percent of graduates from the highest income quartile were enrolling, a gap of over 26 percent.[9] In 1992, that gap had grown to 34 percent (53 percent versus 87 percent). Regarding enrollment in a postsecondary institution within two years of high-school graduation, the gap grew from 24 percent to 30 percent. Gaps between lowest-quartile graduates and graduates in the middle two quartiles are less dramatic, but grew similarly over the decade (from 11 to 16 percent for attendance directly after graduation as well as for attendance within two years of graduation).

Clearly, all income groups grew in their participation rates, but raw growth in rates was smallest in the lower-income group. These data must be taken cautiously for two reasons. In proportionate terms, one could draw the conclusion that growth has been equally impressive among the lower-income group. For example, growth from a 49 per-

---

[6]Data for assertion 1, unless otherwise noted, are from Adelman (forthcoming). Adelman used nationally representative data from the High School and Beyond [HS&B] study's sophomore cohort (1982 high-school graduates) and the National Education Longitudinal Study [NELS-88] cohort of (1992 high-school graduates).

[7]Data for assertion 2, unless otherwise noted, are from Adelman (forthcoming).

[8]Interestingly, the improvements are even more dramatic within race/ethnicity groups (Adelman, forthcoming). In 1982, 48 percent of black recent high-school graduates enrolled in a traditional postsecondary institution within two years of high-school graduation. In 1992, the figure was 71 percent. In 1982, 42 percent of black recent high-school graduates enrolled in a postsecondary institution directly after high-school graduation. In 1992, the figure was 60 percent. Patterns were similar for Latino students.

[9] Data for assertion 3, unless otherwise noted, are from Adelman (forthcoming).

cent to a 63.5 percent rate in attendance within two-years by lower-income students is roughly equivalent proportionately to growth from a 73 percent rate to a 93 percent rate among the highest-income group. In addition, the absence of controls for academic qualifications in these data necessitates great caution in drawing conclusions about equity. Still, regardless of whether one views the enrollment gap as growing or merely persisting, its continuing existence is troubling.

Other authors have noted the same pattern: improvement within the lower-income group but, relative to other groups, mere stability or loss for that population. McPherson and Schapiro (1998) attribute this growing gap to the decreasing affordability of education. As loans have grown relative to need-based grant aid, they argue: "The considerable increases in net tuition for low-income students have led to a growing gap between enrollment rates for high-income and low-income students and to an increased concentration of low-income students at the least costly institutions (p. 140)."[10]

4. The gap between expectations and actual enrollment is far greater among lower-income students than others, and has grown since 1982. Taken together, the first and third points above highlight a troubling pattern. In 1982, 70 percent of graduates in the lowest income quartile stated an expectation to attend postsecondary education at some time and 49 percent actually enrolled within two years. In 1992, 94 percent of graduates in the lowest income quartile stated an expectation to attend postsecondary education at some time but only 63.5 percent actually enrolled within two years. The raw gap between expectations and behavior thus grew from 21 percent to 30.5 percent. In the highest income quartile, the same gap actually shrank from 13 percent to 6 percent. In that group, expectations had come to be almost universally translated into enrollment. Among graduates in the middle-income quartile, the gap was essentially stable, going from 19 percent to 18 percent. Thus, the graduates in the lowest income group are alone in their pattern of a growing gap between expectations and enrollment. Strikingly, their relative disadvantage in this respect was greater in 1992 than in 1982. Put simply, lower-income students seemed in 1992 to be notably less likely than others to translate their expectations into enrollment. Their postsecondary expectations had risen far more than their postsecondary enrollments. There is no evidence to suggest that this trend has changed substantially since 1992.

5. The addition of statistical controls for academic qualifications and other factors does not remove the gap in enrollment between high- and low-income students. Multiple factors other than parental income influence high-school graduates' postsecondary attendance, including not only parents' educational and occupational attainments (often linked with parental income in a construct termed socioeconomic status, or SES) but also students' ability test scores, race/ethnicity, gender, high-school peers, high-school grades, high-school course-taking, and high-school track (Akerhielm et al., 1998). All these factors tend to be correlated with parental income and their influences intersect

---

[10]The argument that access is harmed by the growing federal emphasis on loans and de-emphasis of grants has been stressed also by others. Spencer (1999, pp. 116-117), for example, states, "Plainly, the federal commitment to 'access' for low-income students can no longer be taken for granted ... The erosion of a functional commitment to promoting access, backed by programs and funds actually designed to achieve that goal, threatens the role of education as an engine of economic opportunity in this country."

with it. Yet, when these other factors are statistically controlled, the enrollment influence of parental income and related socioeconomic factors does not disappear.

Hearn (1990, 1991, 1992), in a series of studies of the high-school graduates of 1980, found that SES played a secondary but still significant role in postsecondary access and a more notable role in postsecondary choice among different institutions. More recently, Akerhielm et al. (1998, p. 19) report that, among 1992 high-school graduates with lowest-quartile test scores, postsecondary attendance rates were twice as high among the high-income group as among the low-income group. Even when additional controls were added, the participation rate gap persisted in these data.[11]

Clearly, although academic qualifications and other factors are associated with socioeconomic status, there is something embedded in socioeconomic status that *distinctively* influences postsecondary enrollment, independent of those associations. Is that "something" a factor so simple as a lack of funds? That question can be addressed through examination of the effects on access of providing student financial aid.

The Equity Influences of Need-Based Student Aid

In the midst of the analytic and political whirlwind surrounding Hansen's 1982 paper, economist David Breneman provided wise counsel (1982, p. 13):

> This paper has the potential to be destructive....The potential also exists, however, to turn this study and the questions that it raises to good account. Rather than getting trapped into a sterile and unproductive debate about whether student aid makes a difference, we should attempt to pinpoint more precisely the differences that it does make, and debate the value of those effects.

Fortunately, the analytic community has been true to Breneman's charge. Below are some summary assertions on what has been learned about the effects of aid since 1982.

1. The massive investment in federal, state, and institutional financial aid has improved enrollment rates among lower-income students. Unquestionably, exogenous trends in society and the labor market have lifted enrollment rates nationally. Nevertheless, sophisticated econometric studies of the effects of student financial aid on enrollment have consistently concluded that aid programs have distinctive and significant positive influences on the postsecondary participation of recent high-school graduates from lower-income backgrounds (Cabrera et al., 2000; Heller, 1997; Kane, 1999; McPherson, 1988; Paulsen, 1998; St. John, 1991). Grant, loan, and work-study programs all serve to lower students' net costs of attendance, and thus help facilitate access. The current empirical evidence clearly contradicts Hansen's 1982 conclusion that the behavioral effects of federal aid programs are negligible.

2. The policy shift in recent years away from need-based grants and toward loans

---

[11]As Michael Paulsen has suggested (personal communication), what remains for further exploration is the mystery of the distinctions in the causal factors and mechanisms affecting expectations and aspirations and those affecting actual enrollments. In analyses in earlier periods, little distinction could be drawn between the two, and expectations and aspirations were very strong predictors of enrollment. Current trends suggest, however, that the link between expectations/aspirations and enrollment is eroding, at least among lower-income groups.

and merit aid has tended to disadvantage lower-income students relative to others. Students from different backgrounds tend to react differently to aid awards. Not surprisingly, grants tend to have more positive effects on high-school graduates' enrollment than loans. Also not surprisingly, lower-income students are more sensitive than other students in their enrollment decisions to prices and aid, including the grants/loans distinction (see Cabrera et al., 2000; Heller, 1997). Therefore, as national policy has moved away from funding grants, it has moved away from funding the kind of aid most positive for ensuring lower-income students' access.

Although the nation's total amount of student aid has not fallen, or even lost ground to tuition over the past decade, and although growth in aid per FTE student has exceeded growth in tuition, this growth has been less and less focused on need and thus less and less focused on lower-income students (Baum, Chapter 2). Since 1988-89, federal aid has tilted dramatically to loans, with loan aid rising as a proportion of all federally supported aid and as a proportion of all aid (College Board, 1999). Much of this growth in loans has come in the form of unsubsidized, non-need-based loans. On top of that trend has come the rise in state and institutional merit-based aid (see McPherson and Schapiro, 1998). Together, the two trends have helped produce a significant decline in the proportion of overall aid based on need. According to the College Board (1999), need-based aid fell from 80 percent of all aid a decade ago to just under two-thirds now.

In that period, the maximum Pell Grant fell dramatically in purchasing power, continuing a trend begun earlier. McPherson and Schapiro (1998, p. 141) note, "[While] gross tuition at the average public four-year school increased by 86% in real terms between 1980 and 1994 (77% at private four-year colleges and 70% at public two-year schools), the real value of the maximum Pell Grant fell by 27% over that period." Furthermore, the average Pell award and average Stafford Subsidized loan, after adjustment for inflation, remained nearly constant over the past ten years, while the costs of attendance at private and public four-year institutions increased by 33 and 29 percent, respectively (College Board, 1999, pp. 8-13).

While institutional aid has more than doubled in constant-dollar terms in the past decade, helping to compensate somewhat for the decline in federal grant support (College Board, 1999), the overall landscape is still dominated by loans. "Over the past quarter century, federal student aid has drifted from a grant-based to a loan-based system, producing a sea-change in the way many students and families finance postsecondary education (ibid., p. 4)."

In summary, the growth of aid in recent years has been substantial, but it is less targeted on equity for the disadvantaged than in the past. Increasingly, aid for lower-income students comes in a form requiring repayment. This pattern continues their legacy of disadvantage relative to students whose families can afford to use savings and current income to pay for college attendance. There is no evidence in the research literature that loan aid is as effective in improving lower-income students' access as grant aid (e.g., see St. John and Noell, 1989; St. John, 1994a, b).

3. Much of what remains of the enrollment gap may be attributed to social and cultural factors not addressed by the student financial-aid programs. Regardless of the potential gains in lower-income enrollments that might be obtained through increased investment in grants, it is apparent that finances alone will not do the job of equalizing access. The financial-aid environment of the mid-1970s was far more oriented to grants than our present environment, and gaps in enrollment between income-groups remained large nonetheless. What is more, we have convincing evidence that the logic of the decision to attend college is more complex than is typically assumed in financial-aid policy.

Hossler et al. (1999), Levine and Nidiffer (1996), and many others argue that college participation patterns are only partly, and sometimes only peripherally, affected by financial-aid programs. From the perspective of comprehensive, empirically based models of students' college decision-making, policymakers and others should never have expected that aid programs would by themselves have effects powerful enough to offset other factors discouraging students' from attending. As noted earlier, before the final year in high school, students experience a host of influences on their beliefs about themselves and life, their aspirations, and their plans for education and work. Parents' own educational backgrounds, their life experiences, and their level of available resources for securing books, encyclopedias, and computers for the house are important influences on young children's thinking. Likewise, teachers, counselors, and peers in the neighborhood and in school can have powerful influences. To the extent these other individuals do not reflect the goals of the student-aid programs, the influence of those programs may be contradicted and muted.

4. Lower-income high-school students face different contexts from other students, and the influential factors for students as a whole may play out in special ways in the distinctive contexts of lower-income students' lives. Lower-income students may very well consider educational issues in a different light from others, and may be influenced by somewhat different factors. There is evidence that, as they think about college attendance, lower-income students tend to rely less than others on parents, other students, college catalogues, college representatives, and private guidance counselors, and more on their high-school counselors (Cabrera et al., 2000). As is well known, lower-income students are also more likely to come from families without prior experiences in college (Akerhielm et al., 1998; Cabrera et al., 2000).

5. For lower-income students and their families, the financial aid system has become more complex and difficult to understand. As detailed in Chapter 7 of this volume, analysts have long bemoaned the complexity of the financial-aid system. Yet that complexity continues, and may well affect student decision-making. Kane (1999, p. 152) has perceptively argued, "We have built a system so complicated that it nearly requires a college degree simply to understand the full range of subsidies available. Although any form of means-testing implies some level of complexity, much of that complexity is currently situated at the front end of the college application process, taking the form of financial aid forms and complicated need-analysis calculations, rather than later in a student's career."

Not surprisingly in this context, unawareness and lack of knowledge concerning financial aid may well be deterrents to enrollment. Akerhielm et al. (1998, p. 19) report that, nationally, there are income-based disparities in parental attitudes and knowledge about financial aid, and those disparities may have significant influences on educational experiences and postsecondary outcomes. Fortunately, the analysis by Akerhielm et al.

suggests most parents in all income groups have read about financial aid and talked about it with a teacher, counselor, or other knowledgeable person. Nevertheless, lower-income parents are far more likely than others to harbor unwarranted doubts about the financial accessibility of postsecondary education: 28 percent of low-income parents of low-test score students stated "I do not see any way of getting enough money for my eighth grader to go to college" and 12 percent of low-income parents of high-test score students stated that belief.

WHAT IS DIFFERENT NOW?

The question of how governments can best spend their resources to promote access to postsecondary education has become more challenging in the past twenty years. Post-secondary education as a whole is changing quickly in a variety of ways.

As is well known and was noted earlier, *students* in higher education are quite different from those of the early 1980s. Many more than before come from lower-income backgrounds and from communities of color, and women have surpassed men by a good margin in enrollment rates and overall undergraduate enrollment (Martinez and Day, 1999; *Chronicle of Higher Education*, 1999, August 27).

One trend of special relevance for this analysis is the growth of enrollment among adults older than the traditional college age of 18-24. In this group, parental finances play a less direct role in postsecondary access. As Baker and Velez (1996, p. 95) argue, "since more and more college students are adults who are no longer economically dependent on their families of origin and whose own SES's are largely undetermined, the significance of the social-class position of one's family is relevant for only part of the body of college students." This argument may downplay the "deep" effects of parental status on students' aspirations and plans for attendance, but certainly bears investigation. For adults contemplating postsecondary attendance, compared with other prospective students, the role of parents is less immediate and less facilitative or constraining.

The adult student population also brings distinctive attitudes toward access and enrollment. According to Levine (2000), who conducted interviews with a variety of adult students on what they seek in postsecondary education, older students today are growing resistant to fees that are assessed across the board for all students, and in many cases, they are seeking access to a scaled-back, tailored product, not the full-service, one-cost product that was typical before the current era. Levine (2000) suggests these students want their educational experiences to be like their experiences with banks, with features like high quality, low cost, service orientation, access on every corner (an ATM analogy), and no requirement of payments for services or goods not received. For those interested in questions of access and aid policy, the pursuit by older students of unbundled, user-fee-style pricing rather than full-package pricing is especially noteworthy.

In concert with changes in students and their attitudes toward attendance have come changes in *providers*. Traditional universities are moving toward increased "virtual" offerings for students, and changing the face of their curricula in keeping with changing technologies (Gladieux and Swail, 1999b). In addition, new institutions, if "institutions" is indeed the appropriate term, are emerging that lie "off the books" from our usual higher-education data sources. Most are profit-oriented, many provide only distance education, all rely heavily on electronic forms of delivery, some lie outside U.S. borders, and some offer only courses and certificates, with no degrees (see the review by Adelman, 2000).

Relatedly, we are also seeing some blurring of institutional boundaries, even among the most established institutions. We may be entering an era of decreasing distinctions among the various institutional and non-institutional providers of education and related services and goods. Phrased in the converse, it appears to Levine (2000) and others that we are witnessing a convergence and combining of knowledge providers. Note for example, the disparate entities involved in recently headlined across-sector alliances: major universities, libraries, museums, certificate providers, proprietary institutions, and a variety of cable, software, and multimedia companies.[12]

Parallel to the changes in students and providers are changes in the nature of *enrollments*. The question of postsecondary access is increasingly becoming intertwined with the questions of postsecondary choice and persistence. In the 1970s and even into the 1980s, it was straightforward and defensible to draw clear distinctions between the questions of whether or not one attended a postsecondary institution (access), which institution one attended (choice), and how long one attended (persistence). Increasingly, however, the distinctions are growing blurred. As students enroll in a more and more diverse pool of institutions (now including "e-institutions"), and as they enroll in more and more unusual ways, the familiar definitions and measures of enrollment grow less reliable. In concert, the definitions of access and equity grow more ambiguous. Adelman (1999b, p. 21) has put it bluntly: "The available...data suggest that 'attending college' today means something very different from what it meant as recently as 1985." Some examples illuminate the point. Partly in response to new federal tax-credits, there is increased non-credit enrollment (Adelman, forthcoming). In addition, many students are attending more than one institution at a time, are constructing educational careers out of movement from one institution to another, and are targeting their course-taking and certification-seeking on particular career needs which change rapidly in content and intensity (Adelman, 2000; Levine, 2000). There is increased volume of "occasional students" who enroll for brief periods to upgrade employment skills and often at non-credit-bearing places, e.g., corporate training centers (Adelman, 1999b). Enrollments are thus more likely than before to be part-time and episodic (Adelman, 1999a).

For part-time attenders, federal, state, and institutional aid resources are all more limited. Because older students are especially likely to attend part-time, they are likely to face a somewhat different aid system from that facing younger students. But younger students are also attending part-time in increasing numbers, and for both groups, the shift to part-time attendance since the 1980s creates a distinctively changed context for assessing access and equity.

Enrollments are also more likely than before to be part-year. In 1995-96, fully one half of the enrollments in community colleges and one fourth of the enrollments in four-

---

[12]E.g., see the recent for-profit joint venture of Columbia University, the British Library, the Smithsonian Institution, the New York Public Library, the London School of Economics, and Cambridge University Press, detailed in Carr and Kiernan (2000).

year institutions were part-year (Horn, 1998). These figures are surprising now, and would have been thoroughly startling fifteen to twenty years ago.[13]

Another area of change in enrollment is the timing of initial postsecondary entry. Interestingly, students are now more likely both to enroll late and to enroll early, relative to two decades ago. On the former point, students now are more likely than in earlier times to enroll for the first time several years after high-school graduation (Hearn, 1992; Adelman, 1999a). On the latter point, many states now offer high-school students the opportunity to enroll in postsecondary classes while still in high school (Adelman, 1999b), and students are taking advantage of those opportunities.

Examining these and other enrollment trends, former University of Michigan president James Duderstadt (1998) has commented that we are abandoning prior eras' orientation toward "just-in-case education" in favor of a new focus on "just-in-time education." That is, we may be moving away from a defensive stance toward obtaining, early on, an education "for all seasons" and moving toward a stance viewing education as lifelong, pervasive, adaptive, and need-based. Duderstadt's inference may or may not hold over time, but it is in keeping with enrollment trends during the fast-growing economy of the past decade: enrollment growth has historically tended to slow a bit when unemployment is low and the economy is healthy (Heller, 1999), implying some people see higher education as an investment to be made in lean times, but both enrollments and the economy have surged in the recent boom years, perhaps implying a new, more aggressive attitude toward enrollment.

Even when one focuses on one clear-cut institution of attendance at one point in time, *student aid and tuition and fees policies* have become more complex in recent years. This growing complexity has made the calculation of a student's net price of attendance more difficult. As noted earlier, loan and merit aid together have risen as a proportion of all aid. What is more, in state-supported institutions, tuition levels have risen without parallel rises in aid levels, belying the promise of high-tuition/high-aid models for ensuring equity and efficiency in postsecondary financing (Mumper, Chapter 8; Paulsen, Chapter 4). In private institutions, as many have noted, we are in a new era marked by heavy price discounting (Breneman, Doti and Lapovsky, Chapter 12; Kane, 1999; McPherson and Schapiro, 1998). In some private colleges, paying the full "sticker price" is rare. Merit aid and other new forms of aid are widely awarded, in an effort to reduce financial burdens and enroll a student body with certain desired characteristics. The increasing proclivity in colleges and universities to charge different prices for different students is making tuition and fees, in some senses, chimerical.

Parents of traditionally aged, dependent college students are also playing a somewhat different role from the past. One of the core tenets of the aid programs before the late 1970s was the notion that parents had a responsibility for a major portion of the costs of their children's postsecondary educations. Need and eligibility calculations for the grant and work-study programs assumed substantial parental contributions and left little room for the substitution of federal aid for those expected contributions. Now,

---

[13]It is important to stress that part-year enrollments are a distinct phenomenon from part-time enrollments: 34 percent of first-time postsecondary students in 1995-96 were part-year, and these were evenly split between part-time and full-time students (Kojaku and Nunez, 1998).

however, students are clearly paying for more of their college educations. The shift to loans may be viewed as a shift in generational responsibility for paying for college. Hartle (1994, p. A52) puts the point succinctly: "The United States, in effect, has decided to shift the burden of financing higher education to students themselves. The social compact that assumed that the adult generation would pay for the college education of the next generation has been shattered."[14]

Faculty, at the heart of the prices faced by students because they are central to institutional cost profiles, are also changing. Increasingly, the faculty encountered by undergraduates are off the tenure track, working part- or full-time on time-bound contracts (Gappa, 1996). From the perspective of access issues, these new faculty may raise or lower institutional costs, and thus contribute to rises or declines in tuition levels. The indeterminacy stems from the fact that it's arguable whether such faculty ultimately cost institutions *less* because institutions achieve efficiencies when not locked in by tenure or *more* because certain valued faculty services may be lost by their hire and because contract faculty may demand higher salaries to offset the benefits lost by not working in tenured positions.[15] Similar issues arise from the fact that students are increasingly encountering "virtual" faculty offering much of their coursework online or via CD-ROM or DVD.

Another complicating factor is the growing realization that we are moving into an era of *fluid, global educational markets*. The U.S. postsecondary system is no longer alone in its openness to others and its offering of advanced options in a wide variety of fields. As barriers between states and nations in education fall, there is growing mention of the notion of an educational passport (Levine, 2000). Such a document, already being provided on a limited basis by some organizations, summarizes individuals' capabilities and experiences and reduces lengthy applications and transcripts. Movement in and out of educational experiences would potentially be greatly facilitated by such a system. The growing fluidity and cross-border character of postsecondary education may be profoundly important for access. It may not be too glib to conclude that, at least gradually and in some sense, access is being disassociated from time and space.

The *desired outcomes* of postsecondary education may also be changing in important ways. Specifically, formal academic degrees, such as the bachelor's degree, may become less valued by students and less valuable in the labor force. Some analysts have suggested that, in the future, we will be seeing strong growth among those who seek certificates, rather than degrees, from their postsecondary experiences (Levine, 2000; Adelman, 1999b, 2000). It is at least arguable that students are increasingly focused on practical outcomes and knowledge and decreasingly focused on specific institutions as providers of prestigious degrees.

Finally, the new era is bringing *increasing numbers of people seeking access* to postsecondary education. The size of traditional-age high-school graduating classes will grow by roughly half a million students over the next decade (WICHE/College Board, 1998). Making the conservative assumption of only moderate improvements in enroll-

---

[14]This topic is considered in more detail in Hearn (1998).

[15]See Hearn and Anderson (2001) for a discussion of some of the issues involving contract faculty.

ment rates and no change in retention rates, that's roughly an additional two million traditional-age students in college, compared with current numbers, according to an analysis by Adelman (1999b). Adelman's estimate does not consider the nontraditional students and nontraditional forms of enrollment discussed earlier: assuming growth in those areas as well, the capacity of higher education to offer adequate access arises as an even more pressing issue. Most analyses of postsecondary access in the U.S. take capacity as a given, focusing instead on expanding demand to the point of equity. In a potential context of inadequate capacity, the problem of lack of access for certain populations becomes more critical: how will capacity be rationed, and specifically, how will the rationing system deal with the ongoing problem of lower-income students' access?

The Increasing Challenges of Studying Access

The new kinds of students, enrollment, parents, pricing, aid, providers, and faculty are all making access more difficult to analyze and understand than in earlier years. In the realm of student aid, analysis of the effects of aid programs has been complicated by the initiation of new tax-incentive programs at the federal and state levels; by increasing use of credit card debt, home-equity lines, and consumer loans to finance postsecondary attendance; by a rise in student employment and a parallel rise in student wages that are not part of college work-study programs; by growing use of the federal government's unsubsidized loans; and by the rise of various forms of employer-provided aid, which is usually unknown and invisible to external analysts.

Another challenge for analysis lies in the evolving core technology of education.[16] Until recently, most observers would agree that they knew postsecondary education experiences when they saw them. A physical classroom with a board, a professor, and a group of students qualified, and a television set or a computer hook-up alone did not. Now, there is blur in place of clarity.[17] Where before, the question of access focused on whether students would sit in such a classroom, we must now consider whether postsecondary education can occur without any classroom experiences. For example, are we achieving universal access when all students can obtain a certificate via an online curriculum? At the extreme, when the content-delivering instructor is a contracted expert whose lectures are preserved on electronic media and the grading instructor is a graduate student, can a student remotely accessing such instruction be said to have access to postsecondary education?[18]

In the context of the multi-organization provider cooperatives noted earlier, with prestigious institutions working with less prestigious institutions, libraries, and corpora-

---

[16] The term "technology" is used here in the way it is often used in sociology, economics, and anthropology, i.e. as the modal form of production in a social group. Although a narrower, electronically oriented definition is often used currently, the point here is more general.

[17] For a lucid and more extended discussion of these issues, see Gladieux and Swail (1999b).

[18] Similar questions could be asked about equity in postsecondary choice. Where before, the question of choice focused on institutional differences (e.g., elite, high-priced universities versus other four-year institutions), we now must consider delivery differences. For example, does a course delivered online from Harvard represent a more desirable and valuable experience than a similar course delivered in a classroom on the campus of a state college? Is there inequity to be found in such comparisons?

tions, similar questions arise. At what point, among the range of possible contacts with University X, may we say that a student has access to that institution of postsecondary education?[19]

The new "off the books" institutions pose additional challenges for analysis of access. For example, none of the new providers in information technology described by Adelman (2000) are included in "higher education" in the usual definition and none are in the U.S. Department of Education's IPEDS system or the Department's various student-aid databases, and none report their curricula to the American Council on Education or other associations. There is no incentive for them to be involved in any of these data-gathering efforts, given their profit-seeking status and their indifference to aid systems. Indeed, there is not even much incentive for them internally to know much about their students, other than what might be helpful for marketing purposes. Incentives for ascertaining socioeconomic, racial/ethnic, and gender characteristics are minimal. Moreover, the global nature of this kind of education (e.g., Italian students earning certificates from Sun Microsystems, without leaving Italy) means governments and associations will never know much about these students unless they manage to fashion cost-effective data-collection agreements with international agencies.

The problems of the understanding the new patterns of enrollment extend as well to the traditional brick and mortar institutions. For example, non-credit students are important for a full sense of access to postsecondary education, yet this kind of enrollment poses special problems not considered in most existing data-gathering systems (Adelman, 1999b). In addition, when students access courses at traditional institutions from remote locations, enrollments are not easy to count (Adelman, 1999b). At present, despite the importance of this kind of enrollment, such students cannot be easily included in analyses of access.

Adelman (2000, p. 22) notes that people in traditional higher education institutions no longer work in a world of predictable boundaries:

> We have universities, colleges, community colleges, and trade schools, all accredited by one body or another, all granting credit hours and traditional degrees, all participating in the federal student financial aid system, all reporting data on enrollments, degrees, staffing, salaries, and so forth to the U.S. Department of Education through the Integrated Postsecondary Education Data System (IPEDS). Even when they offer virtual instruction, credit-by-examination, and other variations on the delivery of knowledge, they are still recognizably parts of the American postsecondary system. [But now a] new class of postsecondary providers has come on the scene—boundary-breaking and border-crossing every step of the way—to scramble institutional and governmental assumptions about the future.

Adelman focuses on these new providers' inroads into instruction in the field of

---

[19]Not surprisingly, in light of this trend, institutions themselves are changing. Levine (2000) has argued that we will soon have three kinds of institutions: "brick" (i.e., traditional campus-based institutions), "click" (i.e., institutions existing solely in cyberspace), and "brick and click" (i.e., campus-based institutions also offering online learning opportunities). Of these, Levine argues, the "sweet spot" for higher education is brick and click: having both an electronic and a physical presence. Traditional institutions may be in trouble if they resist online education and corporations move into their niche offering both a physical presence and web-delivered content.

information technology. It seems prudent to wonder whether we may soon see similar developments in other fields.

RECASTING QUESTIONS AND RECASTING POLICY FOR A NEW ERA

The U.S. public believes that access to postsecondary education for all citizens is more important than ever.[20] A growing number of educational leaders and analysts agree.[21] Work is becoming more professionalized, productivity and education are becoming increasingly interconnected, and nations' control over their economic fates is decreasing as competition grows more globalized. Higher education can help the nation adjust to economic, social, cultural, demographic, and technological changes, and it is fundamental to equalizing socioeconomic opportunity.

So, what can we say about this critically important topic? The changes in our understanding of lower-income students' postsecondary access since Hansen's 1982 paper are striking. On the positive side, we have learned much about aid effects, and the evidence is strong and mounting that grants and other forms of aid do influence traditional forms of postsecondary enrollment by lower-income students in ways sought by policymakers. Grants, work-study, and loans do provide equity benefits. Both postsecondary expectations and postsecondary participation rates are up among lower-income students, and there is solid evidence that aid programs played a notable role in these improvements. The Hansen thesis cannot be supported, at least in the terms in which it was presented.

Yet, on the less positive side, enrollment gaps between lower-income students and others remain and, in some respects, have grown. What is more, current aid programs seem too complex, too diluted, and too modest to remove these gaps. Much lies beyond their reach, in the early years of schooling well before families become aware of their students' enrollment and aid options.

Neither positive nor negative, but certainly hovering over these conclusions, is the fact that we are entering a new era in which access itself is losing its clarity as a driving construct for policymaking in postsecondary equity. As noted above, if access was ever a clear-cut question, it most certainly is less so now. How do we operationalize access, and thus equity, in this new context? When we argue about access, what do we mean? What should we mean? Access to what? Access for whom? Access by what means? Institutions and other providers are changing, as are students, patterns of enrollment, tuitions, and much else. As a consequence, access to what, by whom, and by what means are more legitimate questions than ever for policymakers, as is the very definition of access. In a context of definitional and policy uncertainty regarding access, measuring its adequacy and refining the role of financial aid in ensuring adequacy are extremely difficult.

---

[20]See the surveys and reports of the American Council on Education (1998) and, more recently, a consortium of public policy organizations (Immerwahr and Foleno, 2000).

[21]E.g., see the report of the American Association of State Colleges and Universities (Chandler, 1997) and the report of the Institute for Higher Education Policy, the Education Resources Institute, and the Council for Opportunity in Education (Institute for Higher Education Policy, 1999).

There is good reason to worry that, in this new era, lower-income students are more vulnerable than ever. Loans and tuition discounting tend to advantage other students more than lower-income students, and the new providers, new venues, new styles of enrollment, and new students each may lie somewhat beyond the reach of the current policies. As a result, sorting and access may proceed inequitably, without ready policy oversight and solutions. McPherson and Schapiro (1998, pp. 135-6) argue, "[T]he group most likely to be placed at risk by the shifting environment of American higher education is the group of low-income students who do not have the strong qualifications needed to qualify for selective private colleges.... [F]or increasing numbers of children from low-income families, the only educational choice they can meaningfully consider is the local community college"[22] For this group, wishing to avoid heavy loan burdens, lower-cost options are the most affordable, feasible choice. Of course, online educational options can also be relatively low in cost. As costs and loan burdens rise, lower-income students may increasingly head to such offerings.

To the extent policymakers allow the intensified sorting of lower-income students into lower-cost options such as community colleges, proprietary institutions, and online providers, access is served only in the broadest sense. If such a pattern indeed emerges, it would be only the most contemporary example of the society's tendency to expand the definition of access while not really intruding on the societal influence of elite institutions of greater power and privilege (see Hearn, 1990, 1992). The expansion of status-differentiated postsecondary education systems, however effective from the standpoint of broadening postsecondary educational opportunity, is not by itself a sufficient antidote to enduring social-class differences in educational attainments. Few of us would be comfortable with a system in which some form of postsecondary access is available to everyone, but in which people are sorted into institutional sectors on the basis of their socioeconomic resources.

Fortunately, there are policy solutions available to help guard against such a scenario. Existing research points in some directions worth exploration. Of course, we do not have optimal studies of the effects of student aid and other government policy initiatives on postsecondary participation, because the most powerful potential designs for studying such matters (e.g., field experiments) are expensive, complex, and politically infeasible. Nevertheless, we can make some judgments and suggest some approaches.

A first, rather obvious policy solution is indicated by research findings as well as by common sense: provide *more grant funding* for lower-income students. Specifically, expanding the population covered by need-based grants, moving the Pell Grants further toward full entitlement status, and raising the maximum Pell Grant all would most likely raise attendance rates among disadvantaged students. All evidence suggests that substantial additional federal and state investment in need-based grants could make a notable dent in the persistent SES-gaps in attendance rates.

In concert with the above initiative is a second policy option: the federal government and states wishing to deal effectively with issues of access need to begin *moving*

---

[22]See Voorhees, Chapter 13 in this volume, for a thorough consideration of issues in the finance of community colleges.

away from, and countering when possible, policies that do not serve the access goal. For example, governments and institutions may wish to provide targeted need-based aid to counter the growing movement to use tax concessions to fund access to postsecondary education. To the extent tax-based policies tend to serve families already having the resources to attend, those policies detract attention and funding from need-based approaches. Similarly, merit-based aid tends to go to students already able financially and academically to attend, and may detract from funding for need-based aid. As McPherson and Schapiro (1998) argue, if states continue to increase funding of merit-centered programs, relative to means-tested programs, then the federal government should offset that unhealthy trend by concentrating on need-based aid.

Even if significantly increasing federal and state funding for need-based grants is impossible, there is good reason to consider *"front-loading" Pell Grants* as a third policy option: i.e., tilting Pell funding toward the initial postsecondary years, when dropout is a particular threat to attainment. Kane (1999) argues that, given the unlikelihood of major increases in available Pell funding, we need to target Pell resources to raise the maximum grant for the most price-sensitive young people. Thus, he supports the idea of front-loading Pell Grants into the first two years of postsecondary education and, if necessary to support this approach, shifting grant funding away from the later college years. This would bring a larger effect of the grant funds on those on the border about college attendance and persistence.[23]

A fourth area for policy development is related but more ambitious: *across-level policy development relating to educational opportunity.* This effort begins with a conceptual shift. All available research suggests that students and their families tend to think of their education as a whole, rather than as something chunked into discrete elementary, secondary, and tertiary sectors. Yet, most states have long relied on separate departments for K-12 and postsecondary education, with little across-department communication or policy dialogue. Multilevel policy development should replace this narrow-vision approach. We are in an era of increasing attention to P-16 issues, i.e., issues that cross over the borders between levels of education. It was noted earlier that low enrollment rates among certain groups are rooted deep in young people's personal histories and are not easily solvable by finances. The adoption of a P-16 focus, and the concomitant encouragement of across-level dialogue and policy development, will not be easy. Yet, the challenge is worth pursuing.

One domain of special appeal here is joint efforts to provide all students improved information on postsecondary education, from middle school (or before) into the last year of high school. Akerhielm et al. (1998), Hossler et al. (1999), Kane (1999), King (1996), and numerous others put strong faith in information as an antidote to the problems of income-based gaps in enrollments. Indeed, leading analysts of access-related policies have long endorsed making understandable, accurate information on aid and tuition more widely available to young people in elementary and secondary schools.

---

[23]Of course, such an approach should be evaluated carefully. A state policy official recently suggested to the author that front-loading runs the danger of appearing to be a "bait-and-switch" operation, luring students into the system with generous grants, then holding their completion of four-year degrees hostage to their willingness and ability to take on substantial debt in their junior and senior years.

An aspect of this is increasing support for effective college-participation programs delivered by high schools, community agencies, postsecondary institutions, or some combination of those organizations. Such programs address the growing realization that postsecondary attendance is a product of a variety of forces, many of which are beyond the influence of student financial aid. Analysts are beginning to identify the features of such programs most conducive to successfully raising attendance rates among disadvantaged populations (see various chapters in Tierney and Hagedorn, forthcoming).

Additional *investment in K-12 schooling* is a fifth, somewhat broader domain for improvement. Here, an array of initiatives is possible. Rigorous courses, excellent teachers, and high expectations of students are particularly critical for the college attendance of lower-income students (Adelman, 1999a; King 1996). As Gladieux and Swail (1999a, p.194) note:

> Everyone knows that aid is not enough; that to equalize college opportunities for the poor requires more fundamental, complementary strategies. But debates on student aid policy tend to be insular....The roots of unequal educational opportunity are deep. There appear to be huge and growing disparities in the capacity of K-12 educational systems to prepare young people for the world beyond high school. Higher education, much less student aid as a financing strategy, cannot by itself redress social deficits and imbalances that appear to threaten our country's future. But neither can colleges stand apart. All of us—policymakers, educators, analysts, citizens—are challenged to try to make a difference.

A sixth domain for potential policy development is pursuing an *incentives-sensitive approach* in aid programs and related policy arenas. Gladieux and Hauptman (1995) have argued that incentives should be used far more productively, and regulations less aggressively, in federal policies. Along these lines, it seems worthwhile to explore not only incentives for students, through various forms of discounting, but also incentives for aid officers and institutions to award aid to lower-income students and keep them in school, incentives to high-school counselors to point students toward postsecondary attendance, and incentives to parents to plan, save, learn more about aid, and encourage attendance as a realistic option for their children.

A corollary suggestion is to be more aware and planful regarding manifest and latent incentives in existing educational policies and programs. As McPherson and Schapiro (1998) suggest, incentives-based thinking needs to be forward-looking: because federal policies create incentives for colleges and universities to react in certain ways in their funding and pricing, federal officials should take such incentives and consequences into account as they plan policies. In some cases, counterincentives may be needed. More broadly, policies create incentives for students and their parents that may need to be corrected. The classic example is the putative disincentives for parental and student savings built into federal and state aid programs.

Gladieux and Hauptman (1995), McPherson and Schapiro (1998), and others suggest a seventh way in which access policies could be improved: movement toward *improved integration of institutional and governmental efforts in postsecondary education*. McPherson and Schapiro (1998) suggest that federal funding for the Pell program arguably leads not only to increased access but also to increased institutional aid, so students receive a leveraged benefit from Pell increases. This observation arises out of a holistic, empirically based perspective. Such a perspective is too rare, and perhaps too much discouraged, in the current aid arena. Old hands in student-aid policy report there was a short period in the 1970s in which a coherent, across-sector, across-government "aid coalition" emerged (Hearn, Chapter 7). That coalition emphasized working together to foster student opportunity and deemphasized the expression or pursuit of organizational self-interest.[24] Memories may make this period less conflicted than it was, but the goal remains worthy. It merits renewed pursuit.

An eighth policy initiative worth serious consideration has long been advocated by a variety of leaders and researchers: *expanding analysis and evaluation* of access-related policies.[25] Funding for research on aid-related topics seems to have decreased in recent years, at the very time such work may be most needed. Kane (1999, pp. 144-5) observes that,

> [L]ow-income youth often behave as if their decisions to attend college were limited by their financial position. Observers may all have guesses about the likely effects of different polices, but they are just that, guesses. One can only go so far by analyzing the economic incentives implicit in a policy. Perceptions matter, and parents and student may not always think like good economists when it comes to investing in a college education. In fact, whether the problem is an aversion to debt or lack of knowledge of the complicated financial aid system or the limits to borrowing under the student loan programs, the source of the constraint is not clear. But the solutions—providing better high school counseling or raising the loan limits or raising the Pell Grant maximum—have very different costs. Currently, there is no empirical basis for claiming that one is more effective per dollar spent than the other.

One form of analysis not often attempted has been to view policies from a systems perspective. Individual policies and programs like the Pell program are too often evaluated as if they served only one purpose. Conversely, policy arenas are too often viewed as if they had only one initiative directed at them. In fact, programs often serve multiple goals, and multiple programs serve individual goals. In light of that, analyses need to take into account the broad context of policies and programs, and seek system-level conclusions and solutions. In a provocative recent article taking this approach, Stampen and Hansen (1999) argue that analyses of postsecondary access require a more ambitious scope less tied to individual programs, as well as a more sustained level of attention to the broad goals of postsecondary education.

Of course, policy analysis is no cure-all. *Expanding dialogue on postsecondary opportunity* is also critical, and comprises a ninth policy option. As Gladieux bluntly put it (1983, p. 1), "Social scientists and policy researchers may believe their data and investigations could improve the quality and soundness of decision-making, if government officials would pay heed. But research is only one variable in the diffuse, disjointed process of public policy-making. No policy study, no matter how apparently dispassionate and compelling, can displace the fundamentally political exercise of reconciling competing interests and decisions through political institutions." Expanded dialogue on access can help policymakers and analysts avoid the too prevalent mismatches

---

[24]For more on this period in aid policy, see Chapter 7 in this volume.

[25]See Chapter 7 for discussion of this issue.

between analysts' products and policymakers' needs and preferences. Ideally, new conversations and exchanges of views can take place across postsecondary stakeholder and constituency groups, via symposia, conferences, legislative hearings, task forces and the like. Unfortunately, there is cause to worry that we will be seeing less rather than more in this vein: familiar, valued sponsors and organizers of policy dialogue are coming under increasing fiscal and organizational pressures.[26]

Any new dialogue should pay special attention to the evolving context of postsecondary education. However commonplace the phrasing may be, postsecondary education may indeed be entering a new era. As discussed earlier, this new era will feature new providers, new students, new styles of enrollment, new technologies, and new faculty. Certainly, it will require new thinking and new policies.[27] Policymakers and analysts should initiate a dialogue reconsidering what we have too often taken for granted: the definition and measurement of access. Old definitions and old measures may well be of shrinking usefulness. The new dialogue must necessarily be rather open-ended and sensitive to rapidly changing environments. Decades ago, lengthy philosophical disputes, analytic efforts, testimony, lobbying, and negotiations were needed before federal aid policies were revised to focus more on students than on institutions and to include proprietary offerings as well as traditional two- and four-year institutions. Such time-consuming, intense work is necessary again now. The need for rethinking access for new societal and educational conditions is apparent. That need should be addressed soon, for the sake of equity.

References

Adelman, C. (1999a). *Answers in the Toolbox: Academic Intensity, Attendance Patterns, and Bachelors' Degree Attainment*. U.S. Department of Education, Office of Educational Research and Improvement. Washington, DC: Government Printing Office.

Adelman, C. (1999b). Cross-currents and riptides: Asking about the capacity of the higher education system. *Change Magazine*, January/February, pp. 21-27.

Adelman, C. (2000). A parallel universe: Certification in the information technology guild. *Change Magazine*, May/June, pp. 20-29.

Adelman, C. (forthcoming). Urbanicity and census division in the educational "fate" of disadvantaged students. In W.G. Tierney and L.S. Hagedorn (eds.), *Extending Their Reach: Strategies for Increasing Access to College*.

Akerhielm, K., Berger, J., Hooker, M., and Wise, D. (1998). *Factors related to college enrollment: Final report*. Office of the Undersecretary, U.S. Department of Education. Washington, DC: Government Printing Office. Report ED 421 053.

American Council on Education, The. (1998). *Too Little Knowledge Is a Dangerous Thing*. Washington, DC: American Council on Education.

Baker, T.L., and Velez, W. (1996). Access to and opportunity in postsecondary education in the United States: A review. *Sociology of Education*, extra unnumbered issue, 82-101.

Breneman, D.W. (1982). Comments on Lee Hansen's paper. Paper presented at the National Institute of Education Conference on Education, Productivity, and the National Economy, Leesburg, Virginia, November 12.

Cabrera, A.F., Terenzini, P.T., and Bernal, E.M. (2000). *Leveling the Playing Field: Low-Income Students in*

---

[26]A case in point is the recent termination of the policy-related efforts of the Washington, DC office of the College Board (*Chronicle of Higher Education*, 2000, February 11).

[27]Some important early thinking is taking place on broad policy implications of the new context. See, for example, Noam (1995) and Matthews (19983).

Postsecondary Education. Report from the College Board. Washington, DC: The College Board.

Carr, S., and Kiernan, V. (2000). For-profit web venture seeks to replicate the university experience online. *Chronicle of Higher Education*, April 14, 2000, p. A59.

Chandler, A. (1997). *Access, Inclusion, and Equity: Imperatives for America's Campuses*. A report from the American Association of State Colleges and Universities. Washington, DC: American Association of State Colleges and Universities.

Chronicle of Higher Education, The. (1999, August 27). 1999-2000 Almanac Issue.

Chronicle of Higher Education, The. (2000, February 11). College Board president fires 4 top figures in Washington office. P. A28.

College Board, The. (1999). *Trends in Student Aid*. Washington, DC: The College Board.

Duderstadt, J.J. (1998). The future of the university. *Issues in Science and Technology* 14(2): 7-8.

Gappa, J.M. (1996). *Off the tenure track: Six models for full-time, nontenurable appointments*. Working Paper Series on Faculty Roles and Rewards, Inquiry #10, American Association for Higher Education. Washington, DC: American Association for Higher Education.

Gladieux, L.E., and Hauptman, A.M. (1995). *The College Aid Quandary: Access, Quality, and the Federal Role*. Washington, DC: The Brookings Institution and the College Board.

Gladieux, L., and Swail, W.S. (1999a). Financial aid is not enough: Improving the odds for minority and lower-income students. In J. King (ed.), *Financing a College Education: How It Works, How It's Changing*. Phoenix, AZ: American Council on Education and Oryx Press.

Gladieux, L., and Swail, W.S. (1999b). *The virtual university and educational opportunity: Issues of access and equity for the next generation*. College Board Policy Perspectives. Washington, DC: The College Board.

Hansen, W.L. (1982). *Economic growth and equal opportunity: Conflicting or complementary goals in higher education*. Discussion Paper #706-82, Institute for Research on Poverty, University of Wisconsin.

Hansen, W.L. (1983). In J. Froomkin (ed.), *The Crisis in Higher Education*. New York: The Academy of Political Science, 1983.

Hartle, T.W. (1994, November). How people pay for college: A dramatic shift. *The Chronicle of Higher Education*, p. A52.

Hearn, J.C. (1990). Pathways to attendance at the elite colleges. In P.W. Kingston and L. S. Lewis (eds.), *The High Status Track: Studies of Elite Schools and Stratification*. Albany, New York: SUNY Press.

Hearn, J.C. (1991). Academic and nonacademic influences on the college destinations of 1980 high school graduates. *Sociology of Education* 63(4): 158-171.

Hearn, J.C. (1992). Emerging variations in postsecondary attendance patterns: An investigation of part-time, delayed, and non-degree enrollment. *Research in Higher Education* 33(6): 657-687.

Hearn, J.C. (1998). The growing loan orientation in federal financial-aid policy: A historical perspective. In R. Fossey and M. Bateman (eds.), *Condemning Students to Debt: College Loans and Public Policy*. New York: Teachers College Press.

Hearn, J.C. and Anderson, M.S. (2001). Clinical faculty in schools of education: Using staff differentiation to address disparate goals. In W. Tierney, Ed., *Faculty Work in Schools of Education: Rethinking Roles and Rewards for the 21st Century*. Albany, NY: SUNY Press.

Heller, D.E. (1997). Student price response in higher education: An update to Leslie and Brinkman. *Journal of Higher Education* 68(6): 624-659.

Heller, D.E. (1999). The effects of tuition and state financial aid on public college enrollment. *Review of Higher Education* 23(1): 65-89.

Horn, L. (1998). *Profile of Undergraduates in U.S. Postsecondary Institutions, 1995-96*. Washington, DC: National Center for Education Statistics.

Hossler, D., Schmit, J. and Vesper, N. (1999). *Going to College: How Social, Economic, and Educational Factors Influence the Decisions Students Make*. Baltimore: Johns Hopkins.

Immerwahr, J., and Foleno, T. (2000). *How the Public and Parents—White, African American and Hispanic —View Higher Education*. A report of the National Center for Public Policy and Higher Education, Public Agenda, the Consortium for Policy Research in Education, and the National Center for Postsecondary Improvement, May 2000. San Jose: National Center for Public Policy and Higher Education and Public Agenda.

Institute for Higher Education Policy, The. (1999). *What Is Opportunity?: Defining, Operationalizing, and Measuring the Goal of Postsecondary Educational Opportunity*. A joint report of the Institute for Higher Education Policy, the Education Resources Institute, and the Council for Opportunity in Education.

Washington, DC: Institute for Higher Education Policy.

Kane, T.J. (1999). *The Price of Admission: Rethinking How Americans Pay for College.* Washington, DC: Brookings Institution.

King, J.E. (1996). *The Decision to Go to College: Attitudes and Experiences Associated with College Atten-dance Among Low-Income Students.* A report from the College Board. Washington, DC: The College Board.

Kojaku, L., and Nunez, A. (1998). *Descriptive Summary of 1995-96 Beginning Postsecondary Students.* Washington, DC: National Center for Education Statistics.

Levine, A. (2000). Restructuring higher education to meet the demands of a new century. Twenty-second annual Pullias Address, University of Southern California, Los Angeles, July 1, 2000.

Levine, A., and Nidiffer, J. (1996). *Beating the Odds: How the Poor Get to College.* San Francisco: Jossey-Bass.

Martinez, G. and Day, J.C. (1999). School enrollment—Social and economic characteristics of students. *Current Population Reports,* P20-516. Washington, DC: U.S. Department of Commerce, Census Bureau.

Matthews, D. (1998). Transforming higher education: Implications for state higher education finance pol-icy. *Educom Review,* September/October, pp. 48-57.

McPherson, M.S. (1988). *How Can We Tell if Student Financial Aid Is Working?* A report from the College Board. Washington, DC: The College Board.

McPherson, M.S. and Schapiro, M.O. (1998). *The Student Aid Game: Meeting Need and Rewarding Talent in American Higher Education.* Princeton: Princeton University Press.

Noam, E.M. (1995). Electronics and the dim future of the university. *Science* 270: 247-249.

Paulsen, M.B. (1998). Recent research on the economics of attending college. *Research in Higher Educa-tion* 39(4):471-489.

Postsecondary Education Opportunity. (2000, July). College participation for students from low income families by state, 1992 to 1998. Pp. 1-5. Oskaloosa, IA: Mortenson Research Seminar on Public Policy Analysis of Opportunity for Postsecondary Education.

Spencer, A.C. (1999). The new politics of higher education. In J. King (ed.), *Financing a College Educa-tion: How It Works, How It's Changing.* Phoenix, AZ: American Council on Education and Oryx Press.

St. John, E.P. (1991). The impact of student financial aid: A review of recent research. *Journal of Student Financial Aid* 21(1): 18-32.

St. John, E.P. (1994a). Assessing tuition and student aid strategies: Using price-response measures to simu-late pricing alternatives. *Research in Higher Education* 35: 301-34.

St. John, E.P. (1994b). Prices, Productivity, and Investment: Assessing Financial Strategies in Higher Edu-cation. *ASHE/ERIC Higher Education Report,* No. 3. Washington, DC: The George Washington Univer-sity.

St. John, E.P., and Noell, J. (1989). The effects of student financial aid on access to higher education: An analysis of progress with special consideration of minority enrollment. *Research in Higher Education* 30: 563-81.

Stampen, J.O., and Hansen, W.L. (1999). Improving higher education access and persistence: New direc-tions from a "systems" perspective. *Educational Evaluation and Policy Analysis* 21(4): 417-426.

Tierney, W.G., and Hagedorn, L. S. (eds.). (forthcoming). *Extending their reach: Strategies for Increasing Access to College.*

Chapter 12

FINANCING PRIVATE COLLEGES AND UNIVERSITIES:
The Role of Tuition Discounting[1]

David W. Breneman, James L. Doti, and Lucie Lapovsky

INTRODUCTION

The financing of private colleges and universities, never easy, has become particularly difficult to manage and understand in recent years as fewer and fewer students actually pay the posted tuition price. This fact is of more than passing interest, for this sector of higher education relies heavily upon tuition as its most important revenue source (Tout-koushian, Chapter 1). As Table 1 shows, this reliance has grown steadily over the past twenty years, with tuition and fees accounting for 36.6 percent of total revenues in 1980-81, 40.4 percent in 1990-91, and 43.0 percent in 1995-96.

In this paper, we examine the analytics of "tuition discounting," the means by which many private institutions manage to fill their entering classes. A clear understanding of the role, and limitations, of this enrollment management technique is essential to awareness of the future of this sector of higher education. We also explore the response of "net tuition revenue" to changes in price and enrollment, and examine the differential effects of discounting among highly selective colleges and universities, and those that are less selective. We begin by discussing the growing role that institutional financial aid plays in helping private institutions recruit an entering class.

TUITION DISCOUNTING EXPLAINED

Institutional financial aid, often referred to as tuition discounting, has taken on heightened importance in higher education as it has become a critical strategic tool in enroll-

---

[1]The authors are grateful to Ann Cameron for her invaluable research assistance related to the study on which this chapter is based.

Table 1. Percentage of Current-Fund Revenue for Private Institutions, By Source

Source of Revenue	1980-81	1990-91	1995-96
Tuition and Fees	36.6	40.4	43.0
Federal Government	18.8	15.4	13.8
State Government	1.9	2.3	1.9
Local Government	0.7	0.7	0.7
Private Gifts, Grants, and Contracts	9.3	8.6	9.1
Endowment Income	5.1	5.2	5.2
Sales and Services	23.3	22.9	21.0
Other Sources	4.2	4.5	5.3

SOURCE. — Table 333, *Digest of Education Statistics, 1999.*

ment management. In the past, financial aid was largely used to make it possible for colleges and universities to matriculate students who might not otherwise have been able to afford the costs of a particular institution. In more recent years, it has been used as a merit-based incentive to recruit students who have demonstrated academic, athletic, artistic and other skills or attributes that an institution uses to mold a "desirable" student profile.

The growth of institutional aid is reflected in the results of the NACUBO *Institutional Student Aid Survey* (1993 and 1998). For the 223 colleges and universities that provided data for the 1993 and 1998 surveys, total institutional grants for full-time freshmen[2] at independent colleges and universities increased 56.4 percent between fall 1993 and fall 1998, or at an average annual compounded rate of 9.3 percent. Over the same period, these schools increased tuition and fees 27.9 percent, or at an average annual compounded rate of 5.0 percent. Hence, institutional grants increased at almost twice the rate of tuition increase.

These findings are mirrored in a larger sample surveyed by the College Board. The results reported in *Trends in Student Aid* (1999) suggest that institutional grants increased at an average annual compounded rate of 9.3 percent, the same as that indicated in the NACUBO study, while tuition and fees increased at a 5.9 percent rate.

The fact that tuition discounting is increasing at a significantly greater rate than tuition poses many challenging questions. Among them is the extent to which different tuition rates and enrollment levels affect tuition discounting. As merit-based aid has increased, what has been the effect on financial aid for students with need? And what are the characteristics of those institutions that will be able to more effectively engage in tuition discounting?

---

[2]The total amount of institutional financial aid grants awarded to full-time freshmen for the fiscal years specified on the survey. This figure does not include the institution's match for other externally funded student aid grants or transfers from the current fund to student loan funds. It does include restricted endowment grants, athletic scholarships and tuition remission.

In answering these questions, one needs data that more precisely measure the relationships between tuition discounting and tuition, enrollment and other aspects of a college or university. To generate such data, the elasticities of tuition discounting with respect to those institutional characteristics will need to be estimated.

In the analysis to follow, a graphic interpretation of the model is presented. Multiple linear regression tests of that model are then used to estimate the relevant elasticities that can be used in measuring the impact on tuition discounting resulting from changes in tuition and enrollment levels as well as changes in student selectivity.

Graphic Interpretation of the Model

As described by Breneman (1994) in his volume on liberal arts colleges, tuition discounting can be graphically illustrated as shown in Figure 1. It is postulated that demand on the part of students admitted to a particular institution, dt0, is inversely related to that institution's tuition, pt, where the subscript "t" refers to a given time period. The supply offered by each institution is assumed for simplicity to be at a desired fixed level of enrollment given by qt0. If tuition were set at pt0, the college would be able to enroll only qt1 students paying the full tuition (full-pay students).

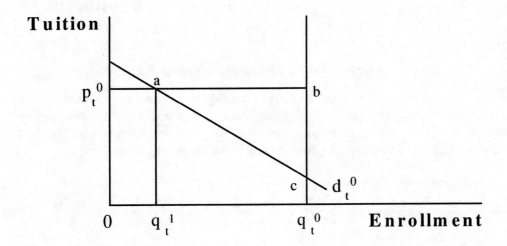

Figure 1. Tuition Discounting

In the case of perfect price discrimination, where the college is able to selectively offer discounts to admitted students not willing to pay the full tuition, scholarships and financial aid (discounts) can be offered as shown by the difference between p_t^0 and the demand curve d_t^0 beyond q_t^1. These discounts can be increased to the point where the desired enrollment q_t^0 is reached.

In that case, total discounts would be given by the area "abc" as shown in Figure 1. The discount rate is given by the ratio of total discounts "abc" to total gross revenue $(p_t^0 * q_t^0)$.

For example, as shown in figure 2, College X with a freshman admission pool of 1,000 students in fall '98 may charge tuition and fees of $16,000. In order to matriculate 500 of the 1,000 admitted students (i.e., $q_t^0 = 500$), total discounts of $3.2 million would be given. The discount rate of 0.4 would be the ratio of total discounts of $3.2 million to total revenue of $8 million ($16,000 * 500).

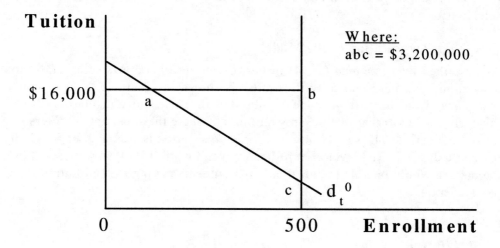

Figure 2. Tuition Discounting at College X

The above model can be used to analyze the impact of changes in tuition, enrollment and other qualitative factors on the magnitude of tuition discounting. For such an analysis, it will be necessary to measure more precisely the relevant elasticities of tuition discounting with respect to tuition, enrollment and other factors.

Data and Regression Estimates

The empirical data used in this study are derived from the NACUBO *Institutional Aid Survey for Independent Institutions* as well as data published annually by *U.S. News & World Report* in *America's Best Colleges*.

In the empirical tests to follow, TIGF is total institutional grants in dollars for entering full-time freshmen, ITF is the tuition and mandatory fee rate, FTF is the number of entering full-time freshmen, ACR is the acceptance rate for full-time freshmen and MSAT is the midpoint of the first and third quartiles of SAT scores for entering full-time freshmen, hereafter referred to as the "average SAT," with each variable relating to a given institution.

The general and specific functional forms of the regression tests are shown below where the prefix P refers to the percentage change in a particular variable from 1993 to 1998. The stochastic error terms in Equation 2 and subsequent equations have been suppressed, but are assumed to be normally distributed with standard properties. $a_1...a_4$ measure the functional relationships in a linear equation and a_0 is a constant.

(1) $PTIGF = f(PITF, PFTF, PACR, PMSAT)$, or

(2) $PTIGF = a_0 + a_1 (PITF) + a_2 (PFTF) + a_3 (PACR) + a_4 (PMSAT)$

The regression test of the above functional relationship is shown in Table 2. The high t-statistics for the estimated coefficients for the change in the tuition and mandatory fee rate (PITF) and the change in the number of entering full-time freshmen (PFTF) of 8.6 and 15.5, respectively, indicate a high degree of statistical significance for these explanatory variables. The low t-statistics for the change in the acceptance rate for full-time freshmen (PACR) and the change in the average SAT score (PMSAT) suggest there is no statistically significant relationship between these variables and tuition discounting.

Table 2. LS/Dependent Variable Is Change in Total Institutional Grants for Entering Full-time Freshmen (PTIGF)

Sample (adjusted): 1 223
Included observations: 217
Excluded observations: 6 after adjusting endpoints

Change in Variable, 1993 to 1998:	Coefficient	Std. Error	t-Statistic	Prob.
Constant	26.95340	33.46473	0.805427	0.4215
Tuition and mandatory fee rate (PITF)	2.341665	0.273562	8.559906	0.0000
Number of entering full-time freshmen (PFTF)	1.482245	0.095355	15.54454	0.0000
Acceptance rate for full-time freshmen	-0.477173	0.981059	-0.486386	0.6272
Midpoint of 1st and 3rd quartiles of SAT scores (PMSAT)	-0.841557	3.136381	-0.268321	0.7887

R-squared	0.653223	Mean dependent variable	207.7508
Adjusted R-squared	0.646680	S.D. dependent variable	452.1439
S.E. of regression	268.7575	Akaike info criterion	11.21039
Sum squared residual	15312887	Schwarz criterion	11.28827
Log likelihood	-1519.237	F-statistic	99.83610
Durbin-Watson stat	2.129636	Prob (F-statistic)	0.000000

Since the variables are in percentage change form, the estimated coefficients also represent estimated elasticities. That is, the estimated coefficient (elasticity) of 2.34 for PITF suggests that a 5 percent increase in tuition (ITF) from '93 to '98 will lead to an 11.7 percent (5 * 2.34) increase in tuition discounting (TIGF) over that same period. Similarly, the estimated coefficient of 1.48 for PFTF suggests that a 5 percent increase in freshman enrollment (FTF) will lead to a 7.4 percent (5 * 1.48) increase in tuition discounting (TIGF).

The estimated elasticities for PITF and PFTF can be used to measure the impact on net tuition revenue as a result of changes in tuition and enrollment. Figure 3 illustrates the impact of a 5 percent increase in tuition at College X while holding enrollment constant. A 5 percent increase in tuition at College X from $16,000 to $16,800 will lead to an 11.7 percent increase in tuition discounting from $3,200,000 to $3,574,400—an increase of $374,400. This compares with an increase in gross tuition revenue of $400,000 from $8,000,000 ($16,000 * 500) to $8,400,000 ($16,800 * 500). Net tuition revenue for College X would therefore increase only $25,600 ($400,000 - $374,400). As a result, a 5 percent increase in the tuition rate led to an increase of 0.5 percent ($25,600/ $4,800,000) in net tuition revenue.

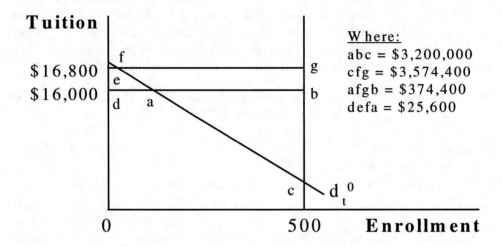

Figure 3. The Impact of a Tuition Increase on Discounting at College X

Figure 4 illustrates the impact of a 5 percent increase in enrollment at College X from 500 to 525 while holding tuition constant. As noted above, the estimated coefficient (elasticity) of 1.48 for PFTF suggests that tuition discounting will increase 7.4 percent from $3,200,000 to $3,436,800 – an increase of $236,800. This compares with an increase in gross tuition revenue of $400,000 ($16,000 * 25) and an increase in net revenue of $163,200 ($400,000 - $236,800). Hence, a 5 percent increase in freshman enrollment led to an increase in net tuition revenue of 3.4 percent ($163,200/ $4,800,000).

While the higher elasticity of discounts with respect to tuition (2.34) compared with enrollment (1.48) led to greater growth in net tuition revenue for enrollment vs. tuition changes, it should be noted that the additional enrollment will lead to greater costs, thereby having a more negative impact on an institution's net margin.

Everything else being held constant, one would expect an inverse relationship between an institution's tuition discounting and its acceptance rate. As shown in Figure 5, an increase in College X's acceptance rate should increase the pool of accepted students, thereby shifting the demand curve to the right from d_t^0 to d_t^1. Such a shift would

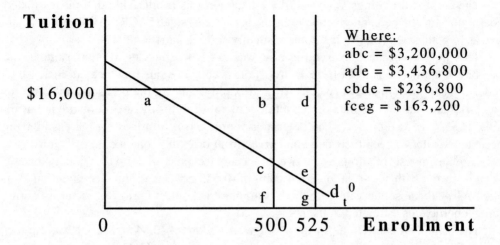

Figure 4. The Impact of an Enrollment Increase on Discounting at College X

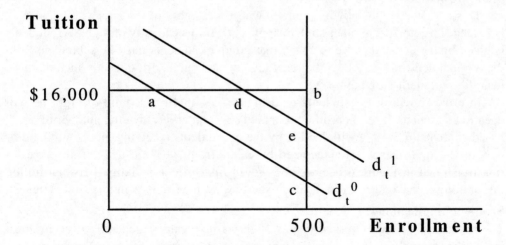

Figure 5. The Impact of a Higher Acceptance Rate on Tuition Discounting at College X

decrease tuition discounts from the area "abc" to "dbe."i

The empirical findings, however, do not support this result. Although the estimated coefficient for the percentage change in the acceptance rate (PACR) in Table 1 is negative as hypothesized (-0.48), it s not statistically significant (t = – 0.49).

This may be because everything else was not held constant. If, for example, the number of applications to College X drops, the acceptance rate may need to increase in order to keep the demand curve, d_t^0, from dropping. Indeed, there is some evidence to support that result. While data on the number of applications by institution are not available, *U.S. News* data on SATs can be used as a proxy. If institutions are increasing their acceptance rates to keep their demand curves from dropping, one would expect to see a measurable inverse relationship between acceptance rates and SATs. That is exactly what occurred with a correlation coefficient of -0.54 between acceptance rates and average SATs—the absolute value of which is among the highest for any of the cross correlation coefficients estimated in the study.

The estimated coefficient for the average SAT score of -0.84 in Table 1 was another insignificant variable with a t-statistic of -0.27. This empirical result runs counter to an intuitive expectation that a measurable relationship exists between changes in tuition discounting and SATs. One would expect that institutions that increase their average SATs over time also increase their tuition discounting to attract those students.

This would not be the case, however, if institutions that increase merit-based aid do so at the expense of financial aid for needy students. Since the NACUBO data do not distinguish between merit-based and need-based aid, the lack of a significant empirical relationship between total discounting and average SATs indicates that substitution is occurring between the two types of aid.

This is shown graphically in Figure 6, where a category of students with high SATs is treated separately from other student applicants. If this category of high SAT students is given by the demand curve d_t^2, then that group of students must be subtracted from the original demand curve d_t^0. The resulting demand curve, d_t^1, does not include those identified for merit-based aid.

In order to recruit q_t^* students with high SATs, merit-based aid of "fgp_t^0h" will need to be granted. If total enrollment is held constant at q_t^0, then the number of need-based students ($q_t^0 - q_t^1$) will decline by the q_t^* students receiving merit-based aid or $(q_t^0 - q_t^1) - (q_t^*)$. This will reduce need-based aid from "abc" to "aed". If the substitution illustrated in Figure 6 occurs, one would find little association between tuition discounting and average SATs. That is exactly what the findings in this study suggest.

Strategic Implications

The robustness of the empirical results suggests they can be generally used by most institutions to analyze the implications of various changes in tuition and enrollment on the level and rate of tuition discounting.

In the case of College X, for example, it had a tuition discount rate of 0.4, which was about one standard deviation above the average discount rate of 0.3 for all schools included in the 1998 NACUBO sample. Given that the empirical results show that the estimated elasticities are about the same at institutions with high and low discount rates, the impact of a tuition change on the discount rate at College X using the elasticities shown in Table 2 can be examined.

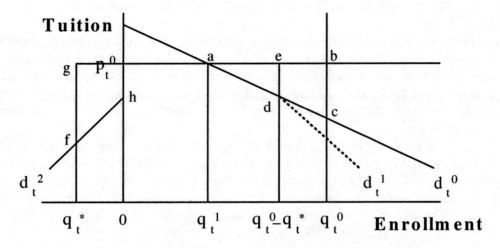

Figure 6. Substituting Need-based Aid with Merit-based Aid

Recall in Figure 2 that College X had in period t tuition of $16,000 and enrollment of 500 with tuition discounting of $3,200,000 and a tuition discount rate of 0.4 ($3,200,000/ $8,000,000). When tuition increased 5 percent in Figure 3, the estimated elasticity of tuition discounting with respect to tuition and fees of 2.34 suggested that tuition discounts would increase from $3,200,000 to $3,574,400. This, in turn, suggests that the discount rate for College X would increase from 0.4 ($3,200,000/ $8,000,000) to 0.425 ($3,574,400/$8,400,000)—an increase of 0.025 or 2.5 percent in the discount rate.

This result can be compared with a "low" discount rate institution, College Y, whose discount rate of 0.2 is about one standard deviation below the average of 0.3 for all colleges and universities. If College Y, like College X, increases its tuition 5 percent from $16,000 to $16,800, it too will be subject to the same tuition discount elasticity of 2.34.

As a result, its tuition discounts will increase, as shown in Figure 7, 11.7 percent

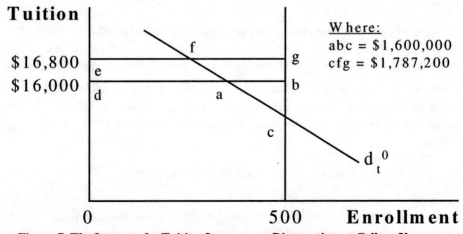

Figure 7. The Impact of a Tuition Increase on Discounting at College Y

from \$1,600,000 to \$1,787,200. Its discount rate will therefore increase from 0.2 (\$1,600,000/\$8,000,000) to 0.212 (\$1,787,200/\$8,400,000)—an increase of 0.012 or 1.2 percent.

In the case of an enrollment increase, recall that Figure 4 illustrated the impact of a 5 percent increase in enrollment at College X from 500 to 525. Since the estimated elasticity of tuition discounting with respect to enrollment is 1.48, tuition discounts increased from \$3,200,000 to \$3,436,800. The discount rate, therefore, increased from 0.4 (\$3,200,000 /\$8,000,000) to 0.409 \$3,436,800/\$8,400,000)—an increase of 0.009 or about 1 percent.

Figure 8 shows the impact of that same 5 percent increase in enrollment on College Y, whose tuition discount rate is at a lower 0.2. Assuming that the elasticity of tuition discounting with respect to enrollment for College Y is the same as that of College X (1.48), then the enrollment increase will lead to an increase in discounts of 7.4 percent from \$1,600,000 to \$1,718,400 and the discount rate from 0.2 (\$1,600,000/\$8,000,000) to 0.205 (\$1,718,400/ \$8,400,000)—an increase of a half of one percent.

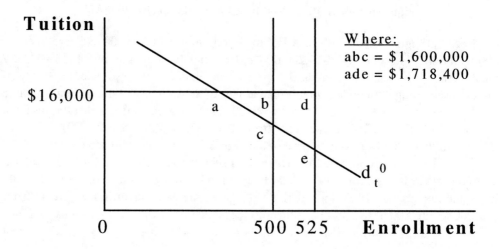

Figure 8. The Impact of an Enrollment Increase on Discounting at College Y

These results suggest that for those institutions with higher tuition discount rates, holding everything else constant, either a tuition or an enrollment increase (decrease) will result in larger increases (decreases) in the discount rate than it will for low discount rate schools.

RECENT TRENDS IN DISCOUNTING

The theoretical model presented in this study and empirical results that test it help answer a number of critical questions relating to the impact of tuition rates and enrollment levels on tuition discounting. But we have also been questioning where the higher education industry is moving in terms of its pricing and financial aid strategies. Is tuition going to continue to increase? Are schools going to continue their practice of providing scholarships to significant numbers of students? Will the published price continue to lose meaning and if "yes," what will the consequence of this be? What impact do pricing and discounting strategies have on access to higher education?

There now exist ten years of tuition, financial aid and enrollment data from a large sample of independent institutions. The data show that on average, and for an overwhelming majority of the individual institutions, decisions have been made to increase financial aid faster than stated tuition rates, resulting in real revenue (net tuition) growth which has been decidedly lackluster if not, in many instances, negative. In fall 1999 the average discount rate across participating institutions was 37 percent. Interestingly however, the pace of growth in the rate of tuition discounting was clearly reduced this year at all institutions, not just the "best" institutions. The "best" institutions, for purposes of this analysis are defined as the top national liberal arts colleges and the top private universities according to *U.S. News and World Report.* The data also suggest that more institutions are becoming more financially effective in their use of discounting and thus have been able to combine tuition and aid increases with increases in enrollment so that net revenue increases.

While need unmet by federal and state aid has driven much of the increase in institutional financial aid over the past ten years, a recent and, we believe, increasingly pervasive, trend has been the addition or substitution of merit- or characteristic-based aid to enhance the marketing of high-priced educational services to the price-sensitive middle-class and affluent families. At the heart of this issue is, quite simply, the confluence of each institution's need for a robust revenue stream to pay for the things that keep their institution competitive, and families' willingness or in many cases unwillingness to pay the published price. The core of the strategy is to provide incentives to those desirable students who are able to pay, according to the traditional need-based aid formulas, but are unwilling to pay the sticker price to attend the institution.

To the extent that the merit aid or characteristic-based aid strategy has been substitutive and not incremental, this enrollment management approach has reduced educational access to the economically disadvantaged (Hearn, Chapter 11) while providing financial subsidies to those with the ability to pay and has reduced resources available for educational programming.

Many of us believe that the continuing increase in tuition discounting is in part a response to the increased use of it and the increased consumer understanding of it. In addition, discounting continues to grow, in part as a logical consequence of the increasingly fierce competition for academically stellar students, and in part as a reflection of the increased quality and competition for these students from public institutions, particularly the flagship universities. But discounting also increases as a result of the commodity-like marketing presentation and comparison of educational services through rankings and lists, in combination with an increasing consumer mentality focusing on convenience, service, quality and cost. Certainly, whatever the driving forces underlying this shift towards characteristic-based aid, the strategy of using aid to attract and retain the unwilling to pay, will feed upon itself. Because this approach goes beyond more objectively measured need (however flawed and flexible the federal and institutional methodologies may be for determining family contribution) into the discretionary application of funds, characteristic-based aid can, and predictably will, be much more subject to escalation in response to the vicissitudes of competition and strategic response.

Discounting is also clearly no longer the strategy for private institutions only. More and more public institutions are offering high quality honors programs and many are now offering scholarships to these students; they too are discounting! Furthermore, studies have indicated that the average income of the students and their families at many of the public institutions now exceeds the income of those attending independent colleges and universities. This points to an increasing economic stratification of the education industry.

Fewer and fewer students are paying the published tuition price.

Enrollment continues to grow at independent institutions in the United States and the number of students who are receiving institutional financial aid continues to grow significantly at all institutions except the "best." In fall 1990, 63.7 percent of the students received institutional financial aid compared with 79.4 percent in fall 1999 (see Table 3). Reviewing the data by type of institution indicates that at the best institutions, less than 50 percent of the students received institutional grants in 1999. The growth in institutional grant aid to students at the best institutions has been much less than at the "other" private institutions.

Table 3. Percent of Freshmen Receiving Institutional Grants: 1990-1999

Percent of Freshmen on Grants	1990	1993	1996	1999
"Best" LA Institution	44.5%	48.3%	52.7%	49.3%
"Best" University	38.9%	41.2%	44.3%	46.2%
Other Institutions	66.8%	74.1%	80.1%	83.8%
All Institutions	63.7%	70.6%	76.3%	79.4%

Looking further at this data, one finds that the percentage of students who receive no institutional financial aid decreased significantly between 1990 and 1999. Table 4 below shows the percent of freshmen aided at the independent institutions grouped by institutions. In 1990, 5.1 percent of the institutions aided less than 30 percent of the freshmen who enrolled and 28.4 percent of the institutions aided more than 80 percent of their freshmen. By comparison, in 1999 less than one percent of the institutions aided fewer than 30 percent of their freshmen and more than 60 percent of the institutions aided more than 80 percent of their freshmen.

Institutional aid used to be granted primarily to students to enhance access to higher education for those without the financial resources to attend and this is still true to a large extent at the "best" institutions. Today, most institutions are providing institutional grants to shape their classes. Today many, if not most, institutions employ financial aid as a necessary tool to recruit and retain students.

Table 4. Frequency Distribution of Percent of Freshmen Receiving Institutional Grants

Percent of Freshmen Aided	Percent of Independent Institutions		
	1990	**1995**	**1999**
0-30%	5.1%	1.5%	0.7%
30.1-40%	12.0%	6.5%	3.6%
40.1-50%	14.5%	7.6%	8.7%
50.1-60%	12.0%	9.5%	6.5%
60.1-70%	11.6%	7.6%	7.6%
70.1-80%	16.4%	17.8%	12.0%
80.1-90%	14.2%	27.3%	17.5%
90.1%+	14.2%	22.2%	43.3%

The average grant has been relatively stable across the last decade.

A second critical component of how financial aid is operating is the average size of the financial aid award. Table 5 below indicates that for those freshmen who receive institutional aid, their grant as a percent of tuition at all the institutions has increased from 45.2 percent of tuition in 1990 to 48.1 percent in 1999. This represents an increase of only 6.5 percent over this ten-year period and an increase of less than a half of a percent over 1998. Thus, while aid has become much more widely dispersed across an entering class, the average award as a percent of tuition has not changed significantly. The data also indicate that the average award at the "best" institutions is significantly larger as a percent of tuition than at the "other" institutions. At the "best" liberal arts institutions, the average institutional grant exceeds 60 percent of tuition compared with less than 50 percent of tuition at the "other" institutions.

Table 5. Institutional Grants to Freshmen as a Percent of Tuition: 1990-1999

Freshmen Grants as Percent of Tuition	1990	1993	1996	1999
"Best" LA Institution	65.2%	62.5%	61.5%	64.4%
"Best" University	56.3%	58.3%	58.1%	58.5%
Other Institutions	42.8%	43.9%	44.9%	46.1%
All Institutions	45.2%	46.1%	46.8%	48.1%

What is happening to gross and net tuition?

Between 1990 and 1999, the published tuition price at the independent colleges in this data base has increased from $9,838 to $16,493, an increase of 67.6 percent (see Table 6 below). In 1999, there was only one institution among the survey respondents which decreased tuition from the 1998 level and one institution which did not increase its tuition; this is in marked contrast to the previous year when six institutions decreased tuition and 13 institutions held their tuition constant at the 1997 level. There were only five institutions which increased their tuition more than 10 percent this year compared with 12 last year. The average increase in 1999, across all schools, was 4.6 percent compared with 4.0 percent at the "best" institutions.

Table 6. Tuition and Tuition Increases

	Net Tuition Rates and Percent Increase			
	1990	*1999*	*Percent increase 1990-1999*	*Percent increase 1998-1999*
"Best" LA Institution	$14,329	$23,008	60.6%	4.0%
"Best" University	$14,518	$23,603	62.6%	4.0%
Other Institutions	$9,178	$15,258	69.2%	4.6%
All Institutions	$9,838	$16,493	67.6%	4.6%

Table 7. Tuition Rates and Percent Increases

	Net Tuition Rates and Percent Increase			
	1990	*1999*	*Percent increase 1990-1999*	*Percent increase 1998-1999*
"Best" LA Institution	$10,240	$15,789	54.2%	4.2%
"Best" University	$11,435	$17,395	52.1%	2.5%
Other Institutions	$6,608	$9,476	43.4%	4.1%
All Institutions	$7,121	$10,335	45.1%	4.0%

A comparison of Tables 6 and 7 shows that the increase in net tuition per student at the "best" institutions has lagged only slightly behind the increase in tuition over this ten-year period while the increase in net tuition at the other institutions has increased 43 percent compared with an increase of 69 percent in tuition. Net tuition has grown from $7,121 in 1990 to $10,335 in 1999 at all institutions while at the "best" institutions, net tuition now exceeds $15,000. Between 1998 and 1999, net tuition and tuition increased at about the same rate at all types of institutions except the "best" universities. This is a clear indicator that institutions are getting much better at strategically discounting in order to accomplish their enrollment and revenue goals.

Notwithstanding improvements in rates of growth of financial aid, the fundamental conclusion from the survey data remains that less and less of the stated price of attending a college or university is ultimately reflected in real revenue available to institutions to support educational services. In 1990, the average net tuition of $7,121 was 75.9 percent of the average gross tuition rate of $9,838. By 1999, the average net tuition rate of $10,335 was a significantly lower 62.7 percent of the gross rate.

Discussing the average changes at institutions masks the significant differences that individual institutions are experiencing. For example, between 1998 and 1999, 27 percent of the institutions experienced decreases in their net tuition per student; a year earlier, only 25 percent of the institutions experienced decreases in net tuition per student. These rates are, however, a real improvement over the experience in institutions earlier in this decade where, between 1990 and 1991, 35 percent of the institutions experienced a decrease in net freshman revenue. Among the institutions with decreases in net tuition per student in 1999, more than a third experienced decreases of more than five percent. On the other hand, 16 percent of the institutions experienced increases in net tuition per student of more than 10 percent.

Relationship between changes in tuition, net tuition and freshman enrollment—1998-1999

Between 1998 and 1999, freshman enrollment increased 2.7 percent overall at the 348 independent institutions in this data base while gross tuition rates increased 4.7 percent and net tuition increased 4.1 percent (see Table 8). The gap between the increase in tuition and net tuition has been narrowing in recent years; this indicates that as institutions increase tuition, financial aid has been increased only slightly more than the increase in tuition. In earlier years, more of the increase in tuition was being offset by even larger increases in institutional financial aid.

Table 8. Comparison of Tuition, Net Tuition and Freshmen Enrollment: 1998-1999

	1998	*1999*	*Percent Change*
Freshmen Enrollment	494	507	2.7%
Tuition	$15,283	$15,995	4.7%
Net tuition	$9,485	$9,871	4.1%

Among these institutions, freshmen enrollment increased at 193 institutions (55%), tuition increased at 346 institutions (99%) and net tuition increased at 275 institutions (75%). In addition, net freshman revenue increased at 255 institutions (73%).

Tuition Discount Rate at the Independent Institutions

The tuition discount rate in this study is defined as the institutional financial aid dollars divided by the gross tuition and fee revenue. The discount rate may also be calculated by multiplying the percent of students receiving institutional financial aid by the average grant awarded as a percent of tuition. Both methods lead to the same result. The percent of students receiving aid has increased by 28.9 percent between 1990 and 1999 while the average grant as a percent of tuition has increased 6.3 percent over this same period. Clearly, both variables contribute to the increasing discount rate displayed below in Table 9.

Table 9. Tuition Discount: 1990-1999

Tuition Discount for Freshmen	*1990*	*1993*	*1996*	*1999*
"Best" LA Institution	29.0%	30.2%	31.5%	31.6%
"Best" University	21.0%	23.3%	24.6%	26.3%
Other Institutions	28.0%	32.0%	34.8%	38.4%
All Institutions	27.7%	31.5%	34.0%	37.3%

Overall, the discount rate is 37.3 percent in 1999 compared with 27.7 percent in 1990. The discount rates at all but the best universities are comparable in 1990 while in 1999, the discount rates at the "best" institutions are significantly lower than the discount rate at the "other" institutions. The discount rate at all the institutions has increased 35 percent between 1990 and 1999 while the discount at the "best" liberal arts institutions has increased 8.9 percent. The discount rate at the "best" universities has increased 25.2 percent over this period but is still less than the average discount rate of all institutions in 1990.

The relationship between the endowment and the discount rate

It has often been assumed that there is a positive correlation between a college's endowment and its ability to provide financial aid. Table 10 demonstrates that there is no significant relationship between endowment size and the tuition discount. While there is a slight shift to higher levels of tuition discounting as endowment values decline, the difference between the $1+ billion endowments schools and the less than $50 million endowment schools is only 6.2 percent—much less than the relative difference in their institutional wealth. Further, there are wide ranges in discounting levels in each tier of endowment making the averages for each tier less indicative of individual experience.

Table 10. Comparison of Endowment and Freshmen Tuition Discount

Endowment Size	Freshman Discount Rate	Number of Institutions
$1 billion+	31.8%	13
$500m - $999m	33.7%	19
$250m - $499m	35.1%	24
$100m - $249m	37.6%	54
$50m - $99m	41.4%	50
0 - $49m	38.0%	188

More simply, relative institutional wealth or poverty does not sharply affect the level of financial aid. Institutional aid is an enrollment management tool. The granting of aid to a significant percent of the class is a necessary tool to fill the class with the number and quality of students that are necessary. Most institutions today are unable to enroll an adequate number of qualified students at their published price. We must continue to ask if we are on a pricing merry-go-round or is the pricing strategy being employed a rational method for most appropriately attracting the best mix of students to each institution?

Historically, the wealthiest colleges and universities in the country espoused "need blind" admissions policies and promised to meet the full need of all accepted applicants. "Need blind" admissions policies meant that a students' ability to pay was not considered in the admissions process. Today at many institutions the new term is "need aware" meaning that an applicant's financial need is a consideration in the admissions process. Meeting full need meant that an institution would provide all aid that one of the accepted formulas for calculating need stated was required by that student to attend the institution. Today, most institutions engage in what is called "strategic packaging." This means that an institution will consider both the financial need of the student and the attractiveness of that student to the institution in meeting its enrollment goals in developing the package of aid which will be offered to that student. Students with similar financial need but different academic or other characteristics are likely to get different aid packages; the student who is more desirable to that institution will be awarded significantly more grant aid than the other student who may be offered much more of his package as a loan. Some institutions take the concept of strategic packaging beyond a sorting for academic credentials to attempt to explicitly measure willingness to pay and to adjust aid up or down on the basis of probability of enrollment.

SUMMARY

These findings from the ten years of tuition, financial aid and enrollment data are also supported by the theoretical model and empirical tests presented earlier in this study. In summary, those findings include the following:

- Increases in tuition and enrollment lead to greater increases in institutional aid.
- On average, increases in institutional aid offset most of the revenue gains resulting from increases in tuition and enrollment.
- Colleges that increase their acceptance rates, in general, do so not to reduce institutional aid but to keep application pools from falling.
- Merit-based aid is growing at the expense of need-based aid.
- Increases in tuition and enrollment lead to even higher aid rates for those colleges that already have relatively high aid rates.

Charging a higher tuition by offering less institutional aid to higher income families or to less "desirable students" may work in the short run, when a prospective student has few alternatives. In the longer run, however, our empirical results suggest colleges are luring full-pay students away from other schools by increasing the level of institutional aid offered to them. This competitive response to external market forces results in colleges giving ever-higher levels and rates of institutional aid to attract more students. Our empirical findings suggest that this longer-run competitive impact is now in high gear.

THE DATA

The data for this paper come from the NACUBO tuition discounting surveys of independent institutions. The surveys are sent to all four-year accredited independent institutions. Responses were received from more than 350 independent institutions. There are complete data for 1998 and 1999 from 349 institutions; while there are ten years of data from 276 institutions. The institutions have been divided into three categories for purposes of analysis in this paper:

"best" liberal arts colleges which represent those 40 institutions identified by *U.S. News and World Report* as the best national liberal arts college. Data is included here from 24 of those institutions

"best" private universities come from *U.S. News and World Report*'s 50 "best" national universities. Among the best universities, 33 are private and 17 are public. The data base includes 13 of the 33 private universities.

"other" colleges and universities include the other institutions in the NACUBO base which are not considered "best" as defined above.

References

Banziger, G., Wagner, A.M., and Watts, T. (1997). On the road to ratios. *Business Offi*cer. National Association of College and University Business Officers (NACUBO): From the NACUBO website (www.nacubo.org).

Behind the Price Tag – Explaining the Intricacies of College Cost, Price, Subsidy, and Affordability (1998). Washington, DC: National Association of Independent Colleges and Universities (NAICU).

Breneman, D.W. (1994). *Liberal Arts Colleges: Thriving, Surviving, or Endangered?* Washington, D.C., The Brookings Institution.

Breneman, D.W. (1996). Affordability and the private institution. *The Educational Record* 77:4.

Breneman, D.W. (1993). Student Aid: Price Discount or Educational Investment? *The College Board Review* 167.

Breneman, D., Lapovsky, L., and Meyers, D. (1999). Private college pricing: are current policies sustainable? Paper presented at Futures Forum 1999: Exploring the Future of Higher Education. Yale University.

Carnegie Commission on Higher Education. (1973). *Higher Education: Who Pays? Who Benefits? Who Should Pay?* New York, NY: McGraw-Hill.

Davis, J.S. (1997). *College Affordability – A Closer Look at the Crisis.* Washington, DC: Sallie Mae Education Institute.

Digest of Education Statistics. (1998). Washington, DC: Government Printing Office.

Doti, J.L. (1998). 'Discounts' Make Colleges Much More Affordable for Low-Income Students. *Chronicle of Higher Education,* February 6: B7.

Hanushek, E.A. (1986). The economics of schooling: production and efficiency in public schools. *Journal of Economic Literature,* 24 September: 1141-1177.

Heller, D. (1997). Student price response in higher education. *Journal of Higher Education* (November/ December.

Institutional Aid Survey. (1993 and 1998). Washington, DC: *National Association of College and University Business Officers (NACUBO.*

Lapovsky, L. (1998). Wisdom needed: NACUBO's institutional student aid survey provides pricing data. *NACUBO Business Officer,* February: 17-24.

Lenth, C.S. (1993). *The Tuition Dilemma—State Policies and Practices in Pricing Public Higher Education.* Denver, Co: State Higher Education Executive Officers (SHEEO).

McPherson, M.S., and Schapiro, M. (1998). *The Student Aid Game.* Princeton, NJ: Princeton University Press.

McPherson, M.S., and Winston, G.C. (1993). The economics of cost, price, and quality in U.S. higher education. In M.S. McPherson, M. Schapiro, and G.C. Winston (eds.), *Paying the Piper: Productivity, Incentives, and Financing in U.S. Higher Education.* Ann Arbor, MI: The University of Michigan Press.

National Commission on the Cost of Higher Education. (1998). *Straight Talk About College Costs & Prices.* Phoenix, AZ: Oryx Press.

Trends in Student Aid: 1986 to 1996. (1996). Washington, DC: The College Board.

Trends in College Pricing. (1999). Washington, DC: The College Board.

Trends in Student Aid. (1999). Washington, DC: The College Board.

The Tuition Puzzle: Putting the Pieces Together. (1999). Report prepared for the New Millennium Project on Higher Education Cost, Pricing, and Productivity. Washington, DC: The Institute for Higher Education Policy.

U.S. News & World Report: America's Best Colleges. (1995 and 2000). Washington, D.C.: U.S. News and World Report.

Yanikoski, R.A., and Wilson, R.F. (1984). Differential pricing of undergraduate education. *Journal of Higher Education* 55(6) (November/December): 735-50.

Zemsky, R. (ed.) (1999). *Policy Perspectives* 8(4) April.

Chapter 13

FINANCING COMMUNITY COLLEGES FOR A NEW CENTURY[1]

Richard A. Voorhees

INTRODUCTION

At the beginning of the new century, the nation's public two-year colleges stand at the financial crossroads. On one hand, the need for the services and education they provide in a rapidly changing local, regional, national and international environment continues to accelerate. On the other hand, community colleges now draw less of their total operating revenues from taxpayers than at any other time in their histories. If these recent trends are harbingers, the finance of community colleges will become even more critical and problematic in the foreseeable future. The Center for Higher Education and Educational Finance at Illinois State University reports that states increased their appropriations for operating expenses to public institutions by 13.3 percent from 1996-97 to 1998-99 (Palmer and Hines, 2000). During this same time, total community college appropriations from state and local sources combined increased by only 12.5 percent. While at first blush this difference may seem insignificant, a matter of great concern within this pattern of funding is the failure of local tax revenues to keep pace with state allocation levels. Local tax appropriations for community colleges grew only 7.1 percent during this same period. For community colleges this is more than unsettling because these recent statistics do not represent an aberration; rather, they are the result of a twenty-year trend in shifting public responsibility for all of public higher education, a long slide which, if left unchecked, will radically impact the entire community college sector.[2]

The present analysis of financial trends affecting community colleges begins by comparing expenditures and revenues across sectors. While these gross comparisons are

---

[1]The author is grateful to Richard Allen, Pikes Peak Community College; Robert Toutkoushian, University System of New Hampshire; and James Hearn, University of Minnesota, for their comments on earlier versions of this paper. All opinions expressed herein, however, are solely those of the author.

[2]This chapter focuses on the degree-granting public two-year college and its finances. The other filter employed with respect to the NCES data presented is institutional participation in Title IV, federal financial aid programs. Throughout this work, the term "public two-year college" and "community college" are used interchangeably. Private two-year institutions receive almost no attention in this chapter. Although there are about half as many private two-year institutions as public two-year institutions (n=415 v. n=1,047) they account for less than two percent of nationwide enrollments (NCES, 1999a). In 1995-96, they accounted for two percent of total current-fund expenditures. Public technical colleges are not referred to separately.

useful, they also are somewhat limited because they cannot account for differences in mission and scope between the two-year and four-year sectors, especially since available data, including those data published by the federal government, are not reported in ways that permit exploration of expenditure and revenue differences for lower-division institutional activity. Even given the uneven nature of these data, the differences are remarkable. The most recent data indicate that current fund expenditures per full-time equivalent student at public two-year institutions are only 35 percent of the expenditures per full-time equivalent student at public four-year institutions (National Center for Education Statistics [NCES], 1999a, Table 335). Stated in other words, by the middle of the 1990s the nation's community colleges enrolled 48 percent of all students in public higher education but received only 37 percent of total higher education appropriations (NCES, 1997).[3]   It is ironic that these multifaceted institutions, established to provide access to instruction and services that other sectors of higher education were either unable or unwilling to provide, do not fare more equitably in the competition for public support for higher education.

No other sector in American higher education depends on state and local revenues as much as community colleges. At the same time, the mission of the community college, built in concert with the communities they serve, has resulted in the adoption of many activities and roles not found in other sectors of higher education. A frequent criticism of community colleges is that they attempt to be all things to all people while doing nothing particularly well (see, for example, Dougherty, 1994). Common sense alone would dictate that it is difficult to do many things well. The world is changing, raising expectations for higher education to respond in new ways. Given the financial prospects for community colleges, it will be difficult to deliver the existing menu of services let alone addressing new demands.

This chapter does not intend to dismiss, or even deflect, traditional criticism of the community college. Rather, the intention here is to point out how the mission of the community college, and the evolving roles it must now assume, make it especially vulnerable to reduced public financial support. Because of its ability to respond quickly to new educational demands and its longstanding history of identifying and responding to those demands, the community college will continue to face multiple challenges. The extent to which new public resources can be identified and marshaled to support new and exiting activities in the public interest poses challenges for community college leaders, public officials, and state legislators.

The enrollment growth experienced by community colleges in the 1960s and 1970s was unprecedented in the history of higher education. Community colleges have created a track record of success which other countries have tried to emulate. However, as the 1990s unfolded, the public perception of higher education as isolated and unaccountable institutions gained ascendancy and, despite their origins as "people's colleges," and their deep ties to the communities they serve, community colleges were swept up in this

---

[3]The revenue comparison offered here is based on *total* appropriations, inclusive of federal and state research outlays at four-year institutions. Because it is not based solely on enrollment, this comparison cannot fully account for differences in institutional mission. Even so, the differences in expenditures are a function of available revenue and represent a conspicuous gap.

perception. Apparently, historical ties to local communities count for little in state environments where those legislators who helped establish community colleges in the 1960s are no longer active. The first generations of community college leaders also are retiring, taking with them institutional memories and leaving perhaps the greatest challenge to community colleges just ahead.

A MULTIPLICITY OF ROLES

Richardson and Leslie (1980) traced six roles for the community college: (1) academic transfer programs, (2) vocational-technical education, (3) developmental/remedial programs, (4) continuing education, (5) community service, and (6) assessment, skill training, and placement. These roles still have relevance two decades later, although a rapidly expanding economy and technological advances have caused the addition of one new function to this list, *distance education*, and the relabeling of "assessment, skill training, and placement" as *workforce development*.[4] Collectively, these functions represent useful frameworks for examining community college finance but do not, by themselves, account for the commitments to open access and opportunity that underscore and animate the community college mission. Not only have community colleges admitted "all comers," they also have ensured physical access by maintaining their operations on weekends, evenings, and early mornings, in addition to a "traditional" daytime schedule. The 168-hour week, 52-week schedule continues to gain ground in community colleges as the distinctions between academic terms and even academic years are blurred. This entrepreneurial spirit underlies the community college's commitment to accessibility and is evidenced across each of its multiple roles.

Academic Transfer Programs
This function is the legacy of the junior college model that guided the establishment and organization of the first two-year colleges. Programs in this area are designed to be the academic equivalent of the freshman and sophomore year at four-year colleges and universities. It is here that community colleges are perhaps the most efficient from an expenditure perspective. For example, the cost of a unit of instruction in sociology taught at a community college should not exceed the cost of a unit of sociology taught at a four-year college or university. Given the community college's lower overall faculty pay scales, its greater reliance on part-time faculty, and the differences in part-time and full-time faculty pay scales, the community college course should be less expensive to offer. Such between-sector differences in cost per instructional unit may be offset, however, by a lower average class size in the community college and the use of teaching assistants to teach lower-division courses at many four-year institutions. Instructional costs in the academic transfer area have been essentially stable as a proportion of total budgets since Breneman and Nelson (1981) reported only

---

[4]Workforce development might have been subsumed under the older, more narrow, label; however, it has taken on a larger meaning in today's economy, especially as it represents the efforts of colleges to respond directly to organized federal government efforts to link employment-specific skills with labor market demand.

small differences in public support for lower-division students between the two-year and four-year sectors.[5]

Vocational-technical Education

These programs are designed to provide students with skills which are in demand in the labor market, not necessarily to prepare students for transfer or pursuit of a baccalaureate degree. This distinction, too, is changing as rapid developments in the workplace call for workers who can identify, solve, and broker problems through technology. Acquisitions of these skills obviously do not end with certification programs, at the associate degree level or even at the baccalaureate degree level. Richardson and Leslie (1980) point out that when vocational programs were introduced in community colleges they were almost always accompanied by only incremental funding, based on the cost of providing academic programs, and not on the "true" cost of providing vocational programs. On average, costs in vocational programs are higher than in academic programs because they are linked to more intensive faculty contact and, especially in health and technology-based programs, the need for expensive instructional equipment. A deeper understanding of this important distinction among funding agencies is essential to protect the community college from greater vulnerability to inadequate public financial support in the years ahead.

Developmental/remedial Programs

Developmental/remedial education is an incendiary issue across higher education. NCES reports that 41 percent of all freshmen at community colleges were enrolled in remedial reading, writing, or mathematics in the fall of 1995 (NCES, 1999). Indications are that this proportion will rise in tandem with the declining secondary school completion rates. Although the raw numbers of high school graduates are expected to increase, the survival rate between the freshman year and senior year is decreasing for entering cohorts, resulting in the potential for more younger students to require remediation if and when they enroll in community colleges. Community college educators also express concern about the preparation of those who complete secondary schools and their increasing demand for remediation.

The number of students requiring English as a Second Language training will increase, adding to the cost of total support for remedial services. Because practitioners have linked low student-faculty ratios with student success, the cost of remedial and ESL education is higher than other instructional areas. Remedial and ESL populations also require increasing support from institutions beyond intensive instruction, including counseling, child care, and other assistive institutional activities that likely will add to total costs. A recent survey conducted by the Education Commission of the States (ECS, 2000) indicates that nearly three-quarters of the states do not support remediation with

[5]Estimating the instructional costs per unit of lower-division academic credits at both two-year and four-year institutions has long been a very important, but also very complex and problematic task. For a thorough treatment of the subject—including issues such as the joint production of instruction and either research or service; the relation of public subsidies, instructional expenditures and instructional quality; and questions of intersectoral equity in funding—see Breneman and Nelson's (1981) study, especially chapter three.

separate funding mechanisms. This appears particularly shortsighted because the continuation of current directions in U.S. immigration policy and in economic development throughout the rest of the world, particularly Latin America, will yield a continued influx of non-English speakers. Both trends signal substantial needs for funding to cover accompanying costs of meeting expanding educational needs at the community college.

Continuing Education

Richardson and Leslie included credit instruction offered at times or locations or through delivery systems that differ from the traditional academic or vocational programs in this function. To their definition we add non-credit classes that are chiefly funded by students who enroll in them and do not receive direct taxpayer support. Included here are classes that are recreational in nature and usually of insufficient duration to qualify as either academic or vocational course work. Continuing education activities are commonly thought of as community service in other sectors of higher education, and both terms are combined in this chapter. Community service activities, however, are more internalized at community colleges where closer community ties, born out of local funding models and practices, have created a history of providing facilities and expertise to address community demands. Here, one might find debates for a local or regional election, provision of office space for community groups, and economic development outreach. Most states specifically exclude non-credit courses and activities from state reimbursement, a fact that places pressure on community colleges to offer credit for programs and activities that many might otherwise consider as community service activities. Inasmuch as the distinctions between community service and continuing education may be blurred, one difference is that the cost of continuing education as an activity can be readily described and analyzed. Community service, on the other hand, can consist of a multitude of activities which defy easy description and cost analyses.

Workforce Development

Community colleges have been at the forefront of providing education for the new knowledge society. The pace of economic change at the beginning of this new century is driven by global competition and worldwide flows of information that place a high premium on high skills training. A changing workplace results in a growing number of students with bachelors and other degrees who choose to come back to the community college for specific skill training. Businesses and industries also recognize these changes and are prime consumers for ever more frequent and sophisticated training and retraining of their employees. This connection is drawn tighter by the traditional practice of community colleges in creating formal advisory councils of employers and other experts for individual instructional programs to provide curriculum oversight and to assist program graduates to find jobs.

Most community colleges rely heavily on dollars flowing from the Carl D. Perkins Vocational and Technical Education Act to subsidize their role in workforce development. The Workforce Investment Act of 1998 also has created expectations for community colleges to play a central role in formalized agreements with local One-Stop

Centers to provide assessment and training. The required connections between community colleges that receive Perkins funding and their obligation to provide services to One-Stops is congruent with the historic role of community colleges in training employees for local employers. The revenues generated from enrollments of students from One-Stops will not be substantial for most community colleges, however, since training and education are the last of three mandated services provided to participants.[6]

Distance Education

A recent report by the National Center for Education Statistics (NCES, 1999a) indicates that in 1997-98 public two-year institutions were more likely to offer distance education courses than either public four-year institutions or private institutions at either level. The number of undergraduates enrolled in college-level, credit-granting distance education courses was much greater at public two-year institutions (n=690,700) than at public four-year institutions (n=289,520) (NCES, 1999, p. 16). Most distance education offerings at community colleges are in the form of courses and not degree programs; only 13 percent of those community colleges offering distance education courses had established degree programs by 1997-98, suggesting that considerable activity, and expanded needs for public financial support to cover the attendant costs of such activities, are likely as institutions gear up to capture this market.

The accelerated interest in distance education has resulted in heavy investments by community colleges in new tools including Internet servers, interactive software, and technology infrastructures. Courses and programs already developed by others provide for economies through larger course sizes, increased faculty course loads, or hiring lower wage discussants/facilitators to accompany the video lectures of higher-salaried, more senior faculty. On the other hand, courses delivered through technology can incur large developmental costs and require the installation and maintenance of expensive electronic equipment and infrastructure. The reality is that whenever new costs arise, the inclination is to pass them onto students. The NCES survey indicates, however, that community colleges were least likely to raise tuition and fees to support distance education, thereby exacerbating financial problems for individual colleges, and intensifying their need for additional public funding.

Distance learning and other alternative delivery mechanisms challenge the current systems of student financing. Setting appropriate tuition and fee charges for students in technology-based programs is not straightforward. These students do not use some of the traditional institutional resources, such as libraries, parking lots, and study areas that on-campus students do. However, they may incur unique costs related to computers,

---

[6]The services that One-Stops are required to provide are arrayed as "core services," which include job search and placement, labor market information, initial assessment of skills and needs, information about available services, and some follow-up to help clients keep their jobs once they are placed. The next level of service is "intensive services," which include more comprehensive assessments, development of individual employment plans, group and individual counseling, and short-term pre-vocational services. It is only when qualified clients receive these intensive services and are still not able to find jobs that they may receive training services including vocational training, job readiness training, and adult education and literacy activities in conjunction with training (U.S. Department of Labor, 1999)

Internet access, and other technology-based requirements. Determining "seat time" and other measures of instructional productivity also is much more difficult when students are engaged in these more self-paced, technology-mediated programs. Measuring seat time is a frequent stumbling block in calculating a student's eligibility for federal financial aid and institutional funding levels.

STUDENTS

To understand higher education finance in the context of the community college it is necessary to understand both the size and nature of the total student market served by community colleges. Despite near parity in overall enrollments between two-year and four-year institutions in the public sector, large differences in student demographics enter into play in defining the community college market. As Table 1 indicates, the bulk of student enrollment across various age-range categories is in the public sector. Over half (55.4 percent) of the total enrollment in American higher education aged 29 and younger is enrolled in either public two-year (23.7 percent) or four-year institutions (31.7 percent). And public four-year and two-year institutions enroll 8.2 percent and 6.9 percent, respectively, of the nation's total enrollment in the traditional college-starting ages of 18 to 19. These percentages dispel the common perception that community colleges serve chiefly an older, more nontraditional market. Competition for this traditional-age cohort is intense across sectors of higher education since they consume more credit hours per headcount than older students. However, the community college niche in this overall competition is more racially and ethnically diverse than the four-year sector.

Table 1. Enrollment by Sector, Institutional Control, and Age Ranges, Fall 1995

	Public 4-Year	Private 4-Year	Public 2-Year	Private 2-Year
under 18	0.5%	0.3%	1.1%	0.0%
18 and 19	8.2%	4.2%	6.9%	0.3%
20 to 24	16.9%	7.2%	10.4%	0.4%
25 to 29	6.1%	3.2%	5.3%	0.2%
30 to 39	5.2%	3.2%	7.1%	0.3%
40 to 49	2.8%	1.7%	4.0%	0.1%
50 to 64	0.7%	0.5%	1.3%	0.0%
65 +	0.1%	0.0%	0.4%	0.0%
Unknown	0.2%	0.4%	0.3%	0.0%
Total	40.8%	20.7%	37.0%	1.5%

Source: NCES, 1997, p.186

High School Graduates
More than 3.2 million young Americans will graduate from high school during the 2008-09 school year, a 23 percent rise from 1996-97 (NCES, 1999c). Growth will vary across the states. A few will experience declines, but others will have dramatic increases: California, more than 50 percent; Florida, more than 70 percent; and Nevada, more than 200 percent. This tidal wave of potential college students is now progressing

though the nation's elementary and secondary schools, but only recently have its implications for college opportunity been raised by policy leaders. Moreover, the next generations of high school graduates will be far more ethnically heterogeneous than in the past. As with enrollment demand, the extent of ethnic and cultural diversity will differ among the states, and will be largely influenced by immigration patterns. Given that 48 percent of all U.S. undergraduates are found at a community college, even without new state policies that would direct more enrollment to community colleges, the lion's share of this impact will be felt at the community college. The upward trajectory in younger enrollments will challenge most community colleges, especially if the demand for remedial education continues apace.

Part-time Status

Sixty-six percent of public community college students were enrolled on a part-time basis in the fall of 1995, compared with 24 percent of undergraduate public four-year students (NCES, 1997). The proportion of all part-time students—including undergraduate, professional, and graduate students—enrolled in the public four-year sector was virtually identical in 1975 and again in 1985. In contrast, the proportion of part-time students at public community colleges rose from 57 percent in 1975 to 65 percent in 1985 and has stayed constant since then. The consistency in part-time enrollments since 1985 is remarkable given the tremendous economic expansion in the United States during the 1990s and the inverse relationship between part-time enrollments and economic conditions. The annual increase in part-time students is expected to average just 0.3 percent from 2000 to 2009 (NCES, 1999c).

Older students constitute a major proportion of part-time student enrollments and their projected growth in community colleges mirror the overall projections for part-time students. While the enrollment of older students increased by 19 percent from 1986 to 1994, it is expected to increase by only 4 percent from 1999 to 2009 (NCES, 1999c). An aging student population might result in increasing costs, such as on-campus child care, and night and weekend facility access. At the same time, it is likely that most community colleges are already offering these services. Whether older students will offset any new institutional expenditures they create by producing higher revenues is unknown but as the Boomer generation ages, it is doubtful they would wish to forfeit any accustomed privileges such as reduced tuition for senior citizens granted by many community colleges.

Financial Ability of Students

Community colleges serve a lower-income population than do four-year colleges, yet the proportion of students who receive financial aid is higher at four-year colleges and universities. This is because federal financial aid is sensitive to the cost of attendance among institutions. Since community colleges have been able, for the most part, to constrain their tuition and fee charges, national profiles that trace the number of aid recipients across sectors mask the economic circumstances of most community college students. Among first-time, full-time dependent college freshmen in 1996, for example, median family income for community college students was $43,100, compared with $53,800 in four-year colleges and $62,300 in universities (Mortenson, 1999a).

A high-tuition and high-aid policy became attractive to states during the 1980s especially as the eligibility criteria for federal loans were widened (Mumper, Chapter 8). The original framework of high-tuition and high-aid envisioned nonrepayable grant aid as the bargaining chip for adapting to ever-increasing tuition hikes. However, during the 1980s and the 1990s, the greatest growth in available federal aid was in loan programs and not in grant programs (The College Board, 1999). Thus, the most needy of students found their access to educational opportunity circumscribed by undertaking repayment obligations. The extent to which this eventuality was considered by state legislators and policymakers is unknown, but the appeal of raising the cost of attendance for needy students because of rising federal aid appears to have been irresistible. Tuition charges could be allowed to rise while state appropriations could decrease as a share of institutional revenues (see, for example, Toutkoushian, Chapter 1). The impact of this policy on community colleges has not been so subtle, since students who attend community colleges on less than a half-time basis are not eligible to participate in the federal need-based financial aid programs. The transition from the early days, when little or no tuition was charged to anyone, toward an environment of subsidizing only the neediest of students is pivotal to community colleges. While the level of borrowing from federal loan programs at four-year institutions has accelerated during the past decade, it has declined slightly at community colleges (NCES, 2000).

More recently, the establishment of the Hope Scholarship has widened the focus of federal financial aid programs from the most needy students to those students or their families who possess the resources to benefit from a tax credit. The Hope Scholarship represents the misconception that poor students are currently taken care of in the constellation of federal financial aid programs. It is premature to judge the impact of the Hope Scholarship on enrollments and community college finances, but its establishment holds the potential that less money might be available for other types of federal student aid. This connection may not be a perfect correlation, however, since a tax credit represents forgone income for the federal treasury while increases in financial aid represent direct federal outlays. The former requires essentially no Congressional intervention while the later requires an active, ongoing commitment.

The American Association for Community Colleges estimates that just 1.6 percent of the total enrollment at community colleges receive merit scholarships (Phillippe and Patton, 1999). Those students attending public four-year institutions are three times as likely to receive merit scholarships while students attending private four-year institutions are nine times as likely. These differences are further indication of the financial need as well as academic preparedness of community college students; merit scholarships skew dollars toward the non-needy since traditional merit measures are highly correlated with family income.

Student Diversity

Minorities are projected to be the majority of the U.S. population by the middle of the next century. Community colleges enroll significantly higher proportions of minority populations than other higher education sectors. In 1997, college enrollment rates in two-year institutions were similar for white, black, and Hispanic high school completers ages 18 to 24. In contrast, black and Hispanic high school completers were less likely to be enrolled in four-year institutions (NCES, 1999a). Hispanics are especially represented in two-year colleges where their proportional representation is roughly double what it is in the four-year sector. Over half of all Hispanic-serving institutions of higher education, institutions that serve a Hispanic student population greater than 25 percent, are two-year colleges, as are virtually all of the nation's 30 tribal colleges (Merisotis and O'Brien, 1998). Increasing proportions of underprepared minority populations enrolling in community colleges has particular financial implications for advising, support services, and developmental/remedial education efforts.

Students with Disabilities

The Americans with Disabilities Act, the Individuals with Disabilities Education Act (IDEA), and other changes in federal and state laws have enhanced the educational opportunities for individuals with disabilities. Community colleges serve a higher proportion of students with disabilities than any other sector of higher education (Phillippe and Patton, 1999). The largest category among this group was learning disabilities, suggesting that in addition to modifications to facilities for physically disabled students, community colleges also carry heavy responsibility to provide reasonable accommodations in existing instructional programs, another area in which community colleges are especially vulnerable if additional public financial support is not forthcoming.

Welfare Recipients

The 1996 welfare reform legislation's limitations on the amount of postsecondary education that can count toward the law's work requirements has had a large impact on community colleges. The law permitted states to consider only up to 12 months of job-related education and training as work. While this may restrict enrollments for the future, states have also responded by contracting with community colleges to train welfare recipients with short-term programs. Almost half of all community colleges support welfare-to-work programs in this way (Phillippe and Patton, 1999). Given this short time frame for training, however, it should be no surprise that the focus of these programs is to prepare former welfare recipients for jobs in the service industry or administrative support occupations, not the fastest growing occupations in high technology where training times are typically longer. The issue of student preparedness for more than an entry-level, service industry occupation cuts across this scenario and is connected in no small way to community colleges' efforts in remedial education. In combination, provision of these services is costly, but necessary to meet society's goal of reduced welfare rolls and an improved workforce.

Faculty

Nowhere is the efficiency of the community college captured better than by its reliance on part-time faculty. On average, part-timers at community colleges constitute two-thirds of the total faculty and teach about half of the total classes (NCES, 1999c). In contrast, the proportion of part-time faculty at public four-year institutions is less than 25 percent of the total faculty, including graduate assistants. In the main, this difference in the use of part-time faculty accounts for substantial differences in public support for full-time equivalent students between two-year and four-year institutions. The financial realities facing community colleges have made the employment of a less expensive instructional workforce an imperative; in contrast, the four-year sector has been able to divert savings from employing graduate assistants teaching on the lower-division level to subsidize upper-division and graduate instruction.

FINANCIAL STATUS OF COMMUNITY COLLEGES

A complete discussion of community college financing must acknowledge the interdependencies between the states, the federal government, and community colleges. It appears that the annual federal deficit now has been eliminated, turning the major policy discussions to the surplus and ways that may be used. Current proposals include strengthening Social Security, cutting taxes, paying off the national debt, and discussions about strengthening aid to law enforcement and K-12 education. At the same time, most state governments are flush with new resources brought about by a vibrant economy. Economic growth, however, does not mean balanced growth.

States, too, are contemplating tax cuts while facing increasing demand for prisons and ways to fund Medicaid, the latter is part and parcel of the devolution of the federal role in providing health and welfare for citizens. Although, there is hope that higher education will somehow make up for the ground it lost during the 1990s in most state legislatures, a grim forecast is in store as states search for revenue sources to meet various federal matching requirements and to shore up K-12 education and corrections. Beyond these new demands, states also are obligated to maintain their more stable operations such as personnel systems, building departments, financial processing, and other overhead functions. Hovey (1999) observes that absent a fiscal crisis, elected officials are loath to cut current services, creating a pessimistic picture of the alternatives before higher education leaders. For all of higher education the question will be whether, at the margin, state spending on higher education contributes more to the state's overall well-being than spending at the margin in other programs.

Even though earlier statistics cited in this chapter may indicate that higher education and community colleges receive adequate increases from state governments over the past several years, a truer picture can be drawn by understanding state tax effort. Mortenson (1999b) reports that the national average for tax support to higher education among the states was $11.22 per $1,000 in personal income for Fiscal Year 1979. By Fiscal Year 1999, that statistic had dropped to $7.65, a decrease of 31.8 percent. While total appropriations to higher education have increased, they have not kept pace with personal income. In fact, Hovey (1999) calculates that the current annual gap between state and local revenues and the dollars needed to maintain current services across all programs of government, including higher education, is 0.5 percent nationwide. The resulting backlog is likely to crush higher education's ability to advocate new spending. It is not possible to predict future economic conditions with accuracy, but a downturn in the current economy likely would accelerate a downward spiral, since many citizens do not seem to consider higher education as critical to public well-being in the short term as healthcare, prisons, and maintaining the core services of state and local government.

This picture for community colleges is further clouded because there is no single model to finance them nor is there a single governance model that is readily understood by the public. Community college budgets are ultimately approved by one of five entities: legislatures, local community college boards, state postsecondary boards, state boards of education, or state community college boards (ECS, 2000). Local community college boards are the predominant model for determining budgets, meaning that even if a single method were developed in all 50 states, there is no practical way it could be implemented. Little has changed in enrollment-driven formulas during the two decades since Breneman and Nelson's (1981) observation that traditional financing formulas treat two-year colleges as if they primarily enroll degree-seeking students. State governments most often appropriate dollars to community colleges based on a unit-rate formula. Over one-third of the states recognize differential program costs for setting allocations to community colleges (ECS, 2000). This, however, falls short of a deliberate scheme to target dollars at those community college programs where resource requirements are highest.

What has changed across higher education in the 1990s is the introduction of performance-funding models. These models seek to promote efficiency, usually expressed as accountability, within higher education through development of numerical and qualitative benchmarks which, in turn, drive resources to institutions. The effect of these models on community college financing is only now beginning to be felt, although the accent on efficiency, as opposed to quality, sends chilling overtones across a sector long accustomed to returning maximum outcomes with comparatively minimal resources. Christal (1997) reported that 37 states were actively engaged in some variant of performance indicator systems, and that another seven states were contemplating establishing such systems in the near-term. Only eight states linked their performance systems to budgeting decisions while 15 states reported "consideration" of these measures in budgeting. The threshold amount for performance budgeting varies from state to state but typically ranges from two to three percent of total general fund appropriations, an amount which may seem relatively insignificant in a total scheme but which represents a major portion of total budgets for marginally funded institutions.

Table 2.[a] Distribution of Current Fund Revenues by Public 2-Year Institutions, 1976-77 and 1995-96

	1976-77	*1995-96*	*% Change*
Tuition and Fees	15.5	21.2	+5.7
Federal	7.2	5.6	-1.6
State	45.3	43.3	-1.9
Local	23.5	19.2	-4.3
Private Grants, Gifts, and Contracts	0.5	1.0	-0.5
Endowment Income	0.1	0.1	0.0
Sales and Services	6.3	6.6	+0.2
Other Sources	1.7	3.1	+1.4

Source: NCES, 1979, Table 1 and 1999d, Table 3

a.NCES expanded the universe of colleges from which it collected data for these surveys in 1995-96 to include some "non-accredited" institutions which had been previously omitted. However, accredited institutions receive nearly 99 percent of current fund revenues, making the data for 1995-96 virtually compatible with those for 1976-77.

Table 2 compares current fund revenues for public two-year colleges across two decades. These data demonstrate fundamental shifts in both public support and the corresponding actions taken by colleges to survive. The revenue environment has migrated both to increased user charges in the form of tuition and fee collection and to a greater emphasis on entrepreneurial activities. These implications are discussed below in the context of total revenues.

Local and State Tax Revenue

Local tax appropriations. Twenty-six states support community colleges through local tax appropriations. This total reached nearly $4.5 billion in a 1998-99, including operating expenses and capital outlays, a modest increase of 12.3 over the previous five years (Palmer and Hines, 2000). Idaho and Oregon showed decreases during this time while Virginia community colleges enjoyed an unprecedented 113 percent increase. As a proportion of total revenue available to institutions, however, local appropriations fell by 4.3 percent over two decades (Table 2). This is the largest decrease in the share of total revenue coming from any source over the past twenty years. It is an important and disturbing trend, representing a decrease in local support for America's most "local" institutions of higher education.

State-aided Community Colleges. Twenty-two states appropriate state tax funds for the operating expenses of community colleges which they do not govern directly. These colleges collect both local tax appropriations and state appropriations. In 1998-99 these colleges received nearly $5.7 billion from state legislatures to support their operating expenses, exclusive of any expenditures for buildings or other capital outlay (Palmer and Hines, 2000). This represents a 17.1 percent increase over the previous three years; however, when California, which appropriated nearly half of the total, is removed from these calculations the total increase drops to 13.1 percent.

State-governed community colleges. State-governed community colleges are found in 24 states and received $3.8 billion in 1998-99 (Palmer and Hines, 2000). If the recent trend in support for local community colleges via local tax funds is unremarkable in the five-year period from 1994-95 to 1998-99, the level of state appropriations to state-governed community colleges depicts only a slightly better picture. States increased their appropriations to their "own" community colleges by 12.3 percent over three years, translating into a 4.1 percent yearly increase. Minnesota[7] and Tennessee have decreased their appropriations to state community colleges during this time while the two mega-states that operate state community colleges, Florida and North Carolina, topped the list in increases. Thus while the total state dollars have increased recently, their proportion of total institutional revenue has decreased by 1.9 percent over the past two decades (Table 2). It is noteworthy and even incongruous that in combination, local and state appropriations as a share of total revenue for community colleges—the purely public sources of financial support—have decreased by 6.2 percent during the past twenty-year period.

---

[7]Minnesota's 4 percent decrease during this period includes appropriations for both state community colleges and consolidated state community and technical colleges.

Revenue from Tuition and Fees

Tuition and fee revenue as a proportion of total community college budgets has increased from 16 percent in 1980 to 21 percent in 1996 (NCES, 1999b). Average tuition and fees at community colleges increased 366 percent from 1976-77 ($283) to 1997-98 ($1,318) (NCES, 1999b). Two decades ago, when the first state budget cuts were implemented, many community colleges were charging little or no tuition. The data in Table 2 clearly indicate that tuition and fees have been the most rapidly growing part of institutional revenue over the past two decades.[8] This increase is substantial and especially burdensome for community college students.

Students attending community colleges are more sensitive to tuition increases than students at any other institutional type (Heller, 1997). This is just as one would expect, because community college enrollment is disproportionately made up of low-income, minority, older and part-time students, all of whom are more tuition-sensitive than their respective counterpart groups of students. Kane (1995) has described the level of tuition at community colleges as the "marginal" price of attendance at any college. This "tuition threshold" is the barrier to enrollment and is consistent with the historic role of the community college as America's most accessible postsecondary institution. Halstead (1998) refers to tuition at community colleges in each state as an indicator of how accessible higher education is in that state, as part of his well-known cross-state comparisons of access to and funding of higher education in America.

Increases in community college tuition would be highly likely to reduce participation in higher education among those groups who are already the most under-represented groups in higher education. A policy of continued increases in tuition at community colleges appears at the apex of shortsightedness and would work against promoting the value and expanding the opportunities of educating the "new majority" (Rendon and Hope, 1996).

Revenue from the Federal Government

Aside from direct support to the nation's tribal colleges, most of which are two-year colleges, direct federal support for current operating expenses of community colleges is rare. Since almost no community colleges compete directly for federal research dollars and no community college enjoys "land grant" status, direct federal outlays are virtually nonexistent in the overall scheme of community college financing. The proportion of institutional revenues from federal grants and contracts also decreased from 1976-77 to 1995-96, meaning that there were fewer opportunities to supplement state and local revenues with either federal grant support or indirect cost recovery. Direct revenue from the federal government, exclusive of indirect revenues derived from student federal financial aid, constitutes about 5 percent of total institutional revenue for public two-year institutions (NCES, 1999b), a figure which has been constant over the past two decades.

Revenue from Self-Help

The entrepreneurial or self-help side of community college revenue presents a hopeful picture over two decades for those concerned with the failure of all levels of government

---

[8]Only two states ran counter to this trend: Massachusetts and 7'Vermont decreased their tuition and fee revenue between academic years 93-94 and 97-98.

to keep pace with community college revenue needs. Table 2 indicates modest increases in two areas: "Sales and Services" and "Other Sources." Together, these categories represent efforts to engage external entities in contracted services including sales of services and goods. Employers are increasingly turning to community colleges as essential centers of worker training (Zeiss, 1997). Accelerated interest in workforce development and technological improvements in delivering content have brought competition from temporary employment agencies, publishing conglomerates, and corporate universities resulting in corresponding efforts at the community college to deliver education to all types of learners, any time at any place. As noted above, this entrepreneurial spirit is not limited to the workforce development arena, but certainly is spurred further by increased employer interest in moving beyond the traditional delivery of instruction according to a term-long schedule. Despite almost universal employer interest, funding polices across states for workforce development vary enormously. Given the demands of the workplace and the clear connection between employee training and a state's economic health, it seems almost implausible that some states have restricted funding for workforce development (Grubb, Badway, Bell, Bragg, and Russman, 1997). Less than half of the states provide funding to support workforce development as part of routine appropriations to community college; nearly two-thirds of the states make resources available which colleges may seek outside the funding formula (ECS, 2000). Another two-thirds of the states report that they have access to non-state funding sources to support workforce development, an external source that may explain, at least in part, the increases in the "Other Sources" and "Sales and Services" categories in the last two decades, and why connections between businesses and community colleges have flourished in recent years.

Fundraising by community colleges under the auspices of institutional foundations has become an important institutional activity. Phillippe and Patton (1999) report that the number of community colleges with endowments increased by nearly 40 percent, to 420 colleges, from 1991-92 to 1996-97. During the same time, the median value of individual institutional endowments increased to $503,355 at public two-year colleges versus $4,826,616 at public four-year colleges. Ultimately, little has changed in the picture of endowment revenue as a proportion of overall institutional budgets over the preceding two decades (Table 2).

Expenditures

Without controlling for differences in role and mission, the contrast in expenditures between the public two-year and four-year sectors is especially conspicuous. In 1995-96, public four-year institutions reported current fund expenditures of $15,342 per full-time equivalent student. The corresponding figure for public two-year colleges was $6,346 (NCES, 1999b, Table 83). Expenditure trends within community colleges portray a more complex interaction of factors. The fastest growing expenditure categories have been administration, student services, and scholarships and fellowships, the latter perhaps due to an attempt on behalf of institutions to mitigate the effects of price increases on low-income students (Table 3). The administration category includes both academic support and institutional support, two areas which are sensitive to increased enrollment. Increases in academic support and student services may be attributable to efforts to serve a growing number of students who require higher levels of assistance, a prominent feature of the mission and special roles of community colleges, as described at some length in previous sections. No single cause can be advanced for increases in administration, a stumbling block for many state policymakers who question community college efficiency while pointing to elevated numbers of administrators over time. But probable causes include administrative adaptations and responses to expanding reporting and accountability requirements; changes in other regulatory, technological and economic factors in an increasingly complex environment; the growing use of management styles that are more participatory; and the expanded efforts of public-sector administrations—like their private-sector counterparts—to engage in more diligent fund-raising and lobbying activities. On the other hand, expenditures for instruction have decreased over this period, suggesting that community colleges have been able to achieve cost savings by employing larger numbers of part-time faculty or by increasing

Table 3. Distribution of Current Funds Expenditures by Public 2-Year Institutions, 1976-77 and 1995-96

Area	1976-77	1995-96	Change in%
Instruction	51.1	48.1	-3.0
Administration	18.1	21.6	+3.5
Student Services	8.4	10.7	+2.3
Research	0.3	0.1	-0.2
Library	3.5	2.2	-1.3
Public Service	2.0	2.3	+0.3
Operating and Physical Plant	11.2	10.3	-0.9
Scholarships	2.9	3.9	+1.0

Source: NCES, 1999b, Table 344

class sizes.

PROSPECTS FOR FINANCING COMMUNITY COLLEGES IN A NEW CENTURY

If the proportion of state and local government's budgets earmarked for community colleges would increase even fractionally, community colleges might be more adequately funded and certainly would be better able to meet the accelerated demand for the services they can provide. ECS (2000) reports that more than half of the states currently are in various stages of investigating enhancements to existing funding models for community colleges. In addition to discussions on performance-funding models, these discussions also include developing allocation factors that recognize customized industry training, creation of factors which provide for a minimum foundation of funding for all community colleges (known as base-plus), and changes to existing funding schemes which would permit local tax payers to deduct as a credit the dollars they pay for local millage. While these discussions may prove fruitful, it is difficult to imagine that substantial new resources for community colleges would result. In reality, many states will find it impossible to maintain current public services within existing tax structures.

Several dramatic steps need to occur before the current funding impasse for community colleges is surmounted. First, legislators and policymakers who make decisions about how community colleges are funded appear to be uninformed by, and disconnected from, what actually happens at most community colleges. Community colleges appear to have been generally unsuccessful in their efforts to demonstrate their unique contributions to the public. Although community colleges have become expert at delivering courses and programs that serve the demands of their diverse constituents with courses and programs delivered in a functional and cost-effective manner, it is fair to say that they still are regarded as "junior colleges," in the minimizing sense of this expression and have failed to overcome this connotation. The narrowness of the junior college perspective clouds the fact that demands on community colleges are escalating, creating corresponding pressures on their infrastructures, so that they now resemble educational "general stores." This transformation has promoted an increasing dependence on revenue from diversified activities apart from the allocation of public funds that reward them for junior college activities.

A central challenge therefore is the extent to which community colleges can demonstrate their value-added beyond a simplistic view of their mission as providing the first two years of college. The junior college label castigates community colleges as inferior. In this world view, the inputs of the community college are thought to be less-qualified or ambitious students who nonetheless seek a four-year degree, but are not perhaps academically able or financially able to begin their academic careers at their desired destination, a four-year college or university. Despite recent evidence that when the effects of gender, race, and economic status are controlled, students who enter community colleges achieve learning outcomes equal to those achieved by students who begin their career at public four-year institutions (see, for example, Pascarella, Bohr, Nora, and Terenzini, 1995, and Voorhees, 1997), legislators and other policymakers seldom turn away from their rigidly traditional and myopic junior-college view when making funding decisions. So entrenched is this perspective that it is doubtful that in the foreseeable future, a battle of perceptions between sectors can be won by community colleges. Instead, community colleges should try to demonstrate the ways in which they are different from other public institutions and seek to articulate their economic and educational advantages.

Although interest in performance funding across states shows no signs of diminishing, it is clear after several years of implementation that, as currently conceived, it promises no tangible hope of improving community college financing. The penultimate measures across states and sectors are persistence rates and graduation rates, two measures on which community colleges do not achieve at the same rate as four-year institutions because of the special nature of the students and the multidimensional mission of the community college.

When policymakers and legislators rush to the least-common-denominator schemes for establishing funding across public higher education, community colleges can best demonstrate their competitive advantages by trying to focus attention on value-added measures and through an explicit articulation of their cost advantages. What community colleges have long known is that students vote with their feet and, by this measure alone, the enrollment gains experienced by community colleges over three decades have been proof positive of superior performance. Enrollment growth, however, is the antithesis to performance indicator systems as states attempt to derive more efficiency from their public institutions.

Performance indicator systems seek to homogenize differences between sectors by instituting indicators that treat all students as if they have the same goals, a dubious stance given the overwhelming diversity of goals of community college students.[9] At the same time, an indicator system that adequately captures community college student goals might be so complex as to annoy, rather than inform, state-level decision-makers. A focus on success as expressed by enrollment increases and the types of students served rather than conformity to stringent mechanisms which lead to marginalization appears as good advice for community college leaders. Systems which appear to submerge differences between sectors cannot be productive for community colleges in the long term. It is doubtful that performance indicator systems can coexist alongside the impending community college enrollment boom since states may be unable to fund both.

Yet, to advocate for community colleges as willing receptacles for processing ever-increasing enrollments is a disservice. Two decades ago, before the advent of performance indicator systems, Richardson and Leslie (1980) recommended that community colleges seek modifications in funding formulas so that the actual cost of providing services might be isolated and recognized. In the meantime, they suggested that community colleges should avoid performing services for which they do not receive adequate funding. To continue to serve all that enter, given the funding systems existing during the time they made their recommendations, and which for the most part are still operative today, signals legislators that quantity is more important than quality. While most community college educators would be loath to turn away prospective students at a time when state allocation schemes suggest that "more is better," preparing to offer external policymakers data that accurately portrays the cost of operating a multiplicity of programs rings as sage advice.

Within this context, how can states best ensure adequate resources for community colleges? The central challenge is to determine how much subsidy states wish to provide institutions to cover an appropriate portion of the cost of educating their students, a calculation which might be based on current cost or educational and general expenditure per student. Such a cost-based subsidy would be provided to all public institutions irrespective of current enrollment levels. This approach would ensure equality of funding between two-year and four-year sectors, setting the stage for price and value competition. Here, it is suggested that these calculations be based on average *lower-division* costs per student, for each field of study, at all public institutions; students who choose to pursue upper-division study would be eligible for an institutional subsidy based on the actual cost of providing that level of service across all fields of study. The effect of a "differentiated" cost-based subsidy would be to preserve role and mission differences between two- and four-year institutions in the public sector, while simultaneously driv-

---

[9]For a longer discussion of the connections between community college student goals and performance indicator systems, see Voorhees and Zhou (2000).

ing efficiencies across the educational marketplace. In other words, four-year institutions would receive per-unit state subsidies that would correspond to differences in the average costs of educating upper- and lower-division students, as well as to differences between the costs of educating undergraduate, graduate and professional school students. At a time when funding higher education is not high on the priority list of most state legislatures, it makes little sense for community colleges to continue to embrace state systems that provide the largest subsidies to the highest-cost public institutions.

Community colleges may have much to gain in this scenario because presumably all current state appropriations per full-time equivalent lower-division students would be averaged, resulting in a subsidy amount which would likely exceed current state allocation levels for community colleges. This would drive new money into community colleges and ameliorate the tendency to rely on financial aid to partially close the difference in tuition costs. Externally, the role of state agencies then becomes that of acquiring, assembling, and providing relevant and validated data for the necessary calculations and to inform all institutions and potential students of the opportunities provided through the new cost-based appropriations program.

How can the federal actions support an increase in necessary community college costs? If recent actions constitute a trend, it is unlikely that community colleges can rely on the federal government to lead required changes in financing. Congress continues to authorize hefty increases in the Pell Grant program but fails to appropriate dollars to its authorized maximums. In 1997-98, the maximum Pell Grant was $2,700 while its authorized level was $4,500. In 1997-98 constant dollars, this maximum level brought the Pell Grant program back to levels last funded in 1992-93. In fact, when maximum Pell Grants are held constant, the highest maximum level of Pell Grants was experienced twenty-five years ago during the program's third year, 1975-76 (College Board, 1999). While the share that community college students derive from Pell Grants has increased to one-third of the total available to higher education since 1985-86, the community college share from other federal programs, including Stafford Loans and PLUS loans, has actually decreased. The volume of borrowing is probably suppressed since students who attend any institution on less than a half-time basis are ineligible for federal loans. As this chapter recommends at the state level, community colleges should seek to reform the uniform methodology to eliminate differential student budgets and allow price competition. This change would increase the share gained by community colleges and would moderate incentives to raise tuition.

The Hope Scholarship also marks a watershed in federal support for students. The Hope Scholarship provides a federal tax credit to students and their families some months after they first pay their tuition bill. Tax credits probably serve as a reward for those who already would have enrolled in college since one must have the financial wherewithal in the first place to pay tuition bills and to be able to wait to receive a credit. There also is some suspicion that community college tuitions might rise, as tuitions may rise throughout higher education, to fully capture the $1,500 tuition credit from students, although recent evidence does not support this conjecture.

Even if there were universal agreement about the cost structure of public higher education, the massive changes required would be difficult to implement with speed.

Movement on the public policy front in adjusting budgets and allocations tends to be gradual, almost glacial. In the meanwhile, community colleges should continue their efforts to cooperate with other educational providers, especially high schools and universities. Community colleges cannot stand alone; they must reach out to create liaisons with other institutions in the public sector to jointly identify prospects for service and funding. Questions about who pays for developmental/remedial education between community colleges and the K-12 system and the success of those students who transfer to four-year colleges create opportunities to meld the agendas of community colleges with the legitimate interests of policymakers.

Multiple sources of financing will accelerate in importance; especially supplemental financing at the local level, where it now appears stalled. If the community college is a service provider for its local area then local businesses and philanthropic agents must assist in paying the cost. In the case of business relationships, an emphasis must be placed on market transactions and value-added strategies rather than contributions to maintain current operations. Community colleges always have been dynamic institutions that seek to challenge the status quo. If activity levels and expansion of roles are true indicators of institutional health and if community colleges can articulate their differences in ways that attract greater proportional funding, the financial futures of community colleges may be more promising than the current financial conditions and policies indicate.

References

Breneman, D.W., and Nelson, S.C. (1981). Financing community colleges: An economic perspective. Washington, D. C.: Brookings Institution.

Christal, M.E. (1997). *Survey on Performance Measures*. Denver: State Higher Education Executive Officers.

College Entrance Examination Board (1999). *Trends in Student Aid*. Report #23612. New York: College Board.

Dougherty, K.J. (1994). *The Contradictory College: The conflicting Origins, Impacts, and Futures of the Community College*. Albany: State University of New York Press.

Education Commission of the States (2000). *Community College Finance Policy Survey, Preliminary Findings*. Denver: Education Commission of the States.

Grub, W.N., Badway, N., Bell, D., Bragg, D., and Russman, M. (1997). *Workforce, Economic, and Community Development: the Changing Landscape of the Entrepreneurial Community College*. Washington, D.C.: League for Innovation in the Community College, National Center for Research in Vocational Education, and National Council on Occupational Education.

Halstead, D.K. (1996). *Higher Education Report Card 1995*. Washington, DC: Research Associates.

Heller, D.E. (1997). Student price response in higher education: An update to Leslie and Brinkman. *Journal of Higher Education 68* (6): 624-659.

Hovey, H.A. (1999). *State spending for higher education in the next decade: The battle to sustain current support*. National Center Report 99-3. San Jose, CA: National Center Public Policy and Higher Education.

Kane, T.J. (1995). *Rising Public College Tuition and College Entry: How Well Do Public Subsidies Promote Access to College? Cambridge, MA: National Bureau of Economic Research Working Paper Series No. 5164*.

Merisotis, J.P., and O'Brien, C.T (1998). *Minority-serving institutions: Distinct purposes, common goals*. New Directions for Higher Education No. 102. San Francisco: Jossey-Bass, Inc.

Mortenson, T. (1999a). *State outreach efforts to students from low income families, 1996*. Report No. 80 Oskaloosa, IA: Postsecondary Education Opportunity.

Mortenson, T. (1999b). *State Tax Fund Appropriations for Higher Education, FY 2000*. Report No. 90 Oskaloosa, IA: Postsecondary Education Opportunity.

National Center for Education Statistics (2000). *Trends in Undergraduate Borrowing: Federal Student Loans in 1989-90, 1992-93, and* 1995-96. NCES Publication #2000-151. Washington, D.C.: U.S. Government Printing Office.

National Center for Education Statistics (1999a). *Distance Education at Postsecondary Educations Institutions: 1997-98.* NCES Publication #2000-013. Washington, D.C.: U.S. Government Printing Office.

National Center for Education Statistics (1999b). *Digest of Education Statistics, 1998.* NCES Publication #1999-036. Washington, D.C.: U.S. Government Printing Office.

National Center for Education Statistics (1999c). *Projections of Education Statistics to 2009.* NCES Document #1999-038. Washington, D.C.: U.S. Government Printing Office.

National Center for Education Statistics (1999d). *Current Funds Revenues and Expenditures of Degree-Granting Institutions: Fiscal Year 1996.* NCES Document #1999-161. Washington, D.C.: U.S. Government Printing Office.

National Center for Education Statistics (1998). *State Comparisons of Education Statistics: 1969_70 to 1996_97.* NCES Publication #98018. Washington, D.C.: U.S. Government Printing Office.

National Center for Education Statistics (1979). *Financial Statistics of Institutions of Higher Education: Fiscal Year 1977.* NCES Publication #017-080-02018-1. Washington, D.C.: U.S. Government Printing Office.

Palmer, J.C., and Hines, E.R. (2000). *Grapevine.* Illinois State University: Center for Higher Education and Educational Finance. www.coe.ilstu.edu/grapevine.

Pascarella, E.T., Bohr, L., Nora, A., and Terenzini, P.T. (1995). Cognitive effects of 2-Year and 4-year colleges: new evidence. *Educational Evaluation and Policy Analysis* 17:83-96.

Phillippe, K.A., and Patton, M. (1999). *National Profile of Community Colleges: Trends and Statistics.* 3rd Edition. Washington, D.C.: Community College Press, American Association of Community Colleges.

Rendon, L.I., and Hope, R.O. (1996). *Educating a New Majority: Transforming America's Educational System for Diversity.* San Francisco: Jossey-Bass.

Richardson, R.C., Jr., and Leslie, L. (1980). *The Impossible Dream: Financing Community College's Evolving Mission.* ERIC Report 197783. Washington, D.C.: ERIC Document Reproduction Service.

U.S. Department of Labor (1999). *Workforce Investment Act of 1998.* Washington, D.C.: U.S. Department of Labor.

Voorhees, R.A. (1997). Student learning and cognitive development in the community college. In J. C. Smart (Ed.), *Higher Education: Handbook of Theory and Research.* New York: Agathon.

Voorhees, R.A., and Zhou, D. (2000). Intentions and goals at the community college: Associating student perceptions and demographics. *Community College Journal of Research and Practice.* 24: 219-232.

Zeiss, T. (1997). Developing the World's Best Workforce: An Agenda for America's Community College. Eric Document Reproduction Service #ED407034. Annapolis Junction, MC: Community College Press.

Chapter 14

COLLEGE AND UNIVERSITY BUDGETING: What Do We Know? What Do We Need to Know?[1]

William F. Lasher and Deborah L. Greene

INTRODUCTION/OVERVIEW

This chapter reviews what we know and what we don't know about budgeting in American institutions of higher education, and where budgeting is going. We shall revisit the various types of institutional budgets and the institutional budget process. Next, economic, political, and other factors that affect institutional budgets will be explored. Seven approaches to institutional budgeting will then be described, and their strengths and weaknesses highlighted. Since American colleges and universities are not exempt from financial stress—as is all too apparent on so many campuses these days—we shall also examine the issues influencing resource retrenchment and reallocation. Finally, some thoughts will be offered on areas for future research on institutional budgeting.

Webster's New Collegiate Dictionary (1981) defines a budget as "a statement of the financial position of an administration for a definite period of time based on estimates of expenditures during the period and proposals for financing them; a plan for the coordination of resources and expenditures; the amount of money that is available for, required for, or assigned to a particular purpose." Wildavsky (1988, p. 2) defines a budget as a "link between financial resources and human behavior in order to accomplish policy objectives." Simply put, a budget is a spending plan for a given period of time.

Developing a budget is both an art and a science. Since there are never enough resources to satisfy every institutional need, a budget helps to set and communicate institutional priorities (Meisinger and Dubeck, 1984) within the limited resources available. It serves both as an institutional action or operating plan for a given period of time and as a contract. Funders expect specified activities to be accomplished with their funds. For example, students purchase classes with their tuition, legislators purchase a public good, donors purchase a sense of well-being and, perhaps, immortal-

---

[1]This chapter was originally published in Volume IX of *Higher Education: Handbook of Theory and Research,* © 1993 by Agathon Press. It has been updated with an Epilogue written especially for this volume

ity. A budget doubles as an accountability and control device, against which expenditures can be monitored for compliance. A budget is the result of many political battles, replete with offer and counter-offer, negotiation, and compromise. A budget "lives" over multiple fiscal periods: as last year's actual expenditures, as this year's estimates, and as next year's projections.

The budget process actually consists of multiple budget cycles, overlapping and intersecting each other. While one budget is being developed, another budget is being executed. Still another is being evaluated and audited. The single most critical determinant of the budget for a given fiscal period is the budget from the previous cycle (Meisinger and Dubeck, 1984). Budgets "tend to be altered incrementally to reflect marginal changes" (p. 5), rather than be modified through wholesale changes. Regardless of the latest policy fad or changes in terminology, this year's budget at a college or university will look remarkably similar to last year's.

It has often been argued that there should be strong ties between an institution's planning function and its budget process. William G. Bowen (1986) has argued this need by enumerating five specific measures that budget officers can take to foster success in reaching hard decisions during the budget process. First, the budget process should be organized so that all elements likely to compete for institutional resources can be considered at the same time. It is critical that resource commitments be made simultaneously, not separately, so that all elements have an equal opportunity of being considered. Second, financial data should "be organized according to the logic of decision making as well as the logic of control" (p. 16). Bowen advocates program budgeting in the sense that all resources that support a broad objective should be identified with that objective. Additional groupings of resources or expenditures may be necessary, but not for the purpose of assuring that there are sufficient resources budgeted to meet a specific programmatic objective. Third, program data such as the number of students enrolled should be provided along with financial data for each program. Fourth, in addition to the budget year, financial and program data should be provided for several years into the future. Bowen supports long-term planning and using the budget process as one of several planning tools. The picture derived from multiyear budgets helps to highlight areas of institutional commitment and may provide sufficient time to identify the source of necessary resources. Fifth and last, the budget process should be closely coordinated and integrated with institutional planning and control processes.

However, this crucial relationship between planning and budgeting is often confounded by the very nature of planning. Planning is conducted to reduce uncertainty. But the ability of planning to provide a durable, accurate, precise, program of action is constrained by a number of conditions that may be beyond its control. Among these conditions are "the uncertain nature of future conditions and difficulties in predicting opportunities and threats, the politics of institutional decision making, the distribution of power within the institutions, the potential rigidity of formal planning processes, and the time and cost for comprehensive planning" (Schmidtlein, 1989). Planning and budgeting operate on different horizons; a planning cycle may run one to five years while a budgeting cycle generally is limited to one to two years (Meisinger, 1989).

The impact of these intangible, but existing, conditions causes an incongruity between planning and budgeting that is more apparent when looking at the relationship between specific types of planning and the budget process. For example, strategic plans seldom provide specific guidance for budget decisions and program plans. While they delineate which programs and activities should be included in the budget, they do not include the exact amount of funding necessary to operate them. Separate capital budgets usually deal with facilities plans, but there is substantial spillover into the operating budget for utilities, maintenance, and related expenditures. Operational planning may parallel, then converge with, budget planning, but it too may lack the specificity in cost and revenue estimates that is required by budgeting. Issue-specific plans may include more details regarding financing, but lack the comprehensiveness that budgeting requires to encompass all campus programs and activities.

Although the link between planning and budgeting is described and encouraged in the literature, planning rarely provides the detailed operational direction for particular budget decisions. Planning is fixed in the theory side of an institution's program and activities, while budgeting exists more on the application or practice side.

TYPES OF BUDGETS

Meisinger and Dubeck (1984, p. 7-9) have identified six types of budget components: (1) operating budgets, (2) capital budgets, (3) restricted budgets, (4) auxiliary enterprise budgets, (5) hospital operations budgets, and (6) service center budgets. An operating budget generally includes all of the unrestricted funds, and those restricted funds (from endowments and sponsored programs) specified for instruction and departmental support. It is generally viewed as the institution's core budget, and it is the most sensitive to changes in academic program priorities.

A capital budget generally consists of expenditures for major facilities construction, repair, and renovation. The link between the capital budget and the operating budget, though often neglected, is critical to completeness and accuracy in budget development. New facilities burden the operating budget with additional expenditures for utilities and maintenance, while renovated facilities usually lessen the burden.

Expenditures supported by federal and other sponsored research grants and contracts, non-government grants, specified endowment and gift income, and externally-provided student aid generally comprise the restricted budget. This budget affects the operating budget through its support of graduate research assistantships and graduate training grants. The revenue in this budget is generally referred to as "soft money," due to the temporary nature of the projects supported. The level of this budget is the most volatile of the various components, reflecting the uncertainty of project continuation and the potential for the initiation of new projects.

Auxiliary enterprise budgets generally include those institutional support activities that enjoy a dedicated income stream, usually from student user fees and charges to the public for admission to institutional events, activities, or facilities. Auxiliary enterprise units (e.g., dormitories, book stores, intercollegiate athletic programs) are expected to "pay their own way" without receiving support from the tuition or appropriation revenues that support the core operating budget.

A special type of auxiliary enterprise is the institutionally affiliated teaching hospital. The hospital's operating budget includes expenditures for noninstructional hospital services and activities. Its revenues are derived from collected fees that are charged to patients and other users of hospital services. Also, direct legislative appropriations or contracts with state agencies may provide additional income to support the delivery of health care services to indigent patients.

Service centers are support units (e.g., printing shops, telephone systems) that operate within an institution. Revenues for these units typically originate as transfers from other departments or offices within the institution as payment for services rendered. Generally, these budgets are not reflected in the institution's total budget, since the funds have already been counted in the original budgets of transferring departments.

BUDGET PROCESS

Traditionally, budgets have been constructed in successive steps that start with the current year's approved budget (Whalen, 1991). This current approved budget is then adjusted to reflect necessary changes in activities during the fiscal year. (Examples include new appointments, faculty promotions, new programs or activities initiated during the year, reorganizations, and permanent cuts.) This base budget for the next year is then adjusted further to reflect budget policies and planned changes in activities for the upcoming fiscal year.

The budget cycles for public and private colleges and universities are quite similar with the exception that the cycle for public institutions takes more time to allow for state-level, and perhaps system-level, involvement (Meisinger and Dubeck, 1984). Both sectors have phases during which the highest authority (i.e., a state agency or a governing board) establishes the overall procedures that will guide the development of budget requests. The cycle of a public institution generally coincides with state or local government budget cycles (Caruthers and Orwig, 1979). States usually issue technical instructions or guidelines for submitting appropriation requests as many as 9 to 18 months prior to final adoption of the state budget, and 12 to 21 months prior to the beginning of the institution's fiscal year. Some states require a preliminary request and a final request document. At this stage, university activities compete with each other and with other state services such as public education, criminal justice, and mental health.

In public institutions, the state's budget instructions are used as the basis for the development of a set of institution-specific instructions, guidelines, or policies. At private institutions, these instructions are developed to reflect the economic and policy environment and the plans of the institution. In either sector, these guidelines indicate that budget *development* is generally a "top-down" activity, initiated from the central administration and imposed on the departments and units lower in the hierarchy. *Budget preparation*, on the other hand, is then begun at the budgetary units and rises to the central administration in a "bottom-up" fashion. This communication can be characterized as information transference within the university's hierarchy. There is, however, an imbalance in the directional flow of information—more information tends to flow upward to central administration than returns to subordinate levels (Meisinger and Dubeck, 1984). Central administration usually requires more information from subordinate levels than is actually necessary for decision making, but rarely provides sufficient feedback to the initiating unit. (At least that is typically the view from the units lower in the hierarchy.)

Expenditure estimates for new and proposed activities are developed. These estimates are affected by the policies outlined in the request guidelines, the effects of inflation, changes in enrollment, new or renovated buildings scheduled to come on-line, and other major developments, as well as the requirements for continuing activities. The resulting request documents are reviewed, possibly modified, prioritized, and summarized at each level as they are transmitted up the institution's hierarchy. In the public sector, the requests are reviewed by campus-level, perhaps system-level administrators, and the institution's governing board before they are submitted to a state-level postsecondary education agency, the legislature, and the governor for their evaluation and review. After submission of the request documents, budget hearings are held to provide additional information about intended activities and related expenditures and to respond to any other inquiries the funders may decide to include. State funding is determined through the normal legislative process and is provided to the institutions through an enacted appropriations bill. At private institutions, the requests are reviewed at the campus level and then submitted to the institutional governing board.

Once the state has determined the level of higher education funding, the funds may be allocated to the state's postsecondary agency for subsequent allocation to institutions; they may be appropriated directly to institutions in a lump sum; or they may be appropriated by line item to specific institutional functions, units, or activities. In any case, the institution revises its operating budget to reflect the differences between the requested amount and the appropriated amount. Since an institution rarely receives 100 percent of the amount it requested, it must recast its budget and may allocate funds to instructional, administrative, and support units differently than originally requested.

At this point in the process, both public institutions and private institutions consider final revenue estimates from all sources, including: tuition and fees, governmental appropriations, investment income, sponsored programs, auxiliary enterprises, and others. Available fund balances from prior year activities are also included as appropriate. Expenditure requests are evaluated against these revenue estimates and tentative budget amounts are allocated to all units. These allocations often set maximum budget levels for each unit. The units then develop more detailed budgets that will be used for the day-to-day operation of the institution. These budgets are reviewed up the institutional hierarchy, summarized by budget staff members, and finally presented to the governing board by the institution's president. Upon receiving board approval, the budget is disseminated to all units.

The budget, once adopted and disseminated, is implemented and monitored. Since the annual operating budget is closely linked to the institution's day-to-day activities, it serves as a control device to keep a rein on expenditures. Expenditure forecasts are typically required throughout the fiscal year (perhaps as often as monthly, but usually no less than quarterly). In public institutions, there are normally reporting requirements to inform state treasury officials about actual expenditures. There may also be reporting requirements before appropriated funds are transferred from the state treasury to institutional current accounts so they can be spent. Transfers among line item appropriations may require approval from the executive and/or legislative branches. In the event of a mid-year adjustment, caused by underrealized income or additional unanticipated expenditures, budget staff members may have to develop information on possible alternative adjustments.

After the close of the fiscal year, the institution will be required to develop an annual financial report concerning its revenue and expenditure activities during the year. This report will then be audited by state, federal, or other officials depending on the institution's governance system and the degree to which it is involved in sponsored activities. These audits will verify the accuracy of the financial reports to assure compliance with various state and federal regulations, as well as generally accepted accounting procedures, and the adequacy of institutional controls and performance.

As has been stated previously, these audit and evaluation activities actually overlap with budget cycles for other years. While last year's budget is being evaluated and audited, this year's budget is being executed and administered, and next year's budget is being planned and developed. Unfortunately, the activity that typically gets short-changed in all of this activity is budget evaluation. Most institutions do not spend sufficient time evaluating the prior year budget to determine whether the objectives of the institution's short-range plans were achieved.

FACTORS THAT INFLUENCE BUDGETS

There are both external and internal factors that affect higher education budgets. External factors include economic, political, and demographic factors, plus the regulatory environment; while internal factors include institutional history, mission, and other characteristics.

Economic Environment

The state of the economy is directly relevant to the fiscal health of higher education. High inflation means that: a static budget will purchase fewer goods and services over time; the real value of faculty salaries will be reduced; and the value of income generated by endowments will be eroded (Layzell and Lyddon, 1990). The strength of the economy also directly affects the level of private contributions to institutions of higher education. In good economic times, monies flow relatively easily to university operating and capital funds. In hard times, not only is charitable giving reduced, but there is more competition among nonprofit sectors for the philanthropic dollar.

During times of rising unemployment, higher education faces a triple threat from more competition for scarcer resources. First, high unemployment signals the demand for additional services, which increases the competition for resources among state services, including higher education. Second, in an economic recession, consumers purchase fewer goods, which leads to fewer tax dollars being collected to pay for federal and state services. In addition, enrollment tends to rise during periods of high unemployment and recession as people take the opportunity to increase their skills in hopes of attaining higher employment levels after the economy starts growing again.

Institutions are directly affected by recession-related problems in federal student aid. Students use the funds from these aid programs to pay the cost of tuition and mandatory fees. As more people enroll in college because they cannot find work and more students become eligible for aid, there is an increase in demand on Pell Grants and College Work-Study Programs. Since the level of federal appropriation has not increased to keep up with demand (there was a $1.4 billion shortfall for the 1991-92 federal fiscal year), the increase in eligible students results in smaller grants for individual students. In some cases, colleges and universities are using institutional funds to make up the shortfall in students' aid packages so they can continue their studies. Also, the rise in student loan defaults, approaching $3.4 billion nationally, has been attributed to the 1992 recession. An institution with a high default rate could be denied future eligibility for federal aid programs for its students, which could harm its tuition and fee revenues (Chronicle of Higher Education, 1992a).

In some states, local economies play a key role for public junior and community colleges, providing one-third to one-half of their operating funds and 100 percent of their capital funds. During an economic downturn, operating budgets at these institutions may be affected simultaneously by decreased state appropriations and static or decreased local support. Taxes linked to local property values generally cannot be raised to equal the entire shortfall from state cutbacks.

Political Environment
The national, state, and local levels of government also affect higher education indirectly through the development of public policy and the imposition of regulations, and directly through special interest appropriations.

National
In July 1992, the Congress reauthorized the Higher Education Act. This will have a wide impact on policy and funding levels providing aid for federal student financial assistance programs, libraries, building construction, renovation, and repair, historically black colleges, and special-purpose institutions. Institutional budgets are also affected by federal research and training grant programs. In addition to the direct costs of these grants, indirect costs are also recovered through institutionally negotiated indirect cost recovery rates. Public and private institutions that receive any kind of federal funds also have to ensure that all programs on campus that benefit from federal funds comply with federal legislation pertaining to civil rights and employment, age, disability, and gender discrimination.

State
A state's legislature, the governor, and the structure of its higher education system all have a tremendous influence on budgeting for public and private higher education (Layzell and Lyddon, 1990). Legislatures are becoming increasingly active in determining higher education policy. As issues become more localized, they try to balance what is good for the state as a whole with what best serves their constituents. While for many states, much of the budget is restricted by federal or state law, (and increasingly by court order), higher education budgets have recently become viewed as a discretionary item (Zusman, 1986). This makes higher education a likely target for legislative scrutiny during difficult economic times. For example, 54 percent of the 1992-93 budget cuts in Ohio came from higher education, while postsecondary spending represents only 12 percent of that state's budget (Chronicle of Higher Education, 1992b). The notion of higher education as a discretionary budget item has also been discussed in the states of California, Illinois, and Texas. This idea is a relatively recent phenomenon, within the last four to six years (Chronicle of Higher Education, 1992c).

Many state legislatures also retain the authority of setting tuition rates. This has a serious effect on the level of tuition revenue institutions can generate. Most states consider tuition as a user fee that supports higher education activities only. They do not view it as a general tax that can be used to support other items in the state budget, such as highways, health care, or the criminal justice system.

Governors also play an important role in influencing the development of higher education policy. In addition to the authority to approve or veto legislation (including appropriations) that is directly related to higher education, the governor's influence is fully exercised through both his or her leadership on particular issues and through the appointments that he or she makes to cabinet-level positions and to the governing boards of public institutions and systems. The focused attention of the governor on higher education issues may serve as a beacon for other elected officials and the public to take up these issues.

Regulatory Environment

All public and private higher education institutions must comply with various governmental regulations and programs. These requirements represent imposed costs that must be borne by the institution. Bowen (1980) refers to these costs as part of "an educational institution's total cost of doing business." He identified several areas of compliance common to all organizations (personal security, work standards, personal opportunity, participation and due process, public information, and environmental protection) and a few that are critical to the higher education enterprise (emancipation of youth, federal grants and contracts, teaching hospitals, and tax reform). Most recently, disability has been added to this list. Each requirement has a direct and an indirect cost: an actual cost for the program or activity and a compliance cost for maintaining records and reporting on the program or activity. Further, some compliance costs are incurred only one time, while others are recurring. Regardless of whether these costs are direct or indirect, one time or recurring, they must be considered as real costs to be offset either through a corresponding increase in revenue or a corresponding reduction in expenditures in some other area of the budget.

Demographic Characteristics

Several demographic conditions exist that can affect higher education budgets. A state's overall population and its composition has a direct impact on its higher education institutions. Nationally, the traditional 18-to-24 age cohort is contracting. There will be fewer individuals from this cohort to enroll in postsecondary educational institutions in the near term. However, not all states will be affected equally; the traditional college-going populations of the sunbelt states are growing, while those in the Midwest have experienced little or no growth (Layzell and Lyddon, 1990). Enrollment declines have both visible and invisible effects on institutional budgets. The loss of tuition is most easily identified. Although the impact of this loss may be partially alleviated by increasing tuition rates, at a certain point the institution will begin to lose enrollment if the increased cost of attendance becomes unaffordable for some students.

The ethnic composition of a state's population can also directly affect institutions of higher education because of variance in persistence to high school graduation. For whatever reasons, minority students tend to drop out of high school at higher rates than majority students. This situation is improving in some states, but it is worsening in others. Fewer high school graduates implies fewer students interested in and eligible for admission to colleges and universities.

Changes in state funding practices may also have an impact on institutions of higher education. Public institutions may experience reductions in state appropriations that result when lower enrollments are factored into the state's formula funding system. For example, Indiana experienced a loss of enrollment in the late 1970s. As a result, the Indiana Commission for Higher Education developed marginal cost factors in its budget process for enrollment changes. Marginal cost factors tend to minimize the funding losses caused by enrollment declines and thereby provide greater funding stability for institutions than do average cost factors. The Indiana Commission also used an actual full-time student equivalent adjustment, rather than esti-mated annual head count enrollment figures, to make appropriations more accurate in their sen-sitivity to enrollment (Seitz, 1981).

A less conspicuous but nonetheless real effect of changes in a state's demographic com-position is the institution's response. Changes in priorities and internal resources usually accompany an institution's perceived need to approach new markets. An institution may find it necessary to add more resources to recruitment and retention activities to attract and keep more students. To reverse potential declines in traditional cohorts, many institutions look to new markets to attract students. These include part-time students, older students returning to complete a degree or take specific courses, and foreign students (Caruthers and Orwig, 1979).

Institutional Factors

An institution's mission, age, tradition, legal history, and special character shape its budget. The institution's mission, established early in its history by constitution, statute, or governing board, guides much of its instructional, research, and service activity. The mission dictates the scope and breadth of its degree programs and its curriculum, and thus, influences its instructional budget. Different missions require curricula that vary in terms of program mix, level of instruction, method of instruction (e.g., laboratory, clinical, or lecture), and class size. Curriculum requirements also dictate minimum resources for equipment and library hold-ings. The curriculum also prescribes the level of faculty training. For example, the accrediting body for baccalaureate nursing programs requires that nursing faculty minimally be mas-ter's-prepared, while master's level nursing program faculty must be doctorally-prepared. Taken together, these requirements impose a minimum level of resources necessary to provide nursing instruction.

The character of the student body is partially prescribed by an institution's mission through its admission standards. Whether an institution is extremely selective or open to all who apply results in different mixes of students and different levels of academic prepared-ness. The less prepared a student body is for college-level work, the more remediation will need to be provided by the institution.

Instructional level, the mix of academic disciplines, the nature of the student body, and institutional policies regarding student/faculty ratio determine the size of the fac-ulty, and thus, the cost of faculty compensation (salary and benefits). Most colleges and universities try to keep faculty salaries competitive with like academic institutions while keeping pace with the cost of living (Bowen, 1980). Personnel costs account for a sig-nificant portion of higher education costs. Faculty and staff compensation together rep-resent approximately 80 percent of educational and general costs (Halstead, 1991). Faculty compensation alone is estimated to account for at least 64 percent of educational and general expenditures. (Educational and general expenditures include operating expenditures for such core institutional functions as instruction, research, public service, academic support, student services, institutional support, operation and maintenance of physical plant, scholarships, and fellowships.)

Public and private institutions operate under governing boards that are selected under different conditions. A private institution operates with a self-perpetuating board of trustees whose membership is generally nominated and elected by the existing board or by the alumni, whereas the governing boards of public institutions are either elected by the state's voters or appointed by the governor. The governing boards of private institutions usually have significant fund-raising responsibilities in addition to their policy-making duties.

Institutional tradition is related to institutional mission. Nevertheless, different types of institutions have different budget characteristics. For example, historically black colleges and universities, which emerged in reaction to the segregated American society of the 19th century, receive some federal support that is unavailable to other institutions. Similarly, land grant institutions collect noncompetitive federal funds for certain research and service activities. Many private institutions have been adopted wholly or partially by their states and have special funding relationships. A few institutions, such as the service academies and other special purpose institutions, are supported entirely by the federal government. Numerous, separate public institutions have been reconfigured as multicampus systems operating under single governing boards. All these examples demonstrate traditional conditions that affect the preparation and implementation of institutional budgets.

An institution's budget is also affected by its overall financial condition, including its level of debt. A limited repertoire of revenue sources affects an institution's ability to support its budget. Public institutions, once completely reliant on state appropriations, now have expanded their funding base to include higher tuition levels, significant fund-raising efforts, and increased indirect cost revenues from government and private grants and contracts. These increased development activities at public sector institutions are in direct competition for philanthropic funds with those of private institutions. While public institutions increasingly look to private contributions to support their activities, private institutions seek additional support from states to support instructional activities for resident students, research, and some construction projects. These trends are evidence that institutions of higher education will seek revenues from whatever sources seem available. This concept will be discussed further later.

Institutional age is also a significant factor. Older institutions are more likely than younger institutions to have greater physical resources, more degree programs, and more alumni to support them. The age of the physical plant of the campus as well as its size and location also influences the budget. Older buildings require proportionately more funds for maintenance and utilities; larger and urban campuses tend to require additional funds for increased security measures.

Capital renewal and replacement is a topic of growing concern. Postsecondary institutions have tended to balance their budgets during difficult fiscal times by deferring building maintenance, and thereby reducing the physical plant portion of their budgets (Jenny, 1981). The accumulation of deferred maintenance has been identified as a threat to the stability of higher education funding because of the generally poor understanding of capital budgeting, especially maintenance of capital assets (Allen, 1981). In a national survey, Halpern (1987) found that 50 percent of college and university structures will require significant renovation within the next 20-25 years due to age. The cost of backlogged renovation and repairs nationwide was estimated at $60-70 billion, of which one-third was considered "critical" (Rush and Johnson, 1988). The growth of deferred maintenance nationally has been linked to reductions in the level of capital investment in existing facilities and in the level of funding for operations and maintenance (Kraal, 1992). To avoid continued growth in the level of deferred maintenance, the Association of Physical Plant Administrators, the National Association of College and University Business Officers, and the Society for College and University Planning have developed and adopted capital renewal and replacement standards that recommend annual expenditures of 1.5 to 3 percent of the "existing investment in plant and equipment" for postsecondary institutions (Dunn, 1989). Obviously, the deferred maintenance problem will significantly affect institutional budgets in the future if appropriate measures are not taken.

Other Contextual Factors

Howard Bowen, in his far-reaching research on the economics of higher education, formulated the revenue theory of costs and several associated "laws" to help explain higher education financial matters and why institutions budget the way they do. In his 1980 book, *The Costs of Higher Education*, Bowen stated that, "The basic concept underlying the revenue theory of cost is that an institution's educational cost per student unit is determined by the revenues available for educational purposes" (p. 17). In public institutions, this revenue comes primarily from tuition and state appropriations. In private institutions, it is derived mainly from tuition. In other words, at any given time, the unit cost of education at a particular college or university is determined by the amount of revenue that institution has available to it relative to enrollment.

From this theoretical base, Bowen developed a set of "laws" of higher education costs that describe the motivations and activities of higher education institutions from year to year. These "natural laws" of higher education costs are as follows (Bowen, 1980, pp. 19-20):

1. *The dominant goals of institutions are educational excellence, prestige, and influence.* Attainment of these goals is measured by student/faculty ratios, faculty salaries, qualifications of students, the number of library holdings, the quality of facilities, and the amount of equipment available. These things are all resource inputs, not educational outcomes.
2. *In the quest for excellence, prestige, and influence, there is virtually no limit to the amount of money an institution could spend for seemingly fruitful educational ends.* No matter how much an institution has, there is always something else that it needs to meet its mission, improve its programs, or enhance its quality.
3. *Each institution raises all the money it can.* No institution of higher education ever admits to having enough money.
4. *Each institution spends all it raises.* An exception to this is the endowments that are raised where the endowment principal is not spent, but the annual income is. However, these arrangements are designed for the long-term enhancement of the institution, and in that sense are also part of the institution's quest for excellence, prestige, and influence.
5. *The cumulative effect of the preceding four laws is toward ever increasing expenditures.* Questions concerning what higher education ought to cost, or whether higher education could oper-

ate more efficiently, are usually raised from outside the institution rather than inside. As a result, there is a basic assumption that institutional budgets must ever increase.

Bowen also noted that these laws were also applicable to other nonprofit organizations such as schools, hospitals, and churches, as well as government agencies.

These laws help explain why private institutions have increased their tuitions so dramatically in recent years. They also indicate why public institutions will naturally turn to students to fund an increasing share of their budgets as state legislatures reduce state appropriations. Bowen would argue that if higher education budgets are to be controlled, the external revenue-providers for higher education—that is, state legislators, the federal government, local governments, students and their families, and donors—must be the source of that control. There are simply too few incentives within colleges and universities to operate with great efficiency or to cut costs.

Three other reasons for the continuation of rapidly increased costs in higher education have been identified by Massy (1989) as cost disease, growth force, and organizational slack. First, due to its high labor intensity, higher education has not been able to accrue great savings nor increase productivity from technological improvements in the workplace. Thus, higher education suffers from a cost disease: its inability to increase productivity means costs will continue to increase. Hopefully, recent advances in the use and sophistication of telecommunications for instruction may provide one remedy to this situation. Second, given its reluctance to eliminate old programs and activities before adding new ones, postsecondary institutions are always moving toward a net increase in programs and activities. This growth force also leads to ever-increasing costs. Finally, the waste and inefficiency common to all organizations, organizational slack, is no kinder to higher education than to other organizations. Additional costs often result from handling the problems that arise from these inefficiencies.

These three reasons and the "natural laws" combine to explain the widespread perception in higher education that budgets must always increase—next year's budget must be higher than this year's—and that the solution to all problems in higher education is more money. Obviously, in the financial environment of the 1990s, the reality at many institutions is that the budget is not going to increase. The additional resources necessary to make that happen are simply not available.

TOOLS FOR INSTITUTIONAL BUDGETING

Caruthers and Orwig (1979) have identified three distinct eras in the evolution of budgeting: (1) the era of executive budgeting, which emphasized control and responded to the perception of waste and inefficiency in organizations; (2) the era of performance-based budgeting, which emphasized management using work measures and cost accounting and responded to a demand for precision in cost attribution and outcome assessment; and (3) the era of programming, planning, and budgeting systems, which emphasized planning and its link to budgeting and responded to the perception of linking dollars to objectives. We may now be in a fourth era, one of budget reform, in response to increasing demands for accountability and reduced public revenues. Many of the reform measures are characterized by aspects of performance budgeting and a strong relationship (at least from a rhetorical standpoint) with strategic planning. Rubin (1988) also suggests that environmental factors will have an impact on the budget process, that this process will affect outcomes, and that budgets will mirror policy. As in the past, the current drive to overhaul the budget process will no doubt require that institutions continually add on, not substitute, new budgeting requirements.

Over the years, various techniques, methodologies, and approaches have been used by colleges and universities to prepare budgets. In this section, we shall describe several of the better-known approaches, and list some of their strengths and weaknesses.

Incremental Budgeting ("the Science of Muddling Through")

The oldest and most common approach to budgeting is incremental budgeting, which is defined as a "budgeting method that uses essentially the same budget from one year to the next, allowing only minor changes in revenue levels and resource distribution" (Vandement, 1989). Increments or decrements from the base budget are either positive or negative dollar amounts or percentages. Each budget line or group of budget lines is considered separately from others (Caruthers and Orwig, 1979). This approach generally assumes that the basic objectives of the institution, the department, or the program have not changed markedly from the current year, and that they will continue into the next year. New initiatives can be started, and reflected in the budget, but most of the units and programs will see budget changes that reflect only minor changes in existing salary and operating expense levels. Lindblom (1959) referred to this process of determining realistic, successive, budget alternatives that differ only marginally from existing conditions as "the science of muddling through."

The strengths of incremental (decremental) budgeting include the following (Vandement, 1989; Welzenbach, 1982):

- It is relatively simple and easy to understand;
- Budget alternatives are limited to a reasonable set;
- It increases the ability to predict the consequences of budget alternatives with accuracy and confidence;
- It conserves time and energy;
- Its pragmatic approach provides an alternative to other more theoretical approaches;
- It generates limited conflict among resource competitors; every budget item is treated the same;
- It complements long-term organizational commitments during times of fiscal stability;
- It is generally accepted by governing boards and legislators.

The weaknesses of this approach include (Hossler, Kuh, and Bateman, 1989; Vandement, 1989; Welzenbach, 1982):

- It is a nonaggressive approach to management and budget decision making;
- There is a general assumption that the base budget is the absolute minimum, below which the institution cannot function;
- It may easily be affected by internal institutional politics ("the squeaky wheel gets the grease") or by the administration's preferences (budgeting by "king's degree");
- Little incentive is provided to justify continuing programs, to assess their quality, or to cut unproductive programs;
- It is based on inputs, rather than outputs;
- It minimizes conflict rather than selecting the best policy.

Nevertheless, for all of its flaws and "warts," incremental budgeting has been the most widely used approach in institutions of higher education. To paraphrase Winston Churchill, "Incremental budgeting is the worst budgeting approach, except for all the others."

Formula Budgeting

As the name implies, formula budgeting is the application of one or more formulas in the budgeting process (Caruthers and Orwig, 1979). Each formula manipulates certain institutional data based on mathematical relationships between program demand and costs to derive an estimated dollar amount to support future program operation. Formulas are based on historical data, projected trends, and negotiated parameters to provide desired levels of funding. Put another way, formula budgeting is a method that calculates the amount of funding a program requires by applying selected measures of unit costs to selected output measures (Vandement, 1989). As such, formula budgeting is "a combination of technical judgments and political agreements" (Meisinger and Dubeck, 1984, p. 186). This form of budgeting is used mostly at the state level as a method for public institutions to develop their appropriations requests. It is seldom used at the institutional level, although, as discussed later in this section, this may change if cost center budgeting becomes more widely used.

The strengths of formula budgeting include the following (Brinkman, 1984; Meisinger and Dubeck, 1984; Morgan, 1984; Welzenbach, 1982; Caruthers and Orwig, 1979):

* It provides of an equitable distribution of funds among institutions;
* It enhances uniformity and ease of budget preparation;
* It provides for a useful framework through which colleges and universities communicate with the state legislature;
* It depoliticizes the budgeting process by relying on technical decision making rather than power and influence associated with the traditional political process;
* The quantitative nature of formula budgeting makes decision making appear to be more objective and more routine.

The weaknesses of formula budgeting include (Hossler, Kuh, and Bateman, 1989; Brinkman, 1984; Welzenbach, 1982; Caruthers and Orwig, 1979):

* Although the process may appear to be less political, formula budgeting just shifts the level of political judgments from a traditional program and issues orientation to the level of technical judgments concerning the nature of the mathematical relationships involved in the formula(s);
* Formula approaches are typically enrollment-driven, which may become problematic during periods of enrollment downturns;
* The quantitative nature of formula approaches makes it difficult to include qualitative issues;
* Mechanisms to fund new or innovative programs are typically lacking in formula approaches;
* Formulas perpetuate the status quo because they are based on historical relationships involving existing programs;
* The approach encourages institutions to develop high-cost programs such as engineering or doctoral programs, because the formula generates more funds from such programs;

- Merit-based decisions are typically excluded;
- Many formula approaches do not recognize differences in institutional mission or program;
- Formula approaches tend to have a leveling effect on institutions;
- Formula approaches tend to focus on what can be measured and modeled quantitatively;
- Formulas tend to be overly simplistic and rigid;
- Unintended incentives and disincentives are built-in (such as always rewarding higher enrollment);
- Formulas generally do not recognize economies of scale;
- Such approaches can unintentionally serve as devices of institutional budget control.

This last point deserves additional comment. In those states where formula budgeting approaches are used, institutions insist that the use of appropriated funds not be tied to the unit that generated the funds through the formula. That is, they want the formula used as a revenue generation mechanism, but not as an internal budgeting technique. For the most part, the institutions have been successful in this argument, leaving administrators great discretion in allocating appropriated funds among budgetary units. Of course, the basic amount of support appropriated, and the fact that legislatures rarely appropriate 100 percent of the amount generated by the formula, limits internal allocation to a large extent. Nevertheless, this decoupling of state appropriation and institutional allocation continues to be a source of distrust between higher education and some public officials in states that utilize formula funding approaches.

Program Budgeting

Many budgeting approaches have been designed in response to the weaknesses found in incremental budgeting. Program budgeting was one of the first attempts to develop a more output-oriented approach. It is defined as a budgeting method "in which budgets are created for specific programs or activities, rather than departments, and each program's budget is apportioned among the several departments that contribute to the program's activities" (Vandement, 1989, p. 129). It is based on allocating funds to related activities that have been grouped together based on their common goals and objectives (Green, 1971).

The primary components of this approach are the program plan, the program budget, and cost-benefit analysis. The process includes developing program goals and objectives, developing alternative activities to meet these objectives, costing each alternative, identifying benefits to each alternative, and selecting the best alternative. These alternatives are forwarded to the next higher administrative unit for review.

A well-known example of program budgeting is Planning, Programming, and Budgeting Systems (PPBS). PPBS strives to match and allocate the appropriate resources that lead to institutionally-desired outputs (Robins, 1986). The concepts of PPBS include (1) a systematic long-range planning process (5-15 years), (2) a selection process for examining mid-range alternatives and objectives (1-5 years), (3) a short-term translation of selected objectives into budgetary data (0-1 year), and (4) a recognition of the costs and benefits of alternatives and objectives over time (Balderston and Weathersby, 1972).

PPBS was used in the early 1960s in the U.S. Department of Defense. By 1965, PPBS was required for budget preparation in most federal agencies (Bowen, 1975). However, the system was not fully integrated into the federal bureaucracy. At the state level, PPBS was thought to provide governors and legislators with the opportunity to achieve specified goals through the reallocation of state resources. However, in 1966, the American Council on Education rejected PPBS as not being conceptually suited to higher education (Robins, 1986). While PPBS was employed at one time by institutions such as the University of California, Princeton University, and the University of Utah, it is no longer used in higher education. However, because of its theoretical attractiveness, program budgeting still has its proponents. The strengths of program budgeting are (Morgan, 1984; Caruthers and Orwig, 1979):

- It focuses on ends rather than means;
- It relates means to desired ends;
- It provides a sense of institutional direction;
- It does contain qualitative dimensions;
- It creates a better understanding of institutional data bases.

The weaknesses of program budgeting include the following (Hossler, Kuh, and Bateman, 1989; Vandement, 1989; Meisinger and Dubeck, 1984; Morgan, 1984; Welzenbach, 1982):

- It is often difficult in higher education to define what constitutes a program;
- There is often little agreement on specific goals and objectives;
- It is often difficult to identify and measure specific outcomes (many of higher education's outcomes are joint products);
- While it may make sense conceptually to aggregate activities into programs, most organizations are not structured that way;
- Program budgeting is considered an irrelevant operating tool for institutional managers who are responsible for implementing policies and programs;
- The approach focuses on what should be done, rather than how to do it;
- It is unwieldy when used regularly for annual budgeting;
- It fails to take into account institutional missions;
- It falsely assumes that the program cost and other data necessary to make decisions already exist;
- Since programs normally involve several units, it is difficult for institutions to control resources when they are allocated by program;
- It is easier to budget resources to organizational units on the basis of functional need, and to control the resources by unit.

Zero-Base Budgeting

Zero-base budgeting (ZBB) was originally developed by Peter A. Pyhrr, used by Texas Instruments in Dallas in the late 1960s, and exported to Georgia in 1971 for developing the state's FY 1973 budget (Green, 1971). The basic premise behind ZBB is that every activity and program is significant and must be rejustified each year through a series of "decision packages" (Caruthers and Orwig, 1979). It is a microeconomic approach to budgeting (i.e., program and activity objectives are directly translated into elements of the operating plan), whereas program budgeting has a macroeconomic focus (i.e., broad policies are transformed into operating plan elements through a centralized, vertical decision-making process). Under ZBB, each budget unit evaluates its goals and objectives, justifies the need for various activities and their costs and benefits, and develops decision packages for each activity at each level of output. A priority rank is established for each decision package at each hierarchical level. ZBB is a useful approach for developing preliminary budgets for new programs and "start-up" activities. However, it has not been used widely in higher education.

The strengths of zero-base budgeting include:

- It is focused on results and outcomes;
- It is a highly rational, objective approach to budgeting;
- Preparing the decision packages provides an excellent understanding of activities, programs, and organizational units.

The weaknesses of zero-base budgeting include (Morgan, 1984):

- The fact that no budget history is assumed does not recognize continuing commitments, such as faculty tenure, that cannot be changed quickly;
- The process is highly time-consuming and generates a great deal of paperwork;
- The judgments used during the preparation of the decision packages tend to be *ad hoc* in nature;
- The validity and reliability of the criteria and measures used to rank the decision packages may be questionable.

Performance Budgeting

As indicated previously, performance budgeting emerged historically as the second stage in the evolution of budgeting. It is a budgeting approach based on funding desired outcomes or accomplishments (Green, 1971). Although implemented by few states (Banta, 1988; Ewell, 1988, 1985), performance funding developed originally as a cost reimbursement model for resource allocations (Morgan, 1984). It addresses activities rather than objectives, and relies on activity classifications, performance measures, and performance evaluations. It is clearly an approach where institutional funding depends on performing in certain ways and meeting certain expectations.

Performance budgeting was largely unused for many years, but is currently experiencing a renaissance as a state-level budgeting practice that relates resources to activities and outcomes (Banta, 1986; Banta and Fisher, 1984; Bogue and Brown, 1982). Recently, several state legislatures have demonstrated renewed interest in performance funding to ensure accountability by postsecondary institutions.

Some barriers to implementation exist, however. There is disagreement regarding definition and measurement of performance measures. It is often difficult to identify appropriate, measurable criteria on which to judge performance (Caruthers and Orwig, 1979). There is not always a proven relationship between the cause and effect of the criteria and the measures used as proxies for the desired accomplishments. Political reality may prohibit its full implementation, since performance budgeting tends to have little "pork barrel appeal." That is, since objective measures are used to appropriate funds to institutions, legislators feel they no longer have the ability to provide appropriations to specific institutions, particularly those in the area they represent. Another problem is the potential for establishing easily achievable criteria that require little advancement for some institutions. For example, colleges and universities could easily increase the percent of students that graduate by relaxing their grading standards.

Other critical questions in recent cases where performance budgeting has been used include: how much of an institution's appropriation should depend on performance funding, and secondly, should performance budgeting be applied to base funding or incremental funds. If performance criteria are applied to base funds, institutions will not know from year to year (or biennium to biennium) what level of funding to expect. The resulting uncertainty makes it difficult for academic and operational planning to take place. On the other hand, if performance funding is supplemental—that is, provided in addition to base funding—it serves as an incentive to institutions to accomplish the objectives for which the performance funding is provided.

Although some states (e.g., Colorado, Florida, Kentucky, Missouri, South Carolina, Virginia, and West Virginia) have moved toward developing performance measures for their institutions of higher education (Lenth, 1992; Ewell, 1988), only Tennessee has implemented performance budgeting (Lenth, 1992; Banta, 1988). Texas is an example of a state that is moving toward performance budgeting at the present time. The Texas Legislative Budget Board plans to develop an appropriations bill for the 1994-1995 biennium that is based, to some degree, on agency performance for all state agencies and all institutions of higher education. As a result, Texas is in the planning stages of developing performance funding methods for health-related institutions, universities, and community and technical colleges. In 1991, the Texas Legislature instructed the Texas Higher Education Coordinating Board (THECB) to develop a method for distributing state funds to health-related institutions using an outcome-based performance approach. The THECB (1992a) adopted an advisory committee recommendation that would establish core performance measures based on common institutional missions and goals for admission, graduation, licensure, certain postgraduate training, continuing education, research, model training and education projects, and professional, hospital, and clinical services that are defined as unsponsored charity care. Additional measures were provided for enhancements beyond institutional missions and goals that contributed to broader state goals, such as minority participation and training in geographic areas and in particular disciplines where shortages exist within the state. No recommendations were made regarding the percentage of institutional appropriations that should be funded based on these performance measures, nor on whether these funds should be considered part of an institution's base funding or as a supplement.

Although not required to develop a performance funding approach for senior academic institutions, the THECB also recommended that supplemental funds be added to base funding to reward performance in senior universities. The Board proposed that these funds be distributed based on institutional achievement of state goals for instruction, research, and public service as represented by thirteen measures: degrees awarded, course completion, student remediation, minority student enrollment and graduation, community college transfers and graduates, critical skills, graduate/professional study, lower division tenure track teaching, externally funded research, intellectual property income, and faculty service. It is recommended that the Legislature establish thirteen pools of funds from which performance funding can be drawn. Institutions would share proportionately in these pools based on their performance during a given period. The THECB recommended that the total performance funding amount not exceed two percent of base funding for the 1994 fiscal year, five percent of base funding for fiscal 1995, and ten percent in future years.

The THECB also accepted a recommendation from the Texas Public Community/Junior Colleges Association regarding performance funding for those institutions. The Association recommended that 50 percent of performance funding be based on course completion, and 50 percent be based on credentials (certificates and degrees) awarded, transfers to senior institutions, employed course completers, licensure, successful remediation, minority participation, and economic development contribution (i.e., total earnings of all community college students over a base period). While the Association's report made no recommendation regarding the overall percentage of institutional budgets that should be based on these performance measures, it did recommend that these funds be supplemental to community college base funding, which is currently formula-based.

The strengths of performance budgeting include (Morgan, 1984, Caruthers and Orwig, 1979):

- The approach focuses on accomplishments and results rather than on inputs and processes;
- Once defined, it is a relatively simple approach;
- It promotes an equitable allocation of resources to those institutions that meet performance criteria.

The weaknesses of performance budgeting include (THECB, 1992b; Hossler, Kuh, and Bateman, 1989):

- It is difficult to define performance criteria and performance measures;
- There is a tendency to measure that which is measurable and perhaps not deal adequately with important issues (for example, using multiple-choice tests as the only measure of learning);
- Legislators are less able to influence decisions concerning institutions in the areas they represent;
- The time gap between an accomplishment, the measurement of it, and the receipt of the funds may be considerable;
- It is difficult to measure long-term outcomes;
- The approach does not take into account the diversity of various institutional missions in setting universal performance criteria;
- The budgeting and reporting documentation is complex and voluminous.

Incentive Budgeting
Incentive budgeting, like performance budgeting, continues higher education's pursuit of output-oriented budgeting, especially at the state level. Some states are using their budgets to provide incentives to their institutions of higher education for achieving state goals for educational quality. Typically, they set aside a pool of funds earmarked for the achievement of these goals, and once they are met, institutions share proportionately in these funds. Other states operate initiative programs, which provide the funds in advance of goal achievement, based on proposals submitted by institutions. A state's priorities may include specific outcomes, efficient and effective management, decentralized decision making, formula funding (Allen, 1984), remediation, and/or scholarships. Incentive programs give institutions the opportunity to move in the direction of state goals through increased motivation (i.e., additional funding),

rather than through coercion (i.e., the threat of funding reductions) and regulation. Colleges and universities are relatively free to participate in those programs where they have the highest likelihood of achieving the objectives.

It may be argued that every budget contains incentives for certain activities and disincentives for others (Folger, 1989). Incentive funding is a mechanism more states are using to encourage institutions of higher education to conduct activities that meet state goals by either adding value to inputs, assuring that certain activities occur, or rewarding specific results. Although terminology varies from state to state, the major types of incentive funding include those programs that reward results after performance has occurred, and those programs that provide prospective funding for new programs and activities that promise the desired results (Berdahl and Holland, 1989). Funding that is awarded based on results is usually referred to as primary incentive funding whereas funding that is allocated prior to achieving the results is referred to as secondary incentive funding. A Texas committee has defined programs that fund results as "incentive funding" and those that fund prospective results as "initiative funding" (THECB, 1990).

Most existing incentive programs concentrate on funding inputs (e.g., centers of excellence, recruitment of eminent faculty, equipment funds), activities and processes (e.g., assessment programs, minority student recruitment/retention, business partnerships), and outputs (e.g., learning outcomes, improved graduation rates). A 1989 survey of fiscal incentive practices by the National Center for Postsecondary Governance and Finance found that the purpose most often served by incentive programs was economic growth, including technology transfer and applied research to solve state problems. Recruitment of minority students, faculty, and staff was the second most popular category, followed by eminent scholars programs, improvement in undergraduate education, equipment support, and support of basic research. Thirty-two states reported having established some type of incentive funding program. Florida and New Jersey have established the largest number of individual programs, but other states such as Ohio and Tennessee have also been very active in this area (Berdahl and Holland, 1989).

As in the case of performance budgeting, the question of whether the funds for incentive programs will be taken from higher education's base funding or will be added as supplemental funding is critical to institutions. If the incentive programs are supported from funds taken from the base, institutions will be uncertain as to what their basic level of support is. They will be forced to compete for funds that they had previously received. Incentive programs that are supported by funding that is supplemental to basic appropriations truly provide incentives for institutions to achieve the state's specific goals.

The strengths of incentive budgeting include (Holland and Berdahl, 1990; Berdahl and Holland, 1989; Folger, 1984):

- It is a method whereby states can encourage institutions to achieve specific state goals;
- It is an approach that focuses on results and outputs;
- Qualitative issues, such as the quality of educational programs, can be addressed rather than only quantitative issues, such as enrollment levels;
- Incentive programs are most effective when faculty members (i.e., "those closest to the action") are directly involved;
- Incentive programs that use matching funds to leverage private fund raising are especially effective.

The weaknesses of incentive budgeting include (Berdahl and Holland, 1989):

- Measurement of outputs or outcomes in higher education is difficult;
- The tendency is to measure that which is measurable, i.e., that which is quantifiable;
- Since many higher education objectives are difficult to measure directly, proxies (such as test scores) are used; in many cases these proxies then become the objective;
- Incentive budgeting is much more effective when supported by funding that is additional to higher education base appropriations, rather than taken from that base;
- Incentive programs tend not to be very useful as accountability measures;
- Incentive programs are not very effective unless a state has developed a comprehensive strategy for higher education improvement; incentive programs should be one part of such as strategy;
- Fiscal incentives tend to emphasize short-term goals rather than long-term planning.

Cost Center Budgeting

Cost center budgeting originated with Harvard's president James Conant who stated that "Every tub stands on its own bottom, each dean balances his own budget" (Caruthers and Orwig, 1979). Under this budgeting approach, academic departments and support units are considered cost centers for fiscal purposes, and are expected to be self-supporting. That is, in each cost center, projected expenditures must be supported by sufficient revenues raised by that center. In an academic department or college, for example, this means that the unit's faculty and staff salaries, its operating expenses, and a share of physical plant costs and other overhead expenditures must be covered by the unit's income from tuition and fees, endowments, gifts, and grants. Some support units are allowed to charge for their services. Nevertheless, under this budgeting approach, any revenue shortfalls in a particular unit must be accompanied by a scaling back of expenditures in order that unit operations can fall within available income.

Currently, some institutions are using an approach called Responsibility Center Budgeting (RCB). This approach is essentially cost center budgeting by another name. Until recently, RCB had only been implemented at private institutions, such as Cornell University, Harvard University, Johns Hopkins University, University of Miami, University of Southern California (where it is known as Responsibility Center Management), University of Pennsylvania, Vanderbilt University, and Washington University. When Thomas Ehrlich became president of Indiana University in 1989, the former provost of the University of Pennsylvania and former dean of the Stanford University Law School brought this innovation to a public institution. The University of Vermont and the University of Alabama-Birmingham have also implemented some form of RCB, but to date, Indiana is the only major research university (as per the Carnegie classification) to do so.

The key concept in responsibility center budgeting is the financial autonomy provided to each budgetary unit (Leslie, 1984). According to Ehrlich, three principles serve as the basis for RCB: "(1) all cost and income attributable to each school and other academic unit should be assigned to that unit; (2) appropriate incentives should exist for each academic unit to increase income and reduce costs to further a clear set of academic priorities; and (3) all costs of other units, such as the library or student counseling, should be allocated to academic units" (Whalen, 1991).

In responsibility center budgeting, tuition and fee income is attributed to the academic unit that generates it, while charges to academic units provide income to support units (Whalen, 1991). Each academic unit is assessed a formula-derived tax for university-wide support services such as libraries, academic computing, academic affairs, student services, physical facilities, and central administration. After all academic and support unit income is estimated for the year, the central administration allocates state appropriated funds among the academic units to offset remaining expenditures.

Among the incentives that make it possible for Indiana University to implement RCB without external interference is the fact that it retains its fund balances at the end of the fiscal year; that is, unspent general revenue funds (i.e., state tax dollars) do not revert back to the state treasury. In addition, Indiana University has legislative authority to use student tuition and fees as well as local funds to supplement state appropriations; that is, these funds are not considered part of the university's appropriation. Finally, the legislature authorized the university to manage its own funds, thus demonstrating a healthy level of trust between the university and the state.

The strengths of cost center budgeting or responsibility center budgeting are as follows (Whalen, 1991; Leslie, 1984; Morgan, 1984; Zemsky, Porter, and Oedel, 1978; Hoenack, 1977):

- It provides a rational approach to budgeting;
- It provides a method for distributing resources that demonstrates an institution's objectives;
- It facilitates accountability (it is easy to track the use of appropriated state funds as they relate to specific state funding decisions);
- There is closer proximity between budget responsibility and control and the institution's operating units;
- Decisions regarding academic changes are made closer to the instructional level;
- Resources can be moved within the institution in direct relation to enrollment patterns;
- The approach is responsive to both public policy and institutional needs;
- It increases competition among "players" (which is good for the consumer);
- It increases the effective use of resources;
- It enhances cooperation among campus units,
- Students have more influence across campus because they can "vote with their feet."

The weaknesses of cost center budgeting include (Whalen, 1991; Hossler, Kuh, and Bateman, 1989; Leslie, 1984; Meisinger and Dubeck, 1984):

- It is difficult to apply in many institutions because many academic units have considerable service components (e.g. liberal arts departments);
- It may be difficult to classify units as responsibility centers;
- It requires tedious and complex calculations for the allocation of support unit costs to academic units;
- Institutional politics may affect the determination of which unit receives credit for some course offerings or services, or the algorithms that allocate indirect costs;
- Academic programs may become budget-driven;
- Academic units may vie to offer inappropriate service courses just to generate income;
- Central controls may be lacking;

- New fees may be developed to provide dedicated revenue streams for support units;
- It is sometimes difficult to develop equitable cost algorithms for taxing academic units.

Summary

In examining these seven institutional budgeting approaches, it should be remembered that they are not mutually exclusive. Some aspects of one approach may overlap with those of another. The terminology used at a particular institution or in a particular state may contain elements of each approach. This is partly because higher education seems to be constantly trying to move away from incremental budgeting—at least conceptually. Nevertheless, budgeting systems exist that contain decision packages (from zero-base budgeting) within program areas, each with its own formula, and supported by performance measures, with separate incentive funding programs. In the final analysis, however, most institutional administrators are interested in maintaining the funds they were budgeted for this year, and then arguing for the additional funds they need for next year. They frame their requests within the specific budget approach or combination of approaches they are required to use, but their goal is the same, nevertheless.

RETRENCHMENT AND REALLOCATION

Financial stress and uncertainty represent special conditions for budgeters—no more "business as usual." Regardless of whether the stress confronting the institution occurs suddenly or gradually, regardless of whether it is caused by unstable or declining enrollments, reductions in financial support (i.e., tuition, appropriations, fund raising, or endowment income) or other factors, difficult fiscal decisions lay ahead. The basic goal of institutional efforts during these times is to minimize the negative impact on instruction and academic program quality. Institutions respond by using both adaptive and resistive practices to control where reductions take place.

Of course, different types of institutions are affected by financial stress in different ways. Public colleges and universities, for example, feel the greatest impact from declining state and local tax revenues. However, many private institutions that receive direct or indirect public support are also affected. Enrollment declines are most keenly felt at the undergraduate level, largely affecting public state colleges and universities and private, nonselective liberal arts colleges that depend primarily on tuition revenues to support the bulk of their budget revenue. At the graduate level, enrollment declines create difficulties for major research universities that need a critical mass of students to maintain high quality graduate programs (Breneman, 1981). However, at community colleges, open admissions policies and the responsiveness of vocational programs to local community needs help to maintain enrollment levels.

Institutions whose students rely heavily on financial aid are most affected by declines in federal financial assistance programs. Curtailment of federally supported research centers and programs affects major research universities. All postsecondary institutions are affected by inflation, especially as it boosts the cost of those goods and services that are especially relevant to higher education, such as salaries, fringe benefits, scientific equipment, scholarly books and journals, and utilities.

An institution's ability to respond to financial crises as well as financial opportunities depends on several elements. Among those critical abilities are the institution's financial flexibility, including prior development of reserve funds to meet contingencies, a regular review of the costs and benefits of instructional programs, a regular review of institutional priorities, the diversity of revenue sources, and enhanced communications with faculty, staff, students, and such interest groups as alumni and industry representatives (Vandement, 1989). These elements allow an institution to respond more positively to enrollment fluctuations and financial emergencies and to take advantage of unforeseen opportunities.

Volkwein's (1988) review of state regulatory practices over public postsecondary educational institutions also revealed that there is a relationship between state deregulation and financial flexibility. He found that public universities generally operate more efficiently when subjected to fewer regulations. This underscores the need for flexibility when times are less than ideal. Public universities rely less on state appropriations when they are given incentives for good management. Relief from state control through lump-sum appropriations, campus retention and control of tuition and non-tuition revenues, campus retention of year-end balances, flexibility to shift funds among budget categories, authority to finance capital construction, and biennial budgeting lead to increased flexibility at public research universities. High levels of state control directly and negatively affect institutional efficiency and adaptability, as well as educational effectiveness (Volkwein, 1986).

Under ideal conditions, a postsecondary institution would have the ability to respond to a crisis (Brinkerhoff, 1981). This ability would include having both adequate time to react and the financial flexibility to reallocate funds and make changes in operations without irreparably harming instructional programs. However, the fact that a large proportion of the annual budgets of most colleges and universities are relatively fixed makes it difficult to make quickly the fiscal changes necessary to shift resources from lower priority to higher priority programs and activities. Unfortunately, the conditions associated with the fiscal crises facing many institutions are rarely ideal.

When confronted with a fiscal crisis, colleges and universities generally try to either resist or adapt depending on their assessment of the severity and the duration of the crisis. Like budgeters in other settings, higher education officials have three basic methods of responding—increasing revenues, reducing expenditures, or some combination of the two. Increasing revenue is a resistive option that allows institutions to maintain current programs and activities. However, campuses may shift energies that should be focused on expenditure savings, retrenchment, and reallocation to increasing revenue as a defense mechanism to avoid difficult decisions. Increasing revenue is not a feasible option for all institutions in all conditions of financial duress. Another related resistive option used to lessen the impact of loss of income from a single source is diversification of funding sources. A broadened base of funds spreads the risk of revenue shortfalls among many revenue sources, rather than relying on only a few.

How colleges and universities allocate resources among units is closely related to each unit's centrality (i.e., the match between the unit's purpose and the institution's mission), its relational power among units within the institution and outside the institution, and the repertoire of resource negotiation strategies it uses (Hackman, 1985). Campus administrators usually review peripheral units first during times of fiscal distress, since it is perceived that their reduction or elimination can occur without harming the integrity of the institution's academic mission.

Bowen and Glenny (1981) have categorized short-term, adaptive responses to fiscal crisis as being either selective or across-the-board reductions of expenditures. Five examples of these techniques include:

- Operational responses that are temporary and have limited impact on instructional programs (e.g., reductions in vacant staff positions, building maintenance, travel, etc.);
- Academic program responses that have little impact on faculty (e.g., reductions in vacant faculty positions, travel to professional meetings, equipment funds, etc.);
- Faculty adjustments that rely mainly on attrition;
- Faculty adjustments that rely mainly on academic program considerations (e.g., shifting faculty to service courses as a way of responding to declining majors);
- Procedural responses within the organization (e.g., increased centralization of decision making).

Bowen and Glenny also discuss the fact that several of these reactions erode an institution's budget flexibility over time and limit its options for responding to the problem on a long-term basis. Ordinarily, institutions maintain a certain degree of flexibility through budget and salary savings, the use of part-time and temporary faculty, and the difference between the average costs by which academic programs are typically funded and the marginal costs of additional students. During periods of financial crisis, vacant positions and contingency reserves are usually the first things cut, followed by reductions in support units, supplies, and equipment. Over the short term, these adjustments may allow an institution to withstand brief financial turmoil, but they do not provide long-term solutions. As these types of cuts are made, the institution's budget flexibility is reduced. If the fiscal crisis is short-term, the institution will, over a few years, rebuild a measure of this flexibility. However, if the crisis is long-term, the flexibility will soon be used up, and the institution will be forced to consider more drastic measures.

It is also true that during the early stages of a fiscal dilemma, institutions may choose to make budgets cuts across-the-board, with the budgets of all affected campus units being reduced by the same amount or percent. Before long, however, and especially if it becomes clear that the duration of the crisis will be longer term, a realization develops that deeper, more selective reductions are necessary to avoid a slow erosion in the overall quality of institutional programs.

When colleges and universities are confronted with significant reductions in revenues and/ or when the duration of the financial crisis appears to be long-term, they must consider more substantive and fundamental changes, such as retrenchment and reallocation. These approaches usually involve reductions in course offerings, program review, and ultimately the release of faculty and staff in order to achieve financial equilibrium. Obviously, this last option is a painful process for any institution, and one that is entertained only after other alternatives have been exhausted. Nevertheless, this is the situation in which many institutions find themselves in the decade of the 1990s.

Retrenchment, defined as "the dismissal or layoff of tenured faculty, or non-tenured faculty in mid-contract" (Mortimer and Taylor, 1984, p. 70), is an adaptive response to long-term fiscal crisis. Since higher education is a labor-intensive enterprise, it stands to reason that any significant reductions in expenditures will ultimately involve reducing personnel. Random faculty attrition is unlikely to provide the necessary budgetary flexibility during a long-term financial dilemma. Rather, reductions in the number of faculty positions in selected programs will probably be required. In her review of institutional experiences in program reduction, Dolan-Green (1981) found that retrenchment occurs as a result of three broad categories of decisions: program elimination, reallocation of positions, and financial exigency [which the American Association of University Professors has defined as "an imminent financial crisis which threatens the survival of the institution as a whole and which cannot be alleviated by less drastic means (AAUP, 1976)].

One adaptive retrenchment tool that helps institutions identify in which program cutbacks should occur is the review of doctoral programs. In the early 1980s, the Board of Regents of the State University of New York reviewed doctoral programs in both public and private universities in that state. More recently, the Texas Higher Education Coordinating Board completed a statutorily mandated sunset review of more than 600 doctoral programs at the state's public institutions. This resulted in institutions (voluntarily) eliminating 112 low priority programs. Many other institutions have used this technique in recent years to meet fiscal crises. However, it is difficult to complete this process quickly. When a fiscal crisis is imminent, launching a systematic review of doctoral programs will probably not be sufficient to meet the budget challenges associated with the crisis. It can, however, be a useful long-term solution.

Another adaptive aid for institutions experiencing retrenchment is strategic planning, in which the institution identifies its academic niche by reviewing its mission, role and scope, and strengths and weaknesses and eliminating those weak programs that fall outside the mission. An institution may also adopt a resistant approach by redefining its mission so that it is more in line with market demands and by tailoring new programs and recruitment activities to match. Like program review, initiating a strategic planning process is a longer-term solution to dealing with financial crisis.

Reallocation, another long-term, adaptive response to fiscal distress, is a "process whereby resources are distributed according to a plan" (Hyatt and Santiago, 1986, p. 91). A review of estimated revenues and expenditures suggests alternatives for the reallocation of institutional resources through a series of trade-offs. Additional resources may be provided to some units for selective enhancement and improvement while resources may be reduced for those units identified as "revenue bloated." Other units that have adequate resources that match current activities may have their resource levels maintained. Institutional decisions are made based on academic program quality, unit efficiencies and enrollment fluctuations, revenue options, identification of fixed and variable costs, the spillover effect on other programs, the degree to which programs are in line with the institution's overall mission, and institutional goals and ambitions.

A key issue when an institution is faced with a fiscal crisis and is considering major budget changes is who participates in the decision process and assists in the identification of policy alternatives. During stable economic times, college and university administrators, with advice from the faculty, make decisions regarding the development and maintenance of academic and support programs and activities (Zammuto, 1986). Given the deep cuts that confront many institutions during periods of fiscal crisis, however, many administrators do more than seek advice from the faculty by adopting a decision-making process and style that both informs the college community and invites participation in decision making from various constituencies. The process and the degree to which various campus constituencies are involved in decision making is critical (Hardy et al, 1983). In many cases, how retrenchment and reallocation decisions are made is as important as what decisions are made (Dill and Helm, 1988).

During difficult financial periods, administrators generally communicate with and seek advice from members of various constituencies from all areas of the institution concerning the nature of the crisis, potential solutions, and the process by which decisions will be made (Hardy et al, 1983; Powers and Powers, 1983; Mortimer and McConnell, 1978). At certain times, institution-wide newsletters or memoranda may be sufficient to provide this information. At others, face-to-face meetings are necessary. The administration may use existing institution-wide committees or establish ad hoc committees for strategic discussions concerning retrenchment or reallocation strategies. These process decisions depend in large measure on the campus situation itself—including governance tradition, financial history, and general institutional character. Consultation and advice usually are obtained from all campus groups that have a stake in the outcome of the decisions, including administrators (especially deans and department chairpersons), faculty, staff, and students. Many institutions also maintain effective communication with other constituencies such as alumni, key donors, and community leaders, and the media. Of course, members of the governing board must give final approval to any major retrenchment or reallocation plans, but it is important that they be kept informed as these plans are developed. Implementation of a decision is at risk of failure if appropriate and adequate communication and participation have been denied to stakeholders (Vroom, 1984).

Bowen and Glenny (1981) suggest that the difficulty in preparing an institutional plan in times of "pervasive uncertainty" and the fact that many educational leaders refuse to acknowledge economic problems both contribute to the institutional paralysis that often occurs in response to a fiscal crisis. They suggest, instead, that by developing a series of alternative resource scenarios in the midst of uncertainty and incomplete information, institutions are better prepared to function under various funding levels. The state of readiness of an institution in anticipation of funding cuts directly affects its ability to respond. Preparation of multiple budget options minimizes the potential disruption of academic and support programs and activities, if anticipated revenues are not realized. Despite the fear that preparation of several budget options will result in lower funding, the existence of multiple funding strategies does not necessarily invite a self-fulfilling prophecy of financial doom. Contingency plans provide immediate options in both hard and good economic times. Such plans strengthen an institution's state of preparedness and its ability to respond to whatever level of financial austerity occurs.

Identifying those academic and support programs and activities that are to be reduced or eliminated is almost always painful and controversial. It is a step that usually occurs only after all other policy alternatives have been examined. When such cuts cannot be avoided, however, institutions are better served when they anticipate carefully how such reassignments, lay offs, or dismissals will be made. As established committees prepare prioritized lists of non-essential academic and support programs and activities that are deemed to be weak and/or peripheral to the institution's mission, many administrators simultaneously develop criteria to determine how faculty and staff from these areas will be selected for reassignment or termination. These criteria usually include such items as tenure status, program need, performance, academic custom and usage, affirmative action, and age.

Tenured and nontenured faculty who are dismissed from their positions have certain rights.

In situations involving financial exigency, program reductions, or program discontinuation, these rights include reassignment, retraining, appeal, and reinstatement. Colleges and universities forced to take these actions generally strive to ensure that adequate personnel policies are in place and are followed to guarantee appropriate due process.

Human nature being what it is, and institutions of higher education being the kind of organizations they are, it is only natural that when a college or university is confronted with a fiscal crisis, its leadership will choose to make easy cuts first. As indicated previously, this usually involves such things as reducing travel expenditures, equipment purchases, library acquisitions, funds for long-distance telephone calls, contingency funds; deferring building maintenance; reducing course offerings; not filling faculty and staff positions that become vacant; and increasing revenues, especially tuition and student fees. Normally, cuts in support areas such as physical plant, student services, and administrative areas are emphasized before core academic units are touched. During such periods, it is not unusual for many examples of innovative cost-cutting strategies to be found on the campus.

Nevertheless, as the crisis worsens, more severe actions may be necessary. In the tradition of shared governance, and in an effort to "share the blame/pain," the president or chancellor may choose to request recommendations from vice presidents, deans, faculty members, students, and representatives from other campus stakeholders. Budget priority committees—usually consisting of administrators, faculty members, and student leaders—may be formed (if they do not already exist) to provide recommendations about specific cuts, reorganizations, or programs to be considered for elimination. Normally, however, the last cuts considered will be to tenured faculty members. A "siege mentality" may develop as faculty are forced to consider whether a colleague's program should be reduced or cut all together. The institution may also experience a "brain drain" as faculty members with established reputations receive offers from other institutions to leave and move to financially greener pastures. Unfortunately, this scene is being repeated over and over again as institutions are confronted with expenditure increases and revenue reductions of magnitudes rarely witnessed in higher education in the past.

IMPLICATIONS FOR FURTHER RESEARCH

As colleges and universities learn to function in this new era of financial restraint, and as they are confronted with new levels of distrust on the part of the American public, there are questions concerning whether the budgeting models and approaches that have been used in the past will continue to be appropriate. In general, the question is: Where is higher education budgeting going in these times of persistent uncertainty? More specific questions relate to how higher education budgeting will change as institutions cope with an environment of increasing costs and severe revenue shortfalls. How will they deal with the renewed interest in performance funding? Will more institutions turn to cost center budgeting (or responsibility center budgeting)? How will capital budgeting be changed so that institutions can deal more effectively with the notion of capital renewal and solve the problem of deferred maintenance? Each of these questions provides avenues of future research for scholars interested in higher education finance and governance.

Probably the question that will affect most institutions of higher education in the 1990s is what budget and governance processes will they use to respond to the fiscal crises which will confront them. Although earlier research (such as Hyatt, Schulman, and Santiago, 1984; Leslie, 1984; and Mingle, 1981) offers some insights into how institutions have behaved in the past during such periods, the methods used in those situations may no longer be appropriate because current funding cuts are larger and of longer duration. Budget reductions in the early 1980s were in the range of 2-3 percent. Current reductions are ranging more in the 10-20 percent area. Not only are overall expenditures being trimmed, but entire degree programs and whole colleges are being eliminated. In this new environment, one wonders whether institutions will continue to "take the easy cuts first." Will they continue to make across-the-board cuts first? Will they continue to cut non-academic support areas and non personnel-related costs before they turn to core academic areas? Or will the size or degree of the revenue shortfalls cause them to consider eliminating academic programs that are no longer deemed as being central to the completion of the institution's mission earlier in the process? Case analyses should be completed and the results compared to the earlier literature to answer these questions.

As mentioned previously, institutions have also responded to fiscal crisis in recent years by attempting to increase revenue from other sources to make up for short-falls. Will these attempts continue? For example, students are being asked to carry a significantly larger share of the burden of financing higher education. In the private sector, this trend has been in existence for many years—to a point where many wonder whether the costs are now so high that students cannot afford to attend. The trend is more recent in the public sector. Yet, in response to reductions in appropriations, many states have either raised tuition levels or allowed institutions to raise them. These tuition increases, coupled with reductions in course offerings, have led many students to argue that they are being forced to pay more for less service, especially if they must extend their college careers because they cannot get the necessary coursework to complete their degrees.

Institutions of higher education, both public and private, both four-year and two-year, are increasing the amount of development and fund-raising activities in which they participate. Billion dollar capital campaigns are announced at an increasing rate. Can this continue? Bristol has reported that corporations, foundations and religious organizations, non-alumni individuals, and alumni have each contributed one quarter of all gifts to higher education since 1950 (Bristol, 1991). He also forecast that the average gift from an alumnus would increase from $94.93 in 1990 to $116.52 in 2010. Alumni gifts totaled $2.8 billion in 1990 and are estimated to increase to $11.2 billion by 2010. Bristol identifies five factors that will affect the reliability and likelihood of this prediction: (1) the rate of inflation between now and 2010, (2) the graduation rate for baccalaureate degrees, (3) the average age of alumni in the base (i.e., the number of years that have passed since graduation), (4) history (i.e., the hidden variables cause change in attitudes over time), and (5) the mix of alumni from public and private institutions (since alumni from private institutions tend to support their institutions more generously than alumni from public institutions). Nevertheless, questions remain: Are there sufficient philanthropic dollars available to meet all the perceived needs? Will the competition from other sectors of society, including public elementary and secondary education, reduce the amount of these funds on which colleges and universities can rely?

For public colleges and universities, especially, the proportions of financial support which come from various sectors are changing. At some major research universities, for example, state tax dollars provide around one-third of total operating budgets, down from the 50-65 percent levels of years ago. The proportions paid from tuition, outside research support (mostly federal), and gift income have increased greatly. These institutions are becoming "state-assisted" institutions instead of state institutions. What types of governance changes will result from such changes? What impact will those changes have on institutional budgeting processes and approaches?

The history of higher education budgeting is filled with attempts to move from the orientation of incremental budgeting on inputs (e.g., the cost of faculty members, staff, supplies, equipment, travel, etc.) to an orientation on outcomes (e.g., goals, objectives, performance measures). Program budgeting, zero-base budgeting, performance budgeting, and incentive budgeting are all more focused on outcomes than is the much-maligned technique of incremental budgeting. Generally, these methods have been used for a time by a few institutions or states and subsequently discarded. However, will institutions continue to try new approaches, only to return to incremental budgeting (perhaps in the current environment it should be called decremental budgeting)? Will those states that have tried incentive budgeting be able to continue their programs if revenues decline? Will the current popularity of performance budgeting continue as a reflection of the accountability movement?

A related question is, how much government oversight is necessary to ensure the quality of higher education? Given the growing distrust of all institutions (including colleges and universities), given the general mood concerning the inadequacy of the public K-12 educational system, and given recent scandals concerning the misuses of public funds (e.g., Stanford University) or exorbitant compensation packages for top officials (e.g., University of California), it is only natural that the quality of institutions of higher education would be called into question. When this is combined with the perception that higher education costs only increase, the fact that benefits are not fully understood, and the realization that fewer funds are available to fund government services in general, it stands to reason that states, especially, will want to have more control over how their appropriations will be spent by public colleges and universities and what they will produce—i.e., they will turn to performance funding systems. If the institutions want this money (and Bowen's revenue theory of cost would lead us to predict that they will always want it), they will have to continue to develop their information systems to collect and report the necessary performance indicators and measures to show their compliance or progress. Implementation of these requirements may be counterproductive in that they shift institutional resources away from core academic activities to peripheral compliance activities.

Perhaps responsibility center budgeting will lead the way to the development of the next generation of budget approaches that simultaneously address the need for stability in a highly volatile environment and the externally-driven demand for increased accountability. While this technique may lead to "the rich getting richer," it may also provide a new mechanism for making difficult reallocation decisions. Many private institutions of higher education have used cost center budgeting for years—with varying degrees of success. Public colleges and universities may want to keep a watchful eye on the progress of Indiana University, and any other institutions that may decide to try this technique, as it implements this budgeting approach.

For the most part in this section, we have focused on the implications for further analysis and research on financial, governance, and procedural aspects of budgeting approaches as they relate to institutional operating budgets. There are, of course, equally important issues related to capital budgeting. While there may be little new building on campuses that are facing funding shortages, there are nevertheless matters of renovation, meeting building maintenance needs that have been too long deferred, and renewing physical plants that are reaching the end of their useful lives. Institutional operating budgets are directly affected by additions of space for classrooms, offices, instructional and research laboratories, recreation, and maybe even parking. Changes in institutional infrastructure automatically impact the operating budget. Since this relationship is often neglected or ignored, new procedures may be necessary to guarantee that operating requirements embedded in capital budget decisions receive consideration during the budget process that is equal to other items. As mentioned, deferred maintenance and capital renewal and replacement should occupy a more prominent place among budget needs. Additional analyses should be carried out to examine such questions as: (1) Will building maintenance and custodial services continue to be deferred as institutions adapt to fiscal constraints? (2) Will the work that has already been done in the area of capital renewal and replacement (Dunn, 1989) provide a useful standard? and (3) Will new financing methods for capital budgeting and asset management be explored?

In the final analysis, however, we return to the general financial outlook for the 1990s, and what that means for budgeting in institutions of higher education. This environment will require that every college and university reevaluate its mission and—using that mission as a framework—examine the academic programs it offers, the management and care of its capital assets, its policies regarding student admissions and financial aid, its practices with regard to faculty tenure, promotion, and workload, and the allocation of its financial, human, and capital resources. To the extent that their leaders can get outside the bounds of psychological constraints (such as the "business as usual" commitment to traditional ways), and contextual constraints (including the organizational characteristics and cultural boundaries of higher education institutions), more creative budgeting solutions will be identified.

Unfortunately, it seems that many of the decisions being made these days are providing new answers to the age-old questions of, "Who pays for higher education?" and its companion, "Who gains from higher education?" However, these new answers are not being offered as a result of a public policy debate on higher education finance. Rather, they are the corollary results of decisions designed to solve serious economic and political problems. That students and others should shoulder more of the costs of higher education may indeed be a reasonable solution to these problems. However, one would hope that those individuals who make higher education budget decisions would understand that these solutions can change long-standing public policies in addition to meeting current economic needs.

References

Allen, R. (1981). Capital budgeting overview. In L. Leslie and J. Hyatt (eds.), *Higher Education Financing Policies: State/Institutions and Their Interactions.* Tucson, AZ: Center for the Study of Higher Education, University of Arizona.

Allen, R. (1984). New approaches to incentive funding. In L. Leslie (ed.), *Responding to New Realities in Funding.* San Francisco: Jossey-Bass.

American Association of University Professors. (1976). Recommended institutional regulations on academic freedom and tenure. 62 AAUP Bulletin 186: 184-191.

Balderston, F., and Weathersby, G. (1972). PPBS in higher education planning and management: part II, the University of California experience. *Higher Education* 1(3): 299-319.

Banta, T. (ed.). (1988). *Implementing Outcomes Assessment: Promises and Perils.* (New Directions in Institutional Research, No. 59.) San Francisco: Jossey-Bass.

Banta, T. (1986). *Performance Funding in Higher Education: A Critical Analysis of Tennessee's Experience.* Boulder, CO: National Center for Higher Education Management Systems.

Banta, T., and Fisher, H. (1984). Performance funding: Tennessee's experiment. In J. Folger (ed.), *Financial*

Incentives for Academic Quality. (New Directions for Higher Education, No. 48.) San Francisco: Jossey-Bass.

Berdahl, R., and Holland, B. (eds.). (1989). *Developing State Fiscal Incentives to Improve Higher Education.* Proceedings from a national invitational conference. College Park, MD: National Center for Postsecondary Governance and Finance, University of Maryland.

Bogue, G., and Brown, W. (1982). Performance incentives for state colleges. *Harvard Business Review* Nov./Dec.: 123-128.

Bowen, F. (1975). Making decisions in a time of fiscal stringency: the long-term implications. Paper presented at a seminar for state leaders in postsecondary education, Denver, CO. ED 202 282.

Bowen, H. (1980). *The Costs of Higher Education: How Much Do Colleges and Universities Spend per Student and How Much Should They Spend?* San Francisco: Jossey-Bass.

Bowen, W. (1986). The role of the business officer in managing educational resources. In L. Leslie and R. Anderson (eds.), *ASHE Reader on Finance in Higher Education.* Lexington, MA: Ginn Press.

Bowen, F., and Glenny, L. (1981). The California study. In L. Leslie and J. Hyatt (eds.), *Higher Education Financing Policies: State/Institutions and Their Interactions.* Tucson, AZ: Center for the Study of Higher Education, University of Arizona.

Breneman, D. (1981). In J. Mingle (ed.), *Challenges of Retrenchment: Strategies for Consolidating Programs, Cutting Costs, and Reallocating Resources.* San Francisco: Jossey-Bass.

Brinkerhoff, J. (1981). The chief institutional officer perspective. In L. Leslie and J. Hyatt (eds.), *Higher Education Financing Policies: State/Institutions and Their Interactions.* Tucson, AZ: Center for the Study of Higher Education, University of Arizona.

Brinkman, P. (1984). Formula budgeting: the fourth decade. In L. Leslie (ed.), *Responding to New Realities in Funding.* New Directions in Institutional Research, No. 43. San Francisco: Jossey-Bass.

Bristol, R. Jr. (1991). How much will alumni give in the future? *Planning for Higher Education* 20, Winter 1991-92: 1-12.

Caruthers, J.K., and Orwig, M. (1979). *Budgeting in Higher Education.* (AAHE/ERIC Higher Education Research Report No. 3. ED 167 857.) Washington, DC: American Association for Higher Education.

Chronicle of Higher Education. (1992a, June 10). Recession takes toll on U.S. aid. 38(40): A1, 20-21.

Chronicle of Higher Education. (1992b, September 9). Drop in state support leaves Ohio colleges wondering how much farther they can fall. 39(3): A23-24.

Chronicle of Higher Education. (1992c, October 7). Budget outlook prompts some college leaders to speak out for higher state taxes. 39(7): A22.

Dill, D., and Helm, K. (1988). Faculty participation in strategic policy making. In J.C. Smart (ed.), *Higher Education: Handbook of Theory and Research.* Vol. IV. New York: Agathon Press.

Dolan-Green, C. (1981). What if the faculty member to be laid off is the governor's brother? In S. Hample (ed.), *Coping with Faculty Reduction.* (New Directions for Institutional Research. No. 30.) San Francisco: Jossey-Bass.

Daughterly, E. (1981). Should you starve all programs or eliminate a few? In S. Hample (ed.), *Coping with Faculty Reduction.* (New Directions for Institutional Research. No. 30.) San Francisco: Jossey-Bass.

Dunn, J. (1989). *Financial Planning Guidelines for Facility Renewal and Adaption.* (A joint project of The Society for College and University Planning, The National Association for College and University Business Officers, The Association of Physical Plant Administrators of Colleges and Universities, and Coopers and Lybrand) Ann Arbor, MI: Society for College and University Planning.

Ewell, P. (1988). Outcomes, assessment, and academic improvement: in search of usable knowledge. In J.C. Smart (*ed.*), *Higher Education: Handbook of Theory and Research,* Vol. IV. New York: Agathon Press.

Ewell, P. (ed.). (1985). *Assessing Educational Outcomes.* (New Directions for Institutional Research, No. 47.) San Francisco: Jossey-Bass.

Folger, J. (1989). Designing state incentive programs that work. In R. Berdahl and B. Holland (eds.), *Developing State Fiscal Incentives to Improve Higher Education.* (Proceedings from a national invitational conference.) College Park, MD: National Center for Postsecondary Governance and Finance, University of Maryland.

Folger, J. (ed.). (1984). *Financial Incentives for Academic Quality.* (New Directions for Higher Education, No. 48.) San Francisco: Jossey-Bass.

Green, J.L., Jr. (1971). *Budgeting in Higher Education.* Athens, GA: University of Georgia Business and Finance Office.

Hackman, J. (1985). Power and centrality in the allocation of resources in colleges and universities. *Administrative Science Quarterly* 30: 61-77.

Halpern, D. (1987). *The State of College and University Facilities.* Ann Arbor, MI: Society for College and

University Planning.

Halstead, D.K. (1991). *Higher Education Revenues and Expenditures: A Study of Institutional Cost.* Washington, D.C.: Research Associates of Washington.

Hample, S. (ed.), (1981). *Coping with Faculty Reduction.* (New Directions for Institutional Research, No. 30.) San Francisco: Jossey-Bass.

Hardy, C., Langley, A., Mintzberg, H., and Rose, J. (1983). Strategy formation in the university setting. *Review of Higher Education* 6: 407-433.

Hoenack, S. (1984). Direct and incentive planning within a university. *Socio-Economic Planning Sciences* 11(4): 191-204.

Holland, B., and Berdahl, R. (1990). Green carrots: a survey of state use of fiscal incentives for academic quality. A paper presented at the annual meeting of the Association for the Study of Higher Education. Nov. 1-4. Portland, OR.

Hopkins, D., and Massy, W. (1981). *Planning Models for Colleges and Universities.* Stanford, CA: Stanford University Press.

Hossler, D., Kuh, G., and Bateman, J.M. (1989). An investigation of the anticipated effects of responsibility center budgeting at a public research university: the first year. Paper presented at the annual meeting of the American Educational Research Association, March 27-31. San Francisco.

Hyatt, J., and Santiago, A. (1986). *Financial Management of Colleges and Universities.* Washington, D.C.: National Association of College and University Business Officers.

Hyatt, J., Schulman, C., and Santiago, A. (1984). *Reallocation: Strategies for Effective Resource Management.* Washington, D.C.: National Association of College and University Business Officers.

Jenny, H. (1981). The capital margin. In L. Leslie and J. Hyatt (eds.), *Higher Education Financing Policies: State/Institutions and Their Interactions.* Tucson, AZ: Center for the Study of Higher Education, University of Arizona.

Kaludis, G. (ed.) (1973). *Strategies for Budgeting.* (New Directions in Higher Education, No. 2.) San Francisco: Jossey-Bass.

Kraal, S. (1992). A comparative analysis of funding models used to estimate the renovation and renewal costs of existing higher education facilities. Ph.D. dissertation. The University of Texas at Austin.

Layzell, D., and Lyddon, J. (1990). *Budgeting for Higher Education at the State Level: Enigma, Paradox, and Ritual.* (ASHE-ERIC Higher Education Report No. 4.) Washington, D.C.: The George Washington University, School of Education and Human Development.

Lenth, C. (1992). Telephone conversation with D. Greene. October 30.

Leslie, L., and Anderson, R. (eds.), (1986). *ASHE Reader on Finance in Higher Education.* Lexington, MA: Ginn Press.

Leslie, L. (ed.), (1984). *Responding to New Realities in Funding.* (New Directions in Institutional Research, No. 43.) San Francisco: Jossey-Bass.

Leslie, L., and Hyatt, J. (eds.). (1981). *Higher Education Financing Policies: State/ Institutions and Their Interactions.* Tucson, AZ: Center for the Study of Higher Education, University of Arizona.

Lindblom, C. (1959). The science of "muddling through." *Public Administration Review* 19: 79-88.

Massy, W. (1989). Budget decentralization at Stanford University. *Planning for Higher Education* 18(2): 39-55.

Meisinger, R., and Dubeck, L. (1984). *College and University Budgeting: An Introduction for Faculty and Academic Administrators.* Washington, D.C.: National Association of College and University Business Officers.

Mingle, J., and Associates. (1981). *Challenges of Retrenchment: Strategies for Consolidating Programs, Cutting Costs, and Reallocating Resources.* San Francisco: Jossey-Bass.

Morgan, A. (1992). The politics and policies of selective funding: the case of state-level quality incentives. *The Review of Higher Education* 15(3): 289-306.

Morgan, A. (1984). The new strategies: roots, context, and overview. In L. Leslie (ed.), *Responding to New Realities in Funding.* (New Directions in Institutional Research, No. 43.) San Francisco: Jossey-Bass.

Mortimer, K., and McConnell, T. (1978). *Sharing Authority Effectively.* San Francisco: Jossey-Bass.

Mortimer, K., and Taylor, B. (1984). Budgeting strategies under conditions of decline. In L. Leslie (ed.), *Responding to New Realities in Funding.* (New Directions in Institutional Research, No. 43.) San Francisco: Jossey-Bass.

Powers, D., and Powers, M. (1983). *Making Participatory Management Work.* San Francisco: Jossey-Bass.

Robins, G. (1986). *From* Understanding the college budget. In L. Leslie and R. Anderson (eds.), *ASHE Reader on Finance in Higher Education.* Lexington, MA: Ginn Press.

Rubin, I. (ed.), (1988). *New Directions in Budget Theory.* Albany, N.Y.: State University of New York Press.

Rush, S., and Johnson, S. (1988). *The Decaying American Campus: A Ticking Time Bomb.* (A joint report of the Association of Physical Plant Administrators of Universities and Colleges and the National Association of College and University Business Officers in cooperation with Coopers and Lybrand).

Schmidtlein, F. (1989). Why linking budgets to plans has proven difficult in higher education. *Planning for Higher Education* 18(2): 9-23.

Seitz, C. (1981). The Indiana experience. In L. Leslie and J. Hyatt (eds.), *Higher Education Financing Policies: State/Institutions and Their Interactions.* Tucson, AZ: Center for the Study of Higher Education, University of Arizona.

Texas Higher Education Coordinating Board. (1990). Report of the Initiative and Incentive Subcommittee, March. Austin, TX.

Texas Higher Education Coordinating Board. (1992a). Board agenda item IV-A, Minutes from July Board Meeting. Austin, TX.

Texas Higher Education Coordinating Board. (1992b). Report from Committee on Performance Based Funding for the Health-Related Institutions, July. Austin, TX.

Vandement, W. (1989). *Managing Money in Higher Education: A Guide to the Financial Process and Effective Participation Within It.* San Francisco: Jossey-Bass.

Volkwein, J. (1988). State regulation and campus autonomy. In J.C. Smart (ed.), *Higher Education: Handbook of Theory and Research,* Vol. IV. New York: Agathon Press.

Volkwein, J. (1986). State financial control of public universities and its relationship to campus administrative elaborateness and cost: results of a national study. *The Review of Higher Education* 9(3): 267-286.

Vroom, V. (1984). Leaders and leadership in academe. In J.L. Bess (ed.), *College and University Organization: Insights from the Behavioral Sciences.* New York: New York University Press.

Webster's New Collegiate Dictionary. (1981). Springfield, MA: G. & C. Merriam.

Welzenbach, L. (1982). *College and University Business Administration.* Washington, D.C.: National Association of College and University Business Officers.

Whalen, E. (1991). *Responsibility Center Budgeting: An Approach to Decentralized Management for Institutions of Higher Education.* Bloomington, IN: Indiana University Press.

Wildavsky, A. (1988). *The New Politics of the Budgetary Process.* Glenview. IL: Scott, Foresman and Company.

Zammuto, R. (1986). Managing decline in American higher education. In J.C. Smart (ed.) *Higher Education: Handbook of Theory and Research,* Vol. IV. New York: Agathon Press.

Zemsky, R., Porter, R., and Oedel, L. (1978). Decentralized planning: to share responsibility. *Educational Record* 59: 229-253.

Zusman, A. (1986). Legislature and university conflict: the case of California. *The Review of Higher Education* 9(4): 397-418.

Epilogue

INTRODUCTION

Our chapter was first published in 1993 and reflected the higher education environment of that time. Many aspects of that environment have changed, while several trends have continued. Some of these have directly affected higher education budgeting, both in terms of the level of resources available for allocation and the processes used to make those allocations. In this Epilogue we will review and summarize what in our view are the most important of these changes and trends.

Changes in the Financial Environment

Tuition inflation: Tuition continues to increase at roughly twice the rate of inflation (Paulsen, Chapter 6; Toutkoushian, Chapter 1). Although the rate of increase is slowing, at both public and private institutions, the fact that the "sticker price" for higher education is increasing faster than most other items American families pay for has brought complaints from students and their parents as well as the interest of investigative journalists, policy makers, and the financial community. Newspapers, national magazines, and network news programs regularly carry stories about tuition trends. The fact that these stories tend to concentrate on the costs at elite private institutions gives the public a somewhat biased perception of the situation.

Nevertheless, the fact that tuition is increasing faster than median family income means that there are affordability issues (Baum, Chapter 2), and this brings the problem to the attention of policy makers. Congress has commissioned several reports that have analyzed the situation, and in 1997 established the National Commission on the Cost of Higher Education to study the problem and surrounding issues in depth. The Commission's report was more balanced than many expected. Nevertheless, it left little doubt that institutions of higher education must do better jobs of: 1) explaining their financial structures, and 2) keeping their charges in line. Several legislatures have also weighed in on the problem by freezing tuition levels or capping the rates of possible increases at their public colleges and universities.

The trends in tuition prices have also sparked the interest of policy makers and financial institutions in helping families save for college. What has resulted is an almost mind-boggling set of savings options, including state college savings plans (Mumper, Chapter 9), prepaid tuition plans, Education Individual Retirement Accounts (IRA's), Roth IRA's, and custodial accounts. Each of these options has its own advantages and disadvantages depending on a student's or family's financial situation. Choices made may affect the ability to secure financial aid and eligibility for the HOPE Scholarship and Lifetime Learning tax credits enacted as part of the Taxpayer Relief Act of 1997.

State Appropriations: In 1993 when our original chapter was written, the economic environment for many states was much worse than it is today. Many states had cut their appropriations to higher education. In fact, appropriations nationwide for 1993 were actually lower than they were for 1992. This was the first (and so far, the only) time that public appropriations had not increased year over year. State economies have since improved, but until recently, states continued to reduce the proportion of their budgets allocated to public institutions of higher education. This is one of the reasons that tuition levels in public institutions have continued to increase. Moreover, indicators of a slowdown in economic activity in early 2001 may, once again, make the outlook for public institutions less rosy.

The cost burden in public higher education has increasingly shifted from states to students and their families. This represents a fundamental shift in the philosophical argument of whether the principal gains of a higher education accrue to the individual student or to society (who gains?), and as a result, who should pay the basic costs (who pays?) (Paulsen, Chapter 4). Largely however, this trend has resulted from economic pressures on state budgets, rather than fundamental philosophical discussions. Higher education has had to compete with other compelling state interests, such as public education, prisons and the criminal justice system, and Medicaid. However, the situation may be changing. States appropriated about $56.7 billion for higher education for fiscal year 2000, an increase of 7.3 percent. There is also evidence that the proportion of state budgets being allocated to higher education has stopped decreasing. Nevertheless, public higher education continues to be funded at levels that suggest its priority among the states is still low.

Financial Aid: During the 1990s there was also a fundamental shift in federal financial aid policy away from grants toward loans (Baum, Chapter 2). The College Board has estimated that of the $64.1 billion available for financial aid during 1998-99, 52.6 percent, or $33.7 billion, was available from federal loan programs. When added to the 3.7 percent ($2.4 billion) available from non-federal loan programs, over 56 percent of the financial aid was in the forms of loans. Add to this the notion that the purchasing power of the Pell Grant has declined since the 1970s, and this fundamental change in the financial aid landscape becomes more evident. These loan dollars do allow access. Students can pay their higher education bills when they need to. However, the true cost of their higher education is spread out over many years as the loans are paid off. This affects their economic well-being over time. Research also shows that this shift from grants to loans has had considerable impact on enrollment rates of economically disadvantaged students. For these students, although grant funds do seem to influence college-going decisions, loan funds do not.

A second major change in financial aid is the recent tendency for many colleges and universities (primarily private) to use student aid as a strategic tool to help attract students with desired characteristics and qualities. The increasing use of merit aid and tuition discounting indicates a trend away from the need-based financial aid philosophy that has characterized American higher education for the last four decades (Breneman, Doti and Lapovsky, Chapter 12). The extent to which institutions engage in these techniques can have major impacts on their budgeting and their financial stability. Some institutions, typically not the most selective or the best endowed, are moving toward an approach that Michael McPherson and Morton Schapiro have called "strategic maximization," where they follow a financial aid policy that seeks to admit the best students available while gaining from them as much revenue as possible. (McPherson and Schapiro, pp. 16-17). This is a fundamentally different philosophy from not restricting the admission of any student because of his or her ability to pay.

Changes in the Applicant Pool

Unemployment in the United States reached historically low rates in the late 1990s. It is well understood that higher education enrollment is indirectly related to economic conditions (Paulsen, Chapter 3). The impact of low unemployment in the economy is a general reduction in the number of degree program applicants. Because they have other choices, some high school graduates do not seek admission to college immediately after high school, and many college undergraduates leave college prior to graduation because they are able to obtain satisfying employment without a degree.

The implications for public higher education institutions that depend on formula funding for state support are unsettling in times of near full employment. With already low graduation rates in many states, lower enrollments and semester credit hours generated mean fewer funds appropriated to these institutions. To compensate for those students who traditionally would have chosen to attend college but who are now leaving the educational pipeline for jobs, institutions of higher education are establishing new relationships and programs with grade schools, middle schools, and high schools, to expand the pool of high school graduates who might be considering college. This technique is also being used to increase the pool of adequately prepared minority students. As another strategy in enrollment management, four-year colleges are continuing to establish transfer curricula with community colleges at increasing rates to ensure a stable and diverse student body in these times of low unemployment.

Changes in the Delivery Of Higher Education

In addition to the impact of enrollment trends on higher education finance, colleges and universities are confronted with new media for delivering traditional curricula. Increased access to higher education through distance education now allows students to be enrolled at remote locations and attend class far from the main campus where lectures are being given. New technology makes it possible for students to take courses at their convenience—not at the times dictated by course schedules. Web-based courses allow students to progress at their own pace, and cover material in more depth than was previously possible in traditional lecture-seminar formats. Higher education has responded with a proliferation of new offerings for students, ranging from single courses to entire degree programs. This change has resulted in the creation of new fees to cover the costs of updating antiquated infrastructure. Higher education is still baffled by the cost differential for delivering the same course electronically and traditionally. Public policy makers are still debating how to address these differentials. New investment in distance education equipment and technologies is expected to be less costly than constructing campus facilities to accommodate the anticipated surge in the college student population in some states. New markets—and the resulting discretionary income—are being explored as institutions determine which student niche they will target. For some institutions, campus location is no longer a relevant issue for consideration.

Changes Affecting Health Professions Education

These are particularly turbulent times for higher education institutions whose missions include educating the next generation of health professionals. The Federal Balanced Budget Act (BBA) of 1997 put in place $16 billion in cuts over five years, severely affecting graduate medical education and educational programs in three rehabilitation therapy disciplines across the country. The BBA reduced the rates of payment for direct and indirect medical education for all physician residency training programs, which resulted in a decrease in the number of residents in training. The Act, as implemented through rules promulgated by the Health Care Financing Administration, required stringent attending physician oversight of clinical care being provided by physicians-in-training, which reduced the income to medical schools and teaching hospitals generated through patient care fees for physician services. The cumulative effect of these cuts has been a reduced ability to generate the discretionary dollars necessary to continue to maintain the levels of excellence in some educational programs.

The BBA also set reimbursement limits of $1,500 per year per individual for Medicare reimbursement for occupational therapy, physical therapy, and speech and language therapy. This limit resulted in many hospitals, home health-care facilities, and nursing homes reducing their employment of these therapists, which in turn contributed to reducing the attractiveness of these professions to potential students. This situation, coupled with the impact of managed care, also led to many affiliated teaching facilities reducing the number of students they would accept for clinical training, or completely eliminating their facilities as training sites for students in these disciplines. Many educational programs were forced to reduce their class sizes significantly, and some actually closed their programs entirely.

In late 1999, Congress restored many of the budget cuts. Among the funds restored were support to graduate medical education, elimination of caps for physical, occupational, and speech therapy, and adjusted payment rates to physicians for services provided under Medicare. Among the provisions, Congress provided a two-year $600 million freeze on payments for indirect medical education and a mechanism to increase funds in FY 2001 for direct graduate medical education to teaching hospitals. The lesson learned from the past four years is that institutions whose missions include educating the next generation of health professionals must remain vigilant and continue to advocate for complete restoration of the federal support that was eliminated through the BBA of 1997.

Changes in Accreditation

Recent changes in accreditation standards of both regional and specialized accreditation agencies have resulted in institutions of higher education directing more resources toward compliance efforts to retain their accreditation status. An increasing amount of faculty, staff, and financial resources are necessary to develop and update the costly databases and tracking systems that are required to maintain compliance. Other curricular requirements dictate changes in teaching space. For example, recent changes in dental and medical accreditation standards have resulted in curricular changes that have forced many schools to alter their physical teaching space to accommodate required problem-based learning modalities. This approach requires small-group settings and increased faculty participation in place of traditional lecture halls and high student-faculty ratios. Although they may be phased in over time, these accreditation requirements can add unanticipated costs to an institution's annual operating budget—not unlike unfunded legislative mandates—and demand additional academic resources.

Changes in Accountability Requirements

Despite the fact that American higher education is generally regarded as the best in the world, all is not well in the halls of academia. Accountability has become a buzzword in legislative halls, among accreditors, and from the general public. The furor over tuition increases was discussed previously. In addition, many believe that institutions, particularly major research institutions, have lost touch with their primary mission—teaching undergraduates. They read about faculty members spending more time on research and less time teaching. They see a faculty reward structure that is based on research more than teaching. They hear of faculty members increasingly interested in narrower areas of specialization and their greater loyalty to their research disciplines than to their institutions. They perceive faculty tenure as job security that makes people lazy and unproductive and out of touch with the reality of layoffs and job cutbacks in certain industries in corporate America.

In addition to the increasing range of accountability measures developed to address specific standards for various stakeholders, another continuing trend is the growth in the number of required reports to these groups. Institutions are subjected to reporting burdens that do not add value to their educational product, but are intended solely as accountability mechanisms for the public and for funding agencies. For example, the U.S. Department of Education annually requests mountains of data from each college and university. These data may not vary in substance but do vary significantly in format from those required by state legislatures and executive offices, university system offices, and even the institution's own planning and administrative offices. Additional compliance reporting is being placed on institutions that conduct research concerning human and animal subjects. Over the last two years, the Office for Protection from Research Risks has conducted site visits examining the function and structure of Institutional Review Boards for adequacy of space and staff as well as the substance of research protocol reviews. As a result, research on human subjects was shut down for some period of time at eight universities where deficiencies were cited. PATH (Physicians Attending in Teaching Hospitals) audits, under billing rules promulgated by the Health Care Financing Administration, have resulted in fines and penalties being collected from at least ten academic health centers for allegations of upcoding, lack of physician-in-training oversight, and lack of adequate documentation. Medical schools and research universities have created and implemented rigorous mandatory training programs for faculty engaged in clinical care and research, whereby faculty must attend and demonstrate sufficient knowledge of the rules and regulations governing clinical and research activities before privileges in these areas are given or restored. There is an enormous bureaucracy associated with these compliance enterprises, one that does not necessarily add to the quality or enhance the outcome of the clinical care provided or the research conducted.

Performance Funding

In our original chapter, we discussed the various approaches (we called them "tools" then) to budgeting used by colleges and universities. We discussed the advantages and disadvantages of incremental budgeting, formula budgeting, program budgeting, zero-base budgeting, performance budgeting, incentive budgeting, and cost center budgeting. We said that incremental budgeting was the most widely used by institutions of higher education, and was probably "the worst budgeting approach, except for all the others." Although much of that statement continues to be true, there have been changes in budgeting approaches since 1993. Probably the most significant and visible change has been the increase in interest in performance budgeting. This has resulted from the increased interest in accountability on the part of legislators for reasons explained previously. It is clear that legislators in many states want their public colleges and universities to improve their behavior in certain areas. It is also clear that they are interested in tracking institutional progress in these areas (e.g., graduation rates, student performance on licensure and other examinations, enrollment of minority students, attraction of research funding, etc.) and in some cases tying appropriations to these performance measures.

This situation is being monitored closely by Dr. Joseph Burke and his colleagues at the Nelson A. Rockefeller Institute of Government, Higher Education Program. The numbers change each year, but by 1999, 60 percent of the states had adopted programs that linked their funding of public institutions of higher education to campus performance in some way. An important distinction that Burke has made is in differentiating between those states that are involved in performance funding from those that use performance budgeting. Performance funding is defined as "special state funding tied directly to the achievements of public colleges and universities on specific performance indicators" (Burke and Serban, p. 3). In this case the relationship between performance and state funding is direct. Performance budgeting, on the other hand, is defined as the use of "reports of institutional achievements on performance indicators as a general context in shaping the total budgets for public colleges and universities" (*ibid.*). In this case, the relationship between performance and state funding is indirect. The performance information is available and used during the appropriations process, but dollars are not tied directly to it. Obviously, the link between performance and funding is harder to discern.

Currently, a small percentage (5% or less) of total higher education state appropriations are allocated through performance funding mechanisms. However, in 1996, the South Carolina General Assembly passed a law that mandated that 37 quality indicators be used to rate institutional performance, and that by FY 2000, 100 percent of their state support would be allocated according to performance on these measures. The eyes of the finance officers around the country have been trained on South Carolina to see if in fact it is possible to implement this plan. Available evidence suggests that after four years, there has been no significant increase in higher education appropriations; not all of the 37 indicators are being used; and only a small proportion of dollars are actually being allocated based on campus performance.

Suffice it to say, performance funding/budgeting is a very active area of higher education finance, and one that needs to be watched closely by everyone who has an interest in how colleges and universities, and especially those in the public sector, are funded. In fact, discussions concerning incentive budgeting have largely been subsumed into discussions of performance budgeting. In our opinion this is largely a matter of the attitudes of those external to higher education. When policy makers and others are pleased with higher education or see colleges and universities in a positive light, they are more likely to speak in terms of "incentives." However, when the attitude is more negative and questions are asked concerning how colleges and universities manage their finances or why they pursue certain policies (e.g. continually raising tuition), these same individuals are more likely to speak in terms of "performance" or "accountability."

Responsibility Center Budgeting

In the original chapter, we also discussed cost center budgeting, an approach under which academic and support units are considered costs centers for fiscal purposes and are expected to be self-supporting (i.e., "Each tub on its own bottom"). This approach was largely confined to private institutions until the late 1980s, when Thomas Ehrlich moved from the University of Pennsylvania to become president of Indiana University. Since then, several major public universities in the U.S. and Canada (e.g., Indiana University, the University of Michigan, UCLA, Ohio State University, the University of Illinois, and the University of Toronto) have adopted an approach variously known as responsibility center budgeting, responsibility center management, value center management, incentive based budgeting, mission focused budgeting and planning, revenue center management, and school-based budgeting. The basic operating principles of these approaches are as follows:

- All costs and income generated by each college, faculty, or department are attributed to that unit, appear in its budget, and are under its control.
- Incentives are created and barriers are removed to allow each academic unit to increase income and reduce costs according to its own academic plans and priorities.
- All costs of administrative and service units are allocated to academic units.
- Decisions about prices (tuition, fees) and volume (enrollment) are devolved to the academic units.
- Decisions about optimal balances between costs and revenue are made by the academic units. They set priorities and link plans to budgets.
- Restrictions on line-by-line budgets are relaxed or eliminated. Each academic unit allocates the global revenue base available to it (Lang, p. 2).

The strengths and weaknesses identified in the original chapter have been found to be largely replicated in these public institutions. For example, entrepreneurial behavior is encouraged for increased revenue generation, and decisions about resource allocation are located at a level where there is more knowledge to make them. However, some additional disadvantages have been found: higher level and more sophisticated financial information systems are required than may be available; higher departmental and unit level managerial skills may be required than exist; and any disconnects between government funding formulas and institutional cost structures become highlighted. Nevertheless, the fact that this approach is now being used in various forms in public institutions is an important development.

CONCLUSION: WE'RE NOT IN KANSAS ANYMORE

Budget and financial officers at today's colleges and universities are wrestling with the problem of creating responsible approaches to financing their institutions during times of enormous ambiguity and uncertainty. Changes in the higher education environment (e.g., the evolving student body composition, newly available methods for financing capital expenditures, and the delivery of more and varied educational products through the Internet) make the identification of new budgeting tools essential for institutional advancement. The key is to maintain as much budget flexibility as possible in the face of the uncertainty of many external factors.

These financial professionals must be increasingly creative in stretching their limited—and often restricted—resources. The art of "doing more with less" is more important than ever, as conflicting priorities lead to harder decisions. In addition, many institutions are actively seeking new sources of revenue to support expanded initiatives rather than reducing expenditure choices. For example, more public institutions are developing or enhancing their fundraising capabilities. Public and private institutions are privatizing various functions such as dormitories, food service, and custodial services to mention only three from what is a growing list. Advertising is being sold at athletic events at institutions that have "big time" programs. Some institutions are entering into "preferred beverage partner" contracts, and targeted computer purchase arrangements. Research universities are developing research parks and business incubators. Many are doing applied research supported by particular corporations. Many institutions are entering into e-business arrangements, thereby unlocking the marketing potential of their stakeholders and their corporate identities. While many of these examples involve controversial activities, they are symptomatic of institutional efforts to develop new streams of revenue to help contend with changing economic, demographic, and political environments.

The times are changing in higher education finance—and at an increasing pace. New budgeting approaches will undoubtedly continue to be developed in response to new environmental stimuli and our intellectual abilities to make sense out of all the change. It is an interesting time in higher education finance, but it is a time full of challenges.

References

Burke, J.C. (2000). *Performance Funding: Popularity and Volatility.* Conference presentation at the 40th Annual Forum of the Association for Institutional Research. Cincinnati, OH, May 21-24, 2000.

Burke, J.C. and Serban, A.M. (1998). *Current Status and Future Prospects of Performance Funding and Performance Budgeting for Public Higher Education: The Second Survey.* Albany, NY: Rockefeller Institute of Government.

Hines, E.R. (1998). *State Higher Education Appropriations, 1997-98.* Denver, CO: State Higher Education Executive Officers.

Lang, D.W. (1999). *A Primer on Responsibility Centre Budgeting and Responsibility Centre Management.* Professional File #17, Canadian Society for the Study of Higher Education. Winter 1999. Toronto, ON.

McPherson, M.S. and Schapiro, M.O. (1998). *The Student Aid Game: Meeting Need and Rewarding Talent in American Higher Education.* Princeton, NJ: Princeton University Press.

McKeown-Moak, M.P. (2000). *Financing Higher Education in the New Century: The Second Annual Report from the States.* Denver. CO: State Higher Education Executive Officers.

National Commission on the Cost of Higher Education (1998). *Straight Talk about College Costs and Prices.* Phoenix, AZ: Oryx Press.

Watt, C.E. and Fleming, D.B. (2000). *The Best Laid Plans… The Evolution of Performance Funding in South Carolina.* Conference presentation at the 40th Annual Forum of the Association for Institutional Research. Cincinnati, OH, May 21-24, 2000.

PART V

The Finance of Higher Education in the Twenty-first Century

Chapter 15

THE FINANCE OF HIGHER EDUCATION:
Implications for Theory, Research, Policy, and Practice

Edward P. St. John and Michael B. Paulsen

Higher education finance is maturing as a field of inquiry, which means that there are competing theories and methods being used. This situation complicates efforts to design research that can inform policymakers about new policy challenges. The chapters in this volume provide thoughtful analyses, reviews, and policy perspectives, as well as a thorough treatment of the concepts and models from the economics of human capital, the public sector, and the microeconomics of costs, productivity, demand, supply and pricing in the marketplace, that are relevant to the study of higher education finance. In combination, this wide range of analytic perspectives can help us to better understand the financial challenges facing the higher education research community, and inform us about possible ways of addressing these challenges with a new generation of research. This concluding chapter starts with an overview of challenges that are emerging in higher education policy research. Then it explores new understandings of theory that emerge from these chapters and related studies and the ways policymakers and researchers might address the new challenges.

NEW CHALLENGES FOR POLICYMAKERS AND POLICY RESEARCH

Over time, states and the federal government have changed the ways they finance higher education. The emphasis placed on funding public institutions and students changed in the past two decades, as voters and politicians responded to new issues and beliefs (Callan and Finney, 1997). As we step back and look at the analyses from the previous chapters within the context of the national discourse on higher education finance, three challenges seem particularly important for policymakers and scholars who are concerned about policy in higher education finance in the next decade or so.

Development, Productivity, and Investment

For most of the twentieth century, the primary state concern was the development of state systems of higher education. Originally, many states approached this task with an emphasis on subsidizing institutions as a means of providing low-cost higher education. Several of the authors in this volume examined the changes in patterns of funding in public systems of higher education (Lasher and Greene, chapter 14; Mumper, chapter 8; Paulsen, chapters 3 and 4; Toutkoushian, chapter 1; and Voorhees, chapter 13). In combination, these analyses provide evidence that state support for public institutions has substantially eroded over the past two decades. As a direct consequence of this underlying change in state finance, there was a steady pattern of tuition increases in public colleges. In spite of rising tuition, enrollments did not drop during the last two decades of the twentieth century, as had once been predicted (e.g., Breneman, Finn, and Nelson, 1978; Carnegie Commission on Higher Education, 1973).

Now, after two decades of relative stability in enrollment, states are again faced with growing enrollment demand for their state systems due to growth in the traditional college-age population and to the need to open the doors to a greater portion of this population (Council for Aid to Education, 1997). Zumeta (chapter 9) argues that increased state investment in student aid provides a lower cost method of meeting demand than the traditional pattern of subsidizing public colleges. Hearn (chapter 11) and Mumper (chapter 8) also ponder how states will respond to this new challenge in the face of fiscal constraints.

These analyses raise serious questions for policymakers about whether states can find more economical ways to reinvest in higher education systems. Given the erosion in traditional patterns of support, the states are again confronted by basic questions about who pays for and who benefits from higher education (Paulsen, chapter 4). More of the burden of paying for college has shifted from taxpayers in states to students; affordability now looms as a larger problem (Baum, chapter 2; Hearn, chapter 11; Paulsen, chapters 4 and 6; St. John, Asker, and Hu, chapter 10). Yet, states' decisions about alternative strategies for expanding higher education will also be influenced by concerns about improving productivity within higher education.

Indeed, for the past two decades there have been calls for greater efficiency in the public sector (Lasher and Greene, chapter 14; Lewis and Dundar, chapter 5; Paulsen, chapters 4 and 6). However, diverse patterns of productivity have emerged. In community colleges, Voorhees (chapter 13) reminds us, there has been a tightening of the economic belt, an uneasy emphasis on improving efficiency. Yet in public four-year colleges expenditures for education and related purposes rose in the last two decades as the portion of these expenses paid by states declined (Touthoushian, chapter 1).

In the early twenty-first century, more states will begin to look at the methods they use to invest in the higher education of their citizens (the combinations of institutional and student subsidies) and the types of institutions in which they invest (two-year or four-year campuses, or new high technology delivery systems). These new debates will undoubtedly reconsider productivity and the state's role in promoting it. Ideally, these debates should also be informed by evaluative information that considers the effects of prices and student subsidies on access and the opportunity to persist by diverse groups.

Access, Affordability, and Accountability

The interrelated questions of access, affordability, and accountability (Heller, 2000) are also important to states and the federal government. The questions of access and affordability have been closely linked in the past (Baum, chapter 2), but in the current policy context, it is also important to consider the role of state accountability systems when considering affordability and access. In particular, it is troubling that with the decline in the purchasing power of federal grant aid per student, many states have incorporated persistence rates into their accountability systems without considering the influence of adequate student aid on the opportunity to persist (St. John, Kline, and Asker, 2000).

There is substantial evidence that inadequate grants have influenced the gaps in college attendance between lower- and higher-income and between minority and white students (Kane, 1999; Paulsen, chapters 3 and 4; Paulsen and St. John, in press). The research suggests that interventions aimed at improving K-12 schools, providing information on postsecondary opportunities, and student aid have important roles to play in promoting aspirations and expanding opportunities to attend, or access (Hearn, chapter 11; Paulsen, chapter 3). However, student aid has not received as much attention from policymakers as have other strategies that can reduce the disparity in opportunity. In the last two decades of the twentieth century, there was an increase in federal support for providing postsecondary information (e.g., GEAR UP) and for school reform (e.g., comprehensive school reform and the *Reading Excellence Act*), but the purchasing power of federal need-based grants per student declined. This suggests there are reasons for the federal government to reconsider its investment in grants. When federal funds decline, then states must spend more just to maintain affordability for low-income students (St. John, Hu, and Weber, 2000, in press).

The current movement toward accountability in many states (Lasher and Greene, chapter 14; Zumeta, chapter 9, 2000) can complicate efforts to maintain affordability and access. In particular, federal requirements that institutions report on six-year persistence rates have influenced many states to use persistence rates as an integral part of accountability reporting (St. John, Kline, and Asker, 2000; Zumeta, 2000). However, as long as colleges are not affordable for students from poor families nationally (Baum, chapter 2; Kane, 1999; Paulsen, chapters 3 and 4; Paulsen and St. John, in press), states cannot maintain equal opportunity to persist without making substantial investments in need-based grants (St. John, 1999; St. John, Hu, and Weber, 2000, in press). When there is not an adequate state investment in need-based grants, having high persistence rates probably means that institutions attract more economically advantaged students. If states provide institutions more funding for having high persistence or graduation rates, as part of performance-based funding (Lasher and Greene, chapter 14), then they run the risk of rewarding institutions that attract students with little financial need, rather than rewarding institutions that improve students' chances of persisting. To adjust for this prospect, a state's accountability system would need to take into account the initial probabilities of student enrollment and persistence, controlling for the level of public investment in the state (St. John, Kline, and Asker, 2000). Indeed, states need to develop better ways to assess the impact of their own investments in higher education, as well as methods of holding institutions accountable.

Adapting to Privatization and the New Market: Global and Ideological Forces

There is growing evidence that a new set of market forces emerged in the 1990s. The essays in this volume document growth in tuition (Paulsen, chapter 6; Toutkoushian, chapter 1) and in institutional grant aid (Breneman, Doti and Lapovsky, chapter 12), along with an expansion in federal loans relative to need-based grants (Baum, chapter 2; Paulsen, chapters 3, 4 and 6). These trends indicate that there has been substantial change in the market; however, there are other ways that higher education is adapting to changes in the global economy.

Slaughter and Leslie (1997) point to changes in the global economy that influenced changes in higher education finance in the late twentieth century. Not only is the shift from need-based grants to loans a global pattern but so is the decline in investment in public systems of higher education. The result is incremental movement toward privatization of public universities on a global scale, along with overt efforts to encourage entrepreneurial behavior in colleges (Slaughter and Leslie, 1997). The national pattern of increasing total revenues from sources other than state appropriations and tuition (Toutkoushian, chapter 1), means the new pattern of institutional finance also involves seeking revenues from alternative sources. In addition, there have been efforts to introduce market forces into budgeting within colleges and universities (Massy, 1997; Lasher and Greene, Epilogue, Chapter 14), a development that further promotes entrepreneurial practices.

Changes in the labor market have also influenced the demand for higher education (Paulsen, chapters 3 and 6). National study groups are increasingly calling for expanding access, especially for technical education (e.g., Boesel, 1999; Council for Aid to Education, 1997). Grubb (1996) argues that new types of community colleges are needed: institutions that respond to the need for mid-skilled workers. And Voorhees (chapter 13) described how these forces are transforming community colleges, especially the ways they respond to local labor market demands.

This movement toward a new market approach was influenced by the new conservative political ideologies that argued for cutting back on public investment in social programs. This ideology dominated higher education policy at the turn of the century (St. John, 1994; Slaughter and Leslie, 1997). After twenty years of drift toward decreasing public investment in higher education, it is time to reconsider the role of political ideologies in higher education finance and the ways policy research can better inform policy discourse. This means it is important to examine the ways liberal assumptions are linked to mainstream theories, as well as how the new ideologies have influenced more changes in policy.

THE ROLE OF THEORY IN POLICY ANALYSIS

Originally, most of the research in the field of higher education finance was situated in the discipline of economics, with some contributions from sociology and other social sciences. Economists and other social scientists viewed the higher education enterprise as a topical area to which they could apply the substance and syntax of their disciplines toward the conduct of research and the development and testing of theory. A few decades ago, emergent leaders in the higher education research community began to argue for more paradigm development within the field of higher education (e.g., Peterson, 1985) and, over time, some areas of higher education research became more paradigmatic. For example, the concept of student price response evolved within higher education finance research (Paulsen, chapter 4).

However, as postmodernists and critical theorists began to question the foundational assumptions of the theories used in the disciplines (e.g., Foucault, 1980; Habermas, 1984, 1987), the role of theory came into question in higher education as well (Tierney, 1992; St. John and Elliott, 1994). For more than fifteen years, the annual volumes of *Higher Education: Handbook of Theory and Research* helped the higher education research community to examine the relations between theory and research, as they apply to specific topical areas. As we reflected on the contributions made by the chapters in this volume and related research, it became evident that theory played a crucial role in the ways scholars have addressed policy issues. Below we examine the central role theory has played in scholarship on finance.

Economic Theories

While economic theories provide a substantial and important basis for the analysis of financial policy in higher education, this area of theory is far from monolithic (Paulsen, chapters 3, 4 and 6; Lewis and Dundar, chapter 5). There are different areas of theory and competing explanations of economic phenomena within economic theory. We focus on how theory and research in this volume informs our collective understanding of three areas of thought about the economics of higher education: human capital theory, public sector economics, and the microeconomics of costs, productivity and the marketplace (Lewis and Dundar, chapter 5; Paulsen, chapters, 3, 4 and 6).

Human capital theory has provided a broad framework for assessing public investment decisions (Becker, 1964) in the last half of the twentieth century. Paulsen (chapter 3) reviews and illustrates the role of human capital theory and the ways in which new research has served to better inform our understanding of this area of theory. Some of the economic concepts, principles, and models from human capital theory that have been, or could be, helpful in the construction of productive frameworks for the study of higher education finance include the following: (1) the earnings differentials between college and high school graduates, the earnings forgone while attending college, and the out-of-pocket costs of college have consistent and predictable effects on students' college-going behavior; (2) the private returns to baccalaureate and sub-baccalaureate investment in college are substantial and significant; (3) the marginal benefits of investment in college vary among students according to their academic ability and socioeconomic and family background, the quality of pre-college and college-level schooling, and discriminatory experiences; (4) the marginal cost of funds to invest in college varies among students according to family income and wealth and the availability of financial aid; and (5) in combination, variations in the marginal benefits and marginal costs of investments in college provide a useful framework for understanding and studying the effects of public policies on students' college investment behavior.

Theory and research from *public sector economics*, an area of research reviewed by

Paulsen in Chapter 4, provides an important framework for inquiry into the nature and effectiveness of policies in higher education finance. Concepts, principles, and models from the economics of the public sector that have been, or could be, useful in research on higher education finance include the following: (1) the criterion of Pareto efficiency to inform the development and evaluation of policies related to the allocation of resources to higher education; (2) equity criteria to inform the development and evaluation of policies related to the distribution of the benefits and costs of higher education; (3) the economic rationales for government intervention in the application of public policies to influence the behavior of demanders or suppliers in the marketplace, such as externalities, quasi-public goods, attractive social rates of return on investment, and market imperfections; (4) market models to examine the use and effectiveness of public policy interventions, such as subsidies to students or institutions, to promote the socially optimum level of investment in higher education; (5) principles for the efficient use of subsidies in higher education finance; and (6) the benefits-received and ability-to-pay principles as criteria for efficient and equitable pricing in higher education.

Microeconomic theories of costs and productivity also play an important role in framing research in this area, especially research on institutional finance. Lewis and Dundar reviewed this economic literature in chapter 5. Some of the economic concepts and principles in these areas that can better inform the development and assessment of the financial policies and practices of institutions include the following: (1) when average costs exceed marginal costs, average costs will decrease, and vice versa; (2) substantial cost advantages due to economies of scale occur over a range of production where long-run average costs are decreasing (a phenomenon observed for all types of institutions); (3) there are significant marginal and average cost differences between production units (e.g., departments such as social sciences versus physical or laboratory sciences) and between products (e.g., lower- and upper-level or graduate-level students, or teaching and research); (4) cost-related price-setting policies or practices can promote efficiencies in resources allocation; (5) cost advantages or economies of scale occur when institutions jointly utilize resources (e.g., faculty, administrators, staff, equipment and services) to produce multiple products (e.g., both teaching and research); and (6) costs of production depend on both the quantity of resources employed as well as the prices of needed resources, the latter of which reflect the interplay between the supply of, and demand for, each type of resource in its respective external marketplace.

Microeconomic theories of demand and supply in the marketplace have been used as frameworks within which to examine a range of phenomena in the area of higher education finance. Paulsen has reviewed this literature in chapter 6. Some of the economic concepts and principles that have been useful in the study of financial policies and behavior (e.g., price setting) among institutions in the marketplace environment include the following: (1) prices (e.g., tuition) are influenced by both demand-side and supply-side (cost-related) factors; (2) prices of services in nonprofit organizations such as colleges and universities depend on a combination of increases in costs of providing services and the subsidies received from government or private sources; (3) increases in the supply-side factors related to subsidies to institutions (e.g., state appropriations or private giving and endowment income) reduce upward pressure on prices; (4) increases in institutional costs or expenditures (e.g., for instruction, administration, student services) put upward pressures on prices; (5) increases in productivity in the use of resources (e.g., a higher student-faculty ratio) can reduce unit costs, but often at the expense of reductions in the quality of services provided; and (6) prices of services are directly related to the benefits consumers expect from purchase of the product (e.g., future earnings), demographic factors that affect the number of consumers in the market (e.g., larger numbers of students of traditional age), increases in the incomes of consumers (e.g., the incomes of students and their families), increases in the price of substitutes (e.g., prices or tuition charged by other institutional types), and decreases in the price of complements (e.g., room and board, books, transportation, living expenses).

Higher Education Finance

The study of higher education finance has led to the development of new applications of economic concepts and theories. Below we examine several examples—price response, revenue theory, and the role of market forces—that are distinct applications of economic theories and concepts within the field of higher education finance. Indeed, research on these topics is evolving at the intersection of the discipline of economics and research on the finance of higher education in a way that creates a distinct area of inquiry—higher education finance—an applied professional field of study. Below we consider these examples as distinct in ways that are derived from three of the major strands of economic theory and research that are frequently applied to higher education.

Price-response analyses have become a central concern in the study of higher education finance. This area of theory and research represents an application of the economic concept of price elasticity of demand (Paulsen, chapter 4), but has become important within the field of higher education finance. It has evolved within the applied field of higher education finance research—through a series of efforts to apply the idea that students respond to price discounts—into the expanded construct of differentiated student price response (Paulsen, chapter 4).

Net price has been the dominant approach to research in this area. This approach not only assumes tuition and grants have equal but opposite effects, but also assumes that students respond to a *net price* (tuition minus grants). These common assumptions have been carried forward in this volume, particularly as Breneman, Doti and Lapovsky (chapter 12) report on their research, which clearly documents that these assumptions are appropriate and workable as they apply to the widespread price-discounting practices of private colleges and universities. When institutions treat student aid as a price discount, they have a direct method for linking analysis of aid strategies to budgeting. The notion of net price implicit in tuition discounting links directly to net tuition revenue in the institutional budget—that is, net tuition revenue equals the amount of gross tuition revenue minus the amount of grant aid from institutional sources. Clearly, the net price approach is effective in explaining institutional pricing behavior and student enrollment behavior relative to the tuition discounting practices of institutions.

However, the net price construct does not fully consider the roles of loans and tax credits in inducing enrollment and persistence. While earlier chapters reviewed the research related to net price (e.g., Paulsen in chapter 4), it is important also to consider the policy aspects of the possible limitations of this concept. In particular the assumption of net price has potential shortcomings when it is applied uniformly across a range of public policy contexts.

One lingering indicator of the limitations of the net price construct is that it did not explain the relatively modest impact that the implementation of the Pell grant program had on enrollment (Hansen, 1983; Kane, 1995), compared with predictions for a substantial impact (National Commission on the Financing of Postsecondary Education, 1973). To understand the impact that the massive new Pell program had, when it was implemented as the Basic Educational Opportunity Grant Program in fall 1973, we need to use a more flexible way of conceptualizing and measuring the impact of prices and price subsidies.[1] One alternative is to treat the effects of different prices and subsidies as distinct but interdependent (e.g., Dresch, 1975; St. John and Starkey, 1995). In a study of first-time enrollment decisions by students who graduated in the high school class of 1980, St. John (1990a) tested this alternative method of assessing the impact of aid. He found that low-income students were more responsive to grants than to tuition, middle-income students were about as responsive to grants as they were to tuition[2], and upper-income students were not responsive to grant awards, but they were moderately responsive to tuition. If we consider these differences in response to prices and subsidies, along with the fact that a substantial portion of Pell grants went to students who would have enrolled anyway, then the modest impact that the Pell program had on enrollment is explainable.

However, implementation of the Pell program resulted in a notable reduction in the gap in enrollment rates for African-Americans and Hispanics compared with whites (St. John, 1994). In fact, there was near equality in opportunity for African-Americans and Hispanics compared to whites in the late 1970s (National Center for Education Statistics, 1998). In the early 1980s, African-Americans were more responsive to packages with grants only than to packages with loans only (St. John and Noell, 1989) and low-income students were more responsive to grants than to tuition and were not responsive to loans (St. John, 1990a). Thus, the fact that a gap appeared in participation rates for African-Americans and Hispanics compared with whites in the early 1980s (U. S. Department of Education, NCES, 1998), after the federal grants were reduced, can also be explained using a differentiated price response approach (Paulsen, Chapter 4).

A second problem with the concept of net price is that it does not explain why

[1]Readers are reminded that the concept of student price response was developed by the National Commission on the Financing of Postsecondary Education in its efforts to estimate the impact of BEOG. Dresch (1975) was one of the critics who objected to the idea of abstracting elasticities from economic studies and creating price response measures. Standardized price response measures were created (Jackson and Weathersby, 1975) in response to criticisms, but did not adequately deal with problems associated with this data transformation (Paulsen, chapter 4).

[2]Thus the concept of net price was most applicable to middle-income students because such students would need to be equally responsive to both grants (tuition reductions) and tuition for the concept to work well. Low-income students were more responsive to the grant award and upper-income students were not responsive to the grant awards (or the tuition reduction). Thus, the tuition discounting method (Breneman et al., chapter 12) might be most appropriately applied in colleges and universities attempting to attract middle-income students, such as private colleges.

enrollment remained high when the federal government expanded loans and cut grants as a means of finding a lower cost method of promoting educational opportunity.[3] Indeed, net price theory either ignores the direct effects of loans, or considers only the government subsidy and subtracts this amount from tuition in the calculation of net price (McPherson and Schapiro, 1991, 1998). Dresch (1975) argued that the effects of loans should be considered as distinct from the effects of grants, an approach that is consistent with Becker's theory (1964). The study of students who enrolled in the fall of 1980 (St. John, 1990a) found that middle-income students were more responsive to loans than they were to tuition or grants. Research studies using this alternative perspective provide evidence that loans kept enrollment at higher levels than expected, because middle-income and white students respond to loans (Paulsen, chapter 4; St. John, 1990a). However the gap in opportunity between whites and African-Americans has persisted, at least in part, because of inadequacy of grants. Indeed, the purchasing power of federal grants per student declined in the last two decades of the twentieth century, a period when this gap emerged and persisted.

Finally, it should be noted that the net-price logic typically used in policy research on higher education finance carries forward a new liberal rationale that argues it is more appropriate to invest in low-income students than in middle- and high-income students (Paulsen, chapter 4).[4] The HEA Title IV programs were created in the liberal period of the 1960s, which argued for more rational ways of promoting social equity and economic opportunity.

Revenue theories: Developed in higher education research, revenue theories have the potential of informing policy researchers who are interested in the financial challenges facing higher education. Pfeffer's (1977) resource-dependency theory and Bowen's revenue theory (1980) of costs hold the potential of informing a further rethinking of finance policy in higher education.

Pfeffer's resource-dependency theory (1977) provided an explanation of why some academic units in colleges and universities attracted more internal resources than other units. For example, he argued that the strength of disciplines, as measured by the number of prerequisite courses, was thought to be an indicator of resource competitiveness. Slaughter and Leslie (1997) have extended this theory to argue that it explains why institutions have sought revenues from private sources to replace losses in state support. This argument merits further examination.

Bowen's revenue theory of cost (1980) argued that in their pursuit of excellence, institutions would raise all the revenues they could which, in turn, would determine their level of expenditures or costs. Based on a review of research on finance, St. John (1994)

---

[3]We distinguish here between "educational opportunity" and "equal educational opportunity." Adequate grant aid would be needed to equalize educational opportunity, controlling for disparities in academic preparation. Loans did not equalize educational opportunity in this way. However, they did have an influence on educational opportunity, influencing enrollment increases.

[4]We distinguish here between the old liberal argument that states and the federal government should support higher education directly through institutional subsidies and the new liberal argument that high tuition, high grants provide a less expensive means of promoting equal opportunity (Hansen and Weisbrod, 1969; Hearn and Anderson, 1995).

concluded that the emphasis on incentives embedded in revenue theory held up well, as did their basic idea of revenue generation. Indeed, this not only provides an explanation for rising tuition, but also for the emphasis on generating revenue from alternative sources (Paulsen, Chapter 6). St. John (1994) also speculated that a corollary of revenue theory could be that incentive structures for faculty, including the emphasis on rewarding research in promotion and salary reviews, also implicitly reinforced cost increases.

A better understanding of the relationship between strategic behavior within colleges and universities and the incentives provided by public finance strategies is clearly needed, especially given the changes in higher education finance. Research focusing on these relationships may provide a better foundation for addressing the challenges noted above. More critical thinking about theory, coupled with empirical research, is needed on these topics.

Market forces need to be better understood in higher education, and there is room for new models that better explain the roles of market forces and budget incentives in higher education. Few researchers have focused on this issue (e.g., Weathersby and Jacobs, 1977), but it merits further study. Clearly the notion of price response that was commonly used in higher education was too narrowly conceived and tightly constructed. And while the alternative, differentiated price-response theory (Dresch, 1975; St. John and Starkey, 1995) explained student behavior better than did net price theory, it does not entirely solve the problem. Better and more workable explanations of the role of market forces are needed. At the very least, there is a need to conceptualize and assess how changes in the environment and public policies link to changes in faculty and institutional behavior (e.g., Paulsen, 1990b).

In a sense we are caught between new and old notions of market forces in higher education. The dominant perspective in the higher education community has been to apply an economic theory that holds liberal values, such as arguments by Becker (1964) and Hansen and Weisbrod (1969) about the social returns from investment in higher education (Paulsen, chapter 4). This led to an applied economic theory of price response that implicitly valued subsidies to students (e.g., grants) because they promoted equity more efficiently than subsidies to institutions (e.g., low tuition). However, this approach ignored, or at best underestimated, the effects of loans. A new conservative ideology has dominated for more than two decades, resulting in policies that emphasize loans and tax credits as means of further expanding opportunity for the middle class. In some ways, loans for the middle class have become a substitute for direct institutional subsidies. Now a new generation of merit-based grant programs in Georgia and other states (see Mumper, chapter 8) has extended the equivalent of tuition subsidies to only students who meet specific academic achievement standards. This approach not only favors middle class students, but also adds to the burdens of students who are at greatest risk academically. This essentially means state support has been incrementally redirected from subsidies for all students (i.e., block grants to institutions) to subsidies for middle class students whose enrollment decisions can be influenced by the latest form of merit-based aid. Clearly a better theory and better set of empirical studies is needed to assess the effects of these policies. The dominant theory of net price is ineffective and the differentiated price response theory is more effective, but still not fully adequate for this task.

In addition, if there is further expansion of responsibility center management (Lasher and Greene, chapter 14) and of related incentive-based budget models, then market forces will be more deeply embedded into governance and budgeting. A few higher education scholars have begun to argue for a new balance between market and structural strategies in higher education (Callan and Finney, 1997). In addition, a few economists have begun to address this as a theoretical question (Becker and Theobald, in preparation; Wilson, in preparation). Perhaps it is time to explore these questions further.

Social and Cultural Theories

Social and cultural theories are also important for the study of higher education finance because they provide an alternative, more complete explanation of the role of non-monetary factors that foster and inhibit access. They also provide possible foundations for conceptualizing and evaluating policies aimed at increasing equity in postsecondary opportunity. Below we consider and compare sociological attainment theory and Bourdieu's social reproduction theory, which introduces cultural capital and habitus as alternate explanation for the ways families influence educational opportunity. Both of these theories assume that family background—parental income and occupation—have an influence on attainment (i.e., first-time and continued enrollment), but they offer different explanations for how background fosters or inhibits attainment. Hearn (chapter 11) reviewed some of the research that considered both the sociological and economic perspectives. He concluded that social and cultural factors explain much of the disparity in opportunity. Thus, there is reason to consider the extent to which the disparity is attributable to social and cultural factors not often addressed by student aid researchers. Clearly, the role of social forces needs to be better understood if institutions, states, and the federal government are going to revise their strategies to increase opportunities.

Social attainment theory is widely used to frame research on the social factors that influence college attendance and postsecondary attainment. Social attainment theory implicitly assumes that across generations, families aim to improve professional status and educational attainment across generations (Blau and Duncan, 1967; Alexander and Eckland, 1974, 1977). However, the social-class measures used in much of this research were hierarchically constructed, which can make it difficult to test some of the assumptions that are frequently made about the role of prior schooling, as well as to test assumptions about the influence of separate dimensions or aspects of family background.

Moreover, using a single measure of socioeconomic status (SES) can limit insight into how background factors influence enrollment behavior by diverse groups. To untangle how social background variables influence enrollment behavior, it is necessary to break down the component variables included in general measures of SES. Specifically, it is important to unbundle different levels of income and different levels of parent education into design sets of predictor variables because these variables may not have a linear relationship with attainment, as measures by college choice and persistence. When this approach is used, then differences in the patterns of choice across groups are more evident (Paulsen and St. John, in press).

Social reproduction theory, as articulated by Bourdieu (1977, 1990), provides an alternative way to conceptualize how social and cultural forces influence educational attainment. He argues that the "habitus" in which individuals are situated—a class-based, internalized set of beliefs and viewpoints about the social world which individuals get from their immediate cultural, social and family environments and experiences—influences one's attitudes, aspirations, behaviors, and life choices, and helps explain social and cultural reproduction. Bourdieu distinguished among three forms of capital formation that influence reproduction of social class within families: *economic capital*, which refers to financial means, *symbolic capital*, which refers to social status and symbols of status, and *cultural capital*, which refers to the capacity to transmit values that influence educational attainment. McDonough (1997) has used the logic of habitus and cultural capital to explore the reasons why children from inner-city Los Angeles had constrained postsecondary opportunities. Her research illuminated how the lack of cultural capital in families, schools, and community settings constrained opportunity, thus promoting reproduction of class.

Thus, there are at least two competing explanations of the ways social and cultural factors combine to influence educational opportunity. One explanation emphasizes uplift across generations, while the other emphasizes class reproduction. Further research in this area, especially research that tests these two competing notions of social and cultural influences, is important because it can add to our understanding of the ways public policies might be developed or revised to further address inequities in educational opportunity. The student-choice construct (St. John, Asker, and Hu, chapter 10) can potentially be used to address some of these questions; it can also be used to frame studies that compare how different theories explain student choice behavior. By unbundling the roles of parent education, occupational status, and income in promoting class reproduction and cross-generation uplift, it may be possible to identify both factors that inhibit and promote attainment of diverse groups. Further research is definitely needed in these areas.

Policy Sciences

The study of policy processes and the role of policy analysis in informing policy development also evolved over the last half of the twentieth century. Based on the successes with the Allies' war efforts in World War II, systems approaches to policy gained credibility in social policy formation (Schultz, 1968) and were influential in the creation of the Great Society Programs, including the *Higher Education Act*. Early critics of systems approaches argued that policy was essentially political and social in nature (Lindblom, 1963; Wildavsky, 1979). While the tension continues between rational, research-based notions of policy and more social views, the chapters in this volume add to our collective understanding of the role of research in higher education policy.

Politics Prevails in the Policy Process: Hearn (chapter 7) examined alternative explanations for a paradox in policy. He examined the paradox that government policy has continued to support student aid in spite of a lack of evidence on the effects of aid policy. He concludes that the social and political aspects of the policy process have greater influence than rational analysis. His essay continues to be important nearly a decade after it was written, not only because it is thought-provoking, but also because it captures apparent truths about the policy process. Because of its importance, we want to separately examine two aspects of his argument: the political nature of policy and the role of evidence.

Regarding the political nature of policy, there should be little doubt of Hearn's conclusion. Mumper's interviews with state policymakers (chapter 8) illustrate that state policymakers make choices in political environments with many competing expectations. Clearly higher education policy over the last half of the twentieth century has been constructed within political environments at the state and national levels. Clearly there are periods of major policy shifts. The passage of the *Higher Education Act*, the *Education Amendments of 1972*, and the neoconservative turn in higher education policy symbolized by the election of Ronald Reagan (St. John, 1994; St. John and Elliott, 1994) each represent major shifts in federal policy on higher education. Thus, there are good reasons to accept Hearn's conclusion about the political nature of policy.

Second, Hearn's paradox points to the need to generate research that can better inform policymakers about the impact of student aid and tuition charges. Gladieux and Wolanin (1976) have documented that economic research had a substantial influence on the *Education Amendments of 1972*, which increased the market emphasis in student aid. Further, a reanalysis of trends in student aid and enrollment and trends in all types of student aid (grants and loans from both specially directed and generally available federal programs) reveals that enrollment generally has followed patterns we might expect (St. John and Elliott, 1994). Additionally, several other researchers have documented that the changes in federal student aid have influenced enrollment (Kane, 1999; McPherson and Schapiro, 1991, 1998; St. John, 1991; St. John and Noell, 1989). However, such evidence does not seem to have had an influence on federal decisions about student aid, especially need-based grants. Thus, questions remain. How can evaluative information on the impact of finance policies be used to inform policy decisions in states and on the federal level? Or is ideology, coupled with advocacy by interest groups, too compelling a force to make use of evaluative information?

Ideology and Advocacy Influence Policy Decisions: During the past two decades, research that explicitly holds advocacy positions has become much more common. The new conservative ideology of the Reagan-Bush-Clinton years has essentially moved student aid away from being focused on equal educational opportunity and toward promoting opportunity for the middle class. The purchasing power of federal grants per student was reduced after 1980, while loans, and more recently tax credits, have been expanded (Baum, chapter 2; College Board, 1998; St. John and Elliott, 1994; St. John, 1994). The extreme conservative argument of Milton Freidman (1962) had a substantial influence on the initial arguments for these policies during the Reagan administration (St. John, 1994), and this agenda has been followed to its logical path in the Clinton years with implementation of tax credits.

In the late 1970s, theorists began to argue that researchers and policy analysts should take an advocacy position (Linblom and Cohen, 1979). The new conservatives took this approach in the 1980s, arguing that student aid had gone too far, that it influenced institutions to raise tuition (Carnes, 1987) and that institutions were greedy and unproductive (Finn, 1988a, 1988b). However liberals did not substantially adapt their arguments about student aid, in part because net-price theory combined economic theory and ideological beliefs in a way that disguised the ideological aspect of the rationale. Thus, mainstream finance research essentially held a liberal position. Using the net-price approach led to the conclusion that need-based grant aid was necessary to promote equal opportunity, as is illustrated by the summary statements of policy options that emerge from this area of research (Paulsen, chapter 4). The conclusion that more grant aid would improve opportunity was inevitable. However the research ignored the effects of loans, and researchers using this approach found it hard to explain why enrollment was higher than predicted (e.g., Hansen, 1983; Kane, 1995, 1999). The theories and metrics used by most analysts simply were not easily adapted to assess the effects of new conservative strategies. The alternative, examining the independent effects of prices and subsidies for students in different levels of need, was less frequently used.

Now there is a new wave of arguments about market approaches that reconstruct the new liberal (or old market) rationales that were widely used by liberals. For example, Zumeta (chapter 9) argues that expanding state student aid programs to encourage enrollment in private colleges provides a more economical alternative for states than does expanding subsidies to public colleges. Advocates of high technology solutions, such as the Western Governors' University, argue that states can expand opportunity at lower costs than building new institutions that use technology better (Norris, 1997). However, there is a tendency among mainstream analysts to link theory and liberal ideology in ways that make advocacy (and ideology) implicit rather than explicit, as has been the case with using human capital rationales to lobby for funding higher education programs (Slaughter, 1991).

Thus, the current period of policy research is enmeshed in ideological debates about policy alternatives, but many analysts essentially ignore the phenomenon. The ideological nature of the debate is less visible than it should be, at least if our aim is to inform policymakers. This is not to argue that policy analysts should not hold ideological positions about new policies. But it is important that policy analysts, especially analysts who are independent of government, make it clear when their analyses take advocacy positions. Unfortunately, many of the studies conducted under contract with the U. S. Department of Education and many advocacy groups often hold inherent advocacy positions (St. John and Elliott, 1994). Thus, it is important that researchers in higher education finance begin to think critically about the role of theory and ideology in policy analysis, as well as to think critically about the influence of ideology on policy changes. If this happens, then perhaps it will be possible for policy researchers to maintain their own points of view while constructing analyses that inform policymakers (legislators, executives, and their staffs).

Theory in Higher Education

While higher education researchers originally borrowed their theories from other fields, a number of recent theories generated from within the field of higher education can inform understanding of higher education finance. Below, we examine how theory in higher education, including contributions in this volume and related research, contribute to framing research on higher educational policy, including finance policy. Specifically, we consider three related areas of inquiry in higher education—theory and research on framing assumptions, strategic behavior, and student choice—that might inform research on higher education finance.

Understanding the Role of Framing Assumptions in Colleges and Universities: Higher education research has contributed substantially to the understanding of universities as organizations and of organizations in general. In particular, higher education research that focuses on frames for viewing organizations is particularly germane to the purposes of this chapter. There has been a line of inquiry, starting with Baldridge's (1971) analysis of universities as political organizations, that informs our understanding of the policy issues facing universities and states.

Baldridge (1971) argued that while the literature had historically viewed organizations as collegial environments or bureaucratic organizations, the university as a political organization better explained the ways universities adapted in the 1960s. Then Deal, one of the early scholars to introduce the concept of culture as a way of viewing organizations (Deal and Kennedy, 1982), teamed up with Bolman to articulate four frames: structural (or bureaucratic), human resources (or collegial), political, and cultural (Bolman and Deal, 1991). Several higher education scholars have used the four frames to examine the ways college administrators think about their organizations (e.g., Bensimon, 1989).

Extending this perspective, Smart and St. John (1996) speculated about the ways the four frames related to public policy on higher education. In a structural model, policymakers would emphasize regulation and control, including rigid systems of accountability. In a human resources frame, policymakers would emphasize students and professional development, a view that would be compatible with an emphasis on equal opportunity. In a political frame, policymakers would emphasize strategic adaptation to changing environments, including the introduction of incentives into budgeting. In a symbolic frame, policymakers would be more concerned about the symbolic meaning of new strategies in building coalitions, if not in developing new visions to guide the development of education systems.

These frames have two implications for research on higher education financial strategy. First, the frames illustrate another way in which different ways of believing can influence the ways policy issues are viewed. Like political ideologies, the frames provide ways of discerning different types of claims about the ways specific policies link to outcomes. Second, the idea that there are different frames further illustrates that it is important for researchers to think about the underlying assumptions held by policymakers as part of their research on the impact of new policies or when they design research to address new policy challenges.

Contributions to Strategic Thinking: Higher education scholars have also made substantial contributions to the general understanding of strategy that can inform research on higher education policy. Starting with Burton Clark's organizational sagas (1972), higher education scholars contributed to the general understanding of strategy and culture. For example, Keller (1983) introduced the concept of strategic planning and thinking into the discourse on universities and public policies. And Chaffee (1985; 1984) defined different ways of viewing strategies that were highly compatible with the frames.

In the 1980s, colleges and universities widely adopted strategic planning models, a practice that changed the traditional approaches to planning and finance. These developments had a substantial direct influence on the emergence of the new higher education market. Faced with the prospect of declining enrollment, private colleges developed new academic and financial strategies that enabled them to compete better with public colleges for prospective students (Paulsen, chapter 6, 1990b; Paulsen and Pogue, 1988; St. John, 1992a, 1992b). By the late 1990s, sophisticated approaches to tuition discounting (Breneman et al., chapter 12) and budgeting (Lasher and Greene, chapter 14) had been introduced into public as well as private universities. At a minimum, this new pattern of strategic adaptation needs to be considered when states and the federal government attempt to assess alternative finance policies.

The original economic theories of human capital and the public sector (Paulsen, chapters 3 and 4) did not take this type of adaptive behavior into account. And while the newer market theories hold this prospect (e.g., Paulsen, chapter 6), we still lack an economic theory of the market that fully accommodates this type of strategic behavior. James Hearn (1987) examined strategic issues in budgeting, as do Lasher and Greene (chapter 14). More inquiry is needed to explain the interactions between institutional behavior, the incentive structures for faculty and administrators, and public policy on higher education finance.

Patterns of Student Choice: The fact that student-choice behavior is more complex than can be explained by economic theories alone is well established in the field of higher education (Hossler, Bean and associates; Hossler, Schmit, and Vesper, 1999; Pascarella and Terenzini, 1991; Paulsen, 1990a; Tinto, 1987; Braxton, 2000). However, the models used to assess the impact of financial strategies often do not discuss an understanding of student choice processes. The student-choice construct introduced in this volume (St. John, et al., chapter 10) holds some potential in this regard. Specific suggestions are made in that chapter about future directions in research on the role of finances in student choice.

The student-choice construct provides a more comprehensive framework for examining student responses to tuition and subsidies, along with the impact of other institutional and public policies, including academic preparation and postsecondary information. Most economic and finance research on student choice has focused on discrete choices—that is, enrollment, college choice, and persistence—but has tended to overlook the patterns across choices and the impact of previous educational choices on current expectations and choices. Researchers who have begun to examine continuities have found that prior choices and family experiences do have a substantial influence on college choice and persistence (Hossler, Schmit, and Vesper, 1999; McDonough, 1997; Paulsen, 1990a; Paulsen and St. John, in press). To untangle further how institutional and government policies can be redesigned to promote gains in postsecondary attainment, it is important to begin to explore these continuities.

Understanding the Role of Theory

The theories researchers hold play a central role in policy research, just as the frames (political ideologies and ways of viewing policy) are central to the political nature of policy development. Clearly economic theories are the dominant area of theory as far as finance policy is concerned in higher education. However, social-cultural theories, policy sciences, and higher education theories are also important because they help provide a more complete explanation for the pattern of behavior that policymakers attempt to influence as they craft finance strategies.

Indeed, because economic theories alone have not provided a fully sufficient explanation for the ways students respond to prices or the ways universities react to reductions in public funding, other theoretical explanations are needed. The full range of theories discussed above can potentially inform the reconstruction of policy research on higher education finance. However, this may require new approaches to policy research.

THE PRACTICE OF POLICY RESEARCHERS

This examination of research on higher education finance can inform the practice of policy researchers, especially their decisions about the use of theory and selection of methods. Given the complex challenges now facing policymakers in government and higher education, we need new approaches in policy research, as well as a continuation of approaches that have provided sound explanations. Policy researchers need to find better ways of comparing the explanations provided by different theories, as they apply to the critical challenges now facing policymakers concerned about the future of higher education. We examine two ways of thinking about policy research below.

Paradigmatic Approaches

Most researchers have typically used paradigmatic approaches in the study of higher education finance and policy. These approaches involve specifying research problems within an area of theory and conducting research to extend knowledge within that paradigm (Kuhn, 1962). Replication studies within an area of inquiry provide a way of building a body of knowledge, which has been the case with research on college students (Pascrella and Terrenzini, 1991). However, there are limitations with the paradigmatic approach, which are evident in the pattern of research on price response.

Any serious attempt to study financial issues in higher education should certainly include an understanding of the related economic literature precisely because economics is the discipline that provides productive frames for most inquires on financial issues in higher education. Chapters 3 and 4 (Paulsen) in this volume provide reviews of the theory and research on human capital and public sector economics precisely because these areas of theory and research should be given more attention by researchers who conduct studies on higher education finance. However, the contributions of higher education finance research are also important precisely because researchers in this field have the freedom to step outside the assumptions made by economists and test new ways of framing policy problems.

In higher education finance, price response theory—originally grounded in the economic concept of price elasticity of demand—is one area of applied research that has evolved and been expanded with substantial input from the community of higher education finance researchers. However, a relatively rigid theory of price response has evolved, and this theory has been used for several integrative reviews (Heller, 1997; Jackson and Weathersby, 1975; McPherson, 1978; Leslie and Brinkman, 1988). Perhaps because of this large body of work, the basic assumptions of net price went largely unquestioned between the middle 1970s and the late 1990s. In the early 1970s, there was conflict about the use of student surveys to study college choice and the adaptation of econometric analysis, in the form of standardized price response measures (e.g., Jackson and Weathersby, 1975; Leslie and Brinkman, 1988), became an acceptable alternative. In recent decades, the statistical methods used in higher education research on price response parallel those used in economics (Paulsen, chapter 4), even if scholars in the two fields view and use the concept differently—that is, economists view and apply the concept of price elasticity as highly generalizable, while a few higher education researchers have focused on the more context-specific, differentiated concept of student price response. However, the need to rethink the meaning of price response research has implications for economics (Paulsen, chapter 4), as well as for higher education finance as a specialized field of study.

This example exposes one of the potential problems with paradigmatic approaches to research in higher education or any other applied field. Postmodern and critical theories have provided a counterview of paradigmatic approaches in the study of higher education (e.g., Tierney, 1992; Slaughter, 1991), as they have in other fields, but they have not provided a workable approach to finance policy. This ongoing tension between mainstream and critical thought serves as a reminder that there is a constant need to generate and test different theoretical explanations. For example, Slaughter and Leslie (1997) provide a rich critique based in empirical study of trends and research that enlightens our general understanding of global markets.

Researchers who use paradigmatic approaches in their research can make adaptations that allow for more complete exploration of the issues. For example, one of the reasons why Hearn's paradox (chapter 7) cannot be simply explained away is that he has compared different ways of viewing the problem and the comparisons themselves are of great value to policy researchers, providing an exemplar for other analysts and researchers. By looking across explanations of problems we gain new insights. This suggests that researchers who work within paradigms need to be open-minded. They need to be explicit about the assumptions they make and to think critically about the meaning of their research when their findings are not congruent with their initial theories.

The Critical-Empirical Approach

The critical-empirical approach provides an alternative to paradigmatic approaches to policy research. The critical-empirical approach is compatible with critical and postmodern theories, but it is less locked into neo-Marxist assumptions about reproduction. The critical-empirical approach evolved out of reviews of policy research on student aid (St. John and Elliott, 1994) and desegregation policy (St. John and Hossler, 1998). St. John and Hossler (1998) developed the critical-empirical approach in their analysis of alternative desegregation remedies. Charles Teddlie (1998), the series editor for *Reading on Equal Education*, has argued that the critical-empirical approach could also be used to generate new research on school desegregation. More recently the approach has been used to examine reading reforms (St. John, Bardzell, and Associates, 1999) and urban school reform (Miron and St. John, forthcoming). While this approach has only developed recently, it provides an alternative way of framing policy and evaluation studies. There are three key elements of the critical-empirical approach.

1. Discerning Claims: First, based on a critical reading of different explanations for the policies that might influence an outcome, the researcher can discern different claims about the factors, forces, or variables that can influence an outcome, or even multiple outcomes related to a policy goal. For example in desegregation, the courts were concerned about how alternative remedies might influence student choice, with a specific intent of influencing white enrollments on historically black campuses and African-American enrollment on traditionally white campuses. By discerning the claims various proponents of reforms make, it was possible to generate a set of hypotheses that can be examined in relation to empirical evidence (St. John and Hossler, 1998).

2. Testing Claims: The process of testing claims involves reviewing whether research evidence supports claims. The review process involves carefully assessing whether research by independent analysts actually confirms the specific claims made by reform advocates, which is not always the case. In the initial study, St. John and Hossler (1998) first specified a set of claims based on a review of proposals presented to the court in *Knight v. Alabama*, reviewed related research and conducted both case studies and survey of high school students to further examine certain key propositions. More recent studies have used large-scale reviews (Miron and St. John, in preparation; St. John and Hossler, 1998) and quantitative studies (Paulsen and St. John, in press; St. John, Manset, Hu, Simmons, and Michael, 2000).

3. Building New Understandings: The third step in the process involves examining the evidence by looking at evidence that relates to the various sets of claims that are derived from different types of proposals. This approach makes it easier to build new understandings of the problem and the ways policy influences intended and unintended outcomes. Based on the analysis of desegregation remedies, it became apparent that student choice research, and especially research that tested different propositions, could help inform policy decisions that influenced diversity (St. John and Hossler, 1998). Based on this understanding, a new set of studies further examined how different admissions practices influence diversity (St. John, Simmons, et al., 1999; St. John, Hu, et al., 1999).

COLLABORATIONS BETWEEN POLICYMAKERS AND POLICY RESEARCHERS

This volume provides a comprehensive treatment of theory and research on higher education finance policy. In this chapter, the studies in the volume were reviewed to identify the issues that confront policymakers, policy researchers, administrators and professors of higher education. The conclusions from this review are:

- Policymakers at the state and federal levels face a new set of challenges that defy the old logic of higher education finance.

- Economic theory and research is an essential for policy and research on higher education finance; however, by itself, it is not sufficient to fully address the challenges that currently face higher education, states, and the federal government.
- Social and cultural theory, policy sciences, and higher education theory also provide valuable insights that can inform policy research.
- It is possible to rethink policy research approaches to better address the new challenges facing policymakers.
- If paradigmatic approaches are used in policy research and applied policy studies, then the researchers need to think more critically about research findings that are incongruent with their framing assumptions.
- A critical-empirical approach to applied policy research potentially provides a basis for designing policy studies that might address critical challenges facing policymakers in states, if not at the federal level.

This set of conclusions flows directly from the review. However, we would like to add one further proposition: *collaborations between policymakers and policy researchers can hasten breakthroughs in policy*. This proposition is based in part on the conclusions outlined above. If researchers engage in studies that test the propositions made by the advocates of various reforms, they have an increased capacity to work with and inform policymakers. Indeed, research that tests theoretical and ideological claims could enable policymakers to craft more workable policies precisely because it allows advocates of different approaches to work with evidence that relates to their propositions, along with evidence related to the propositions of their opponents. When this type of research evidence is made publicly available, it is possible for political advocates with different points of view to reach new, possibly shared, understandings.

We also make this proposition because a new way of approaching research may now be politically feasible. Education policy in the United States has recently entered a new period in which research is once again informing the development of new policies and programs. For example, the GEAR UP program, which funds programs that provide information to students in middle school and high school, was developed based on sound basic research (e.g., Hossler, Schmit, and Vesper, 1999). In addition, the *Reading Excellence Act* and the Comprehensive School Reform Demonstration Project, major new federal K-12 reforms being implemented across the United States, were designed based on research, and states are being encouraged to use research to guide the development of new state and local reforms. These developments suggest preconditions for increased collaboration between researchers and policymakers.

In conclusion, although the field of higher education finance is maturing, researchers in the field still face challenges in the conceptual designs they use in their research studies. An understanding of the most relevant economic concepts and theories can serve to better inform research and policy analysis in higher education finance. However, there are also needs to test competing claims about the ways public policy influences student outcomes and to communicate findings in ways that are understandable by policymakers. Researchers in higher education finance have an important role to play in the development of informed finance policies, especially in states. In particular, there is a need to translate and test the claims of university lobbyists for government analysts, as well as to translate, and test the implicit claims of, economic research for both government analysts and lobbyists. Finance researchers can help create a new common ground for communication about finance policy. However, movement in this direction will require critical thinking about theory, methods, and political ideology. In the midst of the current turmoil about higher education finance we need more high quality analyses that address state and institutional policy issues to complement the plethora of studies of national finance issues.

References

Alexander, K.L., and Eckland, B.K. (1974). Sex differences in the educational attainment process. *American Sociological Review* 59: 668-82.

Alexander, K.L., and Eckland, B.K. (1977). High school context and college selectivity: Institutional constraints in educational stratification. *Social Forces* 56: 166-88.

Alexander, K.L., and Eckland, B.K. (1978). Basic attainment processes: A replication and extension. *Sociology of Education* 48: 457-95.

Baldridge, J.V. (1971). *Power and Conflict in the University.* New York: Wiley.

Becker, G.S. (1964). *Human Capital: A Theoretical and Empirical Analysis with Special Reference to Education.* New York: Columbia University Press.

Becker, W.E. and Theobald, N. (in preparation). Academic behavior given uncertain outcomes and a stochastic reward structure. In Priest, D., Becker, W. E., Hossler, D., and St. John, E. P. (eds.) *Responsibility Center Budgeting Systems In Public Universities.*

Bensimon, E.M. (1989). Measuring good presidential leadership: A frame analysis. *The Review of Higher Education* 12: 107-123.

Blau, P., and Duncan, O. D. (1967). *The American Occupational Structure.* New York: Wiley.

Bolman, L. and Deal, T. E. (1991). *Reframing Organizations.* San Francisco: Jossey Bass.

Bosel, D. (1999). *College for All? Is There Too Much Emphasis on Betting a 4-year College Degree.* Washington, D.C.: US Department of Education.

Bourdieu, P. (1977). *Outline of a Theory of Practice.* Cambridge: Cambridge University Press.

Bourdieu, P. (1990). *The Logic of Practice.* Stanford, CA: Stanford University Press.

Bowen, H.R. (1980). *The Cost of Higher Education.* San Francisco: Jossey-Bass.

Breneman, D.W. (1994). *Liberal Arts Colleges: Thriving, Surviving or Endangered?* Washington D.C.: Brookings.

Breneman, D.W., Finn, C.E., and Nelson, S. (eds.) (1978). *Public Policy and Private Higher Education.* Washington D.C.: Brookings.

Callan, P.M. and Finney, J.E. (1997). *Public and Private Financing of Higher Education: Shaping Public Policy for the Future.* Phoenix: Oryx.

Carnegie Commission on Higher Education. (1973). *Priorities for Action: Final Report.* New York: McGraw-Hill.

Carnes, B.M. (1987). The campus cost explosion: College tuitions are unnecessarily high. *Policy Review* 40: 68-71.

Chaffee, E.E. (1984). Successful strategic management in small private colleges. *Journal of Higher Education* 55(2): 212-241.

Chaffee, E.E. (1985). The concept of strategy. In John C. Smart, ed. *Higher education: Handbook of Theory and Research.* New York: Agathon.

Clark, B.R. (1977). *Academic Power in Italy: Bureaucracy and Oligarchy in a National University System.* Chicago: University of Chicago Press.

Clark, B.R. (1972). The organizational saga in higher education. *Administrative Science Quarterly* 17: 178-82.

College Board. (1998). *Trends in Student Aid.* Washington, D.C.: College Board.

Council for Aid to Education. (1997). *Breaking the social contract: The Fiscal Crisis in Higher Education.* Santa Monica, CA: RAND.

Deal, T.E., and Kennedy, A.A. (1982). *Corporate cultures: The rites and rituals of corporate life.* Reading, MA: Addison-Wesley.

Dresch, S.P. (1975). A critique of planning models for postsecondary education: Current feasibility, potential relevance and a prospectus for future research. *Journal of Higher Education* 46: 246-86.

Finn, C.E. (1988a). Judgment time for higher education: In the court of public opinion. *Change* 20 (4): 35-38.

Finn, C.E. (1988b). Prepared statement and attachments. Hearing before the Subcommittee on Postsecondary Education, Committee on Education and Labor, House of Representatives, 100th Congress, 1st Session, No. 100-47, September 25. Washington, D. C.: U.S. Government Printing Office.

Finn, C.E., and Manno, B.V. (1996). Behind the curtain. *Wilson Quarterly* Winter: 44-53.

Fischer, F.G. (1990). State financing of higher education: A new look at an old problem. *Change* 22(1): 42-56.

Foucault, M. (1972). *The Archaeology of Knowledge and the Discourse on Language.* Trans. A. M. Sheridan Smith. New York: Phantheon.

Friedman, M. (1962). *Capitalism and Freedom.* Chicago: University of Chicago Press.

Gladieux, L.E., and Wolanin, T.R. (1976). *Congress and the Ccolleges.* Lexington, MA: Heath.

Grubb, W.N. (1996). *Working in the Middle: Strengthening Education and Training for the Mid-Skilled Labor Force.* San Francisco: Jossey-Bass.

Habermas, J. (1984). *The Theory of Communicative Action, Volume1: Reason and the Rationalization of Society.* Trans. T. McCarthy. Boston: Beacon Press.

Habermas, J. (1987). *The Theory of Communicative Action, Volume 2: Lifeworld and System: A Critique of Functionalist Reason.* Trans. T. McCarty. Boston: Beacon Press

Hansen, W.L. (1983). Impact of student financial aid on access. In J. Froomkin (ed.). *The Crisis in Higher Education.* New York: Academy of Political Science.

Hansen, W.L., and Weisbrod, B.A. (1969). *Benefits, Costs, and Finance of Public Higher Education.* Chicago: Markham Pub. Co.

Hearn, J.C. (1987). Strategy and resources: economic issues in state planning and management in higher education. In J. C. Smart (ed.). *Higher Education: Handbook of Theory and Research.* Vol. 4. New York: Agaton.

Hearn, J.C., and Anderson, M.S. (1995). The Minnesota financing experiment. In E. P. St. John (ed.) *Rethinking Tuition and Student Aid Strategies,* New Directions for Higher Education, no. 89. San Francisco: Jossey-Bass.

Hearn, J.C., and Griswold, C.P. (1994). State-level centralization and policy innovation in U.S. post-secondary education. *Educational Evaluation and Policy Analysis* 16: 161-90.

Hearn, J.C., and Longanecker, D. (1985). Enrollment effects of alternative post-secondary pricing policies. *Journal of Higher Education* 56: 485-508.

Heller, D.E. (1997). Student price response in higher education: An update of Leslie and Brinkman. *Journal of Higher Education.* 23, 65-89.

Heller, D.E. (Ed.). (2000). *State Policy and Public Higher Education: Affordability, Access, and Accountability.* Baltimore: Johns Hopkins University Press.

Hossler, D., Bean, J.P. and Associates. (1990). *The Strategic Management of College Enrollment.* San Francisco: Jossey-Bass.

Hossler, D, Schmit, J. and Vesper, N. (1997). *Going to college.* Baltimore: Johns Hopkins University Press.

Jackson, G.A., and Weathersby, G.B. (1975). Individual demand for higher education. *Journal of Higher Education* 46: 623-52.

Kaltenbaugh, L.S., St. John, E.P., and Starkey, J.B. (1999). What difference does tuition make? An analysis of ethnic differences in persistence. *Journal of Student Financial Aid* 29(2): 21-32.

Kane, T.J. (1995). *Rising Public Tuition Levels and Access to College.* Cambridge, MA: National Bureau of Economic Research.

Kane, T.J. (1999). *The Price of Admission: Rethinking how Americans Pay for College.* Washington, D.C.: Brookings.

Keller, G. (1983). *Academic strategy.* Baltimore, MD: Johns Hopkins University Press.

Leslie, L.L., and Brinkman, P. T. (1988). *The Economic Value of Higher Education.* New York: Oryx Press.

Lindblom, C.E. (1963). *The Policy Making Process.* Englewood Cliffs, NJ: Prentice Hall.

Lindbom, C.E. and Cohen, D.K. (1979). *Usable Knowledge: Social Science and Social Problem Solving.* New Haven, CT: Yale University Press.

McDonnough, P.M. (1997). *Choosing Colleges: How Social Class and School Structure Opportunity.* Albany: State University of New York Press.

McPherson, M.S., (1978). The demand for higher education. In D. W. Breneman, C. E. Finn, and S. Nelson (eds.). *Public Policy and Private Higher Education.* Washington, DC: Brookings.

McPherson, M.S., and Schapiro, M.O. (1991). *Keeping College Affordable.* Washington, D.C.: Brookings.

McPherson, M.S., and Schapiro, M.O. (1998). *The Student Aid Game: Meeting Needs and Rewarding Talent in American Higher Education.* Princeton, NJ: Princeton University Press.

Miron, L.F. and St. John, E.P. (eds.) (forthcoming). *Reinterpreting Urban School Reform: A Critical-Empirical Review.* Albany: State University of New York Press.

National Commission on the Financing of Postsecondary Education. (1973). *Financing Postsecondary Education in the United States.* Washington, DC: Government Printing Office.

Norris, D.M. (1997). *Revolutionary Strategy for the Knowledge Age.* Ann Arbor, MI: Society for College and University Planners.

Pascarella, E.T., and Terenzini, P.T. (1991). *How College Affects Students.* San Francisco: Jossey-Bass.

Paulsen, M.B. (1990a). *College Choice: Understanding Student Enrollment Behavior.* ASHE-ERIC Higher Education Report no. 6. Washington, D.C.: The George Washington University, School of Education and Human Development.

Paulsen, M.B. (1990b). Enrollment management with academic portfolio strategies: Preparing for environment-induced changes in student preferences. *Journal of Marketing for Higher Education* 3(1): 107-119.

Paulsen, M.B., and Pogue, T.F. (1988). Higher education enrollment: The interaction of labor market conditions, curriculum and selectivity. *Economics of Education Review* 7(3): 275-290.

Paulsen, M.B., and St. John, E.P. (in press). Social class and college costs: Examining the financial nexus between college choice and persistence. *Journal of Higher Education* 72.

Peterson, M.S. (1985). Emerging developments in postsecondary organization theory and research: Fragmentation or integration. *Educational Researcher* 14(3): 5-12.

Pfeffer, J. (1977). Power and resource allocation in organization. In B. M. Staw. And G. R. Salancik (eds.) *New Directions in Organization Behavior.* Chicago: St. Clair Press.

St. John, E.P. (1990). Price response in enrollment decisions: An analysis of the high school and beyond sophomore cohort. *Research in Higher Education* 31: 161-76.

St. John, E. P. (1991). What really influences minority attendance? Sequential analyses of the high school and beyond sophomore cohort. *Research in Higher Education* 32: 141-58.

St. John, E. P. (1992a). Changes in pricing behavior during the 1980s: An analysis of selected case studies. *Journal of Higher Education* 63(2): 13-26.

St. John, E. P. (1992b). The transformation of private liberal arts colleges. *The Review of Higher Education* 15: 83-106.

St. John, E. P. (1994). *Prices, Productivity and Investment: Assessing Financial Strategies in Higher Education.* ASHE/ERIC Higher Education Report, no. 3. Washington, D. C.: George Washington University.

St. John, E. P. (1999). Evaluating state grant programs: A study of the Washington state grant programs. *Research in Higher Education* 40:149-70.

St. John, E. P., Bardzell, J. and Associates. (1999). *Improving Early Reading and Literacy: A Guide for Development Research-Based Programs.* Bloomington, IN: Indiana Education Policy Center.

St. John, E. P., and Elliott, R. J. (1994). Reframing policy research: A critical examination of research on federal student aid programs. In J. C. Smart, (ed.). *Higher Education: Handbook of Theory and Research,* vol. 10. New York: Agathon Press.

St. John, E. P., and Hossler, D. (1998). Higher education desegregation in the post-*Fordice* legal environment: A critical-empirical perspective. In R. Fossey (ed.) *Race, the Courts, and Equal Education: The limits of the Law, vol. 15, Readings in equal education.* (123-156) New York: AMS-Press.

St. John, E. P., Hu, S., Simmons, A., and Musoba, G. D. (1999). *Aptitude v. merit: What matters in persistence.* Policy Research Report #99-1. Bloomington, IN: Indiana Education Policy Center.

St. John, E. P., Hu, S. and Weber, J. (2000). Keeping public colleges affordable: A study of persistence in Indiana's public colleges and universities. *Journal of Student Financial Aid.* 30(1): 21-32.

St. John, E. P., Hu, S. and Weber, J. (in press) State policy and the affordability of public higher education: The influence of state grants on persistence in Indiana. *Research in Higher Education.*

St. John, E. P., Kline, K., and Asker, E. H. (2000). The call for accountability: Rethinking the linkages to student outcomes. In D. E. Heller (ed.). *State Policy and Public Higher Education: Affordability, Access and Accountability.* Baltimore: Johns Hopkins University Press.

St. John, E. P., Manset, G., Hu, S. Simmons, A., and Michael, R. (2000). Assessing the impact of reading interventions: Indiana's Early Literacy Intervention Grant Program. *Policy Research Report* 00-01, Bloomington, IN: Indiana Education Policy Center.

St. John, E. P., and Noell, J. (1989). The effects of student financial aid on access to high education: An analysis of progress with special consideration of minority enrollment. *Research in Higher Education*

30: 563-81.

St. John, E. P., Paulsen, M. B. and Starkey, J. B. (1996). The nexus between college choice and persistence. *Research in Higher Education* 37: 175-220.

St. John, E. P., Hu, S., Simmons, A. and Musoba, G. D. (1999 October). Merit-aware admissions in public universities: Increasing diversity without considering race. *Policy Bulletin. PB-25*, Bloomington, IN: Indiana Education Policy Center.

St. John, E.P., and Starkey, J.B. (1995). An alternative to net price: Assessing the influences of prices and subsidies on within-year persistence. *Journal of Higher Education* 66: 156-86.

Schultz, C.E. (1968). *The Politics and Economics of Public Spending.* Washington, DC: Boookings.

Slaughter, S. (1991). The official 'ideology' of higher education: Ironies and inconsistencies. In W. G. Tierney (ed.). *Culture and Ideology in Higher Education.* New York: Praeger.

Slaughter, S. and Leslie, L.L. (1997). *Academic Capitalism: Politics, Policies, and the Entrepreneurial University.* Baltimore: Johns Hopkins University Press.

Smart, J.C., and St. John, E.P. (1996). Organizational culture and effectiveness in higher education: A test of the 'culture type' and culture strength' hypotheses. *Educational Evaluation and Policy Analysis* 18, 219-242.

Teddlie, C. (1998). Four literatures associated with the study of equal education and desegregation in the United States. In R. Fossey (ed.) *Race, the Courts, and Equal Education. Vo. 15, Readings on Equal Education* (237-258). New York: AMS Press.

Tierney, W.G. (1992). An anthropological analysis of student participation in college. *Journal of Higher Education* 63: 603-618.

Tinto, V. 1987. *Leaving College: Rethinking the Causes and Cures of College Attrition.* Chicago: University of Chicago Press.

U.S. Department of Education, National Center for Educational Statistics. (1998). *The Condition of Education 1998.* Washington, D.C.: NCES.

Weathersby, G. B., and Jacobs, F. (1977). *Institutional Goals and Student Costs.* ASHE/ERIC Higher Education Research Report, no. 2. Washington, D. C.: American Association for Higher Education.

Wildavsky, A. (1979). *Budgeting: A Comparative Theory of Budgetary Processes.* Boston: Little Brown.

Wilson, J. (in preparation). The effects of incentive-based budgeting systems on academic departments. . In Priest, D., Becker, W.E., Hossler, D., and St. John, E.P. (eds.) *Responsibility Center Budgeting Systems in Public Universities.*

Zumeta, W.F. (1997). How did they do it? The surprising enrollment success of private nonprofit higher education from 1980 to 1995: Presented at the Association for the Study of Higher Education Annual Meeting. San Antonio, TX

Zumeta, W.F. (2000). Public accountability in higher education: Lessons from the past and resent for the new millenium. In D. E. Heller (ed). *State Policy and Public Higher Education: Access, Affordability, and Accountability.* Baltimore: Johns Hopkins University Press.

Author Index

Subject Index

cost analysis 140, 146, 219
dismissals 527
part-time 489
retrenchment 525
salaries as cost factor 14
teaching loads 220
time allocation 152
wages 167
workload 2
Family background
college choice and 430
and future earnings 75
Family income
and educational opportunity 78
growth rates 41
relative to attendance cost 42
Federal appropriations
community colleges 493
definition 35
Federal Balanced Budget Act (BBA) of 1997
537
Federal policy making
anarchic qualities 302
Fellowships
economic categorization 18
Financial accounting 135
Financial Accounting Standards Board 18
Financial aid
"access" vs. "affordability" 2
federal policy 535
sources of 44
system complexity 446
see also Institutional aid; Grants; Loans;
Student aid; Subsidies; Tuition
discounts
Financial equilibrium 198
Financial report auditing 506
Firm, theory of the 13
Fiscal crisis, responses to 524, 528
Florida
community college support 492
incentive funding 332, 520
Ford, William 287
Forgone earnings 115
Formula budgeting 514
Framing assumptions, role of 559
Freshmen
enrollment rates 475

institutional grants for 465
Fund raising
and donative subsidies 242
effectiveness 200
sources 529

G
GEAR UP program 430, 431, 564
General Accounting Standards Board 18
Georgia
higher education funding 336
HOPE scholarships 351, 488, 498
GI Bill 375(ff.)
Giving behavior, determinants of 242
Global education 450
Government role in higher education 98 (ff.)
Government support
declining levels 327
decreases in 214
foundational vs. institution-focused 280
low tuition strategy 346
public colleges 327
sources 233
Graduate education
choices about 426
dual role 149
influence of finances 434
Graduate students
costs of 146
as teaching assistants 153
Grants and contracts, definitions 35
Grants
compared with loans, *see* Loans
guaranteed 284
see also Need-based grants; Pell grants
Green, Edith 280
Growth force 222, 512
Guaranteed Student Loans 284

H
Habitus 75
Hansen, Lee 440 (ff.)
Hauptman, Arthur 271
Health professions education 537
High school
aspirations 425
graduation rates 358, 360
graduation statistics 330
High school completers

Printed in the United States
2547